CROATIA & SLOVENIA

Rick Steves & Cameron Hewitt

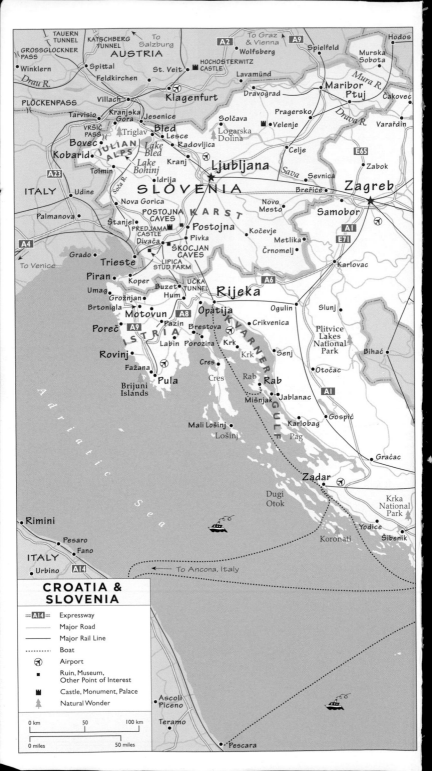

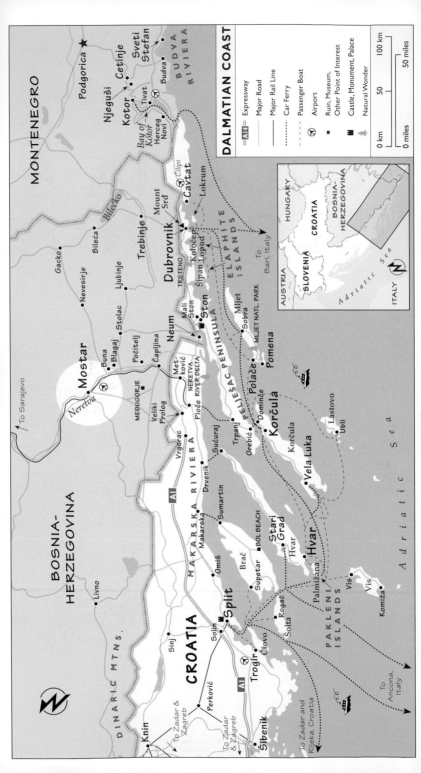

Rick Steves'

CROATIA & SLOVENIA

AVALON
TRAVEL

CONTENTS

INTRODUCTION

Set sail on the shimmering Adriatic, to a remote island whose name you can't pronounce, but whose wonders you'll never forget. Corkscrew your way up impossibly twisty mountain roads to panoramic vistas of cut-glass peaks. Lie on a beach in the hot summer sun, listening to the lapping waves as a Venetian-style bell tower overhead clangs out the hour. Ponder the fading scars of a recent war, and admire how skillfully the locals have revitalized their once-troubled region. Dine on a seafood feast and sip a glass of local wine as you watch the sunset dip into the watery horizon... feeling smug for discovering this place before all your friends did. Unfamiliar as they might seem, Croatia and Slovenia have what you've been looking for: some of Europe's most spectacular natural wonders, a fascinating recent history, and a spirit of adventure—much of it still off the beaten path.

Here in the land where the Adriatic meets the Alps, there are countless ways to have fun. Begin your adventure by flipping through this book, which covers Croatia's and Slovenia's best big-city, small-town, and back-to-nature destinations. You'll get all the specifics and opinions necessary to wring the maximum value out of your limited time and money. If you're planning a trip of four weeks or less, this book is all you need.

Less than two decades ago, Croatia and Slovenia—two of Europe's youngest nations—belonged to the union called Yugoslavia. Today they're proudly independent and racing toward the future. Carefree Croatia, with a long and varied coastline, beckons vacationers with its dramatically scenic terrain, romantic old towns, sunshine-bathed pebbly beaches, and irrepressible seafaring spirit. Perky Slovenia surprises travelers with its tidy quaintness, breathtaking mountainscapes, colorful towns, and impossibly friendly natives. And for good measure, I've also included detours into two other parts of the former Yugoslavia, each one offering a striking contrast to Croatia or Slovenia: the craggy coast of Montenegro, and the diverse and fascinating town of Mostar, in Bosnia-Herzegovina.

Experiencing Europe's culture, people, and natural wonders economically and hassle-free has been my goal for three decades of traveling, tour guiding, and writing. With this book, I pass on to you all of the lessons I've learned.

Rick Steves' Croatia & Slovenia covers the predictable biggies and adds a healthy dose of "Back Door" intimacy. Along with strolling the walls around Dubrovnik's peerless Old Town, you'll poke your way into a hidden little tavern clinging like a barnacle over the sea. I've been selective, including only the top destinations and sights. For example, Croatia has over a thousand islands. But why not focus on the very best? That's Korčula, Hvar, Rab, and Mljet.

The best is, of course, only my opinion. But after spending half of my adult life researching Europe, I've developed a sixth sense for what travelers enjoy. Just thinking about the places featured in this book makes me want to polka.

About This Book

Rick Steves' Croatia & Slovenia is a personal tour guide in your pocket. Better yet, it's actually two tour guides in your pocket: The co-author of this book is Cameron Hewitt. Cameron edits guidebooks and leads Eastern Europe tours for my travel company, Rick Steves' Europe Through the Back Door. Inspired by his Slavic roots and by the enduring charm of the Croatian and Slovenian people, Cameron has spent the last decade closely tracking the exciting changes in this part of the world. Together, Cameron and I keep this book up-to-date and accurate (though for simplicity we've shed our respective egos to become "I" in this book).

This book is organized by destination, each one a mini-vacation on its own, filled with exciting sights, strollable neighborhoods, affordable places to stay, and memorable places to eat. I update this book regularly, but things change. For the latest, visit www.ricksteves.com/update, and for reports and experiences—good and bad—from fellow travelers, check www.ricksteves.com/feedback.

In the following chapters, you'll find these sections:

Planning Your Time suggests a schedule, with thoughts on how best to use your limited time.

Orientation includes specifics on public transportation, helpful hints, local tour options, easy-to-read maps, and tourist information (abbreviated **TI** in this book).

Self-Guided Walks take you through interesting neighborhoods, with a personal tour guide in hand.

Map Legend

⌐	Viewpoint	✈	Airport			Pedestrian Zone
↑	Entry Point	Ⓣ	Taxi Stand	○⊢⊢⊢⊢⊢○	Funicular
⊕	Tourist Info	Ⓜ	Metro Stop	- - - - -	Railway
WC	Restroom	Ⓣ	Tram Stop	⊢——⊣	Tram Line
♜	Castle	Ⓑ	Bus Stop	⁚⁚⁚⁚⁚⁚	Stairs
⌂	Church	⛴	Boat Stop	- - - - -	Trail
☾	Mosque	Ⓟ	Parking	)⁚⁚⁚⁚(	Tunnel

Use this legend to help you navigate the maps in this book.

Sights, described in detail, are rated:

▲▲▲—Don't miss.
▲▲—Try hard to see.
▲—Worthwhile if you can make it.
No rating—Worth knowing about.

Sleeping describes my favorite places to stay, from good-value deals to cushy splurges.

Eating serves up a range of options, from inexpensive take-out joints to fancy restaurants.

Connections explains your options for reaching nearby destinations by train, bus, and boat. In car-friendly regions, I've also included route tips for drivers.

Country Introductions, for both Croatia and Slovenia, give you an overview of each country's culture, customs, money, history, current events, cuisine, language, and other useful practicalities.

The **Understanding Yugoslavia** chapter sorts out the various countries and conflicts, giving you a good picture of why Yugoslavia was formed, and why it broke apart.

The **appendix** is a traveler's tool kit, with telephone tips, useful phone numbers, transportation basics (on trains, buses, boats, car rentals, driving, and flying), recommended books and films, a festival list, climate chart, handy packing checklist, useful Croatian and Slovenian phrases and pronunciations, and a hotel reservation form.

Browse through this book and choose your favorite sights. Then have a great trip! Traveling like a temporary local and taking advantage of the information here, you'll get the absolute most out of every mile, minute, and dollar. I'm happy you'll be visiting places I know and love, and meeting some of my favorite Croatians and Slovenes.

Croatia & Slovenia at a Glance

Croatia

▲▲Zagreb Croatia's underrated capital city, with interesting museums (especially the Croatian Museum of Naive Art), lush parks, and a lively urban bustle, plus the nearby town of Samobor.

▲▲▲Plitvice Lakes National Park Arguably Europe's most breathtaking natural wonder: a forested canyon filled with crystal-clear lakes, stunning waterfalls, and easy-to-hike boardwalks and trails.

▲▲Istria Croatia's most Italian-feeling corner, with the super-romantic, Venetian-flavored coastal town of Rovinj; top Roman ruins in the city of Pula; and a rolling interior of vineyards and picturesque hill towns (including Motovun and Grožnjan).

The Kvarner Gulf Sparsely populated coastline between Istria and Dalmatia, with the genteel Habsburg resort of Opatija, the port city of Rijeka, and the island of Rab.

▲▲Split Unofficial capital city and transit hub of the Dalmatian Coast, with a people-filled seaside promenade and a lived-in warren of twisting lanes sprouting out of a massive Roman palace, plus the nearby town of Trogir.

▲▲Hvar Ritzy island and old town known for its jet-set appeal, high prices, and easy access to beaches and smaller islands.

▲▲Korčula Low-key island and peninsular Old Town with a fjord-like backdrop, a fish-skeleton street plan, and quirky offbeat museums.

▲▲▲Dubrovnik The "Pearl of the Adriatic": a giant walled Old Town with a scenic wall walk, tons of crowds, great beaches, an epic past and difficult but inspiring recent history, and a well-earned reputation as Croatia's single best destination.

Near Dubrovnik Boat excursions from Dubrovnik's Old Port, the nearby Trsteno Arboretum, the walled town of Ston, and the giant national park at Mljet Island.

Bosnia-Herzegovina

▲▲▲**Mostar** The most accessible destination in Bosnia-Herzegovina, with a striking setting, vital Muslim culture, old Turkish architecture, evocative war damage, and an inspiring, rebuilt Old Bridge.

Međugorje Famous Catholic pilgrimage site in the countryside near Mostar.

Montenegro

▲▲**The Bay of Kotor** Steep bay with fjord-like inlets, visit-worthy towns and sights, and the remarkably fortified Old Town of Kotor.

The Montenegrin Interior Rugged mountain road leading up the cliffs into the Montenegrin heartland, ending at the historic capital of Cetinje.

The Budva Riviera Glitzy emerging beach resort zone.

Slovenia

▲▲**Ljubljana** Slovenia's vibrant yet relaxing capital, with a fun-to-browse riverside market, scintillating architecture, and inviting riverside promenade.

▲▲▲**Lake Bled** Photogenic lake resort huddled in the foothills of the Julian Alps, with a church-topped island, cliff-hanging castle, lakefront walkway, tasty desserts, and appealing side-trips.

▲▲**The Julian Alps** Cut-glass peaks easily conquered by a twisty and scenic mountain road over the Vršič Pass, ending in the tranquil Soča River Valley, with the fine WWI museum in Kobarid.

▲**Logarska Dolina and the Northern Valleys** Remote mountain valleys with traditional farming lifestyles.

Ptuj and Maribor In Ptuj, a charming-if-sleepy historic town topped by a castle; and Slovenia's "second city" of Maribor.

▲**The Karst** Windblown limestone plateau with world-class caves (Škocjan and Postojna), the Lipizzaner Stallion stud farm at Lipica, and the dramatically situated Predjama Castle.

▲**Piran** Slovenia's leading seaside resort town.

Planning

This section will help you get started on planning your trip—with advice on trip costs, when to go, and what you should know before you take off.

Travel Smart

Your trip to Croatia and Slovenia is like a complex play—easier to follow and really appreciate on a second viewing. While no one does the same trip twice to gain that advantage, reading this book in its entirety before your trip accomplishes much the same thing.

Design an itinerary that enables you to visit the various sights at the best possible times. Note holidays, festivals, and days when sights are closed. Hotels are most crowded on Fridays and Saturdays, especially in resort towns.

Sundays have the same pros and cons as they do for travelers in the US (special events, limited hours, banks and many shops generally closed, limited public-transportation options, no rush hours). Rowdy evenings are rare on Sundays. Saturdays are virtually weekdays, with earlier closing hours and no rush hour (though transportation connections can be less frequent than on weekdays).

Be sure to mix intense and relaxed periods in your itinerary. To maximize rootedness, minimize one-night stands. Hotels are more likely to give a good price to someone staying more than one night. Every trip (and every traveler) needs at least a few slack days (for picnics, laundry, people-watching, and so on). Pace yourself. Assume you will return.

Reread this book as you travel, and visit local TIs. Upon arrival in a new town, lay the groundwork for a smooth departure; write down (or print out from an online source) the schedule for the train, bus, or boat you'll take when you depart. Drivers can study the best route to their next destination.

While traveling, take advantage of the Internet and phones to make your trip run smoothly. By going online (at Internet cafés or your accommodations) and using the phone (buy an insertable phone card or carry a mobile phone), you can get tourist information, learn the latest on sights (special events, tour schedules, etc.), book tickets and tours, make reservations, reconfirm hotels, research transportation connections, and keep in touch with loved ones.

Connect with the culture. Set up your own quest for the best bell tower, mountain vista, or scenic seafront perch. Enjoy the hospitality of the Croatians and Slovenes. Slow down and be open to unexpected experiences. Ask questions—most locals are eager to point you toward their idea of the right direction. Keep a notepad in your pocket for organizing your thoughts. Wear your money belt, and learn the local currency and how to estimate prices in dollars. Those who expect to travel smart, do.

Trip Costs

Croatia and Slovenia—while just under two decades removed from communism—are no longer Europe's bargain basement. Although local economies are struggling along with everyone else's due to the global crisis, the cost of living in Croatia and Slovenia has come close to their European neighbors. Things aren't exactly cheap here—but they're still more affordable than similar, better-established tourist countries, such as Italy or Switzerland. If you're careful to avoid inflated tourist-trap prices (by following my tips on where to stay and where to eat), a trip to this region can be a good value.

Five components make up your total trip cost: airfare, surface transportation, room and board, sightseeing and entertainment, and shopping and miscellany.

Airfare: A basic round-trip flight from the US to Ljubljana or Dubrovnik costs $1,400 to $1,900 (cheaper in winter), depending on where you fly from and when. Always consider saving time and money in Europe by flying "open jaw"—into one city and out of another. The additional cost of flying into Ljubljana and out of Dubrovnik is often cheaper than the added expense (and wasted time) of an overland return trip to Ljubljana.

Surface Transportation: For the two-week whirlwind trip described in this chapter, allow $150 per person for public transportation (train, bus, and boat tickets). Train travelers will probably save money by simply buying tickets along the way, rather than purchasing a railpass (see "Transportation," page 559). A basic car rental costs about $300 per week (including tolls, gas, and basic insurance). Long-term car rental is cheapest when arranged in advance from the US, but exorbitant fees for dropping off in a different country can make long-term car rental prohibitively expensive if you're going to both Croatia and Slovenia (see "Renting a Car," page 564).

Room and Board: You can thrive in Croatia and Slovenia on an average of $100 a day per person for room and board. A $100-a-day budget per person allows $15 for lunch, $25 for dinner, and $60 for lodging (based on two people splitting the cost of a $120 double room that includes breakfast). That's doable. Students and tightwads eat and sleep for $50 a day ($30 per hostel bed, $20 for groceries and snacks).

Sightseeing and Entertainment: Sightseeing is cheap here. Major sights generally cost $3–6. Figure $10–25 for splurge experiences (e.g., watching the *Moreška* sword dance in Korčula, or seeing Slovenia's Lipizzaner stallions). You can hire your own private guide for four hours for about $100–150—a good value when divided among two or more people. An overall average of $20 a day works for most people. Don't skimp here. After all, this category is the driving force behind your trip—you came to sightsee, enjoy, and experience Croatia and Slovenia. Fortunately for you, the region's best attractions—the sea, mountains, and sunshine—are free.

Shopping and Miscellany: Figure $2 per postcard, coffee, beer, and ice-cream cone. Shopping can vary in cost from nearly nothing to a small fortune. Good budget travelers find that this category has little to do with assembling a trip full of lifelong and wonderful memories.

When to Go

Tourist traffic in this part of Europe (especially the coastal towns) is extremely seasonal. The peak season hits suddenly and floods the towns like a tidal wave, only to recede a couple months later—leaving empty streets and dazed locals. In general, the tourist season runs roughly from May through September, reaching a peak in early August.

Peak Season: July and especially August are top season, when just about everything is likely to be open very long hours daily (occasionally closed for a midday siesta). It's also the busiest time of year—boats, buses, and budget accommodations are packed to the gills. Visiting Croatia in July or August is like spending spring break in Florida—fun, but miserably crowded and hot. Hotels charge top dollar, and you'll miss out on the "undiscovered" quality that pervades most of the region the rest of the year.

Shoulder Season: Early May through June and September through mid-October are shoulder season. Within this time span, late June and early September are nearly, but not quite, as crowded as peak season, but the rush subsides substantially in May and October. Shoulder season is my favorite time to visit—I enjoy the smaller crowds, milder weather, and ability to grab a room almost whenever and wherever I like.

Off-Season: Mid-October through early May are dead as a doornail. Many small coastal towns close down entirely, with only one hotel and one restaurant remaining open during the lean winter months, and most of the town's residents move to the interior to hibernate. Anything that's open keeps very limited hours (weekday mornings only). The weather can be cool and dreary, and night will draw the shades on your sightseeing before dinnertime. You may find the climate chart in the appendix helpful.

Seasonal Changes: Because of this region's extreme seasonality, specifics such as opening times and prices are especially flexible. It's not unusual for a hotel to charge six different rates for the same room, depending on the time of year. (A hotel recep-

Major Holidays and Weekends

Popular places are even busier on weekends, and holidays can bring many businesses to a grinding halt. Plan ahead and reserve your accommodations and transportation well in advance, especially for the month of August. Mark these dates in red on your travel calendar: Easter (April 4 in 2010, April 24 in 2011), Ascension Day (May 13 in 2010, June 2 in 2011), Whitsunday and Whitmonday (May 23–24 in 2010, June 12–13 in 2011), Christmas, December 26, and New Year's Day. Also check the list of holidays and festivals in the appendix.

tionist once showed me an entire book with literally hundreds of potential rates they could charge, based on room size, type, views, and season.) With every visit, I dutifully hike around these towns trying to pin down hours for tourist offices, travel agencies, and museums. And every time, they change. If you're here anytime outside of midsummer, don't rely on my hours—call a day or two ahead to double-check that the place you need (like a room-booking agency) will actually be open when you arrive.

Sightseeing Priorities

Depending on the length of your trip, here are my recommended priorities. Assuming you're traveling by public transportation, I've taken geographical proximity into account.

3 days:	Dubrovnik
5 days, add:	Mostar, Split
7 days, add:	Korčula or Hvar (for a relaxing island experience) or Montenegro's Bay of Kotor (for diverse culture/history)
9 days, add:	Lake Bled and the Julian Alps
10 days, add:	Plitvice Lakes
12 days, add:	Ljubljana, more time for Dalmatian islands
14 days, add:	Istria
16 days, add:	The Karst, Zagreb
18 days, add:	More mountains (Logarska Dolina) or coastal villages (Piran, Rab, Mljet)
21 days or more, add:	Ptuj, Opatija, and even more islands and coastal villages

The map on page 11 and the two-week itinerary on page 10 include all of the stops in the first 14 days.

As you plan your trip, don't underestimate the long distances. People tell me, "I've got four days, and I want to see Lake Bled and Dubrovnik"—not realizing they'll waste at least a full day connecting those two sights. If you have less than a week, consider focusing either on the Dalmatian Coast (plus Mostar and Montenegro)

Croatia and Slovenia:
Best Two-Week Trip by Car

Day	Plan	Sleep in
1	Arrive Ljubljana's airport and take a taxi to Lake Bled	Lake Bled
2	Relax at Lake Bled	Lake Bled
3	Pick up car, drive through Julian Alps, end in Ljubljana	Ljubljana
4	Ljubljana	Ljubljana
5	Drive through the Karst and Piran to Rovinj*	Rovinj
6	Tour Istria	Rovinj
7	Drive to Plitvice Lakes via Istria's hill towns	Plitvice
8	Hike the lakes, then drive to Split and drop car	Split
9	Split	Split
10	To Hvar or Korčula	Hvar/Korčula
11	Relax on Hvar or Korčula	Hvar/Korčula
12	To Dubrovnik	Dubrovnik
13	Dubrovnik	Dubrovnik
14	Rent a car to day-trip to Mostar or to Montenegro's Bay of Kotor	Dubrovnik

* To save the substantial extra cost of picking up your car in one country and then dropping it off in another (see page 564), come up with a strategy for turning in your rental car in Slovenia, then taking public transportation to Croatia, where you can pick up a different rental car for your Croatia time. For example, you could take the bus from Ljubljana or Portorož (near Piran) to Rovinj, then pick up a rental car in Pula; or take the train from Ljubljana to Zagreb or Rijeka, then pick up your rental car in one of those cities. It can be a bit of a puzzle to figure out, but it could save you plenty.

in the south, or on Slovenia and Istria (and maybe Venice) in the north. For more details, see "Getting to the Dalmatian Coast" on page 170.

Where Should I Go?

The perfect Croatian vacation is like a carefully refined recipe—a dash of this, a pinch of that, a slow simmer...and before long, you've got a delicious feast. Overwhelmed with options, people often ask me how to prioritize their time. Here's my tried-and-true recipe:

By Public Transportation

This itinerary can be done entirely by public transportation, with a few modifications. Skip the Julian Alps, and take the bus from Lake Bled to Ljubljana. Skip Istria; instead, take the train from Ljubljana to Zagreb, see that city, then take a bus to Plitvice. The bus connects Plitvice to Split, and from there, you'll continue down the Dalmatian Coast by boat or bus.

Even if you're using public transportation, seriously consider periodically renting a car for the day to see the Julian Alps, Istria, Mostar, or Montenegro's Bay of Kotor.

Begin with the biggies. Dubrovnik is a must, period. If you like big cities, Split is entertaining. Plitvice Lakes National Park, while difficult to reach, rarely disappoints.

Fold in one or two seafront villages. Croatian coastal towns are all variations on the same theme: A warm stone Old Town with a Venetian bell tower, a tidy boat-speckled harbor, ample seafood restaurants, a few hulking communist-era resort hotels on the edge of town, and *sobe* and *apartman* signs by every other doorbell. Of course, each town has its own personality and claims

Top 10 Small Coastal Towns

1. Rovinj (Croatia)
2. Korčula (Croatia)
3. Hvar (Croatia)
4. Piran (Slovenia)
5. Kotor (Montenegro)

6. Rab (Croatia)
7. Trogir (Croatia)
8. Perast (Montenegro)
9. Sveti Stefan (Montenegro)
10. Poreč (Croatia)

to fame (for a quick run-down of my favorites—including Rovinj, Hvar, Korčula, and Rab—see the "Croatia & Slovenia at a Glance" sidebar). Beach bums, sightseers, yachters, historians, partiers—everyone you'll talk to has their own favorite town. Don't trust this advice blindly. Try out a few and choose your own top town.

Sprinkle liberally with Slovenia. You won't regret splicing Slovenia into your itinerary. Its spectacular mountain scenery, colorful capital (Ljubljana), Germanic efficiency, and extremely friendly natives are a pleasant contrast to Croatia. In hindsight, many travelers wish they'd budgeted more time for Slovenia.

Add some spice. This is my secret ingredient. After you've been to one or two of the coastal resorts, you could head for another one…or you could use that time for something completely different. Some of these options are easy and convenient—the Roman ruins of Pula, the hilltop hamlets of the Istrian interior, the imported-Austrian-resort feel of Opatija. But my favorites involve crossing borders and broadening horizons: the city of Mostar, in Bosnia-Herzegovina; and Montenegro's spectacular Bay of Kotor. A year from now, you'll barely remember the difference between all those little seaside towns you toured. But you'll never forget the mosques of Mostar.

Know Before You Go

Your trip is more likely to go smoothly if you plan ahead. Check this list of things to arrange while you're still at home.

You need a **passport**—but no visa or shots—to travel in Croatia, Slovenia, Bosnia-Herzegovina, and Montenegro. You may be denied entry into certain European countries if your passport is due to expire within three to six months of your ticketed date of return. Get it renewed if you'll be cutting it close. It can take up to six weeks to get or renew a passport (for more on passports, see www.travel.state.gov). Pack a photocopy of your passport in your luggage in case the original is lost or stolen.

Book your rooms in advance if you'll be traveling during **peak season** (July and August), any major **holidays** and festivals (see page 575 of appendix), and definitely for your first night.

Call your **debit- and credit-card companies** to let them know the countries you'll be visiting so that they won't deny your international charges. Confirm your daily withdrawal limit; consider asking to have it raised so you can take out more cash at each ATM stop. Ask about international transaction fees.

If you're interested in **travel insurance,** do your homework before you buy. Compare the cost of the insurance to the likelihood of your using it and your potential loss if something goes wrong. For details on the many kinds of travel insurance, see www.ricksteves.com/plan/tips/insurance.htm.

If you're planning on **renting a car** in Croatia or Slovenia, bring your US driver's license. It's also recommended that you carry an International Driving Permit (IDP), available at your local AAA office ($15 plus two passport-type photos, www.aaa.com).

Because **airline carry-on restrictions** are always changing, visit the Transportation Security Administration's website (www.tsa.gov/travelers) for an up-to-date list of what you can bring on the plane with you...and what you have to check. Remember to arrive with plenty of time to get through security.

Croatia is known for its glimmering **beaches.** However, most are pebbly or rocky rather than sandy—and spiny sea urchins are not uncommon. In addition to your swimsuit, you may want to pack (or buy in Europe) a pair of water shoes for wading. Bring good sunscreen, and—if you'll be **hiking** on Croatia's many scenic coastal trails, which can be rugged and often lack shade—a sun hat and sturdy shoes.

Practicalities

Emergency Telephone Numbers: For medical or other emergencies, dial 112 in Croatia, Slovenia, and Montenegro; or 124 in Bosnia-Herzegovina. For police, dial 92 in Croatia, 113 in Slovenia, or 122 in Bosnia-Herzegovina and Montenegro.

Borders: Even though Croatia and Slovenia used to be part of the same country, you will have to stop and show your passport when you cross the border between them. Whether by car, train, or bus, you'll find that border crossings are generally a nonevent—flash your passport, maybe wait a few minutes, and move on. Now that Slovenia has joined the Schengen open-borders agreement, you don't have to stop or show a passport when crossing between

Where Do I Find Information On...?

Credit-Card Theft	See page 18.
Packing Light	See the packing list on page 579.
Phoning	See "Telephones" on page 552.
Language	See page 550.
Making Hotel Reservations	See page 28.
Tipping	See page 18.
Tourist Information Offices	See page 549.
Updates to This Book	See www.ricksteves.com /update

Slovenia and Austria, Italy, or Hungary. If you're crossing from Croatia into Bosnia-Herzegovina or Montenegro, you'll find the border crossing fairly straightforward, if occasionally a bit slow. (When entering Montenegro, you'll be required to pay a €10 "eco-tax" and must declare if you're carrying more than €2,000 in cash.) When you change countries, you change phone cards, postage stamps, and, in most cases, money.

Time: In Europe—and in this book—you'll use the 24-hour clock. It's the same through 12:00 noon, then keep going—13:00, 14:00, and so on. For anything after 12, subtract 12 and add p.m. (14:00 is 2:00 p.m.).

Croatia and Slovenia are generally six/nine hours ahead of the East/West Coasts of the US. The exceptions are the beginning and end of Daylight Saving Time: Europe "springs forward" the last Sunday in March (two weeks after most of North America) and "falls back" the last Sunday in October (one week before North America). For a handy online time converter, try www.timeanddate.com/worldclock.

Watt's Up? Europe's electrical system is different from North America's in two ways: the shape of the plug (two round prongs) and the voltage of the current (220 volts instead of 110 volts). For your North American plug to work in Europe, you'll need an adapter, sold inexpensively at travel stores in the US. As for the voltage, most newer electronics or travel appliances (such as hair dryers, laptops, and battery chargers) automatically convert the voltage—if you see a range of voltages printed on the item or its plug (such as "110–220"), it'll work in Europe. Otherwise, you can buy a converter separately in the US (about $20).

Discounts: While discounts are not listed in this book, youths (under 18) and students (with International Student Identity Cards, www.isic.org) often get discounts—but only by asking.

Business Hours: Particularly in seasonal resort areas along the coast, business hours can be very unpredictable—dictated entirely by demand. (I've tried to list hours throughout this book, but these are just rough guidelines.) A shop may be open daily from 9:00 to 24:00 in August, with its hours becoming progressively shorter in the shoulder season until it closes entirely in mid-October. In larger, less touristy cities and towns—and in most of Slovenia—hours are a bit more predictable (typically open Mon–Fri from around 8:00 or 9:00 until 17:00, Sat mornings from 8:00 or 9:00 until 12:00 or 13:00, and closed Sun); however, there's no clear and consistent set of hours from place to place. Both Croatia and Slovenia recently enacted, then modified or repealed, laws that compelled most shops to close entirely on Sundays; these days, you will find some (but not many) businesses open on Sundays, but generally only in touristy areas or at bus or train stations. If you have business or shopping chores to take care of, try to avoid doing them on Sunday.

Smoking Bans: Croatia recently enacted a smoking ban on indoor public spaces, including restaurants, cafés, and bars; however, within months the law was modified to permit smoking in larger establishments, provided they have adequate ventilation. Stay tuned to see how successfully this ban is enforced. Slovenia's smoking ban, which permits indoor smoking only in specially designated rooms, seems to be more successful.

News: Americans keep in touch in Europe with the *International Herald Tribune*, published almost daily throughout Europe and online at www.iht.com. Other newsy sites are http://news.bbc.co.uk and www.europeantimes.com. Every Tuesday, the European editions of *Time* and *Newsweek* hit the stands with articles of particular interest to travelers in Europe. Sports addicts can get their fix from *USA Today*. News in English will be sold only where there's enough demand: in big cities and tourist centers. Many hotels have CNN or BBC television channels available.

Money

This section offers advice on getting cash, using credit and debit cards, dealing with lost or stolen cards, and tipping.

Cash from ATMs

Throughout Europe, cash machines (ATMs) are the standard way for travelers to get local currency. Bring plastic—credit and/or debit cards. It's smart to bring two cards, in case one gets demagnetized or eaten by a temperamental machine. As an emergency backup, bring several hundred dollars in hard cash (in $20 bills rather than hard-to-exchange $100 bills). Don't use traveler's checks—they're a waste of time (long waits at slow banks) and a waste of money in fees.

Exchange Rates

Croatia and Slovenia use different currencies. For currency information on Bosnia-Herzegovina and Montenegro, see those chapters.

Croatia

Croatia still uses its traditional currency, the kuna (abbreviated kn locally, HRK internationally):

5 Croatian kunas (kn) = about $1

A kuna is broken into 100 smaller units, called lipas. There are coins of 1, 2, 5, 10, 20, and 50 lipas; and 1, 2, and 5 kunas. To roughly convert Croatian kunas into dollars, double the amount and drop the final zero (e.g., 5 kn = about $1; 70 kn = about $14; 200 kn = about $40).

Even though Croatia doesn't officially use the euro, many businesses (especially hotels) quote prices in euros for the convenience of their international guests. In some towns, most accommodations tend to list prices in euros; in others, it's in kunas; and in Dubrovnik, it's a pretty even mix of both. In order to make it easier for you to compare your options, in a few cases I've converted the rates they gave me into the other currency, so you might notice some variation between the actual prices and those listed in this book.

If you need to convert prices between kunas and euros (7 kunas = about €1), it's simple: just divide the kuna price by 7 to get euros, or multiply the euro price by 7 to get kunas.

Slovenia

Slovenia uses the euro currency:

1 euro (€) = about $1.40

Like dollars, one euro (€) is broken down into 100 cents. You'll find coins ranging from one cent to two euros, and bills from five euros to 500 euros. To convert prices in euros to dollars, add 40 percent: €20 is about $28, €45 is about $63, and so on.

So, that 50-kn bottle of Croatian wine is about $10, the €25 Slovenian feast is about $35, and the 300-kn taxi ride through Zagreb is...uh-oh.

You'll find cash machines (called *Bankomat* in Croatia and Slovenia) all over, always open and providing quick transactions. To withdraw money, you'll need a debit card—ideally with a Visa or MasterCard logo for maximum usability—plus a PIN (Personal Identification Number). Know your PIN code in numbers; there are only numbers—no letters—on European keypads.

Before you go, confirm with your bank that your card will work overseas, and alert them that you'll be making withdrawals in Europe; otherwise, the bank may not approve transactions if it perceives unusual spending patterns. (Your credit-card company may do the same thing—let them know about your travel plans, too.) Also ask about international transaction fees; see "Credit and Debit Cards," later.

When using a cash machine, try to take out large sums of money to reduce your per-transaction bank fees. If the machine refuses your request, try again and select a smaller amount (some cash machines limit the amount you can withdraw—don't take it personally). If that doesn't work, try a different machine.

Bank machines often dispense high-denomination bills, which can be difficult to break (especially at odd hours). My strategy: Request an odd amount of money from the ATM (such as 450 kn instead of 500 kn); or, if that doesn't work, go as soon as possible to a bank or a large store (such as a supermarket) to break the big bills.

Because Croatia and Slovenia have different currencies, you may wind up with leftover cash when you're leaving a country. Coins can't be exchanged once you leave the country, so try to spend them before you cross the border. But bills are easy to convert to the "new" country's currency. Regular banks have the best rates for changing currency. Post offices and train stations usually change money if you can't get to a bank.

To keep your cash safe, use a money belt—a pouch with a strap that you buckle around your waist like a belt, and wear under your clothes. Thieves target tourists. A money belt provides peace of mind, allowing you to carry lots of cash safely. Don't waste time every few days tracking down a cash machine—withdraw a week's worth of money, stuff it in your money belt, and travel!

Credit and Debit Cards

For purchases, Visa and MasterCard are more commonly accepted than American Express. Just like at home, credit or debit cards work easily at larger hotels, restaurants, and shops, but smaller businesses prefer payment in local currency. If receipts show your credit-card number, don't toss these thoughtlessly.

Fees: Credit- and debit-card transactions—whether used for purchases or ATM withdrawals—often charge additional, tacked-on "international transaction" fees of up to 3 percent plus $5 per transaction. Note that if you use a credit card for ATM transactions, it's technically a "cash advance" rather than a "withdrawal"—and subject to an additional cash-advance fee.

To avoid unpleasant surprises, call your bank or credit-card company before your trip to ask about these fees. Ask your bank if it has agreements with any Croatian or Slovenian banks for lower withdrawal fees. If the fees are too high, consider getting a card just for your trip: Capital One (www.capitalone.com) and most credit unions have low-to-no international transaction fees.

If merchants offer to convert your purchase price into dollars (called dynamic currency conversion, or "DCC"), refuse this "service." You'll pay even more in fees for the expensive convenience of seeing your charge in dollars.

Damage Control for Lost Cards

If you lose your credit, debit, or ATM card, you can stop people from using it by reporting the loss immediately to the respective global customer-assistance centers. Call these 24-hour US numbers collect: Visa (410/581-9994), MasterCard (636/722-7111), and American Express (623/492-8427).

At a minimum, you'll need to know the name of the financial institution that issued you the card, along with the type of card (classic, platinum, or whatever). Providing the following information will allow for a quicker cancellation of your missing card: full card number, whether you are the primary or secondary cardholder, the cardholder's name exactly as printed on the card, billing address, home phone number, circumstances of the loss or theft, and identification verification (your birth date, your mother's maiden name, or your Social Security number—memorize this, don't carry a copy). If you are the secondary cardholder, you'll also need to provide the primary cardholder's identification-verification details. You can generally receive a temporary card within two or three business days in Europe.

If you promptly report your card lost or stolen, you typically won't be responsible for any unauthorized transactions on your account, although many banks charge a liability fee of $50.

Tipping

A decade ago, tipping was unheard of in Croatia and Slovenia. But then came the tourists. Today, some waiters and taxi drivers are beginning to expect Yankee-sized tips when they spot an American. Tipping the appropriate amount—not feeling stingy, but also not contributing to the overtipping epidemic—is nerve-wracking to conscientious visitors. Relax! Many locals still don't tip at all, so any tip is appreciated. As in the US, the proper amount depends on your resources, tipping philosophy, and the circumstances, but some general guidelines apply.

Restaurants: Tipping is an issue only at restaurants that have table service. If you order your food at a counter, don't tip.

At restaurants that have a waitstaff, round up the bill 5–10 percent after a good meal. My rule of thumb is to estimate about 10 percent, then round down slightly to reach a convenient total (for a 70-kn meal, I pay 75 kn—a tip of 5 kn, or about 7 percent). A 15 percent tip is overly generous, verging on extravagant. At some tourist-oriented restaurants, a 10 or 15 percent "service charge" may be added to your bill, in which case an additional tip is not necessary. If you're not sure whether your bill includes the tip, just ask.

Taxis: To tip the cabbie, round up about 5 percent (for a 71-kn fare, pay 75 kn). If the cabbie hauls your bags and zips you to the airport to help you catch your flight, you might want to toss in a little more. But if you feel like you're being driven in circles or otherwise ripped off, skip the tip.

Special Services: Tour guides at public sites sometimes hold out their hands for tips after they give their spiels. If I've already paid for the tour, I don't tip extra unless they've really impressed me. At hotels, porters expect the local equivalent of 50 cents for each bag they carry (another reason to pack light). Leaving the maid a dollar's worth of local cash per overnight at the end of your stay is a nice touch. In general, if someone in the service industry does a super job for you, a small tip (the equivalent of a dollar or two) is appropriate...but not required.

When in doubt, ask: If you're not sure whether (or how much) to tip for a service, ask your hotelier or the TI; they'll fill you in on how it's done on their turf.

VAT Refunds for Shoppers

Wrapped into the purchase price of your souvenirs is a Value-Added Tax (VAT) of 23 percent in Croatia and 20 percent in Slovenia. You're entitled to get most of that tax back if you make a purchase of more than a certain amount (501 kn in Croatia, €50 in Slovenia) at a store that participates in the VAT refund scheme.

Getting your refund is usually straightforward and, if you buy a substantial amount of souvenirs, well worth the hassle. If you're lucky, the merchant will subtract the tax when you make your purchase. (This is more likely to occur if the store ships the goods to your home.) Otherwise, you'll need to:

Get the paperwork. Have the merchant completely fill out the necessary refund document, called a "cheque." You'll have to present your passport at the store.

Get your stamp at the border or airport. Process your cheque(s) at your last stop in the country with the customs agent who deals with VAT refunds. It's best to keep your purchases in your carry-on for viewing, but if they're too large or dangerous (such as knives) to carry on, track down the proper customs agent to inspect them before you check your bag. To qualify, your purchased goods should be unused. If you show up at customs wearing your Slovenian shoes, officials might look the other way—or deny you a refund.

Collect your refund. You'll need to return your stamped document to the retailer or its representative. Many merchants work with a service that has offices at major airports, ports, and border crossings, such as Global Refund (www.globalrefund.com) or Premier Tax Free (www.premiertaxfree.com). These services, which extract a 4 percent fee, usually can refund your money immediately in your currency of choice or credit your card (within two billing cycles). If the retailer handles VAT refunds directly, it's up to you to contact the merchant for your refund. You can mail the documents from home, or quicker, from your point of departure (using a stamped, addressed envelope you've prepared or one that's been provided by the merchant). You'll then have to wait—it could take months.

Customs for American Shoppers

You are allowed to take home $800 worth of items per person duty-free, once every 30 days. The next $1,000 is taxed at a flat 3 percent. After that, you pay the individual item's duty rate. You can also bring in duty-free a liter of alcohol (slightly more than a standard-size bottle of wine; you must be at least 21), 200 cigarettes, and up to 100 non-Cuban cigars. You may take home vacuum-packed cheeses; dried herbs, spices, or mushrooms; and canned fruits or vegetables, including jams and vegetable spreads. Baked goods, candy, chocolate, oil, vinegar, mustard, and honey are OK. Fresh fruits or vegetables are not. Meats, even if canned, are generally not allowed. Remember that you'll need to carefully pack any bottles of *vino, šnops,* or other liquid-containing items in your checked luggage, due to the three-ounce limit on liquids in carry-on baggage. To check customs rules and duty rates before you go, visit www.cbp.gov, and click on "Travel," then "Know Before You Go."

Sightseeing

Sightseeing can be hard work. Use these tips to make your visits to Croatia's and Slovenia's finest sights meaningful, fun, efficient, and painless.

Plan Ahead

Set up an itinerary that allows you to fit in all your must-see sights. Most sights keep stable hours in the summer months, but hours tend to fluctuate in the winter. If you have your heart set on visiting particular sights, it's always smart to confirm the latest hours by checking their websites or asking at the local TI.

When possible, visit major sights first thing (when your energy is best) and save other activities for the afternoon. Hit the highlights first, then go back to other things if you have the stamina and time.

Study up. To get the most out of the self-guided walks and sight descriptions in this book, read them before your visit.

At Sights

Here's what you can typically expect:

At **churches**—which often offer interesting art (usually free) and a welcome seat—a modest dress code (no bare shoulders or shorts) is encouraged, but rarely enforced.

Major **museums** and sights require you to check daypacks and coats. They'll be kept safely. If you have something you can't bear to part with, stash it in a pocket or purse. To avoid checking a small backpack, carry it under your arm like a purse as you enter. From a guard's point of view, a backpack is generally a problem, while a purse is not.

Photography is sometimes banned at major sights. Look for signs or ask. If cameras are allowed, flashes or tripods usually are not. Flashes damage oil paintings and distract others in the room. Even without a flash, a handheld camera will take a decent picture (or buy postcards or posters at the museum bookstore). If photos are permitted, video cameras generally are, too.

A few sights rent **audioguides** offering recorded descriptions in English, but they're rarely worth the cost (about $6–8). If you bring along your own pair of headphones and a Y-jack, you can sometimes share one audioguide with your travel partner and save money.

Some sights have **videos** about the attraction. These are generally worth your time. I make it standard operating procedure to ask when I arrive at a sight if there is a video in English.

The WCs at many sights are free and clean. Many places sell postcards that highlight their attractions. Before you leave, scan the postcards and thumb through the biggest guidebook (or skim its index) to be sure you haven't overlooked something that you'd like to see.

Most sights stop admitting people 30–60 minutes before **closing time,** and some rooms close early (often 45 minutes before the actual closing time). Guards usher people out, so don't save the best for last.

Every sight or museum offers more than what is covered in this book. Use the information in this book as an introduction—not the final word.

Sleeping

The accommodations scene in Croatia and Slovenia is quirky and complicated. You have two basic choices: either a big hotel

or what locals call "private accommodations"—a rented apartment *(apartman)* or a room in a private home *(soba,* pronounced SOH-bah; plural *sobe,* SOH-bay). I've explained the ins and outs of each in this section.

I look for places that are friendly, comfortable, professional-feeling, centrally located, English-speaking, and family-run. I'm more impressed by a handy location and a fun-loving philosophy than hair dryers and shoeshine machines. I also like local character and simple facilities that don't cater to American "needs." Obviously, a place meeting every criterion is unusual, and all of my recommendations fall short of perfection—sometimes miserably. But I've listed the best values for each price category. My favorites are small, family-run hotels (which are rare) and friendly local people who rent "hotelesque" private rooms without a reception desk (which are, thankfully, abundant).

In Croatia, most hotels are outrageously expensive, but private accommodations are an excellent value. My recommendations range from $15 bunks to $300-plus splurges, but most cluster around the same price range: For a well-located standard double room in peak season on the Croatian coast, plan on spending $125–200 in a big resort hotel; $60–110 in a small hotel or a "hotelesque" private room or apartment (with

Sleep Code

To help you sort easily through the listings, I've divided the rooms into three categories based on the price for a standard double room with bath:

$$$ **Higher Priced**
$$ **Moderately Priced**
$ **Lower Priced**

Prices listed in this book are per room, not per person. Hotels usually accept credit cards and include a buffet breakfast (unless otherwise noted); private accommodations rarely do either. Virtually all of my recommended accommodations are run by people who speak English; if they don't, I mention it in the listing.

When there is a range of prices in one category, that means the prices fluctuate with the season; the prices and seasons are posted at or near the hotel desk. To give maximum information in a minimum of space, I use the following code to describe the accommodations.

S = Single room (or price for one person in a double).

D = Double or twin. Double beds are usually big enough for nonromantic couples.

T = Triple (often a double bed with a single).

Q = Quad (usually two double beds).

b = Private bathroom with toilet and shower or tub.

s = Private shower or tub only (the toilet is down the hall).

According to this code, a couple staying at a "Db-480 kn, cash only" place in Dubrovnik would pay a total of 480 Croatian kunas (about $96) for a double room with a private bathroom. Credit cards are not accepted, but you can assume the staff speaks English.

If I mention "Internet access" in a listing, there's a public terminal in the lobby for guests to use. If I specify "Wi-Fi" or "cable Internet," you can generally access it in your room (usually for free), but only if you have your own laptop.

your own bathroom, TV, and other amenities); or $45–65 for a more basic private room with a shared bathroom.

Slovenia has a wider range of affordable small hotels (about $90–120 in Ljubljana, and $70–90 in small towns and the countryside), which make private accommodations a lesser value there.

Remember that some Croatian accommodations quote their rates in euros, while others use kunas. Regardless of how they quote their rates, when you check out, they generally expect payment in kunas (or by credit card).

At either type of accommodation, rates vary wildly by season, with August being the most expensive. Also at both types, short stays (of less than three nights) are discouraged, especially in peak season. Expect to pay 20–50 percent extra if you're staying just one or two nights, and don't be surprised if some places have a multi-night minimum in summer. But if you can fill a gap in their reservations schedule, they might be willing to waive this surcharge.

Three or four people can save money by requesting one big room. Traveling alone can be expensive: A single room is often only 20 percent cheaper than a double.

Discos and nightclubs are proliferating in the old town centers of many cities in this book—including Dubrovnik, Split, and Ljubljana. I've noted the specific hotels that suffer the worst noise. If you're a light sleeper, make a point of requesting a quiet room.

Perhaps because they tend to be located in musty old stone buildings, many hotels and *sobe* in Croatia use heavily perfumed air fresheners in their rooms. It's usually easy to locate and unplug these when you arrive, but if you are very sensitive to fragrances, you can try asking your *sobe* host to remove them before you arrive.

Window screens are rare in this area, so in warm weather be prepared to share your room with mosquitoes and other bugs.

In Slovenia, a recent smoking ban forced many accommodations to become non-smoking, though some larger hotels have designated smoking rooms. Croatia's new smoking ban is still in flux and often not enforced. For this reason, be very specific and assertive if you need a room that's strictly non-smoking.

If there seems to be no hot water, try flipping the switch with a picture of a water tank, usually next to the light switch. In many *sobe,* the hot-water tank is tiny—about big enough for one American-length shower. So two people traveling together may want to practice the "navy shower" method (douse yourself, turn off water, soap up, then turn water back on for a quick rinse)...or the second one may be in for a chilly surprise. The incredibly high water pressure in most Croatian showers just makes the hot water go that much faster (turn the faucet on only partway to help stretch the precious hot water).

For environmental reasons, towels are often replaced in hotels only when you leave them on the floor. In private accommodations and some cheap hotels, they aren't replaced at all, so hang them up to dry and reuse. The cord that dangles over the tub or shower in big resort hotels is not a clothesline—you pull it if you've fallen and can't get up.

Before accepting a room, confirm your understanding of the complete price (including, for example, surcharges for short stays). Pay your bill the evening before you leave to avoid the time-wasting crowd at the reception desk in the morning, especially if you need to rush off to catch your boat. The only tip my recommended accommodations would like is a friendly, easygoing guest. And, as always, I appreciate feedback on your experiences.

Types of Accommodations
Private Accommodations (*Sobe* and Apartments)
Private accommodations offer travelers a characteristic and money-saving alternative for a fraction of the price of a hotel. You have two options: a *soba* (room; plural *sobe,* SOH-bay) or *apartman* (apartment).

Often run by empty-nesters, private accommodations are similar to British bed-and-breakfasts...minus the breakfast (ask your host about the best nearby breakfast spot). Generally the more you pay, the more privacy and amenities you get: private bathroom, TV, air-conditioning, kitchenette, and so on. The simplest *sobe* allow you to experience Croatia on the cheap, at nearly youth-hostel prices, while giving you a great opportunity to connect with a local family. The fanciest *sobe* are downright swanky and offer near-hotel anonymity. Apartments are bigger and cost more than *sobe,* but they're still far cheaper than hotels.

Registered *sobe* are rated by the government using a system that assigns stars based on amenities. Three or more stars means that you'll have your own bathroom, two stars means that the bathroom's down the hall, and one star is rock-bottom basic. If you don't like the idea of sharing a toilet with strangers, look for three stars and you'll do fine. (Apartments always have private bathrooms, plus modest kitchen facilities.) Many, but not all, three-star *sobe* also have TV and air-conditioning (but usually no telephone). The prices for private accommodations generally fluctuate with the seasons, and remember that stays of fewer than three nights usually come with a 20–50 percent surcharge (though this is often waived outside of peak season).

You can reserve most *sobe* in advance by email or by phone. In fact, since the best-value *sobe* deservedly book up early, reser-

vations are highly recommended. But keep in mind that holding you a room represents a major financial risk for your host, who loses money if you don't show up. For this reason, some hosts may ask for your credit-card number to secure the reservation. (They'll generally ask for payment in cash when you're there; your credit card won't be charged, and is used only as a convenience to secure your reservation.) Other hosts might ask you to wire or mail money to them as a deposit. Because wiring money can come with substantial fees—which you (rather than the *sobe* host) will incur—it usually works better to mail them a check or travelers check. Ask your *sobe* host which options they accept. If their request seems too complicated for you, reserve elsewhere.

Sobe hucksters who accost you on the street can be very aggressive about luring travelers away from their reserved rooms. But if you've already booked a room at a particular place, you owe it to them to show up.

If you like to travel spontaneously, during most of the year you'll have no problem finding *sobe* as you go (though August can be extremely crowded). Locals hawking rooms meet each arriving boat, bus, and train. Many of these *sobe* have not been classified by the government, but they can sometimes turn out to be a good deal. The person generally shows photos of her place, you haggle for a price, then she escorts you to your new home. Be sure you understand exactly where it's located (i.e., within easy walking distance of the attractions) before you accept—ask to see the location on a map, and find out how long it takes to walk into town.

You can also keep an eye out for rooms as you walk or drive through town—you'll see blue *sobe* and *apartman* signs everywhere. It's actually fun to visit a few homes and make a deal. While it takes nerve to just show up without a room, this is standard operating procedure for backpackers.

As a last resort, you can enlist the help of a travel agency to find you a room—but you'll pay 10–30 percent extra (various agencies are listed in this book; to search from home, try www.dubrovnikapartment source.com for Dubrovnik, or www.adriatica.net for all of Croatia).

I'm accustomed to staying in hotels. But a few years ago, I found all of the hotels in Dubrovnik booked up. With some trepidation, I stayed in a *soba*...and I'll never go back to a Croatian resort hotel again. I've made it my mission to convince you to sleep in *sobe,* too.

Note that *sobe* aren't as common or as much of a good value in Slovenia, but the Slovenes have their own cheap option: tourist farms *(turistične kmetije)*. At these working farms, you can get a hotelesque room, plus breakfast and dinner, for a surprisingly low cost. For more on tourist farms, see page 488.

Hotels

For most travelers, Croatian hotels are a bad value. You basically have two options: Over-the-top, fancy, overpriced splurge hotels catering to the international jet set crowd; or run-down, communist-era, overpriced resort hotels desperate for a renovation. Whether old or new, Croatian hotels all seem to carry on the old Yugoslav aesthetic of mass tourism: crowded "beach" access (often on a concrete pad), typically surly staff, a travel-agency desk selling excursions in the lobby, corny live music in the lobby a few nights each week, and a seaview apéritif bar. More money buys you a friendlier, more polished staff and newer decor. These hotels are just fine with the busloads of European tourists who head south for a week-long summer holiday. But Americans are appalled at how much you have to spend for such low quality.

Fortunately, *sobe* and apartments are stepping up to fill the mid-budget accommodations void. Another promising development is that a handful of new, smaller, family-run hotels are opening around Croatia. These are usually much more reasonably priced than the big resorts—and friendlier, to boot. I've listed my favorites. Note that the fine line that separates small, family-run guest houses and top-end *sobe* can be blurry.

The hotel situation is more straightforward in Slovenia, which has a wider range of small, reasonably priced hotels. While you will find some hulking, overpriced, communist-era holdover hotels in resorty parts of Slovenia, they don't dominate the scene as they do in Croatia.

Hostels

For $25–35 a night, travelers of any age can stay at a youth hostel. While official IYHF hostels admit nonmembers for an extra fee, it can be easier to join the club and buy a youth hostel card before you go (call Hostelling International at US tel. 202/783-6161 or order online at www.hiayh.org). However, to increase your options, consider the many independent hostels that don't require a membership card.

Throughout Croatia, hostels are a relatively new concept. Usually official IYHF hostels are poorly located, in bad repair, and institutional, while independent hostels are loosely run, tend to attract a youthful party crowd, and are a bit grungier than the European norm. If you need a cheap bed and aren't into the party scene, you'll probably do better for only a little more money by sleeping in basic private accommodations (rooms in private homes with shared bathrooms, described earlier).

Slovenia has a more appealing range of hostels. For example, the official hostel at Lake Bled (Penzion Bledec, described on page 455) is particularly well-run. And one of Europe's most innovative hostels is Ljubljana's Celica, a renovated former prison (see page 429).

In each town, I've tried to list the best-established, most reputable hostel options, both independent and official. But this scene is evolving so fast that avid hostelers will do better getting tips from fellow travelers and searching on sites such as www.hostels.com, www.hostelworld.com, www.hostelz.com, and www.hostelseurope.com.

At any hostel, cheap meals are sometimes available, and kitchen facilities are usually provided for do-it-yourselfers. Expect crowds in the summer, snoring, and lots of noisy backpacker bonding in the common room while you're trying to sleep. Hosteling is ideal for those traveling single: Prices are per bed, not per room, and you'll have an instant circle of friends. At most hostels, you can reserve online or by phoning ahead (usually with a credit card).

Phoning

To make international calls to line up hotel reservations, you'll need to know the country codes. For detailed instructions on telephoning, see page 552 in the appendix.

Making Reservations

It's possible to travel most of the year without reservations, especially if you arrive early in the day (however, popular tourist towns can be completely full in August). But given the erratic accommodations values and the quality of the places I've found for this book, I'd highly recommend that you reserve your rooms in advance. Book several weeks ahead, or as soon as you've pinned down your travel dates. Note that some holidays jam things up and merit your making reservations far in advance (see "Major Holidays and Weekends" sidebar on page 9). Just like at home, holidays that fall on a Monday, Thursday, or Friday can turn the weekend into a long holiday, so book the entire weekend well in advance.

Because my favorite accommodations tend to be small-time entrepreneurs renting only a few rooms, they book up fast with my readers. I've tried to list several good options, so if your first choice is full, you can simply try others on the list. Sometimes one of my listings might offer to find you somewhere else to stay. This is convenient, and these alternatives can be just as good as the ones I've listed, but don't feel obligated—you'll have more control over your options if you book direct, using my recommendations.

Requesting a Reservation: To reserve, contact hotels and *sobe* directly by email, phone, or fax. Email is the clearest and most economical way to make a reservation. Or you can go straight to the hotel website; many hotels have secure online reservation forms and can instantly inform you of availability and any special deals. But be sure you use the hotel's official site and not a booking agency's site—otherwise you may pay higher rates than you should. If you're phoning from the US, be mindful of time zones (see page

14). Most recommended accommodations are accustomed to guests who speak only English.

Your hotelier or *sobe* host wants to know these key pieces of information (also included in the sample request form on page 580):

- number and type of rooms
- number of nights
- date of arrival
- date of departure
- any special needs (e.g., bathroom in the room or down the hall, twin beds vs. double bed, air-conditioning, quiet, view, ground floor, etc.)

When you request a room in writing for a certain time period, use the European style for writing dates: day/month/year. Hoteliers need to know your arrival and departure dates. For example, for a two-night stay in July I would request: "1 double room for 2 nights, arrive 16/07/11, depart 18/07/11." (Consider in advance how long you'll stay; don't just assume you can tack on extra days once you arrive.)

If you don't get a reply to your email or fax, it usually means the place is already fully booked (but you can try sending the message again, or call to follow up).

Confirming a Reservation: If the hotel's response tells you its room availability and rates, it's not a confirmation. You must tell them that you want that room at the given rate. Many hoteliers will request your credit-card number for a one-night deposit to hold the room. While you can email your credit-card information (I do), it's safer to share that personal info via phone call, fax, two successive emails, or secure online reservation form (if the hotel has one on its website).

Canceling a Reservation: If you must cancel your reservation, it's courteous to do so with as much advance notice as possible—at least three days. Simply make a quick phone call or send an email. Family-run hotels and *sobe* hosts lose money if they turn away customers while holding a room for someone who doesn't show up. Understandably, many hoteliers bill no-shows for one night.

Hotels sometimes have strict cancellation policies: For example, you might lose a deposit if you cancel within two weeks of your reserved stay, or you might be billed for the entire visit if you leave early. Ask about cancellation policies before you book.

If canceling via email, request confirmation that your cancellation was received to avoid being accidentally billed.

Reconfirm Your Reservation: Always call to reconfirm your room reservation a day or two in advance from the road. Smaller hotels and *sobe* appreciate knowing your estimated time of arrival. At any accommodation, let them know if you'll be arriving after 16:00. On the small chance that a hotel loses track of your reservation, bring along a hard copy of their emailed or faxed confirmation.

Reserving Rooms as You Travel: If you enjoy having a fluid itinerary, you can make reservations as you travel, calling hotels or *sobe* a few days to a week before your visit. If you prefer the flexibility of traveling without any reservations at all, you'll have greater success snaring rooms if you arrive at your destination early in the day. When you anticipate crowds (weekends are worst), call hotels at about 9:00 on the day you plan to arrive, when the hotel clerk knows who'll be checking out and just which rooms will be available. If you encounter a language barrier, ask the fluent receptionist at your current hotel to call for you.

Eating

Croatia and Slovenia offer good food for reasonable prices—especially if you venture off the main tourist trail. This is affordable sightseeing for your palate.

While not exactly high cuisine, the food of this region is surprisingly diverse. Choosing between strudel and baklava on the same menu, you're constantly reminded that this is a land where East meets West. I've listed the specific specialties in each country introduction, but throughout Croatia and Slovenia you'll sink your teeth into lots of tasty Italian-style food (pizzas and pastas), as well as seafood and fine local wines. You'll also find some

pan-Balkan elements that distinguish the cuisine throughout the former Yugoslavia (see sidebar).

At fish restaurants, seafood is often priced by weight—either

by kilogram or by hectogram (100 grams, or one-tenth of a kilogram). A one-kilogram portion feeds two hungry people or three light eaters. When I list price ranges for main dishes at restaurants, I don't include the super-top-end seafood splurges (such as lobster). For more tips on ordering seafood here, see "Croatian Food" on page 48.

While bread, cover, and service charges haven't traditionally been applied in these countries, a few tourist-oriented restaurants have started to pad their bills with these extra fees. If you're concerned about this, ask up front.

Balkan Flavors

All of the countries of the Balkan Peninsula—basically from Slovenia to Greece—have several foods in common. The Ottomans from today's Turkey, who controlled much of this territory for centuries, imported some goodies that remained standard fare here long after they left town. Whether you're in Slovenia, Croatia, Bosnia-Herzegovina, Montenegro, Serbia, Kosovo, or Albania, here are some local tastes worth seeking out.

A popular, cheap fast food you'll see everywhere is *burek* (BOO-rehk)—phyllo dough filled with meat, cheese, spinach, or apples. The more familiar *baklava* is phyllo dough layered with honey and nuts.

Grilled meats are a staple of Balkan cuisine. You'll most often see *čevapčići* (cheh-VAHP-chee-chee), or simply *čevap* (cheh-VAHP)—minced meat formed into a sausage-link shape, then grilled; and *ražnjići* (RAZH-nyee-chee)—small pieces of steak on a skewer, like a shish kebab. Sometimes you'll come across *pljeskavica* (plehs-kah-VEET-suh)—similar to *čevapčići*, except the meat is in the form of a hamburger-like patty.

While Balkan cuisine favors meat, a nice veggie complement is *duveđ* (JOO-vedge)—a spicy mix of stewed vegetables, flavored with tomatoes and peppers.

And you just can't eat any of this stuff without the ever-present condiment *ajvar* (EYE-var). Made from red bell pepper and eggplant, *ajvar* is like ketchup with a kick. Many Americans pack a jar of this distinctive, flavorful sauce to remember the flavors of the Balkans when they get back home. And these days, you can often find it at specialty grocery stores in the US (look for "eggplant/red pepper spread").

When restaurant-hunting, choose a spot filled with locals, not the place with the big neon signs boasting, "We Speak English and Accept Credit Cards." Venturing even a block or two off the main drag leads to local, higher-quality food for less than half the price of the tourist-oriented places. Most restaurants tack a menu onto their door for browsers and have an English menu inside. Only a rude waiter will rush you. Good service is relaxed (slow to an American).

When you're in the mood for something halfway between a restaurant and a picnic meal, look for bakeries selling *burek* (the savory phyllo-dough pastry) and other goodies, or shops advertising "pizza cut" (pizza by the slice). Many grocery stores sell pre-made sandwiches, and others might be willing to make one for you from what's in the deli case.

Traveling as a Temporary Local

We travel all the way to Europe to enjoy differences—to become temporary locals. You'll experience frustrations. Certain truths that we find "God-given" or "self-evident," such as cold beer, ice in drinks, bottomless cups of coffee, hot showers, cigarette smoke being irritating, and bigger being better, are suddenly not so true. One of the benefits of travel is the eye-opening realization that there are logical, civil, and even better alternatives.

Americans are enjoying a surge in popularity these days. But if there is a negative aspect to the image Europeans have of Americans, it's that we are big, loud, aggressive, impolite, rich, superficially friendly, and a bit naive.

Americans tend to be noisy in public places, such as restaurants and trains. My European friends place a high value on speaking quietly in these same places. Listen while on the bus or in a restaurant—the place can be packed, but the decibel level is low. Try to remember this nuance, and soften your speaking voice as a way of respecting their culture.

Meanwhile, most Americans traveling in this region find Slovenes to be extremely gregarious, but tend to be disappointed with the brusqueness of many Croatians they encounter. While tourism is big in Croatia, the finer points of service and hospitality sometimes get lost. Before losing your patience (as I often do), try to remember that these people lived under a communist regime 20 years ago, weathered a devastating war 15 years ago, and today are coping with an unprecedented tourist crush. They're scrambling to keep up.

While Europeans look bemusedly at some of our Yankee excesses—and worriedly at others—they nearly always afford us individual travelers all the warmth we deserve.

Judging from all the happy feedback I receive from travelers who have used this book, it's safe to assume you'll enjoy a great, affordable vacation—with the finesse of an independent, experienced traveler.

Thanks, and *sretan put*—happy travels!

How Was Your Trip?

Were your travels fun, smooth, and meaningful? If you'd like to share your tips, concerns, and discoveries, please fill out the survey at www.ricksteves.com/feedback. I value your feedback. Thanks in advance—it helps a lot.

Back Door Travel Philosophy
From *Rick Steves' Europe Through the Back Door*

Travel is intensified living—maximum thrills per minute and one of the last great sources of legal adventure. Travel is freedom. It's recess, and we need it.

Experiencing the real Europe requires catching it by surprise, going casual..."Through the Back Door."

Affording travel is a matter of priorities. (Make do with the old car.) You can eat and sleep—simply, safely, and enjoyably—anywhere in Europe for $120 a day plus transportation costs. In many ways, spending more money only builds a thicker wall between you and what you traveled so far to see. Europe is a cultural carnival, and time after time, you'll find that its best acts are free and the best seats are the cheap ones.

A tight budget forces you to travel close to the ground, meeting and communicating with the people. Never sacrifice sleep, nutrition, safety, or cleanliness to save money. Simply enjoy the local-style alternatives to expensive hotels and restaurants.

Connecting with people carbonates your experience. Extroverts have more fun. If your trip is low on magic moments, kick yourself and make things happen. If you don't enjoy a place, maybe you don't know enough about it. Seek the truth. Recognize tourist traps. Give a culture the benefit of your open mind. See things as different, but not better or worse. Any culture has plenty to share.

Of course, travel, like the world, is a series of hills and valleys. Be fanatically positive and militantly optimistic. If something's not to your liking, change your liking.

Travel can make you a happier American, as well as a citizen of the world. Our Earth is home to six and a half billion equally precious people. It's humbling to travel and find that other people don't have the "American Dream"—they have their own dreams. Europeans like us, but with all due respect, they wouldn't trade passports.

Thoughtful travel engages us with the world. In tough economic times, it reminds us what is truly important. By broadening perspectives, travel teaches new ways to measure quality of life.

Globetrotting destroys ethnocentricity, helping us understand and appreciate other cultures. Rather than fear the diversity on this planet, celebrate it. Among your most prized souvenirs will be the strands of different cultures you choose to knit into your own character. The world is a cultural yarn shop, and Back Door travelers are weaving the ultimate tapestry. Join in!

CROATIA

CROATIA

Hrvatska

Sunny beaches, succulent seafood, and a taste of *la dolce vita*...in Eastern Europe?

With thousands of miles of seafront and more than a thousand islands, Croatia's coastline is Eastern Europe's Riviera. Holidaymakers love its pebbly beaches, predictably balmy summer weather, and melt-in-your-mouth seafood. Croatia is also historic. From ruined Roman arenas and Byzantine mosaics to Venetian bell towers, Habsburg villas, and even communist concrete, past rulers have left their mark.

Croatia feels more Mediterranean than "Eastern European." Historically, Croatia has more in common with Venice and Rome than Vienna or Budapest. Especially on the coast, it's sometimes difficult to distinguish this lively, chaotic place from Italy. If you've become accustomed to the Germanic efficiency of Slovenia, Croatia's relaxed and unpredictable style can come as a shock.

Aside from its fun-in-the-sun status, Croatia is also known as one of the sites, just over a decade and a half ago, of the most violent European war in generations. Thankfully, the bloodshed is in the past. While a trip to Croatia offers thoughtful travelers the opportunity to understand a complicated chapter of recent history, most visitors focus instead on its substantial natural wonders: mountains, waterfalls, sun, sand, and sea.

Croatia's 3,600 miles of coastline—its main draw for visitors—is loosely divided into three regions. Most people flock to the Dalmatian Coast, in the south—where dramatic limestone cliffs rise from the deep and islands are scattered just offshore (the most appealing are Hvar and Korčula). Here you'll find Croatia's top tourist town, Dubrovnik, and the big city of Split, with its impressive Roman ruins. Way up at the northern corner of the country is the wedge-shaped peninsula called Istria, which has

Croatia

100 Kilometers
100 Miles

AUSTRIA

Drava · Maribor   HUNGARY   *Danube*

Bled · Ptuj   · Pécs
Ljubljana · Varaždin   SERBIA

ITALY   SLOVENIA   **Zagreb**   Osijek·
· Samobor   S L A V O N I A   Vukovar·
Trieste·   *Sava*
Piran·   · Karlovac
· Opatija · Rijeka   Slunj·
Motovun   Krk · Senj   ■ Plitvice Lakes   BOSNIA-
Poreč·   **ISTRIA**   National Park   HERZEGOVINA
Rovinj· Pula   Cres   Otočac
· **Rab**   · Sarajevo
Brijuni   *Pag*
Islands   Knin·
· Zadar
Dugi   · Šibenik
Otok   · Trogir **Split**   **Mostar**
· Makarska   · Medugorje   MONTE-
Hvar· Hvar   ■   Neum   NEGRO
Korčula   Ploče   · Trebinje **Kotor**
Korčula   Ston·   Mljet
Dubrovnik   · Cetinje
ITALY   *Bay of*   Budva·
Kotor   Sveti
Stefan

Adriatic
DALMATIAN COAST
Sea

less dramatic scenery but arguably even more romantic towns—including my favorite, the Venetian-flavored Rovinj—along with the city of Pula (more great Roman ruins) and a hilly interior blanketed with vineyards and topped with hill towns (Motovun is the

best). Wedged between Dalmatia and Istria is the Kvarner Gulf, a windy, arid no-man's-land that has few worthwhile attractions, but a few fine islands offshore (including Rab).

Enjoy the coast, but don't ignore the interior. The bustling capital of Zagreb is urban, engaging, and full of great museums. And Croatia's single best natural wonder (in this country that's so full of them) are the stunning waterfalls at Plitvice Lakes National Park.

If you want to blow through a lot of money here, you can. Croatian hotels, especially on the coast, are a terrible value, and there are plenty of touristy restaurants happy to overcharge you.

But if you know where to look, you can find some wonderful budget alternatives—foremost among them *sobe* (rooms in private homes). *Sobe* are a comfortable compromise: new-feeling, fresh, hotelesque doubles with a private bathroom and TV, for half the cost of a moldy room in a crumbling resort hotel just down the beach (for details, see page 25).

Europeans are reverent sun-worshippers, and on sunny days, virtually every square inch of coastal Croatia is occupied by a sunbather on a beach towel. Nude beaches are a big deal, especially for vacationing Germans and Austrians. If you want to work on an all-around tan, seek out a beach marked *FKK* (from the German *Freikörper Kultur,* or "free body culture"). First-timers get comfortable in a hurry, finding they're not the only pink novices on the rocks. But don't get too excited—these beaches are most beloved by people you'd rather see with their clothes on.

Perhaps because sunshine is so important to the economy, Croatians often seem particularly affected by weather. They complain that the once-predictable climate has become erratic, with surprise rainy spells or heat waves in the once perfectly consistent, balmy summer months. Historically, the Dubrovnik senate was legally forbidden from making any major decision if the hot, humid Jugo wind was blowing, as that wind tended to make people cranky and ill-tempered. And today, the weather report includes a *biometeorološka prognoza* that indicates how the day's weather will affect your mood. Weather maps come with smiley or frowny faces, and forecasts predict, "People will be tired in the afternoon and not feel like working." Hmm...good excuse.

Every Croatian coastal town has two parts: The time-warp old town, and the obnoxious resort sprawl. Main drags are clogged with gift shops selling shell sculptures and tasteless T-shirts. While European visitors enjoy this tacky-trinket tourism, Americans are generally more interested in Old World charm. Fortunately, it's relatively easy to ignore the touristy scene and instead poke your way into twisty old medieval lanes, draped with drying laundry and populated by gossiping housewives, humble fishermen's taverns, and soccer-playing kids.

Croatian popular music, the mariachi music of Europe, is the ever-present soundtrack of a Dalmatian vacation. Oliver Dragojević—singing soulful Mediterranean ballads with his gravelly, passionate voice—is the Croatian Tom Jones. Known simply as "Oliver," this beloved crooner gets airplay across Europe and has spawned many imitators (such as the almost-as-popular Gibonni).

More traditional is the hauntingly beautiful *klapa* music—men's voices harmonizing a cappella, like barbershop with a sooth-ing Adriatic flavor. Typically the leader begins the song, and the rest of the group (usually 3 to 12 singers) follow behind him with a slight delay. You'll see mariachi-style *klapa* groups performing in touristy areas; a CD of one of these performances (or of a professional group—Cambi is great) is a fun souvenir.

Croatia may be Europe's second most ardently Catholic country (after Poland). Under communism, religion was downplayed and many people gave up the habit of attending Mass (or mosque) regularly. But as the wars raged in the early 1990s, many Croatians rediscovered their religion. You may be surprised by how many people you see worshipping in Croatia's churches today.

In the Yugoslav era, Croatia was flooded with tourists—both European and American—who fell in love with its achingly beautiful beaches and coves. In its heyday, Croatia hosted about 10 million visitors a year, who provided the country with about a third of its income. But then, for several years after the war, Croatia floundered. Just a decade ago, the streets of Dubrovnik were empty, lined with souvenir shops tended by desperate-looking vendors. But in the last few years, locals are breathing a sigh of relief as the number of visitors returns to pre-war highs. With astonishing speed, Croatia is becoming one of Europe's top destinations.

Even so, the standards for service (at restaurants, hotels, and so on) are lower than you might expect. While you'll meet plenty of wonderfully big-hearted Croatians, many of my readers have characterized the Croatian waiters or hotel receptionists they've encountered as "rude." Be prepared for two universal gestures: the classic eye-roll, directed at anyone asking someone to do something that's not precisely in their job description—or, all too often, something that is; and the "Croatian Shrug"—a simple gesture meaning, "Don't know, don't care."

Maybe this attitude is understandable, even forgivable. After all, how would you like it if a tidal wave of sweaty, ill-behaved, clueless tourists took over your entire town for the nicest months of each year? The one-two punch of several decades of communism, followed by a devastating war, wasn't exactly the best preparation for being the perfect host. On the other hand, it can be a bit jarring in a place so dependent upon tourism to find such a stubborn disregard for some of the fundamentals of hospitality. My advice:

CROATIA

Croatia Almanac

Official Name: Republika Hrvatska, or just Hrvatska for short.

Snapshot History: After losing its independence to Hungary in 1102, Croatia watched as most of its coastline became Venetian and its interior was conquered by Ottomans. Croatia was "rescued" by the Habsburgs, but after World War I it became part of Yugoslavia—a decision many Croats regretted until they finally gained independence in 1991 through a bitter war with their Serbian neighbors.

Population: Of the country's 4.5 million people, 90 percent are ethnic Croats (Catholic) and 4.5 percent are Serbs (Orthodox). (The Serb population was more than double that before the ethnic cleansing of the 1991–1995 war.) About 1.3 percent of Croatians are Bosniak (Muslim). "Croatians" are citizens of Croatia; "Croats" are a distinct ethnic group made up of Catholic South Slavs. So Orthodox Serbs living in Croatia can be Croatians, but they can't be Croats (since they're not Catholic).

Latitude and Longitude: 45°N and 15°E (similar latitude to Venice, Italy; Ottawa, Canada; or Portland, Oregon).

Area: 22,000 square miles, similar to West Virginia.

Geography: This boomerang-shaped country has two terrains: Stretching north to south is the long, rugged Mediterranean coastline (3,600 miles of beach, including more than 1,100 offshore islands), which is warm and dry. Rising up from the sea are the Dinaric Mountains (which also cover virtually all of neighboring Bosnia-Herzegovina). To the northeast, beginning at about Zagreb, Croatia's flat, inland "panhandle" (called Slavonia) has hot summers and cold winters.

Biggest Cities: The capital, Zagreb (in the northern interior), has 780,000 people; Split (along the Dalmatian Coast) has 189,000; and Rijeka (on the northern coast) has 150,000.

Economy: Much of the country's wealth ($70 billion GDP, $18,300 GDP per capita) comes from tourism, banking, and trade with Italy. Unemployment is a stiff 14 percent.

Currency: 1 kuna (kn, or HRK) = about 20 cents, and 5 kunas = about $1. One kuna is broken down into 100 lipa. *Kuna* is Croatian for "marten" (a foxlike animal), recalling the long-ago era when

Expect the worst, then be pleasantly surprised by the positive interactions you have, rather than getting hung up on the frustrating ones.

Today's Croatia is crawling with a Babel of international guests speaking German, French, Italian, every accent of English...and a smattering of Croatian. And yet, despite the tourists, this place remains distinctly and stubbornly Croatian. You'd have to search pretty hard to find a McDonald's.

fur pelts were used as currency. A *lipa* is a linden tree.

Government: The country's prime minister (currently Jadranka Kosor, head of the majority party in parliament) is conservative, while the directly elected (but more figurehead) president—Stipe Mesić through 2010—is left-of-center. The single-house assembly (Sabor) of 152 legislators is elected by popular vote.

Flag: The flag has three horizontal bands (red on top, white, and blue) with a traditional red-and-white checkerboard shield in the center.

The Average Croatian: The average Croatian will live to age 74 and have 1.4 children. One in four uses the Internet. The average Croatian absolutely adores the soccer team Dinamo Zagreb and absolutely despises Hajduk Split...or vice versa.

Notable Croatians: A pair of big-league historical figures were born in Croatia: Roman Emperor Diocletian (A.D. 245–313) and explorer Marco Polo (1254?–1324). More recently, many Americans whose names end in "-ich" have Croatian roots, including actor John Malkovich and Ohio politicians Dennis Kucinich and John Kasich, not to mention baseball legend Roger Marich...I mean, Maris. More Croatian athletes abound: NBA fans might recognize Toni Kukoč or Gordan Giricek, and at the 2002 and 2006 Winter Olympic Games, the women's downhill skiing events were dominated by Janica Kostelić. Actor Goran Višnjić (from TV's *ER*) was born and raised in Croatia, and served in the army as a paratrooper. You've likely never heard of the beloved Croatian sculptor Ivan Meštrović, but you'll see his expressive works all over the country (see page 188). Inventor Nikola Tesla (1856–1943)—who, as a rival of Thomas Edison's, invented alternating current (AC)—was a Croatian-born Serb. And a band of well-dressed 17th-century Croatian soldiers stationed in France gave the Western world a new fashion accessory—the *cravate*, or necktie (for the full story, see page 185).

Helpful Hints

Stow Your Euros: Tourists are notorious for confusing euro bills with Croatian kuna bills (both modeled after the old German *Deutschmark* and therefore similar). Make a point of deep-storing all euros while outside the euro zone, or you'll pay about seven times more than you should to enjoy Croatia. While some merchants accept euros in payment, most prefer to be paid in kunas (even if they list prices in euros).

Telephones: Croatia's phone system uses area codes. If you're dialing within an area code, just dial the local number; but if you're calling outside an area code, dial both the area code (which starts with a 0) and the local number. To call Croatia from another country, dial the international access code (00 if calling from Europe, 011 from US or Canada), 385 (Croatia's country code), the area code (without the initial zero), and the local number. To call out of Croatia, dial 00, the country code of the country you're calling (see chart in appendix), the area code if applicable, and the local number.

Croatia's pay phones take insertable phone cards (buy at newsstands or kiosks). Mobile phone numbers begin with 091, 098, or 099. Numbers beginning with 060 are pricey toll lines.

Free Tourist Help by Phone: The "Croatian Angels" service gives free information in English over a toll-free line (tel. 062-999-999, daily June–Aug 8:00–24:00, April–May and Sept–mid-Oct 9:00–17:00, closed mid-Oct–March).

Addresses: Addresses listed with a street name and followed by "b.b." have no street number. In most small towns, locals ignore not only street numbers but also street names—navigate with a map or by asking for directions.

Slick Pavement: Old towns, with their well-polished pavement stones and many slick stairs, can be quite treacherous, especially after a rainstorm. (On a recent trip, one of your co-authors almost broke his arm slipping down a flight of stairs.) Tread with care.

Siesta: Croatians eat their big meal at lunch, then take a traditional Mediterranean siesta. This means that many stores, museums, and churches are closed in the mid-afternoon.

Business Closures on Sundays: During the busier tourist months, from June through December, stores are allowed to be open on Sundays. Off-season, from January through May, most shops are legally required to close.

Croatian History

For nearly a millennium, bits and pieces of what we today call "Croatia" were batted back and forth between foreign powers: Hungarians, Venetians, Ottomans, Habsburgs, and Yugoslavs. Only in 1991 did Croatia (violently) regain its independence.

Early History

Croatia's first inhabitants were the Illyrians (ancestors of today's Albanians). During antiquity, the Greeks and Romans both sailed ships up and down the strategic Dalmatian Coast, founding many towns that still exist today, and littering the Adriatic seabed with shipwrecks. Romans built larger settlements on the Dalmatian

After the War

Some Americans shy away from Croatia, clinging to outdated memories of wartime images on the nightly news. But those who venture here are, without exception, amazed by how peaceful and stable today's Croatia feels. Croatia's primary tourist region—the coast—was barely touched by the war (except Dubrovnik, which has been painstakingly restored). The interior is sprinkled with destroyed homes and churches, but even these villages are gradually being refurbished.

The only actual danger is that much of the Croatian interior was once full of landmines. Most of these mines have been removed, and fields that may be dangerous are usually clearly marked. As a precaution, stay on roads and paths, and don't go wandering through overgrown fields and deserted villages.

The biggest impact from the war has been on the people. Throughout the country, but especially in the war-torn interior, sadness and resentment hang heavy in the air. Though the country is repairing itself admirably, the Croatians' souls will take the longest to heal.

For more on Croatia during and after the war, see the Understanding Yugoslavia chapter.

Coast as early as 229 B.C., and in the fourth century A.D., Emperor Diocletian built his retirement palace in the coastal town of Split. As Rome fell in the fifth century, Slavs (the ancestors of today's Croatians) and other barbarians flooded Europe. The northern part of Croatia's coast fell briefly under the Byzantines, who slathered churches with shimmering mosaics (the best are in the Euphrasian Basilica in Poreč, Istria).

Beginning in the seventh century, Slavic Croats began to control most of the land that is today's Croatia. In A.D. 925, the Dalmatian Duke Tomislav united the disparate Croat tribes into a single kingdom. By consolidating and extending Croat-held territory and centralizing power, Tomislav created the first "Croatia."

Loss of Independence

By the early 12th century, the Croatian kings had died out, and neighboring powers (Hungary, Venice, and Byzantium) threatened the Croats. For the sake of self-preservation, Croatia entered an alliance with the Hungarians in 1102, and for the next 900 years, Croatia was ruled by foreign states. The Hungarians gradually took more and more power from the Croats, exerting control over the majority of inland Croatia. Meanwhile, the Venetian Republic conquered most of the coast and peppered the Croatian Adriatic with bell towers and statues of St. Mark. Through it all, the tiny

Republic of Dubrovnik flourished—paying off whomever necessary to maintain its independence and becoming one of Europe's most important shipbuilding and maritime powers.

The Ottomans conquered most of inland Croatia in the 15th century and challenged the Venetians—unsuccessfully—for control of the coastline. Most of the stout walls, fortresses, and other fortifications you'll see all along the Croatian coast date from this time, built by the Venetians to defend against Ottoman attack. In the 17th century, the Habsburgs forced the Ottomans out of inland Croatia. Then, after Venice and Dubrovnik fell to Napoleon in the early 19th century, the coast also went to the Habsburgs—beginning a long tradition of Austrians basking on Croatian beaches.

The Yugoslav Era, World War II, and the Ustaše

When the Austro-Hungarian Empire broke up at the end of World War I, Croats banded together with the Serbs, Bosniaks, and Slovenes in the union that would become Yugoslavia. But virtually as soon as Yugoslavia was formed, many Croats began to fear that the Serbs would steer Yugoslavia to their own purposes. So when the Nazis invaded and installed a puppet government—run by the homegrown fascist Ustaše party—many Croats supported them, believing that fascism could provide them with greater independence from Serbia. The Ustaše operated one of the most brutal Nazi puppet states during World War II. Ustaše concentration camps were used to murder not only Jews and Roma (Gypsies), but also Serbs. Hot-tempered debate rages even today about how many Serbs died at the hands of the Ustaše—estimates vary wildly, from 25,000 to over a million, but most legitimate historians put the number in the hundreds of thousands.

Cardinal Alojzije Stepinac was one Croat who made the mistake of backing the Ustaše. By most accounts, Stepinac was a mild-mannered, extremely devout man who didn't agree with the extremism of the Ustaše...but also did little to fight it. When Tito came to power, he arrested, tried, and imprisoned Stepinac, who died under house arrest in 1960. In the years since, Stepinac has become a martyr for Catholics and Croat nationalists. But even though he's the single most revered figure of Croatian Catholicism, Stepinac remains highly controversial and unpopular among Serbs.

At the end of World War II, the Ustaše were forced out by Yugoslavia's homegrown Partisan Army, led by a charismatic war hero named Josip Broz, who went by his nickname, "Tito." Tito became "president for life," and Croatia once again became part of a united Yugoslavia. The union would hold together for more than

40 years, until it broke apart under Serbian President Slobodan Milošević and Croatian President Franjo Tuđman.

For all the details on Yugoslavia and its breakup, see the Understanding Yugoslavia chapter, page 532.

Independence Regained

Croatia's declaration of independence from Yugoslavia in 1991 was met with fear and anger on the part of its more than half-million Serb residents. Even before independence, the first volleys of a bloody war had been fired. The war had two phases: First, in 1991, Croatian Serbs declared independence from the new nation of Croatia, forming their own state and forcing out or murdering any Croats in "their" territory (with the thinly disguised support of Slobodan Milošević). Then a tense cease-fire fell over the region until 1995, when the second phase of the war ignited: Croatia pushed back through the Serb-dominated territory, reclaiming it for Croatia and forcing out or murdering Serbs living there. For details on this bloody war, see the Understanding Yugoslavia chapter.

Imagine becoming an independent nation after nine centuries of foreign domination. The Croatians seized their hard-earned freedom with a nationalist fervor that bordered on fascism. This was a heady and absurd time, which today's Croatians recall with disbelief, sadness...and maybe a tinge of nostalgia.

In the Croatia of the early 1990s, even the most bizarre notions seemed possible. Croatia's first post-Yugoslav president, the extreme nationalist Franjo Tuđman (see sidebar on page 46), proposed implausible directives for the new nation—such as privatizing all of the nation's resources and handing them over to 200 super-elite families (which, thankfully for everyone else, never happened). The government began calling the language "Croatian" rather than "Serbo-Croatian" and creating new words from specifically Croat roots. The Croats even briefly considered replacing the Roman alphabet with the ninth-century Glagolitic script to invoke Croat culture and further differentiate Croatian from Serbia's Cyrillic alphabet. Fortunately for tourists, this plan didn't take off.

After Tuđman's death in 1999, Croatia began the new millennium with a more truly democratic leader, Stipe Mesić. The popular Mesić, who was once aligned with Tuđman, had split off and formed his own political party when Tuđman's politics grew too extreme. Tuđman spent years tampering with the constitution to give himself more and more power, but when Mesić took over, he reversed those changes and handed more authority back to the parliament.

Franjo Tuđman
(1922–1999)

Independent Croatia's first president was the controversial Franjo Tuđman (FRAHN-yoh TOOJ-mahn). Tuđman began his career fighting for Tito on the left, but later had a dramatic ideological swing to the far right. His anticommunist, highly nationalistic HDZ party was the driving force for Croatian statehood, making him the young nation's first hero. But even as he fought for independence from Yugoslavia, his own ruling style grew more and more authoritarian. Today Tuđman remains a polemical figure.

Before entering politics, Tuđman was a historian. He revered the Ustaše, Croatia's Nazi-affiliated government during World War II, who murdered hundreds of thousands of Serbs and Jews in concentration camps. (Because the Ustaše governed the first "independent" Croatian state since the 12th century, Tuđman figured that these quasi-Nazis were the original Croatian "freedom fighters.") When Croatia voted for independence and Tuđman was elected president in 1990, he immediately reintroduced many Ustaše symbols, including their currency (the kuna, still used today). His actions raised eyebrows worldwide and raised alarms in Croatia's Serb communities.

Tuđman espoused many of the same single-minded attitudes about ethnic divisions as the ruthless Serbian leader Slobodan Milošević. Croat forces—which may or may not have been acting under Tuđman's orders—carried out wide-scale ethnic cleansing, targeting Serb and Muslim minorities. Tuđman and Milošević had secret, Hitler-and-Stalin-esque negotiations even as they were ripping into each other rhetorically. According to some reports, at one meeting they drew a map of Bosnia-Herzegovina on a

Croatia Today

In 2003, Croatia applied for membership in the European Union. It's officially an EU candidate country, and may join as early as 2011.

Initially, Croatia's biggest hurdle to EU membership was its human-rights record during the recent war. Several Croatian officers were indicted for war crimes by the International Criminal Tribunal for the Former Yugoslavia (ICTY) in The Hague, Netherlands. But many Croatians feel that the soldiers branded as "war criminals" by The Hague are instead heroes of their war of independence. The highest-profile Croatian figure to be arrested was Ante Gotovina, a lieutenant general accused of atrocities

GENERAL
ANTE GOTOVINA

cocktail napkin, then drew lines divvying up the country between themselves. When Tuđman's successor moved into the president's office, he discovered a top-secret hotline to Milošević's desk.

To ensure that he stayed in power, Tuđman played fast and loose with his new nation's laws. He was notorious for changing the constitution as it suited him. By the late 1990s, when his popularity was slipping, Tuđman extended Croatian citizenship to anyone in the world who had Croatian heritage—a ploy aimed at getting votes from Croats living in Bosnia-Herzegovina, who were sure to line up with him on the far right.

Through it all, Tuđman kept a tight grip on the media, making it illegal to report anything that would disturb the public—even if true. When Croatians turned on their TV sets and saw the flag flapping in the breeze to the strains of the national anthem, they knew something was up...and switched to CNN to get the real story. In this oppressive environment, many bright, young Croatians fled the country, causing a "brain drain" that hampered the postwar recovery.

Tuđman died of cancer at the end of 1999. While history will probably judge him harshly, the opinion in today's Croatia is qualified. Most agree that Tuđman was an important and even admirable figure in the struggle for Croatian statehood, but he ultimately went too far and got too greedy. Tuđman's political party is still active, frequently naming streets, squares, and bridges for this "hero" of Croatian nationalism. But if he were alive, Tuđman would be standing trial before the International Criminal Tribunal in The Hague.

against Serb civilians. After four years in hiding, Gotovina was found and arrested in Spain in December 2005 and sent to stand trial in The Hague. As a sign of support, photos of Gotovina appeared in towns throughout Croatia. Gotovina's name means "cash." Many Croatians grouse, "To get into the EU, we have to pay cash *(gotovina)!*"

Some Croatians remain skeptical about joining the EU for other reasons. One Croatian said to me, "We were just badly divorced. We're not ready to be married again." For the other countries that recently joined the EU, a concern with EU membership was that the new members' citizens would flood to the West. Some Croatians are worried about the opposite: Westerners buying up Adriatic beachfront property.

Perhaps not surprisingly for a post-communist country, Croatia's government can be excessively bureaucratic. Expats who want to work here find it a tough place to do business. Laws tend

CROATIA

to be implemented, then quickly overturned. In the last few years, a ban on shops being open on Sundays, a smoking ban, and a zero blood-alcohol limit for drivers have all come and gone. (The last one was contested by priests, who pointed out that if the blood-alcohol limit is zero, their parishioners can't take the wine at communion.)

Despite the country's false starts, pro-EU President Stipe Mesić's re-election in 2005 was a clear signal that most Croatians are optimistic about becoming a part of a united Europe. Mesić is viewed both by most Croatians and by international observers as precisely the kind of moderate, modern, European-minded leader a fledgling country needs to lead it into the 21st century. When Mesić's second—and, constitutionally, last—term is up in 2010, Croatia will need to decide which direction to take in the future.

Croatian Food

Croatian food is good, but tends to be fairly expensive and unimaginative—and all too often comes with less than cheerful service. The country's tourist board has gone to great lengths to promote its cuisine and wines as major components of any trip. This seems to have backfired, as many visitors find themselves disappointed by Croatian restaurants. Adjust your expectations and you'll eat well here—it ain't Tuscany, but it ain't bad, either.

Like its people, the food in Croatia's different regions has been shaped by various influences—predominantly Italian, Turkish, and Hungarian. And yet, the cuisine here is surprisingly uniform: 90 percent of coastal restaurants have a similar menu of seafood, pasta, and pizza. Because it's so easy to get into a culinary rut here, I've also tried to recommend a few more exotic alternatives.

Two staples of Croatian food, as in most Mediterranean lands, are wine and olive oil. You'll see vineyards and olive groves blanketing the Croatian countryside and islandscapes. Croatians joke that grapes are like a new bride—they demand a lot of attention, while olives are like a mother—low-maintenance. Another major part of the local diet is the air-dried ham called *pršut* (a.k.a. prosciutto—see sidebar on page 392).

On the coast, seafood is a specialty, and the Italian influence is obvious. According to Dalmatians, "Eating meat is food; eating fish is pleasure." They also say that a fish should swim three times: first in the sea, then in olive oil, and finally in wine—when you eat it.

You can get all kinds of seafood: fish, scampi, mussels, squid,

CROATIA

Croatian Wine

The quality of Croatia's wine declined under the communists, as much of the industry was state-run and focused on mass production. Now that the communists are gone, vintner families are returning to their roots—literally—and bringing quality back to Croatian wine.

The northern part of the country primarily produces whites *(bijelo vino)*, usually dry *(suho)* but sometimes semi-dry *(polusuho)* or sweet *(slatko)*. The sunny mountains just north of Zagreb are covered with vineyards producing whites. From Slavonia (Croatia's inland panhandle), you'll find *graševina*—crisp, dry, and acidic (like Welsh Riesling); Krauthaker and Enjingi are well-respected brands. The Istrian Peninsula corks up some good whites, including *malvazija*, a very popular, light, mid-range wine (Muscat is also popular).

As you move south along the Dalmatian Coast, the wines turn red—which Croatians actually call "black wine" *(crno vino)*. The most common grape here is *plavac mali* ("little blue")—a distant ancestor of Californian Zinfandel grapes. Generally speaking, the best coastal reds are produced on the long Pelješac Peninsula, across from Korčula (the most well-respected regions are Dingač—literally, "Donkey"—and Postup). But each island also produces its own good wines. Korčula makes *pošip* (near the town of Čara), *grk*, and *korčulanka*, and Hvar has *bogdanuša*.

Miljenko Grgić (a.k.a. "Mike Grgich"), a Croatian-American who has started a Croatian branch of his California wine empire, is putting Croatian wines on the map. Grgić grows his red wines (*plavac mali* grapes) at Postup and Dingač on the Pelješac Peninsula, and his white wines on Korčula Island. The prices for Grgić's wines match his reputation; for producers that are comparable but a bit more affordable, look for these red-wine alternatives: Madirazza (they make a great Postup), Frano Miloš (try the full-bodied Stagnum), and Matuško and Skaramuća (good Dingač).

octopus, you name it. Remember that prices for fish dishes are listed either by the kilogram (1,000 grams) or by the 100-gram unit (figure about a half-kilo, or 500 grams—that's about one pound—for a large portion). When ordering, be prepared for surprises. For example, *škampi* (shrimp) often come still in their shells (sometimes with crayfish-like claws), which can be messy and time-consuming to eat. Before you order shrimp, ask if it's shelled. The menu item called "small fried fish" is generally a plate of deep-fried minnows. If you're not clear on exactly what something is, feel free to ask for clarification (though some waiters are more forthcoming than others).

Sometimes it's a pleasant surprise. Many menu items that

don't sound appetizing can be delicious. Jump at the chance to sample a good, fresh anchovy—which, when done right, has a pleasant flavor and a melt-in-your-mouth texture that's a world away from the salty, withered little fish you might find topping a pizza back home. Those not accustomed to eating octopus might want to try octopus salad—a flavorful mix of octopus, tomatoes, onions, and spices. In the interior, trout is popular.

If you're not a seafood-eater, there are plenty of meat options. A Dalmatian specialty is *pašticada*—braised beef in a slightly sweet wine-and-herb sauce, usually served with gnocchi. Dalmatia is also known for its mutton. Since the lambs graze on salty seaside herbs, the meat—often served on a spit—has a distinctive flavor. The most widely available meat dish is the "mixed grill"—a combination of various Balkan grilled meats, best accompanied by the eggplant-and-red-pepper condiment *ajvar* (see "Balkan Flavors" on page 31).

The best meat dish in Croatia is veal or lamb prepared under a *peka*—a metal baking lid that's covered with red-hot coals, to allow the meat to gradually cook to tender perfection. Available only in traditional restaurants, this dish typically must be ordered in advance and for multiple people. You'll also find a break from seafood in the north (Zagreb) and east (Slavonia), where the food has more of a Hungarian flavor—heavy on meat served with cabbage, noodles, or potatoes.

Many tourists reserve meat and fish for splurge dinners and mostly dine on cheaper and faster pastas and pizzas. You'll see familiar dishes, such as spaghetti Bolognese (with meat sauce) and spaghetti carbonara (with an egg, parmesan, and bacon sauce), gnocchi (*njoki*, potato dumplings), and lasagna. Risotto (a rice dish) is popular here, often mixed with squid ink and various kinds of seafood.

There are many good local varieties of cheese made with sheep's or goat's milk. Pag, an island in the Kvarner Gulf, produces a famous, very salty, fairly dry sheep's-milk cheese *(paški sir)*, which is said to be flavored by the herbs the sheep eat.

A common side dish is boiled potatoes and mangold *(blitva)*, similar to Swiss chard. When ordering salad, choose between mixed (typically shredded cabbage, tomatoes, and maybe some beets and a little lettuce) or green (mostly lettuce). Throughout Croatia, salad is typically served with the main dish unless you request that it be brought beforehand.

For dessert, look no further than the mountains of delicious, homemade ice cream *(sladoled)* that line every street in Dalmatia. I've worked hard to sample and recommend the best ice-cream parlors in each town. (Poor me.) Dalmatia's typical dessert is a flan-like, crème caramel custard, which they call *rozata*. *Prošek* is a sweet dessert wine.

Water is *voda*, and mineral water is *mineralna voda*. Jamnica is the main Croatian brand of bottled water, but you'll also see Bistra and Studenac. Many restaurants—especially fancier ones—might not want to bring you a glass of tap water, but you can try asking for *voda iz slavine*. For coffee *(kava)*, the easiest choice is *bijela kava* (BEE-yeh-lah KAH-vah)—"white coffee," or espresso with lots of milk (similar to a *caffè latte*). To get it black, ask for *crna kava*.

The most popular Croatian beers *(pivo)* are Ožujsko and Karlovačko, but you'll also see the Slovenian brand Laško (which is also brewed here in Croatia). Fans of dark beer *(crno pivo)* enjoy Tomislav.

Even more beloved in Croatia is wine *(vino;* see "Croatian Wine" sidebar). Along the coast, locals find it refreshing to drink wine mixed with mineral water (called, as in English, *špricer*). When toasting with some new Croatian friends, raise your glass with a hearty *"Živjeli!"* (ZHEE-vyeh-lee).

To request a menu, say, *"Meni, molim"* (MEH-nee, MOH-leem; "Menu, please"). To get the attention of your waiter, say *"Konobar"* (KOH-noh-bahr; "Waiter"). When he brings your food, he'll likely say, *"Dobar tek!"* ("Enjoy your meal!"). When you're ready for the bill, ask for the *račun* (RAH-choon).

Croatian Language

Croatian was once known as "Serbo-Croatian," the official language of Yugoslavia. Most Yugoslav republics—including Croatia, Serbia, and Bosnia-Herzegovina—spoke this same language (though Slovene is quite different). And while each of these countries has tried to distance its language from that of its neighbors since the war, the languages spoken in all of these places are still very similar. The biggest difference is in the writing: Croatians and Bosniaks use our Roman alphabet, while Serbs use Cyrillic letters.

In recent years, Croatia has attempted to artificially make its vocabulary different from Serbian. A decade ago, you'd catch a plane at the *aerodrom*. Today, you'll catch that same flight at the *zračna luka*—a new coinage that combines the old Croatian words for "air" and "port." These new words, once created, are artificially injected into the lexicon. Croatians watching their favorite TV show will suddenly hear a character use a word they've never heard before...and think, "Oh, we have another new word."

Remember, *c* is pronounced "ts" (as in "bats"). The letter *j* is pronounced as "y." The letters *č* and *ć* are slightly different, but they both sound more or less like "ch"; š sounds like "sh," and ž sounds like "zh" (as in "leisure"). One Croatian letter that you won't see in other languages is đ, which sounds like the "dj" sound in "jeans." In fact, this letter is often replaced with "dj" in English.

When attempting to pronounce an unfamiliar word, remember that the accent is usually on the first syllable (and never on the last). Confusingly, Croatian pronunciation—even of the same word—can vary in different parts of the country. This is because modern Croatian has three distinct dialects, called Kajkavian, Shtokavian, and Chakavian—based on how you say "what?" (kaj?, što?, and ča?, respectively). That's a lot of variety for a language with only five million speakers.

For a smoother trip, take some time to learn a few key Croatian phrases (see "Croatian Survival Phrases," page 581).

CROATIA

ZAGREB

In this land of time-passed coastal villages, Zagreb (ZAH-grehb) offers a welcome jolt of big-city sophistication. You can't get a complete picture of modern Croatia without a visit here—away from the touristy resorts, in the lively and livable city that is home to one out of every six Croatians (pop. 780,000). In Zagreb, you'll find historic neighborhoods, worthwhile museums, a thriving café culture, my favorite urban people-watching in Croatia, and virtually no tourists.

Zagreb began as two walled medieval towns, Gradec and Kaptol, separated by a river. As Croatia fell under the control of various foreign powers—Budapest, Vienna, Berlin, and Belgrade—the two hill towns that would become Zagreb gradually took on more religious and civic importance. Kaptol became a bishopric in 1094, and it's still home to Croatia's most important church. In the 16th century, the Ban (Croatia's governor) and the Sabor (parliament) called Gradec home. The two towns officially merged in 1850, and soon after, the railroad connecting Budapest with the Adriatic port city of Rijeka was built through the city. Zagreb prospered.

After centuries of being the de facto religious, cultural, and political center of Croatia, Zagreb officially became a European capital when the country declared its independence in 1991. In the ensuing war with Yugoslavia, Zagreb was hardly damaged—Yugoslav bombs hit only a few strategic targets. Today, just a decade and a half later, Zagreb has long since repaired the minimal damage, and the capital is safe, modern, lively, and fun.

Planning Your Time

Most visitors just pass through Zagreb, but the city is worth a look. Throw your bag in a locker at the station and zip into the center for a quick visit—or consider spending the night.

You can get a decent sense of Zagreb in just a few hours. With whatever time you have, make a beeline for Jelačić Square to visit the TI and get oriented. Take the funicular up to Gradec, visit the excellent Museum of Naive Art, and stroll St. Mark's Square. Then wander down through the Stone Gate to the lively Tkalčićeva scene (good for a drink or meal), through the market (closes at 14:00), and on to Kaptol and the cathedral.

With more time, visit some of Zagreb's museums, wander the series of parks called the "Green Horseshoe," or head to the enjoyable nearby town of Samobor (see the end of this chapter).

If you're moving on from Zagreb to Plitvice Lakes National Park (see next chapter), be warned that the last bus leaves in the mid-afternoon (usually 16:00); confirm your bus departure carefully to ensure that you don't get stranded in Zagreb.

Orientation to Zagreb

(area code: 01)
Zagreb, just 30 minutes from the Slovenian border, stretches from the foothills of Medvednica ("Bear Mountain") to the Sava River. In the middle of the sprawl, you'll find the modern **Lower Town** (Donji Grad, centered on **Jelačić Square**) and the historic **Upper Town** (Gornji Grad, comprising the original hill towns of **Gradec** and **Kaptol**). To the south is a U-shaped belt of parks, squares, and museums that make up the **"Green Horseshoe."** The east side of the U is a series of three parks, with the train station at the bottom (south) and Jelačić Square at the top (north).

Zagrebians have devised a brilliant scheme for confusing tourists: Street names can be depicted several different ways. For example, the street that is signed as ulica Kralja Državislava ("King Državislav Street") is often called by locals simply Državislavova ("Državislav's"). So if you're looking for a street, don't search for an exact match—be willing to settle for something that just has a lot of the same letters.

Tourist Information

Zagreb has Croatia's best-organized TI, right on Jelačić Square (Mon–Fri 8:30–20:00, until 21:00 in summer, Sat 9:00–17:00, Sun 10:00–14:00, Trg bana Jelačića 11, tel. 01/481-4052, www.zagreb -touristinfo.hr). The TI offers piles of free, well-produced tourist brochures; highlights include the one-page city map (with handy

Zagreb Essentials

English	Croatian	Pronounced
Jelačić Square	Trg bana Jelačića	turg BAH-nah YEH-lah-chee-chah
Gradec (original civic hill town)	Gradec	GRAH-dehts
Kaptol (original religious hill town)	Kaptol	KAHP-tohl
Café street between Gradec and Kaptol	Tkalčićeva (or "Tkalči" for short)	tuh-KAHL-chee-chay-vah (tuh-KAHL-chee)
Main train station	Glavni Kolodvor	GLAHV-nee KOH-loh-dvor
Bus station	Autobusni Kolodvor	OW-toh-boos-nee KOH-loh-dvor

transit map and regional map on back), the *Zagreb Info* booklet (including accommodations and restaurant listings), the monthly events guide, and the great *City Walks* brochure (with a couple of mildly diverting self-guided walking tours). I'd skip the TI's Zagreb Card (free transportation and discounts at most Zagreb museums, 60 kn/24 hrs, 90 kn/72 hrs).

Arrival in Zagreb

By Train: Zagreb's main train station (Glavni Kolodvor) is conveniently located a few blocks south of Jelačić Square on the Green Horseshoe. The straightforward arrivals hall has a train information desk, ticket windows, luggage lockers (15 kn/day), ATMs, WCs, Konzum grocery store, and newsstands. To reach the city center, go straight out the front door. You'll run into a taxi stand, and then the tracks for **tram #6** (direction: Črnomerec zips you to Jelačić Square; direction: Sopot takes you to the bus station—the third stop, just after you turn right and go under the big overpass). You can also take tram #13 to Jelačić Square (direction: Žitnjak). For the trip to Jelačić Square, you don't need a ticket—since it's within Zagreb's free-ride zone, you can just hop on. If going to the bus station, buy an 8-kn ticket from the kiosk before boarding. If you **walk** straight ahead through the long, lush park, you'll wind up at the bottom of Jelačić Square in 10 minutes.

By Bus: The user-friendly but inconveniently located bus station (Autobusni Kolodvor) is a few long blocks southeast of the

ZAGREB

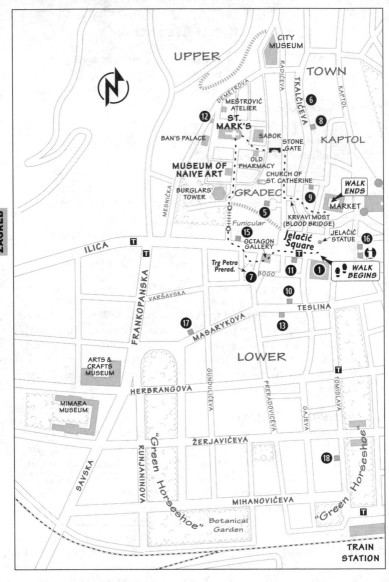

main train station. The station has all the essentials—ATMs, post office, mini-grocery store, left-luggage counter...everything from a smut store to a chapel. Upstairs, you'll find ticket windows and access to the buses (follow signs to *perone;* wave ticket in front of turnstile to open gate). Tram #6 (direction: Črnomerec) takes you to the main train station, then on to Jelačić Square. Walking from the bus station to Jelačić Square takes about 25 minutes.

Zagreb

1. Hotel Dubrovnik
2. Hotel Astoria
3. Hotel Central
4. Hotel Jadran
5. Apartments Lessi & Fulir Backpackers Inn
6. Tkalčićeva St. Eateries
7. Trg Petra Preradovića Eateries
8. Pivnica Medvedgrad Pub
9. Nokturno Restaurant
10. Vinodol Restaurant
11. Sora Restaurant
12. Konoba Didov San
13. Sandwich Bar Pingvin
14. Mimice Restaurant
15. Slastičarnica Vincek Ice Cream
16. Gradska Kavana Café
17. Marko Polo Travel Agency
18. Plitvice Lakes Office

By Plane: Zagreb's small airport is 10 miles south of the center (tel. 01/626-5222, www.zagreb-airport.hr). Once you get through security, your only food and drink option is one very expensive bar. While a shuttle bus connects the airport to the bus station (2/hr, 30 min, 30 kn), it's more convenient to pay for a taxi right to your hotel (30 min; the fair metered rate is around 180–200 kn, but some crooked cabbies might try to charge you more).

Getting Around Zagreb

The main mode of public transportation is the **tram,** operated by ZET (Zagreb Electrical Transport). You can ride free for up to two stops in any direction from Jelačić Square (including the train station); people over age 65 can ride free anywhere. For longer rides, a single ticket (good for 90 min in one direction, including transfers) costs 10 kn if you buy it from the driver (8 kn at kiosk, ask for *ZET karta*—zeht KAR-tah). A day ticket *(dnevna karta)* costs 25 kn. The most useful tram for tourists is #6, connecting Jelačić Square with the train and bus stations.

Taxis start at 19 kn, then run 7 kn per kilometer (20 percent more Sun and 22:00–5:00, 3 kn extra for each piece of baggage; beware of corrupt cabbies—ask for an estimate up front, or call Radio Taxi, tel. 01/661-0200 or 060-800 800). A typical ride within the city center shouldn't run more than about 30 kn, and the trip to the airport should cost no more than 200 kn (agree on a price first).

Helpful Hints

Schedule Quirks: Virtually all of Zagreb's museums are closed on Sunday afternoon and all day Monday. Some museums stay open late one night a week in summer (usually Thu). On Sunday morning, the city is thriving—but by afternoon, it's extremely quiet.

Ferry Tickets: If you're heading for the coast, you can reserve and buy Jadrolinija ferry tickets at the **Marko Polo** travel agency (Mon–Fri 9:00–17:00, Sat 9:00–13:00, closed Sun, Masarykova 24, tel. 01/481-5216).

Plitvice Lakes Office: If you're going to Plitvice Lakes National Park, you can get a preview and ask any questions at their information office in Zagreb (Mon–Fri 8:00–16:00, closed Sat–Sun, a block in front of main train station at Trg Kralja Tomislava 19, tel. 01/461-3586).

Tours in Zagreb

Local Guide—Dijana Bebek Miletić is an energetic, knowledgeable guide who helps visitors appreciate Zagreb's charms (500 kn/3-hour walking tour, mobile 091-303-3979, dijana.bebek@vip.hr).

Bus-plus-Walking Tours—This option, which combines a two-hour town walk with a one-hour bus tour, is a good way to get your bearings in this city. Unfortunately, there's no set schedule, so you'll have to ask for details at the TI (165 kn, www.ibus.hr).

Self-Guided Walk

▲▲Zagreb's Upper Town

The following one-way circular orientation walk begins at Jelačić Square. The entire route takes about an hour at a leisurely pace (not counting museum stops).

▲Jelačić Square (Trg bana Jelačića)

The "Times Square" of Zagreb bustles with life. Watching the crowds pile in and out of trams and seeing the city buzz with activ-

ity, you feel the energy of an on-the-rise capital of a vibrant new nation. The city's busy pedestrian scene, sense of style, and utter lack of tourists make it arguably Croatia's best people-watching destination.

Believe it or not, this frenetic Donji Grad ("lower town") once held the townspeople's farm fields. Today, it features a prominent equestrian statue of national hero **Josip Jelačić** (YOH-seep YEH-lah-cheech, 1801–1859), a 19th-century governor who extended citizens' rights and did much to unite the Croats within the Habsburg Empire. In Jelačić's time, the Hungarians were exerting extensive control over Croatia, even trying to make Hungarian the official language. Meanwhile, Budapesters revolted against Habsburg rule in 1848. Jelačić, ever mindful of the need to protect Croatian cultural autonomy, knew that he'd have a better shot at getting his way from Austria than

from Hungary. Jelačić chose the lesser of two evils and fought alongside the Habsburgs to put down the Hungarian uprising. In the Yugoslav era, Jelačić was considered a dangerously nationalistic symbol, and this statue was dismantled and stored away. But when Croatia broke away in 1991, Croatian patriotism was in the air, and Jelačić returned. Though Jelačić originally faced his Hungarian foes to the north, today he's staring down the Serbs to the south.

Get oriented. As you face Jelačić's statue, down a long block to your left is a funicular that takes you up to one of Zagreb's original villages, Gradec. To the right, look for the TI. At the top-right corner of the square is the **Gradska Kavana,** Zagreb's top café (with an elegant white-and-purple Art Deco interior that was recently renovated with gleaming style). If you leave the square ahead and to the right, you'll reach the other original village, Kaptol, and the cathedral (you can't miss its huge, pointy, Neo-Gothic spires—visible from virtually everywhere in Zagreb). The small street behind Jelačić and a little to the left leads to the market (Dolac) and the lively café street, Tkalčićeva.

For now, we'll head up to Gradec. Go a long block down the busy Ilica, then enter the big **"Octagon" shopping gallery** on the left (at #5, enter under *Privedna Banka Zagreb* sign). This was the ultimate in iron-and-glass shopping elegance a century ago, and still features a few of the city's top shops (including Croata, the tie store that loves to explain how Croatians invented the necktie; for the whole story, see page 185).

Walk all the way through the gallery, exiting into the inviting café-lined square called **Trg Petra Preradovića.** Survey your options for a coffee break, then turn right and head back out to Ilica street, where you'll turn left and continue the way you were headed before (noticing, at #18, the popular and recommended ice cream and cake shop Slastičarnica Vincek).

After another block, cross the tram tracks and turn right up Tomičeva, where you'll see a small **funicular** (ZET Uspinjača) crawling up the hill. Dating from the late 19th century, this funicular is looked upon fondly by Zagrebians—both as a bit of nostalgia and as a way to avoid some steps. You can walk up if you want, but the ride is more fun and takes only 55 seconds (4 kn, validate ticket in orange machine before you board, leaves every 10 min daily 6:30–21:00).

Gradec

From the top of the funicular, you'll enjoy a fine panorama over Zagreb. The tall tower you face as you exit is one of Gradec's original watchtowers, the **Burglars' Tower** (Kula Lotrščak). After the Tatars ransacked Central Europe in the early 13th century, King Béla IV decreed that towns be fortified—so Gradec built a wall and guard towers (just like Kraków and Budapest did). Look for the little cannon in the top-floor window. Every day at noon, this cannon fires a shot, supposedly to commemorate a 15th-century victory over the besieging Ottomans. Zagrebians hold on to other traditions, too—the lamps on this hill are still gas-powered, lit by a city employee every evening.

Head up the street next to the tower. Little remains of medieval Gradec. When the Ottomans overran Europe, they never managed to take Zagreb, but the threat was enough to scare the nobility into the countryside. When the Ottomans left, the nobles came back, and they replaced the medieval buildings here with

Baroque mansions. At the first square, to the right, you'll see the Jesuit **Church of St. Catherine.** It's not much to look at from the outside, but the interior is intricately decorated. The same applies to several mansions on Gradec. This simple-outside, ornate-inside style is known as "Zagreb Baroque."

As you continue up the street, notice that the old-timey **street signs** are a holdover from the Austro-Hungarian era: in both Croatian (Gospodska ulicza) and German (Herren Gasse).

On the left you'll see the **Croatian Museum of Naive Art**—Zagreb's best museum, and well worth a visit (listed later, under "Sights in Zagreb"). In the next block, on the left, look for the monument to Nikola Tesla (1856–1943), a prominent Croatian-born Serb scientist who moved to America and championed alternating current as a better electrical system than Thomas Edison's direct current.

At the end of the block, you'll come to **St. Mark's Square** (Markov trg), centered on the **Church of St. Mark.** The origi-

nal church here was from the 13th century, but only a few fragments remain. The present church's colorful tile roof, from 1880, depicts two coats of arms. On the left, the red-and-white checkerboard symbolizes north-central Croatia, the three lions' heads stand for the Dalmatian Coast, and the marten (*kuna,* like the money) running between the two rivers (Sava and Drava) represents Slavonia—Croatia's northern, inland panhandle. On the right is the seal of Zagreb, featuring a walled city. (The seal typically shows wide-open doors—to demonstrate that Zagreb is strong, but still welcoming to visitors—but on this seal, the doors are closed.) The church interior (open sporadically) features frescoes with Bible scenes, and was redecorated in the early 20th century by local artists. Sculptures by the talented artist Ivan Meštrović flank the main altar: a *pietà* on the left, and Madonna and Child on the right (sitting cross-legged, in a typical Meštrović pose). He also sculpted the crucifix over the main altar. If you like these works, consider visiting Meštrović's nearby former home, which is now a museum of his works (it's about a block away: go down the street behind the church on the left-hand side, and you'll see the museum on the right; see Ivan Meštrović Atelier listing later, under "Sights in Zagreb").

As you face the church, to the right is the **Sabor,** or parliament. From the 12th century, Croatian noblemen would gather here to make important decisions regarding their territories. This gradually evolved into today's modern parliament. (If you walk along the front of the Sabor and continue straight ahead two blocks, you'll run into the excellent Zagreb City Museum, described later, under "Sights in Zagreb.")

Across the square from the Sabor (to your left as you face the church) is **Ban's Palace** (Banski Dvori), today the offices for the prime minister. This was one of the few buildings in central Zagreb damaged in the war following Croatia's independence. In October of 1991, Yugoslav forces shelled it from afar, knowing that Croatian President Franjo Tuđman was inside...but Tuđman survived. (Notice the different-colored tiles where the roof had to be patched.)

Walk from Gradec to Kaptol

For an interesting stroll from St. Mark's Square to the cathedral, head down the street (Kamenita ulica) to the right of the parliament building. Near the end of the street, on the right, you'll see the oldest **pharmacy** in town—recently restored and gleaming (c. 1355, marked *gradska ljekarna*).

Just beyond, you'll reach Gradec's only surviving town gate, the

Stone Gate (Kamenita Vrata). Inside is an evocative chapel. The focal point is a painting of Mary that miraculously survived a major fire in the adjoining house in 1731. When this medieval gate was reconstructed in the Baroque style, they decided to turn it into a makeshift chapel. The candles (purchased in the little shop and lit in the big metal bin) represent Zagrebians' prayers. Notice the  soot-blackened ceiling over the forest fire of blazing candles in the bin. The stone plaques on the wall give thanks *(hvala)* for prayers that were answered. You may notice people making the sign of the cross as they walk through here, and often a crowd of worshippers gather, gazing intently at the painting. Mary was made the official patron saint of Zagreb in 1990.

As you leave the Stone Gate and come to Radićeva, turn right and walk downhill. Take the next left, onto the street called **Krvavi Most**—"Blood Bridge." At the end of Krvavi Most, you'll come to Tkalčićeva. This lively café-and-restaurant street used to be a river—the natural boundary between Gradec and Kaptol. The two towns did not always get along, and sometimes fought against each other. Blood was spilled, and the bridge that once stood here between them became known as Blood Bridge. By the late 19th century, the towns had united, and the polluted river began to stink—so they covered it over with this street.

As you cross the pedestrian drag called **Tkalčićeva,** you enter the old town of Kaptol. Consider taking a detour up delightful, in-love-with-life Tkalčićeva to scout your options for a coffee, beer, or meal (I've listed a few recommendations under "Eating in Zagreb," later).

Just beyond Tkalčićeva is the **market** *(dolac),* packed with colorful stalls selling produce of all kinds (Mon–Sat 7:00–14:00, Sun 7:00–13:00). At the back-left corner is the fragrant fish market *(ribarnica),* and under your feet is an indoor part of the market *(tržnica),* where farmers sell farm-fresh eggs and dairy products (same hours as outdoor market, entrance below in the direction of Jelačić Square).

Your walk is over. On the other side of the market, you can visit the cathedral (described later, under in "Sights in Zagreb").

Sights in Zagreb

▲▲▲Croatian Museum of Naive Art (Hrvatski Muzej Naivne Umjetnosti)

This remarkable spot, founded in 1952 as the "Peasant Art Gallery," is one of the most enjoyable little museums in Croatia. It features expressionistic paintings by untrained peasant artists (called "autodidacts" because they are self-taught). On one easy floor, the museum displays 80 paintings made mostly by Croatians from the 1930s to the 1980s.

Cost, Hours, Location: 20 kn, pick up the English explanations as you enter, Tue–Fri 10:00–18:00, Sat–Sun 10:00–13:00, closed Mon, ulica Sv. Ćirila i Metoda 3, tel. 01/485-1911, www.hmnu.org.

Background: Starting in the late 19th century, the art world began to broaden its definition of great art, seeking out worthy

art originating outside the esteemed academies and salons of the day. Their goal: to demonstrate that art was not simply a trained skill, but an inborn talent. Intellectuals began to embrace an "anti-intellectual" approach to art. Interest grew in the indigenous art of Africa, Mesoamerica, and Polynesia (Picasso went through an African mask phase, and Gauguin went to live in Tahiti); composer Béla Bartok collected traditional folk melodies from the Hungarian countryside; the "art brut" movement preserved artwork by people deemed "insane" by mainstream society; the self-taught painter Grandma Moses became well-known in the US and Europe; and art by children gained acclaim.

Here in Croatia in the 1930s, the focus was on art by untrained peasants. At that time, as in much of rural Europe, 85 percent of Croatians lived virtually medieval lifestyles—with no electricity or other modern conveniences—and about 60 percent were illiterate and uneducated. These artists captured this humble reality, creating figurative works in an increasingly abstract age. By the 1950s and 1960s, Croatian "naive art" had emerged at the forefront of a Europe-wide phenomenon.

This museum presents an easily digestible sampling of the top names from this movement. Viewing these evocative works, it's important to remember that this isn't considered "folk art" or "amateur art"—but top-quality works by great artists who were, by fluke of fate, never formally trained.

●Self-Guided Tour: Buy your ticket and follow the one-way route through the six numbered rooms, which you'll circle counter-clockwise.

Room 1: Immediately to the right as you enter is the first of many paintings by **Ivan Generalić** (1914–1992), the founder

and star of Croatian naive art (his self-portrait, with a blue background, dominates the room). Generalić was discovered in the 1930s by a Paris-trained Croatian artist. The first few paintings show his evolution as an artist (and the evolution of Croatian naive art in general): While his early works came with a social or political agenda (such as *The Requisition,* where two policemen repo a cow from an impoverished couple), he eventually mellowed his focus to simply show typical village scenes. These start out as purely representational of peasant life *(Village Dance),* gradually become more and more fantastical *(Harvesters),* and eventually strip away people entirely to focus on the land (1939's *Landscape*). In 1953, Generalić—still relatively unknown outside his homeland—did a show in Paris, sold everything, and came home rich. This put Croatian naive art on the international map and kick-started a new vigor in the movement. *Woodcutters,* from 1959, shows the next phase, as Generalić's works became even more rich with

fantasy—the peacock, the men clinging to tree tops, and the trademark "coral trees." Instead of showing, Generalić is evoking; naive art strove to capture the spirit and emotion of peasant life. Paintings such as this one inspired Generalić's

followers (called the "Hlebine School," for the village where Generalić lived).

Flanking the door are works by the next generation of naive art—two big-name followers who were inspired (if not trained) by Generalić: on the left, the gruesome *Evangelists at Cavalry* crucifix, by **Ivan Večenaj,** who focused on religious scenes; and on the right, *Winter Landscape with Woman,* by **Mijo Kovačić,** who specialized in peasant landscapes.

Room 2: The next room features more works by Večenaj and Kovačić. Studying Kovačić's many landscapes, notice how he took a style of painting pioneered by Generalić and brought it to the next level. Winter scenes were most common, because the peasant artists were busy working the fields the rest of the year. (Early on, such artists were sometimes called "Sunday painters," because they had to work their "real" jobs from Monday to Saturday.) Kovačić also enjoyed winter scenes for the evocative black-and-white contrast they allowed. Like Dalí, Magritte, and other surrealists, Kovačić juxtaposed super-realism (look at each individual hair on the swine in his painting *Swineherd,* pictured below) with fantastical, almost otherworldly settings. Also in this room are some landscapes by **Dragan Gaži,** a friend and neighbor of Generalić's.

You may notice that these supposedly "untrained" artists seem to borrow from other painters—most notably, the countryside peasant scenes often feel ripped from a Pieter Bruegel canvas.

While not formally schooled, there's no doubt that these artists were aware of, and often inspired by, their artistic forebears.

Also notice that naive artists frequently painted on glass. It was cheaper and more readily available in rural areas than art canvases, and—because it required no special technique—was an easier medium for the untrained naive artists to work on.

Room 3: On the right, find the portraits of Roma (Gypsy) people by **Martin Mehkek.** For the one depicting his cross-eyed neighbor Steve, Mehkek mostly painted with his fingers, using brushes only for fine details (such as the Hitler-style moustache). On the other side of the door is *Guiana '78*—by **Josip Generalić,** the founder's less-talented son—showing the gruesome aftermath of the Jim Jones mass suicide, with a pair of monkeys surveying the smiling corpses. (While vivid, this painting doesn't reflect the Croatian peasant experience, and the curator admits it's not the best representative of naive art.) Filling out the room are more of those distinctive coral-style trees that per-vade naive works, these by **Ivan Lacković.**

Room 4: This room shows off two big names from the latter part of the move-ment. On the left are lyrical landscapes by **Ivan Rabuzin,** arguably second only to Ivan Generalić in importance to this movement. Like a visual haiku, Rabuzin's dreamlike world of hills, trees, and clouds is reminis-cent of Marc Chagall. Rabuzin's works are especially popular among the museum's many Japanese visitors. On the right are **Emerik Feješ**'s colorful scenes of famous monu-

ments from around Europe—Paris, Venice, Vienna, Milan, and more. In fact, Feješ never traveled to any of these places—his paintings are based on romantic black-and-white postcards of the era, which Feješ "colorized" in his unique style.

Rooms 5 and 6: Room 5 displays works mostly by naive art-ists from other countries. And Room 6 features pencil sketches used by naive artists to create their works. After the sketch was complete, the artist would put it against a pane of glass to paint the scene—small details first, gradually filling in more and more of the background. Then the glass painting would literally be flipped over to be viewed. All of the works on glass you've seen in this collection were actually painted backwards.

Other Museums in Gradec

▲**Ivan Meštrović Atelier**—Ivan Meštrović—Croatia's most famous artist—designed, built, and decorated this house, and lived here from 1922 until 1942 (before he fled to the US after World War II). The house has been converted into a delightful gallery of the artist's works, displayed in two parts: residence and studio. Split's Meštrović Gallery (described on page 187) is the definitive museum of the 20th-cen-tury Croatian sculptor, but if you're not going there, Zagreb's gallery is a convenient place to gain an appreciation for this prolific, thought-

ZAGREB

ful artist (30 kn, 20-kn English catalog, Tue–Fri 10:00–18:00, Sat–Sun 10:00–14:00, closed Mon, behind St. Mark's Square at Mletačka 8, tel. 01/485-1123, www.mdc.hr/mestrovic). For more on Meštrović, see page 188.

▲Zagreb City Museum (Muzej Grada Zagreba)—This collection, with a modern, well-presented exhibit that sprawls over two floors of an old convent, traces the history of the city through town models, paintings, furniture, clothing, and lots of fascinating artifacts. After buying your ticket, head through the door and turn left, then work your way up through the ages. Each display has a fine English description. The 19th-century wing is like a folk museum. Find the giant map on the floor, punctuated with models of key buildings. The coverage of the tumultuous 20th century is perhaps most engaging, with an understandably bad attitude about the Serb-dominated first Yugoslav period, followed by stirring videos, a hall of propaganda posters, and artifacts from World War II and the Tito period (when Croatia was a player in Belgrade). The finale is a room dedicated to the creation of independent Croatia, including an exhibit on damage sustained during the warfare (20 kn, Tue–Fri 10:00–18:00, Thu until 22:00, Sat 11:00–19:00, Sun 10:00–14:00, closed Mon, at north end of Gradec at Opatička 20, tel. 01/485-1361, www.mgz.hr).

▲Cathedral (Katedrala)

By definition, Croats are Catholics. Before the recent war, relatively few people practiced their faith. But as the Croats fought against their Orthodox and Muslim neighbors, Catholicism took on a greater importance. Today, more and more Croats are attending Mass. This is Croatia's single most important church.

In 1094, when a diocese was established at Kaptol, this church quickly became a major center of high-ranking church officials. In the mid-13th century, the original cathedral was destroyed by invading Tatars, who actually used it as a stable. It was rebuilt, only to be destroyed again by an earthquake in 1880. The current version—undergoing yet another renovation for the last several years—is Neo-Gothic (about a hundred years old inside and out). Surrounding the church are walls with pointy-topped towers (part of a larger archbishop's palace) that were built for protection against the Ottomans. The full name is the Cathedral of the Assumption of the Blessed Virgin Mary and the Saintly Kings Stephen and Ladislav (whew!)—but most locals just call it "the cathedral."

As you stand out front, appreciate the stately facade and modern tympanum (carved semicircular section over the door). Then step inside and wander down the nave (free, Mon–Sat 10:00–17:00, Sun 13:00–17:00). Look closely at the silver relief on the main **altar:** a scene of the Holy Family doing chores around the house (Mary sewing, Joseph and Jesus building a fence...and angels helping out).

In the front-left corner (on the wall, between the confessionals), find the modern tombstone of **Alojzije Stepinac.** He was the Archbishop of Zagreb during World War II, when he shortsightedly supported the Ustaše (Nazi puppet government in Croatia)—thinking, like many Croatians, that this was the ticket to greater independence from Serbia. When Tito came to power, he put Stepinac on trial and sent him to jail for five years. But Stepinac never lost his faith, and he remains to many the most important inspirational figure of Croatian Catholicism. (He's also respected in the US, where some Catholic schools bear his name. But many Serbs today consider Stepinac a villain who cooperated with the brutal Ustaše.)

Facing the nearby altar, on the right look for the grave of **Josip Jelačić,** the statesman whose statue adorns Zagreb's main square.

As you leave the church, look high on the wall to the left of the door. This strange script is the **Glagolitic alphabet** *(glagoljca),* invented by Byzantine missionaries Cyril and Methodius in the ninth century to translate the Bible into Slavic languages. Though these missionaries worked mostly in Moravia (today's eastern Czech Republic), their alphabet caught on only here, in Croatia. (Glagolitic was later adapted in Bulgaria to become the Cyrillic alphabet—still used in Serbia, Russia, and other parts east.) In 1991, when Croatia became its own country and nationalism surged, the country flirted with the idea of making this the official alphabet.

The Green Horseshoe

With extra time, stroll around the Green Horseshoe (the U-shaped belt of parks and museums in the city center). The museums here aren't nearly as interesting as those on Gradec, but may be worth a peek on a rainy day.

Mimara Museum (Muzej Mimara)—This grand, empty-feeling building displays the eclectic collection of a wealthy Dalmatian, ranging from ancient artifacts to paintings by European masters. While the names are major—Rubens, Rembrandt, Velázquez, Renoir, Manet—the paintings themselves are minors. Still, art buffs may find something to get excited about (10 kn, 90 kn English guidebook, otherwise virtually no English, Tue–Sat 10:00–17:00, Thu until 19:00, Sun 10:00–14:00, closed Mon, Rooseveltov trg 5, tel. 01/482-8100).

Arts and Crafts Museum (Muzej za Umjetnost i Obrt)—This decorative arts collection of furniture, ceramics, and clothes is well-displayed. From the entry, go upstairs, then work your way clockwise and up to the top floor—passing through each artistic style, from Gothic to the present. It's mostly furniture, with a few paintings and other items thrown in (30 kn, some rooms have laminated English descriptions to borrow, otherwise very limited English, Tue–Sat 10:00–19:00, Thu until 22:00, Sun 10:00–14:00, closed Mon, Trg Maršala Tita 10, tel. 01/488-2111, www.muo.hr).

Botanical Garden (Botanički Vrt)—For a back-to-nature change of pace from the urban cityscape, wander through this relaxing garden, run by the University of Zagreb (free, Mon–Tue 9:00–14:30, Wed–Sun 9:00–18:00—or until 19:00 in summer, at southwest corner of the Green 'Shoe).

Sleeping In Zagreb

Hotels in central Zagreb are very expensive. I prefer sleeping in Ljubljana or at Plitvice Lakes National Park, both of which offer better values. But if you must stay in Zagreb, these are the best deals right in the main tourist zone. If you show up without a reservation, the TI can help you find a hotel room or *soba* for no fee.

$$$ Hotel Dubrovnik is a professional-feeling, business-class hotel with 268 rooms, ideally located at the bottom of Jelačić Square (small Sb-820 kn, bigger Sb-980 kn, Db with 1 big bed-1,200 kn, twin Db-1,300 kn, suite-1,500–1,600 kn, extra bed-250 kn, rooms overlooking the square don't cost extra but come with some tram noise, often cheaper on weekends, prices soft, air-con,

Sleep Code

(5 kn = about $1, country code: 385, area code: 01)
S = Single, **D** = Double/Twin, **T** = Triple, **Q** = Quad, **b** = bathroom. English is spoken at each place. Unless otherwise noted, credit cards are accepted, breakfast is included, and the modest tourist tax (7 kn per person, per night) is not.

To help you sort easily through these listings, I've divided the rooms into three categories based on the price for a standard double room with bath:

$$$ Higher Priced—Most rooms 800 kn or more.
$$ Moderately Priced—Most rooms between 500–800 kn.
$ Lower Priced—Most rooms 500 kn or less.

ZAGREB

non-smoking floors, elevator, free Internet access and Wi-Fi, Gajeva 1, tel. 01/486-3555, fax 01/486-3506, www.hotel-dubrovnik .hr, reservations@hotel-dubrovnik.hr).

$$$ Hotel Astoria, a Best Western, offers 100 smallish but plush, recently renovated rooms and a high-class lobby. It's on a grimy street near the train station, so I wouldn't splurge here unless I was in town on a weekend, when rates drop by a third (Sb-880–900 kn, Db-1,140 kn; Fri–Sun: Sb-610–690 kn, Db-785 kn; rates can be soft on some weekdays, various discounts offered—including military, fancier suites also available, air-con, elevator, free Internet access and Wi-Fi, Petrinjska 71, tel. 01/480-8900, fax 01/480-8908, www.bestwestern.com, recepcija@hotelastoria.hr).

$$ InZagreb, run by Ivana and Ksandro Kovačić, rents nine well-furnished, mostly one-bedroom apartments in various buildings around the city. While locations vary, most are within a 10- to 15-minute walk of the main square. Visit their website, find the apartment that appeals to you, and make a reservation. Clearly communicate your arrival time, and they'll pick you up at the train or bus station (no extra charge) or at the airport (150 kn extra) and take you to your home-away-from-home in Zagreb (Db-475–625 kn depending on apartment and location, no 1-night stays, 50 percent extra for 2-night stays, no breakfast, kitchenettes, air-con, free Wi-Fi, laundry machine, mobile 091-652-3201, fax 01/652-3201, www.inzagreb.com, info@inzagreb.com).

$$ Hotel Central's 76 overly perfumed rooms are comfortable and modern, and the price is right. This place seems to get a little better every year, and the location—right across from the main train station—is convenient for rail travelers (Sb-530 kn, larger Sb-660 kn, Db with one big bed-800 kn, twin Db-870 kn, Tb-1,100 kn, air-con, elevator, free Wi-Fi, Branimirova 3, tel.

01/484-1122, fax 01/484-1304, www.hotel-central.hr, info@hotel -central.hr).

$$ Hotel Jadran has 49 outdated, throwback rooms two urban blocks from the cathedral, and about a 10-minute walk east of Jelačić Square (Sb-520 kn, Db-730 kn, Tb-900 kn, some street noise—request quiet room, air-con, elevator, pay Wi-Fi, Vlaška 50, tel. 01/455-3777, fax 01/461-2151, www.hup-zagreb.hr, jadran @hup-zagreb.hr).

$ Apartments Lessi, run by youthful and English-speaking Tin, are three rooms that share a centrally located courtyard with a bar and the Fulir Backpackers Inn (see next listing). The rooms (one of which is up a tight spiral staircase) have pleasantly rustic decor with modern comforts (smaller room: Sb-200 kn, Db-360 kn; apartments: Sb-350 kn, Db 450 kn, Tb-550 kn, Qb-600 kn; cash only, no breakfast, air-con, free Wi-Fi, tucked down the courtyard at Radićeva 3a, mobile 091-288-8858, www.lessi.com.hr, info@lessi.com.hr).

$ Fulir Backpackers Inn, a funky slumbermill named for a legendary Zagrebian bon vivant, is loosely run by Davor and Leo, a pair of can-do Croats who lived in Ohio. It's colorful, friendly, and youthful, with a big 10-bunk dorm, three six-bed rooms, and a quad. Just a few steps from Jelačić Square, this hostel puts you in the heart of Zagreb (130–145 kn/bunk depending on season— cheaper Oct–April, includes sheets, no breakfast, free lockers, free Internet access and Wi-Fi, self-service laundry, upstairs at the end of the courtyard at Radićeva 3a, tel. 01/483-0882, mobile 098-193-0552, www.fulir-hostel.com).

Eating in Zagreb

People-Watching and Coffee-Sipping

One of my favorite Zagreb pastimes is nursing a drink along its thriving people zones, watching an endless parade of fashionable locals saunter past, and wondering why they don't create such an

inviting space in my hometown. The best place is on **Tkalčićeva street,** Zagreb's main café street and urban promenade rolled into one. It's a parade of fashionable locals and *the* place to see and be seen (starts a block behind Jelačić Square, next to the market). I've listed my favorite Tkalčićeva eat- eries next. Honorable mention goes to **Trg Petra Preradovića,** an inviting square just a short walk from Jelačić Square (up Ilica street) that bustles with appealing outdoor cafés and bars.

Eating on or near Tkalčićeva Street

Most places along Tkalčićeva serve only drinks. For a meal, consider these options.

Pivnica Medvedgrad is a brewpub serving five different in-house beers and heavy, stick-to-your-ribs pub grub that feels closer to Prague than to Dubrovnik. The food offers a welcome break from the pizzas-pastas-and-seafood rut you'll encounter on the coast, and the outdoor seating right on Tkalčićeva's most colorful stretch will seduce you into staying for another beer (25–50-kn meals, daily 10:00–24:00, food served until 22:00, Tkalčićeva 36, tel. 01/492-9613).

Nokturno, just off of Tkalčićeva, serves up good pizza and pasta in a lively interior and has ample outdoor seating on a terrace cascading down the street (cheap 20–30-kn pizzas, pastas, and salads; 30–50-kn meat and fish dishes; daily 9:00–1:00 in the morning, Skalinska 4, tel. 01/481-3394).

At the Market **(Dolac):** Zagreb's busy market offers plenty of options (Mon–Sat 7:00–14:00, Sun 7:00–13:00). Assemble a fresh picnic direct from the producers. Or, for something already prepared, duck into one of the many cheap restaurants and cafés on the streets around the market. The middle level of the market, facing Jelačić Square, is home to a line of places with cheap food and indoor or outdoor seating.

Elsewhere in Zagreb

Vinodol is your white-tablecloth classy dinner spot, with a peaceful covered terrace and a smartly appointed dining room under an impressive vaulted ceiling. The good, reasonably priced cuisine includes veal prepared *peka*-style, in a pot covered with hot coals (*peka* portion costs 80 kn, served only at certain times—generally at 12:30 and 18:30; 60–100-kn main courses, open daily 10:00–24:00, Teslina 10, tel. 01/481-1427).

Sky-High Asian: To dine on trendy Japanese fare atop a skyscraper with Zagreb's best view, ride up to the 16th floor of the Ilica Tower (just a block off Jelačić Square) and grab a table at **Sora.** The restaurant has mod, air-conditioned, jazzy ambience and enjoys fantastic views over the rooftops of Zagreb, though the stout security bars shatter some of the appeal (35–50-kn sushi, 30–70-kn light dishes, 70–90-kn noodles, 80–170-kn main courses, Mon–Sat 11:30–1:00 in the morning, closed Sun, reservations smart, Ilica 1a, tel. 01/482-8940).

In the Upper Town (Gradec): For a lunch or dinner break from sightseeing in the upper town, **Konoba Didov San** serves up traditional food from the Dalmatian hinterland. You'll find the normal Dalmatian specialties, plus eel, frogs, and snails. Choose between the homey, traditional interior and the outdoor tables

(25–40-kn starters, 60–100-kn main courses, daily 10:00–24:00, a few steps up from the Ivan Meštrović Atelier at Mletačka 11, tel. 01/485-1154).

Fast and Cheap: **Sandwich Bar Pingvin,** busy with locals dropping by for take-away, is a favorite for quick, cheap, tasty sandwiches with chicken, turkey, steak, fish, and even salmon. They'll wrap it all in a piece of grilled bread and top it with your choice of veggies and sauces to go—or, to eat here, sit at one of the few tiny tables or stools. There are so many options that ordering can be tricky, but the menu is in English, and the staff generally speaks English, too (20–30 kn, open long hours daily, about a block below Jelačić Square at Teslina 7).

Fried and Fishy: **Mimice** is a local institution and an old-habits-die-hard favorite of the older generation. While a bit tired and dreary, it's a cheap and memorable time-warp serving up simple fish dishes (15–35 kn, order starches and sauces separately). Choose what you want from the limited menu (if confused, survey the room for a plate that looks good and ask what it is), pay, and take your receipt to the next counter to claim your food. Order the smelt to get a plate of tiny deep-fried fish (Mon–Fri 7:00–22:00, Sat 7:00–18:00, closed Sun, Jurišićeva 21). As Zagreb is a Catholic town, you'll have to wait in line if you're here on a Friday.

Dessert: As the long line out front suggests, Zagreb's favorite *sladoled* (Italian gelato-style ice cream) is at **Slastičarnica Vincek,** two blocks west of Jelačić Square. Choose from a wide variety of flavors (6 kn/scoop), giving special consideration to the Vincek flavor—chocolate and walnuts. They also have other desserts, including *Zagrebačka kremšnita*—a variation on the famous cream-and-custard cake from Lake Bled (see page 456), but with chocolate (Mon–Sat 8:00–23:00, closed Sun, on the busy tram-lined Ilica street at #18).

Zagreb Connections

From Zagreb by Train to: Rijeka (3/day, 4 hrs), **Pula** (3/day, 6 hrs, transfer in Rijeka; in summer also 1 night train, 8 hrs), **Split** (3/day, 2/day off-season, 5.5 hrs, plus 1 direct night train, 8 hrs), **Mostar** (1/day, 12 hrs, bus is faster), **Ljubljana** (8/day, 2.5 hrs), **Vienna** (4/day, 5.5–7 hrs, 2 direct, others with 1–2 changes), **Budapest** (2/day, 5 or 7 hrs), **Lake Bled** (via Lesce-Bled, 5/day, 3.5 hrs).

By Bus to: Samobor (about 3/hr, 30 min), **Plitvice Lakes National Park** (about hourly until around 16:00, 2–2.5 hrs), **Rijeka** (hourly, 3.5 hrs), **Rovinj** (6–9/day, 5–8 hrs), **Pula** (almost hourly, 3.75–6 hrs), **Split** (about 2/hr, 5–9 hrs), **Mostar** (1/day, 8 hrs, plus 1 night bus, 9.5 hrs), **Dubrovnik** (7/day including some overnight options, 10 hrs), **Korčula** (1/night, 13.5 hrs).

Bus schedules can be sporadic (e.g., several departures clustered around the same time, then nothing for hours)—confirm your plans carefully (inquire locally, or use the good online schedules at www.akz.hr). The TI is very helpful with providing bus information. Popular buses, such as the afternoon express to Split, can fill up quickly in peak season. Unfortunately, it's impossible to buy bus tickets anywhere in the center, so to guarantee a seat, you'll have to get to the station early (locals suggest even two hours in advance). Better yet, call the central number for the bus station to check schedules and reserve the bus you want, ideally at least 24 hours ahead: tel. 060-313-333 (from abroad, dial +385-1-611-2789). If you can't get an English-speaker on the line, and the TI isn't too busy, they might be willing to call for you.

Near Zagreb: Samobor

This charming little town, tucked between Zagreb and the Slovenian border, is where city dwellers head to unwind, get away from the clattering trams, and gorge themselves on sausages and cream cakes. Cuddled by hiker-friendly hills, bisected by a picturesque stream, favored by artists and poets, and proud of its tidy square, Samobor is made to order for a break from the big city.

Orientation to Samobor

Samobor (with 15,000 people, plus 20,000 more in the surrounding area) has a pleasantly compact tourist zone. Virtually anything you'd want to see or do is within sight of its centerpiece, King Tomislav Square (Trg Kralja Tomislava). A stream called Gradna cuts through the middle of town.

Tourist Information

The eager TI is dead center on the main square (Mon–Fri 8:00–19:00, Sat 9:00–17:00, Sun 10:00–17:00, Trg Kralja Tomislava 5, tel. 01/336-0044, www.samobor.hr). Pick up the free, handy map-guide, and get suggestions for restaurants and hikes.

Getting There

By public transportation, you'll have to arrive by **bus** via Zagreb (about 3/hr, 20 kn, 30-min trip). Once at Samobor's bus station, go to the end of the station that has all the kiosks. From there, walk five minutes (past the covered produce market) toward the big, yellow steeple that marks the main square.

By **car,** Samobor is just off the main Zagreb–Ljubljana

expressway. Exit following signs for Samobor, then follow the bull's-eyes to the *Centar*. Once at the main square, drive over the little covered bridge to reach the parking lot (5 kn/hr, put ticket on dashboard).

Sights in Samobor

Samobor is more about ambience than about sightseeing. Stroll the main square, sit at a café, gaze at the surrounding hills, and contemplate a hike. For extra credit, you can drop into the town's sleepy Samobor Museum (10 kn, Tue–Fri 8:00–15:00, Sat 9:00–13:00, Sun 9:00–18:00, closed Mon, across the covered bridge from the main square at Livadićeva 7, tel. 01/336-1014).

Sleeping in Samobor

(5 kn = about $1, country code: 385, area code: 01)
Both of central Samobor's hotels are more welcoming and a much better deal than anything in downtown Zagreb. Rail or bus travelers might find it too much of a hassle to sleep in Samobor, but drivers may prefer to avoid urban traffic by sleeping here, then day-tripping by bus (30 min) into Zagreb.

$ Hotel Livadić, named for a Croatian patriot and Samobor native, has 23 rooms with elegant, old-fashioned décor over a classy café right on the main square (Sb-360–410 kn, Db-465 kn, bigger Db-530 kn, Tb-531 kn, 6 percent cheaper if you pay cash, free Internet access, Trg Kralja Tomislava 1, tel. 01/336-5850, fax 01/332-5588, www.hotel-livadic.hr, info@hotel-livadic.hr).

$ Hotel Lavica, more businesslike and less personal, rents 33 slightly worn rooms next to a pleasant park just across the covered bridge from the main square (Sb-225 kn, Db-300 kn, Tb-375 kn, Livadićeva 5, tel. 01/336-8000, fax 01/336-6611, www.lavica-hotel.hr, info@lavica-hotel.hr).

Eating in Samobor

Samobor is highly regarded among Zagrebians for its cuisine, and the TI loves to recommend specific restaurants. First, an apéritif: Samobor's own Bermet is a sweet red wine made with fruits and grasses from the Samobor hills. As it's an acquired taste, start with just a sip. The local sausage, *češnjovke,* is traditionally eaten with the town's own mustard, *Samoborska Muštarda* (sold in little ceramic pots). Round out your meal with a piece of cream cake, or *kremšnita* (curiously similar to Lake Bled's specialty).

PLITVICE LAKES NATIONAL PARK

Nacionalni Park Plitvička Jezera

Plitvice (PLEET-veet-seh) is one of Europe's most spectacular natural wonders. Imagine Niagara Falls diced and sprinkled over a heavily forested Grand Canyon. There's nothing like this lush valley of 16 terraced lakes, laced together by waterfalls and miles of pleasant plank walks. Countless cascades and water that's both strangely clear and full of vibrant colors make this park a misty natural wonderland. Years ago, after eight or nine visits, I thought I really knew Europe. Then I discovered Plitvice and realized you can never exhaust Europe's surprises.

Planning Your Time

Plitvice deserves at least a few good hours. Since it takes some time to get here (two hours by car or bus from Zagreb), the most sensible plan is to spend the night in one of the park's hotels (no character, but comfortable and convenient) or a nearby private home (cheaper, but practical only if you're driving). If you're coming from the north (e.g., Ljubljana), you can take the train to Zagreb in the morning, spend a few hours seeing the Croatian capital, then take the bus (generally no buses after about 16:00) or drive to Plitvice in the late afternoon to spend the night at the park. Get up early and hit the trails (ideally by 8:30); by early afternoon, you'll be ready to move on (by bus to the coast, or back to Zagreb). The most interesting and accessible part of the park can be seen very efficiently, in

a three- to four-hour hike; while there are other hiking opportunities, they pale in comparison to this "greatest hits" section.
Therefore, two nights and a full day at Plitvice is probably overkill
for all but the most avid hikers.

Crowd-Beating Tips: Plitvice is swamped with international
tour groups, many of whom aren't shy about elbowing into position
for the best photos. The park's trails are most crowded between
10:00 and 15:00. It's essential to get an early start to get in front of
the hordes. I try to hit the trails by 8:30; that way, the crowds are
moving in just as I'm finishing up.

Getting to Plitvice

Plitvice Lakes National Park, a few miles from the Bosnian border, is two hours by car south of Zagreb on the old highway #1
(a.k.a. D-1).

By **car** from Zagreb, you'll take the A-1 expressway south
for about an hour, exiting at Karlovac (marked for *1* and *Plitvice*).
From here, D-1 takes you directly south about another hour to the
park. If you're staying at the park hotels, you can park for free at
the hotel lot; to park at the lots at Entrance 1 or Entrance 2, you'll
have to pay (7 kn/hr). For information about driving onward from
Plitvice, see "Route Tips for Drivers" at the end of this chapter.

Buses leave from Zagreb's main bus station in the direction
of Plitvice. Various bus companies handle the route; just go to
the ticket window and ask for the next departure (about 75–95 kn
depending on company, trip takes 2–2.5 hours). Buses run from
Zagreb about hourly until about 16:00; while sporadic buses run
late at night, they'll get you to the park extremely late and should
be avoided. Confirm that your bus will actually stop at Plitvice.
(The official Plitvice bus stop is along the main road, about a 5- to
10-minute walk beyond the hotels.) Confirm the schedule online
(www.akz.hr) or at the Plitvice office in Zagreb (Mon–Fri 8:00–
16:00, closed Sat–Sun, Trg Kralja Tomislava 19, tel. 01/461-3586).

By car or bus, you'll see some thought-provoking terrain
between Zagreb and Plitvice. As you leave Karlovac, you'll pass
through the village of **Turanj,** part of the war zone from almost
two decades ago. The destroyed, derelict houses belonged to Serbs
who have not come back to reclaim and repair them. Farther along,
about 25 miles before Plitvice, you'll pass through the striking village of **Slunj,** picturesquely perched on travertine formations (like
Plitvice's) and surrounded by sparkling streams and waterfalls. If
you're in a car, this is worth a photo stop. This town, too, looks very
different than it did before the war—when it was 30 percent Serb.
As in countless other villages in the Croatian interior, the Orthodox
church has been destroyed...and locals still seethe when they describe
how occupying Serbs "defiled" the town's delicate beauty.

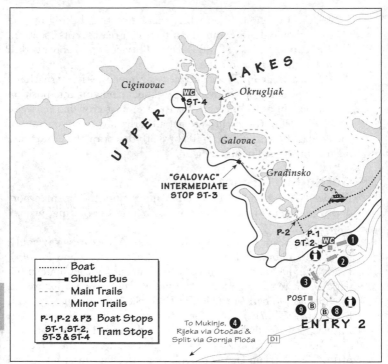

Orientation to Plitvice

(area code: 053)

Plitvice's 16 lakes are divided into the Upper Lakes (Gornja Jezera) and the Lower Lakes (Donja Jezera). The park officially has two entrances *(ulaz)*, each with ticket windows and snack and gift shops. Entrance 1 is at the bottom of the Lower Lakes, across the busy D-1 road from the park's best restaurant, Lička Kuća (described later, under "Eating in Plitvice"). Entrance 2 is about 1.5 miles south, below the cluster of Plitvice's three hotels (Jezero, Plitvice, and Bellevue; see "Sleeping in Plitvice," later). There is no town at Plitvice. The nearest village, Mukinje, is a residential community mostly for park workers (boring for tourists, but has some good private room options).

Cost: The price to enter the park during peak season (April–Oct) is 110 kn (80 kn Nov–March; covers park entry, boat, and shuttle bus). Park hotel guests pay the entry fee only once for their entire stay; if you're staying off-site and want to visit the park on several days, you'll have to buy separate tickets each day.

Hours: The park is open every day, but the hours vary by season. In summer, it's generally open 7:00–20:00 (last ticket sold at

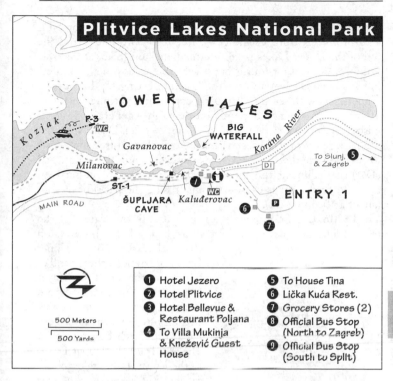

Plitvice Lakes National Park

L O W E R   L A K E S

Kozjak   P-3   WC

BIG WATERFALL

Korana River

Gavanovac

Milanovac

To Slunj & Zagreb ⑤

ST-1

D1

ŠUPLJARA CAVE   Kaluđerovac   WC   ⑦   ①

E N T R Y   1

MAIN ROAD

P

⑥

⑦

500 Meters
500 Yards

① Hotel Jezero
② Hotel Plitvice
③ Hotel Bellevue & Restaurant Poljana
④ To Villa Mukinja & Knežević Guest House

⑤ To House Tina
⑥ Lička Kuća Rest.
⑦ Grocery Stores (2)
⑧ Official Bus Stop (North to Zagreb)
⑨ Official Bus Stop (South to Split)

16:00); in spring and fall, 8:00–18:00 (last ticket sold at 14:00); and in winter, 8:00–16:00 (last ticket sold at 12:00). Night owls should note that the park never really "closes"; these hours are for the ticket booths and the boat and shuttle bus system. You can just stroll right into the park at any time, provided that you aren't using the boat or bus. Again, for fewer tour-group crowds, visit early or late in the day.

Tourist Information

A handy map of the trails is on the back of your ticket, and big maps are posted all over the park. The big map is a good investment; the various English-language guidebooks are generally poorly translated and not very helpful (both sold at entrances, hotels, and shops throughout the park). The park has a good website: www.np-plitvicka-jezera.hr.

Getting Around Plitvice

Of course, Plitvice is designed for hikers. But the park has a few ways (included in entry cost) to help you connect the best parts.

By Shuttle Bus: Buses connect the hotels at Entrance 2 (stop ST2, below Hotel Jezero) with the top of the Upper Lakes (stop ST4) and roughly the bottom of the Lower Lakes (stop ST1, a 10-min walk from Entrance 1). Between Entrance 2 and the top of the Upper Lakes is an intermediate stop (ST3, at Galovac Lake)—designed for tour groups, available to anyone, and offering a convenient way to skip the less interesting top half of the Upper Lakes. Buses start running early and continue until late afternoon (frequency depends on demand—generally 3–4/hr; buses run from March until the first snow—often Dec). Note that the park refers to its buses as "trains," which confuses some visitors. Also note that no local buses take you along the major road (D-1) that connects the entrances. The only way to get between them without a car is by shuttle bus (inside the park) or by foot (about a 40-min walk).

By Boat: Low-impact electric boats ply the waters of the biggest lake, Kozjak, with three stops: below Hotel Jezero (stop

P1), at the bottom of the Upper Lakes (P2), and at the far end of Kozjak, at the top of the Lower Lakes (P3). From Hotel Jezero to the Upper Lakes, it's a quick five-minute ride; the boat goes back and forth continuously. The trip from the Upper Lakes to the Lower Lakes takes closer to 20 minutes, and the boat goes about twice per hour—often at the top and bottom of every hour. (With up to 10,000 people a day visiting the park, you might have to wait for a seat on this boat.) Unless the lake freezes (about every five years), the boat also runs in the off-season—though frequency drops to hourly, and it stops running earlier.

Sights in Plitvice

Plitvice is a refreshing playground of 16 terraced lakes, separated by natural travertine dams and connected by countless waterfalls. Over time, the water has simultaneously carved out, and, with the help of mineral deposits, built up this fluid landscape.

Plitvice became Croatia's first national park in 1949, and was a popular destination during the Yugoslav period. On Easter Sunday in 1991, the first shots of Croatia's war with Yugoslavia were fired right here—in fact, the war's first casualty was a park policeman, Josip Jović. The Serbs occupied Plitvice until 1995, and most of the Croatians you'll meet here were evacuated and lived near the coastline as refugees. During those five years, the park saw virtually no tourists, and was allowed to grow wild—allowing the ecosystem to recover from the impact of so many visitors. Today, the war is a fading memory, and the park is again a popular tourist destination, with nearly a million visitors each year (though relatively few are from the US).

▲▲▲Hiking the Lakes

Plitvice's system of trails and boardwalks makes it possible for visitors to get immersed in the park's beauty. (In some places, the path leads literally right up the middle of a waterfall.) The official park map and signage recommend a variety of hikes, but there's no need to adhere strictly to these suggestions; invest in the big map and create your own route.

Most visitors stick to the main paths and choose between two basic plans: uphill or downhill. Each one has pros and cons. Park officials generally recommend hiking uphill, from the Lower Lakes to the Upper Lakes, which offers slightly better head-on views of the best scenery (this is the route described below). It also saves the most scenic stretch of lakes and falls—the Upper Lakes—for last. Hiking downhill, from Upper to Lower, is easier (though you'll have to hike steeply up out of the canyon at the end), and since most groups go the opposite way, you'll be passing—but not stuck behind—the crowds. Either way you go, walking briskly and with a few photo stops, figure on an hour for the Lower Lakes, an hour for the Upper Lakes, and a half-hour to connect them by boat.

Lower Lakes (Donja Jezera)—The lower half of Plitvice's lakes are accessible from Entrance 1. If you start here, the route marked *G2* (intended for groups, but doable for anyone) leads you along the boardwalks to Kozjak, the big lake that connects the Lower and the Upper Lakes (described later).

From the entrance, you'll descend a steep path with lots of **switchbacks,** as well as thrilling views over the canyon of the Lower Lakes. As you reach the lakes and begin to follow the boardwalks, you'll have great up-close views of the travertine formations that make up Plitvice's many waterfalls. Count the trout. If you're tempted to throw in a line, don't. Fishing is strictly forbidden. (Besides, they're happy.)

After you cross the path over the first lake, an optional

The Science of Plitvice

Virtually every visitor to Plitvice eventually asks the same question: How did it happen? A geologist once explained to me that Plitvice is a "perfect storm" of unique geological, climatic, and biological features you'll rarely find elsewhere on earth.

Plitvice's magic ingredient is calcium carbonate ($CaCO_3$), a mineral deposit from the limestone. Calcium is the same thing that makes "hard water" hard. If you have hard water, you may get calcium deposits on your cold-water faucet. But these deposits build up only at the faucet, not inside the pipes. That's because when hard water is motionless (as it usually is in the pipes), it holds on to the calcium. But at the point where the water is subjected to pressure and movement—as it pours out of the faucet—it releases the calcium.

Plitvice works the same way. As water flows over the park's limestone formations, it dissolves the rock, and the water becomes supersaturated with calcium carbonate. When the water is still, it holds on to the mineral—which helps create the beautiful deep-blue color of the pools. But when the water speeds up and spills over the edge of the lakes, it releases carbon dioxide gas. Without the support of the carbon dioxide, the water can't hold on to the calcium carbonate, so it gets deposited on the lake bed and at the edges of the lakes. Eventually, these deposits build up to form a rock called travertine (the same composition as the original limestone, but formed in a different way). The travertine coating becomes thicker, and barriers—and eventually dams and new waterfalls—are formed. The moss and

10-minute detour (to the right) takes you down to the **Big Waterfall** (Veliki Slap). It's the biggest of Plitvice's waterfalls, where the Plitvica River plunges 250 feet over a cliff into the valley below. Depending on recent rainfall, the force of the Big Waterfall varies from a light mist to a thundering deluge.

If you're a hardy hiker, consider climbing the steep steps from the Big Waterfall up to a **viewpoint** at the top of the canyon (marked *Sightseeing Point/Vidikovac*; it's a strenuous 10-min hike to the top). Take the stairs up, bearing to the right at the top (near the shelter) to find a nice viewpoint overlooking the Big Waterfall. From here, you can carry on along the road that actually goes up over the top of the Big Waterfall, offering more views over the park. (Go as far as you like, then return grass serve as a natural foundation for the calcification. In other words, the stone hangs down like the foliage because the foliage guides the growth of the stone. Because of this ongoing process, Plitvice's landscape is always changing.

And why is the water so clear? For one thing, it comes directly from high-mountain runoff, giving it little opportunity to become polluted or muddy. And because the water calcifies everything it touches, it prevents the creation of mud—so the bottoms of the lakes are entirely stone. Also, a different mineral in the water, magnesium carbonate, both gives the water its special color (which, park rangers brag, changes based on the direction of the sunshine) and makes it highly basic, preventing the growth of plant life (such as certain algae) that could cloud the water.

The park contains nearly 1,300 different species of plants. Wildlife found in the park include deer, wolves, wildcats, lynx, wild boar, voles, otters, 350 species of butterflies, 42 types of dragonflies, 21 species of bats, and more than 160 species of birds (including eagles, herons, owls, grouse, and storks). The lakes (and local menus) are full of trout, and you'll also see smaller, red-finned fish called *klen* ("chub" in English). Perhaps most importantly, Plitvice is home to about 40 or 50 brown bears—a species now extremely endangered in Europe. You'll see bears, the park's mascot, plastered all over the tourist literature (and in the form of a scary representative in the lobby of Hotel Jezero).

the way you came.) The giant mill perched at the top of the Big Waterfall was used to grind grains; this very poor part of Croatia was traditionally inhabited by farmers.

After seeing the Big Waterfall, backtrack up to the main trail and continue on the boardwalks. After you pass another bank of waterfalls, a smaller trail branches off (on the left) toward **Šupljara Cave.** You can actually climb through this slippery cave all the way up to the trail overlooking the Lower Lakes (though it's not recommended). This unassuming cavern is a surprisingly big draw. In the 1960s, several German and Italian "Spaghetti Westerns" were filmed at Plitvice and in other parts of Croatia (which, to European eyes, has terrain similar to the American West). The most famous, *Der Schatz im Silbersee (The Treasure in Silver Lake)*, was filmed here at Plitvice, and the treasure was hidden in this cave. The movie—complete with *Deutsch*-speaking "Native Americans"—is still a favorite in Germany, and popular theme tours bring German tourists to movie locations here in Croatia. (If you drive the roads near Plitvice, keep an eye out for strange, Native American–sounding names such as Winnetou—fictional characters from these beloved stories of the Old West, by the German writer Karl May.)

After Šupljara Cave, you'll stick to the east side of the lakes, then cross over one more time to the west, where you'll cut through a comparatively dull forest. You'll emerge at a pit-stop-perfect clearing with WCs, picnic tables, a souvenir shop, and a self-service restaurant. Here you can catch the shuttle boat across Lake Kozjak to the bottom of the Upper Lakes (usually every 30 min).

Lake Kozjak (Jezero Kozjak)—The park's biggest lake, Kozjak, connects the Lower and Upper Lakes. The 20-minute boat ride between Plitvice's two halves offers a great chance for a breather. You can hike between the lakes along the west side of Kozjak, but the scenery's not nearly as good as in the rest of the park.

Upper Lakes (Gornja Jezera)—Focus on the lower half of the Upper Lakes, where nearly all the exotic beauty is. From the boat dock, signs for C and G2 direct you up to Gradinsko Lake through the most striking scenery in the whole park. Enjoy the stroll, taking your time...and lots of photos.

After Gradinsko Lake, when you reach the top of Galovac Lake, you'll have three options:

1. Make your hike a loop by continuing around the lake (following H and G1 signs back to the P2 boat dock), then take the boat back over to the hotels (P1 stop).

2. Hike a few steps up to the ST3 bus stop to catch the shuttle bus back to the hotels (more efficient, but doesn't give you a second look at the lakes).

3. Continue hiking up to the top of the Upper Lakes; you'll get away from the crowds and feel like you've covered the park thoroughly. From here on up, the scenery is less stunning, and the waterfalls are fewer and farther between. At the top, you'll finish at shuttle bus stop ST4 (with food stalls and a WC), where the bus zips you back to the entrances and hotels.

Nice work!

Sleeping in Plitvice

At the Park

The most convenient way to sleep at Plitvice is to stay at the park's lodges, which are run by the same office (reservation tel. 053/751-015, fax 053/751-013, www.np-plitvicka-jezera.hr, info @np-plitvicka-jezera.hr; reception numbers for each hotel listed below). Warning: Because of high volume in peak season, the booking office often doesn't respond to emails. Instead, to make a reservation, use the park's website to book your room (look for the "Online booking" box). In a pinch, try calling the book-

---

Sleep Code

(€1 = about $1.40, country code: 385, area code: 053)
English is spoken, credit cards are accepted, and breakfast is included at each place. The tourist tax (€1 per person, per day) is not included in these prices.

To help you sort easily through these listings, I've divided the rooms into three categories based on the price for a standard double room with bath in peak season:

$$$ **Higher Priced**—Most rooms €100 or more.
$$ **Moderately Priced**—Most rooms between €50-100.
$ **Lower Priced**—Most rooms €50 or less.

---

ing office or the hotel directly (they speak English), or emailing the park information office in Zagreb (np.zg.info@np-plitvicka-jezera.hr), which is more likely to respond in the busy summer months.

$$$ Hotel Jezero is big and modern, with all the comfort—and charm—of a Holiday Inn. It's well-located right at the park entrance and offers 200 rooms that feel newish, but generally have at least one thing that's broken. Rooms facing the park have big glass doors and balconies (July–Aug: Sb-€83, Db-€118; May–June and Sept–Oct: Sb-€76, Db-€108; Nov–April: Sb-€61, Db-€86; elevator, reception tel. 053/751-400).

$$ Hotel Plitvice, a better value than Jezero, offers 50 rooms and mod, wide-open public spaces on two floors with no elevators. For rooms, choose from economy (fine, older-feeling; July–Aug: Sb-€72, Db-€96; May–June and Sept–Oct: Sb-€65, Db-€82; Nov–April: Sb-€50, Db-€70), standard (just a teeny bit bigger; July–Aug: Sb-€77, Db-€106; May–June and Sept–Oct: Sb-€70, Db-€96; Nov–April: Sb-€55, Db-€74), or superior (bigger still, with a sitting area; July–Aug: Sb-€82, Db-€116; May–June and Sept–Oct: Sb-€75, Db-€106; Nov–April: Sb-€60, Db-€84, reception tel. 053/751-100).

$$ Hotel Bellevue is simple and bare-bones (no TVs or elevator). It has an older feel to it, but the price is right and the 80 rooms are perfectly acceptable (July–Aug: Sb-€55, Db-€74; May–June and Sept–Oct: Sb-€50, Db-€68; Nov–April: Sb-€40, Db-€54; reception tel. 053/751-700).

Sobe near the Park

While the park's lodges are the easiest choice for non-drivers, those with a car should consider sleeping at a $–$$ *sobe* (room in a private home). You'll see *sobe* signs for miles on either side of the park. A few that have good reputations include **Villa Mukinja** (in the village of Mukinje just south of the park, tel. 01/652-1857, www .plitvice-lakes.com, info@plitvice-lakes.com), **House Tina** (just north of the park in the village of Grabovac, tel. 04/778-4197), and **Knežević Guest House** (also in the village of Mukinje, tel. 053/774-081, mobile 098-168-7576, www.knezevic.hr, guest _house@vodatel.net, daughter Kristina speaks English).

Eating in Plitvice

The park runs all of the restaurants at Plitvice. These places are handy, and the food is affordable and decent. If you're staying at the hotels, you have the option of paying for half-board with your room (lunch or dinner, €12 each). This option is designed for the restaurants inside hotels Jezero and Plitvice, but you can also use the voucher at other park eateries (you'll pay the difference if the bill is more). The half-board option is worth doing if you're here for dinner, but don't lock yourself in for lunch—you'll want more flexibility as you explore Plitvice (excellent picnic spots and decent food stands abound inside the park).

Hotel Jezero and **Hotel Plitvice** both have big restaurants with adequate food and friendly, professional service (half-board for dinner, described above, is a good deal; or order à la carte; both open daily until 23:00).

Lička Kuća, across the pedestrian overpass from Entrance 1, has a wonderfully dark and smoky atmosphere around a huge open-air wood-fired grill (pricey, daily 11:00–24:00, tel. 053/751-024).

Restaurant Poljana, behind Hotel Bellevue, has the same boring, park-lodge atmosphere in both of its sections: cheap, self-service cafeteria and sit-down restaurant with open wood-fired grill (same choices and prices as the better-atmosphere

Lička Kuća, above; both parts open daily but closed in winter, tel. 053/751-092).

For **picnic** fixings, there's a small grocery store at Entrance 1 and another one with a larger selection across road D-1 (use the pedestrian overpass). At the P3 boat dock, you can buy grilled meat and drinks. Friendly old ladies sell homemade goodies (such as strudel or hunks of cheese) throughout the park, including at Entrance 1.

Plitvice Connections

To reach the park, see "Getting to Plitvice," earlier in this chapter. Moving on from Plitvice is trickier. **Buses** pass by the park in each direction—northbound (to **Zagreb,** 2–2.5 hrs) and southbound (to coastal destinations such as **Split,** 4–6 hrs).

There is no bus station—just a low-profile *Plitvice Centar* bus stop shelter. To reach it from the park, go out to the main road from either Hotel Jezero or Hotel Plitvice, then turn right; the bus stops are just after the pedestrian overpass. The one on the hotel side of the road is for buses headed for the coast (southbound); the stop on the opposite side is for Zagreb (northbound). Try to carefully confirm the bus schedule with the park or hotel staff, then head out to the bus stop and wave down the bus. (It's easy to confuse public buses with private tour buses, so don't panic if a bus doesn't stop for you—look for a bus with your final destination marked in the windshield.)

But here's the catch: If the bus is full, they won't stop to pick you up at Plitvice. This is most common on days when the buses are jammed with people headed to or from the coast. For example, on Fridays—when everyone is going from Zagreb to Split—you'll have no luck catching a southbound bus at Plitvice after about 12:00, as they are likely to be full. Similarly, on Sunday afternoons, northbound buses are often full.

While this sounds risky, and there is a chance that you'll miss a bus and have to wait for the next one, in practice it usually works...if you're patient.

Route Tips for Drivers

Plitvice's biggest disadvantage is that it's an hour away from the handy A-1 expressway that connects northern Croatia to the Dalmatian Coast. You have three ways to access this expressway from Plitvice, depending on which direction you're heading.

Going North: If you're heading north (to Zagreb or Slovenia), you'll get on the expressway at **Karlovac:** From Plitvice, drive about one hour north on D-1 to the town of Karlovac, where you can access A-1 northbound. Alternatively, you can take A-1 southbound to A-6, which leads west to Rijeka, Opatija, and Istria (though this route is more boring and only slightly faster than the route via Otočac, next).

Going to Central Croatia: If you're going to central destinations, such as Istria, Rijeka, Opatija, or Rab, get on the expressway at **Otočac.** From Plitvice, go south on D-1, then go west on road #52 to the town of Otočac (about an hour through the mountains from Plitvice to Otočac). After Otočac, you can get on A-1 (north to Zagreb, south to the Dalmatian Coast); or continue west and twist down the mountain road to the seaside town of Senj, on the main coastal road of the Kvarner Gulf. From Senj, it's about an hour north along the coast to Rijeka, then on to Opatija or Istria; or an hour south to Jablanac, where you can catch the ferry to Rab Island.

During the recent war, the front line between the Croats and Serbs ran just east of **Otočac** (OH-toh-chawts), and bullet holes

still mar the town's facades. (Watch for minefield warning signs just east of Otočac, but don't be too nervous—it's safe to drive here, but not safe to get out of your car and wander through the fields.) Today Otočac is putting itself back together, and it's a fine place to drop into a café for a coffee, or pick up some produce at the outdoor market. The Catholic church in the center of town, destroyed in the war but now rebuilt, has a memorial out back with its damaged church bells. Notice that the crucifix nearby is made of old artillery shells. Just up the main street, beyond the big, grassy park, is the Orthodox church. Otočac used to be about one-third Serbian, but the Serbs were forced out during the war, and this church fell into disrepair. But, as Otočac and Croatia show signs of healing, about two dozen Serbs have returned to town and reopened their church (for more on the Serbian Orthodox Church, see page 278).

Going South: If you're heading south (to Split and the rest of Dalmatia) from Plitvice, catch the expressway at **Gornja Ploča.** Drive south from Plitvice on D-1, through Korenica, Pećane, and Udbina, then follow signs for the A-1 expressway (and *Lovinac*) via Kurjak to the Gornja Ploča on-ramp. Once on A-1, you'll twist south through the giant Sveti Rok tunnel to Dalmatia.

ISTRIA

Rovinj • Pula • The Brijuni Islands • Poreč • Hill Towns

Idyllic Istria (EE-stree-ah; "Istra" in Croatian), at Croatia's northwest corner, reveals itself to you gradually and seductively. Pungent truffles, Roman ruins, striking hill towns, quaint coastal villages, carefully cultivated food and wine, and breezy Italian culture all compete for your attention. The wedge-shaped Istrian Peninsula, while not as famous as its southern rival (the much-hyped Dalmatian Coast), is giving Dalmatia a run for its money.

The Istrian coast, with gentle green slopes instead of the sheer limestone cliffs found along the rest of the Croatian shoreline, is more serene than sensational. It's lined with pretty, interchangeably tacky resort towns, such as the tourist mecca Poreč (worthwhile only for its Byzantine mosaic-packed basilica). But one seafront village reaches the ranks of greatness: romantically creaky Rovinj, my favorite little town on the Adriatic. Down at the tip of Istria is big, industrial Pula, offering a bustling urban contrast to the rest of the time-passed coastline, plus some impressive Roman ruins (including an amphitheater so remarkably intact, you'll marvel that you haven't heard of it before). Just offshore are the Brijuni Islands—once the stomping grounds of Maršal Tito, whose ghost still haunts a national park peppered with unexpected attractions.

But Croatia is more than the sea, and diverse Istria offers some of the country's most appealing reasons to head inland. In the Istrian interior, between humble concrete towns crying out for a paint job, you'll find vintners painstakingly reviving a delicate winemaking tradition, farmers pressing that last drop of oil out of their olives, trained dogs sniffing out truffles in primeval forests, and a smattering of fortified medieval hill towns with sweeping

views over the surrounding terrain—including the justifiably popular village of Motovun and the artists' colony of Grožnjan.

Planning Your Time

Istria offers an exciting variety of attractions compared to the relatively uniform, if beautiful, string of island towns farther south. While some travelers wouldn't trade a sunny island day for anything, I prefer to sacrifice a little time on the Dalmatian Coast for the diversity that comes with a day or two exploring Istria's hill towns and other unique sights.

Istria's main logistical advantage is that it's easy to reach and

Istria at a Glance

▲▲▲**Rovinj** Extremely romantic, Venetian-style coastal town with an atmospheric Old Town and salty harbor. See page 93.

▲▲**Pula** Big, industrial port town with one of the world's best-preserved Roman amphitheaters. See page 116.

▲▲**Motovun** Touristy but enjoyable hill town with a fun rampart walk offering sweeping views over inland Istria. See page 136.

Brijuni Islands Tito's former summer residence, now a national park with a Tito museum, mini-safari, and other offbeat sights. See page 128.

Grožnjan Sleepy artists' colony hill town in the interior. See page 142.

Hum Miniscule, touristy town deep in the interior. See page 145.

Poreč Big coastal resort squeezed full of European holiday-makers, plus a church with remarkably intact Byzantine mosaics. See page 132.

ISTRIA

to explore by car. Just a quick hop from Venice or Slovenia, compact little Istria is made-to-order for a quick, efficient road trip.

With a car and two weeks to spend in Croatia and Slovenia, Istria deserves two days, divided between its two big attractions: the coastal town of Rovinj and the hill towns of the interior. Ideally, make your home base for two nights in Rovinj or in Motovun, and day-trip to the region's other attractions. To wring the most out of limited Istrian time, the city of Pula and its Roman amphitheater are well worth a few hours. If you have a car, it's easy to go for a joyride through the Istrian countryside, visiting a few hill towns en route. The town of Poreč and the fun but time-consuming Brijuni Islands merit a detour only if you've got at least three days.

Getting Around Istria

Istria is a cinch for **drivers,** who find distances short and roads and attractions well-marked (though summer traffic can be miserable, especially on weekends). While Istria has no four-lane expressways, it is neatly connected by a speedy two-lane highway nicknamed the *ipsilon* (the Croatian word for the letter Y, which

Istrian Food and Wine

Foodies consider Istria the best part of Croatia. Though much of the country is arid and barren, Istria is noticeably greener—its fertile soil bursts with a cornucopia of delicious ingredients. Like the Istrian people, Istrian cuisine is a mix of various cultural influences, including Italian-style elements, farmer fare, and seafood. Truffles are used liberally, if only to please the many tourists who come here for their pungent flavor (see sidebar on page 141). Dishes such as gnocchi, risotto, and fusilli are popular, as is *pršut*, the air-cured ham that's Istria's answer to prosciutto (see sidebar on page 392).

Food here is distinctly Mediterranean, with lots of olives and wine. You'll often find game on the menu.

Istria is also a major wine-growing region, producing about 80 percent whites. Istrian vintners are particularly proud of their *malvazija* (mahl-VAH-zee-yah; better known to English-speakers as Malvasia)—a light white wine that can be either sweet *(slatko)* or dry *(suho)*. *Malvazija* wines are produced throughout Europe, but Istria's *malvazija* is indigenous. The red *teran* is also popular, as is Merlot. *Teran,* a heavy wine from *refošk* grapes, is sometimes blended with Merlot to soften its flavor. *Teran* pairs well with *pršut*. Because many Istrian vintners are relatively recent to the job—having gotten into the craft when the industry was privatized at the end of communism—the focus is on quality, not quantity...so few Croatian wines are exported.

ISTRIA

is what the highway is shaped like). One branch of the "Y" (A-9) runs roughly parallel to the coast from Slovenia to Pula, about six miles inland; the other branch (A-8) cuts diagonally northeast to the Učka Tunnel (leading to Rijeka). You'll periodically come to toll booths, where you'll pay a modest fee for using the *ipsilon.* Following road signs here is easy (navigate by town names), but if you'll be driving a lot, pick up a good map to more easily navigate the back roads. My favorite is the Kod & Kam 1:100,000 *Istra* map (available in local bookstores and some TIs).

If you're relying on **public transportation,** Istria can be frustrating: The towns that are easiest to reach (Poreč and Pula) are less appealing than Istria's highlights (Rovinj and Motovun). Linking up the coastal towns is doable if you're patient and check schedules carefully, but the hill towns probably aren't worth the hassle. Even if you're doing the rest of your trip by public transportation, consider renting a car for a day or two in Istria.

Driving from Istria to Rijeka (and the Rest of Croatia): Istria meets the rest of Croatia at the big port city of Rijeka (described in the Kvarner Gulf chapter). There are two ways to get to Rijeka: The faster alternative is to take the *ipsilon* road via Pazin to the Učka Tunnel (28-kn toll), which emerges just above Rijeka and Opatija (for Rijeka, you'll follow the road more or less straight on; for Opatija, you'll twist down to the right, backtracking slightly to the seashore below you). Or you can take the slower but more scenic **coastal road** from Pula via Labin. After going inland for about 25 miles, this road jogs to the east coast of Istria, which it hugs all the way into Opatija, then Rijeka. From Rijeka, you can easily hook into Croatia's expressway network (for example, take A-6 east to A 1, which zips you north to Zagreb or south to the Dalmatian Coast).

By Boat to Venice: Venezia Lines sporadically connects Venice with Rovinj, Poreč, and Pula, as well as Piran (in Slovenia) and other Adriatic destinations. While designed for day-trippers from Istria to Venice, this service can also be used one-way. Since the schedule tends to change from year to year, check their website for details: www.venezialines.com.

Rovinj

Rising dramatically from the Adriatic as though being pulled up to heaven by its grand bell tower, Rovinj (roh-VEEN, Rovigno/roh-VEEN-yoh in Italian) is a welcoming Old World oasis in a sea of tourist kitsch. Among the villages of Croatia's coast, there's something particularly romantic about Rovinj—the most Italian town in Croatia's most Italian region. Rovinj's streets are delightfully twisty, its ancient houses are characteristically crumbling, and its harbor—lively with real-life fishermen—is as salty as they come. Like a little Venice on a hill, Rovinj is the stage set for your Croatian seaside dreams.

Rovinj was prosperous and well-fortified in the Middle Ages.

It boomed in the 16th and 17th centuries, when it was flooded with refugees fleeing both the Ottoman invasions and the plague. Because the town was part of the Republic of Venice for five centuries (13th to 18th centuries), its architecture, culture, and even language are strongly Venetian. The local folk groups sing in a dialect actually considered more Venetian than what the Venetians themselves speak these days. (You can even see Venice from Rovinj's church bell tower on a very clear day.)

After Napoleon seized the region, then was defeated, Rovinj became part of Austria. The Venetians had neglected Istria, but the Austrians invested in it, bringing the railroad, gas lights, and a huge Ronhill tobacco factory. (This factory—recently replaced by an enormous, state-of-the-art facility you'll pass on the highway farther inland—is one of the town's most elegant structures, and is slated for extensive renovation in the coming years.) The Austrians chose Pula and Trieste to be the empire's major ports—cursing those cities with pollution and sprawl, while allowing Rovinj to linger in its trapped-in-the-past quaintness.

Before long, Austrians discovered Istria as a handy escape for a beach holiday. Tourism came to Rovinj in the late 1890s, when a powerful Austrian baron bought one of the remote, barren islands offshore and brought it back to life with gardens and a grand villa. Before long, another baron bought another island... and a tourist boom was underway. In more recent times, Rovinj has become a top destination for nudists. The resort of Valalta, just to the north, is a popular spot for those seeking "southern exposure"...as a very revealing brochure at the TI illustrates (www.valalta.hr). Whether you want to find PNBs (pudgy nude bodies), or avoid them, remember that the German phrase *FKK* (*Freikörper Kultur*, or "free body culture") is international shorthand for nudism.

Rovinj is the most atmospheric of all of Croatia's small coastal

towns. Maybe that's because it's always been a real town, where poor people lived. You'll find no fancy old palaces here—just narrow streets lined with skinny houses that have given shelter to humble families for generations. While it's becoming known on the tourist circuit, Rovinj retains the soul of a fishermen's village; notice that the harbor is still filled not with glitzy yachts, but with a busy fishing fleet.

Planning Your Time

Rovinj is hardly packed with diversions. You can get the gist of the town in a one-hour wander. The rest of your time is for enjoying the ambience or pedaling a rental bike to a nearby beach. When you're ready to overcome your inertia, there's no shortage of day trips (the best are outlined in this chapter). Be aware that much of Rovinj closes down from November through Easter.

Orientation to Rovinj

(area code: 052)

Rovinj, once an island, is now a peninsula. The Old Town is divided in two parts: a particularly charismatic chunk on the oval-shaped peninsula, and the rest on the mainland (with similarly time-worn buildings, but without the commercial cuteness that comes with lots of tourist money). Where the mainland meets the peninsula is a broad, bustling public space called Tito Square (Trg Maršala Tita). The Old Town peninsula—traffic-free except for the occasional moped—is topped by the massive bell tower of the Church of St. Euphemia. At the very tip of the peninsula is a small park.

Tourist Information

Rovinj's helpful TI, facing the harbor, has several handy, free materials, including a town map and an info booklet (June–Sept daily 8:00–22:00; Oct–May Mon–Fri 8:00–15:00, Sat 8:00–13:00, closed Sun; along the embankment at Obala Pina Budičina 12, tel. 052/811-566, www.tzgrovinj.hr).

Arrival in Rovinj

By Car: To make a beeline to the Old Town, follow *Centar* signs through the little roundabout to the big parking lot on the waterfront (5 kn/hr, or 4 kn/hr from 1:00–6:00 in the morning). While this lot is the most convenient—and comes with the classic Rovinj view—the cost adds up fast if you're parking overnight. If it's full, you'll be pushed to another pay lot farther out, along the bay northwest of the Old Town (a scenic 15-minute walk from town; 5 kn/hr in summer, 2 kn/hr off-season). If you're sleeping at a hotel away from the Old Town, carefully track individual blue hotel signs as you approach town.

By Bus: The bus station is on the south side of the Old Town, close to the harbor. Leave the station to the left, then walk on busy Carera street directly into the center of town. Note that there are plans to move the bus station to the other side of the Old Town, just above the long waterfront parking lots. If your bus stops here instead, simply head down to the main road and walk along the parking lots into town.

By Boat: The few boats connecting Rovinj to Venice, Piran, and other Istrian towns dock at the long pier protruding from the Old Town peninsula. Just walk up the pier, and you're in the heart of town.

ISTRIA

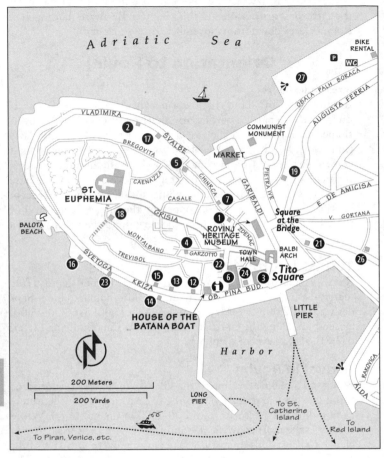

ISTRIA

Helpful Hints

Internet Access: A-Mar Internet Club has several terminals and long hours (40 kn/hr, Mon–Fri 8:00–22:00, Sat–Sun 9:00–23:00, on the main drag in the mainland part of the Old Town, Carera 26, tel. 052/841-211).

Laundry: The full-service **Galax** launderette hides up the street beyond the bus station. You can usually pick up your laundry after 24 hours, though same-day service might be possible if you drop it off early enough in the morning (70 kn/load wash and dry, daily 6:00–20:00, even longer hours in summer, closed Sun Oct–Easter, up Benussia street past the bus station, on the left after the post office, tel. 052/816-130).

Local Guides: Vukica Palčić is a very capable guide who knows her town intimately and loves to share it with visitors (€50 for a 2-hour tour, mobile 098-794-003, vukica.palcic@pu.t-com.hr).

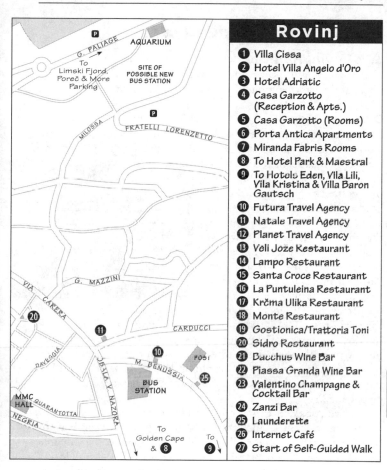

Rovinj

1. Villa Cissa
2. Hotel Villa Angelo d'Oro
3. Hotel Adriatic
4. Casa Garzotto (Reception & Apts.)
5. Casa Garzotto (Rooms)
6. Porta Antica Apartments
7. Miranda Fabris Rooms
8. To Hotel Park & Maestral
9. To Hotels Eden, Vila Lili, Vila Kristina & Villa Baron Gautsch
10. Futura Travel Agency
11. Natale Travel Agency
12. Planet Travel Agency
13. Veli Joze Restaurant
14. Lampo Restaurant
15. Santa Croce Restaurant
16. La Puntuleina Restaurant
17. Krčma Ulika Restaurant
18. Monte Restaurant
19. Gostionica/Trattoria Toni
20. Sidro Restaurant
21. Bacchus Wine Bar
22. Piassa Granda Wine Bar
23. Valentino Champagne & Cocktail Bar
24. Zanzi Bar
25. Launderette
26. Internet Café
27. Start of Self-Guided Walk

ISTRIA

Renato Orbanić is a laid-back musician (sax) who also enjoys wandering through town with visitors. While light on heavy-hitting facts, his casual tour somehow suits this easy-going little town (€60 for a 2-hour tour, mobile 091-521-6206, rorbanic@inet.hr).

Best Views: The town is full of breathtaking views. Photography buffs will be busy in the "magic hours" of early morning and evening, and even by moonlight. The postcard view of Rovinj is from the parking lot embankment at the north end of the Old Town (at the start of the "Self-Guided Walk," next). For a different perspective on the Old Town, head for the far side of the harbor on the opposite (south) end of town. The church bell tower provides a virtual aerial view of the town and a grand vista of the outlying islands.

Self-Guided Walk

▲▲▲Rovinj Ramble

This orientation walk introduces you to Rovinj in about an hour. Begin at the parking lot just north of the Old Town.

Old Town View

Many places offer fine views of Rovinj's Old Town, but this is the most striking. Boats bob in the harbor, and behind them Venetian-looking homes seem to rise from the deep. (For an aerial perspective, notice the big billboard overhead and to the left.)

The Old Town is topped by the church, whose bell tower is capped by a weathervane in the shape of Rovinj's patron saint, Euphemia. Local fishermen look to this saintly weathervane for direction: When Euphemia is looking out to sea, it means the stiff, fresh Bora wind is blowing, bringing dry air from the interior...a sailor's delight. But if she's facing the land, the humid Jugo wind will soon bring bad weather from the sea. After a day or so, even a tourist learns to look to St. Euphemia for the weather report. (For more on Croatian winds and weather, see the sidebar on page 152.)

As you soak in this scene, ponder how the town's history created its current shape. In the Middle Ages, Rovinj was an island, rather than a peninsula, and it was surrounded by a double wall—a protective inner wall and an outer seawall. Because it was so well-defended against pirates and other marauders (and carefully quarantined from the plague), it was extremely desirable real estate. And yet, it was easy to reach from the mainland, allowing it to thrive as a trading town. With more than 10,000 residents at its peak, Rovinj became immensely crowded, explaining today's pleasantly claustrophobic Old Town.

Over the centuries—as demand for living space trumped security concerns—the town walls were converted into houses, with windows grafted on to their imposing frame. Gaps in the wall, with steps that seem to end at the water, are where fishermen would pull in to unload their catch directly into the warehouses on the bottom level of the houses. (Later you can explore some of these lanes from inside the town.) Today, if you live in one of these houses, the Adriatic is your backyard.

• *Now head into town. In the little park near the sea, just beyond the end of the parking lot, look for the big, blocky...*

ISTRIA

Communist-Era Monument

Dating from the time of Tito, this celebrates the Partisan Army's victory over the Nazis in World War II and commemorates the

victims of fascism. The minimalist reliefs on the ceremonial tomb show a slow prisoners' parade of victims prodded by a gun in the back from a figure with a Nazi-style helmet. Notice that one side of the monument is in Croatian, and the other is in Italian. With typical Yugoslav grace and subtlety, this jarring block shatters the otherwise harmonious time-warp vibe of Rovinj. Fortunately, it's the only modern structure anywhere near the Old Town.

• *Now walk a few more steps toward town, stopping to explore the covered...*

Market

The front part of the market, near the water, is for souvenirs. But natives delve deeper in, to the local produce stands. Separating the gifty stuff from the nitty-gritty produce is a line of merchants aggressively pushing free samples. Everything is local and mostly homemade. Consider this snack-time tactic: Loiter around, joking with the farmers while sampling their various tasty walnuts, figs, cherries, grapes, olive oils, honey, *rakija* (the powerful schnapps popular throughout the Balkans), and more. If the sample is good, buy some more for a picnic. In the center of the market, a delightful and practical fountain from 1908 reminds locals of the infrastructure brought in by their Habsburg rulers a century ago. The hall labeled *Ribarnica/Pescheria* at the back of the market is where you'll find fresh, practically wriggling fish. This is where locals gather ingredients for their favorite dish, *brodet*—a stew of various kinds of seafood mixed with olive oil and wine...all of Istria's best bits rolled into one dish. It's slowly simmered and generally served with polenta (unfortunately, it's rare in restaurants).

• *Continue up the broad street, named for* **Giuseppe Garibaldi**—*one of the major players in late-19th-century Italian unification. Imagine: Even though you're in Croatia, Italian patriots are celebrated in this very Italian-feeling town (see the "Italo-Croatia" sidebar). After one long block, you'll come to the wide cross-street called...*

Square at the Bridge (Trg na Mostu)

This marks the site of the medieval bridge that once connected the fortified island of Rovinj to the mainland (as illustrated in the small painting above the door of the Kavana al Ponto—"Bridge

Italo-Croatia

Apart from its tangible attractions, one of Istria's hallmarks is its biculturalism: It's an engaging hybrid of Croatia and Italy. Like most of the Croatian Coast, Istria has variously been controlled by Illyrians, Romans, Byzantines, Slavs, Venetians, and Austrians. After the Habsburgs lost World War I, most of today's Croatia joined Yugoslavia—but Istria became part of Italy. During this time, the Croatian vernacular was suppressed, while the Italian language and culture flourished. This extra chapter of Italian rule left Istrians with an identity crisis. After World War II, Istria joined Yugoslavia, and Croatian culture and language returned. But many people here found it difficult to abandon their ties to Italy.

Today, depending on who you ask, Istria is the most Italian part of Croatia...or the most Croatian part of Italy. Istria pops up on Italian weather reports. A few years ago, Italy's then-Prime Minister Silvio Berlusconi declared that he still considered Istria part of Italy—and he wanted it back. When I wrote an article about Istria for a newspaper recently, some Italian readers complained that I made it sound "too Croatian," while some Croatians claimed my depiction was "too Italian."

People who actually live here typically don't worry about the distinction. Locals insist that they're not Croatians and not Italians—they're Istrians. They don't mind straddling two cultures. Both languages are official (and often taught side-by-side in schools), street signs are bilingual, and most Istrians dabble in each tongue—often seeming to foreign ears as though they're mixing the two at once.

As a result of their tangled history, Istrians have learned how to be mellow and take things as they come. They're gregarious, open-minded, and sometimes seem to thrive on chaos. A twentysomething local told me, "My ancestors lived in Venice. My great-grandfather lived in Austria. My grandfather lived in Italy. My father lived in Yugoslavia. I live in Croatia. My son will live in the European Union. And we've all lived in the same town."

ISTRIA

Café"). Back then, the island was populated mostly by Italians, while the mainland was the territory of Slavic farmers. But as Rovinj's strategic importance waned, and its trading status rose, the need for easy access became more important than the canal's protective purpose—so in 1763, it was filled in. The two populations integrated, creating the bicultural mix that survives today.

Notice the breeze? Via Garibaldi is nicknamed Val de Bora ("Valley of the Bora Wind") for the constant cooling wind that blows here. On the island side of Trg na Mostu is the Rovinj Heritage Museum (described later, under "Sights in Rovinj"). Next door, the town's cultural center posts lovingly hand-lettered signs in

Croatian and Italian announcing upcoming musical events (generally free, designed for locals, and worth noting and enjoying).

Nearby (just past Kavana al Ponto, on the left), the Viecia Batana Café—named for Rovinj's unique, flat-bottomed little fishing boats—has a retro interior with a circa-1960 fishermen mural that evokes an earlier age. The café is popular for its chocolate cake and "Batana" ice cream.

• *Now proceed to the little fountain in the middle of the square (near Hotel Adriatic).*

Tito Square (Trg Maršala Tita)

This wide-open square at the entrance to the Old Town is the crossroads of Rovinj. The **fountain,** with a little boy holding a water-spouting fish, celebrates the government-funded water system that finally brought running water to the Old Town in 1959. Walk around the fountain, with your eyes on the relief, to see a successful socialist society at the inauguration of this new water system. Despite the happy occasion, the figures are pretty stiff—conformity trumped most other virtues in Tito's world.

Now walk out to the end of the concrete pier, called the **Mali Molo ("Little Pier").** From here, you're surrounded by Rovinj's crowded harbor, with fishing vessels and excursion boats that shuttle tourists out to the offshore islands. If the weather's good, a **boat trip** can be a memorable way to get out on the water for a different angle on Rovinj. In Rovinj's own little archipelago, the two most popular islands to visit are St. Catherine (Sv. Katarina—the lush, green island just across the harbor, about a 5-min trip, boats run about hourly in summer, 20 kn) and Red Island (Crveni Otok—farther out, about a 15-min trip, boats run hourly in summer, 30 kn). Each island has a hotel and its own share of beaches. If you're more interested in the boat trip than the destination, it's also fun to simply go for a cruise to the various coves and islands around Rovinj. Your two basic options are a straightforward 1.5-hour loop trip around the offshore islands for around 100 kn; or a four-hour, 150-kn sail north along the coast and into the disappointing "Limski Canal" (a.k.a. "Limski Fjord"), where you'll have two hours of free time. To sort through your options, chat with the captains nearby hawking excursions.

Scan the **harbor.** On the left is the MMC, the local meeting and concert hall (described later, under "Nightlife in Rovinj"). Above and behind the MMC, the highest bell tower inland marks the Franciscan monastery, which was the only building on the mainland before the island town was connected to shore. Along the waterfront to the right of the MMC is Hotel Park, a typical monstrosity from the communist era, now tastefully renovated on the inside. A recommended bike path starts just past this hotel,

ISTRIA

leading into a nature preserve and the best nearby beaches (which you can see in the distance; for more on bike rental, see "Activities in Rovinj," later).

Now head back to the base of the pier. If you were to walk down the **embankment** between the harbor and the Old Town (past Hotel Adriatic), you'd find the TI and a delightful "restaurant row" with several tempting places for a drink or a meal. Many fish-

ermen pull their boats into this harbor, then simply carry their catch across the street to a waiting restaurateur. (This self-guided walk finishes with a stroll down this lane.)

Backtrack 10 paces past the fountain and face the Old Town entrance gate, called the **Balbi Arch.** The winged lion on top is a reminder that this was Venetian territory for centuries.

• *Head through the gate into the Old Town. Inside and on the left is the red...*

Town Hall

On the old Town Hall, notice another Venetian lion, as well as other historic crests embedded in the wall. The Town Hall actually sports an Italian flag (along with ones for Croatia and Rovinj) and faces a square named for Giacomo Matteotti, a much-revered Italian patriot.

Continue a few more steps into town. Gostionica/Trattoria Cisterna faces another little square, which once functioned as a cistern (collecting rainwater, which was pulled from a subterranean reservoir through the well you see today). On your left, the building with a *batana* boat out front is the Italian Union—yet another reminder of how Istria has an important bond with Italy.

• *Now begin walking up the street to the left of Gostionica/Trattoria Cisterna.*

Grisia Street

The main "street" (actually a tight lane) leading through the middle of the island is choked with tourists during the midday rush and lined with art galleries. This inspiring town has attracted many artists, some of whom display their works along this colorful stretch. Notice the rusty little nails speckling the walls—each year in August, an art festival invites locals to hang their best art on this street. With

paintings lining the lane, the entire community comes out to enjoy each other's creations.

As you walk, keep your camera cocked and ready, as you can find delightful scenes down every side lane. Remember that, as crowded as it is today, little Rovinj was even more packed in the Middle Ages. Keep an eye out for arches that span narrow lanes (such as on the right, at Arsenale street)—the only way a walled city could grow was up. Many of these additions created hidden little courtyards, nooks, and crannies that make it easy to get away from the crowds and claim a corner of the town for yourself. Another sign of Rovinj's overcrowding are the distinctive chimneys poking up above the rooftops. These chimneys, added long after the buildings were first constructed, made it possible to heat previously underutilized rooms...and squeeze in even more people.
• *Continue up to the top of Grisia. Capping the town is the can't-miss-it...*

▲Church of St. Euphemia (Sv. Eufemija)

Rovinj's landmark Baroque church dates from 1754. It's watched

over by an enormous 190-foot-tall campanile, a replica of the famous bell tower on St. Mark's Square in Venice. The tower is topped by a copper weathervane with the weather-predicting St. Euphemia, the church's namesake.

Go inside (free, generally open May–Sept daily 10:00–18:00, Easter–April and Oct–Nov open only for Mass and with demand, generally closed Dec–Easter). The vast, somewhat gloomy interior boasts some fine altars of Carrara marble (a favorite medium of Michelangelo's). Services here are celebrated using a combination of Croatian and Italian, suiting the town's mixed population.

To the right of the main altar is the church's highlight: the chapel containing the relics of St. Euphemia. Before stepping into the chapel, notice the altar featuring Euphemia—depicted, as she usually is, with her wheel (a reminder of her torture) and a palm frond (symbolic of her martyrdom), and holding the fortified town of Rovinj, of which she is the protector.

St. Euphemia was the virtuous daughter of a prosperous early fourth-century family in Chalcedon (near today's Istanbul). Euphemia used her family's considerable wealth to help the poor. Unfortunately, her pious philanthropy happened to coincide with anti-Christian purges by the Roman Emperor Diocletian. When she was 15 years old, Euphemia was arrested for refusing to worship the local pagan idol. She was brutally tortured, her bones broken on a wheel. Finally she was thrown to the lions as a public spectacle. But, the story goes, the lions miraculously refused to attack her—only nipping her gently on one arm. The Romans murdered Euphemia anyway, and her remains were later rescued by Christians. In the year 800, a gigantic marble sarcophagus containing St. Euphemia's relics somehow found its way into the Adriatic and floated all the way up to Istria, where Rovinj fishermen discovered it bobbing in the sea. They towed it back to town, where a crowd gathered. The townspeople realized what it was and wanted to take it up to the hilltop church (an earlier version of the one we're in now). But nobody could move it...until a young boy with two young calves showed up. He said he'd had a dream of St. Euphemia—and, sure enough, he succeeded in dragging her relics to where they still lie.

The small chapel behind the altar is dominated by Euphemia's famous sarcophagus. The front panel (with the painting of Euphemia) is opened with much fanfare every September 16, St. Euphemia's feast day, to display the small, withered, waxen face of Rovinj's favorite saint. The sarcophagus is flanked by frescoes depicting her most memorable moment (protected by angels, as a bored-looking lion tenderly nibbles at her right bicep) and her arrival here in Rovinj (with burly fishermen looking astonished as the young boy succeeds in moving the giant sarcophagus). Note the depiction of Rovinj fortified by a double crenellated wall—looking more like a castle than like the creaky fishing village of today. At the top of the hill is an earlier version of today's church.

• *If you have time and energy, consider climbing the...*

Bell Tower

Scaling the church bell tower's creaky wooden stairway requires an enduring faith in the reliability of wood. It rewards those who brave the climb with a commanding view of the town and surrounding islands (10 kn, same hours as church, enter from inside church—to the left of the main altar). The climb doubles your altitude, and from this perch you can also look down—taking advantage of the quirky little  round hole in the floor to photograph the memorable staircase you just climbed.

• *Leave the church through the main door. A peaceful café on a park terrace (once a cemetery) is a bit to your right. Farther to the right, a winding lane leads down toward the water, then forks. A left turn zig-*

zags you past a WWII pillbox and leads along the "restaurant row," where you can survey your options for a drink or a meal (see "Eating in Rovinj," later). A right turn curls you down along the quieter northern side of the Old Town peninsula. Either way, Rovinj is yours to enjoy.

Sights in Rovinj

▲**House of the Batana Boat (Kuća o Batani)**—Rovinj has a long, noble shipbuilding tradition, and this tiny but interesting museum gives you the story of the town's distinctive *batana* boats. Locals say this museum puts you in touch with the soul of this town.

The flat-bottomed vessels are favored by local fishermen for their ability to reach rocky areas close to shore that are rich with certain shellfish. The museum explains how the boats are built, with the help of an entertaining elapsed-time video showing a boat built from scratch in five minutes. You'll also meet some of the salty old sailors who use these vessels (find the placemat with wine stains, and put the glass in different red circles to hear various seamen talk in the Rovinj dialect). Another movie shows the boats at work. Upstairs is a wall of photos of *batana* boats still in active use, a tiny library (peruse photos of the town from a century ago), and a video screen displaying *bitinada* music—local music with harmonizing voices that imitate instruments. Sit down and listen to several (there's a button for skipping ahead). The museum has no posted English information, so pick up the comprehensive English flyer as you enter (5 kn; June–Sept daily 9:00–13:00 & 19:00–22:00; Oct–Dec and March–May Tue–Sun 10:00–13:00 & generally also 15:00–17:00, closed Mon; closed Jan–Feb; Obala Pina Budicina 2, tel. 052/812-593, www.batana.org).

The museum, which serves as a sort of cultural heritage center for the town, also presents a variety of engaging *batana*-related

activities. On some summer evenings, you can take a boat trip on a *batana* from the pier near the museum. The trip, which is accompanied by traditional music, circles around the end of the Old Town peninsula and docks on the far side, where a traditional wine cellar has a fresh fish dinner ready, with local wine and more live music (June–mid-Sept, generally 2 days per week—likely Tue and Thu at 20:30, boat trip-50 kn, dinner-120 kn extra, visit or call the museum the day before to reserve). Also on some summer evenings, you can enjoy an outdoor food market with traditional Rovinj foods and live *bitinada* music. The center-piece is a *batana* boat being refurbished before your eyes (in front of museum, 20–30-kn light food, mid-June–early Sept generally Tue and Sat 20:00–23:00—but confirm details at museum). Even if you're here off-season, ask at the museum if anything special is planned.

Rovinj Heritage Museum (Zavičajni Muzej Grada Rovinja)—This ho-hum museum combines art old (obscure classic painters) and new (obscure contemporary painters from Rovinj) in an old mansion. Rounding out the collection are some model ships and a small archaeological exhibit (15 kn; summer Tue–Fri 9:00–15:00 & 19:00–22:00, Sat–Sun 9:00–14:00 & 19:00–22:00, closed Mon; winter Tue–Sat 9:00–15:00, closed Sun–Mon; Trg Maršala Tita 11, tel. 052/816-720, www.muzej-rovinj.com).

Aquarium (Akvarij)—This century-old collection of local sea life is one of Europe's oldest aquariums. Unfortunately, it's also tiny (with three sparse rooms holding a few tanks of what you'd see if you snorkeled here), disappointing, and overpriced (20 kn, daily June–Aug 9:00–21:00, Sept 9:00–20:00, Oct–May 10:00–16:00 or longer depending on demand, across the street from the end of the waterfront parking lot at Obala G. Paliage 5, tel. 052/804-712).

Activities in Rovinj

▲Swimming and Sunbathing—The most central spot to swim or sunbathe is at **Balota Beach,** on the rocks along the embank-ment on the south side of the Old Town peninsula (no showers, but scenic and central). For bigger beaches, go to the wooded **Golden Cape** (Zlatni Rt) south of the harbor (past the big, waterfront Hotel Park). This cape is lined with walking paths and beaches, and shaded by a wide variety of trees and plants. For a scenic and  memorable sunbathing spot, choose a perch facing Rovinj on the north side of the Golden Cape. Another beach, called **Kuvi,** is beyond the Golden Cape. To get away from it all, take a boat to an island on Rovinj's little archipelago (described earlier, on my self-guided walk).

▲Bike Ride—The TI's free, handy biking map suggests a variety of short and long bike rides. The easiest and most scenic is a quick loop around the Golden Cape (Zlatni Rt, described above). You can do this circuit and return to the Old Town in about an hour

(without stops). Start by biking south around the harbor and past the waterfront Hotel Park, where you leave the cars and enter the wooded Golden Cape. Peaceful miniature beaches abound. The lane climbs to a quarry (much of Venice was paved with Istrian stone), where you're likely to see beginning rock climbers inching their way up and down. Cycling downhill from the quarry and circling the peninsula, you hit the Lovor Grill (open daily in summer 10:00–16:00 for drinks and light meals)—a cute little restaurant housed in the former stables of the Austrian countess who planted what today is called "Wood Park." From there, you can continue farther along the coast or return to town (backtrack two minutes and take the right fork through the woods back to the waterfront path).

Bike Rental: Bikes are rented at subsidized prices from the city parking lot kiosk (5 kn/hr, open 24 hours daily except no rentals in winter, fast and easy process; choose a bike with enough air in its tires or have them pumped up, as the path is rocky and gravelly). Various travel agencies around town rent bikes for quadruple the price (20 kn/hr); look for signs or ask around.

Nightlife in Rovinj

Rovinj After Dark

Rovinj is a delight after dark. Views that are great by day become magical in the moonlight and floodlight. The streets of the Old Town are particularly inviting when empty and under stars.

Concerts—Lots of low-key, small-time music events take place right in town (ask at the TI, check the events calendar at www.tzgrovinj.hr, and look for handwritten signs on Garibaldi street near the Square at the Bridge). Groups perform at various venues around town: right along the harborfront (you'll see the bandstand set up); in the town's churches (especially St. Euphemia and the Franciscan church); in the old cinema/theater by the market; at the House of the Batana Boat (described earlier, under "Sights in Rovinj"); and at the Multi-Media Center (a.k.a. the "MMC," which locals call "Cinema Belgrade"—its former name), in a cute little hall above a bank across the harbor from the Old Town.

Wine Bars—Rovinj has two good places to sample Istrian and Croatian wines, along with light, basic food—such as prosciutto-like *pršut*, truffles, and olive oil. Remember, two popular local wines worth trying are *malvazija* (a light white) and *teran* (a heavy red). At **Bacchus Wine Bar,** owner Paolo is happy to explain how the local wine has improved since communist times, when wine production stagnated (15–40 kn per deciliter, most cost around 20–30 kn, 70–250-kn bottles, daily 7:00–23:00, Carera 5, tel. 052/812-154). **Piassa Granda,** on a charming little square right in the heart of the Old Town, has a classy, cozy interior and 140 types of wine (18–25-kn glasses, 30–70-kn Istrian small plates, more food than Bacchus, daily 10:00–24:00, Veli trg 1, mobile 098-824-322, Helena).

Lounging—Valentino Champagne and Cocktail Bar is a memorable, romantic, justifiably pretentious place for a late-

night waterfront drink with jazz. Fish, attracted by its underwater lights, swim by from all over the bay...to the enjoyment of those nursing a cocktail on the rocks (literally—you'll be given a small seat cushion and welcomed to find your own seaside niche). Or you can choose to sit on one of the terraces. Classy candelabras twinkle in the twilight, as couples cozy up to each other and the view. Patricia opens her bar nightly from 19:00 until as late as there's any action. While the drinks are extremely pricey, this place is unforgettably cool (50–65-kn cocktails, 50-kn non-alcoholic drinks, Via Santa Croce 28, tel. 052/830-683). **La Puntuleina**—next door and listed later, under "Eating in Rovinj"—has a similarly rocky ambience, with lower prices (30–40-kn drinks) but a bit less panache than Valentino. **Zanzi Bar,** while named for an African archipelago, has a Havana ambience. Stepping over its threshold, you enter a colonial Caribbean world, with seating indoors or out on the tropical veranda (80 different cocktails for 45–60 kn each, nightly until 1:00 in the morning, near the TI on Obala Pina Budicina).

***Batana* Boat Activities**—In summer, the House of the Batana Boat often hosts special events such as a boat trip and traditional dinner, and an outdoor food court. For details, see the listing earlier, under "Sights in Rovinj."

Sleeping in Rovinj

Most Rovinj accommodations (both hotels and *sobe*) prefer longer stays of at least four or five nights, so in peak season (mid-July–mid-Sept), you'll likely run into strict minimum-stay requirements or high surcharges for shorter stays. Unfortunately, you'll probably have to simply eat this extra cost for a short stay. Hoteliers and *sobe* hosts are somewhat more flexible in the shoulder season. Don't just show up here without a room in August—popular Rovinj is packed during that peak month.

In the Old Town

All of these accommodations are on the Old Town peninsula, rather than the mainland section of the Old Town. Rovinj has no real hostel, but *sobe* are a good budget option.

$$$ Hotel Villa Angelo d'Oro is your Old Town splurge. The location—on a peaceful street just a few steps off the water—is ideal, and the public spaces (including a serene garden bar and sauna/whirlpool area) are rich and inviting. The 23 rooms don't quite live up to the fuss, but if you want your money to talk your way into the Old Town, this is the place (mid-July–Aug: Sb-950 kn, Db-1,600 kn; June–mid-July and Sept: Sb-860 kn, Db-1,450 kn; cheaper Oct–Dec and March–May, closed Jan–Feb, pricier suites also available, no extra charge for 1-night stays, no elevator, air-con, free Wi-Fi in lobby, bike rental for guests, Vladimira Švalbe 38–42, tel. 052/840-502, fax 052/840-111, www.angelodoro .hr, hotelangelo@vip.hr).

Sleep Code

(5 kn = about $1, country code: 385, area code: 052)

S = Single, **D** = Double/Twin, **T** = Triple, **Q** = Quad, **b** = bathroom. The modest tourist tax (7 kn per person, per night, lower off-season) is not included in these rates. Hotels accept credit cards and include breakfast in their rates, while most *sobe* accept only cash and don't offer breakfast. Everyone listed here speaks at least enough English to make a reservation (or knows someone nearby who can translate).

To help you sort easily through these listings, I've divided the rooms into three categories based on the price for a standard double room with bath in peak season:

$$$ Higher Priced—Most rooms 800 kn or more.
$$ Moderately Priced—Most rooms between 500–800 kn.
$ Lower Priced—Most rooms 500 kn or less.

$$$ Porta Antica rents 15 comfortable, nicely decorated apartments in five different buildings around the Old Town (two houses—Porta Antica and Marco Polo—are on the peninsula, while the others are on the mainland). Review your options on their website and be specific in your request—though in busy times (July–Aug), they might not be able to guarantee a particular apartment. The underwhelming sea views aren't worth the extra expense. You'll pay less per night the longer you stay; I've listed rates per night for two-night stays, but you can check specific rates on their website (most of Aug: Db-1,000 kn; July: Db-920 kn; late May–June and late Aug–late Sept: Db-675 kn; rest of year: Db-570 kn; sea views-70–140 kn extra, extra person-180 kn, no breakfast, air-con, tries to be non-smoking, open year-round, reception and main building next door to TI on Obala Pina Budičina, tel. 052/812-548, mobile 099-680-1101, www.portaantica.com, porta antica@yahoo.it).

$$$ Hotel Adriatic, a lightly renovated holdover from the communist days, features 27 rooms overlooking the main square, where the Old Town peninsula meets the mainland. The quality of the drab, worn rooms doesn't justify the outrageously high prices...but the location might. Of the big chain of Maistra hotels, this is the only one in the Old Town (rates flex with demand, in top season figure Sb-1,125 kn, Db-1,700 kn; these prices are per night for 1- or 2-night stays—cheaper for 3 nights or more, all Sb are non-view, most Db are twins and have views—otherwise 150 kn less, closed mid-Oct–March, no elevator, air-con, pay Wi-Fi, some nighttime noise—especially on weekends, Trg Maršala Tita, tel. 052/803-520, fax 052/813-573, www.maistra.hr, adriatic @maistra.hr).

$$ Villa Cissa, run by Zagreb transplant Veljko Despot, has three apartments with tastefully modern, artistic decor above an art gallery in the Old Town. Kind, welcoming Veljko—who looks a bit like Robin Williams—is a fascinating guy who had an illustrious career as a rock-and-roll journalist (he was the only Eastern Bloc reporter to interview the Beatles) and record-company executive. Now his sophisticated, artistic style is reflected in these comfortable apartments. Because the place is designed for longer stays, you'll pay a premium for a short visit (50 percent extra for 2-night stays, prices double for 1-night stays), and it comes with some one-time fees, such as for cleaning. Veljko lives off-site, so be sure to clearly communicate your arrival time (July–early Sept: Db-700 kn; most of Sept: Db-625 kn; May–June and late Sept–Oct: Db-550 kn; April: Db-480 kn; rest of the year: Db-410 kn; about 650–700 kn more for bigger apartment; cash only, air-con, free Wi-Fi, some night noise from café across the street, Zdenac 14, tel. 052/813-080, www.villacissa.com, info@villacissa.com).

$$ Casa Garzotto is an appealing mid-range option, with four apartments, four rooms, and one large family apartment in three different Old Town buildings. These classy and classic lodgings have modern facilities but old-fashioned charm, with antique furniture and historic family portraits on the walls. Thoughtfully run by a friendly staff, it's a winner (rooms—mid-June–late Sept: Sb-370 kn, Db-520 kn; rest of year: Sb-300 kn, Db-450 kn; apartments—mid-July–Aug: 1,030 kn, mid-June–mid-July and Sept: 920 kn, mid-May–mid-June and early Oct: 780 kn, less off-season; 2-bedroom family apartment—mid-June–Sept: Db-890–1,030 kn, Tb-1,110 kn, Qb-1,470 kn; mid-May–mid-June and early Oct: Db-780 kn, Tb-960 kn, Qb-1,180; includes breakfast, off-site parking, loaner bikes, and other thoughtful extras; no extra charge for 1-night stays, air-con, lots of stairs, free Wi-Fi in main building, reception and most apartments are at Garzotto 8, others are a short walk away, tel. 052/811-884, mobile 098-616-168, www.casa-garzotto.com, casagarzotto@gmail.com).

$ Miranda Fabris is an outgoing local teacher who rents four cheap, basic, tight apartments with kitchenettes. While rough around the edges, the rooms are affordable and pleasantly located in the thick of the Old Town (July–Aug: Db-370 kn; Sept–June: Db-300 kn; no extra charge for 1- or 2-night stays, cash only, no breakfast, lots of steep stairs, across from Villa Val de Bora at Chiurca 5, mobile 091-881-8881, miranda_fabris@yahoo.com).

$ *Other* Sobe: Try looking for your own room online (www.inforovinj.com is helpful). Several agencies rent private rooms in the Old Town for good prices (figure Db-150–300 kn, depending on season, location, and size). But remember that in peak season, you'll pay about 70 percent extra for a one-night stay, and 30 percent extra for a two- or three-night stay. Just about everyone in town has a line on rooms. These two agencies are English-friendly and handy to the bus station (open sporadic hours, based on demand): **Futura Travel** (across from bus station at Benussi 2, tel. 052/817-281, fax 052/817-282, www.futura-travel.hr) and **Natale** (Carducci 4, tel. & fax 052/813-365, www.rovinj.com). In the Old Town, try **Planet,** near the TI (Sv. Križa 1, tel. 052/840-494, www.planetrovinj.com).

On the Mainland

To escape the high prices of Rovinj's Old Town, consider the resort neighborhood just south of the harbor. While the big hotels themselves are an option, I prefer cheaper alternatives in the same area. The big hotels are signposted as you approach town (follow signs for *hoteli,* then your specific hotel). Once you're on the road to Hotels Eden and Park, the smaller ones are easy to reach: Villa Baron Gautsch is actually on the road to Hotel Park (on the right, brown *pansion* sign just before Hotel Park itself); Hotel Vila Lili and Vila Kristina are a little farther on the main road toward Eden (to the left just after turnoff for Hotel Park, look for signs). All of these options are about a 15-minute uphill walk from the Old Town.

$$$ *Maistra Hotels:* The local hotel conglomerate, Maistra, has several hotels in the lush parklands just south of the Old Town. Most of my readers—looking for proximity to the Old Town rather than predictable rooms, a big lounge, and hotel-based activities—will prefer to save money and stay at one of my other listings. These hotels have extremely slippery pricing, based on the hotel, the type of room, the season, and how far ahead you book (for starters, in July–Aug figure non-view Sb-925 kn, non-view Db-1,240 kn, view Db-1,450 kn, more for 1- or 2-night stays, cheaper off-season), but you'll have to call or check the website for specifics (www.maistra .hr). **Hotel Park** has 202 thoroughly renovated but dull rooms in a colorized communist-era hull, and a seaside swimming pool with sweeping views to the Old Town. From here, you can walk in about 15 minutes along the scenic harborfront promenade into town (tel. 052/811-077, fax 052/816-977, park@maistra.hr). **Hotel Eden** offers 325 upscale, imaginatively updated rooms with oodles of contemporary style behind a brooding communist facade. This flagship hotel is the fanciest one in the Maistra chain, but it's a bit farther from the Old Town—frustrating without a car (10 percent extra for fancier rooms, tel. 052/800-400, fax 052/811-349, eden@maistra.hr). Both hotels have air-conditioning, elevators, free parking, and pay Internet access. The Maistra chain also has several other properties (including the Old Town's Hotel Adriatic, described earlier, and other more distant, cheaper options). Only one branch of the Maistra chain remains open through the winter.

$$$ Hotel Vila Lili, a lesser value, is a family-run hotel with 20 overpriced rooms above a restaurant on a quiet, leafy lane (April–Oct: Sb-450 kn, Db-800 kn; shoulder season: Sb-370 kn, Db-550 kn; cheaper off-season, pricier suites also available, 10 percent discount with this book except in July–Aug, no extra charge for 1-night stays, elevator, air-con, parking-30 kn/day, Mohorovičića 16, tel. 052/840-940, fax 052/840-944, www.hotel -vilalili.hr, info@hotel-vilalili.hr, Petričević family).

$$ Vila Kristina, run by friendly Kristina Kiš and her family, has 10 rooms and five apartments along a busy road (July–Aug: Db-590 kn, extra bed-295 kn; Sept–June: Db-520 kn, extra bed-260 kn; includes breakfast, air-con, no elevator, free Wi-Fi, Luje Adamovića 16, tel. 052/815-537, www.kis-rovinj.com, kristinakis @mail.inet.hr).

$$ Villa Baron Gautsch, named for a shipwreck, is a German-owned pension with 17 comfortable rooms and an invit-

ISTRIA

ing, shared terrace with a view (late July–early Sept: Db-570 kn; late June–late July and early Sept–early Oct: Db-500 kn; off-season: Db-400–440 kn; they also have two Sb for half the Db price, 20 percent more for 1- or 2-night stays, 35 kn less without balcony, non-balcony rooms have air-con, closed Nov–Easter, cash only, no elevator, free Wi-Fi, Ronjgova 7, tel. 052/840-538, fax 052/840-537, www.baron-gautsch.com, baron.gautsch@gmx.net).

Eating in Rovinj

It's expensive to dine in Rovinj—don't expect great value for your money. Interchangeable restaurants cluster where Rovinj's Old Town peninsula meets the mainland, and all around the harbor. Be warned that most eateries—like much of Rovinj—close for the winter (roughly November to Easter).

Along Rovinj's "Restaurant Row"

The easiest dining option is to stroll the Old Town embankment overlooking the harbor (Obala Pina Budičina), which changes its name to Svetoga Križa and cuts behind the buildings after a few blocks. Window-shop the pricey but scenic eateries along here, each of which has its own personality (all open long hours daily). I've listed these in the order you'll reach them. You'll pay top dollar, but the ambience is memorable.

Veli Jože, with a few outdoor tables and a rollicking, folksy interior decorated to the hilt, is in all the guidebooks but still delivers on its traditional, if overpriced, Istrian cuisine (35–80-kn pastas, 60–120-kn main courses, Sv. Križa 1, tel. 052/816-337).

Lampo is simpler, with scenic seating right on the water—fine for a big salad, pizza, or pasta at a reasonable price (30–45-kn pastas, 60–100-kn main courses, Sv. Križa 22).

Santa Croce, with tables scenically scattered along a terraced incline that looks like a stage set, is well-respected for its pricey seafood and pastas (50–70-kn pastas, 70–160-kn main courses, daily 18:00–24:00, Sv. Križa 11, tel. 052/842-240).

La Puntuleina, at the end of the row, is the most scenic option. This upscale restaurant/cocktail bar/wine bar features pricey Italo-Mediterranean cuisine served in the contemporary dining room, or outside—either on one of the many terraces, or at tables literally scattered along the rocks overlooking a swimming hole. The menu is short, and the selection each day is even less, since Miriam and Giovanni insist on serving only what's fresh in the market. I wouldn't pay these prices unless I got a nice table out on a terrace. Reservations are recommended (80–100-kn pastas, 100–160-kn main courses, Thu–Tue 12:00–15:00 & 18:00–22:00, closed Wed except in peak season, closed Nov–Easter, on the Old Town embankment past the harbor at Sv. Križa 38, tel. 052/813-186). You can also order just a drink to sip while sitting down on the rocks.

Just before La Puntuleina, don't miss the inviting **Valentino Champagne and Cocktail Bar**—with no food but similar "drinks on the rocks" ambience (described earlier, under "Nightlife in Rovinj"). If you're on a tight budget, dine cheaply elsewhere, then come here for an after-dinner finale.

International Fare in the Old Town Peninsula

Offering upscale, international (rather than strictly Croatian) food and presentation, these options are expensive but memorable.

Krčma Ulika, a classy hole-in-the-wall run by Inja Tucman, has a mellow, cozy, art-strewn interior. Inja enjoys surprising diners with unexpected flavor combinations. While the lack of a real kitchen in the back makes this less than a gourmet experience, the food preparation area in a corner of the tight, six-table dining room adds to the ambience. The food is a bit overpriced and can be hit-or-miss, but the experience feels like an innovative break from traditional Croatian fare. Explore your options with Inja's help before ordering (12-kn cover, 100–130-kn main courses, daily 19:00–1:00 in the morning, Sun–Thu also 13:00–15:00, until 23:00 in shoulder season, closed Nov–Easter, cash only, Vladimira Švalbe 34, tel. 052/818-089, mobile 098-929-7541).

Monte Restaurant is your upscale, white-tablecloth splurge—made to order for a memorable dinner out. With tables strewn around a covered terrace just under the town bell tower, this atmospheric place features inventive cuisine that melds Istrian products with international techniques. Come here only if you value a fine dining experience, polished service, and the chance to learn about local food and wines more than you value the price tag (plan to spend 300–500 kn per person for dinner, daily 12:00–14:30 & 18:30–23:00, reserve ahead in peak season, Montalbano 75, tel. 052/830-203, Đekić family).

Affordable Alternatives on the Mainland

These options are a bit less expensive than those described above. I've listed them in the order you'll reach them as you walk around Rovinj's harbor.

Gostionica/Trattoria Toni is a hole-in-the-wall serving up small portions of good Istrian and Venetian fare. Choose between the cozy interior (tucked down a tight lane), or their terrace on a bustling, mostly pedestrian street (40–60-kn pastas, 50–120-kn main courses, Thu–Tue 12:00–15:00 & 18:00–22:30, closed Wed, just up ulica/via Driovier on the right, tel. 052/815-303).

Sidro offers a break from pasta, pizza, and fish; it's well-respected for its Balkan meat dishes such as *ćevapčići* (see "Balkan Flavors" on page 31) and a spicy pork-and-onion stew called *mućkalica*. With unusually polite service and a long tradition (run by three generations of the Paoletti family since 1966), it's a popular local hangout (45–70-kn pastas, 55–90-kn grilled meat dishes, 75–140-kn steaks and fish, daily 11:00–23:00, closed Nov–Feb, harborfront at Rismondo 14, tel. 052/813-471).

Maestral combines affordable, straightforward pizzas and seafood with Rovinj's best view. If you want an outdoor table overlooking bobbing boats and the Old Town's skyline—without breaking the bank—this is the place. It fills a big building surrounded by workaday shipyards about a 10-minute walk from the Old Town, around the harbor toward Hotel Park (30-kn sandwiches, 45–60-kn pizzas and pastas, 45–100-kn fish and meat dishes, May–Sept open long hours daily, Oct–April drinks only and open until 20:00, obala N. Nazora b.b., look for *Bavaria* beer sign).

Breakfast

Most rental apartments come with a kitchenette handy for breakfasts (stock up at a neighborhood grocery shop). Cafés and bars along the waterfront serve little more than an expensive croissant with coffee. The best budget breakfast (and a fun experience) is a picnic. Within a block of the market, you have all the necessary stops: the Brionka bakery (fresh-baked cheese or apple strudel); mini-grocery stores (juice, milk, drinkable yogurt, and so on); market stalls (cherries, strawberries, walnuts, and more, as well as an elegant fountain for washing); an Albanian-run bread kiosk/café between the market and the water...plus benches with birds chirping, children playing, and fine Old Town views along the water. For a no-fuss alternative, you can shell out 60 kn for the buffet breakfast at Hotel Adriatic (daily 7:00–10:00, until 11:00 July–Aug; described earlier, under "Sleeping in Rovinj").

Rovinj Connections

From Rovinj by Bus to: Pula (about hourly, 45 min), **Poreč** (6–9/day, 1 hr), **Umag** (5/day, 1.5 hrs), **Rijeka** (4–7/day, 3 hrs), **Zagreb** (6–9/day, 5–8 hrs), **Venice** (1/day Mon–Sat departing very early in the morning, none Sun, 5 hrs). In the summer, you can reach Slovenia—including **Piran** (2.5 hrs) and **Ljubljana** (5.5 hrs)—by hopping on the 8:00 bus from Rovinj (June–late Sept only, no buses off-season). You can also reach Piran (and other Slovenian destinations) with a transfer in Umag and Portorož. A bus departs Rovinj every evening at 19:00 for the Dalmatian Coast, arriving in **Split** at 6:00 and **Dubrovnik** at 11:00. (If this direct bus isn't running, you might have to take an earlier bus to Pula, from where this night bus leaves at 20:00; also note that Pula has two daytime connections to Split.) As always, confirm these times before planning your trip. Bus information: tel. 052/811-453.

Route Tips for Drivers

Just north of Rovinj, on the coastal road to Poreč, you'll drive briefly along a seven-mile-long inlet dubbed the **Limski "Fjord"** (Limski Zaljev). Supposedly the famed pirate Captain Morgan was so enchanted by this canal that he retired here, founding the nearby namesake town of Mrgani. Local tour companies sell boat excursions into the fjord, which is used to raise much of the shellfish that's slurped down at local restaurants. Calling this little canal a "fjord" outrages Norwegians—it's not worth going out of your way to see. Along the road above the canal, you'll pass kiosks selling grappa (firewater, a.k.a. *rakija*), honey, and other homemade concoctions.

Pula

ISTRIA

Pula (POO-lah, Pola in Italian) isn't quaint. Istria's biggest city is an industrial port town with traffic, smog, and sprawl...but it has the soul of a Roman poet. Between the shipyards, you'll discover some of the top Roman ruins in Croatia, including its stately amphitheater—a fully intact mini-Colosseum that marks the entry to a seedy Old Town with ancient temples, arches, and columns.

Strategically situated at the southern tip of the Istrian Peninsula, Pula has long been a center of industry, trade, and military might. In 177 B.C., the city became an important outpost of the Roman Empire. It was destroyed during the wars following Julius Caesar's death and rebuilt by Emperor Augustus. Many of Pula's most important Roman features—including its amphitheater—date from this time (early first century A.D.). But as Rome fell, so did Pula's fortunes. The town changed hands repeatedly, caught in the crossfire of wars between greater powers—Byzantines,

Venetians, and Habsburgs. After being devastated by Venice's enemy Genoa in the 14th century, Pula gathered dust as a ghost town...still militarily strategic, but otherwise abandoned.

In the mid-19th century, Italian unification forced the Austrian Habsburgs—whose navy had been based in Venice—to look for a new home for their fleet. In 1856, they chose Pula, and over the next 60 years, the population grew thirtyfold. (Despite the many Roman and Venetian artifacts littering the Old Town, most of modern Pula is essentially Austrian.) By the dawn of the 20th century, Pula's harbor bristled with Austro-Hungarian warships, and it had become the crucial link in a formidable line of imperial defense that stretched from here to Montenegro. As one of the most important port cities of the Austro-Hungarian Empire, Pula attracted naval officers, royalty...and a young Irishman named James Joyce on the verge of revolutionizing the literary world.

Today's Pula, while no longer quite so important, remains a vibrant port town and the de facto capital of Istria. It offers an enjoyably urban antidote to the rest of this stuck-in-the-past peninsula.

Planning Your Time

Pula's sights, while top-notch, are quickly exhausted. Two or three hours should do it: Visit the amphitheater, stroll the circular Old Town, and maybe see a museum or two. As it's less than an hour from Rovinj, there's no reason to spend the night.

Orientation to Pula

(area code: 052)
Although it's a big city, the tourist's Pula is compact: the amphitheater and, beside it, the ring-shaped Old Town circling the base of an old hilltop fortress. The Old Town's main square, the Forum, dates back to Roman times.

Tourist Information

Pula's well-organized TI overlooks the Old Town's main square, the Forum. It offers a free map and information on the town and all of Istria (May–Oct daily 9:00–21:00, July–Aug until 22:00; Nov–April Mon–Sat 9:00–18:00 or 19:00, Sun 10:00–16:00; Forum 3, tel. 052/219-197, www.pulainfo.hr).

Arrival in Pula

By Car: Pula is about a 45-minute drive south of Rovinj. Approaching town, follow *Centar* signs, then look for the amphitheater. You'll find a large pay lot just below the amphitheater, toward the waterfront (4 kn/hr, 20 kn/all day).

By Bus: As you exit the bus station, walk toward the yellow mansion, then turn left onto the major street (ulica 43 Istarske Divizije); at the roundabout, bear left again, and you'll be headed for the amphitheater (about a 10-min walk total).

By Train: The train station is a 15-minute walk from the amphitheater, near the waterfront (in the opposite direction from the Old Town). Walk with the coast on your right until you see the amphitheater.

By Plane: Pula's small airport, which is served by various low-cost airlines, is about 3.5 miles northeast of the center. Since there's no convenient public bus option, count on paying 100 kn for the taxi ride into town. Airport info: tel. 052/530-105, www.airport-pula.com.

Helpful Hints

Car Rental: To rent a car in Pula, **Avis** is the most central (Riva 14, tel. 052/224-350). Several other companies have offices at the airport, which is a 100-kn taxi ride outside of town (see "Arrival in Pula," above).

Local Guide: If you'd like a local guide to help you uncover the story of Pula, **Mariam Abdelghani** leads great tours of the major sites (€80 for a 2-hour city tour, €160 for an all-day tour of Istria, mobile 098-419-560, mariam.abdelghani@gmail.com).

Self-Guided Walk

Welcome to Pula

This walk is divided between Pula's two most interesting attractions: the Roman amphitheater and the circular Old Town. About an hour for each is plenty. More time can be spent sipping coffee al fresco or dipping into museums.

• *Begin at Pula's main landmark, its...*

Amphitheater (Amfiteatar)

Of the dozens of amphitheaters left around Europe and North Africa by Roman engineers, Pula's is the sixth-largest (435 feet long and 345 feet wide) and one of the best-preserved anywhere. This is the top place in Croatia to resurrect the age of the gladiators.

Cost and Hours: 40 kn, daily June–Aug 8:00–22:00, May and Sept 8:00–20:30, Oct 8:00–17:00, shorter hours Nov–April. The 30-kn audioguide narrates 20 stops

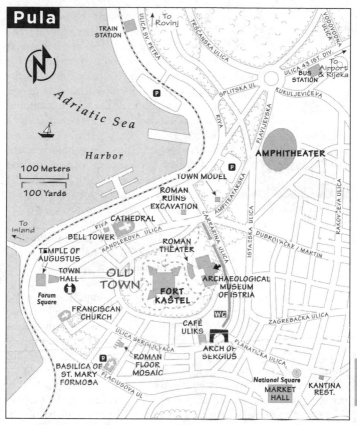

with 30 minutes of flat, basic data on the structure.

⊙ Self-Guided Tour: Go inside and explore the interior, climbing up the seats as you like. An "amphi-theater" is literally a "double theater"—imagine two theaters, without the back wall behind the stage, stuck together to maximize seating. Pula's amphitheater was built over several decades (first century A.D.) under the reign of three of Rome's top-tier emperors: Augustus, Claudius, and Vespasian. It was completed around A.D. 80, about the same time as the Colosseum in Rome. It remained in active use until the beginning of the fifth century, when gladiator battles were outlawed. The location is unusual but sensible: It was built just outside town (too big for tiny Pula, with just 5,000 people) and near the sea (so its giant limestone blocks could more easily be transported here from the quarry six miles away).

Notice that the amphitheater is built into the gentle incline of a hill. This economical plan, unusual for Roman amphitheaters, saved on the amount of stone needed, and provided a natural

foundation for some of the seats (notice how the upper seats incorporate the slope). It may seem like the architects were cutting corners, but they actually had to raise the ground level at the lower end of the amphitheater to give it a level foundation. The four rectangular towers anchoring the amphitheater's facade are also unique (two of them are mostly gone). These once held wooden staircases for loading and unloading the amphitheater more quickly. At the top of each tower was a water reservoir, used for powering fountains that sprayed refreshing scents over the crowd to mask the stench of blood.

And there was plenty of blood. Imagine this scene in the days of the gladiators. More than 25,000 cheering fans from all social classes filled the seats. The Romans made these spectacles cheap or even free—distracting commoners with a steady diet of mindless entertainment prevented discontent and rebellion. (Hmm... *American Idol,* anyone?) Canvas awnings rigged around the top of the amphitheater shaded many seats. The fans surrounded the "slaying field," which was covered with sand to absorb blood spilled by man and beast, making it easier to clean up after the fight. This sand *(harena)* gave the amphitheater its nickname...arena.

The amphitheater's "entertainers" were gladiators (named for the *gladius,* a short sword that was tucked into a fighter's boot). Some gladiators were criminals, but most were prisoners of war from lands conquered by Rome, who dressed and used weapons according to their country of origin. A colorful parade kicked off the spectacle, followed by simulated fights with fake weapons. Then the real battles began. Often the fights represented stories from mythology or Greek or Roman history. Most ended in death for the loser. Sometimes gladiators fought exotic animals—gathered at great expense from far corners of the empire—which would enter the arena from the two far ends (through the biggest arches). There were female gladiators, as well, but they always fought other women.

While the life of a gladiator seems difficult, consider that it wasn't such a bad gig—compared to, say, being a soldier. Gladiators were often better paid than soldiers, enjoyed terrific celebrity (both in life and in death), and only had to fight a few times each year.

Ignore the modern seating, and imagine when the arena (sandy oval area in the center) was ringed with two levels of stone seating and a top level of wooden bleachers. Notice that the outline of the arena is marked by a small moat—just wide enough to

Amphorae

In museums, hotels, and restaurants all along the Croatian coast, you'll see amphorae. An amphora is a jug that was used to transport goods when the ancient Greeks ruled the seas, through about the second century B.C. Later, the Romans also used their own amphorae. These tall and skinny ceramic jugs—many of them lost in ancient shipwrecks—litter the Adriatic coastline.

Amphorae were used to carry oil, wine, and fish on long sea journeys. They're tapered at the bottom because they were stuck into sand (or placed on a stand) to keep them upright in transit. They also have a narrow neck at the top, often with two large handles. In fact, the name comes from the Greek *amphi pherein*, "to carry from both sides." The taller, skinnier amphorae were generally used for wine, while the fat, short ones were for olive oil. Because amphorae differ according to their purpose and nationality, archaeologists find them to be a particularly useful clue for dating shipwrecks and determining the country of origin of lost ships. This is made easier by later Roman amphorae, which are actually stamped with the place they came from and what they held.

keep the animals off the laps of those with the best seats, but close enough so that blood still sprayed their togas.

After the fall of Rome, builders looking for ready-cut stone picked apart structures like this one—scraping it as clean as a neat

slice of cantaloupe. Sometimes the scavengers were seeking the iron hooks that were used to connect the stone; in those oh-so "Dark Ages," the method for smelting iron from ore was lost. Most of this amphitheater's interior structures—such as steps and seats—are now in the foundations and walls of Pula's buildings...not to mention palaces in Venice, across the Adriatic. In fact, in the late 16th century, the Venetians planned to take this entire amphitheater apart, stone by stone, and reassemble it on the island of Lido on the Venetian lagoon. A heroic Venetian senator—still much revered in Pula—convinced them to leave it where it is.

Despite these and other threats, the amphitheater's exterior has been left gloriously intact. The 1999 film *Titus* (with Anthony Hopkins and Jessica Lange) was filmed here, and today the amphitheater is still used to stage spectacles—from Placido Domingo to Marilyn Manson—with seating for about 5,000 fans. Recently, the loudest concerts were banned, because the vibrations were damaging the old structure.

Before leaving, don't miss the museum exhibit (in the "subterranean hall," down the chute marked #17). This takes you to the lower level of the amphitheater, where gladiators and animals were kept between fights. When the fight began, gladiators would charge up a chute and burst into the arena, like football players being introduced at the Super Bowl. As you go down the passage, you'll walk on a grate over an even lower tunnel. Pula is honeycombed with tunnels like these, originally used for sewers and as a last-ditch place of refuge in case of attack. Inside, the exhibit—strangely dedicated to "viniculture and olive-oil production in Istria in the period of antiquity" instead of, you know, gladiators—is surprisingly interesting. Browse the impressive collection of amphorae (see sidebar), find your location on the replica of a fourth-century A.D. Roman map (oriented with east on top), and ogle the gigantic grape press and two olive-oil mills.

• *From the amphitheater, it's a few minutes' walk to Pula's Old Town, where more Roman sights await. Exit the amphitheater to the left and walk one long block up the busy road (Amfiteatarska ulica) along the small wall, bearing right at the fork. When you reach the big park on your right, look for the little, car-sized...*

Town Model

Use this handy model of Pula to get oriented. Next to the amphitheater, the little water cannon spouting into the air marks the blue house nearby, the site of a freshwater spring (which makes this location even more strategic). The big star-shaped fortress on the hill is Fort Kaštel, designed by a French architect but dating from the Venetian era (1630). Read the street plan of the Roman town into this model: At the center (on the hill) was the *castrum,* or military base. At the base of the hill (the far side from the amphitheater) was the forum, or town square. During Pula's Roman glory days, the hillsides around the *castrum* were blanketed with the villas of rich merchants. The Old Town, which clusters around the base of the fortress-topped hill, still features many fragments of the Roman period, as well as Pula's later occupiers. We'll take a counterclockwise stroll around the fortified old hill through this ancient zone.

The huge anchor across the street from the model celebrates Pula's number-one employer—its shipyards.

• *Continue along the street. At the fork, again bear right (on Kandlerova ulica—level, not uphill). Notice the* **Roman ruins** *on your right. Just about any time someone wants to put up a new building, they find ruins like these. Work screeches to a halt while the valuable remains are excavated. In this case, they've discovered three Roman houses, two churches, and 2,117 amphorae—the largest stash found anywhere in the world. (Notice the harbor just behind, which suggests this might have been a storehouse for off-loaded amphorae.) I guess the new parking garage has to wait.*

After about three more blocks strolling through gritty, slice-of-life Pula, on your right-hand side, you'll see Pula's...

Cathedral (Katedrala)

This church combines elements of the two big Italian influences on Pula: Roman and Venetian. Dating from the fifth century A.D., the

Romanesque core of the church (notice the skinny, slitlike windows) marks the site of an early-Christian seafront settlement in Pula. The Venetian Baroque facade and bell tower are much more recent (early 18th century). Typical of the Venetian style, notice how far away the austere bell tower is from the body of the church. The bell tower's foundation is made of stones that were scavenged from the amphitheater. On the square is an instructive poster illustrating the physical development of the town through the ages. The church's interior features a classic Roman-style basilica floor plan, with a single grand hall—the side naves were added in the 15th century, after a fire (free, generally open daily 7:00–12:00 & 16:00–18:00, but often closed).

• *Keep walking through the main pedestrian zone, past all the tacky souvenir shops and Albanian-run fast-food and ice-cream joints. After a few more blocks, you emerge into the...*

Forum

Every Roman town had a forum, or main square. Twenty centuries later, Pula's Forum not only serves the same function but has kept the old Roman name.

Two important buildings front the north end of the square, where you enter. The smaller building (on the left, with the columns) is the first-century A.D. Roman **Temple of Augustus** (Augustov Hram). Built during the reign of, and dedicated to, Augustus Caesar, this temple took a direct hit from an Allied bomb in World War II. After the war, the Allied occupiers rebuilt

ISTRIA

it as a sort of mea culpa—notice the patchwork repair job. It's the only one remaining of three such temples that once lined this side of the square. Inside the temple is a single room with fragments of ancient sculptures (10 kn, daily June–Aug 9:00–22:00, Sept 9:00–20:00, early-Oct–mid-Oct 9:00–19:30, May 9:00–21:00, closed mid-Oct–April, sparse English labels). The statue of Augustus, which likely stood on or near this spot, dates from the time of Christ. Other evocative chips and bits of Roman Pula include the feet of a powerful commander with a pathetic little vanquished barbarian obediently at his knee (perhaps one of the Histri—the indigenous Istrians that the Romans conquered in 177 B.C.).

Head back out on to the square. As Rome fell, its long-subjugated subjects in Pula had little respect for the former empire's symbols, and many temples didn't survive. Others were put to new use: Part of an adjacent temple (likely dedicated to Diana) was incorporated into the bigger building on the right, Pula's medieval **Town Hall** (Gradska Palača). If you circle around behind this building, you can still see Roman fragments embedded in the back. The Town Hall encapsulates many centuries of Pula architecture: Romanesque core, Gothic reliefs, Renaissance porch, Baroque windows...and a few Roman bits and pieces. Notice the interesting combination of flags above the door: Pula, Croatia, Istria (with its mascot goat), Italy (for the large ethnic minority here), and the European Union (since Croatia is a candidate country).

• *Consider dropping by the **TI** on this square before continuing our circular stroll down the main drag, Sergijevaca. You'll pass by a small park on your right, then a block of modern shops. Immediately after the Kenvelo shop on the right (with a red-and-black K sign), turn right into the white, unmarked doorway. Emerging on the other side, turn left, walk to the metal grill, and look down to see the...*

Roman Floor Mosaic (Rimski Mozaik)

This hidden mosaic is a great example of the Roman treasures that lie below the old center of Pula. Uncovered by locals who were cleaning up from World War II bombs, this third-century floor was carefully excavated and cleaned up for display right where it was laid nearly two millennia ago. (Notice that the Roman floor level was about six feet below today's.) The centerpiece of the mosaic depicts the punishment of Dirce. According to the ancient Greek legend, King Lykos of Thebes was bewitched by Dirce and abandoned his pregnant queen. The queen gave birth to twin boys (depicted in this mosaic), who grew up to kill their deadbeat dad and tie Dirce to the horns of a bull to be bashed against a mountain. This same story is famously depicted in the twisty *Toro Farnese* sculpture partly carved by Michelangelo (on display in Naples' Archaeological Museum).

• *For an optional detour to Byzantine times, walk into the parking lot just beyond the mosaic. Near the end of the lot, on the left-hand side, is a fenced-off grassy field. At the far end of the field is the small...*

Basilica of St. Mary Formosa (Kapela Marije Formoze)

We've seen plenty of Roman and Venetian bric-a-brac, but this chapel survives from the time of another Istrian occupier: Byzantium. For about 170 years after Rome fell (the sixth and seventh centuries A.D.), this region came under the control of the Byzantine Empire and was ruled from Ravenna (now in Italy, across the Adriatic, south of Venice). Much of this field was once occupied by a vast, richly decorated basilica. This lonely chapel is all that's left, but it still gives a feel for the architecture of that era—including the Greek cross floor plan (with four equal arms) and heavy brick vaulting. An informational sign posted nearby outlines the original basilica and floor plan.

• *Back on the main drag (Sergijevaca), continue a few more blocks through Pula's most colorful and most touristy neighborhood, until you arrive at the...*

Arch of Sergius (Slavoluk Sergijevaca)

This triumphal arch, from the first century B.C., was Michelangelo's favorite Roman artifact in Pula. Marking the edge of the original Roman town, it was built to honor Lucius Sergius Lepidus. He fought on the side of Augustus in the civil wars that swept the empire after Julius Caesar's assassination. The proto-feminist inscription proudly explains, "Silvia of the Sergius family paid for this with her own money." Statues of Silvia's husband, Lucius, plus her son and her brother-in-law, once stood on the three blocks at the top of the arch. (Squint to see the *Sergivs* name on each block.) On the  underside of the arch is a relief of an eagle (Rome) clutching an evil snake in its talons.

• *Before going under the arch, look to your left to see a famous Irishman appreciating the view from the terrace of...*

Café Uliks

In October 1904, a young writer named James Joyce moved from Dublin to Pula with his girlfriend, Nora Barnacle. By day, he

taught English to Austro-Hungarian naval officers at the Berlitz language school (in the yellow building just behind). By night, he imagined strolling through his hometown as he penned short stories that would eventually become the collection *Dubliners*. But James and Nora quickly grew bored with little Pula and moved to Trieste in March 1905. Even so, Pula remains proud of its literary connections.

• *Now pass through the arch, into a square next to remains of the town wall. Continue straight ahead (up two bustling blocks, along the in-love-with-life Flanatička street) to...*

National Square (Nardoni Trg) and Market Hall

Pula's market hall was an iron-and-glass marvel when inaugurated in the 19th century. This structure is yet another reminder

of the way the Austro-Hungarian Empire modernized Pula with grace and gentility. You'll find smelly fish on the ground floor (Mon–Sat 7:00–13:30, Sun 7:00–12:00) and an inviting food circus upstairs (Mon–Fri 7:00–15:00, Sat 7:00–14:00, Sun 7:00–12:00). All around is a busy and colorful farmers' market that bustles until about 13:00, when things quiet down.

• *Our tour is finished. If you're ready for lunch, consider one of the cheap options inside the market hall, or walk one block to Kantina (see "Eating in Pula," later).*

When you're done here, backtrack to the town wall. As you face the Arch of Sergius, take a right and walk under the leafy canopy next to the wall. Keep an eye out (mostly on your left, along the wall) for more Roman remains. Among these are the **Twin Gates** *(Porta Gemina), marking the entrance to a garden that's home to the* **Archaeological Museum of Istria** *(described next, under "Sights in Pula"). With more time, you can also consider a trip to the hilltop fortress,* **Fort Kaštel.** *Otherwise, we've completed our circular tour—the amphitheater is just around the corner.*

Sights in Pula

Archaeological Museum of Istria (Arheološki Muzej Istre)—If Pula's many ruins intrigue you, here's the place to scratch your Roman itch. This museum, over a century old, shows off some of what you've seen in the streets, plus lots more—stone monuments, classical statues, ancient pottery...you name it (20 kn; May–Sept Mon–Fri 9:00–20:00, Sat–Sun 9:00–15:00; Oct–April Mon–Fri 9:00–14:00, closed Sat–Sun; Carrarina 3, tel. 052/351-301, www.mdc.hr/pula).

On the hill behind the museum (and free to visit even if you don't buy a museum ticket) is its highlight, the remains of a **Roman Theater** (Rimsko Kazalište). Part of the stage is still intact, along with the semicircle of stone seats (some of which are still engraved with the names of the wealthy theatergoers who once sat there). To find it, go up the hill around the right side of the museum. This was the smaller of the two theaters in Roman Pula; the second was south of the center (and is no longer intact).

Fort Kaštel—For a bird's-eye view over the town, head up to its centerpiece fortress. This deserted-feeling place, hosting the Historical Museum of Istria, is worth visiting only for the chance to wander the ramparts. While neither the museum nor the fortress is worth the hike up here, it's a good way to kill some extra time in Pula and sample the views over the town and amphitheater (various trails lead up from the streets below).

Eating in Pula

The best lunch options are in and near the town's **market hall** (which is also where my self-guided walk ends). The top floor of the market is a food circus with a number of cheap and tempting eateries with both indoor and terrace seating (Mon–Fri 7:00–15:00, Sat 7:00–14:00, Sun 7:00–12:00). Upstairs in the back, look for **Laterna,** with unusually classy decor and fish specialties. Back outside, **Pekarna Corona**—a bakery across from the right side of the market (as you face the main entrance)—serves up good, fresh, cheap *burek,* the phyllo-dough pastry (Mon–Fri 6:30–18:00, Sat 6:30–15:00, closed Sun).

Kantina Restaurant, a block away, serves good lunches (including veggie options) and hearty, creative 35-kn salads both in an elegant vaulted cellar and on a lazy shady terrace. The service can be slow—if you're in a rush, eat at the market hall instead (50–75-kn pastas, 90–130-kn meat dishes, daily 12:00–23:00, at the end of the pedestrian zone at Flanatička 16, tel. 052/214-054). They also have a smaller café (drinks only, no food) directly across from the market hall.

Pula Connections

By Bus from Pula to: Rovinj (about hourly, 45 min), **Poreč** (12/ day, 1.5 hrs), **Opatija** (almost hourly, 2 hrs), **Rijeka** (nearly hourly, 2–2.5 hrs), **Zagreb** (almost hourly, 3.75–6 hrs), **Split** (2/day, 10 hrs, plus 1 night bus—described below), **Venice** (1/day departing at 5:30, 5 hrs). A night bus departs Pula at 20:00, going to **Split** (arrives 6:00) and **Dubrovnik** (arrives 11:00). To reach destinations in **Slovenia** (including Piran and Ljubljana), you'll first transfer in Umag; or, in the summer, you can take the 8:00 bus from Rovinj (described on page 115). Be aware that bus connections are more frequent on weekdays (fewer departures Sat–Sun). Bus info: toll tel. 060-300-800.

By Train to: Zagreb (3/day, 6 hrs, transfer in Rijeka; in summer also 1 night train with very early arrival in Zagreb, 8 hrs), **Ljubljana** (1/day Mon–Fri, none Sat–Sun, 3.5 hrs, transfer in Buzet, Croatia, and Divača, Slovenia).

The Brijuni Islands

The Brijuni Islands (bree-YOO-nee, Brioni in Italian)—an archipelago of 14 islands just offshore from the southern tip of the Istrian Peninsula—were a favorite haunt of Maršal Tito, the leader of communist Yugoslavia. The main island, called Great Brijuni (Veli Brijun), was where Tito liked to show off the natural wonders of his beloved Yugoslavia to visiting dignitaries and world leaders. Today the island is a national park that combines serene natural beauty with quirky Yugoslav sights—offering a strange but enjoyable time capsule of the Tito years.

As you'll see from the remains of previous occupants (Romans, Byzantines, Venetians, Austrians—even dinosaurs), Tito wasn't the first to fall in love with Brijuni. Its first tourist boom came at the turn of the 20th century, when Austrian entrepreneur Paul Kupelwieser developed Brijuni into a world-class health resort. Between the World Wars, it hosted many notables, from Douglas Fairbanks and John D. Rockefeller to Richard Strauss and Hirohito. But when Tito took power, he claimed the islands for himself, making Brijuni his summer residence from 1949 until 1979. During this time, the island hosted a steady stream of VIP visitors from the East, West, and the non-aligned world (see sidebar). Just three years after Tito's death, in October 1983, Brijuni opened to the public as a national park.

Getting There: You can get to Great Brijuni Island only on one of the national park's boats. These depart from the town of

Brijuni: Center of the Non-Aligned World

Many visitors to the former Yugoslavia mistakenly assume this country was part of the Soviet Bloc. It most decidedly wasn't. While the rest of "Eastern Europe" was liberated by the Soviets at the end of World War II, Yugoslavia's own, homegrown Partisan Army forced the Nazis out themselves. This allowed the country—and its new leader, the war hero Maršal Tito—a certain degree of self-determination following the war. Though the new Yugoslavia was socialist, it was not Soviet socialism. After formally breaking ties with Moscow in 1948, Tito steered his country toward a "third way" between the strict and stifling communism of the East and the capitalist free-for-all of the West. (For more on Tito's system, see the Understanding Yugoslavia chapter.)

Many other countries also didn't quite fit into the easy East-versus-West dichotomy embraced by the US, USSR, and Europe. On July 19, 1956, the Brijuni Declaration—signed by Tito, Jawaharlal Nehru of India, and Abdel Nasser of Egypt—created the Non-Aligned Movement (NAM). Members recognized each other's sovereignty and respected each leader's right to handle domestic issues however he or she saw fit.

As Tito's international prominence grew, the list of visitors to his Brijuni Islands hideaway began to read like a Who's Who of post-WWII world leaders. In addition to Nehru and Nasser, Tito hosted Haile Selassie (Ethiopia), Yasser Arafat (Palestine Liberation Organization), Fidel Castro (Cuba), Indira Gandhi (India), Muammar al-Gaddafi (Libya), Queen Elizabeth II (Great Britain), Willy Brandt (West Germany), Leonid Brezhnev (USSR)...not to mention Elizabeth Taylor (US) and Sophia Loren (Italy).

In principle, the NAM was envisioned as a competitor of NATO and the Warsaw Pact. But as the world's politics have changed, many NAM members are now closely allied with other, more powerful nations. And when Yugoslavia broke up, most of the countries that emerged preferred to join NATO and the EU.

So whatever happened to the rest of the NAM? It's still going strong, encompassing virtually all of Africa, the Middle East, Southeast Asia, and Latin America. While the EU and the US wrestle for bragging rights as the world's superpower, the NAM represents 55 percent of the world's population.

Fažana, five miles north of Pula and 20 miles south of Rovinj. From Rovinj, drive southeast to Bale, where you'll get on the *ipsilon* highway and continue south. In Vodnjan, watch for the easy-to-miss turnoff (on the right) marked for Fažana and Brijuni. Once in Fažana, follow brown *Brijuni* signs and park along the water (confirm with park ticket office that your parking spot is OK).

Cost and Information: The price varies depending on the time of year: July–Aug-210 kn, June and Sept-200 kn, April–May and Oct-170 kn, Nov–March-125 kn; includes park entry, boat to the island, and a guide (see "English Tour," below). Tel. 052/525-882, www.brijuni.hr, izleti@brijuni.hr.

Hours: From April through October, the first boat departure is at 6:40 and the last trip is at 21:45 (last return from Brijuni at 23:00). The number of departures to the island varies with the time of year: July–Aug about hourly, 14/day; May–June and Sept 12/day; April and Oct 10/day. Sporadic boats run off-season (roughly Nov–Easter), but they're intended for island residents and hotel guests.

English Tour: You're required to go to the island with a four-hour guided tour, much of which is spent on a little tourist train. The only English-language tour usually departs Fažana daily at 11:30. It's essential to call ahead to confirm the schedule and reserve a space on the tour (call at least a day before, or three days ahead in peak season, tel. 052/525-882).

If you can't make it on the English tour, you're welcome to join any tour you like (Croatian, German, Italian, etc.). While it's possible to slip away from your group and explore the island on your own, park officials discourage it. (But, since hotel guests on the island can move about freely, it's generally no problem.) Staying with the tour for most of the trip is wise in any event, as there's lots of ground to cover in a limited amount of time. It's possible to rent bikes at the hotel where the boat puts in. You're technically required to take the same boat back with the rest of your tour, but this isn't closely monitored.

Visiting the Island: Great Brijuni Island can be visited only with a tour. After a 15-minute crossing from the mainland town of Fažana, visitors arrive at the island's main harbor, a hub of activity and the site of its two hotels (Neptun-Istra Hotel and Karmen Hotel, Sb-700–770 kn, Db-1,125–1,350 kn in peak season, www.brijuni.hr). Outside this area, the island is largely undeveloped, with just a few tourist facilities and houses of people who live here. There are virtually no cars—most people get around by bike, golf cart, or the little tourist train you'll board to begin your tour. As you spin around the island, you'll enjoy views over its endlessly twisty coast, with cove after tranquil cove. Your guide will impart both dry facts and eye-rolling legends while you putter past several intriguing sights, periodically giving you a chance to get off the train and explore a few of them up close.

The tour's highlight is the **"Tito on Brijuni"** exhibit. Dating from 1984—four years after his death, but before the end of Yugoslavia—this exhibit celebrates the cult of personality surrounding the head of this now-deceased nation. The museum (with English descriptions) features countless photos of Tito in every Brijuni context imaginable—strolling, sunbathing, skeet shooting, schmoozing with world leaders and movie stars, inspecting military officers, playing with camels given to him by Muammar al-Gaddafi, and so on. (For more on Tito, and why this former dictator remains so beloved in his former lands, see the sidebar on page 538.) Smaller side-exhibits include a taxidermy collection of exotic animals given to Tito by foreign leaders from around the world and photos of Paul Kupelwieser, the Austrian magnate who put Brijuni on the tourist map.

Another high point of the island tour is the **safari,** featuring a diverse menagerie of animals (or their descendants) brought here for Tito as gifts by visiting heads of state. Because many of the non-aligned nations are in Africa, Asia, or other non-European regions, some of these beasts are particularly exotic. Aside from the Istrian ox and Istria's trademark goat, you'll see llamas, Somali sheep, Shetland ponies, chamois, and more. Your train may stop for a visit with Sony and Lanka, a pair of Indian elephants given to Tito by Indira Gandhi, the former prime minister of India. There once were camels, cheetahs, ostriches, monkeys, bears, and bobcats as well, but most of these have gone to the great non-aligned safari in the sky, and their bodies are now preserved at the "Tito on Brijuni" exhibit.

Other attractions you may see on Brijuni: an ancient, gnarled olive tree supposedly dating from the fourth century A.D.; the remains of a mostly first-century A.D. Roman *villa rustica,* or country estate; the ruined street plan of a Byzantine fort; a 15th-century Gothic church with an exhibit on frescoes and Glagolitic (early Croatian) script; a Venetian summer house that hosts an archaeology museum; an Austro-Hungarian naval fort (Brijuni was strategically important back when Pula was Austria's main naval base); and footprints left by a dinosaur who vacationed here 120 million years before Tito.

Birders can look for some of the 250 avian species that live on the island in the summer. Gardeners may spot some exotic, non-native plant species (more gifts, to go along with all those animals), such as Australian eucalyptus. And Republicans can drool over the golf course, a reminder that Brijuni is attempting to cultivate a ritzy image. Your tour's lengthy stop at the bar/gift shop is yet another indication that, while some remember Tito fondly, good ol' capitalism is here to stay.

Poreč

When you tell Europeans you're going to Istria, they say, "Ah, you must go to Poreč!" Poreč (poh-RETCH, Parenzo in Italian), the tourist capital of the Istrian coast, is the kind of resort that brags about how many hotel beds it has, rather than how many museums, churches, or gelato stands are packed into its Old Town. They're also proud to have more than their share of "blue-flag beaches" (which they call *laguna*s)—meaning that the water is crystal-clear for swimming. Finally, Poreč has won several "Croatia's cleanest city" contests. None of this makes for very compelling sightseeing, but...there you go.

Despite the town's appeal to Europeans, most American visitors find Poreč too big to be charming, but too small to be exciting. Its only real sight is the basilica, with its exquisite mosaics. Beyond that, it's mostly interesting as a case study on how Germans like to vacation: Set up camp for a week at a distant resort hotel, bake in the sun, and occasionally trek into the Old Town for dinner. Think of it as the Croatian Acapulco.

Planning Your Time

For the typical speedy American visitor, spending time in Rovinj, Piran, Pula, or the Istrian interior is more satisfying. If you're still curious, see Poreč en route or as a day trip: Zip in, stroll the Old Town, ogle the mosaics in the basilica, then move on. Despite its many hotels, Poreč lacks soul—I prefer sleeping elsewhere.

Orientation to Poreč

(area code: 052)

Like so many Croatian coastal towns, the Old Town of Poreč is on a peninsula. Surrounding it are miles of hotels-and-concrete sprawl. Traffic into the city funnels into Zagrebačka street, which passes the TI and ends at the spacious square named Trg Slobode. From there, Decumanis street marches right through the middle of the Old Town.

Tourist Information

Visit the TI to pick up the information booklet, sightseeing guide, and city map (July–Aug daily 8:00–21:00; progressively shorter hours off-season until winter Mon–Sat 8:00–16:00, closed Sun; a few steps from Trg Slobode at Zagrebačka 9, tel. 052/451-293, www.to-porec.com).

Arrival in Poreč

The bus station and big parking lot straddle the base of the Old Town.

Drivers follow *Centar* and *Parking* signs to reach the big lot nearest the Old Town (take ticket as you enter and bring it with you; when leaving Poreč, pay at the kiosk before returning to your car, then wave paid ticket at exit to open gate). From the lot, walk uphill past the parking kiosk and the market until you reach big Zagrebačka boulevard, with the grass median. Turn right and continue up Zagrebačka, passing the TI (on your right) en route to Trg Slobode and the Old Town.

The **bus** station is at the other end of the Old Town. Exit the station to the right and go through the little park to the seafront and Old Town. Just up the hill is Trg Slobode and the nearby TI.

Sights in Poreč

▲**Euphrasian Basilica (Eufrazijeva Bazilika)**—This sixth-century church is a gold mine for fans of Byzantine mosaics.

The otherwise dull interior is dominated by the mosaics in the apse surrounding the main altar. The top row depicts Jesus surrounded by the 12 apostles, the medallions around the arch celebrate 12 female martyrs, and front and center are Mary and Jesus surrounded by angels and martyrs—including Bishop Euphrasius, holding his namesake basilica in his arms (second from left). These date from the 170-year period after the fall of Rome (roughly 530–700 A.D.), when Istria was part of the Byzantine Empire and was ruled from Ravenna (near Venice, across the Adriatic). The more recent (13th-century) canopy over the altar was inspired by the one in St. Mark's Basilica in Venice. Don't miss another set of mosaics in the floor just inside the door (free entry, open long hours daily, no shorts, a block off the Old Town's main drag on—where else?—Eufrazijeva street).

For more mosaics, drop into the attached **museum,** with several mosaic fragments scattered around two floors (15 kn, May–mid-Oct daily 10:00–17:00, closed mid-Oct–April). Or climb the **bell tower** to get a bird's-eye view of Poreč for 15 kn.

ISTRIA

Poreč Connections

From Poreč by Bus to: Rovinj (6–9/day, 1 hr), **Pula** (12/day, 1.5 hrs), **Piran** (2/day Mon–Fri, 1/day Sun; additional departures to **Portorož**, near Piran).

Hill Towns of the Istrian Interior

Most tourists in Croatia focus on the coast. For a dash of variety, head inland. Some of the best bits of the Croatian interior lie just a short drive from Rovinj. Dotted with picturesque hill towns, speckled with wineries and olive-oil farms, embedded with precious truffles, and grooved by meandering rural roads, the Istrian interior is worth a visit. Tucked below, between, and on top of the many hills are characteristic stone-walled villages, designed to stay cool in summer and warm in winter. The local tourist board is carefully manicuring this region's image as *the* hot new spot to find hill towns, backcountry drives, and a relaxed and relaxing lifestyle. The often-repeated comparisons to Tuscany and Provence are a stretch, if not a little ridiculous. But maybe it's understandable that many visitors find themselves seduced by the *malvazija* wine, truffles, and laid-back ambience of the Istrian hill towns.

Poking around and exploring on your own is a good option here. For a quick visit, focus on the best hill town: Motovun, a popular little burg with sweeping views. With more time, consider visiting the tiny, rugged, relatively untrampled artists' colony of Grožnjan and tiny but touristy Hum. For dinner, stop by Konoba Astarea in Brtonigla.

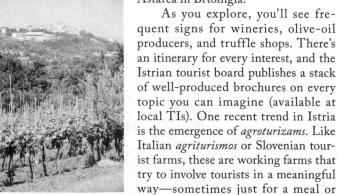

As you explore, you'll see frequent signs for wineries, olive-oil producers, and truffle shops. There's an itinerary for every interest, and the Istrian tourist board publishes a stack of well-produced brochures on every topic you can imagine (available at local TIs). One recent trend in Istria is the emergence of *agroturizams*. Like Italian *agriturismos* or Slovenian tourist farms, these are working farms that try to involve tourists in a meaningful way—sometimes just for a meal or overnight stay, but occasionally actually participating in the daily workings of the farm. For more information, pick up the free brochure (available locally), or visit www.istra.hr.

Getting Around the Istrian Interior

By Public Transportation: While it's possible to see some parts of inland Istria by public transportation, the rewards are not worth the headaches. The large hill town of Pazin is the region's transit hub, with buses to Rovinj, Pula, Poreč, and Motovun—but not Grožnjan, Hum, or Brtonigla.

By Car: The region is ideal by car. For a full day of hill town-hopping in the Istrian interior, follow my suggested clockwise route. Though I've described the trip starting from Rovinj, you can begin wherever you like.

From Rovinj, take the fast *ipsilon* highway (A-9) north to Buje (between the *ipsilon* and Buje, consider stopping for a meal

in **Brtonigla**). From Buje, continue eastward to Krasica and watch for the turn-off to take the twisty back road to **Grožnjan**. After Grožnjan, wind down to the mercifully flat and straight road (#44) that follows the Mirna River Valley farther eastward, to Motovun (well-signed off the main road). Consider dropping by the Zigante truffle shop in **Livade** before leaving the main road

and winding around back of Motovun's hill to find the corkscrew road up. After seeing **Motovun,** you can head back to your home base along the main valley road. Or, with more time, continue farther east to **Hum** (follow the main valley road east to Buzet, then to Roč, then look for the turn-off on the right to Hum, along the **Glagolitic Lane**). From Hum, you're very close to the northeast branch of the *ipsilon* highway (A-8), which leads right back to Rovinj (via Pazin). (Note that Hum is also just a few miles from the Učka Tunnel to Opatija and Rijeka, if you're continuing to the east.)

While you'll traverse some slow and windy roads, this entire trip is quick—you could do the entire circle (including Hum) without stops in less than three hours.

This route is just a rough framework. Venture off it. Run down leads from locals. Follow intriguing signs to wine-tastings, restaurants, and *agroturizams*. Sniff out some truffles in the Motovun Forest. You will see some other tourists, but this area isn't overrun...yet. There may just be some overlooked gems in the Istrian interior waiting for you to discover.

Motovun

Dramatically situated high above vineyards and a truffle-filled forest, Motovun (moh-toh-VOON, Montona in Italian, pop. 593) is the best-known and most-touristed of the Istrian hill towns. And for good reason: Its hilltop Old Town is particularly evocative, with a colorful old church and a rampart walk with the best spine-tingling vistas in the Istrian interior. It's hard to believe that race-car driver Mario Andretti was born in such  a tranquil little traffic-free hamlet. Today Motovun's quiet lanes are shared by locals, tourists, and artists—who began settling here a generation ago, when it was nearly deserted.

Orientation to Motovun

(area code: 052)
Motovun is steep. Most everything of interest to tourists is huddled around its tippy-top. The main, upper entrance gate into town deposits you at the main square, with the church on your left and Hotel Kaštel on the right. From there, you're just about two blocks in every direction from a sheer drop-off. This hilltop zone is circled by an old rampart that today offers Motovun's most scenic stroll.

Tourist Information
Motovun doesn't have an official TI, but the gang at Hotel Kaštel dispenses tourist information. During the day, you can drop into their travel agency on the main square, called Istria Magica (Mon–Fri 8:00–16:00, closed Sat–Sun, to the right as you face Hotel Kaštel, at Trg Andrea Antico 8, tel. 052/681-750); at other times, ask at the hotel reception desk (listed later, under "Sleeping in Motovun").

Arrival in Motovun
Motovun's striking hilltop setting comes with a catch: Visitors usually have to hike up part of the way. A steep, twisty road connects the base of the hill with the Old Town up top. If it's not too crowded, drive as far up this road as possible until you're directed to park in the lot partway up (near the lower church, a steep 10-min uphill walk to the main square, 15 kn/day). In busier peak times, this lot might be full, so you may have to wait a few minutes for a car to leave; or you can park in the big lot at the foot

of the hill and walk all the way up (during very busy times, such as the film festival, a shuttle bus may be taking visitors up the hill). If you're staying at Hotel Kaštel, follow the procedure explained under "Sleeping in Motovun," later. If staying elsewhere, ask your hotelier for advice.

Self-Guided Walk

Welcome to Motovun

The following commentary will bring some meaning to your Motovun hilltop stroll. The walk begins at the traffic barrier halfway up the hill (the highest you can drive unless you're sleeping up top).

The main drag leading up into town is lined with wine-and-truffle shops. My favorite is the Lanča family's **Etnobutiga ČA** (just above the parking lot on the right, at Gradiziol 33). This restored 17th-century house has a beautiful view terrace and a wide selection of local wines, brandies, and truffle products (most of them from the Zigante company, just across the valley). Like many people around here, Livio Lanča makes his own mistletoe brandy laced with honey (daily in season 10:00–20:00, slightly shorter hours in shoulder season, closed Nov–mid-March, tel. 052/681-767).

Hike several more steep minutes up the hill. Soon you'll pass yet another traffic barrier and reach the base of the town's wall (and the recommended Mondo Konoba restaurant). Circling up and around, you'll go through the first of two **defensive gateways.** Inside this passage (under the fortified gate), notice the various insignias from Motovun's history lining the walls—look for the Venetian lion, the Latin family tombstone, and the seal of Motovun (with five towers being watched over by an angel). The area above the gate was a storehouse for weapons in the 15th century, when Motovun first flourished.

Emerging from the gateway, you're greeted by sweeping views of the valley below on your right-hand side. (A coffee or light meal with this view is unforgettable; the town's lone ATM is to your left.) Just up and to the left, you'll find another defensive gateway, which is the main entrance into the heart of the **Old Town.** (Inside this gateway, notice the recommended Konoba pod Voltom restaurant.)

To your left as you come through the main gate is the yellow town church, **St. Stephen's.** The crenellated tower is a reminder of a time when this hilltop town needed to be defended. While unassuming from the outside, this austere house of worship has an impressive pedigree: It was designed by the famous Venetian architect Andrea Palladio (1508–1580), who greatly influenced

the Neoclassical architecture of Washington, DC. The interior is a little gloomy but refreshingly lived-in—used more by locals than by tourists. On the left, notice a painting of the heart of Jesus, its eyes following you around the church (free, generally open daily 10:00–18:00 and during frequent services).

As you stand on the square in front of the church, imagine Motovun during its annual **film festival,** when it's filled with 20,000 movie-lovers from throughout the region and around the world—often including a minor celebrity or two. This square fills to capacity, and films are projected on a giant screen at the far end (generally late July or early Aug, www.motovunfilmfestival.com).

Facing the church is the **Italian Cultural Center,** which fills an important role in this very Italian corner of Croatia. While the building is not open to the public, if your timing is right you'll enjoy beautiful music spilling out from its windows and filling the square. The local *klapa* music troupe—with men's voices harmonizing a cappella—practices here twice weekly (usually Mon and Fri evenings, at 21:00 in summer and 20:00 in winter, www.klapamotovun.com). If you hear them, find a bench and enjoy the show.

At the other end of the square is a leafy little piazza dominated by the big **Hotel Kaštel**—the main industry in town. In addition to its rooms and restaurant, Hotel Kaštel serves as the town TI. This is also where bigwigs in town for the local film festival call home—ask the staff about recent star-sightings of B-, C-, and D-list celebrities. (For example, if you're staying here, you may be showering in the same bathroom once graced by Jason Biggs, star of *American Pie.* Lucky you.) In the fall, they can also arrange truffle-finding excursions for tourists (about 700 kn/person).

Between the church and Hotel Kaštel, follow the lane to the **ramparts.** Take the five-minute stroll around the Old Town on these fortifications. While most of Croatia is overrun by stray cats, Motovun seems populated by dog lovers. If you see or hear dogs in people's backyards, it's a safe bet that they are trained to hunt for truffles in the surrounding forest.

As you breathe in the stunning panorama, notice that well-defended Motovun has been fortified three times—two layers of wall up top, and a third down below.

Sleeping in Motovun

Unlike most small Croatian towns, Motovun's accommodations don't charge extra for one- or two-night stays. In fact, if you're staying for three or more nights, try to score a discount.

$$ Hotel Kaštel, dominating Motovun's hilltop (and its tourist industry), is can-do, ideally located, and the only real hotel in this little burg. Most of the 32 colorful rooms have views. True to its name, the building used to be a castle, so the floor plan can be confusing (July–Aug: Sb-410 kn, Db-690 kn, Tb-950 kn; June and Sept: Sb-380 kn, Db-635 kn, Tb-875 kn; May and Oct: Sb-355 kn, Db-585 kn, Tb-800 kn, 10 percent discount with this book, pricier apartments available, cheaper off-season, elevator, air-con in some rooms, laundry service is handy and affordable if you do it by the kilo, pay Internet access and Wi-Fi, Trg Andrea Antico 7, tel. 052/681-607, fax 052/681-652, www.hotel-kastel-motovun.hr, info@hotel-kastel-motovun.hr). Guests have free access to the new spa facility, with a beautiful indoor pool and a spa offering a wide range of massages (starting at 150 kn/30 min). Guests with cars should tell the attendant at the traffic barrier that you're staying here. If there's room on top, he'll let you drive up. Otherwise he'll tell you where to park and call the hotel, which will send down a free car to shuttle you up.

$ At Bella Vista, just below the lower town gate (a five-minute uphill walk to the main square), the Kotiga family rents five apartments with cute decor and balconies that offer sweeping views across the countryside (Db-360 kn, no breakfast, cash only, Gradiziol 1, check in at gift shop, clearly communicate arrival time if coming after 20:00, tel. & fax 052/681-724, mobile 091-523-0321, www.apartmani motovun.com, info@apartmani motovun .com, Mirjana).

$ Café Antico rents five simple rooms above a lively café/bar, a few steps around the corner from the main square (Db-300 kn, apartment with air-con-400 kn, no breakfast, cash only, some rooms get late-night noise from the café—try requesting a quieter one, Pietra Kandlera 2, tel. 052/681-697, mobile 098-173-0019, antico_motovun@hi.t-com.hr, Tomislav and Sandra).

$ Sobe Nena, run by sweet Doris, is a good budget option at the very bottom of Motovun's hill. It's a steep hike up into town, but you can try catching the shuttle bus from the lower parking lot, or Doris can give you a ride (Sb-215 kn, Db-285 kn, cash only, Kanal 32, tel. 052/681-719, mobile 098-937-2060, sobe.nena@gmail.com).

Eating in Motovun

Considering this is a small hill town with just three real restaurants, all of them are impressively good; the first two listings are particularly notable. Every menu is topped by pricey (but tasty) truffle dishes—but keep in mind that these are a better investment when truffles are in season and the flavors are pungent (see sidebar); otherwise you'll get older, blander truffles.

Mondo Konoba, run by a typical Croatian-Italian hybrid family and located just below the lower town gate (on the left, at the base of the wall), serves up Sicilian-Istrian fusion cuisine. Most diners skip the forgettable dining room in favor of the inviting little outdoor terrace. The Mondo family's pack of five truffle-hunting dogs occasionally pay a visit (60–100-kn pastas, 90–170-kn main courses, Wed–Mon 12:00–15:30 & 18:00–22:00, closed Tue, tel. 052/681-791).

Konoba pod Voltom is actually inside the town's upper, main gate (on the right, with the *Taberna* sign above the door). Motovun's most traditional eatery serves excellent, well-presented Istrian food in a cozy dining room. In good weather (June–Sept only), it's hard to beat their view loggia, just below and outside the gate (40–60-kn pastas, 60–110-kn main courses, 140–220-kn truffle splurges, Thu–Tue 12:00–22:00, closed Wed, tel. 052/681-923).

Hotel Kaštel has its own restaurant, with good food and delightful seating right on the leafy main square (also listed under "Sleeping in Motovun," earlier; daily 7:00–10:00 & 13:00–15:00 & 19:00–21:00).

The simple **Montona Gallery** café, with tables along the rampart between the two gates, serves drinks and ice cream with mammoth views (open long hours daily).

For a pricey truffle feast, head across the valley to **Zigante** in Livade (described next).

Near Motovun, in Livade: Zigante Tartufi

The little crossroads village of Livade, sitting in the valley facing the back of Motovun's hill, is home to the first and last name in Istrian truffles. In 1999, Giancarlo Zigante unearthed the biggest white truffle the world had ever seen—2.9 pounds, as verified by *The Guinness Book of World Records*. (In 2007, the record was broken by a 3.3-pound Tuscan truffle.) This single hunk of fungus—now revered as if a religious relic—kicked off a truffle craze that continues in Istria today (see sidebar). Today Zigante has a virtual monopoly on Istria's truffle industry, producing a wide range of truffle goodies. If you're a connoisseur, or just curious, make a pilgrimage to this truffle mecca.

Truffle Mania

A mysterious fungus with a pungent, unmistakable flavor has been all the rage in Istria for the last decade or so. Called *tartufi* in both Croatian and Italian, these precious tubers have been gathered here since Roman times and were favored by the region's Venetian and Austrian rulers. More recently, local peasants ate them as a substitute for meat (often mixed with polenta) during the lean days after World War II.

In 1999, local entrepreneur Giancarlo Zigante discovered a nearly three-pound white truffle. In addition to making Giancarlo Zigante a very wealthy man (see "Zigante Tartufi" listing on opposite page), this giant truffle legitimized Istria on the world truffle scene. Today, Istria is giving France's Provence and Italy's Piedmont a run for their money in truffle production. Most of Istria's truffles are concentrated in the Motovun Forest, the damp, oak-tree-filled terrain surrounding Motovun, Livade, and Buzet.

A truffle is a tuber that grows entirely underground, usually at a depth of eight inches near the roots of oak trees. Since no part of the plant grows aboveground, they're particularly difficult to find...and, therefore, valuable. Traditionally, Istrian truffle-gatherers use specially trained dogs to find truffles. This is most productive at night, when the darkness forces the dog to rely more on its sense of smell rather than sight.

ISTRIA

There are two general types of truffles: white (more valuable and with a milder flavor—*Tuber magnatum*, known as the "Queen of the Truffles") and black. Each type of truffle has a "season"—a specific time of year when its scent is released, making it easier to find (May–Nov for black, Oct–Jan for white). Once dug up, they look pretty unassuming—like a tough, dirty pinecone.

Truffles can be eaten in a variety of ways. Thanks to their powerful and distinctive kick, they're often used sparingly for flavor—grated like parmesan cheese, or as truffle oil sprinkled over a dish. But you'll also find them in cheese, salami, olive oil, pâté, and even ice cream. Some people find that the pungent, musty aftertaste follows them around all day... and all night, when its supposed aphrodisiac qualities kick in. Because they're so rare and difficult to find, truffles are incredibly expensive—but many people are more than happy to pay royally for that inimitable flavor.

If you're a truffle nut, you'll find yourself in heaven here; if not, you may still appreciate the chance to sample a little taste of truffle. While you do that, ponder how one giant tuber changed the economy of an entire region.

Zigante's large facility here is divided into two parts:

The **Zigante Tartufi shop** offers shelves upon shelves of both fresh and packaged truffle products (plus local wines, olive oils, brandies, and more). There's also a little tasting table where you can sample the earthy goods, and a brain-sized replica of that famously massive chunk of white truffle. A small jar of preserved truffles will run you 50–150 kn, depending on the size, type of truffle, and preparation. You can even pick up a recipe sheet telling you what to do with the precious stuff once you get it home (daily 9:00–21:00, off-season 10:00–20:00, Livade 7, tel. 052/664-030, www.zigantetartufi.com).

The adjacent **Restaurant Zigante,** one of Istria's fanciest (and most expensive), dishes up all manner of truffle specialties. The decor—inside or out on the terrace—is white-tablecloth classy, the service is deliberate but friendly, and the truffles, as if on a cooking game show, are prepared in a dizzying variety of ways. If you want the full dose of this local delicacy from a place that knows its truffles, this is a worthwhile splurge (200–400-kn main dishes, 500-kn-plus fixed-price meals, daily 12:00–23:00, Livade 7, tel. 052/664-302).

Grožnjan

Grožnjan (grohzh-NYAHN, Grisignana in Italian) is your trapped-in-a-time-warp Istrian hill town. Its setting, artfully bal-anced on the tip of a vine-and-olive-tree-covered promontory, is pleasing, if not thrilling. The time-passed character of its sleepy lanes invites you to get lost and leave your itinerary on your dashboard. Not long ago, Grožnjan was virtually forgotten. But now several art-

ists have taken up residence here, keeping it Old World but with a spiffed-up, bohemian ambience.

Grožnjan has virtually no "sights," but it's a delightful place to go for a stroll. The town church's bell tower is its only land-mark. To get the lay of the land, take a 10-minute town wander: Facing the church's front door, go left (past the wine-and-truffle bar) and loop clockwise through town, past the shaded square with Café Pintur, then the Italian Cultural Center. Don't worry about addresses or finding a particular place; whether you want to or not, you'll find yourself walking in circles, and quickly see what there is to see. Instead, let your pulse slow and enjoy being a castaway on this isolated, tranquil hilltop. If gallery-browsing is your idea of fun, you'll like this place.

Tourist Information: The humble TI, in the center of town, doesn't have a lot to do (generally open Sat–Sun 10:00–12:00 & 17:00–19:00, closed Mon–Fri, maybe open longer in peak season, less off-season, Gorjan 3, tel. 052/776-131, www.tz-groznjan.hr).

Arrival in Grožnjan: All roads lead to the convenient and free parking lot, a few steps from the traffic-free village.

Sleeping and Eating in Grožnjan

$ Café Pintur, a nondescript restaurant on a cozy Grožnjan square just downhill from the church, rents four small but comfy top-floor rooms. While there are several other *sobe* in town, I recommend this one because it's run by a restaurant, so someone's usually around. The Černeka family doesn't speak much English, but that's part of the charm (Sb-200 kn, Db-300 kn, about 10 percent less for more than 3 nights; includes breakfast Sept–May, or 25 kn extra June–Aug; cash only, no elevator, Mate Gorjana 9, mobile 098-586-188, tel. & fax 052/776-397, ivan.cerneka@pu.t-com.hr).

Café Pintur's restaurant, open long hours daily in summer, serves up basic pasta and grilled meats. The only other restaurant in town, **Bastia,** is a bit bigger, with a similar menu and hours (across the square and sharing a leafy terrace with Pintur). For a scenic picnic, shop at the grocery store facing the church; nearby is a fine shady terrace with benches.

Enoteka Zigante, a branch of the Istrian truffle empire described earlier, has a gifty little wine-and-truffle bar offering a more genteel nibbling experience. A glass of the best local wine with a plate of cheese and meat makes a good little lunch for about 80 kn. For dessert, step into the adjacent truffle shop and nibble a few samples (Mon–Thu 10:00–20:00, Fri–Sun 10:00–21:00, until 22:00 in peak season, ulica Gorjan 5, tel. 052/721-998).

Since Grožnjan has such limited dining options, consider venturing to a countryside *agroturizam* for dinner. Or head to the restaurants in Brtonigla, Motovun, or Livade.

Brtonigla

Brtonigla (bur-toh-NEEG-lah, Verteneglio in Italian, literally "black soil") is a tiny wine village surrounded by vineyards. It's a bit closer to the sea than the other hill towns in this chapter, and sits above gentle slopes rather than a dramatic hilltop. But this deserted-feeling place is home to a luxurious hotel/restaurant and a well-regarded local eatery. Still, if you're not eating or sleeping here, give it a pass.

Getting There: Brtonigla is well-marked off the main *ipsilon* highway (coming north from Rovinj, but still south of Buje). Once in town, you'll find just a handful of haphazard streets.

Sleeping and Eating in Brtonigla

$$$ San Rocco Hotel and Restaurant is a family-run hotel suitable for a serious splurge. A few years ago this was the abandoned shell of a traditional Istrian house; now, after an extensive renovation, it's a cushy and elegant hotel with traditional beams-and-stone decor and all the modern amenities. With 12 rooms, an outdoor pool, a sauna, and distant views of the Adriatic, it's a welcoming retreat. "Premier" rooms come with views or Jacuzzi tubs, but the simpler "classic" and "comfort" rooms are plenty comfortable (mid-June–mid-Sept: classic Db-1,250 kn, comfort Db-1,300 kn, premier Db-1,450 kn; shoulder season: 300 kn less per room; off-season: 360 kn less per room; Sb costs 35 percent less than Db, no extra charge for 1- or 2-night stays, air-con, elevator, Internet access, loaner bikes, other fun extras explained on their website, Srednja ulica 2, tel. 052/725-000, fax 052/725-026, www.san-rocco.hr, info@san-rocco.hr, Rita and the Fernetich family). Its **restaurant**—open to guests and non-guests alike—features traditional Istrian cuisine in a dressy dining room or outside, with poolside elegance (300–500-kn fixed-price meals, daily 13:00–24:00).

Konoba Astarea, a restaurant down the street and around the corner, is a local favorite for traditional, take-your-time Istrian cuisine with a focus on fish and lamb. Anton and Alma Kernjus don't print an English menu, but they'll explain your options. Choose between the warmly cluttered, borderline-kitschy dining room huddled around the blazing open fire, where Alma does a lot of the cooking, or the cool and welcoming terrace with faraway sea views. It's smart to  reserve ahead (70–120-kn meals, daily 11:00–23:00, closed Nov, tel. 052/774-384).

Hum

According to its marketing plan, Hum (pronounced "hoom," Colmo in Italian) is the "smallest town in the world." While there are, no doubt, hamlets even tinier than its population of 16 people, as of a few decades ago—when first it laid claim to this honor—Hum had a Town Hall, church, school, post office, and all the other trappings of a "town"...so it wins the title on a technicality. Smart gimmick.

Unfortunately, these days Hum is also, per capita, the most touristy town in the world—crammed with visitors who come to stroll through its streets, drop some kunas in its single souvenir shop, or dine at its lone restaurant (**Humska Konoba,** lunch and dinner, open daily mid-May–mid-Oct, closed Mon mid-March–mid-May and mid-Oct–mid-Nov, Sat–Sun only mid-Nov–mid-March, tel. 052/660-005).

But despite its quirks and its one-trick commercialism, Hum is genuinely engaging. At the far corner of Istria—just up the road from Mount Učka, which forms the natural boundary with the neighboring Kvarner Gulf—Hum feels remote, rugged, and (if you don't run into any tour buses) forgotten by modern times.

You'll enter Hum through its main gate, formed by part of its 11th-century castle. Once inside the characteristic Old Town, you'll find cobbled lanes connecting the stone houses and 19th-century town church (with five altars). It's more rustic-feeling than the other villages in this chapter, with rougher paving stones, more overgrowth, and an even more pronounced yesteryear quality. And yet, you'll still spot several *sobe* signs and a souvenir shop. Popular mementos—sold at the restaurant and the shop—are little ceramic tiles with your initials using the Glagolitic alphabet (see below).

Getting There: Coming from Motovun on the road following the Mirna River, you'll pass through Buzet, following signs for *Lupoglav* and *Rijeka*. The turn-off for Hum (and the Glagolitic Lane) is on the right. When you're finished in Hum, you're not far from the A-8 highway back to the south (the coast) or onward to the east (Rijeka or Opatija via the Učka Tunnel).

Near Hum: The Glagolitic Lane

The road leading south to Hum from the Mirna Valley is the **Glagolitic Lane** (Aleja Glagoljaša), commemorating a ninth-century alphabet once used for written Croatian. While the alphabet hasn't been widely used for centuries, Croatians recognize it as an integral and unique part of their cultural heritage. And in the area around Hum, they've clung to the dinosaur alphabet even more than in other parts of the country—claiming it was commonly used here into the 20th century. Today, the alphabet is

ISTRIA

even taught in some schools, and children have poetry contests and spelling bees in Glagolitic. Along the Glagolitic Lane to Hum, you'll see various monuments to this alphabet, including giant Glagolitic characters standing in a field, as well as a sort of "Rosetta Stone" on top of a hill (on the left, just before Hum) comparing the Glagolitic, Cyrillic, and (our) Roman alphabet.

THE KVARNER GULF

Opatija • Rijeka • Rab

The long stretch of Croatian coast from Istria to Dalmatia—between the cities of Rijeka and Zadar—offers twisty seaside roads, functional port towns and fishing villages, some of the country's most rugged scenery, and no real knockout sights. Croatia offers more bang for your buck to the north (Istria) and the south (Dalmatia)—but if you're connecting these areas, the Kvarner Gulf offers several suitable stopovers.

Kvarner's best mainland town is its northern gateway: the former Habsburg resort of Opatija. Shot through with the faded elegance of an upper-crust history, Opatija is, if nothing else, a welcome change of pace from the salty Venetian-flavored towns along the rest of the Croatian coast. Nearby, the big industrial port city of Rijeka is best avoided, unless you're changing buses or boats there.

South of Opatija and Rijeka, the Kvarner coastline is stark and desolate—any traces of settlement long since blown away by the battering Bora wind (see sidebar on page 152). But offshore, sheltered from the elements, are several inviting island getaways. Each of the main islands—Krk, Cres, Lošinj, Rab, and Pag—has its own character and appeal. But the best Kvarner village is Rab, on the island of the same name. Rab's pretty, peninsular Old Town, bristling with Venetian-style bell towers, overlooks a shimmering harbor and beaches full of happy swimmers and sunbathers.

Planning Your Time

The Kvarner Gulf is "passing-through" territory. While destinations in this chapter have their fans, first-timers seeing Croatia in a hurry should give the region a miss. But if you have plenty of

The Kvarner Gulf

time and your own wheels, and you're driving through anyway, Opatija and Rab are worthy overnight stops. Even with less time, Opatija still merits a quick stopover if it's on the way between your destinations.

Driving Between Northern Croatia and Dalmatia

If you're driving between northern Croatia (Zagreb, Plitvice, Istria, or Opatija) and the Dalmatian Coast (Zadar, from where the expressway zips to Split), you have two options: Use the fast inland A-1 expressway, or follow the slow Kvarner Gulf coastal road all the way down.

The **A-1 expressway** option is boring but faster and far more efficient, especially from Zagreb or Plitvice. If you're coming from Zagreb, just take A-1 directly to Split; from Plitvice, drive south through Korenica to access A-1 at Gornja Ploča (see page 88). From Istria or Opatija, you have two options for accessing A-1 that take about the same amount of time: Head east (inland) from

Rijeka on A-6 to join A-1; or, more interesting, drive the Kvarner coastal road as far south as Senj, then cut inland and up over the mountains to Otočac, where you can get on A-1.

The two-lane **Kvarner coastal road** (national road #8, a.k.a. E-65) is twisty and slow, but more scenic. Speedy sightseers won't find it worth the time. Compared to the expressway, you'll lose at least an hour if you're coming from Istria or Opatija, and much more if you're starting in Zagreb or Plitvice. Along this road, you'll enjoy good but not spectacular views—similar to what you'll see in Dalmatia, but less developed. To find this road from Rijeka, just follow signs for *Split* and *Zadar* (being careful not to get on the expressway).

If you want to visit **Rab,** be sure to take the Kvarner coastal road; at Jablanac, catch the car ferry to Rab (see "Route Tips for Drivers" at the end of this chapter).

Opatija

Opatija (oh-PAH-tee-yah) is not your typical Croatian beach town. In the late 19th-century golden age of the Austro-Hungarian Empire, this unassuming village near the port of Rijeka was transformed into the Eastern Riviera, one of the swankiest resorts on the Mediterranean. While the French, British, and German aristocracy sunbathed on France's Côte d'Azur, the wealthy elite from the eastern half of Europe—the Habsburg Empire, Scandinavia, and Russia—partied in Opatija. Baroque, Neoclassical, and Art Nouveau villas popped up along its coastline as it became the sunny playground for barons, dukes, and other aristocrats.

Though the Habsburgs are long gone, Opatija retains the trappings of its genteel past. Most of Croatia evokes the time-passed Mediterranean, but Opatija whispers "belle époque." It

may be the classiest resort town in Croatia, with more taste and less fixation on postcards and seashells. Most people don't come to Croatia for this chic scene. But if rustic seaside villages are wearing on you, Opatija—which hosts equal numbers of tourists and convention-going business-people—is a pleasant return to high-class civilization.

Thanks to its sheltered location nestled under high mountain peaks, Opatija is protected from the Bora wind, enjoying instead a light, refreshing breeze from Učka Mountain.

This gives Opatija a particularly mild and enjoyable climate—the perfect match for its refined ambience.

Orientation to Opatija

(area code: 051)
Opatija is basically a one-street town: Ulica Maršala Tita, lined on both sides by stately hotels, follows the seafront. The town's focal point is its beach area, called Slatina. You can walk from one end of the tourist zone to the other in about 20 minutes.

Tourist Information

Opatija's helpful TI is about a five-minute walk up ulica Maršala Tita from Slatina (walk with the sea on your right, look for TI on the right). Pick up the map, information booklet, and list of hotels (July–Aug Mon–Sat 8:00–21:00, Sun 16:00–21:00; slightly shorter hours May–June and Sept; Oct–April Mon–Fri 8:00–15:00, Sat 8:00–14:00, closed Sun; ulica Maršala Tita 101, tel. 051/271-310, www.opatija-tourism.hr).

Sights in Opatija

Begin at Opatija's centerpiece, the waterfront beach-and-park area called **Slatina,** with sweeping sea views, a marbled Croatian "Walk of Fame" (with one or two names you might recognize), and a seawater swimming pool. From here, Opatija lines up along its main drag, **ulica Maršala Tita,** still fronted by ornate villas that would seem more at home in Vienna than they do in Croatia. Austrians and other tourists stroll here hand-in-hand, taking in the views, dipping into high-class boutiques, and snapping photos of the fancy facades as they go. Joining them, you, too, may soon find yourself thinking of this place as the "Monte Carlo of Croatia."

A few steps toward the sea, stretching in either direction along the

waterfront, is a scenic promenade called the **Lungomare.** This is another wonderful spot for strolling, and it offers striking views across the bay to Rijeka (which looks much better from afar). Near the Slatina end of the Lungomare is one of Opatija's trademarks: a **statue** of a woman surrounded by seagulls, called *Greetings to the Sea.* Much as I'd like to impart some romantic legend behind this evocative monument, the truth is that there's no story behind it—like Opatija itself, it's just pretty to look at.

As for sightseeing...well, Opatija is not that kind of place. If you like, you can drop into the *opatija* (abbey) that gave the town its name, the **Abbey of St. Jacob** (Opatija Sv. Jakov, right along the Lungomare below the TI).

Beyond the abbey, the Lungomare cuts through one of Opatija's many manicured parks and hits the harbor. Here you'll find an outdoor theater that shows movies or concerts nightly in peak season (weather permitting, check with TI for schedule).

Sleeping in Opatija

Opatija is chock-a-block full of swanky resort hotels. While prices are high, you get a lot of luxury for your money (unlike hotels in most small coastal villages). The busiest—and most expensive—times are August (tourists) and September (conventions). Sleeping in Opatija is definitely preferable to overnighting in Rijeka.

$$$ Big and Fancy: These two chain hotels are my favorites of the many opulent Opatija hotels. They have the most striking Habsburg facades in town, and both have luxurious rooms (air-con, elevator, and all the amenities). Each can also refer you to other, similar chain properties (price range depends on season—top price is for Aug). **Hotel Bristol,** part of the Vienna International chain, has 78 rooms. It's gone to great pains to maintain its late 19th-century decor inside and out—mixing modern comfort with period moldings, chandeliers, and a cheery yellow facade (Sb-€77–111, Db-€108–157, free Internet access, pay Wi-Fi, gorgeously restored coffee shop in lobby, €10 parking,

Sleep Code

(€1 = about $1.40, country code: 385, area code: 051)
S = Single, **D** = Double/Twin, **T** = Triple, **Q** = Quad, **b** = bathroom. The modest tourist tax (€1 per person, per night, lower off-season) is not included in these rates. Hotels generally accept credit cards and include breakfast in their rates, while most *sobe* accept only cash and don't offer breakfast. Everyone listed here speaks English.

To help you sort easily through these listings, I've divided the rooms into three categories based on the price for a standard double room with bath in peak season:

$$$ **Higher Priced**—Most rooms €100 or more.
  $$ **Moderately Priced**—Most rooms between €60–100.
    $ **Lower Priced**—Most rooms €60 or less.

The Bora
Or, How to Predict Croatian Coastal Weather

When asked what tomorrow's weather will bring, a salty Croatian fisherman looks to the mountains and feels the stiff wind on his face. "Sun," he says. "The Bora brings good weather."

Like any people whose fate is tied to the sea, coastal Croatians can extrapolate a breeze or a front of clouds into a full-blown weather report. While this is a precise art cultivated over a lifetime, even the casual tourist can learn a few tried-and-tested clues from the natives.

Croatian coastal weather is shaped by a mighty wind called the Bora (named for the Greek Boreas, the North Wind; sometimes called "Bura" in Croatian, or "Burja" in Slovene). Much like the infamous mistral wind that's an unavoidable fact of life in France's Provence, the Bora has an indelible impact on this region's weather, vegetation, architecture, and tourism.

The Dinaric Mountains, which rise sharply up from the sea for nearly the full length of the Croatian Coast, act as a barrier for cold, cloudy weather. As the air on the coastal side of the mountains heats up, the air behind the snow-capped peaks stays cool. Something's gotta give to equalize this temperature and pressure differential. A white fringe of clouds builds up along the ridge of the mountains, as the cool air moves toward the warm air—a sure sign that the Bora is about to blow. When all that pent-up air finally escapes, the Bora comes screaming down the slopes to the sea.

The Bora occurs anywhere that mountains create two different climates in nearby terrains, including Slovenia's Karst. But the Bora's power is at its peak along the Kvarner Gulf—especially where a gap in the mountains provides a natural funnel toward the sea (such as at Senj and at Karlobag). It's strongest in the winter, when the temperature differential between the interior and the coast is most pronounced. Farther south, such as in Dalmatia, the inland remains warmer and the Bora is milder.

The Bora is not constant—it's strongest at midday and made up of intermittent, fierce gusts that can reach 150 miles

ulica Maršala Tita 108, tel. 051/706-300, fax 051/706-301, www.hotel-bristol.hr, info@hotel-bristol.hr). **Hotel Agava,** part of the Milenij chain, also has an impressively restored old shell, but its 76 rooms feel more businesslike and contemporary. The cheaper "economy" rooms are in the attic, with small skylight windows (July–mid-Aug: Sb–€63–91, Db–€90–137; April–June and mid-Aug–mid-Oct: Sb–€55–80, Db–€78–118; mid-Oct–May: Sb–€50–72, Db–€79–109; lower prices are for "economy" rooms, sea view–€5 extra, hotel dinner–€4 extra/person, free cable Internet, ulica Maršala Tita 89, tel. 051/278-200, fax 051/278-

per hour. Young children have been known to "fly" through the air for short distances because of the Bora. The Kvarner coastal road is closed several times each year to trucks, buses, and other high-profile vehicles, which can be tipped over by the gusts. And occasionally Kvarner Gulf ferries (such as the Jablanac–Mišnjak connection to Rab Island) must wait patiently for the Bora to die down. After a day or two of a stiff winter Bora, everything is coated with a thin layer of salt, like ash after a volcano.

The good news: As the Bora rushes toward the coast, it sweeps bad-weather clouds away with it—leaving in its wake clear, cooler air and sunshine.

In summer, the much milder version of this wind—which usually bathes the coast in a refreshing breeze each evening, when the interior cools faster than the sea—is called a Maestral. Sporadic mini-Bora gusts at night are known as Burin.

The Bora's unpopular cousin is the wind called Jugo (YOO-goh, meaning "south," as in "Yugo-slavia"). The Jugo originates as a moist air mass gathering over the Adriatic, which creates a low-pressure vortex. Finally it blows northward toward Croatia, bringing with it hot, humid, and stormy weather. Because humid conditions foster disease, an ancient superstition considers the Jugo wind evil, and the refreshing Bora wind good. Notice that the Bora and the Jugo are the yin and yang of Croatian winds, blowing in opposite directions and with opposite effects.

When all else fails, you can always fall back on the reliable old saying, which also exists in Croatian: "Red sky at night, sailor's delight." If light from the sunset is able to leak through the bottom of a bank of clouds on the western horizon, it's a sign that clearer weather lies just beyond...and should arrive by morning.

Of course, these adages are highly generalized. Croatia's coast is made up of a series of microclimates. Each island has its own very specific weather conditions, which is why one island may grow olives, the next one lavender, the next red wine grapes, and the next white wine grapes. If you really want to know what sort of weather is on the way, ask a local.

THE KVARNER GULF

287, www.milenijhoteli.hr, info@milenijhoteli.hr).

$$$ Smaller and Family-Run: These two small hotels, run by the Brko family, are well-located a few steps from the lively Slatina scene (to the right as you face the water; both have air-con and elevators). **Hotel Galeb,** with 20 comfortable rooms and three stars, has more character than most Opatija hotels (July–Aug: Sb-€100, Db-€125; €15 less May–June and Sept, €25 less Oct–April; €10 more for sea view and balcony, 10 percent less if you pay cash, pricier suites also available, €7 parking—reserve ahead, ulica Maršala Tita 160, tel. 051/271-177, fax 051/711-935, www.hotel-galeb.hr, hotel-galeb@ri.t-com.hr). **Hotel Savoy,** across the street, comes with four stars, more class, 32 nicely appointed rooms, a swimming pool, a private beach, and higher prices (about 20 percent more expensive than Galeb, small standard room with balcony is a good value, ulica Maršala Tita 129, tel. 051/710-500, fax 051/272-680, www.hotel-savoy.hr, info@hotel-savoy.hr).

$ *Sobe:* There are no cheap hotels or hostels in Opatija, but several people rent private rooms (many on or near the main drag). Of the many room-booking agencies in town, the best reputations belong to **GIT** (ulica Maršala Tita 65, tel. 051/273-030, www .tourgit.com, gi-trade@ri.t-com.hr) and **Kvarner Touristik** (ulica Maršala Tita 162, tel. 051/703-723, www.kvarner-touristik.com, office@kvarner-touristik.com).

Eating in Opatija

Many hotels offer a "half-board" option (dinner at the hotel) that can be a good value for a decent, affordable meal. Otherwise, touristy restaurants abound (especially cheap snack and pizza joints). To browse for your own picnic, drop by the old-fashioned indoor market hall (*tržnica*, on the left a 10-minute walk up ulica Maršala Tita from Slatina, past the TI). The town also has many refined Vienna-style coffee houses with late 19th-century appeal.

Opatija Connections

Opatija is connected to the nearby transportation hub of **Rijeka** twice each hour by bus (30-min trip).

THE KVARNER GULF

Rijeka

The industrial city of Rijeka (ree-YAY-kah; it translates as "River") became Croatia's biggest port under Austro-Hungarian rule. It's dainty little Opatija's bigger, burlier brother. Like Opatija, much of Rijeka's architecture is reminiscent of the glory days of the Habsburgs. But unlike Opatija, most of Rijeka's buildings haven't been renovated in the last century or so, giving it a seedy, gritty, past-its-prime feel. Avoid Rijeka if you can. However, since it's a major transportation hub, there's a good chance you'll pass through. Here are the basics.

The bus station, train station, and ferry terminal are within a few blocks of each other in a bustling waterfront business zone. The sector is crossed by two one-way streets (going in opposite directions): Ivana Zajca (or the "Riva," along the waterfront, runs west to east) and Adamićeva (which changes its name a few times as it cuts east to west through town).

A block above these two streets is the **Korzo,** an almost-charming pedestrianized zone packed with shops, restaurants,

and the **TI** (at the widest part of the Korzo, near the well-signed McDonald's; mid-June–mid-Sept Mon–Sat 8:00–20:00, Sun 9:00–14:00; mid-Sept–mid-June Mon–Fri 8:00–20:00, Sat 8:00–14:00, closed Sun; Korzo 33, tel. 051/335-882, www.tz-rijeka.hr).

The **train station** is a few blocks west of the Korzo. On arrival, exit the station to the right and walk 10 minutes to the water. You'll first come to the bus station, then the ferry terminal. The Korzo is just above them.

The **bus station** is basically a big parking lot in the middle of the chaos, near the west end of the Korzo. You'll see the big boats along the waterfront as you exit your bus. To get to the train station, face the water and turn right, following the busy street about 10 minutes.

The **ferry terminal** is at the east end of the waterfront. The Jadrolinija ticket office is in the building with the big *Jadrolinija* sign (at Riva 16, second building east of bus station, ticket office at far right end of building as you face it).

Some of Rijeka's **car-rental** offices are conveniently located right downtown, on the main harborfront street: **Avis** is at Riva 8 (tel. 051/311-135), and **Hertz** is at Zadarska 3B (tel. 051/311-098).

Rijeka Connections

From Rijeka by Boat to: Rab (1/day, 1.5 hrs by passenger catamaran), the **Dalmatian Coast** (slow Jadrolinija car ferry, 2/week year-round, departs in the evening and goes overnight to Split, then onward down the coast; figure 11 hrs to **Split,** 18 hrs to **Korčula,** 21 hrs to **Dubrovnik**).

From Rijeka by Train to: Zagreb (3/day, 4 hrs), **Ljubljana** (2–3/day direct, 2.5 hrs), **Budapest** (1/day, 10 hrs, transfer in Zagreb; plus direct but long night train, 14 hrs).

From Rijeka by Bus to: Opatija (2/hr, 30 min), **Senj** (hourly, 1.5 hrs), **Rab town** (2–3/day, 3.5 hrs), **Pula** (nearly hourly, 2–2.5 hrs), **Rovinj** (4–7/day, 3 hrs), **Zagreb** (hourly, 3.5 hrs), **Split** (10/day including some night buses, 8.5 hrs), **Dubrovnik** (2/day, 12 hrs), **Ljubljana** (2/day, 2.5 hrs). For schedules, see www.autotrans.hr.

Rab

Rab (pronounced "Rob," like the man's name) is the most appealing Croatian island north of the Dalmatian Coast. Though it's one of the greenest islands in the northern Adriatic, its landward half (including where the ferry from the mainland docks) is an eerily dry, rocky moonscape—the result of saltwater blown ashore by harsh Bora winds. But on the seaward side of the island, you'll find lush vegetation, as well as the island's main town, also called Rab. Rab's Old Town peninsula is nestled along a sleepy harbor. Along the spine of the Old Town are four different Venetian-style campaniles (bell towers)—Rab's claim to touristic fame. A relaxing seafront promenade runs behind the Old Town.

Rab was independent and strong in the 14th century, but soon after became a backwater outpost of Venice. In the 19th century, when Rab was part of the Habsburg Empire, Austrians found its beaches a fine place to catch some rays (their descendants still do). In fact, Rab Island kicked off the nude-beach boom that's still going strong in Croatia: In 1936, England's King Edward VIII came to Rab on holiday with his soon-to-be wife, Wallis Simpson. Edward wanted to work on an all-over tan, so he went through the proper channels to have one of Rab's beaches designated for nudists. Inspired by the English monarch's example, other visitors to Rab followed suit (er, dropped suit)...and a phenomenon was born. Keep your eyes peeled for the letters *FKK* (*Freikörper Kultur*, German for "free body culture"), which is pan-European code for nudism.

Orientation to Rab

(area code: 051)
The Old Town of Rab is on a long, tapering peninsula alongside a tidy harbor. Three parallel streets run the length of the peninsula: **"Lower Street"** (Donja ulica, just off the harbor, a narrow lane with a few cafés and discos); **"Middle Street"** (Srednja ulica, a few steps higher, the bustling main drag lined with souvenir shops and ice-cream stands); and **"Upper Street"** (Gornja ulica, a steep climb up at the top of the peninsula, with most of Rab's churches and campaniles). Along the harbor are Rab's two biggest squares: St. Christopher's Square (Trg Svetog Kristofora), with a makeshift

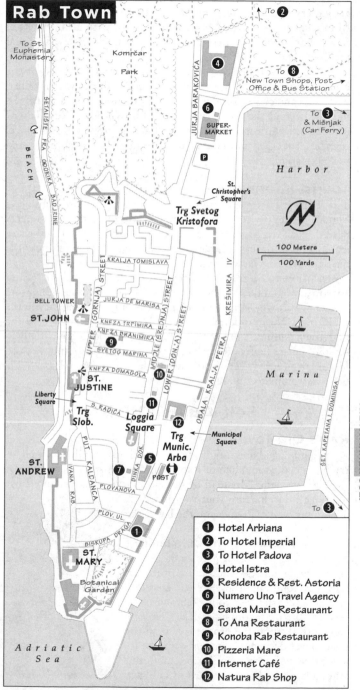

Rab Town

To St. Euphemia Monastery

Komrčar Park

To **2**

To **8**
New Town Shops, Post
Office & Bus Station

JURJA BARAKOVIĆA

4

6

SUPER-MARKET

To **3**
& Mišnjak
(Car Ferry)

P

Harbor

BEACH

ŠETALIŠTE FRA ODORIKA BADURINE

St. Christopher's Square

Trg Svetog Kristofora

100 Meters

100 Yards

KRALJA TOMISLAVA

KREŠIMIRA IV

JURJA DE MARISA

BELL TOWER

ST. JOHN

KNEZA TRPIMIRA

KNEZA BRANIMIRA

UPPER (GORNJA) STREET

SVETOG MARINA

9

Marina

KNEZA DOMAGOLA

10

MIDDLE (SREDNJA) STREET

LOWER (DONJA) STREET

OBALA KRALJA PETRA

ŠET. KAPETANA I. DOMINISA

ST. JUSTINE

Liberty Square

11

S. RADIĆA

Trg Slob.

Loggia Square

12

Trg Munic. Arba

Municipal Square

PUT KALDANCA

ULVANA RAB

ST. ANDREW

DINKA DOK.

7

5

i POST

PLOVANOVA

PLOV. UL.

1

BISKUPA DRAGA

ST. MARY

Botanical Garden

Adriatic Sea

1	Hotel Arbiana
2	To Hotel Imperial
3	To Hotel Padova
4	Hotel Istra
5	Residence & Rest. Astoria
6	Numero Uno Travel Agency
7	Santa Maria Restaurant
8	To Ana Restaurant
9	Konoba Rab Restaurant
10	Pizzeria Mare
11	Internet Café
12	Natura Rab Shop

THE KVARNER GULF

art gallery and steps leading up into the park; and businesslike Municipal Square (Trg Municipium Arba), with a huddle of al fresco café umbrellas surrounded by the TI, the post office, and the Town Hall.

Where the Old Town peninsula attaches to the rest of the island, you'll find the extensive, lush **Komrčar Park,** which is filled with trees and crisscrossed with walking paths. A few steps off the harbor, beyond the park from the Old Town, is a **"New Town"** (called Palit) with modern amenities such as grocery stores, travel agencies, bakeries, an open-air produce market, a post office, and the bus station.

Tourist Information

The **TI,** with a smattering of local brochures, is on Municipal Square (generally open daily June–Sept 8:00–22:00, Oct–May 8:00–14:00, Trg Municipium Arba 8, tel. 051/771-111, www.tzg -rab.hr). In peak season, there's a second, smaller branch near the bus station in the New Town.

Most of Rab's travel agencies—where you can find a *soba* or apartment, rent bikes and scooters, and sign up for excursions—are in the New Town. More convenient is the only travel agency in the Old Town, **Numero Uno,** at the corner of the harbor where the Old Town peninsula meets the mainland (open long hours daily in season, shorter hours off-season, between the big supermarket and Hotel Istra on Šetalište Markantuna de Dominisa, tel. 051/724-688, www.numero-uno.hr).

Self-Guided Walk

Rab's Old Town

Don't get bogged down figuring out which campanile is which, or trying to make too much of Rab's humdrum history. Simply enjoy the lazy ambience. Instead of sightseeing, use Rab as an excuse to take a vacation from your vacation. This 30-minute walk will give you the lay of the land.

Begin at the big **St. Christopher's Square** (Trg Svetog Kristofora). Peruse the starving artists' work and admire the sculpture fountain. These star-crossed lovers, from the island's two big feuding families, are the protagonists of Rab's favorite legend. Kalifront (the bronze guy with the goatee) was desperately in love with a peasant girl named Draga (in the fountain). But since Draga had taken a vow of celibacy to the Roman goddess Diana, she couldn't give in to Kalifront's advances. Draga begged Diana for help, and Diana turned her to stone to prevent any hanky-panky. Tears from the petrified Draga became the spring of a fountain of youth. Diana punished the randy Kalifront by turning him into a half-man-half-tree, fed by the spring of his unrequited lover—and sentenced to watch her eternally from afar.

Look across the harbor to the ridge that runs along the spine of the island. Notice the little **stone walls** climbing up the hill. These walls, called *gromače*—which you'll see throughout the region—traditionally served three purposes: to mark property boundaries, to prevent erosion, and to provide a convenient place for farmers to get rid of big rocks unearthed while tilling.

Continue into town on **Middle Street** (Srednja ulica, near the base of the big staircase). You'll pass restaurants, galleries, tacky souvenir shops (with T-shirts so obscene you can only admire their creativity), and the town's Internet café (look for @ sign on left). Along the way, stop to drool over a few of the ice-cream *(sladoled)* stands—many run by Kosovo Albanians who live on Rab. When you emerge into the little piazza with the pillared loggia, detour through the tunnel on the left.

Municipal Square (Trg Municipium Arba), the second of Rab's two harborfront squares, is home to several outdoor cafés, the recommended Astoria restaurant, and the TI (at the far corner, near the waterfront). On this square, find the family-run **Natura Rab** shop, selling all-organic, all-local products from Rab, including various types of olive oil, honey, lavender, and *rakija*—the local firewater, like Italian grappa (July–Aug daily 9:30–13:00 & 19:00–23:00, shorter hours in shoulder season, closed in winter, www.natura-rab.hr). Just to the right of Natura Rab is the old Rector's Palace (marked with a distinctively carved balcony), the former residence of the Venetian governor.

With your back to the harbor, go to the top-left corner of the square, with the post office (notice the wall of old-fashioned wooden mailboxes inside). Walk down the street the P.O. is on (Biskupa Draga) until you emerge into a sweet little **botanical garden.** This peaceful oasis is watched over by a statue of St. Marin—the Rab-born stonecutter who went to Italy and founded the statelet of San Marino, which remains an independent nation today. (If you continue out the far end of the garden, you'll reach the tip of the Old Town peninsula.)

Take the ramp up from the garden, and find your way to the start of **Upper Street** (Gornja ulica), marked by a big church and a piazza with palm trees. As you stroll along this street with the sea on your left, you'll pass several little monasteries and churches, four of which boast Rab's trademark bell towers (named for, in order, Saints Mary, Andrew, Justine, and John the Evangelist). If a church is open, poke inside (or look through the grate to see the interior); some of them have modest museums attached. You can climb the first **bell tower** (St. Mary, 10 kn, closed for a long mid-day siesta), but it's better to climb the fourth tower, by the ruins of the seventh-century Church of St. John (Sveti Ivan), because it's free and always open.

Halfway along Upper Street, you'll reach **Liberty Square** (Trg Slobode), marked by a single, huge Holm oak. Stairs behind the tree lead down to the embankment that runs behind the peninsula—a fine place for swimming or strolling (see "Activities in Rab").

Beyond the fourth bell tower, Upper Street runs into a small staircase. Go up the stairs and into the garden courtyard, where more stairs on the right lead up to the top of a rampart with a fine view over Rab's rooftops. Continuing past the courtyard leads you into the park—a nicely shaded place to relax.

Activities in Rab

Swimming—As with most beaches in Croatia, Rab's are largely pebbly or rocky. The best swimming area is along the back (non-harbor) side of the Old Town peninsula and park (accessed from Liberty Square/Trg Slobode on Upper Street). This concrete side-walk running along the waterfront has a few low-key cafés and several sets of steps into the sea that make things easy for swimmers. (To stretch your legs, continue along this embankment for about 30 minutes to the Franciscan Monastery of St. Euphemia—not worth going out of your way for, but a suitable excuse for a water-front stroll.)

Reaching the island's sandy beaches (away from the Old Town) takes a little more effort. Sahara Beach, the best beach, is clothing-optional (some people wear swimsuits, but most are nude). It's at the north end of the island, past the town

The Dark History of Rab

For some more serious, somber sightseeing—and a severe contrast to otherwise lighthearted Rab—you can pay your respects at the remains of a **concentration camp** operated by Mussolini's occupying forces during World War II. Tens of thousands of Jews and political prisoners (many of them Slovenes) were interned here; thousands of them died. It's odd to think this facility was Italian, rather than German—making this, for many, a surprising footnote in WWII history. The site is now a graveyard memorial (on the road to Lopar, about three miles northwest of Rab town).

Offshore from Rab Island (to the north) are two smaller islands with a troubled history. After Yugoslav president-for-life Tito split from Moscow in 1948 to pursue his own brand of communism, he arrested Yugoslavs who remained loyal to the Soviet Union. Many of them ended up on the "gulag island" of **Goli Otok** ("Barren Island"). In a strange parallel to the US's McCarthyism, the late 1940s and early 1950s were an era of great anti-Soviet paranoia in communist Yugoslavia. This period—called *Informbiro*, after the Soviet secret police—is the subject of the Oscar-nominated Croatian film *When Father Was Away on Business*. Near Goli Otok, **Grgur Island** hosted a women's prison in the early Yugoslav era. Prisoners were forced to carve Tito's name and a giant star of communism into the hillside (still faintly visible). It's difficult to visit these islands, but you may see them as you drive around Rab Island and along the mainland.

of Lopar (easiest to take the bus to the town of San Marino, then water taxi or walk to Sahara—get details at Rab TI).

Shopping—Trinkets don't get much tackier than the ones on Rab. But with a little searching, you can find some worthwhile souvenirs (try the Natura Rab shop on the Municipal Square—described earlier, in the "Self-Guided Walk"). Look for local honey, grape brandy, and lavender. The next island over, Pag, produces a tasty cheese called *paški sir*—with an herby/salty flavor that is said to come from the sea-air-blown vegetation the sheep graze on.

Other Activities—To get out and see the island, you can rent a bike or scooter, or join an excursion by bus or boat (all are available at hotel reception desks and at travel agencies—see "Tourist Information," on page 158). Boat captains along the harborfront offer cruises to various secluded coves on Rab and nearby islands. With a bike, you can ride the trails in Kalifront and Frkanj (get a good map when you rent your bike).

Sleeping in Rab

(€1 = about $1.40, country code: 385, area code: 051)
I've listed the top-season prices (August). Rab hotels charge progressively less off-season.

$$$ Hotel Arbiana is a splurge hotel with 28 plush rooms at the tip of Rab's Old Town peninsula (Sb-€110, Db-€140, air-con, elevator, free Wi-Fi, Obala Petra Krešimira 12, tel. 051/775-900, www.arbianahotel.com, sales@arbianahotel.com).

$$$ *Imperial Rab Hotels:* Most of Rab's big hotels are run by this company. These communist-era hotels have been nicely renovated, but—as usual for big resort hotels in little island towns—the prices are too high. The best-located option is the **Hotel Imperial,** with 134 rooms in the park just beyond the end of the harbor (Sb-€70, non-view Db-€110, seaview Db-€120, seaview Db with balcony-€125, cheaper off-season, tel. 051/724-522, www.imperial .hr, imperial@imperial.hr). **Hotel Padova** looms across the harbor from the Old Town (a 20-minute walk away; non-view Sb-€85, seaview Sb-€100, non-view Db-€120, seaview Db-€140, cheaper off-season, tel. 051/724-544, www.imperial.hr, padova@imperial .hr). Both hotels have elevators, air-conditioning, and Internet access and Wi-Fi in the lobby.

$$$ Hotel Istra, at the corner of the harbor where the Old Town peninsula meets the mainland, is an old communist-style hotel now run by the Renić family. Its 100 rooms are dingy and not air-conditioned, but the location and lack of other options makes it worth considering (Sb-€63, Db-€106, €4 extra/person for a balcony, elevator, Šetalište Markantuna de Dominisa b.b., tel. 051/724-134, fax 051/724-050, www.hotel-istra.hr, hotel-istra @hi.t-com.hr).

$$ Residence Astoria rents five comfortable apartments over the restaurant of the same name, in a restored Venetian palazzo right in the center of town. It overlooks the bustling Municipal Square, but two rooms have air-conditioning that helps keep things quiet (Db-€60–110 depending on size and amenities, one-week minimum July–Aug, 30 percent extra for 1- or 2-night stays, closed mid-Oct–April, Trg Municipium Arba 7, tel. 051/774-844, www.astoria-rab.com, astoria@astoria-rab.com).

$ Sobe *and Apartments:* As elsewhere in Croatia, the best budget option is to stay in a room in a private home *(soba)* or rent an apartment. Every travel agency in Rab has a line on rooms; Numero Uno is well-located and well-established (see "Tourist Information" on page 158).

Eating in Rab

Rab has a cuisine scene typical for a Croatian resort town—a dozen pizzerias, a half-dozen seafood joints, and some splurges—but a few eateries stand above the rest. All of these recommendations (except Ana) are in the Old Town. As with everything in Rab, opening times flex with the season (long hours daily in summer with a mid-afternoon break, shorter hours or closed entirely off-season).

Astoria is a good choice for a splurge, with lots of delectable seafood options. Sit inside or out on the terrace overlooking the Municipal Square (open daily for lunch and dinner, closed 15:00–18:00, on Trg Municipium Arba 7, tel. 051/774-844).

Santa Maria specializes in grilled meat, but you'll also find fish on the menu. With the most impressive interior in town—including nautical decor reminiscent of its namesake ship and a giant old-fashioned skylight that pulls in a refreshing breeze—it's an enjoyable place for a meal (daily 10:00–14:00 & 17:00–23:00; just beyond the end of Middle Street, continue straight up the narrow alley after the piazza with the loggia, on the right at Dinke Dokule 6, tel. 051/724-196).

Ana Restaurant serves up pastas, seafood, and Balkan-style grilled meats in a residential-feeling area just beyond the New Town commercial center. My only listing outside the Old Town, it lacks the charm—and crowds—of the Old Town eateries, but the food is delicious (daily 11:00–15:00 & 18:00–24:00; go up the New Town's main drag, then turn right just after the open-air produce stalls and look for signs, Palit 80, tel. 051/724-376).

Konoba Rab, run by the father-and-son Vidas family, has good seafood and an over-the-Croatian-village-rooftops interior (daily 10:00–14:00 & 17:00–23:00; about halfway down Middle Street, look for sign leading up the stairway to Upper Street, Kneza Branimira 3, tel. 051/725-666).

Pizza: There's no shortage of pizza and pasta eateries in Rab's Old Town. I enjoy **Pizzeria Mare,** serving up pizza with a soft and tasty crust (daily 9:00–22:00, entrances from both Middle and Lower Streets, Srednja ulica 8).

Rab Connections

By Public Transportation

Getting to Rab can be frustrating by public transportation. It's easy to reach by boat from Rijeka, but it's slow and complicated to continue southward. This makes it difficult to visit Rab efficiently between northern destinations (such as Slovenia or Istria) and the Dalmatian Coast.

Without a car, the easiest way to reach Rab is by **fast passenger catamaran** from Rijeka (1/day in each direction; generally leaves from Rab's harborfront early in the morning, return boat leaves Rijeka in the afternoon; 1.5-hr trip). Rab Island is also connected by other ferries and by taxi boats to nearby islands (such as Krk to the north), and a regular car ferry keeps it linked to the mainland (see "Route Tips for Drivers," next).

Buses connect Rab to the mainland using the Mišnjak–Jablanac ferry. Buses to the north are easy and straightforward: **Rijeka** (2–3/day, 3.5 hrs), **Senj** (partway up the coast to Rijeka—see below; 2–3/day, 1–2 hrs), and **Zagreb** (3/day direct in summer, 5.5 hrs; off-season you'll usually transfer in Senj).

Taking the bus to destinations to the south (such as **Zadar**, at the start of the Dalmatian Coast) is more complex and very slow, since you'll be following the windy coastal road all the way down to Zadar (connections speed up from Zadar to Split). To get on a southbound bus from Rab, you'll have to take one of the northbound buses across to the mainland, then transfer to a southbound bus. After the ferry docks at Jablanac, the bus climbs up to a roadside bus stop called Magistrala, where you can transfer (often requires a long wait for the next bus); or continue another 45 minutes north to **Senj** to transfer. Carefully confirm the transfer schedule at the station before you set out. Rab's bus station is in the New Town (bus info: tel. 051/724-189).

Route Tips for Drivers

Rab is a relatively straightforward stopover if you have a **car.** Driving along the Kvarner coastal road between Rijeka and Zadar, you'll pass above Jablanac (follow signs off the main road down a twisty one-way road to this coastal ferry-port town). In summer, the Rapska Plovidba car ferry makes the 20-minute crossing continuously between Jablanac and Mišnjak, a lonely dock at the very barren end of Rab Island (a 15-minute drive along the length of the island from Rab town). In the busiest times (weekends in July–Aug), you may have to wait up to a few hours to drive your car on. Off-season, the ferry still crosses at least eight times per day.

You'll be struck by how desolate the coast feels as you drive along the Kvarner coastal road. Between Jablanac (with the Rab ferry) and Rijeka, the most appealing spot for a break is **Senj** (pronounced "sehn"—the j is mostly silent, but has a slight *y* sound). Senj has a little harbor and a modest square with a jumble of outdoor cafés. The town is watched over by the boxy fortress of a band of pirates called the Uskoks. These were Croat refugees forced out of their homes in the interior when the Ottomans invaded in the 16th century. After resettling here in Senj, they became pirates and began terrorizing the Adriatic coastline. While they claimed to target only Ottoman ships, they also harassed anyone who traded with the Ottomans—including Venice. Finally the Austrians—bowed by political pressure from the Venetians—put down the Uskoks. Today Senj is the best jolt of civilization along this road, with busloads of tour groups constantly dropping off here for a coffee-and-WC break. This means that the natives of Senj—perhaps harkening back to their pirate ancestors—are adept at overcharging and shortchanging visitors. Check your bill carefully against the posted menu prices.

Senj is also the easiest point where the Kvarner coastal road connects to the speedy A-1 expressway that runs parallel to the coast inland. From Senj, a well-traveled road cuts away from the coast and soon begins twisting up the coastal mountain range. After about an hour, you'll arrive at the A-1 expressway, followed by the war-scarred town of Otočac. (For more on Otočac, see page 88.)

SPLIT

Dubrovnik is the darling of the Dalmatian Coast, but Split (pronounced as it's spelled) is Croatia's "second city" (after Zagreb), bustling with 189,000 people. If you've been hopping along the coast, landing in urban Split feels like a return to civilization. While most Dalmatian coastal towns seem made for tourists, Split is real and vibrant—a shipbuilding city with ugly sprawl surrounding an atmospheric Old Town, which teems with Croatians living life to the fullest.

Though today's Split throbs to a modern, young beat, its history goes way back—all the way to the Roman Empire. Along with all the trappings of a modern city, Split has some of the best Roman ruins this side of Italy. In the fourth century A.D., the Roman Emperor Diocletian (245–313) wanted to retire in his native Dalmatia, so he built a huge palace here. Eventually, the palace was abandoned. Then locals, fleeing seventh-century Slavic

invaders, moved in and made themselves at home, and a medieval town sprouted from the rubble of the old palace. In the 15th century, the Venetians took over the Dalmatian Coast. They developed and fortified Split, slathering the city with a new layer of Gothic-Renaissance architecture.

But even as Split grew, the nucleus remained the ruins of Diocletian's Palace. To this day, 2,000 people live or work inside the former palace walls. A maze of narrow alleys is home to

Split Overview

To Airport & Trogir
HRVATSKE MORNARICE
DOMOVINSKOG RATA
To Bene Beach
KAŠTELANSKA
ZRINSKO FRANKOPANSKA
ARCHAEOLOGICAL MUSEUM
SUBURBAN BUS STATION
MAŽURANIĆEVO ŠET.
LOVREBEK
MATOŠEVA
MANDALINSKA PUT.
VUKOVARSKA
See Detail maps
MARJAN PENINSULA
(TUNNEL)
VAROŠ
OLD TOWN
DIOCLETIAN'S PALACE
MATEJUŠKA (FISHERMEN'S PORT)
KRIŽEVA
MARJON
LUČAC
SENJSKA
RIVA
ZVONIMIRA
TRAIN STATION
MARASOVIĆEVA
MEŠTROVIĆ GALLERY
MIHANOVIĆEVI
JADROLINIJA CATAMARAN
OBALA KNEZA DOMAGOJA
MUS. OF CRO. ARCH. MONUMENTS
OBALA BR. MULICA
City Harbor
KRUO CATAMARAN
BUS STATION
ŠET. IVANA MEŠTROVIĆA
JEŽINAC BEACH
To Kaštelet Chapel
BAČVICE BEACH
MAIN FERRY TERMINAL
Adriatic Sea
500 Meters
500 Yards
To Zadar & Rijeka
To Hvar, Korčula & Dubrovnik

fashionable boutiques and galleries, wonderfully atmospheric cafés, and Roman artifacts around every corner.

Today's Split is struggling to decide how it fits into Croatia's new tourist-mecca image: Is it a big, drab metropolis; a no-nonsense transit point; an impressive destination in its own right, with sights to rival Dubrovnik's...or all three?

Planning Your Time

Split is Dalmatia's hub for bus, boat, train, and flight connections to other destinations in the country and abroad. This means that many visitors to Dalmatia stop in Split only long enough to change boats. But the city is the perfect real-life contrast to the lazy, prettified Dalmatian beach resorts—it deserves a full day. Begin by strolling the remains of Diocletian's Palace, then have a coffee break along the Riva promenade or lunch in the Old Town. After lunch, browse the shops or visit a couple of Split's museums (the Meštrović Gallery, which is a long walk or short bus or taxi ride from the Old Town, is tops). Promenading along the Riva with the natives is *the* evening activity.

With a second day (or en route to or from northern destinations), you could spend some time in nearby Trogir—an enjoyable Dalmatian seaside village (described at the end of this chapter).

SPLIT

Orientation to Split

(area code: 021)

Split sprawls, but almost everything of interest to travelers is around the City Harbor (Gradska Luka). At the top of this harbor is the Old Town (Stari Grad). Between the Old Town and the sea is the Riva, a water-front pedestrian promenade lined with cafés and shaded by palm trees. The main ferry ter-minal (Trajektni Terminal, a.k.a. Trajektna Luka) juts into the har-bor from the east side. Along the harborfront embankment between  the ferry terminal and the Old Town are the long-distance bus station (Autobusni Kolodvor) and the forlorn little train station (Željeznička Stanica). West of the Old Town, poking into the Adriatic, is the lush and hilly Marjan peninsula.

Split's domino-shaped Old Town is made up of two square sections. The east half was once Diocletian's Palace, and the west half is the medieval town that sprang up next door. The shell of Diocletian's ruined palace provides a checkerboard street plan, with a gate at each end. But the streets built since are anything but straight, making the Old Town a delightfully convoluted maze (double-decker in some places). At the center of the former palace is a square called the Peristyle (Peristil), where you'll find the TI, cathedral, and highest concentration of Roman ruins.

Tourist Information

Split's TI is on the square called the Peristyle, in the very center of Diocletian's Palace (Easter–mid-Oct Mon–Sat 8:00–21:00, Sun 8:00–13:00; mid-Oct–Easter Mon–Fri 8:00–20:00, Sat 8:00–13:00, closed Sun; exact location might change due to restoration—ask around, tel. 021/345-606, www.visitsplit.com). Pick up the free town map, monthly *Visit Split* booklet (with information on muse-ums, events, restaurants, and more), and other brochures.

The TI also sells the **Splitcard,** which includes free admis-sion to several sights (including the City Museum, Ethnographic Museum, and cathedral), a 50 percent discount at other sights (including the Meštrović Gallery and Archaeological Museum), and minor discounts at other attractions, shops, and restaurants around town (35 kn/72 hrs). This card might save busy sightse-ers some money—do the arithmetic. The Splitcard is free if you're staying at least three nights in town; to claim yours, bring a note from your hotel to the TI.

Split Essentials

English	Croatian	Pronounced
Old Town	Stari Grad	STAH-ree grahd
City Harbor	Gradska Luka	GRAHD-skah LOO-kah
Harborfront promenade	Riva	REE-vah
Peristyle (old Roman square)	Peristil	PEH-ree-steel
Soccer team	Hajduk	HIGH-dook
Local sculptor	Ivan Meštrović	EE-vahn MESH-troh-veech
Adriatic Sea	Jadran	YAH-drahn

Arrival in Split

For all the details on getting to the Dalmatian Coast, see the next page.

By Boat, Bus, or Train: The **Jadrolinija passenger catamaran** to and from Hvar and Korčula docks at the Obala Lazareta embankment, right in front of the Old Town. The *Krilo* **passenger catamaran** to those destinations uses pier #11, the shorter pier halfway along the harbor. Bigger **car ferries** use various docks along the east side of the harbor (the main terminal, Trajektni Terminal, is at the far end). If you arrive at this ferry terminal, wade through the *sobe* hawkers to the main terminal building, where you'll find ATMs, WCs, a grocery store, and offices for all of the main ferry companies. The large Jadrolinija ticket and information office at the main terminal, which is open long hours daily, generally has a helpful English-speaking staff.

Split's **car ferry** terminal, **main bus station** (Autobusni Kolodvor), and **train station** (Željeznička Stanica) all share a busy and very practical strip of land called Obala Kneza Domagoja, on the east side of the City Harbor. From any of them, you can see the Old Town and Riva; just walk around the harbor toward the big bell tower (about a 10-min walk). Along the way, you'll pass travel

Getting to the Dalmatian Coast

Three recent developments help make the long trip down to Dalmatia nearly painless: an expressway, a high-speed train line, and budget flights.

By Car or Bus: Thanks to Croatia's new A-1 super-expressway, the road trip from Zagreb to Split—which used to take seven hours—now takes less than five. Travelers who used to opt for an all-day journey or a bleary-eyed night bus can now leave Zagreb after an early dinner and arrive in Split before bedtime. In the coming years, the expressway will be extended south to Dubrovnik, making that trip even quicker. For the latest, see www.hac.hr or www.hak.hr. For details on the two different driving routes from northern Croatia to Dalmatia, see page 148. For details on driving south from Split to the rest of the Dalmatian Coast, see page 204.

By Train: Croatian Railways' "tilting train" line connects Zagreb to Split three times a day (2/day off-season, www.hznet.hr). These trains can reach high speeds because the tracks are banked and the cars are designed to tilt slightly, allowing you to make it from the capital to the Dalmatian Coast in just five and a half hours.

By Plane: Several low-cost airlines connect Dalmatia to northern Croatia and the rest of Europe. Even the national carrier, Croatia Airlines, often has surprisingly cheap tickets between Zagreb and Dubrovnik or Split. For more details, see page 571.

By Boat: Overnight boats sail in each direction between Rijeka (on the northern Croatian coast—4 hours by train from Zagreb and 2.5 hours by train from Ljubljana) and Split. But this option is much slower than the alternatives mentioned above.

agencies, left-luggage offices, locals trying to rent rooms, a post office, Internet cafés, shops, and cafés. Arriving or leaving from this central location, you never need to deal with the concrete, exhaust-stained sprawl of outer Split.

By Plane: Split's airport (Zračna Luka Split-Kaštela) is across the big bay, 15 miles northwest of the center, near the town of Trogir (tel. 021/203-305, www.split-airport.hr). A handy airline bus connects the airport with downtown Split (30 kn, 40 min). This bus meets most arriving flights at the airport; to use it to get *to* the airport, catch it at the small "Air Terminal" near the southeast corner of Diocletian's Palace (departs 1.5 hours before each Croatia Airlines flight and some other companies' flights). Cheaper long-distance buses also run regularly between the airport and Split's main bus station on their way to other destinations (15 kn, 7/day Mon–Fri, none Sat–Sun, 40 min). Yet another option is to take public bus #37 (20 kn, 3/hr Mon–Fri, 2/hr Sat–Sun, 45 min; this bus also connects Split and Trogir); the catch is that bus #37 uses the suburban bus station, which is a dreary 10-minute walk north of downtown Split. The most expensive option is a taxi, which costs a hefty 300 kn between the airport and downtown Split.

By Car: Driving around the city center can be tricky—Split is split by its Old Town, which is welded to the harbor by the pedestrian-only Riva promenade. This means drivers needing to get 300 yards from one side of the Old Town to the other must drive about 15 minutes entirely around the center, which can be miserably clogged with traffic. A semicircular ring road and a tunnel under the Marjan peninsula make this better than it might be.

Drivers are treated to the ugly side of Split as they approach town (don't worry—it gets better). From the expressway, you'll pass through an industrial zone, then curl through a few tunnels as you twist your way down into Split's striking, bowl-like setting. While you're still quite a distance from downtown, you'll come to a fork where you'll have to make a decision about which side of town you want to drive to (east or west); ask your hotel in advance for directions, and be ready for your turn. (While many hotels are individually signposted at the fork, it's a long list and hard to read quickly as you zip past.)

At the main fork, turning to the right (marked with *Centar* signs) takes you to the **west end** of the Old Town, including the Varoš neighborhood. Or, if you continue straight (marked *Trajekt*—"ferry"), you'll eventually reach other *Centar* signs and the **east end** of the Old Town, with the ferry terminal, the bus and train stations, and the Lučac neighborhood. You'll pop out right at the southeast corner of Diocletian's Palace (by the Green Market). For handy (but expensive) parking, when the road swings left to the ferry terminal, continue straight and you'll drive right into a parking lot just outside the palace walls (10 kn/hr).

Helpful Hints

Internet Access: Internet cafés are plentiful in the Old Town; look for signs, especially around the Peristyle. Closer to the stations and ferry terminal is **Backpacker C@fé**, which has Internet access, coffee and drinks with outdoor seating, and used paperbacks for sale (30 kn/hr, daily July–Aug 6:00–23:00, shoulder season 6:30–22:00, even shorter hours off-season, near the beginning of Obala Kneza Domagoja, tel. 021/338-548). **Modrulj Launderette** (described later) also has Internet access.

Post Office: A modern little post office is next to the bus station (Mon–Fri 7:30–19:00, Sat 7:30–14:30, closed Sun, on Obala Kneza Domagoja).

Luggage Storage: The train station and adjacent bus station both have safe and efficient left-luggage services *(garderoba)*. If one has a long line, check the other to see if the line is shorter. You can also store your luggage at several places in and near the Old Town, including Modrulj Launderette and Travel49 (both listed below).

Laundry: Modrulj Launderette, a rare coin-operated launderette, is well-run by an Australian couple, Shane and Julie (self-service-50 kn/load, full-service-75 kn/load, air-con, Internet access, left-luggage service; April–Oct daily 8:00–20:00; Nov–March Mon–Sat 9:00–17:00, closed Sun; Šperun 1, tel. 021/315-888). It's conveniently located in the Varoš neighborhood at the west end of the Old Town, near several recommended restaurants—handy if multitasking is your style.

Travel Agencies: Travel49, run by gregarious Josip, is a jack-of-all-trades agency buried deep in the Old Town. Josip offers walking tours (see "Tours in Split," later), bike tours, excursions, a room-booking service, bike and car rental, Internet access, luggage storage, and other services (May–Nov daily 8:00–22:00, shorter hours off-season, mornings only in winter, on Nepotova street, tel. 021/572-772, www.travel49.com). **Turistički Biro,** between the two halves of the Old Town on the Riva, books *sobe* and hotels, sells guidebooks and maps, and sells tickets for excursions (mid-June–Sept Mon–Fri 8:00–21:00, Sat 8:00–20:00, closed Sun except mid-July–mid-Sept Sun 8:00–13:00; Oct–mid-June Mon–Fri 8:00–20:00, Sat 8:00–13:00, closed Sun; Riva 12, tel. & fax 021/347-100, turist.biro.split@st.t-com.hr).

Wine Shop: At **Vinoteka Bouquet,** at the west end of the Riva (near the restaurants and launderette on Šperun street), knowledgeable Denis can help you pick out a bottle of Croatian wine to suit your tastes (Mon–Fri 8:30–12:30 & 17:00–20:30, Sat 9:00–13:30, closed Sun, Obala Hrvatskog Narodnog Preporoda 3, tel. 021/348-031). For a wine primer before you visit, see page 49.

Who's Hajduk?: You'll see the word *Hajduk* (HIGH-dook), and a distinctive red-and-white checkerboard circle design (or red-and-blue stripes), all over town and throughout northern Dalmatia. Hajduk Split is the fervently supported local soccer team, named for a band of highwaymen bandits who rebelled against Ottoman rule in the 17th–19th centuries. Most locals adore Hajduk as much as they loathe their bitter rivals, Dinamo Zagreb.

G'day, *Gospod:* You may notice a surprising concentration of Australians in Split. Many of them are actually Australian-born Croats, returning to the cosmopolitan capital city of their parents' Dalmatian homeland.

Getting Around Split

Most of what you'll want to see is within walking distance, but some sights (such as the Meštrović Gallery) are more easily reached by bus or taxi.

By Bus: Local buses, run by Promet, cost 10 kn per ride (or 9 kn if you buy a ticket from a newsstand or Promet kiosk, ask for a *putna karta;* zone I is fine for any ride within Split, but you need the 20-kn zone IV ticket for the ride to Trogir). For a round-trip within the city, buy a 16-kn transfer ticket, which works like two individual tickets (must buy at kiosk). Validate your ticket in the machine or with the driver as you board the bus. Suburban buses to towns near Split (such as Trogir) generally use the suburban bus station (Prigradski Autobusni Kolodvor), a 10-minute walk due north of the Old Town on Domovinskog rata. Bus information: www.promet-split.hr.

By Taxi: Taxis start at 20 kn, then cost around 10 kn per kilometer. Figure 50 kn for most rides within the city (for example, from the ferry terminal to most hotels)—but if going from one end of the Old Town to the other, it can be faster to walk. To call for a taxi, try Radio Taxi (tel. 021/970).

Tours in Split

Walking Tours—Various companies offer walking tours of Split's Old Town. The most established is **Unique Walking Tours,** which is part of Travel49. Their 1.5-hour tours depart from the Peristyle daily at 10:30, 12:00, and 19:00 (80 kn, tours run May–Nov only, no reservations needed, www.travel49.com).

Local Guides —Consider hiring an insider to show you around. **Maja Benzon** is a smart and savvy local guide who leads good walking tours through the Old Town (500 kn/up to 2 hrs, 600 kn/3 hrs, mobile 098-852-869, maja.benzon@gmail.com). You can also hire a guide through the **guide association,** which has an office at the Peristyle (525 kn/1.5–2 hrs; June–Aug Mon–Fri 9:00–13:00 & 15:00–19:00, Sat 9:00–14:00, closed Sun; May and Sept Mon–Fri 9:00–17:00, Sat 9:00–15:00, closed Sun; Oct–April generally open mornings only but closed Sun; tel. 021/360-058, tel. & fax 021/346-267, mobile 098-361-936, www.guides.hr, info @guides.hr).

Beyond Split

Lifejacket Adventures, run by Australian couple Shane and Julie, works hard to come up with culturally meaningful excursions that

SPLIT

The Dalmatian Coast at a Glance

Trying to decide how to divvy up your Dalmatian days? Here are my favorite spots, listed in order of priority, and with a suggestion of how long to spend at each one on a fast-paced trip.

▲▲▲**Dubrovnik** Croatia's single best attraction is a giant, walled Old Town filled with engaging museums, delicious seafood restaurants, and happy tourists. If you visit one place in Croatia, make it Dubrovnik. Allow two days or more. See Dubrovnik chapter.

▲▲**Split** The perfect big-city antidote to the small-town quaintness on the rest of the Dalmatian Coast, Split's centerpiece is an Old Town built on the goose-pimpling remains of a Roman palace. Long considered merely the "transfer point" of Dalmatia, bustling Split is worth exploring in its own right. Allow a full day. See this chapter.

▲▲**Korčula** This "mini-Dubrovnik" island village features a scenic, walled Old Town peninsula with a looming fjord-like backdrop. Proudly historic Korčula has more than its share of offbeat museums, plus beaches in abundance. Allow a full day or more. See Korčula chapter.

▲▲**Hvar** A low-impact island town with a shimmering harbor, hilltop fortress, and lively nightlife, Hvar is increasingly popular with high-class fun-seekers. Hvar is less immediately striking but more seductively relaxing (and more expensive) than Korčula. Allow a full day or more. See Hvar chapter.

▲**Mljet National Park** If you like your islands without civilization, head for this carefully preserved getaway, great for hiking, biking, and swimming. Allow a day (most convenient as a side-trip from Dubrovnik). See page 309 in the Near Dubrovnik chapter.

Trogir This sleepy little village, across the bay from Split, is best known as a convenient spot to moor your yacht. Less thrilling than the bigger, better Hvar and Korčula, Trogir's biggest advantage is its easy proximity to Split. Allow a half-day. See page 206 in this chapter.

For more on day trips from Dubrovnik, see page 302.

connect travelers to the Croatia they came to see. Many of their trips involve a cruise on an authentic, old-fashioned fishing boat. Options include a sunset cruise, a swim and a picnic on a nearby island, a Jewish-themed walking tour of Split, a cooking trip to Hvar, and longer excursions to Plitvice Lakes National Park. They also arrange custom excursions, with a focus on kayaking, hiking, wine, history, and archaeological sites. Because their schedule is based on demand, get the latest by checking their website (www .lifejacketadventures.com), calling 098-931-6400, or stopping by their office in Split (around the corner from Modrulj Launderette, which Shane and Julie also run; see "Helpful Hints," earlier).

Atlas Travel offers a variety of excursions from Split (mostly full-day, about 300–700 kn). Itineraries include a tour of Split and Trogir, whitewater rafting on the nearby Cetina River, the island of Brač, the island of Hvar, Brač and Hvar together, Međugorje, Krka National Park, Dubrovnik, and Plitvice Lakes National Park. While the guiding is generally disappointing, this can be a quick, convenient way to get to places that are time-consuming to reach by public transportation. Get information and tickets at any travel agency, such as the Turistički Biro on the Riva (see "Helpful Hints," earlier).

Travel49, listed earlier under "Helpful Hints," also runs excursions.

Self-Guided Walk

▲▲▲Diocletian's Palace (Dioklecijanova Palača)

Split's top activity is visiting the remains of Roman Emperor Diocletian's enormous retirement palace, sitting on the harbor in the heart of the city. This monstrous complex was two impressive structures in one: luxurious villa and fortified Roman town. Since the ruins themselves are now integrated with the city's street plan, exploring them is free (though you'll pay to enter a few parts, such as the cellars and the cathedral/mausoleum). Fragments of the palace are poorly marked, and there are no good guidebooks or audioguides for tracking down the remains, making Split a good place to take a walking tour or hire a local guide (see "Tours in Split," earlier). This self-guided tour provides enough information for most visitors. To begin the tour, stand in front of the palace (at the east end of the Riva) to get oriented.

Background: Diocletian grew up just inland from Split, in the town of Salona (Solin in Croatian), which was then the capital of the Roman province of Dalmatia. He worked his way up the Roman hierarchy and ruled as emperor for the unusually long tenure of 20 years (A.D. 284–305). Despite all of his achievements,

SPLIT

DIOCLETIANVS

Diocletian is best remembered for two questionable legacies: dividing the huge empire among four emperors (which helped administer it more efficiently, but began a splintering effect that arguably led to the empire's decline); and torturing and executing Christians, including thousands right here on the Dalmatian Coast.

As Diocletian grew older, he decided to return to his homeland for retirement. Since he was in poor health, the medicinal sulfur spring here was another plus. His massive palace took only 11 years to build—and this fast pace required a big push (more than 2,000 slaves died during construction). Huge sections of his palace still exist, modified by medieval and modern developers alike. To get a sense of the original palace, check out the big illustration posted across from the palace entry. Across the street at the end of the Riva, notice the big car-size model of today's Old Town, which is helpful for orientation. (Both the sign and the model are usually crowded with tour groups.)

Palace Facade

The "front" of today's Split—facing the harbor—was actually the back door of Diocletian's Palace. There was no embankment in front of the palace back then, so the water came right up to this door—sort of an emergency exit by boat. Looking out to the water, appreciate the palace's strategic location, in a place easy to fortify and to watch for enemies approaching either by land or by sea.

Visually trace the outline of the gigantic palace, which was more than 600 feet long on each side. On the corner to the right stands a big, rectangular guard tower (one of the original 16). To the left, the tower is gone and the corner is harder to pick out (look for the beginning of the newer-looking buildings). Mentally erase the ramshackle two-story buildings added 200 years ago, which obscure the grandness of the palace wall.

Halfway up the facade, notice the row of 42 arched window frames (mostly filled in today). Diocletian and his family lived in the seaside half of the palace. Imagine him strolling back and forth along this fine arcade, enjoying the views of his Adriatic homeland. The inland, non-view half of the palace was home to 700 servants, bodyguards, and soldiers.

• *Now go through the door in the middle of the palace (known as the "Brass Gate," located under the* Substructure of Diocletian's Palace *banner). Just inside the door and to the left is the entrance to...*

SPLIT

Diocletian's Palace

Self-Guided Walk

1. Palace Facade View
2. Cellar Entrance (Below)
3. Passage to Peristyle (Below) & Ethnographic Museum (Above)
4. Peristyle Square
5. Entry Vestibule
6. Cathedral of St. Dominus
7. Jupiter's Temple/ St. John's Baptistery
8. View Up Cardo Street
9. Bishop Gregory of Nin Statue

Hotels, Restaurants & Services

10. Peristil Hotel
11. Hotel Vestibul Palace (Above)
12. Hotel Slavija
13. Sobe "Base"
14. Kaleta Apartments
15. Hostel Split
16. Hostel Split the Sequel
17. Marul Konoba Restaurant
18. Apetit Restaurant
19. Zlagogajnica None Pizza
20. Zlatna Vrata Pizza & Pasta
21. Ivona Ice Cream
22. Nadalina Chocolate Shop
23. Luxor Bar
24. Travel49 Travel Agency
25. Turistički Biro Travel Agency
26. Croata Tie Shop
27. Air Terminal Bus Stop

SPLIT

Diocletian's Cellars (Podromi)

Since the palace was built on land that sloped down to the sea, these chambers were built to level out a foundation for the massive structure above (like a modern  "daylight basement"). These cellars were filled with water from three different sources: a freshwater spring, a sulfur spring, and the sea. Later, medieval residents used them as a dump. Rediscovered only in the last century, the cellars enabled archaeologists to derive the floor plan of some of the palace's long-gone upper sections. Today, these underground chambers are used for art exhibits and a little strip of souvenir stands. But before you go shopping, explore the cellars at this end (25 kn, short and dry 10-kn guidebook, some posters inside explain the site; opens daily at 9:00 and closes June–Aug at 21:00, Sept at 20:00, May and Oct at 18:00, April at 17:00; Nov–March Mon–Sat 9:00–14:00, closed Sun).

❸ **Self-Guided Tour:** Use the free map you get at the entry to navigate this labyrinthine complex of cellars. First visit the **western cellars** (to the left as you enter). Near the ticket-seller, notice the big **topographical map** of the Split area, clearly showing the city's easily defensible location—with a natural harbor sheltered by tall mountains. You'll see the former Roman city of Salona, Diocletian's birthplace, just inland.

Then head into the main part of the cellars by going through the door on the right, just past the ticket-seller. This takes you into the complex's vast, vaulted **main hall**—the biggest space in the cellars, with stout pillars to support everything upstairs. When those first villagers took refuge in the abandoned palace from the rampaging Slavs in 641, the elite lived upstairs, grabbing what was once the emperor's wing. They carved the rough holes you see in the ceiling to dump their garbage and sewage. Over the generations, the basement (where you're standing) filled up with layers of waste that solidified, ultimately becoming a once-stinky, then-precious bonanza for 19th- and 20th-century archaeologists. Today this hall is used for everything from flower and book shows to fashion catwalks.

Exit the main hall through either of the doors on the left, turn right down the narrow corridor, and then turn left at the end of the corridor. In this room you'll see a stone olive-oil press. Continue through a small room and into a round room, which has a headless, pawless black granite sphinx—one of 13 that Diocletian brought home from Egypt (only four survive, including a mostly intact one we'll see soon on the Peristyle). Look up to admire the circular brickwork. Then continue straight ahead into the long room, which displays two petrified beams. Looking just overhead, you'll see the holes that once held these beams to support floorboards, making this a two-story cellar.

Exit through the door at the far-right corner (near the mound of ancient garbage) to another round room, featuring a bust of Diocletian (or is it Sean Connery?). Continue straight ahead (near the public WCs), then turn left, left, and right into the second grand hall, with more beam holes and a giant replica of a golden Diocletian coin at the far end. Exiting this hall at the end opposite the coin, you'll find an unexcavated wing—a compost pile of ancient lifestyles, awaiting the tiny shovels and toothbrushes of future archaeologists. Here you'll also see original Roman sewer pipes—square outside and round inside—designed to fit into each other to create long pipes.

From here, head back out to the exit. If you'd like to see more cellars—mostly with their ceilings missing, so they're open to the air—cross over into the **eastern cellars** (same ticket). This section is less interesting than the western part, but worth a quick visit.

• *When you're finished, head back to the main gallery. Ignore the tacky made-in-Malaysia trinket shops as you head down the passage and up the stairs into the...*

Peristyle (Peristil)

This square was the centerpiece of Diocletian's Palace. As you walk up the stairs, the entry vestibule into the residence is above your

head, Diocletian's mausoleum (today's Cathedral of St. Dominus) is to your right, and the street to Jupiter's Temple is on your left. On this square, you'll find the TI (because the old structures on the square are being restored, its exact location might vary). Straight ahead, beyond the little chapel, is the narrow street to the former main entrance to the palace, the Golden Gate.

Go to the middle of the square and take it all in. The red granite pillars—which you'll see all over Diocletian's Palace—are from Egypt, where Diocletian spent many of his pre-retirement years. Imagine the pillars defining fine arcades—now obscured by medieval houses. (As the Peristyle is undergoing a lengthy restoration, you may notice that many of the ruins are lighter-colored than others, and scaffolding may block your view.) The black sphinx is the only one of Diocletian's collection of 13 that's still (mostly) intact.

• *Climb the stairs (above where you came in) into the domed, open-ceilinged...*

Entry Vestibule: Impressed? That's the idea. This was the grand entry to Diocletian's living quarters, meant to wow visitors.

Emperors were believed to be gods. Diocletian called himself "Jovius"—the son of Jupiter, the most powerful of all gods. Four times a year (at the change of the seasons), Diocletian would stand here and overlook the Peristyle. His subjects would lie on the ground in worship, praising his name and kissing his scarlet robe. Notice the four big niches at floor level, which once held statues of the four tetrarchs who ruled the unwieldy empire after Diocletian retired. The empty hole in the ceiling was once capped by a dome (long since collapsed), and the ceiling itself was covered with frescoes and mosaics.

In this grand space, you're likely to run into an all-male band of *klapa* singers, performing traditional a cappella harmonies. Just stand and enjoy a few glorious tunes—you'll rarely find a better group or acoustics. A 100-kn *klapa* CD is the perfect souvenir.

Wander out back to the harbor side through medieval buildings (some with seventh-century foundations), which evoke the way local villagers came in and took over the once-spacious and elegant palace. Back in this area, you'll find the beautifully restored home of the **Ethnographic Museum** (described later, under "Sights in Split").

• *Now go back into the Peristyle and turn right, climbing the steps to the...*

Cathedral of St. Dominus (Katedrala Sv. Duje)

The original octagonal structure was Diocletian's elaborate mausoleum, built in the fourth century. But after the fall of Rome, it was converted into the town's cathedral. Construction of the bell tower began in the 13th century and took 300 years to complete. Before you go inside, notice the sarcophagi ringing the cathedral. In the late Middle Ages, this was prime post-mortem real estate, since being buried closer to a cathedral improved your chances of getting to heaven. On the 13th-century main doors, notice the 14 panels on

each of the two wings—showing 28 scenes from the life of Christ.

Various parts of the cathedral are covered by separate tickets: 15 kn for the "treasury" (actually the fee to enter the cathedral), another 10 kn to climb the tower, and yet another 5 kn for the crypt below. All the sights are open similar hours, but can be closed unexpectedly for services (generally open daily in summer 7:00–19:00, often closed Sat afternoons for weddings and Sun mornings for Mass; in winter daily 7:00–12:00, maybe later on request; Kraj Sv. Duje 5, tel. 021/344-121).

Buy your treasury/cathedral ticket and step inside the oldest—

and likely smallest— building used as a cathedral anywhere in Christendom. Imagine the place in pre-Christian times, with Diocletian's tomb in the center. The only surviving decor from those days are the granite columns and the relief circling the base of the dome (about 50 feet up)—a ring of carvings heralding the greatness of the emperor. The small red-marble pillars around the top of the pulpit (near the entry) were scavenged from Diocletian's sarcophagus. These pillars are all that remain of Diocletian's remains.

Diocletian brutally persecuted his Christian subjects. Just before he moved to the Dalmatian Coast, he had Bishop Dominus of Salona killed, along with several thousand Christians. When Diocletian died, there were riots of happiness. In the seventh century, his mausoleum became a cathedral dedicated to the martyred bishop. The extension behind the altar was added in the ninth century. The sarcophagus of St. Dominus (to the right of the altar, with early-Christian carvings) was once the cathedral's high altar. To the left of today's

main altar is the impressively detailed, Renaissance-era altar of St. Anastasius, who is lying on a millstone that is tied to his neck. On Diocletian's orders, this Christian martyr was drowned in A.D. 302. To the left of St. Anastasius'

altar is the "new" altar of St. Dominus; his relics lie in the 18th-century Baroque silver reliquary, decorated with a relief showing him being beheaded. Posthumous poetic justice: Now Christian saints are entombed in Diocletian's mausoleum...and Diocletian is nowhere to be found.

For another 10 kn, you can climb 183 steep steps to the top of the 200-foot-tall **bell tower.** You'll be rewarded with sweeping views of Split, but it's not for claustrophobes or those scared of heights.

If you circle down and around the right side of the cathedral, you'll find the entrance to the **crypt** (separate 5-kn ticket). This musty, domed cellar (with eerie acoustics) was originally used to level the foundation of Diocletian's mausoleum. Later, Christians turned it into another chapel. The legend you'll likely hear about Diocletian torturing and murdering Christians in this very crypt, which began about the same time this became a church, is probably false.

Jupiter's Temple/St. John's Baptistery

Remember that Diocletian believed himself to be Jovius (that's Jupiter, Jr.). On exiting the mausoleum of Jovius, worshippers would look straight ahead to the temple of Jupiter. (Back then, all of these medieval buildings weren't cluttering up the view.) Make your way through the narrow alley (directly across from the cathedral entry), past another headless, pawless sphinx, to explore the small temple (5 kn, same hours as cathedral; if it's locked, go ask the guy at the cathedral to let you in).

About the time the mausoleum became a cathedral, this temple was converted into a baptistery. The big 12th-century baptismal font—large enough to immerse someone (as was the tradition in those days)—is decorated with the intricate, traditional *pleter* design also used around the border of Croatia's current passport stamp. On the font, notice the engraving: a bishop (on the left) and the king on his throne (on the right). At their feet (literally under the feet of the bishop) is a submissive commoner—neatly summing up the social structure of the Middle Ages. Standing above the font is a statue of St. John the Baptist counting to four, done by the great Croatian sculptor Ivan Meštrović (see page 188). The half-barrel vaulted ceiling, completed later, is considered the best-preserved of its kind anywhere. Every face and each patterned box is different.

• *Back at the Peristyle, stand in front of the little chapel with your back to the entry vestibule. The little street just beyond the chapel (going left to right) connects the east and west gates. If you've had enough Roman history, head right (east) to go through the "Silver Gate" and find Split's busy, open-air Green Market. Or, head to the left (west), which takes you to the "Iron Gate" and People's Square (see "Sights in Split," later) and, beyond that, the fresh-and-smelly fish market. But if you want to see one last bit of Roman history, continue straight ahead up the...*

Cardo

A traditional Roman street plan has two roads: Cardo (the north–south axis) and Decumanus (the east–west axis). Split's Cardo street was the most important in Diocletian's Palace, connecting the main entry with the heart of the complex. As you walk, you'll pass several noteworthy sights: in the first building on the right, a bank with modern computer gear all around its exposed Roman ruins (look through window); at the first gate on the left, the courtyard of a Venetian merchant's palace (a reminder that Split was dominated by Venice from the 15th century on); on the right, an alley to the **City Museum** (described later, under "Sights in Split"); and, on the right, the **Nadalina** chocolate shop, a local artisan chocolatier selling mostly dark chocolate creations with some innovative Dalmatian flavors (30 kn/100 grams, 13-kn chocolate bars, Mon–Fri 9:00–21:00, Sat 9:00–12:00, closed Sun).

• *Before long, you'll pass through the...*

Golden Gate (Zlatna Vrata)

This great gate was the main entry of Diocletian's Palace. Its name wasn't literal—the "gold" instead suggests the importance of this gateway to Salona, the Roman provincial capital at the time. Standing inside the gate itself, you can appreciate the double-door design that kept the palace safe. Also notice how this ancient building is now being used in very different ways from its original purpose. Above, on the outer wall, you can see the bricked-in windows that contain part of a Dominican convent. At the top of the inner wall, notice somebody's garden terrace.

Go outside the gate, where you'll get a much clearer feel for the way the palace looked before so many other buildings were grafted on. Straight ahead from here is Salona (Solin), which was a major city of 60,000 (and Diocletian's hometown) before there was a Split. The big statue by Ivan Meštrović is **Bishop Gregory of Nin,** a 10th-century Croatian priest who tried to convince the Vatican to allow sermons during Mass to be said in Croatian, rather than Latin. People rub his toe for good luck (though only nonmaterial wishes are given serious consideration).

The big building beyond the statue houses Split's new **Gallery of Fine Arts** (described later, under "Sights in Split").

• *Your tour is finished. Now enjoy the rest of Split.*

Sights in Split

In or near the Old Town

In addition to the palace, cellars, and cathedral described on my self-guided walk, you can also enjoy these attractions.

▲**People's Square (Narodni Trg)**—The lively square at the center of the Old Town is called by locals simply *Pjaca*, pronounced the same as the Italian *piazza* (PYAH-tsah). Stand in the center and enjoy the bustle. Look around for a quick lesson in Dalmatian history. When Diocletian lived in his palace, a Roman village popped up here, just outside the wall. Face the former wall of Diocletian's Palace (behind and to the right of the  24-hour clock tower). This was the western entrance, or so-called "Iron Gate." By the 14th century, a medieval town had developed, making this the main square of Split.

On the wall just to the right of the lane leading to the Peristyle, look for the life-size relief of **St. Anthony.** Notice the creepy "mini-me" clutching the saint's left leg—depicting the sculptor's donor, who didn't want his gift to be forgotten. Above this strange statue, notice the smaller, faded relief of a man and a woman arguing.

Turn around and face the square. On your left is the city's grand old café, **Gradska Kavana,** which has been the Old Town's venerable meeting point for generations. Today it's both a café and a restaurant with disappointing food but the best outdoor ambience in town (30-kn breakfasts, 50–75-kn pastas, 70–130-kn main courses, daily 7:00–24:00, Narodni trg 1, tel. 021/317-835).

Across the square, the white building jutting into the square was once the **City Hall,** and now houses temporary exhibitions. The loggia is all that remains of the original Gothic building.

At the far end of the square is the out-of-place **Nakić House,** built in the early 20th-century Viennese Secession style—a reminder that Dalmatia was part of the Habsburg Empire, ruled by Vienna, from Napoleon's downfall through World War I.

The lane on the right side of the Nakić House leads to Split's **fish market** (Ribarnica), where you can see piles of the still-wriggling catch of the day. No flies? It's thanks to the sulfur spring in the nearby spa building (with the gray statues, on the corner). Just beyond the fish market is the pedestrian boulevard Marmontova.

Ethnographic Museum (Etnografski Muzej)—This museum uses well-presented temporary exhibits to show off the culture, costumes, furniture, tools, jewelry, weapons, and paintings of

SPLIT

Dalmatia. It's all displayed in a gorgeously renovated early-medieval palace with a confusing treehouse floor plan. You'll find it in the upper level of the Old Town, behind Diocletian's entry vestibule. Check out the artsy "golden fleece" entry door. The ground floor sports the remains of a seventh-century church, and the exhibits usually include a good look at traditional folk dress. Your ticket also includes access to the roof of the vestibule (find the stairs at the far end of the museum); while it's not high enough to be thrilling, and you can't actually see down into the vestibule, it's a nice view over the rooftops of Split (10 kn, some English explanations; July–mid-Sept Mon–Fri 9:00–21:00, Sat 9:00–13:00, closed Sun; June Mon–Fri 9:00–14:00 & 17:00–20:00, Sat 9:00–13:00, closed Sun; mid-Sept–May Mon–Fri 9:00–14:00, Sat 9:00–13:00, closed Sun; Severova 7, tel. 021/344-164, www.etnografski-muzej-split.hr).

Split City Museum (Muzej Grada Splita)—This museum traces how the city grew over the centuries. It's a bit dull, but it can help you appreciate a little better the layers of history you're seeing in the streets. The ground floor displays Roman fragments (including coins from the days of Diocletian) and temporary exhibits. The upstairs focuses on the Middle Ages (find the terrace displaying carved stone monuments), and the top floor goes from the 16th century to the present (10 kn, some English descriptions, 75-kn guidebook is overkill; May–Sept Tue–Fri 9:00–21:00, Sat–Mon 9:00–16:00; Oct–April Tue–Fri 9:00–16:00, Sat–Sun 10:00–13:00, closed Mon; Papalićeva 1, tel. 021/360-171, www.mgst.net).

The 15th-century Papalić Palace, which houses the City Museum, is a sight all its own. At the end of the palace, near Cardo street, look up to see several typical Venetian-style Gothic-Renaissance windows. The stone posts sticking out of the wall next to them were used to hang curtains.

Radić Brothers Square (Trg Braće Radića)—Also known as Voćni Trg ("Fruit Square") for the produce that was once sold here, this little piazza is just off the Riva between the two halves of the Old Town. Overhead is a **Venetian citadel.** After Split became part of the Venetian Republic, there was a serious danger of attack by the Ottomans, so octagonal towers like this were built all along the coast. But this imposing tower had a second purpose: to encourage citizens of Split to forget about any plans of rebellion.

In the middle of the square is a studious sculpture by Ivan Meštrović of the 16th-century poet **Marko Marulić,** who is considered the father of the Croatian language. Marulić was the first to write literature in the Croatian vernacular, which before then had generally been considered a backward peasants' tongue.

On the downhill (harbor) side of the square is **Croata,** a necktie boutique that loves to explain how Croatian soldiers who fought with the French in the Thirty Years' War (1618–1648) had a distinctive way of tying their scarves. The French found it stylish, adopted it, and called it *à la Croate*—or eventually, *cravate*—thus creating the modern necktie that many people wear to work every day throughout the world. Croata's selection includes ties with traditional Croatian motifs, such as the checkerboard pattern from the flag or writing in the ninth-century Glagolitic alphabet. Though pricey, these ties make nice souvenirs (250–700 kn, Mon–Fri 8:00–20:30, Sat 8:00–13:00, closed Sun, shorter hours off-season). There's also a bigger, second location of this shop on the Peristyle.

Green Market—This lively open-air market bustles at the east end of Diocletian's Palace. Locals shop for produce and clothes here, and there are plenty of tourist souvenirs as well. Browse the wide selection of T-shirts, and ignore the creepy black-market tobacco salesmen who mutter at you: *"Cigaretta?"*

Split Gallery of Fine Arts (Galerija Umjetnina Split)—This collection, beautifully displayed in a finely restored old hospital just behind Diocletian's Palace, features mostly Croatian artwork from the 14th to the 21st centuries. It's basically a hodgepodge with few highlights—best reserved for art-lovers. Cross through the courtyard, climb up the stairs, and follow the one-way route through the chronologically displayed collection, which is heavy on the 20th century (20 kn, Tue–Sat 11:00–19:00, Sun 10:00–13:00, closed Mon, mod café, go straight out the Golden Gate and a bit to the left—behind the statue of Gregory of Nin—to Kralja Tomislava 15, tel. 021/350-110, www.galum.hr).

Archaeological Museum (Arheološki Muzej)—If you're intrigued by all the "big stuff" from Split's past (buildings and ruins), consider paying a visit to this collection of its "little stuff." A good exhibit of artifacts (mostly everyday domestic items) traces this region's history from its Illyrian beginnings chronologically through its notable Roman period (items from Split and Salona) to the Middle Ages. About a 10-minute walk north of the Old Town, it's worth the trip for archaeology fans (20 kn; June–Sept Mon–Sat 9:00–14:00 & 16:00–20:00, closed Sun; Oct–May Mon–Fri 9:00–14:00 & 16:00–20:00, Sat 9:00–14:00, closed Sun; Zrinsko Frankopanska 25, tel. 021/329-340, www.mdc.hr/split-arheoloski). Don't confuse this with the less-interesting Museum of Croatian Archaeological Monuments, on the way to the Ivan Meštrović Gallery.

Ivan Meštrović Sights, West of the Old Town

The excellent Meštrović Gallery and nearby Kaštelet Chapel just outside the Old Town can be reached by foot, bus, or taxi.

▲▲**Meštrović Gallery (Galerija Meštrović)**—Split's best art museum is dedicated to the sculptor Ivan Meštrović, the

most important of all Croatian artists (see sidebar). Many of Meštrović's finest works are housed in this palace, designed by the sculptor himself to serve as his residence, studio, and exhibition space. If you have time, it's worth the 25-minute walk or short bus or taxi ride from the Old Town.

Cost, Hours, Location: 30 kn, includes Kaštelet Chapel entry, free guide booklet, 80-kn guidebook is overkill for most visitors, pricey mobile-phone audioguides available; May–Sept Tue–Sun 9:00–19:00, closed Mon; Oct–April Tue–Sat 9:00–16:00, Sun 10:00–15:00, closed Mon; hours can be sporadic—call to confirm it's open before making the trip, Šetalište Ivana Meštrovića 46, tel. 021/340-800, www.mdc.hr/mestrovic.

Getting There: To get to the gallery, you can take **bus** #12 from the little cul-de-sac at the west end of the Riva (departs hourly, get off at the stop in front of the gallery—just after your bus passes a museum prominently marked *Muzej Hrvatskih Arheoloških Spomenika*). Or you can **walk** about 25 minutes: Follow the harbor west of town toward the big marina, swing right with the road, and follow the park until you see the gallery on your right. A **taxi** from the west end of the Old Town to the gallery costs about 50 kn (much more from the east end of the Old Town).

❂ **Self-Guided Tour:** After buying your ticket (and asking about the time for your return bus to the Old Town), climb the stairs toward Meštrović's house, pausing in the **garden** to admire a smattering of sculptures (including several female nudes, Cyclops hurling a giant shotput, and an eagle).

Climbing another set of stairs, you reach the **Entrance Hall,** displaying sculptures mostly of Carrara marble, which was Michelangelo's favorite medium. Notice the black sculptures by the two staircases: on the left, representing birth, and on the right, representing death—Meštrović strove to capture the full range of human experience in his work.

Go to the left, and enter the **Dining Room** at the end of the main floor. It's decorated with portraits of Meštrović's wife, mother, and children. Meštrović often used his mother as a model for older women and his second wife Olga as a model for younger women. Also look for the self-portrait and two painted portraits of Meštrović (one as a young man, another shortly before his death).

Ivan Meštrović
(1883–1962)

Ivan Meštrović (EE-vahn MESH-troh-veech), who achieved international fame for his talents as a sculptor, was Croatia's answer to Rodin. You'll see Meštrović's works everywhere in the streets, squares, and museums of Croatia.

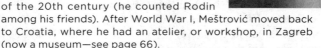

Meštrović came from humble beginnings. He grew up in a family of poor, nomadic farm workers just inland from Split. At an early age, his drawings and wooden carvings showed promise, and a rich family took him in and made sure he was properly trained. He eventually went off to school in Vienna, where he fell in with the Secession movement and found fame and fortune. He lived in Prague, Paris, and Switzerland, fully engaged in the flourishing European artistic culture at the turn of the 20th century (he counted Rodin among his friends). After World War I, Meštrović moved back to Croatia, where he had an atelier, or workshop, in Zagreb (now a museum—see page 66).

Later in life—like Diocletian before him—Meštrović returned to Split and built a huge seaside mansion (today's Meštrović Gallery). The years between the World Wars were Meštrović's happiest and most productive. It was during this time that he sculpted his most internationally famous works, a pair of giant Native American warriors on horseback in Chicago's Grant Park. But when World War II broke out, Meštrović—an outspoken supporter of the ideals of a united Yugoslavia—was briefly imprisoned by the anti-Yugoslav Ustaše (Croatia's Nazi puppet government). After his release, Meštrović fled to Italy, then the US, where he lectured at prominent universities such as Notre Dame and Syracuse. After the war, the Yugoslav dictator Tito invited Meštrović to return, but the very religious artist refused to cooperate with an atheist regime. (Meštrović was friends with the Archbishop Alojzije Stepinac, who was imprisoned by Tito.) Meštrović died in South Bend, Indiana.

Meštrović worked in wood, plaster, marble, and bronze, and dabbled in painting. His sculptures depict biblical, mythological, political, and everyday themes. Meštrović's figures typically have long, angular fingers, arms, and legs. Whether whimsical or emotional, Meštrović's expressive, elongated faces—often with a strong-profile nose—powerfully connect with the viewer.

A painting of the *Last Supper* hangs in virtually every Dalmatian dining room. Meštrović's is no exception—he painted this version himself. At the end of the room are two giant caryatids carved from Dalmatian stone (embedded with fragments of seashells).

Now climb the stairs and go to the right, into the **Secession Room.** Some of these works—including the girl singing and the intimate portrait of a family—show the influence of Meštrović's contemporary, Rodin.

Pass through the room of drawings into the **Long Hall,** lined with life-size figures and a view terrace. The woman sitting with her knees apart and feet together is demonstrating a favorite pose of Meštrović's.

At the end of the hall is the **Study Room,** filled with miniature sculptures Meštrović created to prepare for larger-scale works. Notice the small study of *Job,* then go into the small side-room to see the much larger final version. One of Meštrović's most powerful works, *Job*—howling with an agony verging on insanity—was carved by the artist in exile, as his country was turned upside-down by World War II. Meštrović sketched his inspiration for this piece (displayed on the wall) while he was imprisoned by the Ustaše.

Head down the stairs and turn left into the **Sacral Room.** Meštrović was very religious, and here you can see some of his many works depicting biblical figures. The giant, wood-carved *Adam* and *Eve* dominate the room, but don't miss the smaller side-room, with another of the gallery's highlights: the quietly poignant *Roman Pietà.* Meštrović follows the classical pyramid form, with Joseph of Arimathea (top), Mary (left), and Mary Magdalene (right) surrounding the limp body of Christ. But the harmony is broken by the painful angles of the mourn-

ing faces. While this sculpture is plaster, Meštrović also completed a marble version for the campus of Notre Dame in the US.

▲**Kaštelet Chapel**—If you enjoy the gallery, don't miss the nearby Kaštelet Chapel ("Chapel of the Holy Cross"). Meštrović bought this 16th-century fortified palace to display his 28 wood reliefs of Jesus' life. Because he carved these over a nearly 30-year span (completing the last 12 when he was in the US), you can watch Meštrović's style change over time. (However, note that he didn't carve the reliefs in chronological order—ask for a booklet identifying the topic and year for each one.) While the earlier pieces are well-composed and powerful, the later ones seem more hastily done, as Meštrović rushed to complete his opus. Work

SPLIT

clockwise around the room, tracing the life of Christ. Notice that some of the Passion scenes are out of order (a side-effect of Meštrović's nonlinear schedule). The beautiful *pietà* near the end still shows some of the original surface of the wood, demonstrating the skill required to create depth and emotion in just a few inches of medium. Dominating the chapel is an extremely powerful wooden crucifix, with Christ's arms, legs, fingers, and toes bent at unnatural angles—a typically expressionistic flair Meštrović used to exaggerate suffering.

Cost and Hours: The chapel is covered by the same 30-kn ticket as the gallery, and open the same hours.

Getting There: It's a five-minute walk past the gallery down Šetalište Ivana Meštrovića (on the left, in an olive grove).

Activities in Split

▲▲**Strolling the Riva (Obala Hrvatskog Narodnog Preporoda)**—The official name for this seaside pedestrian drag is the "Croatian National Revival Embankment," but locals just call it "Riva" (Italian for "harbor"). This is the town's promenade, an integral part of Mediterranean culture. After dinner, Split residents collect their families and friends for a stroll on the Riva. It offers some of the best people-

watching in Croatia; make it a point to be here for an hour or two after dinner. At the west end of the Riva, the people-parade of Croatian culture turns right and heads away from the water, up Marmontova. The stinky smell that sometimes accompanies the stroll isn't a sewer. It's sulfur—a reminder that the town's medicinal sulfur spas have attracted people here since the days of Diocletian.

The Riva recently underwent an extensive, costly, and controversial renovation. The old potholed pavement and scrubby gardens were torn up and replaced with a broad, sleek, carefully landscaped people zone. A clean, synchronized line of modern white lampposts and sun screens sashays down the promenade. But many locals miss the colorful quirks of the old version. For example, each café used to have its own tables and umbrellas; now they're forced to buy identical tables and chairs to make everything match. (In protest, some cafés have chosen to offer no outdoor seating at all.) Some locals think that the starkly modern strip is at odds with the rest of the higgledy-piggledy Old Town, while others see this as simply the early-21st century's contribution to the architectural hodgepodge that is Split.

SPLIT

Exploring Matejuška Fishermen's Port—While Split's harborfront Riva is where the beautiful people stroll, the city's

fishermen roots still thrive just to the west. The neighborhood called Matejuška—at the little harbor where the Varoš district hits the water (a five-minute walk beyond the end of the Riva, with the water on your left)—has long been Split's working fishermen's harbor. While the area has received a facelift to match the one along the Riva, it still retains its striped-collar character. You'll notice that the enclosed harbor area is filled with working fishing boats and colorful dinghies that bob in unison. Along the breakwater, notice the new fishermen's lockers, where people who earn their living from the Adriatic still keep their supplies. You'll see the most fisherman action here in the mornings.

The far side of the breakwater—all glitzy white marble—is another world, with a pebbly beach, inviting plaza, and some of the best views looking back on the Riva. After its recent facelift, this jetty has become a popular open-air, after-hours hangout spot for local young people. Like Split itself, these two worlds—that of grizzled fishermen mending nets, and that of teenagers living it up—coexist more smoothly than anyone might have guessed.

Hiking the Marjan Peninsula—This long, hilly peninsula extends west from the center of Split. With out-of-the-way beaches and lots of hiking trails, this is where Split goes to relax. Ask at the TI (or ask any local) for tips on how to enjoy this area. You can walk around the mostly level perimeter of the peninsula, passing the Meštrović Gallery and two of the beaches (Ježinac and Bene) that are described next. Or, if you're up for a serious hike, hoof it up to the top of the peninsula for views back over the city. You can take the slower, more gradual route up through the lanes of the Varoš neighborhood, or find the steeper steps that lead up from the salty Matejuška harbor. If you're in great shape, figure about an hour hike up to the top (third) viewpoint, then another 45 minutes back down.

Hitting the Beach—Since it's more of a big city than a resort, Split's beaches aren't as scenic (and the water not as clear) as small towns elsewhere along the coast. The beach that's most popular—and crowded—is **Bačvice,** in a sandy cove just a short walk east of the main ferry terminal. As it's very shallow, it's especially popular with kids. After dark, it becomes a hopping meat-market nightlife zone for older "kids." You'll find less crowded beaches just to the east of Bačvice.

Or head in the other direction to Marjan, the peninsular city park, which is ringed with several sunbathing beaches. Along the southern edge of Marjan, just below the Meštrović Gallery, is a rocky but more local-feeling and less crowded beach called **Ježinac** (Croatian for "sea urchin"...be sure to wear water shoes). **Bene Beach** is along the northern edge of Marjan—reachable on bus #12 (the same one that goes to the Meštrović Gallery), by bike, or by foot (about a 45-minute walk from the Old Town).

Nightlife in Split

Strolling the Riva—Every night in Split, the sea of Croatian humanity laps at the walls of Diocletian's Palace along the town's pedestrian promenade. Choose a bench and watch life go by, or enjoy a drink at one of the many outdoor cafés.

Visiting Old Town Pubs— Wander the labyrinthine lanes of the Old Town to find the pub of your choice. The **Luxor** bar, right on the Peristyle, often features live music in the evening, with cushions filling the steps surrounding Diocletian's entry hall (if you sit on a cushion, you're expected to order a drink, but you can sit or stand elsewhere for free). Several atmospheric bars cluster along Majstora Jurja (just inside the Golden Gate and—facing outside—to the left about a block) and near Radić Brothers Square (Trg Braće Radića; from the square's statue of Marulić, enter the Old Town and bear right, following the beat).

Clubbing at Bačvice Beach—This family-friendly beach by day becomes a throbbing party area for young locals late at night. Since all Old Town bars have to close by 1:00 in the morning, night owls hike on over to the Bačvice crescent of clubs. The three-floor club complex is a cacophony of music, with the beat of each club melting into the next—all with breezy terraces overlooking the harbor.

Sleeping in Split

Split's sleeps are expensive. Since there aren't enough beds in peak season, many hoteliers are shameless about gouging their customers. Lower your expectations. Split also suffers from perhaps the worst nighttime noise of any destination in this book—bring earplugs, and always ask for a quiet room (if possible). For locations, all of these are on the "Split Hotels & Restaurants" map on page

---

Sleep Code

(5 kn = about $1, country code: 385, area code: 021)

S = Single, **D** = Double/Twin, **T** = Triple, **Q** = Quad, **b** = bathroom. The modest tourist tax (7 kn per person, per night, lower off-season) is not included in these rates. Hotels generally accept credit cards and include breakfast in their rates, while most *sobe* accept only cash and don't offer breakfast. English is spoken at all my recommended accommodations.

To help you sort easily through these listings, I've divided the rooms into three categories based on the price for a standard double room with bath in peak season:

$$$ Higher Priced—Most rooms 800 kn or more.
$$ Moderately Priced—Most rooms between 550–800 kn.
$ Lower Priced—Most rooms 550 kn or less.

194; some also appear on the more detailed "Diocletian's Palace" map on page 177.

Near the Old Town

These good values are within a five-minute walk of the Old Town. They're nearly as convenient as the Old Town options, but cheaper. Note that none of these places has a full-time reception desk; call ahead to arrange your arrival time.

In the Lučac Neighborhood, East of the Old Town

The drab and dull Lučac neighborhood—which lines up along the busy street called Kralja Zvonimira—feels urban and a bit gritty, but it's handy to the Old Town. You'll find more Old World atmosphere (and the recommended Black Cat Bistro) on Petrova street, a block below the main road.

$$$ Villa Diana has six overpriced, mostly small rooms in a stone house over a restaurant (July–Aug: Sb-760 kn, Db-900 kn; May–June and Sept: Sb-630 kn, Db-765 kn; Oct: Sb-560 kn, Db-670 kn; cheaper Nov–April; pricier apartment also available, air-con, free Wi-Fi, Kuzmanića 3, tel. & fax 021/482-460, www.villadiana.hr, info@villadiana.hr).

$$ Villa Ana, my favorite small hotel in Split, has five modern, comfortable rooms in a smart little freestanding stone house. If they're full, try another one of my listings (April–Oct: Sb-600 kn, Db-750 kn, Tb-850 kn; Nov–March: roughly 150 kn less; includes breakfast, air-con, free Wi-Fi, reception open sporadically 7:00–22:00, may be closed mid-Dec–mid-Jan, a few tight free parking spots out front; 2 long blocks east of Old Town up busy Kralja Zvonimira, follow the driveway-like lane opposite Koteks

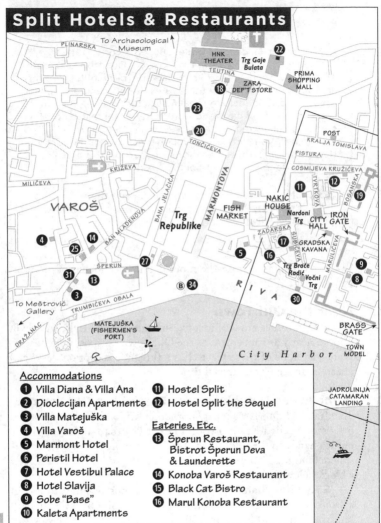

Split Hotels & Restaurants

Accommodations

1 Villa Diana & Villa Ana
2 Dioclecijan Apartments
3 Villa Matejuška
4 Villa Varoš
5 Marmont Hotel
6 Peristil Hotel
7 Hotel Vestibul Palace
8 Hotel Slavija
9 Sobe "Base"
10 Kaleta Apartments
11 Hostel Split
12 Hostel Split the Sequel

Eateries, Etc.

13 Šperun Restaurant, Bistrot Šperun Deva & Launderette
14 Konoba Varoš Restaurant
15 Black Cat Bistro
16 Marul Konoba Restaurant

skyscraper to Vrh Lučac 16; tel. 021/482-715, fax 021/482-721, www.villaana-split.hr, info@villaana-split.hr, Danijel Bilobrk and helpful Branka).

$ Dioclecijan Apartments, run by Tomislav Skalić and his wife Ivana, has two small rooms and one apartment in a pleasant local neighborhood. The decor is a tasteful mix of new and traditional (April–Sept: Db-400 kn, apartment-590 kn; Oct–March: Db-280 kn, apartment-480 kn; 1-night stays cost 40 kn more in rooms or 75 kn more in apartment, prices soft, cash only, no breakfast, air-con, Petrova 19, Tomislav's mobile 091-537-1826, Ivana's

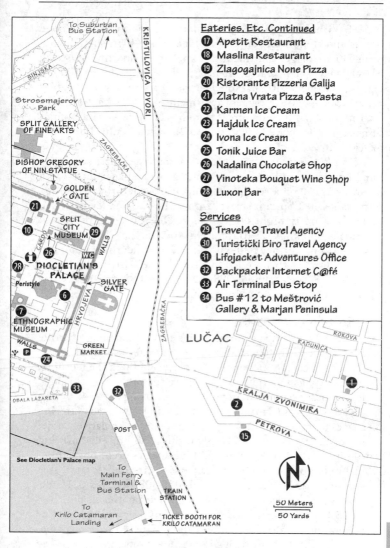

Eateries, Etc. Continued
- ⑰ Apetit Restaurant
- ⑱ Maslina Restaurant
- ⑲ Zlagogajnica None Pizza
- ⑳ Ristorante Pizzeria Galija
- ㉑ Zlatna Vrata Pizza & Pasta
- ㉒ Karmen Ice Cream
- ㉓ Hajduk Ice Cream
- ㉔ Ivona Ice Cream
- ㉕ Tonik Juice Bar
- ㉖ Nadalina Chocolate Shop
- ㉗ Vinoteka Bouquet Wine Shop
- ㉘ Luxor Bar

Services
- ㉙ Travel49 Travel Agency
- ㉚ Turistički Biro Travel Agency
- ㉛ Lifojacket Adventures Office
- ㉜ Backpacker Internet C@fé
- ㉝ Air Terminal Bus Stop
- ㉞ Bus #12 to Meštrović Gallery & Marjan Peninsula

mobile 091-536-7486, tskalic@globalnet.hr). From near the Green Market, head up Kralja Zvonimira, and turn right down Petrova. The apartments are on your left as the road bends.

In the Varoš Neighborhood, West of the Old Town

In addition to hosting the following accommodations, the atmospheric Varoš neighborhood—with twisty lanes climbing up towards the forested peak of the Marjan Peninsula—is also home to several recommended eateries and the local self-service Modrulj Launderette.

$$ Villa Matejuška has six apartments with old-fashioned beams and stone walls on a tight lane (June–Oct: small apartment-740 kn, bigger apartment-810 kn, biggest apartment-935 kn; March–May: small apartment-670 kn, bigger apartment-700 kn, biggest apartment-810 kn; Nov–Feb: small apartment-555 kn, bigger apartment-590 kn, biggest apartment-680 kn; no extra charge for 1-night stays, includes breakfast, air-con, free Wi-Fi, Tomića Stine 3, mobile 098-222-822, www.villamatejuska.hr, info@villa matejuska.hr).

$ Villa Varoš, run with class by Croatian-American Joanne Đonlić and her son Jure, has eight rooms and an apartment (with its own terrace) on a residential lane just beyond the appealing, restaurant-lined Šperun street. Thin walls and echoey halls can make for a noisy night (April–Sept: Db-500 kn, Tb-550 kn, apartment-800 kn; Oct–March: Db-400 kn, Tb-450 kn, apartment-600 kn; optional 20-kn breakfast at nearby restaurant, air-con, stairs with no elevator, free Wi-Fi, Miljenka Smoje 1, tel. 021/483-469, mobile 098-229-408 or 098-469-681, www .villavaros.hr, joanne.d.o.o@st.t-com.hr).

Inside the Old Town

While the Old Town is convenient, it's also a happening nightlife zone, so you're likely to encounter some noise (especially on weekends). Old Town bars are required to close by 1:00 in the morning, so at least things will quiet down before the birds start chirping. To locate these accommodations, see the map on page 194.

$$$ Marmont Hotel is a very inviting new place offering four-star comfort, with 21 mod-feeling rooms in a relatively quiet corner of the Old Town (July–Sept: Sb-1,250 kn, Db-1,670 kn; April–June: Sb-1,070 kn, Db-1,530 kn; Oct–March: Sb-850 kn, Db-1,300 kn; breakfast-75 kn per person, air-con, elevator, free Wi-Fi, sun terrace, Zadarska 13, tel. 021/308-060, fax 021/308-070, www.marmonthotel.com, booking@marmonthotel.com).

$$$ Peristil Hotel has 12 classy rooms over a restaurant just steps from the couldn't-be-more-central square of the same name. Run by the Caktaš family, it's homey and convenient, if pricey (May–Sept: Sb-1,000 kn, Db-1,200 kn; April and Oct: Sb-800 kn, Db-1,000 kn; Nov–March: Sb-700 kn, Db-900 kn; extra bed-100 kn, air-con, stairs with no elevator, free Wi-Fi, some noise from nearby bars, just behind TI and inside the Silver Gate at Poljana Kraljice Jelene 5, tel. 021/329-070, fax 021/329-088, www .hotelperistil.com, hotel.peristil@email.t-com.hr).

$$$ Hotel Vestibul Palace is the swankiest splurge in Split's Old Town, with modern decor in an old shell. Tucked in a corner just behind the entry vestibule on the upper level of Diocletian's Palace, this plush place offers seven rooms with maximum comfort and style for maximum prices. Throughout the day, you'll hear the harmonious voices of the *klapa* singers echoing up from the vestibule below (July–Sept: Sb-1,200–1,420 kn, Db-1,420–1,950 kn; April–June: Sb-1,050–1,250 kn, Db-1,250–1,800 kn; cheaper Oct–March, prices depend on room size and amenities, pricier suites also available, air-con, no elevator, free Internet access and Wi-Fi, valet parking-100 kn, Iza Vestibula 4, tel. 021/329-329, fax 021/329-333, www.vestibulpalace.com, info@vestibulpalace .com). They also have four more rooms in a nearby annex, called Villa Dobrić.

$$$ Hotel Slavija is a lesser value sharing a tiny square with some very popular late-night discos and cafés, so it can be noisy—especially on weekends (double-paned windows attempt, with only some success, to keep out the throbbing dance beat; try requesting a quieter back room). Each of its 25 stark, unimaginative rooms is a little different (June–Sept: Sb-800 kn, Db-1,000 kn, Tb-1,200 kn; March–May and Oct: 100 kn less per room; even cheaper Nov–Feb; 50–250 kn more for balcony or terrace, suites and huge family rooms available, air-con, pay Wi-Fi, a block from Radić Brothers Square at Buvinina 2—look for the low-profile sign at the top of a white staircase, tel. 021/323-840, fax 021/323-868, www .hotelslavija.com, info@hotelslavija.com).

$ Sobe "Base" has three of the nicest rooms in the Old Town. Tina and her dad Ivo offer many amenities unusual for this price range, including free Wi-Fi and Internet terminals in each room. You can't be more central: All of the colorful rooms—located over a gift shop—overlook the front steps of the cute little Jupiter's Temple (July–Aug: Db-510 kn; Sept–June: Db-450 kn; no extra charge for 1- or 2-night stays, cash only, no breakfast, air-con, Kraj Svetog Ivana 3, tel. 021/317-375, Tina's mobile 098-234-855, Ivo's mobile 098-361-387, www.base-rooms.com, mail@base-rooms .com). Because some bustling bars are just around the corner, expect some nighttime noise (even though the double-paned windows do their darnedest to provide silence).

$ Kaleta Apartments consists of two modern, stylish apartments run by the Raić family in a building squeezed between cafés along a tight alley at the back of the Old Town. While it's a lively area, the good windows do a heroic job of keeping the noise to a minimum (June–Sept: Db-500 kn; Oct–May: Db-425 kn; cash only, no breakfast, air-con, free Wi-Fi and Internet terminal in each room, Majstora Jurja 4, mobile 099-509-4299, www.kaleta apartments.hr, kaletaapartments@email.t-com.hr).

$ Other Sobe: Though there are very few *sobe* inside Split's Old Town, there are plenty within a 10-minute walk. As in any coastal town, you can simply show up at the boat dock or bus station, be met by locals trying to persuade you into their rooms, and check out the best offer (about 250 kn for a double). Or you can try booking through a travel agency, such as **Travel49** or **Turistički Biro** (both listed earlier, under "Helpful Hints").

$ Hostel Split is centrally located just off Narodni Trg in the very heart of town. This small, youthful hostel has 23 beds in four cramped rooms, and a shared outdoor terrace to give everyone some much-needed breathing room. Run by a pair of Croat-Aussie women with the simple slogan "booze & snooze," it's Split's most central hostel option (bunk in 6-bed room—June–Sept: 150 kn; mid-April–May: 125 kn; Oct–mid-April: 110 kn; cash only, no breakfast, free Internet access and Wi-Fi, laundry service, excursions, 8 Narodni Trg, tel. 021/342-787, www.splithostel.com, info@splithostel.com). Their second location—Hostel Split the Sequel—has the same prices and a downstairs bar; it's a short walk away, still inside the Old Town (at Kružićeva 5).

Eating in Split

Split's Old Town has oodles of atmosphere, but the street called Šperun, just a couple of blocks west of the Old Town, has several characteristic *konoba*s (traditional restaurants) with good prices (including my first two listings, below). Service in Split's restaurants tends to be a bit grouchy, and you may be unceremoniously turned away if they're very busy (reservations are wise, especially for dinner). All of these eateries are marked on the "Split Hotels & Restaurants" map on page 194; some also appear on the more detailed "Diocletian's Palace" map on page 177.

Šperun Restaurant has a classy, cozy Old World ambience and a passion for good Dalmatian food. Animated owner Zdravko Banović and his son Damir serve a mix of Croatian and "eclectic Mediterranean," specializing in seafood. A "buffet" table of antipasti (starters) in the lower dining room shows you what you're getting, so you can select your ideal meal (not self-service—order from the waiter). This place distinguishes itself by offering a warm welcome and good food for reasonable prices (35–70-kn pastas, 50–120-kn meat and seafood dishes, daily 9:00–23:00, air-con interior, a few sidewalk tables, reservations wise in summer, Šperun 3, tel. 021/346-999). Their annex across the street, **Bistrot Šperun Deva,** has a simpler and cheaper menu, lots of outdoor seating, and a handy à la carte breakfast for *sobe*-dwellers (30–40-kn salads, 50–60-kn main courses, daily 8:00–23:00, Šperun 2).

Konoba Varoš, though bigger and more impersonal than Šperun, is beloved by natives and tourists alike for its great food. Serious waiters serve a wide range of Croatian cooking (including pastas, seafood, and meat dishes) under droopy fishnets in a slightly gloomy throwback interior (50–80-kn pastas, 60–110-kn main courses, daily 9:00–24:00, lots of groups, reservations smart—busiest 20:00–22:00, Ban Mladenova 7, tel. 021/396-138).

Black Cat Bistro, popular with expats, is an innovative eatery offering a range of eclectic flavors, including Tex-Mex, Indian, and Thai—and all are reasonably well-executed. The menu also features several hearty salads that go beyond the cabbage-and-lettuce rut, and breakfast for *sobe*-dwellers (7–16-kn continental breakfast, 16–30-kn cooked breakfast). Choose between the inviting covered terrace out on a local-feeling lane, or the nondescript interior (45–65-kn salads and main courses, 30–35-kn sandwiches and wraps, Mon–Sat 8:00–23:00, closed Sun, corner of Petrova and Šegvića, tel. 021/490-284). It's about a five-minute walk beyond the Old Town: From the Green Market, walk up Kralja Zvonimira and take the first right down Petrova (just past the big, white building); you'll see the restaurant on your right just after the road curves to the left.

Apetit is a new place serving up traditional, home-cooked Dalmatian cuisine in an appealingly modern, second-floor dining room. As there's no outdoor seating, this is a good option in bad weather (45–70-kn pastas, 60–110-kn main courses; 90-kn daily special in summer includes soup, salad, and main dish; daily 9:00–24:00, Šubićeva 5, tel. 021/332-549).

Marul Konoba offers traditional Dalmatian cuisine with delightful outdoor seating on a fine Old Town square, or in an atmospheric, oak-and-stone interior (45–65-kn pastas, 65–110-kn main courses, daily 8:00–24:00, Trg Braće Radića 2, tel. 021/339-068).

Maslina ("Olive"), an unpretentious family-run spot filled with locals, hides behind a shopping mall on the busy Marmontova pedestrian street. They serve a wide range of 40–70-kn pizzas and pastas, plus 65–110-kn meat and fish dishes (Tue–Sat 10:00–24:00, Sun–Mon 12:00–24:00, Teutina 1A, tel. 021/314-988, Pezo family). Approaching the top of Marmontova from the harbor, look for the low-profile wooden archway on the left beyond the café tables (just before the big Zara department store).

Take-Away Pizza: Zlagogajnica None ("Grandma's") is a stand-up or take-away pizza joint handy for a quick bite in the Old Town. In addition to pizzas and bruschettas with various toppings, they serve up a pair of traditional pizza-like specialties (with crust on bottom and top, like a filled pizza): *viška pogača,* with tomatoes, onion, and anchovy; and *soparnik,* with a thin layer of spinach, onion, and olive oil. They can also make you a grilled sandwich—just point to what you want (10–30 kn, Mon–Sat 7:00–23:00, closed Sun, just outside Diocletian's Palace on the skinny street that runs along the wall at Bosanska 4, tel. 021/347-252).

SPLIT

Pizzerias: **Ristorante Pizzeria Galija,** at the west end of the Old Town, has a boisterous local following and good wood-fired pizza, pasta, and salads (35–50 kn, Mon–Sat 9:00–24:00, Sun 12:00–24:00, air-con, just a block off of the pedestrian drag Marmontova at Tončićeva 12, tel. 021/347-932; the recommended Hajduk ice-cream shop is nearby). **Zlatna Vrata** ("Golden Gate"), right in the Old Town, offers wood-fired pizzas and pasta dishes. The food and interior are nothing special, but there's wonderful outdoor seating in a tingle-worthy Gothic courtyard with pointy arches and lots of pillars (40–60 kn, Mon–Sat 7:00–24:00, closed Sun, just inside the Golden Gate and—as you face outside—up the skinny alley to the left, on Majstora Jurja, tel. 021/345-015).

Gelato: Split has several spots for delicious ice cream *(sladoled).* Most ice-cream parlors *(kuća sladoleda)* are open daily 8:00–24:00. To my taste buds, the following three spots are much better than the other options in town. Locals swarm to a pair of places near Trg Gaje Bulata (the modern shopping square—with the big Prima mall and modern-looking church—at the top end of the Marmontova pedestrian drag, just beyond the northwest corner of the Old Town): **Karmen** (hides behind the building in the middle of the square, facing the modern church on Kačićeva) and **Hajduk** (named for Split's soccer team; ask them to dip your cone in milk chocolate for no extra charge; a block west from the top of Marmontova and around the corner from Pizzeria Galija at Matošićeva 4). More central, at the east end of the Riva, look for **Ivona** (near entrance to Diocletian's cellars at Kaštelanska cesta 65).

Smoothies and Fruit Juices: For a healthier energy boost, head for **Tonik Juice Bar,** run by Croat-Aussie Stefanie. You can select from the diverse smoothie menu (25–30 kn), or they'll custom-make a juice combo to your liking (15–40 kn). In summer, they also serve light meals (25-kn wraps and salads, 25-kn muesli for breakfast, June–Sept daily 7:00–23:00, shoulder season 8:00–21:00, less in winter, near the launderette and Šperun street restaurants at Ban Mladenova 5, mobile 098-641-376).

Split Connections

Boat Connections

As the transport hub for the Dalmatian Coast, Split has good boat connections to most anywhere you want to go. Big car ferries use the main ferry terminal at the end of the harbor. The fast passenger catamarans dock a bit closer to the Old Town: the *Krilo* catamaran uses dock #11, which is along the pier halfway between the main ferry terminal and the Old Town. The Jadrolinija catamaran arrives and departs at the handy Obala Lazareta embankment just in front of the Old Town.

Schedules: Be warned that the following boat information is subject to change—always confirm before you make your plans.

To check Jadrolinija schedules, see www.jadrolinija.hr; for *Krilo* catamaran schedules, see www.krilo .hr. Split's helpful Jadrolinija boat ticket office is in the main ferry terminal (open 24/7 in summer, daily 4:15–24:00 off-season, tel. 021/338-333; see "Arrival in Split," page 169), several smaller branch offices are scattered between there and the Old Town. You can buy *Krilo* tickets at the small Jadrolinija kiosk halfway along the harbor, near where that catamaran departs.

Buying Tickets: Tickets for the fast passenger catamarans (either *Krilo* or Jadrolinija) are not sold until 6:00 in the morning on the day of departure. As these boats can sell out quickly in peak season, buy your tickets in the morning (for the 11:30 boat, try to get your tickets by 9:30; for afternoon boats, buy your tickets by noon). If you're a passenger walking onto a car ferry, there's no need to buy tickets in advance. However, if you're driving onto a car ferry, it's smart to buy your tickets and line up early—ask locally about the best advice for your particular boat. For the connections below, I've listed the passenger fare.

Big Jadrolinija Car Ferries: These hulking boats depart twice weekly year-round; they leave Split early in the morning (at 6:30 or 7:00) and head south, stopping at **Stari Grad** on Hvar Island (20-min bus ride from Hvar town; 1.75 hrs, 40 kn; the catamarans described next are faster and take you right to Hvar town), **Korčula town** (5–6 hrs, 97 kn), and **Dubrovnik** (8–9.25 hrs, 115 kn). You can also sleep on the boat as it heads north to **Rijeka** (2/week, 11 hrs overnight, 162-kn deck passage, more if you want a bed). Fares are cheaper off-season.

Other Boats to Hvar Island: Ideally, catch a boat heading to Hvar town, the most interesting part of the island. Speedy **Jadrolinija catamarans** run daily year-round from Split to Hvar town (June–Sept: 2/day, departing Split at 11:30 and 15:00, costs 42 kn in the morning or 22 kn in the afternoon; Oct–May: 1/day, departing Split at 14:00, 50–60 min to Hvar town, 22 kn; occasionally stops at Milna on Brač Island). A different company runs the similar *Krilo* catamaran directly from Split to Hvar town (June–Sept: departs Split daily at 17:00; Oct–May: departs Split daily at 16:00, 50–60 min to Hvar town, 22 kn). You can also reach Hvar Island on the **local car ferries** from Split; these are frequent but more expensive and less convenient, since they take you to the

Sailing Between Croatia and Italy

Many travelers are tempted to splice a little bit of Croatia into their Italian itinerary, or vice versa. But zipping across the Adriatic isn't as effortless as it seems. Most sea crossings involve an overnight on the boat, and the Italian towns best connected to Croatia—Ancona, Pescara, and Bari—are far from Italy's top sights. Plan thoughtfully. For example, if you're in northern Italy and want to sample Croatia, it's much easier to dip into Istria than it is to get all the way down to Croatia's Dalmatian Coast.

If you decide to set sail, you have several options, run by various companies. Split is the primary hub, but you can also go from other cities (usually Dubrovnik or Zadar; some international ferries also call at the small Dalmatian islands). Almost all boats go to Ancona, Italy, which is about two-thirds of the way up the Italian coast (on the calf of Italy's "boot"). Others go to Pescara, about 100 miles south of Ancona; and to Bari, near the southern tip of Italy (the "heel"). Most trips are overnight and last 8–10 hours, but there are faster daytime catamarans. Note that these connections are highly subject to change from year to year— consider doing an Internet search on your own to be confident you know all of your options.

Slow Night Boats: Figure about €55 per person for one-way deck passage (about 10–20 percent more in peak season, roughly July–Aug; sometimes even more on weekends). Onboard accommodation costs extra (about €20 per person for a couchette in a 4-berth compartment, €60–75 per person in 2-bed compartment with private shower and WC). Three different companies operate night boats to Italy:

Jadrolinija goes from Split to Ancona, from Zadar to Ancona, and from Dubrovnik to Bari (tel. 051/211-444 or 021/338-333, www.jadrolinija.hr).

Blue Line sails from Split to Ancona; on weekends in late July–Aug, it stops en route at either Stari Grad (on Hvar Island) or Vis Island (can book at Split Tours travel agency in Split, tel.

---

town of Stari Grad, across the island from Hvar town (3–7/day, 1.75 hrs, 38 kn; from Stari Grad, it's an easy 20-minute bus trip into Hvar town).

Other Boats to Korčula Island: Many of the same boats that go to Hvar town (described previously) continue on to Korčula Island. The most convenient is the *Krilo* catamaran, which takes you right to Korčula town (June–Sept: departs Split daily at 17:00; Oct–May: departs Split daily at 16:00; 2.5–2.75 hrs to Korčula, 55 kn; in summer, it also stops en route at Prigradica on Korčula Island). The other boats leave you at Vela Luka, at the far end of Korčula Island from Korčula town (buses meet arriving boats to take passengers on the one-hour trip into Korčula town). The

021/352-533, www.blueline-ferries.com).

Azzurraline goes between Bari and Dubrovnik, and between Bari and Kotor, Montenegro (Croatian tel. 020/313-178, Montenegrin tel. 085/313-617, Italian tel. 080-592-8400, www.azzurraline.com).

Other companies serving these routes come and go each year—ask the Split TI or poke around Split's main terminal building to discover the latest.

Fast Daytime Boats: Some speedier crossings are available. But because these boats are faster and smaller, they're also weather-dependent—so they don't run off-season. In 2009, due to decreased demand, these boats ran only in August—check online for the 2010 schedule. **SNAV** connects Split and Ancona in just 4.5 hours; they also zip from Split to Stari Grad (on Hvar Island), then on to the Italian town of Pescara (6 hrs total; either trip €60-100 one-way, depending on season; Croatian tel. 021/322-252, Italian tel. 081-428-5555, www.snav.it).

Trains Within Italy: From **Ancona,** you can catch a train to Venice (almost hourly, 4.25-5.25 hrs, most transfer in Bologna), Florence (almost hourly, 3-4.25 hrs, most transfer in Bologna), or Rome (8/day direct, 3-4.5 hrs) From **Pescara,** trains head to Rome (6/day direct, 3.75-4.25 hrs) and Florence (almost hourly, 4.5-5.25 hrs, transfer in Bologna). From **Bari,** you can hop a train to Naples (6/day, 3.75-6 hrs, most transfer in Caserta), Rome (3/day direct, 4.75 hrs), or Florence (8/day, 6.75-8.5 hrs, transfer in Rome or Bologna). For timetables, check www.ferroviedellostato.it or http://bahn.hafas.de/bin/query.exe/en (Germany's excellent all-Europe website).

Northern Italy/Croatia: Venice is connected by boat to several seaside towns in northern Croatia and Slovenia. For details, see page 93.

Note that in Italian, Split is called "Spalato" (which is also the sound you hear if seasickness gets the best of you).

Jadrolinija catamaran goes from Split to Hvar town, then to Vela Luka (departs Split at 15:00 June–Sept, at 14:00 Oct–May, 1.75 hrs to Vela Luka, 27 kn, occasionally stops at Mlina on Brač Island). Jadrolinija's slower **local car ferries** also go from Split to Vela Luka (1–2/day, 2.75 hrs, 46 kn).

Sailing to Italy: See the sidebar.

Overland Connections

By Bus to: Zagreb (at least hourly, 5–8 hrs, depending on route, about 175–200 kn), **Dubrovnik** (almost hourly, less off-season, 4–5 hrs, 105–155 kn), **Korčula** (1 night bus leaves at 1:00 in the morning and arrives at 6:00, 125 kn), **Trogir** (at least hourly, 30 min, about 20 kn), **Zadar** (at least hourly, 3 hrs, about 75 kn), **Mostar** in Bosnia-Herzegovina (7/day, 4–4.5 hrs), **Međugorje** in Bosnia-Herzegovina (4/day, 3.5 hrs), **Rijeka** (10/day including some night buses, 8.5 hrs). Zagreb-bound buses sometimes also stop at **Plitvice** (confirm with driver and ask him to stop at the national park entrance; about 5/day, 4–6 hrs, 130–155 kn). Each of these routes is served by multiple companies, which charge slightly different rates, so the prices listed here are rough estimates. Reservations for buses are generally not necessary, but always ask about the fastest option—which can save hours of bus time. On busy peak-season days, it's smart to arrive about 30 minutes before your bus departs to buy tickets (or, better yet, come to the station to buy them earlier in the day). The generally English-speaking staff at Split's bus station gives out handy little schedules for popular journeys. Bus info: www.ak-split.hr, toll tel. 060-327-777.

By Train to: Zagreb (3/day, 2/day off-season, 5.5 hrs, plus 1 direct night train, 8 hrs), **Ljubljana** (1/day, 8.25 hrs, transfer in Zagreb). Train info: tel. 021/338-525 or toll tel. 060-333-444, www.hznet.hr.

Route Tips for Drivers: Driving in Dalmatia

If you're connecting Split with destinations to the north, the plan is simple: Just drive up out of the city's bowl-like setting and follow signs to the A-1 expressway north (toward Zagreb).

If you're heading south—such as to Dubrovnik, other Dalmatian Coast destinations, or Mostar—it's a bit more complicated, as the expressway southbound from Split is only partially completed (to check the latest progress, see www.hac.hr or www.hak.hr). You have two options. The main **coastal road** twists slowly but scenically along some fantastic scenery, in an area dubbed the "Makarska Riviera." From the town of Drvenik, a ferry plods across to Sućuraj on the island of Hvar, where a surprisingly long and twisty road traverses the length of the island to Hvar town at the opposite end (taking a car ferry directly from Split to Stari Grad on Hvar island is a far faster and less stressful option). Continuing south, you'll wind up in the town of Ploče (described below).

To save some time, most travelers prefer to take the **expressway** part of the way. To do this, as you leave Split, follow blue expressway signs to *Dubrovnik*. You can take A-1 south as far as it goes; it cuts inland from the sea, running behind the tall coastal mountain range, near the Bosnian border. As of early 2010, A-1 was complete to the remote town of Vrgorac, about 100 km (60 miles) south of Split; a small section around the coastal town of Ploče, about 25 km (15 miles) south of Vrgorac, was also complete. To connect Vrgorac to Ploče, you'll transfer to rough and rugged surface roads, or—once A-1 is finished—stay on the expressway the entire way. (Note that if you're headed to Mostar, the fastest way from here is to pass into Bosnia-Herzegovina just south of Vrgorac, at Veliki Prolog, then follow signs to *Mostar* from there.)

Ploče has a ferry that runs to the town of Trpanj, on the landward side of the Pelješac Peninsula—not far from Orebić, where another boat plods across to Korčula town. If you're headed to Korčula and plan your timing to catch this ferry, it could save you some driving.

Just south of Ploče is the dramatic Neretva River Delta, a scenic and lush zone of farmland (described on page 344)—and, likely, the end of the A-1 expressway. Here you'll hop on the main Dalmatian coastal road. Halfway along the delta, you'll see the turnoff to Metković, the gateway town on the main, heavily touristed road between Croatia and Mostar.

South of the Neretva River Delta—after twisting up to a high perch overlooking the delta—you'll reach a border crossing. Here begins an odd little stretch of coastline that's technically in Bosnian rather than Croatian territory. Have your passport ready, but don't panic—the border is generally a quick wave-through. You'll drive along the tiny Bosnian coast, then through the large town of Neum. Its giant concrete hotels are a clue to Neum's reputation as a cut-rate seaside destination that undersells its nearby Croatian coastal competitors. (Age-old tensions combined with pragmatic economic concerns have prompted some Croatian politicians to push for the construction of a bridge from the coastal road to the Pelješac Peninsula, allowing drivers to bypass Bosnia-Herzegovina entirely; you might see some work already going on for this project. For details, see page 308.)

After a few more miles, you'll cross back into Croatia, and shortly come to a crossroads where, if you like, you can turn right and detour a few minutes to the impressively walled little villages of Ston and Mali Ston (described on page 307), at the base of the Pelješac Peninsula. If you're headed to Korčula, continue beyond Ston to the far end of the peninsula, where the ferry goes from Orebić to Dominče, near Korčula town.

After Ston, you're only about an hour from Dubrovnik. Along the way, you'll have fine views of Mljet and the Elaphite Islands. As you're getting close to Dubrovnik, you'll pass through the town of Trsteno, which has a good arboretum (described on page 306). When you cross the giant, modern bridge, you'll know Dubrovnik is just around the bend; for arrival tips, see "Arrival in Dubrovnik," on page 252.

SPLIT

Near Split: Trogir

Just 12 miles northwest of Split across a giant bay is Trogir, a tiny, medieval-architecture-packed town surrounded by water. This made-for-tourists village lacks the real-world heart and soul of Split, and it's reminiscent of a dozen other Croatian coastal resort towns (Hvar and Korčula are bigger and better—see the next two chapters). But its proximity to Split makes it appealing to yachters; the proud masts of tall ships line the harbor three deep. For me, Trogir is nothing to jump ship for, but it's an easy day trip for those looking to get away from urban Split.

Getting There: The easiest option in summer is to take the Sestrice **boat,** which avoids traffic and includes a mini-cruise on the Adriatic. The boat departs from the embankment in front of the Riva (20 kn, 4/day June–mid-Sept only, 1 hr, stops at Čiovo Island en route, www .buraline.com).

You also have two bus options for reaching Trogir from Split, both roughly the same price (20–25 kn): The faster, easier option is to take a bus from Split's **main bus station,** next to the City Harbor. Any bus going north (for example, to Šibenik, Zadar, or even Rijeka) will usually stop at Trogir (2/hr, about 30 min, simply go to ticket window and ask for next bus to Trogir). Note that in the busiest summer months, some long-distance bus drivers may not want to take you (preferring to give your seat instead to someone paying for a longer trip). The other, slower option is **local bus #37.** But, because this bus makes several stops along the way, it can take longer (45–60 min, depending on traffic; 3/hr Mon–Fri, 2/hr Sat–Sun; departs Split's suburban bus station—Prigradski Autobusni Kolodvor, a 10-min walk north of Old Town on Domovinskog rata; buy 20-kn ticket for zone IV at ticket window or on bus). Note that bus #37 also stops at the **airport** on its way between Split and Trogir; if you're sleeping in Trogir before catching a flight, this bus is handy (about 10 min from Trogir; taxis from Trogir to the airport are exhorbitantly priced).

Orientation to Trogir

Trogir is a small island, wedged between the mainland and the much bigger Čiovo Island. Busy bridges connect it to the rest of the world at its east end, and a big soccer field squeezed between imposing watchtowers anchors the west end. In the middle is a tight medieval maze of twisty marble-stone lanes.

Arrival in Trogir: Buses drop you off at the mainland market, just across the canal from the island. Cross the bridge into town and wander straight ahead for two blocks (bearing left); you'll run into the main square.

Tourist Information: At the main square, named for Pope John Paul II (Trg Ivana Pavla II), you'll find the TI (mid-June–Aug Mon–Sat 8:00–23:00, Sun 8:00–12:00; Sept–mid-June Mon–Fri 8:00–20:00, Sat 8:00–13:00, closed Sun; tel. 021/885-628).

Sights in Trogir

On the main square is the town's centerpiece, the **Cathedral of St. Lawrence** (Katedrala Sv. Lovre). Built from the 13th through the 17th centuries, the cathedral drips with history. The bell tower alone took 200 years to build, leaving it a textbook lesson in Dalmatian architecture styles: straightforward Gothic at the bottom, Venetian Gothic in the middle, and Renaissance at the top. The cathedral's front entryway—the ornately decorated, recently restored Radovan's Portal—is worth a gander. Inside, it's dark, very old-feeling, and packed with altars. The treasury features some beautiful 15th-century carved-wood cabinets filled with ecclesiastical art and gear.

The town's other sights are the **Town Museum** (Muzej Grada), a few blocks north (toward the mainland) from the main square; and the **Monastery of St. Nikola** (Samostan Sv. Nikole), a few blocks south (toward Čiovo Island).

But Trogir isn't for museum-going; it's for aimless strolling. And the best place for that is along the wide, beautifully manicured **harborfront promenade** along the southern edge of town (Obala bana Berislavića). Lined with expensive restaurants, and clogged with giddy, ice-cream-licking tourists, this promenade is the highlight of a visit to Trogir. Often the enormous yachts of the rich and famous put in here, giving wanderers something to gaze at and yak about. At the far end of the promenade, the **Kamerlengo Fortress** has a lookout tower with fine views over the town and region.

Sleeping in Trogir

Some travelers prefer sleepy Trogir to bustling Split. But, since Trogir is also lively after-hours, and is in the airport's flight path, it's not the quietest place in Dalmatia.

$$$ Hotel Pašike is a family-run place with lots of character. Situated over a restaurant in the Old Town, its 14 rooms come with over-the-top traditional formality (July–Aug: Sb-650 kn, Db-800; May–June and Sept: Sb-550 kn, Db-700 kn; prices 20–30 percent less off-season, 10 kn cheaper if you pay cash or stay longer than 3 nights, air-con, free Internet access and Wi-Fi, ulica Sinjska, tel. 021/885-185, mobile 091-484-8434, www.hotelpasike.com, info @hotelpasike.com, Buble family).

$$ Hotel Concordia, with 11 outmoded, slightly overpriced rooms at the end of the embankment, is run with warmth by the Bulum family (July–Aug: Sb-450 kn, small Db with view or bigger Db without view-600 kn, big Db with view-730 kn; Sept–June: Sb-450 kn, small Db with view or bigger Db without view-550 kn, big Db with view-650 kn; only partially open in winter, includes breakfast, air-con, free Wi-Fi, Obala bana Berislavića 22, tel. 021/ 885-400, fax 021/885-401, www.concordia-hotel.net, concordia -hotel@st.t-com.hr).

$ Palaća Stafileo has three apartments in a 15th-century Venetian palace buried in a quiet part of town. Well-run by gentle Thomas, it's the best *sobe* option I've seen in Trogir (July–Sept: Db-450 kn; May–June and Oct: Db-400 kn; Nov–April: Db-350 kn; cash only, no breakfast, air-con, lots of stairs, ulica Šubićeva, tel. 021/885-680, mobile 098-131-3171, www.trogironline.com /stafileo, stafileo@vip.hr).

$ Hostel Trogir is a basic, institutional-feeling hostel with four dorm rooms on Čiovo Island, a 10-minute walk across the bridge from downtown Trogir (bunk in 6- to 8-bed dorm-100 kn, air-con, free Internet access, Trg Sv. Jakova 7, tel. 021/884-916, mobile 091-579-2190, www.hosteltrogir.com, hosteltrogir@yahoo .com).

HVAR

Hvar is a rising star in the tourism world. Each year, another magazine or TV show includes it on a list of "world's top 10 most beautiful islands," and a young, international, jet-set crowd whispers its name as the next big thing. Hvar's hip cachet, upscale-ritzy "Croatian Riviera" buzz, and easy proximity to Split have quickly turned this tidy little fishing village into one of the most popular destinations on the Dalmatian Coast.

The island's main town, also called Hvar, lacks the fortified mini-Dubrovnik feel of rival Korčula—Hvar's straightforward Old Town melts into the harbor instead of dominating it. But as you get to know it, Hvar reveals itself to be a fun-loving, easy-going place to be on vacation. Its quirky museums, while far from time-consuming, are enjoyable. The formidable fortress hovering above town provides restless beach bums with a good excuse for a hike and rewards hikers with stunning views. And if you're seeking nightlife, you'll find that happening Hvar can become a party town after hours.

Hvar is aggressively courting the big-money yachting crowd. This means that its hotels and restaurants are pricier than other Croatian destinations (including famous towns like Dubrovnik). And who sails into town on a yacht? Celebrities. Locals claim their laid-back attitude is perfect for high-profile visitors who just want to be left alone.

History? Sure, Hvar's got that, too. Its tongue-twisting name comes from the ancient Greek settlement here: Pharos. Greeks from the island of Paros migrated here in the fourth century B.C., attracted by the fertile farmland. Since then, it's been occupied by Slavs, Venetians, Habsburgs, and—today—tourists, all of whom have left their mark.

But the town is just the beginning. Hvar Island—which insists it's both the sunniest and greenest in Dalmatia—entertains those who stay here long enough to do some exploring. Known for its fragrant fields of lavender and its red and white wines (grapes love the island's perfect combination of wind and sunshine), Hvar Island's gentle climate is appreciated by tourists and farmers alike. Every corner and cove of Hvar has something to offer, but for speedy tourists, the most obvious and easiest side-trip from Hvar town is the Pakleni Islands, a small archipelago just offshore.

Planning Your Time

Don't overdo the Dalmatian islands. On a quick visit, overnighting on one island is enough—choose either Hvar or Korčula, and give it at least two nights and a full day. With a longer visit and a vacation mentality, sleep in both towns.

If time is short, well-connected Hvar is easier to see on the run (for example, a few hours en route between Split and Korčula). But if you're day-tripping here, note that most sights (except the fortress) close for afternoon siesta at 12:00.

With a full day on Hvar, do your sightseeing in the morning, before the weather gets too hot and while the sights are open. Then use the rest of the day to relax, swim at the beaches, explore the Old Town, hike up to the fortress, or take a trip out to Palmižana on the Pakleni Islands (this excursion works well in the late afternoon—take a dip while it's still hot, then hike over to Vlaka for your dinner reservation at Dionis).

Be warned that July and especially August are peak-of-the-peak season. When you ask locals about crowds in August, they roll their eyes and groan. It can be impossible to find a room, and the "undiscovered" back lanes and "hidden" offshore islands are jam-packed with tourists. In August, consider giving Hvar a miss. Conversely, the town is completely dead off-season (roughly mid-Oct–mid-May)—many hotels, restaurants, and even museums shut their doors for winter hibernation. The best times to visit Hvar are mid-May through the end of June, and September through mid-October.

Orientation to Hvar

(area code: 021)

First off, "Hvar" is pronounced like it's spelled, but the H is nearly silent. If you struggle with it, just say "var" (but don't say "huh-var," which just sounds silly to locals).

Hvar town (with about 4,000 residents) clusters around its harbor. The harbor's eastern embankment (to the right, with your

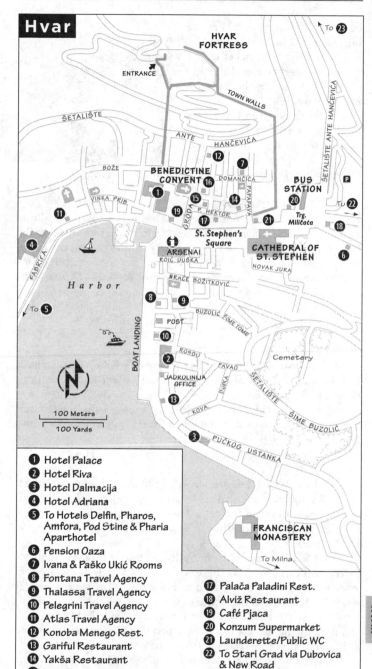

Hvar

HVAR FORTRESS

ENTRANCE

TOWN WALLS

ŠETALIŠTE

ANTE HANČEVIĆA

BOŽE

BENEDICTINE CONVENT

DOMANČIĆA

BUS STATION

VINKA PRIB

GRODA

P. HEKTOR

PATAFAVA

Trg. Miličaća

FABRICA

St. Stephen's Square

ŠETALIŠTE ANTE HANČEVIĆA

To ⑤

Harbor

ARSENAL

KOIĆ DUŠKA

CATHEDRAL OF ST. STEPHEN

NOVAK JURA

BRAĆE BOŽITKOVIĆ

BOAT LANDING

BUZOLIĆ ŠIME TOME

POST

ROSDU

FAVAO

Cemetery

ŠETALIŠTE ŠIME BUZOLIĆ

JADROLINIJA OFFICE

KOVA DURA

100 Meters

100 Yards

PUČKOG USTANKA

FRANCISCAN MONASTERY

To Milna

- ❶ Hotel Palace
- ❷ Hotel Riva
- ❸ Hotel Dalmacija
- ❹ Hotel Adriana
- ❺ To Hotels Delfin, Pharos, Amfora, Pod Stine & Pharia Aparthotel
- ❻ Pension Oaza
- ❼ Ivana & Paško Ukić Rooms
- ❽ Fontana Travel Agency
- ❾ Thalassa Travel Agency
- ❿ Pelegrini Travel Agency
- ⓫ Atlas Travel Agency
- ⓬ Konoba Menego Rest.
- ⓭ Gariful Restaurant
- ⓮ Yakša Restaurant
- ⓯ Luna Restaurant
- ⓰ Macondo Restaurant
- ⓱ Palača Paladini Rest.
- ⓲ Alviž Restaurant
- ⓳ Café Pjaca
- ⓴ Konzum Supermarket
- ㉑ Launderette/Public WC
- ㉒ To Stari Grad via Dubovica & New Road
- ㉓ To Stari Grad via Velo Grablje & Old Road

HVAR

back to the water) is where the
big boats put in, and is home to
the Jadrolinija boat ticket office,
most travel agencies, and the post
office. At the top of the harbor is
Hvar's long, wide main square,
St. Stephen's Square (Trg Svetog
Stjepana). The Old Town scam-
pers up the hills in either direction from St. Stephen's Square.

Overlooking the town and harbor is a mighty hilltop fortress.

Tourist Information

Hvar's informative, no-nonsense TI is in the big Arsenal building
right on the main square, a few steps from the harbor. Pick up the
helpful free map, ask about events, and consider buying the 50-kn
mini-guidebook. Confirm details for your day trips and ferry connections (mid-June–Aug daily 8:00–14:00 & 15:00–22:00; May–
mid-June and Sept–Oct Mon–Sat 8:00–14:00 & 16:00–20:00,
Sun 8:00–12:00; Nov–April Mon–Sat 8:00–14:00, closed Sun; Trg
Svetog Stjepana, tel. 021/741-059, www.tzhvar.hr).

Arrival in Hvar

By Boat: Passenger boats to **Hvar town** arrive on the harbor's
eastern embankment. Simply exit and walk to the left—you'll run
right into St. Stephen's Square.

Car ferries to Hvar Island (including the big Jadrolinija coastal
ferries) arrive just outside the town of **Stari Grad,** across the island
from Hvar town. Buses are timed to meet arriving boats and take
passengers over the island's picturesque spine to Hvar town (20
min, 20 kn).

By Bus: Hvar's bus station is just beyond the far end of St.
Stephen's Square from the harbor. As you get off your bus, you can
see the main tower of the cathedral—marking the town center, a
two-minute walk away. The island's few **taxis** usually hang out at
the bus station.

By Car: Car ferries from Split and most other destinations
arrive on Hvar island at the town of Stari Grad. There are two
ways to drive from Stari Grad to Hvar town: the speedy, newer
road via Dubovica to the south; or the slower, windy road (through
prettier, less-traveled terrain) via Brusje to the north. In Hvar, you
can park by the bus station. Be warned that the car ferries can be
crowded in summer—waiting two hours or more is not unusual.

There's a second ferry crossing at the opposite tip of Hvar
island, connecting the island's settlement of Sućuraj to the mainland town of Drvenik. But be warned that the road connecting

Sućuraj to Hvar town is long, twisty, and challenging to drive—most visitors prefer arriving and departing at Stari Grad instead.

Helpful Hints

Live Music: The Hvar Summer Festival fills the entire peak season (mid-May–mid-Oct) with frequent concerts. Ask the TI for a Summer Festival *Program* with the latest schedule.

Addresses: Everyone in Hvar ignores numbers (you'll constantly see *b.b.*, meaning "without number") and even street names. Navigate with maps (a good one is available free at the TI) and by asking locals for directions.

Post Office: It's along the harbor's main (eastern) embankment, inside a little fenced courtyard (Mon–Fri 7:00–20:00, Sat 7:00–14:00, closed Sun).

Laundry: Hvar has a rare and expensive self-service launderette. You'll find it at the public toilets under the market on the main square (no joke—look for big, blue *toillet* sign; 50-kn wash, 40-kn dry; unpredictable hours, but generally daily June–Aug 6:00–23:00, May and Sept–Oct 8:00–14:00 & 15:00–19:00, Nov–April 8:00–14:00 & 15:00–18:00; to the left as you face the cathedral at Trg Svetog Stjepana 1). If you're day-tripping here and want to swim in the sea, note that this place also has pay showers (25 kn).

Boat Tickets: You can get tickets for most connections at the **Jadrolinija office** (open long hours daily in summer but closed 13:00–15:00 or 12:00–14:00 and Sun after 13:00, along the embankment where the big boats put in, tel. 021/741-132). To buy tickets for the *Krilo* catamaran to Split or Korčula, you'll have to go to the **Pelegrini** travel agency at the opposite end of Hotel Riva (tel. 021/742-743, www.pelegrini-hvar.hr, pelegrini@inet.hr).

Summer Fun: You name it, Hvar has it. Various agencies in town rent cars, scooters, bikes, motorboats, and more—just look for signs or ask at the TI.

Sights in Hvar

▲▲St. Stephen's Square (Trg Svetog Stjepana)—Hvar's main square, which is supposedly Dalmatia's biggest, is a relaxed and relaxing people zone surrounded by inviting cafés filled with deliriously sun-baked tourists. For a quick tour, begin by the harbor and face the cathedral.

To your right is the **Arsenal** building (housing the TI)—a reminder of Hvar's nautical importance through history, thanks to its ideal location on the sailing route between Venice and the Mediterranean. During the town's seafaring heyday, ships were repaired and supplied in this huge building that still dominates the town. Today the Arsenal is nearing the end of a very lengthy and costly renovation. It might be finished in time for your visit; ask at the TI if there's anything to see inside. From near the TI, you can climb the stairs up to the terrace atop the Arsenal for fine views over the square.

Many of Hvar's buildings date from the 16th and 17th centuries, when it was an important outpost of the Venetian Republic. Facing the cathedral, notice that the Old Town spreads out in two directions. During the Venetian period, the population was segregated along this axis. To the left lived the well-to-do patricians, protected within the city wall (looking up the hill to the fortress, you can see the crenellated walls reaching down to embrace this neighborhood). To the right, outside the wall, dwelled the humble plebeians—who worked hard and paid high taxes, but had no say in government. In the 16th century, these two populations came to blows, scuffling sporadically over the course of a century. The Venetians finally decided enough was enough and sent a moderator to restore peace...and this medieval Dr. Phil pulled it off. As a symbol of the reconciliation, part of the Arsenal building was converted into a **communal theater.** Built in 1612, this was the first municipal theater in Europe. It still serves this purpose.

Across the square from the Arsenal, the building with the arches and tower is the **Loggia,** all that remains of a 15th-century palace for the rector (who ruled the island as a representative of Venice). This was the town's court of justice, and important decisions were announced from the stepped pillar in front (with the flagpole). This pillar also served as the town pillory, for publicly humiliating prisoners. During Habsburg control in the early 20th century, most of the palace was torn down to build the town's first resort hotel; today, that building—appropriately called the Palace Hotel—still stands just behind the Loggia.

Walk toward the cathedral, stopping at the first big gap on the left. You can see the top of a never-finished **Venetian palace,** with its distinctive Venetian-style windows. A descendant of the former owner recently bought back this palace, with plans to restore it. But workers began to uncover layer after layer of Hvar's history: blocks of stone from the Greek island of Paros, Illyrian coins, and Roman mosaics. The renovation is planned to continue and may include a small museum to display artifacts found during construction. If you were to head two blocks up this street, you'd run into the yellow Benedictine Convent and its loveable lace museum; if you continued beyond the convent, you'd reach the trailhead for the fortress up above (all described later). But before leaving the square, visit the cathedral (see below).

Then poke around Hvar's **back streets.** As you wander, especially on the left (north) side of the square, look up to find more characteristic Venetian windows. You'll also spot stone tabs jutting from house facades. The ones with holes were used to hang color-coded curtains: white for a birth, black for a death. Also notice the gleaming white limestone everywhere, which is quarried locally. An often-repeated (but false) legend that the US White House was built of this same stone is temptingly plausible.

Cathedral of St. Stephen (Sv. Stjepan)—Hvar's centerpiece is its Renaissance-era cathedral, with a distinctive three-humped

gable (representing the Holy Trinity) and open-work steeple. The interior comes with a few tales from Hvar's storied past (free, daily 8:00–12:00 & 16:30–20:00).

The **bronze entrance doors,** completed by a popular Croatian sculptor in 1990, combine religious themes with important elements of life on Hvar. On the left door, top to bottom, you'll see the Creation; Madonna and Baby Jesus surrounded by the circle of stars (representing the European Union—reflecting Croatians' desire to be considered part of Europe); vineyards (both literal and as a symbol of heaven); and a procession of penitence, a fixture of life among religious locals. On the right door, you'll see a dove (representing peace and the Holy Spirit); the crucified Christ; fishermen (an actual part of Hvar life, but also representing the Church's "fishers of men" evangelical philosophy); and a boat, sailing into the future.

Inside, work your way counterclockwise around the church. At the right-front chapel, the tabernacle behind the yellow cloth (under the big crucifix) holds an important piece of Hvar history: a crucifix that supposedly shed tears of blood on the eve of a major 1510 uprising of the plebeians against the patricians. (This spooked the rebels enough to postpone the uprising a few months.) Behind the main altar, you'll see wooden choir stalls rescued from an earlier Gothic church destroyed during an Ottoman attack in 1571. Notice the two pulpits: The right one, with St. Paul and his sword, is for reading or singing the Epistles; the left one, with the eagle (representing St. John), is used for reading the Gospels. The left-front chapel features the tomb of St. Prosperus, Hvar's "co-patron saint," who shares the credit with the more famous St. Stephen.

People pray to Prosperus for good health. On his feast day, May 10, the lid is opened and you can actually see his preserved body. The figures flanking the tomb represent faith and strength.

▲▲**Benedictine Convent (Benediktinki Samostan) and Lace Museum**—Hvar's most appealing sight is this nun-run attraction, inside a convent where 13 Benedictine sisters spend their lives (they never go outside). When they're not praying, the sisters make lace using fibers from the *agava* (a cactuslike plant with broad, flat, tapered, spiny leaves—see the sample next to the desk as you enter). First, they tease the delicate threads out of the plant, then wash, bleach, and dry them. Finally, they weave the threads into intricate lace designs. The painstaking procedure is made even more challenging by Hvar's unpredictable weather: The humid southerly Jugo wind causes tangles, while the dry northern Bora wind makes the fibers stiff and difficult to work with.

You'll see astonishingly delicate samples of the nuns' work, both new and old—some yellowed specimens date from the late 19th century (the oldest ones are in the back room). The sisters are particularly happy to make lace for bishops and cardinals. And when the *other* Benedict—the XVI—became pope in 2005, they created a lace papal emblem for him as a gift.

Rounding out the museum are ecclesiastical gear, some bishops' vestments (with the Baby Jesus below them wearing an *agava*-lace shirt), ancient kitchenware discovered in this house, a stone sink and baptismal font, an actual well, and some amphora jugs. Out in front of the building is a statue of St. Benedict, the patron saint of Europe, reading his daily routine in a book: *ora et labora* ("pray and work"). You'll notice the museum is also called the Hanibal Lucić Museum for a prominent Renaissance poet whose daughter-in-law donated this property to the church (20 kn, skimpy 20-kn multilingual booklet, extremely expensive samples for sale, June–Aug Mon–Sat 10:00–12:00 & 17:00–19:00, closed Sun; it's generally closed Sept–May, but you can try ringing the bell to the right of the main door to get in during these same hours—use the door in the yellow building; tel. 021/741-052).

▲**Franciscan Monastery (Franjevački Samostan)**—This interesting sight—with an offbeat museum, Hvar's most famous painting, an ancient tree, and a pair of monks—is worth the five-minute stroll from the Old Town (20 kn; May–Oct Mon–Sat 10:00–12:00 & 17:00–19:00, closed Sun; usually closed Nov–April but the TI can call to see if they'll let you in during these hours).

Starting in the 15th century, this monastery was a hospice for sailors who encountered illness on treacherous sea journeys. As you enter, notice that the cloister's floor is slanted inward to capture rainwater. Pipes took this pure water out to the waterfront, where passing ships could use it to replenish their supplies.

The focal point of the monastery is its impressive painting of the **Last Supper** (c. 1640). According to legend, a passing ship had a passenger who was severely ill with scurvy, so they left him on a small offshore island, where monks took pity on him. He asked for the biggest canvas they could find and painted this. (This may be more than a myth—historians recently found a letter inviting the presumed artist to Hvar.) The U-shaped table in the painting provides the framework for some bold experimentation with perspective. Facing Jesus, front and center, is Judas, identified by several clues. In his left hand (hard to see) is a bag of coins, and his right hand is dipping bread into wine (after Jesus had predicted that the one who did this would betray him). The yellow of his garment symbolizes betrayal, and the red indicates that the betrayal led to the spilling of blood. Under the table by Judas is a cat, representing lust. On the lower right, we see a beggar (accompanied by a dog, symbolizing fidelity)—likely a self-portrait by the artist, grateful to the monks who nursed him back to health.

The museum has a few more rooms, including an exhibit of currency from the fourth century B.C. (Greek coins with an image of Zeus) until today (see the rapid evolution of Croatia's currency since its independence); a collection of amphora jugs; and paintings by Venetian artists and modern Croatian artists.

The final attraction, out in the relaxing garden (beyond the museum), is an enormous cypress tree whose gnarled branches are held up by big supports. Scientists believe this ancient tree—probably around 250 years old—was struck by lighting, which caused the branches to spread out and become flatter than usual.

On the way over to the monastery, peek inside the recommended **Gariful Restaurant** to see fish swimming around inside the floor. This is also a good place for a scenic meal.

▲**Hvar Fortress (Fortica Hvar)**—Visiting this mighty castle above the Old Town is a good excuse for a sturdy 20-minute hike

to break up your lazy Hvar day. This huge fortification was built over several generations, beginning in the 13th century. In the 14th century, Spanish engineers did their part to bulk up the fortress (giving it the nickname "Španjola"). In 1571, the townspeople fled here for sanctuary during an attack by the Ottomans (on their way to the famous Battle of Lepanto), but just a few years later, the fortress was devastated when lightning hit a gunpowder store. In the 19th century, the occupying Austrians put their own touches on the castle. Today it's used as a catering facility and tourist attraction (20 kn, daily in summer 8:00–24:00, shoulder season 8:30–21:00, much shorter hours—and sometimes closed—off-season).

From the Old Town, hike up the steep street called Groda to the road passing above town. Once on that road, look for the nearby gate with the picture of a castle for another steep hike up a switchback trail (stay on the main path—side-paths that seem like shortcuts are actually dead-ends). Once inside the fort, there's very little in the way of posted descriptions, but the views over town are terrific. You can also climb down into the prison, sip a drink at the café/bar, and visit the one-room "Marine Archaeological Museum" (hiding inside the blocky central part of the fortress; look for *amphorae* sign). This display features booty found at three different Dalmatian shipwrecks, including a collection of amphora jugs (for more on these jugs, see the sidebar on page 121).

According to the exhibit, one out of every 50 voyages in antiquity ended in a shipwreck. (And you thought flying was dangerous.)

The complex on the higher hill nearby was built by Napoleon (which is also its nickname among locals). In the 1970s, it was converted into an astronomic and seismographic observatory.

Activities in Hvar

Strolling and Swimming—With typically Dalmatian crystal-clear water, Hvar is a great place to swim. Also typically Dalmatian, virtually all of the swimming areas are rocky or pebbly. As you walk along the coastline in either direction from town, you'll spot concrete pads and ladders trying to seduce you into the cool blue (these are generally open to the public, but you may have the option of renting a beach chair).

Whether or not you plan to swim, take a waterfront walk east of town (past the Franciscan Monastery). This delightful path leads past swimmers, sunbathers, and boats bobbing just offshore. After about a 20-minute walk, you'll reach the town's main beach, **Pokonji Dol**, which faces a small, barren island of the same name topped with a lonely little lighthouse. After Pokonji Dol, the path becomes more challenging and not as well-marked, with little shade. Bring water and wear good shoes if planning to venture this far. If you continue eastward along the coast, you'll find more beaches—first the one nicknamed "Robinson," then the even better one at Milna (2.5 miles from Hvar town).

Many people—especially the clothing-optional crowd—prefer to take a water taxi across the bay to the **Pakleni Islands** (described below). The island of Jerolim and the bay of Stipanska (or is it *Strip*anska?) on the island of Marinkovac are particularly good places to spot (or sport?) some bare skin. The beach at Palmižana is another popular swim destination because it's partly "sandy" (translation: smaller pebbles).

Hike from Velo Grablje—For a vigorous but mostly downhill hike on Hvar Island, consider taking the one daily bus that uses the scenic old road to Stari Grad, and get off at the village of Velo Grablje (about 5 miles east of Hvar town). This modest settlement, once famous for its lavender oil production, is now a near-ghost town on a rugged plateau with far-off views of the sea. From Velo Grablje, you can hike back down into Hvar: First you'll descend about two miles (via the abandoned village of Malo Grablje) to the beach at Milna (described previously), then continue about 2.5 miles back to Hvar—with fine views all along the way. The TI can give you details (bus generally departs Hvar town at 11:50—confirm at TI or bus station). As this is a challenging trail with little shade, be prepared (good shoes, water, sunscreen, etc.).

Excursions—Joining a day-trip excursion is a handy way to reach nearby destinations (generally available June–Oct). The best-selling options are trips around Hvar Island and the nearby Pakleni Islands; Vis Island and its "Blue Cave"; Brač Island and the beach at Bol; Korčula; Mljet National Park; Dubrovnik; river rafting; and more. The main operation is **Atlas** (at the top of the harbor); other salespeople along the embankment also hawk various boat excursions.

Near Hvar: The Pakleni Islands (Pakleni Otoci)

These islands, just offshore from Hvar town, are a popular and easy back-to-nature day-trip destination. The name means the

"Devil's Islands" in Croatian, but in the local dialect, *pakleni* refers to the resin used to seal the hulls of ships. As noted above, some of the smaller islands (Jerolim and Marinkovac) are known for their nude beaches, and little else. But for a bit more civilization, set your sights on the biggest island, known as **"Palmižana"** for its main settlement (the island's official name is Svetog Klement, but nobody calls it that). The only real "town" on this island is Palmižana (pahl-mee-ZHAH-nah; sounds like "parmesan-a"), which is basically a modest marina and a handful of cafés huddled

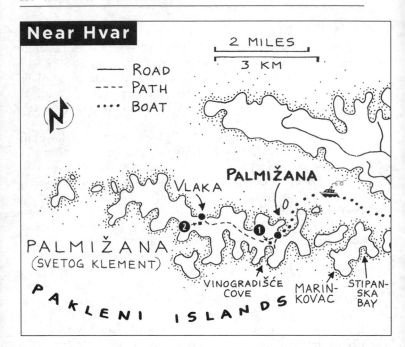

Near Hvar

- —— ROAD
- - - - PATH
- ···· BOAT

2 MILES
3 KM

VLAKA
PALMIŽANA

PALMIŽANA
(SVETOG KLEMENT)

PAKLENI ISLANDS

VINOGRADIŠĆE COVE
MARIN-KOVAC
STIPAN-SKA BAY

around a beach. From there, you can hike through the woods and scramble your way to some postcard-perfect hidden coves.

Getting There: Excursion boats ferry tourists out to the islands every summer morning from the harbor in front of the Hvar TI—just look for signs to the specific island, beach, or cove that you want. It costs about 60 kn round-trip per person to Palmižana; most boats take people over between 9:00 and 11:00, then go back to fetch them home around 16:00 or 17:00 (they run more or less constantly in peak season; figure about 20 min each way to Palmižana). This works well, provided you want to spend the entire day stranded on a tropical island. Visiting Jerolim or Marinkovac costs 35 kn round-trip.

An efficient sightseer might prefer just a few hours of island time—enough for a quick dip, a hike, and maybe a meal. For this purpose, you can pay double for a faster, private **water taxi** to zip you there in just 15 minutes, and then pick you up whenever you like. I had a good experience with one of these speedy taxis, helmed by English-speaking Luka. I called him 15 minutes before I wanted to head over, and again 15 minutes before I came back—door-to-door service to any island you like (100 kn round-trip per person, 2-person minimum—so a single rider pays double, mobile 098-959-5094, www.water-express.com). Luka has two types of boats: the smaller, inflatable boats are built for speed but not comfort, so the ride is rough; the bigger boat is more comfortable.

HVAR

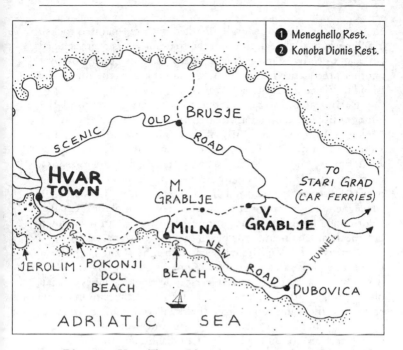

Planning Your Time: If you're relatively fit and have a few hours to spare, try this plan: Ride with Luka to Palmižana, hit the Vinogradišće beach, hike across the island to the settlement of Vlaka, have lunch or dinner at Konoba Dionis, call Luka, and ride with him from Vlaka back to Hvar.

Beach at Vinogradišće Cove: The most popular spot for swimming on the island is the beach at Vinogradišće. To get here from the Palmižana marina, hike up the trail (to the left, past the little cantina). When the road forks, take the middle fork and follow the restaurant signs (they're all at the beach). While it's not as "undiscovered" as you might hope, Vinogradišće is a picturesque spot, with a small patch of semi-sand surrounded by rocks and concrete pads for catching some rays. A smattering of sailboats on the horizon rounds out the idyllic Croatian scene.

Hike to Vlaka: For a hardy 45-minute (2-mile) hike on a rough trail with some pleasant views—and a restaurant reward at the end (Konoba Dionis, described next)—trek across the top of the island to the little settlement of Vlaka (wear good shoes and bring water). From Palmižana, first follow signs to Meneghello. After you pass Meneghello Restaurant and some of its bungalows (described next), there's a fork in the path—go right (following the faint red marking on the wall to *Vlaka*). You'll climb up to the crest of the island, on a very narrow and rocky trail. A few side paths fork down to various bays, but stay on the main trail along

HVAR

the top of the island (generally marked with red-painted rocks). You'll periodically break through the trees for views over secluded coves and nearby islands. Finally, the path leads down along yet another pretty cove before sending you back over the top of the island to Vlaka and Konoba Dionis.

Eating at Palmižana: Several lazy cafés surround the Vinogradišće beach at Palmižana. A bit higher on the hill is **Meneghello,** run by a family of the same name that's been in Palmižana for over a century. They serve mostly seafood on a colorful, funky terrace (100–150-kn combo plates, fishy splurges for a bit more, open long hours daily April–Oct, reservations smart for dinner, follow signs from the Palmižana marina, tel. 021/717-270). Meneghello Restaurant is the centerpiece of a complex of rentable, color-coded bungalows that bunny-hop through an overgrown botanical garden down to the beach (www.palmizana.hr).

Eating at Vlaka: The culinary highlight of the island is at the other end, in Vlaka. **Konoba Dionis** is a charming stone hut with just six tables on a covered terrace, overlooking vineyards, an olive grove, and the distant sea. The electricity comes from a generator, and the water comes from the sky (except during droughts, when it's brought over from the mainland)—so the cuisine is straightforward, traditional Dalmatian dishes, and the focus is on relaxation. Their "aubergine pie" is a tasty eggplant lasagna (figure about 250 kn per person for a meal, mid-May–mid-Oct daily 12:00–23:00, closed off-season, mobile 098-167-1016 or 091-765-6044). Tourists often make the long journey over to Dionis, only to find it's already full—reservations (especially for lunch) are a must. Note that there are boats from Hvar to Vlaka in peak season (but the schedule is sparse; ask at TI).

Shopping in Hvar

You'll see little souvenir kiosks everywhere on Hvar. The big item here is lavender, produced on the island for the last century or so. In addition to making things smell good, lavender is acclaimed by some locals for its medicinal properties: Massage some lavender oil on your temples to cure a headache, or rub it on your chest for asthma. You'll see it sold in bottles or sachets—a fragrant souvenir that helps keep your luggage smelling fresh, too.

Sleeping in Hvar

In keeping with its posh cachet, Hvar has some of the most expensive accommodations in Croatia. As usual, *sobe* are a more affordable option (see page 25), but the variety and quality are lower than

HVAR

Sleep Code

(5 kn = about $1, country code: 385, area code: 021)
S = Single, **D** = Double/Twin, **T** = Triple, **Q** = Quad, **b** = bathroom. The modest tourist tax (7 kn per person, per night, lower off-season) is not included in these rates. Hotels generally accept credit cards and include breakfast, while most *sobe* accept only cash and don't offer breakfast. Everyone listed here speaks at least enough English to make a reservation (or knows someone nearby who can translate).

To help you sort easily through these listings, I've divided the rooms into three categories based on the price for a standard double room with bath in peak season:

$$$ Higher Priced—Most rooms 800 kn or more.
 $$ Moderately Priced—Most rooms between 450-800 kn.
  $ Lower Priced—Most rooms 450 kn or less.

in other Dalmatian destinations. If you don't mind a bit of a walk from the Old Town, there are some fine little private hotels on the outskirts. It can be hard to find a room in July and especially August (when all accommodations boost their rates); book as far ahead as possible for these times. Any time of year, your biggest hurdle is that nearly all of the small (cheaper) places charge 30 percent more for stays less than three nights—try to negotiate your way out of this if it's not peak season.

In the Old Town

$$-$$$ *Sunčani Hvar Hotels:* Most of the big hotels in town are operated by the same company, Sunčani Hvar. These hotels are currently undergoing a long-term, multi-phase renovation to bring them all up to four- and five-star (read: expensive) status, so some of them might be closed for your visit. Those that are fully renovated boast super-modern rooms with strikingly contemporary decor. Prices vary dramatically depending on season, view, size, how recently the rooms were renovated, and the direction the wind is blowing. I've listed the price per night for a two-night stay in a standard double room with no view in peak season (July–Aug). You'll pay more for a sea view, a "superior" room, or other special features, but rates can be much lower off-season—check the specific rates for your visit on their website (www.suncanihvar .com). Here are your options: **Hotel Palace,** a few steps off the main square, at the end of the harbor (not yet fully renovated; Db-770 kn); **Hotel Riva,** along the embankment where the big boats dock (renovated to top-class quality, with artsy mod decor and nude sketches in the halls; Db-1,370 kn); **Hotel Dalmacija,** around the corner from Hotel Riva, just east of the Old Town (unrenovated, Db-815 kn); **Hotel Adriana,** across the harbor from Hotel Riva (recently renovated and even more plush than the Riva; Db-2,560 kn); **Hotel Delfin,** just beyond the Adriana (unrenovated, Db-570 kn); and two others farther along past the Adriana and Delfin, a 5- to 10-minute walk from the Old Town: **Hotel Pharos** (unrenovated; Db-550 kn) and **Hotel Amfora** (nicely renovated but not quite as fancy as the Riva or Adriana; Db-1,550 kn). If you've got deep pockets and are tempted by good locations and big-hotel amenities, you can book any of the Sunčani Hvar hotels through the same office: tel. 021/750-750, fax 021/750-751, www.suncanihvar.com, reservations@suncanihvar.com. But I'd save some kunas and enjoy more local color by sleeping in one of the following options instead.

$$ Pension Oaza is a charming little oasis behind the bus station, a few steps off the main square. The Novak-Bilweis family runs their own little "country farm" in the town center, with five cozy little rooms, plus a big two-bedroom apartment and a small private villa in the corner of the ranch. Because they're planning some changes in the near future, contact them for the latest on prices and availability (Hanibala Lucića 4, tel. & fax 021/741-201, mateo.novak-bilweis@st.t-com.hr). Follow the little steep-walled lane at the end of the bus station parking lot, and you'll spot the sign on your right.

$ Ivana and Paško Ukić offer the best *sobe* I've found in Hvar, with three new-feeling apartments (with kitchens) and one room sharing a quiet square with a little church a few steep blocks above the main square (July–Aug: apartments-480 kn; May–June and Sept: apartments-400 kn; Oct–April: apartments-340 kn; Db about 40 kn less, no breakfast, 30 percent extra for 1-night stays, no extra charge for 2-night stays, cash only, air-con, tel. 021/741-810, Ivana speaks just enough English to make a reservation, or call fluent daughter Lidija at mobile 098-917-0652, www.hvar-apartments-center.com, ivanaukic@net.hr). From the cathedral, walk three blocks up toward the fortress, then look for the little church (Sv. Duh) to your left.

$–$$ *More* Sobe *and Apartments:* Stepping off the boat or bus, you'll be approached by hordes of people hoping to recruit you into their rooms. As you wander the streets, you'll see *sobe* and *apartman* signs everywhere. To find one from home, the TI has a particularly good and user-friendly website for choosing and getting in touch with a *sobe* host on your own (www.tzhvar.hr). Or, once you've arrived, the TI can give you a list of options. For more help, consider going through an agency. Figure anywhere from 200 kn to 500 kn for a double in peak season (30 percent more for

1- or 2-night stays). Most of Hvar's *sobe* and apartments have private bathrooms. Four different agencies in Hvar can book rooms (all are open sporadic hours, based on season; the first three are right along the embankment where the big boats dock, while the last is across the harbor): **Fontana** (tel. 021/742-133, www.happy hvar.com, info@happyhvar.com), **Thalassa** (tel. 021/742-908, thalassa@st.t-com.hr), **Pelegrini** (tel. 021/742-743, www.pelegrini -hvar.hr, pelegrini@inet.hr), and **Atlas** (tel. 021/741-911, atlas -hvar@st.t-com.hr).

In the Residential Area West of the Old Town

These two hotels are in a quiet, nondescript residential neighborhood just beyond the big Hotel Amfora west of the Old Town.

$$$ Pod Stine Hotel ("Under Stones") feels like the sunny hideout of a reclusive writer. At the edge of town overlooking a mini-arboretum and a beautiful cove, this place features smart contemporary decor and 45 upscale-feeling rooms. If you don't mind the 20-minute walk into town, it's a more intimate and enjoyable splurge than the big hotels (mid-July–mid-Sept: non-view Sb-700–950 kn, seaview Sb-1,200–1,600 kn, non-view Db-950–1,300 kn, seaview Db 1,600–2,000 kn; May–mid-July and late Sept: 10–15 percent cheaper; April and Oct: 40–50 percent cheaper; closed Nov–March, higher prices are for rooms with balcony, no extra charge for 1- or 2-night stays, air-con, elevator, free parking, free use of spa facilities—including gym and swimming pool, Podstine b.b., tel. 021/740-400, fax 021/740-499, www .podstine.com, hotel@podstine.com).

$$ Pharia Aparthotel has 10 rooms and 11 apartments in two buildings. The neighborhood is dull and the rooms are straightforward, but they're well-priced for the proximity to the Old Town—about a 15-minute walk away (July–Aug: Sb-460 kn, non-view Db-720 kn, seaview Db-840 kn, non-view apartment-990 kn, seaview apartment-1,070 kn; progressively cheaper off-season, closed mid-Oct–April, air-con, Wi-Fi, Majerovica b.b., tel. 021/778-080, fax 021/778-081, www.orvas-hotels.com, orvas -hotels@orvas.hr).

Eating in Hvar

Hvar is packed with similar places serving up plates of grilled fish and meat, with pasta and pizza rounding out the predictable options. Fortunately—unlike some other small resort towns (such as Korčula)—Hvar also has some more inventive options that provide a nice break from the same old seaside fare. Prices on Hvar are high, but (for the most part) so is quality. No matter where you dine, reservations are smart July through September.

Konoba Menego, run by Dinko and the Kovačević family, offers the chance to try typical cuisine from Dalmatia and throughout Croatia. The user-friendly menu lists the town or region of origin for each specialty. Portions are small, so think of it as Croatian tapas: Two people can order three or four dishes to share, and sample a variety of regional flavors. Dine in the cozy enclosed terrace or in the atmospheric dining room, with air-dried ham *(pršut)* hanging from the rafters (25–60-kn portions, bigger 90-kn combination plates, daily 11:30–14:30 & 17:00–24:00, closed Nov–March, on the steep lane called Groda leading up to the fortress, reservations smart, tel. 021/742-036).

Gariful Restaurant ("Carnation") owns Hvar's best waterfront location, at the end of the yacht-lined embankment. They have a fine outdoor terrace and a small dining room, and the service is crisp and helpful. You know the fish is fresh, because it's swimming around beneath the floor inside (55–95-kn pastas, 85–150-kn meat dishes, 95–190-kn seafood dishes, daily 10:00–23:00; at the end of the embankment, by the green lighthouse; tel. 021/742-999, mobile 098-916-0173).

Yakša is a dressy splurge that oozes style, serving updated Dalmatian cuisine with international flair. They pride themselves on using only the freshest of ingredients and brag that all their produce (and olive oil) is grown right here on Hvar. The dining room is in the heart of a gorgeously restored 16th-century palazzo, with columns and arches between the tables. Or sit outside on the covered sidewalk or in their enclosed patio (70–100-kn pastas, 100–200-kn main courses, daily 9:00–16:00 & 18:00–1:00 in the morning, likely no breakfast in shoulder season, closed mid-Oct–mid-March, just off the cathedral end of the main square at Hektorovićeva b.b.—look for the arches in the illuminated dining room, reservations smart, mobile 091-277-772).

Hvar's "Restaurant Row": The streets just above the main square (to the left, as you face the cathedral) are full of restaurants slinging similar Dalmatian and Mediterranean fare. Outdoor tables make it easy to window-shop and find your favorite. In this zone, three places are particularly well-regarded: **Luna** has colorful, lively decor and a delightful rooftop terrace (70–90-kn pastas, 80–150-kn main courses, 10-kn cover charge, peak season daily 12:00–23:00, shoulder season closed 14:30–18:00, closed Nov–March, free Internet access for diners, tel. 021/741-400). **Macondo** offers fun, tight sidewalk seating and a nondescript dining room (90–100-kn pastas, 90–140-kn main courses; April–Oct Mon–Sat 12:00–14:00 & 18:30–24:00, Sun 18:30–24:00; closed Nov–March, tel. 021/742-850). **Palača Paladini,** in a 500-year-old-palace, has a large enclosed garden courtyard and a small dining room (60–100-kn pastas, 70–130-kn meat dishes, 200–300-kn fish splurges, daily 12:00–24:00, across the street from Luna, tel. 021/742-104).

Alviž, a cheaper option near the bus station, serves pizzas, pastas, and other dishes in a woody interior or outside on a welcoming terrace (30–50-kn pizzas, 50–70-kn pastas, 70–100-kn meat and fish dishes, daily 18:00–24:00, across parking lot from bus station, tel. 021/742-797).

Breakfast: If you're sleeping in a *soba*, you're on your own for breakfast. Small **bakeries** are scattered around town. For something more substantial, drop into **Café Pjaca,** with ideal outdoor seating on the main square across from the TI (50-kn "Arsenal Breakfast" with eggs and meat, daily 7:00–23:00, cool modern decor). **Yakša,** listed previously, serves a pricey breakfast in peak season (40–110 kn).

Picnic Supplies: There's a big, handy **Konzum** supermarket near the bus station (Mon–Sat 7:00–21:00, Sun 8.00–13:00).

Hvar Connections

Boat Connections

Big car ferries use the port at Stari Grad, across the island from Hvar town (a 20-min bus ride; local buses are scheduled to connect Hvar town with these boats). Smaller passenger-only catamarans leave from the harbor in the heart of Hvar town. For non-drivers going to either Split or Korčula, the catamarans are much better, since their departure point is more convenient and they make the trip faster. As always, it's essential to confirm your plans in advance—boat schedules are subject to change.

Boats from Hvar Town to Split and Korčula Island: The handy *Krilo* **catamaran** heads for Split in the morning and for Korčula town in the afternoon (runs daily year-round; to Split: 50–60 min, 22 kn; to Korčula: 1.5 hrs, 33 kn; in summer also stops at Prigradica on Korčula Island en route to Korčula town; in Hvar, buy tickets at Pelegrini travel agency, confirm schedule at www.krilo.hr). In summer (June–Sept), a **Jadrolinija catamaran** connects Hvar town twice daily to Split (50–60 min, 42 kn in the morning or 22 kn in the afternoon) and once daily to Vela Luka (at the far end of Korčula Island, a 1-hr bus ride to Korčula town; 45 min, 22 kn). Off-season (Oct–May), the same boat runs once daily in each direction.

Big Jadrolinija Car Ferries from Stari Grad: These big boats head north, to **Split** (2/week year-round, 1.75 hrs); and south, to **Korčula town** (2/week year-round, 3.5 hrs) and **Dubrovnik** (2/week year-round, 6.5 hrs). Jadrolinija also runs frequent local car ferries from Stari Grad to **Split** (3–7/day, 1.75 hrs, 38 kn).

Overland Connections

Hvar's **buses** only connect you to other parts of the island. For farther-flung destinations (such as Dubrovnik or Zagreb), you'll take a boat to Split, then connect by bus from there. About six buses a day cross the island between Hvar town and Stari Grad, and there's always a bus coordinated to meet the big ferries at Stari Grad (in which case you want Stari Grad's "Trajekt" stop rather than its Old Town stop).

Drivers heading north can drive 20 minutes to Stari Grad and catch the car ferry right to Split (described previously). If you're heading south (or to Mostar), you can also drive the very twisty roads (about 1.5 hrs) down the length of Hvar Island to the town of Sućuraj, where you can catch the car ferry to Drvenik; from Drvenik, you can drive along the mainland, or catch a different ferry to Korčula town (confirm all ferry schedules at Hvar TI before making the trip).

KORČULA

The island town of Korčula (KOHR-choo-lah) boasts an atmospheric Old Town, some surprisingly engaging museums, and a dramatic, fjord-like mountain backdrop. Simpler and humbler than its glitzy big sister Hvar, Korčula—while certainly on the tourist trail—has an often-appealing, occasionally frustrating backwater charm. All things considered, Korčula is the most enjoyable Back Door stopover on the Dalmatian Coast.

Like so many other small Croatian coastal towns, Korčula was founded by the ancient Greeks. It became part of the Roman Empire and was eventually a key southern outpost of the Venetian Republic. Four centuries of Venetian rule left Korčula with a quirky Gothic-Renaissance mix and a strong siesta tradition. Korčulans take great pride in the fact that Marco Polo was born here in 1254—the explorer remains the town's poster boy. Korčula is also known for its traditional *Moreška* sword dance.

You'll discover that there are two Korčulas: the tacky seaside resort and the historic Old Town. Savvy visitors ignore the tourist sprawl and focus on Korčula's medieval quarter, a mini-Dubrovnik poking into the sea on a picture-perfect peninsula. Tiny lanes branch off the humble main drag like ribs on a fish's backbone. This street plan is designed to catch both the breeze and the shade. All in all, this laid-back island village is an ideal place to take a vacation from your busy vacation.

Planning Your Time

Korčula deserves the better part of a day, but you'll quickly exhaust the town's sightseeing options. With a single day, spend the morning wandering the medieval Old Town and exploring the handful of tiny museums (many close for siesta in the early afternoon, especially outside of peak season). In the afternoon, kick back at a café or restaurant and bask on the beach. If you're here on a Thursday, be sure to catch the performance of the *Moreška* dance (also Mon July–Aug). With a second day, unwind more, or consider a one-day package excursion to Mljet Island and its national park (not quite doable in one day by public transportation; see page 309).

If you're trying to choose between Hvar and Korčula, why not do both? For example, if heading south, you can take an early boat from Split to Hvar, have a few hours there, then take the evening boat on to Korčula to set up for a day or two of vacation. If you're in a rush, you can spend one night on Korčula, see the town in the morning, then zip out on the evening *Nona Ana* boat to Dubrovnik (July–Aug 4/week)—but it's much more sane and relaxing to hang out here for two nights.

Orientation to Korčula

(area code: 020)
The long, skinny island of Korčula runs alongside the even longer, skinnier Pelješac Peninsula. The main town and best destination on the island—just across a narrow strait from Pelješac—is also called Korčula.

Korčula town is centered on its compact **Old Town** (Stari Grad) peninsula, which is connected to the mainland at a big staircase leading to the Great Land Gate. In the area in front of this staircase, you'll find ATMs, travel agencies, the Jadrolinija ferry office, Internet cafés, the Konzum supermarket, a colorful outdoor produce market, and other handy tourist services.

Stretching to the south and east of the Old Town is **"Shell Bay,"** surrounded by a strip of tacky tourist shops and resort hotels. This seamier side of Korčula—best avoided—caters mostly to Brits and Germans here to worship the sun for a week or two.

To the west of Old Town is the serene waterfront street **Put Sv. Nikola,** where you'll find a few *sobe* (including Rezi Depolo's—see "Sleeping in Korčula," later), some inviting swimming areas, great views back on the Old Town, and more locals than tourists.

Tourist Information

Korčula's TI, run by Stanka Kraljević, is next to Hotel Korčula on the west side of the Old Town waterfront. Ask about the Korčula brochure and map (mid-June–Sept Mon–Sat 8:00–15:00 &

KORČULA

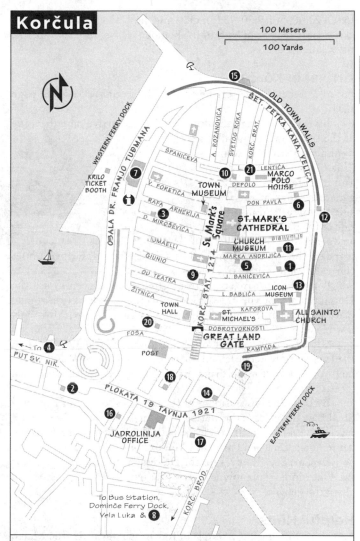

Korčula

100 Meters

100 Yards

N

OBALA DR. FRANJO TUĐMANA

WESTERN FERRY DOCK

KRILO TICKET BOOTH

ŠET. PETRA KANAVELIĆA

OLD TOWN WALLS

ŠPANIĆEVA

A. ROZANOVIĆA

SVETOG ROKA

KORČ. BRAT.

LENTIĆA

MARCO POLO HOUSE

V. FORETIĆA

TOWN MUSEUM

DEPOLO

RAFA ARNEKIJA

St. Mark's Square

DON PAVLA

ST. MARK'S CATHEDRAL

D. MIROŠEVIĆA

ISMAELLI

CHURCH MUSEUM

DIBILVOLIE

GIUNIO

KORČ. STAT. 1214

MARKA ANDRIJIĆA

OD TEATRA

J. BANIĆEVIĆA

ŽITNICA

L. BABLIČA

ICON MUSEUM

TOWN HALL

ST. MICHAEL'S

KAPOROVA

ALL SAINTS' CHURCH

DOBROTVORNOSTI

FOSA

GREAT LAND GATE

RAMPADA

To

PUT SV. NIK.

POST

PLOKATA 19 TRAVNJA 1921

KONZUM

JADROLINIJA OFFICE

EASTERN FERRY DOCK

KORČ. BROD.

To Bus Station,
Dominče Ferry Dock,
Vela Luka & **8**

① Apartments Lenni
② Royal Apartments
③ Vitaić Family Rooms
④ To Depolo Rooms
⑤ Marco Polo Apartments
⑥ Portolan Rooms
⑦ Hotel Korčula
⑧ To Hotels Marko Polo,
   Liburna, Park & Bon Repos
⑨ Pizzeria Amfora
⑩ Adio Mare Restaurant

⑪ Konoba Marinero Rest.
⑫ Konoba Morski Konjic Rest.
⑬ Pizzeria Tedeschi
⑭ Konzum Supermarket
⑮ Buffet "Massimo"
⑯ Cukarin Sweet Shop
⑰ Kiwi Ice Cream
⑱ Atlas Travel
⑲ Korkyra Travel Agency
⑳ Moreška Outdoor Theater
㉑ Marco Polo Gift Shop

KORČULA

16:00–22:00, Sun 9:00–13:00; Oct–mid-June Mon–Sat 8:00–14:00, closed Sun, may be open Sun in shoulder season; tel. 020/715-701, www.korcula.net).

Arrival in Korčula

For all the details on getting to the Dalmatian Coast, see page 170.

By Boat: The big Jadrolinija ferries can arrive on either side of the Old Town peninsula, depending on the wind. (The Orebić passenger ferry and the fast catamarans generally dock at the west side of town.) From either side of the peninsula, it's just a two-minute walk to where  it meets the mainland and all of the services described under "Orientation to Korčula," earlier.

A few boats (car ferries from Orebić and Drvenik) use the Dominče dock two peninsulas east of Korčula, about a five-minute drive from town. Regular buses connect this dock with Korčula town.

Some boats from Split and Hvar town arrive at Vela Luka, at the far end of Korčula Island. Each boat arriving at Vela Luka is met by a bus waiting to bring arriving travelers to Korčula town (about 1 hr).

By Bus: The bus station is at the southeast corner of Korčula's Shell Bay. If you leave the station with the bay on your right, you'll reach the Old Town. If you leave with the bay on your left, you'll get to hotels Liburna, Park, and Marko Polo.

By Car: See "Route Tips for Drivers" at the end of this chapter. Once in Korčula town, there's free parking at the bus station along the marina.

Helpful Hints

Festivals: Korčula has a couple of fun annual festivals. The Marco Polo Festival is in late June and early July, with lots of exhibitions, concerts, dances, and a parade with a costumed Marco Polo returning to his native Korčula after his long visit to China (www.marcopolofest.hr). And for several days at the beginning of September, Korčula remembers the great 1298 naval battle that took place just offshore, when the Genoese captured Marco Polo. The festivities culminate in a 14-ship reenactment, complete with smoke and sound effects.

Jadrolinija Office: This office, essential for sorting through and confirming boat schedules, is located where the Old Town meets the mainland (June–Sept Mon–Fri 8:00–20:00, Sat 8:00–13:30 & 18:00–22:00, Sun 6:00–13:30; Oct–May generally open Mon–Fri 8:00–14:00, Sat 8:00–13:00, Sun 9:00–13:00; tel. 020/715-410, www.jadrolinija.hr). But note that they don't sell tickets for two of the handy, fast catamarans: the *Krilo* catamaran to Hvar town and Split (buy *Krilo* tickets at the small kiosk on the embankment near Hotel Korčula, sold at 18:30–20:00 the night before the boat departs), and the *Nona Ana* catamaran to Mljet and Dubrovnik (buy *Nona Ana* tickets at Korkyra Tours travel agency). For a rundown of the many boat options to and from Korčula, see the end of this chapter.

Travel Agencies: Korčula has several travel agencies where you can book an excursion, browse shelves of books and souvenirs, and get information about car rental and other activities. The most established option is **Atlas Travel** (long hours daily in summer, closed for mid-afternoon break and sometimes closed Sun in shoulder season, open Mon–Sat mornings and closed Sun in winter; a few steps down from the Great Land Gate at Trg 19 Travnja, tel. 020/711-231; main office closed in winter, but second office around the corner stays open). **Korkyra Tours** travel agency is also good (just outside the Great Land Gate, mobile 091-571-4355, www.korkyra.info, info@korkyra.info).

Sights in Korčula

Korčula's few sights cluster within a few yards of each other in the Old Town. I've listed them roughly in order from the Great Land Gate (the Old Town's main entry) to the tip of the Old Town peninsula. All museums are officially "closed" November through April, but most will usually open by request (ask the TI to call for you...or just try knocking on the door).

▲▲**Moreška Dance**—Lazy Korčula snaps to life when locals perform a medieval folk dance called the *Moreška* (moh-REHSH-kah). The plot helps Korčulans remember their hard-fought past: A bad king takes the good king's bride, the dancing forces of good and evil battle, and there's always a happy ending (100 kn, June–mid-Oct every Thu at 21:00, July–Aug also Mon at 21:00, in outdoor theater next to the Great Land Gate—to the left as you face the gate, or in a nearby congress center if bad weather; buy tickets from travel agency, at your hotel, or at the door).

▲**Great Land Gate (Veliki Revelin)**—A noble staircase leads up to the main entrance to the Old Town. Like all of the town's towers, it's adorned with the Venetian winged lion and the coats of arms of the doge of Venice (left) and the rector of Korčula

(right; the offset coat of arms below was the rector who later renovated the gate). Climb the tower to visit a small exhibit with costumes and photos from the *Moreška* dance, then head up to the top level to enjoy panoramic town views (15 kn, daily 10:00–16:00, until 19:00 in summer, generally closed Nov–May, English descriptions).

Just inside the gate is **Franjo Tuđman Square,** renamed in 2001 for the first president of an independent Croatia (see page 46). During the war, Tuđman was considered a hero. In later years, it was revealed that he had held secret negotiations with the Serbian leader Slobodan Milošević about the postwar division of Bosnia-Herzegovina. As the key figure of a recent-but-bygone era that combined both joy and terror, Tuđman remains controversial in today's Croatia. But members of his party are still in power and hold local offices throughout the country, and they sometimes adorn a square or street with his name.

On the left inside the gate is the 16th-century **Town Hall and Rector's Palace.** The seal of Korčula (over the center arch) symbolizes the town's importance as the southernmost bastion of the Venetian Republic: St. Mark standing below three defensive towers. The little church on the other side of the square is dedicated to **St. Michael** (Crkva Sv. Mihovila). Throughout Croatia, many towns have churches dedicated to St. Michael just inside the town gates, as he is believed to offer saintly protection from enemies. Notice that a passageway connects the church to the building across the street—home to the Brotherhood of St. Michael, one of Korčula's many religious fraternal organizations (see "Icon Museum," later).

• *Now begin walking up the...*

Street of the Korčulan Statute of 1214 (Ulica Korčulanskog Statuta 1214)—This street is Korčula's backbone—in more ways than one: While most medieval towns slowly evolved with twisty, mazelike lanes, Korčula was carefully planned to resemble a fish skeleton. The streets to the west (left) of this one are straight, to allow the refreshing northwesterly Maestral winds into town. To the east (right), they're curved (notice you can't see the sea) to keep out the bad-vibe southeasterly Jugo winds.

The street's complicated name honors a 1214 statute—the oldest known written law in Central Europe—with regulations about everyday life and instructions on maintaining the city walls, protecting nature, keeping animals, building a house, and so on.

As you head up the street, look up to notice some interesting decorations on the houses' upper floors.

• *If you continue up the street, you'll reach St. Mark's Square (Trg Sv. Marka). From here, you're a few steps from the next four sights.*

▲**St. Mark's Cathedral (Katedrala Sv. Marka)**—Korčula became a bishopric in the 14th century. In the 19th century—36

bishops later—the Habsburgs decided to centralize ecclesiastical power in their empire, and they removed Korčula's bishop. The town still has this beautiful "cathedral"—but no bishop. On the ornately decorated tympanum above the main door, you'll see another Venetian statue of St. Mark (flanked by Adam and Eve). Inside, above the main altar, is an original Tintoretto painting (recently restored in Zagreb). At the altar to the left, find the statue of St. Rok (better known by his Italian name, San Rocco) pointing to a wound on his leg. This popular-in-Croatia French saint is believed to help cure disease. As you leave, notice the weapons on the back wall, used in some of the pivotal battles that have taken place near strategically situated Korčula (free, May–Oct daily 9:00–14:00 & 17:00–19:00, may be open all day long in peak season, closed during church services, generally closed Nov–April but may be open Mon–Fri 9:00–12:00 after Easter).

▲**Church Museum (Opatska Riznica)**—This small museum has an eclectic and fascinating collection. Go on a scavenger hunt for the following items: a ceremonial necklace from Mother Teresa (who came from Macedonia, not far from here—she gave this necklace to a friend from Korčula), some 12th-century hymnals, two tiny drawings by Leonardo da Vinci, a coin collection (including a 2,400-year-old Greek coin minted here in Korčula), some Croatian modern paintings, three amphora jugs, and two framed reliquaries with dozens of miniscule relics (20 kn; July–Aug daily 9:00–19:00, sometimes later; May–June and Sept–Oct Mon–Sat 9:00–14:00 & 17:00–20:00, closed Sun except sometimes open in the morning; generally closed Nov–April but may be open Mon–Fri 9:00–12:00 after Easter).

▲**Town Museum (Gradski Muzej)**—Housed in an old mansion, this museum does a fine job of bringing together Korčula's various claims to fame. It's arranged like a traditional Dalmatian home: shop on the ground floor, living quarters in the middle floors, kitchen on top. Notice that some of the walls near the entry have holes in them. Archaeologists are continually doing "digs" into these walls to learn how medieval houses here were built.

On the ground floor is a lapidarium, featuring fragments of Korčula's stone past (see the first-century Roman amphora jugs). Upstairs is a display on Korčula's long-standing shipbuilding industry, including models of two modern steel ships built here (the town still builds ship parts today). There's also a furnished living room and, in the attic, a kitchen. This was a smart place for the kitchen—if it caught fire, it was less likely to destroy the whole building. Notice the little WC in the corner. A network of pipes took kitchen and other waste through town and out to sea (20 kn, limited posted English information—pick up the free English brochure at entry; mid-June–Aug Mon–Sat 9:30–21:00, closed Sun; Sept–mid-June Mon–Fri 8:00–15:00—if it's locked, try knocking, closed Sat–Sun; tel. 020/711-420).

Marco Polo's House (Kuća Marka Pola)—Korčula's favorite son is the great 13th-century explorer Marco Polo. Though Polo sailed under the auspices of the Venetian Republic, and technically was a Venetian (since the Republic controlled this region), Korčulans proudly claim him as their own. Marco Polo was the first Westerner to sail to China, bringing back amazing stories and exotic goods (like silk) that Europeans had never seen before. After his trip, Marco Polo fought in an important naval battle against the Genoese near Korčula. He was captured, taken to Genoa, and imprisoned. He told his story to a cellmate, who wrote it down, published it, and made the explorer a world-class and much-in-demand celebrity. To this day, kids in swimming pools around the world try to find him with their eyes closed.

Today, Korčula is the proud home to "Marco Polo's House"— actually a more recent building on the site of what may or may not have been his family's property. The house is in poor repair, but most of the building has been purchased by the city to open to visitors. Currently you can just climb the stubby tower (for an uninspiring view), but in the future, the town hopes to turn the complex into a world-class museum about the explorer (15 kn, daily July–Aug 9:00–21:00, Easter–June and Sept–Oct 9:00–13:30 & 15:30–19:00, closed Nov–Easter, just north of cathedral on—where else?—ulica Depolo).

Across the street from the house's entrance, you'll find a clever **Marco Polo gift shop** selling various items relating to the explorer—herbs, brandies, honey, ice cream, and so on. Each one comes with a little tag telling a legend about M.P.—for example, how the word "million" was based on his middle name, Emilio (because no existing word was superlative enough for his discoveries). There's even a life-size Marco Polo and Kublai Khan keeping an eye on the cash register (daily in summer 9:00–24:00, progressively shorter hours and closed for mid-afternoon break off-season, closed in winter, ulica Depolo 1A, mobile 091-189-8048).

▲**Icon Museum (Zbirka Ikona)**—Korčula is known for its many brotherhoods—centuries-old fraternal organizations that have sprung up around churches. The Brotherhood of All Saints has been meeting every Sunday after Mass since the 14th century, and they run a small but interesting museum of icons. Maja, who lives upstairs, speaks no English but will point out what's worth seeing. These golden religious images were brought back from Greece in the 17th century by Korčulans who had been fighting the Ottomans on a Venetian warship (12 kn, hours depend on demand, but generally May–Oct daily 10:00–14:00 & 17:00–20:00, may be open all day long in peak season, closed Nov–April—but try ringing the bell, on Kaprova ulica at the Old Town's southeast tip).

Brotherhoods' meeting halls are often connected to their church by a second-story walkway. Use this one to step in to the Venetian-style **All Saints' Church** (Crkva Svih Svetih). Under the loft in the back of the church, notice the models of boats and tools—donated by Korčula's shipbuilders. Look closely at the painting to the right of the altar. See the guys in the white robes kneeling under Jesus? That's the Brotherhood, who commissioned this painting.

▲**Old Town Walls**—For several centuries, Korčula held a crucial strategic position as one of the most important southern outposts of the Venetian Republic (the Republic of Dubrovnik started at the Pelješac Peninsula, just across the channel). The original town walls around Korčula date from at least the 13th century, but the fortifications were extended (and new towers built) over several centuries to defend against various foes of Venice—mostly Ottomans and pirates.

The most recent tower dates from the 16th century, when the Ottomans attacked Korčula. The rector and other VIPs fled to the mainland, but a brave priest remained on the island and came up with a plan. All of the women of Korčula dressed up as men, and then everybody in town peeked over the wall—making the Ottomans think they were up against a huge army. The priest prayed for help, and the strong northerly Bora wind blew. Not wanting to take their chances with the many defenders and the weather, the Ottomans sailed away, and Korčula was saved.

By the late 19th century, Korčula was an unimportant Habsburg beach town, and the walls had no strategic value. The town decided to quarry the top half of its old walls to build new homes (and to improve air circulation inside the city). Though today's walls are half as high as they used to be, the town has restored many of the towers, giving Korčula its fortified feel. Each one has a winged lion—a symbol of Venice—and the seal of the rector of Korčula when the tower was built.

Activities in Korčula

Swimming—The water around Korčula is clean and suitable for swimming. You'll find pebbly beaches strewn with holiday-goers all along Put Sv. Nikola, the street that runs west from the Old Town. While this shoreline doesn't have much flat land for sunning yourself, you can generally find a relatively comfy rock to recline on. Another good swimming spot is at the very end of the Old Town peninsula. Or trek to the beaches near Lumbarda (described next).

Lumbarda—For a break from Korčula town, venture about three miles southeast to Lumbarda, a tranquil end-of-the-road village. Lumbarda is known for its wine (the sweet *grk* dessert wine) and for its beaches: the pebbly Bilin Žal, just east of town; and the sandy Vela Pržina, about a 20-minute walk through vineyards to the south. While not worth going out of your way for, Lumbarda and its beaches are fun to explore on a lazy vacation day. From Korčula town, you can get to Lumbarda by water taxi (50 kn) or by bus (hourly Mon–Sat, fewer buses Sun, 15 min, 10 kn).

Excursions—Various companies offer day-long excursions to nearby destinations (generally available June–Oct, each itinerary offered 2–4 times per week). The most popular options are Dubrovnik and the national park on Mljet Island. The biggest, most established operation is Atlas (see "Helpful Hints," earlier). Several new, more active tour companies have popped up recently, offering canoe trips, snorkeling, kayaking, and other "adventures"—look for flyers around town (Sokol is well-regarded, www.korcula-adventures.com).

Other Activities—You'll see travel agencies all over town where you can rent a car, bike, scooter, boat, sea kayak, or anything else

you want for some vacation fun. Local captains take tourists on cruises to nearby bays and islands to get out on the water, swim, and enjoy a local-style "fish picnic." Inquire at any travel agency, or simply talk to a captain at the harbor (near the eastern ferry dock, at Shell Bay; figure about 200 kn per hour regardless of number of people). If you're a wine-lover, consider hiring a driver to take you on a tour of Korčula Island, including stops at some wineries (ask at TI or travel agency).

KORČULA

Sleeping in Korčula

Korčula has only five hotels—all owned by the same company (which is, in turn, government-run). The lack of competition keeps quality low and prices ridiculously high—which makes *sobe* a particularly good alternative.

Sobe

My favorite *sobe* in Korčula offer similar comfort to the hotels at far lower prices—most of them with TVs and air-conditioning, to boot. These are your best *sobe* options, and worth reserving ahead.

$$ Apartments Lenni is run by Lenni and Periša (Peter) Modrinić, both of whom are outgoing and speak good English. They rent three tight, modern, comfortable rooms (one with a private bathroom across the hall) and three apartments in a nicely renovated house right in the heart of the Old Town. Since they live off-site, confirm your reservation the day

before and let them know your arrival time (July–Aug: Db-€60, apartment-€80; shoulder season: Db-€45, apartment €60; cheaper off-season, 2-night minimum unless it's not too busy, cash only,

---

Sleep Code

(€1 = about $1.40, country code: 385, area code: 020)
S = Single, **D** = Double/Twin, **T** = Triple, **Q** = Quad, **b** = bathroom. The modest tourist tax (€1 per person, per night, lower off-season) is not included in these rates. Unless otherwise noted, hotels accept credit cards and include breakfast in their rates, while most *sobe* accept only cash and don't offer breakfast. The accommodations quote their prices in euros, but you'll pay in kunas. Everyone listed here speaks at least enough English to make a reservation (or knows someone nearby who can translate).

To help you sort easily through these listings, I've divided the rooms into three categories based on the price for a standard double room with bath in peak season:

  $$$ **Higher Priced**—Most rooms €100 or more.
   $$ **Moderately Priced**—Most rooms between €55-100.
    $ **Lower Priced**—Most rooms €55 or less.

air-con, near Konoba Marko Polo restaurant at Jakova Baničevića 13, tel. 020/711-400, mobile 091-551-6592, www.ikorcula.net /lenni, perisa.modrinic@du.t-com.hr).

$$ Royal Apartments are some of the most hotelesque (and most expensive) rooms in town. The five apartments are classy and new-feeling, making the place feel more like a small hotel with no real reception desk—arrange your arrival time carefully (July– Aug: small apartment-€80, big apartment-€90; June and Sept: small apartment-€70, big apartment-€80; closed Oct–May, no extra charge for 1- or 2-night stays, cash only, air-con, well-marked with green awning just west of Old Town at Trg Petra Šegedina 4, mobile 098-184-0444, royalapt@ica.net, Jelavić family—Anna- maria speaks English, but Marko doesn't).

$$ The Vitaić family is a father-and-sons operation renting three rooms in the Old Town (July–Aug: Db-€65; Sept–June: Db-€45; 10 percent more for 1- or 2-night stays, cash only, air-con, pay Wi-Fi, Dinko Mirošević 8, tel. 020/715-312, mobile 098-932- 7670, www.familyvitaic.com, info@familyvitaic.com).

$ Rezi and Andro Depolo, probably distant relatives of Marco, rent four comfy rooms on the bay west of the Old Town. Three of the rooms offer beautiful views to the Old Town, and the five-minute stroll into town is pleasant and scenic. English- speaking Rezi is very friendly and works to make her guests feel welcome (July–Aug: Db-€40; Sept–June: Db-€35; room with kitchen-€5 more, 30 percent more for 1-night stays, continental breakfast-€4, big breakfast-€5, cash only, air-con, Put Sv. Nikola 43; walk along waterfront from Old Town with bay on your right, look for *Apartments Depolo* sign at the yellow house set back from the street, just before the two monasteries; tel. 020/711-621, mobile 098-964-3687, tereza.depolo@du.t-com.hr).

$ Marco Polo Apartments has four apartments in the Old Town (July–Aug: Db-€50; Sept–June: Db-€40; cash only or pay online through PayPal, air-con, ulica Marka Andrijica, mobile 099-686-3717, British tel. +44-794-620-8177, www.marcopolo -apartments.com, info@korculainfo.com).

$ Anka Portolan, with her helpful English-speaking grand- daughter Vesna, rents four fine, older-feeling rooms perfectly located near the wall in the Old Town (July–Aug: Db-€35, small apartment-€45, bigger apartment-€50; Sept–June: Db- €30, small apartment-€35, bigger apartment-€40; 30 percent more for 1- or 2-night stays, cash only, air-con, ulica Don Pavla Poše 7, tel. 020/711-711, vesna.stankovic.14@gmail.com).

$ *Booking* Sobe *Through an Agency:* While you can walk along Put Sv. Nikola and generally find a fine deal on a private room, you can also book one through one of Korčula's travel agencies for an additional 20 percent (figure Db-€35–50 in high season, €20–35 off-season, 30 percent more for 1- or 2-night stays). For information on two agencies—Atlas and Korkyra—see "Helpful Hints," earlier.

Hotels

All five of Korčula's hotels are owned by HTP Korčula. If you don't want to stay in a *soba,* these are the only game in town. You can reserve rooms at any of them through the main office (tel. 020/726-336, fax 020/711-746, www.korcula-hotels.com, marketing @htp-korcula.hr). I've listed peak-season prices with breakfast only; rates are progressively lower the farther you get into off-season. You can pay €10 more per person for half-board (dinner at the hotel). It's much cheaper to stay a week or longer. There's a long-term plan to renovate all of these hotels, but so far the Marko Polo is the only one that's seen any progress (and the only one that has air-conditioning).

$$$ Hotel Korčula has by far the best location, right on the waterfront alongside the Old Town. It has a fine seaside terrace restaurant and friendly staff, even if the 20 rooms are outmoded and waaaay overpriced. The rooms are on two floors: The more expensive "first-floor" rooms (actually on the third floor) have big windows and sea views; the cheaper "second-floor" rooms (actually on the fourth floor) have tiny windows and no views (July–Aug: Sb-€120, Db-€160; mid May–June and Sept–mid-Oct: Sb-€85–105, Db-€120–140; cheaper off-season, reception tel. 020/711-078).

$$$ Hotel Marko Polo, the only one of the chain that has been renovated, has 94 crisp rooms, air-conditioning, and an elevator. All of this makes it the town's only real "splurge"...and it's priced accordingly (July–Aug: Sb-€150, Db-€200; mid-May–June and Sept–mid-Oct: Sb-€105–130, Db-€150–170; cheaper off-season, reception tel. 020/726-004).

$$$ *Other Hotels:* Three more hotels cluster a 15-minute walk away, around the far side of Shell Bay. All are rough around the edges, overpriced, and relatively inconvenient to the Old Town, but they share a nice beach. **Hotel Liburna,** with a clever split-level design that reflects the skyline of the Old Town, has 109 rooms, most of them accessible by elevator; half the rooms face the sea and cost an additional 10 percent (July–Aug: Sb-€120, Db-€160; mid-May–June and Sept–mid-Oct: Sb-€85–105, Db-€120–140; cheaper off-season; reception tel. 020/726-006). Dreary **Hotel Park** has 153 cheaper rooms (reception tel. 020/726-100). The fifth hotel, **Hotel Bon Repos**—another 15 minutes by foot from the Old Town—is, in every sense, the last resort.

Eating in Korčula

Korčula is awash in interchangeable seafood restaurants. These are all good options, but everything in town is pretty similar—make your decision based on atmosphere and what looks best to you. The price ranges listed below don't include top-end seafood splurges (which are normally listed in menus by the 100-gram unit or by the kilogram). Note that almost all of these eateries close from about November to Easter.

Pizzeria Amfora, on a side lane off the people-parade up Korčula's main drag in the Old Town, features delicious and well-priced pastas and pizzas. Squeeze into the small dining room or enjoy the sidewalk tables (50–70-kn pizzas and pastas, 60–100-kn main courses, daily 11:00–24:00, closed 15:00–18:00 and Sun dinner in shoulder season, ulica od Teatra 4, tel. 020/711-739).

Adio Mare, with fine seafood, may have the best decor in town: a cavernous stone dining room with long shared tables and a thick vine scaling one wall. Or climb the stairs and cross the little bridge to the delightful rooftop garden terrace (50–110-kn main courses, well-described menu, daily 17:30–24:00, sometimes also 12:00–14:00 in peak season, on the main drag just past Marco Polo's House, tel. 020/711-253).

Konoba Marinero has pleasantly nautical decor, outdoor tables on an atmospherically tight lane, and a simple menu of Dalmatian specialties (60–110-kn main courses, Easter–Oct daily 11:00–24:00, Marka Andrijića 13, tel. 020/711-170).

Along the Seawall: Various restaurants line up scenically along the Old Town's eastern seawall, offering al fresco dining with salty views. Their tables, spilling out along the seafront, are ideal for romantic harborside meals. For traditional fare, consider **Konoba Morski Konjic** ("Moorish Seahorse")—though the crank-'em-out food is disappointing and the service can be jaded (60–110-kn main courses, 10-kn cover, daily 8:00–24:00). For something more affordable, try **Pizzeria Tedeschi,** which serves up good pizzas closer to the base of the peninsula (long hours daily, tel. 020/711-586).

Cheaper Options Around Shell Bay: Prices inside the Old Town are the highest in Korčula. But several cheaper eateries lie just outside the Old Town. Window-shop menus along the harbor, then hang a left at the bus station and continue up the road toward the big resort hotels. You'll find plenty of cafés, pizzerias, and *konoba*s (traditional restaurants), most with outdoor seating.

Picnics: Just outside the main gate, you'll find a lively produce market and a big, modern, air-conditioned **Konzum** supermarket (Mon–Sat 7:00–20:30, Sun 8:00–20:00). A short stroll from there down Put Sv. Nikola takes you to rocky seafront perches with the best Korčula views. Otherwise, there are many inviting picnic spots along the Old Town embankment.

A Scenic Drink: The best setting for drinks is at **Buffet "Massimo,"** a youthful-feeling cocktail bar in a city-wall tower at the very tip of the Old Town peninsula. You can have a drink on one of three levels: the downstairs bar, the main-floor lounge, or climb the ladder (at your own risk) to the tower-top terrace (terrace is only for cocktail-sippers—no beer or wine). If you're up top, notice the simple dumbwaiter for hauling up drinks (35–60-kn cocktails, daily in summer 18:00–2:00 in the morning, shoulder season 17:30–1:00 in the morning, closed Nov–April, tel. 020/715-073).

Sweet Shop: For some good (if pricey) local sweets, stop by **Cukarin,** which sells tasty traditional cookies such as the *amareta* almond cake and the walnut-cream-filled *klašun.* They also sell homemade wine, liqueur, honey, and jam (Mon–Sat 8:30–12:00 & 17:30–20:00, closed Sun and Jan–Feb, a block behind the Jadrolinija office on ulica Hrvatske Bratske Zajednice, tel. 020/711-055).

Ice Cream: My favorite *sladoled* in Korčula is at **Kiwi** (just up the lane across from Konzum supermarket, open long hours daily).

Korčula Connections

Korčula is reasonably well connected to the rest of the Dalmatian Coast by boat, but service becomes sparse in the off-season. If you're here during a lull in the sailing schedule, buses are your ticket out of town (making the short crossing to the Pelješac Peninsula on the Dominče–Orebić ferry). No matter when you travel, it's smart to carefully study current boat schedules, as they are always subject to change.

Boat Connections

Boats big and small depart from the embankment surrounding Korčula's Old Town peninsula. Which side of the peninsula a boat uses can depend on the weather—be flexible and inquire locally about where to meet your boat. Some boats leave from other parts of the island, most notably the town of Vela Luka (at the opposite tip of the island, a 1-hour bus ride from Korčula town—described later). Other boats, including the car ferry to Orebić (described later, under "Route Tips for Drivers"), leave from the Dominče dock, about a five-minute drive east of Korčula town.

Big Jadrolinija Car Ferries: From Korčula town, these huge, handy vessels go north, to **Stari Grad** on Hvar Island (20-min bus ride from Hvar town; 2/week, 3.5 hrs; the catamaran described next is faster and takes you right to Hvar town) and **Split** (2/week,

5–6 hrs—catamaran described next is faster and cheaper); or south, to **Sobra** on Mljet Island (1.25-hr bus ride from the national park, 2–3/week June–Sept, none Oct–May, 2 hrs; for details, see below) and **Dubrovnik** (5/week July–Sept, 4/week June, 2/week Oct–May, 3–4 hrs).

Speedy *Krilo* Catamaran from Korčula Town to Hvar Town and Split: A speedy catamaran called *Krilo* leaves Korčula town at 6:00 in the morning every day year-round, and zips to Hvar town and Split (to Hvar: 1.5 hrs, 33 kn; to Split: 2.5–2.75 hrs, 55 kn; in summer, it also stops en route at Prigradica on Korčula Island). In Korčula, tickets for the *Krilo* are sold at a small waterfront kiosk near Hotel Korčula—not at the Jadrolinija office. While you can buy *Krilo* tickets starting a half-hour before the boat departs (at 5:30), they can sell out—it's much better to buy them the night before (they're sold at the kiosk between 18:30 and 20:00). Since it returns from Split and Hvar the same afternoon, this extremely handy catamaran allows you to effortlessly day-trip to either place (see "Connections" for each town). For the latest schedule, see www.krilo.hr.

Speedy *Nona Ana* Catamaran to Mljet and Dubrovnik: In July and August, this convenient boat zips travelers from Korčula to Polače (on Mljet Island, handy to the national park there), then to Sobra (a less-appealing spot on Mljet) and on to Dubrovnik (4/week, generally departs Korčula at 16:00; to Polače: 1 hr, 30 kn; to Dubrovnik: 2.75 hrs, 55 kn). Unfortunately, the boat doesn't serve Korčula at other times (Sept–June). Confirm schedules at www.gv-line.hr, and buy tickets at Korkyra Tours travel agency (see "Helpful Hints," earlier).

From Vela Luka to Hvar Town and Split: There are additional boats to points north, but they usually require a very early bus from Korčula town (departing at 4:00 in the morning) to the port at Vela Luka, an hour away at the other end of the island. A Jadrolinija **fast catamaran** goes daily from Vela Luka to both Hvar town and Split (Mon–Sat departs at 5:30, Sun at 8:00; to Hvar: 45 min, 22 kn; to Split: 1.75 hrs, 27 kn). A much slower **car ferry** also travels daily from Vela Luka to Split (1–2/day, 2.75 hrs, 46 kn, does not stop at Hvar town). Since reaching Vela Luka from Korčula town is a hassle, carefully confirm these boat schedules and understand all your options (at the Korčula TI or Jadrolinija office) before you get up early to make the trip.

To the National Park on Mljet Island: Unfortunately, day-tripping from Korčula to Mljet National Park by public transportation is not possible (see the Near Dubrovnik chapter). The *Nona Ana* catamaran (described above) gets you there in the evening with no return boat that day to Korčula. However, you can day-trip to Mljet from Korčula by taking an excursion (described on page 238). To do Mljet en route from Korčula to Dubrovnik, you'll have to sleep on Mljet, then take the afternoon catamaran to Dubrovnik the next day.

Bus Connections

All buses from Korčula town (except those to Vela Luka) first drive to Dominče, where they meet the car ferry to cross over to Orebić, on the Pelješac Peninsula. Don't be surprised if you have to get off the bus, walk onto the ferry, and meet a different bus across the channel. It takes just over an hour to drive the length of the Pelješac Peninsula and meet the main coastal road.

From Korčula Town by Bus to: **Dubrovnik** (peak season: 2/day, 3.5 hrs; off-season: Mon–Sat 1/day with an early departure, Sun 2/day; about 100 kn), **Zagreb** (1/day, 9–13.5 hrs depending on route), **Split** (1/day, 5 hrs, same bus goes to Zagreb), **Vela Luka** (at far end of island, Mon–Fri 7/day, Sat 6/day, Sun 4/day, 1 hr, first bus at 4:00 gets you to the early-morning ferries—see above).

Shuttle Bus to Dubrovnik: Korkyra Tours travel agency runs a handy minibus that costs only slightly more than the bus and takes you right to your accommodations in Dubrovnik (125 kn one-way plus 10 kn/bag, runs Mon–Fri at 8:00 year-round, Sat–Sun by request only, 2 hrs, includes light breakfast and room-finding help if needed, reserve ahead, mobile 091-571-4355, www .korkyra.info, info@korkyra.info).

Route Tips for Drivers: Between Korčula and the Mainland

The island of Korčula is connected to the mainland by a small car ferry that runs between Dominče—about a mile east of Korčula town—and Orebić, across the channel on the Pelješac Peninsula (58 kn/car, 12 kn/passenger, 15-min crossing, departs Dominče at the top of most but not all hours—check carefully in Korčula, departs Orebić at :30 past most hours).

If you're driving via the mainland, you'll first cross on this car ferry to Orebić on the vineyard-strewn Pelješac Peninsula. The Pelješac Peninsula is extremely long and narrow, and the roads are very rough, so it can take longer than you'd expect to reach the main coastal road (figure 1–1.5 hrs from Orebić). Where the peninsula meets the mainland, you'll see the cute little "Great Wall of Croatia" town of Ston. For more on the Pelješac Peninsula and Ston, see page 307.

If you're heading south to **Dubrovnik,** the coastal road zips you right there (about an hour from Ston). If you're heading north to **Split,** soon after joining the coastal road you'll actually pass through Bosnia-Herzegovina for a few miles (around the town of Neum—just stop and flash your passport as you enter and exit the country; for more details, see page 205).

Because of the ferry crossing and the long drive along the Pelješac Peninsula, driving **between Split and Korčula** is time-consuming and tiring. Instead, I prefer to take the longer car ferry the whole way between Split and Vela Luka, at the far end of Korčula Island (described earlier; allow 1 hr for the drive from Korčula town to Vela Luka, about 300 kn per car). The scenic and relaxing 2.75-hour boat ride from Vela Luka to Split saves you more than that much driving time.

KORČULA

DUBROVNIK

Dubrovnik is a living fairy tale that shouldn't be missed. It feels like a small town today, but 500 years ago, Dubrovnik was a major maritime power, with the third-biggest navy in the Mediterranean. Still jutting confidently into the sea and ringed by thick medieval walls, Dubrovnik deserves its nickname: the Pearl of the Adriatic. Within the ramparts, the traffic-free Old Town is a fun jumble of quiet, cobbled back lanes; low-impact museums; narrow, steep alleys; and kid-friendly squares. After all these centuries, the buildings still hint at old-time wealth, and the central promenade (Stradun) remains the place to see and be seen. If I had to pick just one place to visit in Croatia, this would be it.

The city's charm is the sleepy result of its no-nonsense past. Busy merchants, the salt trade, and shipbuilding made Dubrovnik rich. But the city's most valued commodity was always its freedom—even today, you'll see the proud motto *Libertas* displayed all over town (see *"Libertas"* sidebar).

Dubrovnik flourished in the 15th and 16th centuries, but an earthquake destroyed nearly everything in 1667. Most of today's buildings in the Old Town are post-quake Baroque, although a few palaces, monasteries, and convents displaying a rich Gothic-Renaissance mix survive from Dubrovnik's earlier Golden Age.

Dubrovnik remained a big tourist draw through the Tito years, bringing in much-needed hard currency from Western visitors. Consequently, the city was never given the hard socialist patina of other Yugoslav cities (such as the nearby Montenegrin capital Podgorica, then known as "Titograd").

As Croatia violently separated from Yugoslavia in 1991, Dubrovnik became the only coastal city to be pulled into the

DUBROVNIK

Libertas

Libertas—liberty—has always been close to the heart of every Dubrovnik citizen. Dubrovnik was a proudly independent republic for centuries, even as most of Croatia became Venetian and Hungarian. Dubrovnik believed so strongly in *libertas* that it was the first foreign state in 1776 to officially recognize an upstart, experimental republic called the United States of America.

In the Middle Ages, the city-state of Dubrovnik (then called Ragusa) bought its independence from whoever was strongest—Byzantium, Venice, Hungary, the Ottomans—sometimes paying off more than one at a time. Dubrovnik's ships flew whichever flags were necessary to stay free, earning the nickname "Town of Seven Flags." As time went on, Europe's big-league nations were glad to have a second major seafaring power in the Adriatic to balance the Venetian threat. A free Dubrovnik was more valuable than a pillaged, plundered Dubrovnik.

In 1808, Napoleon conquered the Adriatic and abolished the Republic of Dubrovnik. After Napoleon was defeated, the fate of the continent was decided at the Congress of Vienna. But Dubrovnik's delegate was denied a seat at the table. The more powerful nations, no longer concerned about Venice and fed up after years of being sweet-talked by Dubrovnik, were afraid that the delegate would play old alliances off each other to re-establish an independent Republic of Dubrovnik. Instead, the city became a part of the Habsburg Empire and entered a long period of decline.

Libertas still hasn't died in Dubrovnik. In the surreal days of the early 1990s, when Yugoslavia was reshuffling itself, a movement for the creation of a new Republic of Dubrovnik gained some momentum (led by a judge who, in earlier times, had convicted others for the same ideas). Another movement pushed for Dalmatia to secede as its own nation. But now that the dust has settled, today's locals are content and proud to be part of an independent Republic of Croatia.

fighting (see "The Siege of Dubrovnik" sidebar). Imagine having your youthful memories of good times spent romping in the surrounding hills replaced by visions of tanks and warships shelling your hometown. The city was devastated, but Dubrovnik has been repaired with amazing speed. The only physical reminders of the war are lots of new, bright-orange roof tiles. Locals, relieved the fighting is over but forever hardened, are often willing to talk openly about the experience with visitors—offering a rare opportunity to grasp the harsh realities of war from an eyewitness perspective.

Though the war killed tourism in the 1990s, today the crowds are most decidedly back. In fact, Dubrovnik's biggest downside is the overwhelming midday crush of multinational tourists who converge on the Old Town when their cruise ships dock. But locals—relieved that all these visitors are finally helping them get their economy back on track—appreciate that the numbers are about back to prewar levels. While Europeans and Australians have been flocking here for years, Americans have only just begun to rediscover Dubrovnik.

Planning Your Time

While Dubrovnik's museums are nothing special, the town is one of those places that you never want to leave. The real attraction here is the Old Town and its relaxing, breezy ambience. While Dubrovnik could easily be "seen" in a day, a second or third day to unwind (or even more time, for side-trips) makes the long trip here more worthwhile.

To hit all the key sights in a single day, start at the Pile Gate, just outside the Old Town. Walk around the city's walls to get your bearings (before it gets too hot and crowded), then work your way down the main drag (following my "Welcome to Dubrovnik" self-guided walk). As you explore, drop in at any museums or churches that appeal to you. To squeeze the most into a single day (or with a second day), consider a boat excursion from the Old Port (Lokrum Island, just offshore, requires the least brainpower).

Dubrovnik also makes an excellent home base for day trips into the surrounding area, including a dizzying array of island getaways, plus a pair of particularly striking international destinations: Bosnia-Herzegovina's Mostar and Montenegro's Bay of Kotor. I enjoy staying three or four nights, for maximum side-tripping flexibility. For options, see the next three chapters.

Orientation to Dubrovnik

(area code: 020)
Nearly all of the sights worth seeing are in Dubrovnik's traffic-free, walled **Old Town** (Stari Grad) peninsula. The main pedestrian promenade through the middle of town is called the **Stradun;** from this artery, the Old Town climbs steeply uphill in both directions to the walls. The Old Town connects to the mainland through three gates: the **Pile Gate,** to the west; the **Ploče Gate,** to the east; and the smaller **Buža Gate,** at the top of the stepped lane called Boškovićeva. The **Old Port** (Gradska Luka), with leisure boats to nearby destinations, is at the east end of town. While

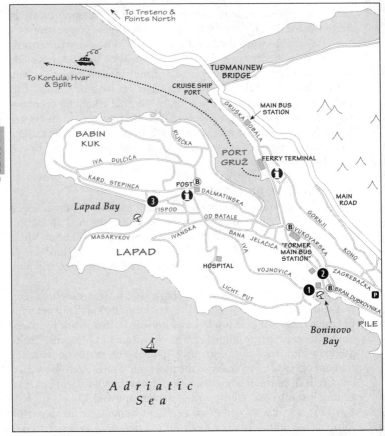

greater Dubrovnik has about 50,000 people, the local population within the Old Town is just a few thousand in the winter—and even smaller in summer, when many residents move out to rent their apartments to tourists.

The **Pile** (PEE-leh) neighborhood, a pincushion of tourist services, is just outside the western end of the Old Town (through the Pile Gate). In front of the gate, you'll find a TI and Internet café (sharing an office), ATMs, a post office, taxis, buses (fanning out to all the outlying neighborhoods), a cheap Konzum grocery store, and the Atlas Travel Agency (described later, under "Helpful Hints"). Just off this strip are some good *sobe* (rooms in private homes—described under "Sleeping in Dubrovnik"). This is also the starting point for my "Welcome to Dubrovnik" self-guided walk.

A mile or two away from the Old Town are beaches peppered with expensive resort hotels. The closest area is **Boninovo Bay** (a 20-min walk or 5-min bus trip from the Old Town), but most

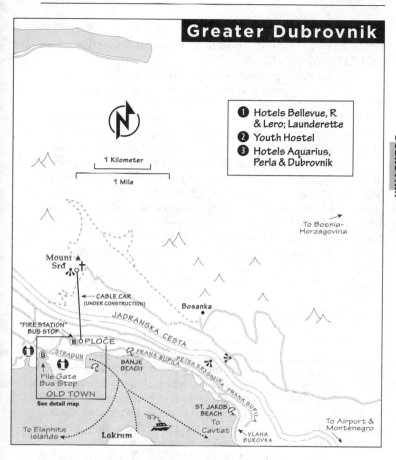

Greater Dubrovnik

1 Hotels Bellevue, R
   & Lero; Launderette

2 Youth Hostel

3 Hotels Aquarius,
   Perla & Dubrovnik

1 Kilometer

1 Mile

To Bosnia-
Herzegovina

Mount
Srđ

← CABLE CAR
(UNDER CONSTRUCTION)

Bosanka

JADRANSKA CESTA

"FIRE STATION"
BUS STOP

B PLOČE

STRADUN

BANJE
BEACH

FRANA SUPILA

PEICA KRSNIKA

FRANA SUPILA

Pile Gate
Bus Stop

OLD TOWN
See detail map

To Elaphite
Islands

Lokrum

ST. JAKOB
BEACH

To
Cavtat

VLAHA
BUKOVKA

To Airport &
Montenegro

cluster on the lush **Lapad Peninsula** to the west (a 15-min bus trip from the Old Town); I've recommended accommodations in each of these areas. Across the bay from the Lapad Peninsula is **Port Gruž,** with the main bus station, ferry terminal, and cruise-ship port.

Tourist Information

Dubrovnik's TI has several branches (www.tzdubrovnik.hr), with hours that tend to fluctuate depending on demand. Plans to consolidate smaller TIs into one larger office just outside the Pile Gate (near the main bus stop) might lead to the closure of some of these branches. Until then, you'll find TIs at the following locations (note that only the Old Town and Port Gruž TIs are likely to stay open through the winter):

• In the **Old Town,** a few steps off the main drag at Široka 1 (July–mid-Sept daily 8:00–22:00; mid-Sept–Oct Mon–Fri

8:00–19:00, Sat–Sun 9:00–14:00; Nov–March Mon–Sat 9:00–19:00, Sun 9:00–14:00; April–June Mon–Sat 9:00–21:00, Sun 9:00–14:00; tel. 020/323-587).

• In the **Pile** neighborhood just outside the Old Town, 100 yards up the street from the Pile Gate (July–mid-Sept daily 8:00–21:00; June and mid-Sept–Oct Mon–Fri 8:00–19:00, Sat 9:00–14:00, closed Sun; April–May Mon–Fri 8:00–15:00, Sat 9:00–14:00, closed Sun; likely closed Nov–March; Branitelja Dubrovnika 7, tel. 020/427-591; Internet access in the same office).

• At **Port Gruž,** across the street from the Jadrolinija ferry dock (July–mid-Sept daily 8:00–20:00; mid-Sept–Oct Mon–Fri 8:00–19:00, Sat–Sun 9:00–14:00; Nov–March Mon–Fri 9:00–16:00, Sat 9:00–14:00, closed Sun; April–May Mon–Fri 8:00–15:00, Sat 9:00–14:00, closed Sun; June Mon–Fri 8:00–20:00, Sat–Sun 9:00–14:00; Gruška obala, tel. 020/417-983).

• In the **Lapad** resort area, at the head of the main drag (July–mid-Sept daily 8:00–21:00; mid-Sept–Oct Mon–Fri 8:00–12:30 & 17:00–19:00, Sat 9:00–14:00, closed Sun; April–May Mon–Fri 9:00–20:00, Sat 9:00–14:00, closed Sun; June Mon–Fri 9:00–20:00, Sat 9:00–14:00, closed Sun; likely closed Nov–March; Šetalište Kralja Zvonimira 25, tel. 020/437-460).

All the TIs are government-run and legally can't sell you anything except the town combo-ticket—but they can answer questions and give you a copy of the free town map and monthly information booklet *The Best in Dubrovnik Riviera,* which contains helpful maps, bus and ferry schedules, museum prices and hours, a current schedule of events and performances, specifics on side-trip destinations, and more. If you need a room and the TI isn't busy, they might be willing to unofficially call around to find a place for you.

Skip the combo-ticket that the TIs sell. A different combo-ticket, sold at participating sights, is a better deal (both described later, under "Sights in Dubrovnik").

Arrival in Dubrovnik

For details on getting to the Dalmatian Coast, see page 170. As is the case throughout Croatia, you'll be met at the boat dock or bus station by locals trying to get you to rent a room *(soba)* at their house. If you've already reserved elsewhere, honor your reservation; if not, consider the offer (but be very clear on the location before you accept—many are nowhere near the Old Town).

By Bus: Long-distance buses and many regional buses use Dubrovnik's **main bus station** (Autobusni Kolodvor), just beyond the ferry terminal along the Port Gruž embankment (about 2.5 miles northwest of the Old Town). It's straightforward and user-friendly, with pay toilets, baggage storage, and a helpful bus information window. To reach the Old Town's Pile Gate, walk straight

Dubrovnik Essentials

English	Croatian	Pronounced
Old Town	Stari Grad	STAH-ree grahd
Old Port	Stara Luka	STAH-rah LOO-kah
Pile Gate	Gradska Vrata Pile	GRAHD-skah VRAH-tah PEE-leh
Ploče Gate	Gradska Vrata Ploče	GRAHD-skah VRAH-tah PLOH-cheh
Main Promenade	Stradun	STRAH-doon
Adriatic Sea	Jadran	YAH-drahn

ahead through the bus stalls, then bear right at the main road to the city bus stop, where you can hop on a bus (#1, #1a, #1b, or #1c) to the Pile stop. A **taxi** from the main bus station to the Old Town and most accommodations runs about 75 kn.

Dubrovnik has two other bus stops that are closer to the Old Town. Some buses (especially regional or local buses) use these stops instead of, or in addition to, the main bus station. The good news is that these stops are more convenient if you're staying in the Old Town. The bad news is that locals call the stops by various names, so it can be confusing to explain which one you're talking about (even if you use the names listed below). Ask your bus driver which stop is best for your destination.

The **"fire station" bus stop** (a.k.a. "cable car" bus stop) is the handiest stop to the Old Town, though it's only used by a few buses to destinations in the south (such as the airport). This stop is just uphill from the Buža Gate, overlooking the old wall, right next to the bottom station of the cable car up to Mount Srđ. From this bus stop, simply walk downhill (and through the pedestrian underpass)—you'll be inside the Old Town walls within a few minutes.

Another transit point is roughly between the Old Town and the main bus station. It's confusingly nicknamed the **"former main bus station"** (locals also call this the "old main bus station," "water polo pool," or "Lapad Stanica"). This station is mostly served by regional, numbered buses (such as bus #10 to Cavtat, or bus #12 or #15 to Trsteno Arboretum). This station is connected to the Pile Gate by local buses #1, #1a, #1b, and #1c (which also go in the opposite direction, to the main bus station), as well as by bus #6.

By Car Ferry or Catamaran: The big car ferries arrive at Port Gruž, two miles northwest of the Old Town. On the road in front of the ferry terminal, you'll find a bus stop (#1, #1a, #1b, and #1c

Dubrovnik at a Glance

▲▲▲**Stradun Stroll** Charming walk through Dubrovnik's vibrant Old Town, ideal for coffee, ice cream, and people-watching. **Hours:** Always open. See page 260.

▲▲▲**Town Walls** Scenic mile-long walk along top of 15th-century fortifications encircling the city. **Hours:** July–Aug daily 8:00–19:30, progressively shorter hours off-season until 10:00–15:00 in mid-Nov–mid-March. See page 267.

▲**Franciscan Monastery Museum** Tranquil cloister, medieval pharmacy-turned-museum, and a century-old pharmacy still serving residents today. **Hours:** Daily April–Oct 9:00–18:00, Nov–March 9:00–17:00. See page 271.

▲**Cathedral** Eighteenth-century Roman Baroque cathedral and treasury filled with unusual relics such as a swatch of Jesus' swaddling clothes. **Hours:** Church—daily 8:00–20:00, treasury—generally open same hours as church, both have shorter hours off-season. See page 273.

▲**Dominican Monastery Museum** Another relaxing cloister with precious paintings, altarpieces, and manuscripts. **Hours:** Daily May–Sept 9:00–18:00, Oct–April 9:00–17:00. See page 274.

▲**Synagogue Museum** Europe's second-oldest synagogue and Croatia's only Jewish museum, with 13th-century Torahs and Holocaust-era artifacts. **Hours:** May–mid-Nov daily 10:00–20:00; mid-Nov–April Mon–Fri 10:00–13:00, closed Sat–Sun. See page 276.

▲**Institute for the Restoration of Dubrovnik** Photos and videos of the recent war and an exhibit on restoration work. **Hours:** June–Sept Mon–Fri 10:00–14:00, closed Sat–Sun; rotating exhibits Oct–May. See page 276.

---

go to the Old Town's Pile Gate; wait on the embankment side of the street) and a taxi stand (figure 70 kn to the Old Town and most accommodations). Across the street is the Jadrolinija office (with an ATM out front) and a TI. You can book a private room *(soba)* at Atlas Travel Agency (room-booking desk in boat terminal building, May–Sept only) or at Gulliver Travel Agency (behind TI). The fast *Nona Ana* catamaran from Mljet and Korčula also arrives near this big ferry dock.

By Cruise Ship: Some ships moor just offshore from the Old Port, then send their passengers into the Old Town on transfer

DUBROVNIK

▲**Serbian Orthodox Church and Icon Museum** Active church serving Dubrovnik's Serbian Orthodox community and museum with traditional religious icons. **Hours:** Church—daily May-Sept 8:00-20:00, Oct-April 8:00-15:00, short services daily at 8:30 and 19:00, longer liturgy Sun at 9:00; museum—May-Oct Mon-Sat 9:00-14:00, closed Sun; Nov-April Mon-Fri 9:00-14:00, closed Sat-Sun. See page 277.

▲**Rupe Granary and Ethnographic Museum** Good folk museum with tools, jewelry, clothing, and painted eggs above immense underground grain stores. **Hours:** Wed-Mon 9:00-16:00, closed Tue. See page 279.

▲**Mount Srđ** Napoleonic fortress capping the mountain above Dubrovnik, now hosting a modest museum to the recent war. **Hours:** Mountaintop—always open; museum—daily 10:00-18:30, maybe until 20:00 in summer. See page 279.

Rector's Palace Sparse antiques collection in the former home of rectors who ruled Dubrovnik in the Middle Ages. **Hours:** Daily May-Oct 9:00-18:00, Nov-April 9:00-16:00. See page 272.

Maritime Museum Contracts, maps, paintings, and models from Dubrovnik's days as a maritime power and shipbuilding center. **Hours:** Vary with demand, usually March-Oct Tue-Sun 9:00-18:00, closed Mon, shorter hours Nov-Feb. See page 275.

Aquarium Tanks of local sea life housed in huge, shady old fort. **Hours:** Daily July-Aug 9:00-21:00, progressively shorter hours off-season until 9:00-13:00 Nov-March. See page 275.

War Photo Limited Thought-provoking photographic look at contemporary warfare. **Hours:** June-Sept daily 9:00-21:00; May and Oct Tue-Sat 9:00-15:00, Sun 10:00-14:00, closed Mon; closed Nov-April. See page 276.

boats. Others actually put in at Port Gruž, generally just beyond the bus station. To reach the Old Town, take a public bus or pay 80 kn for a taxi (described earlier, under "By Bus").

By Plane: Dubrovnik's small airport (Zračna Luka) is in a place called Ćilipi, 13 miles south of the city. A Croatia Airlines bus meets arriving flights for most major airlines at the airport, and brings you to the main bus station (35 kn, 40 min). Legitimate cabbies charge around 220 kn for the ride between the airport and the center (though some cabbies are charging as much as 300 kn; consider arranging your transfer in advance with one of the drivers listed on page 260, or through your *soba* host). Airport info: tel. 020/773-333, www.airport-dubrovnik.hr.

To get *to* the airport, you can take the same Croatia Airlines bus, which typically leaves from Dubrovnik's main bus station 1.5 hours before each Croatia Airlines or Austrian Airlines flight, or two hours before other airlines' international flights (but confirm this schedule at the TI). If you're staying in or near the Old Town, you'll find it more convenient to catch the airport bus at the "fire station" bus stop just above the Old Town. From the Old Town's main drag, hike up steep Boškovićeva lane and go through the wall at the Buža Gate. Once outside, continue straight under the arch and up the stairs, then swing right at the fire station onto the busy Krešimira street; the bus stop is a few steps up the road, by the cable-car station. The airport bus reaches this stop a few minutes after leaving the main bus station—wave it down or it might pass you by. While it's theoretically possible that the bus will be full and not pick you up, locals assure me that it almost always works (and I've done this many times without a problem; in a pinch, call a taxi at tel. 020/970).

By Car: Coming from the north, you'll drive over the super-modern Tuđman Bridge (which most locals, mindful of their former president's tarnished legacy, call simply "the New Bridge"). Immediately after crossing the bridge, you have two options: To get to the main bus station, ferry terminal (with some car-rental drop-off offices nearby), and Lapad Peninsula, take the left turn just after the bridge, wind down to the waterfront, then turn left and follow this road along the Port Gruž embankment. Or, to head for the Old Town, continue straight after the bridge. You'll pass above the Port Gruž area, then take the right turn-off marked *Dubrovnik* (with the little bull's-eye). You'll go through a tunnel, then turn left for *Centar,* and begin following the brown signs for *Grad* (Old Town); individual big hotels are also signed from here. You'll pass the Old Town parking garage (described next), then wind up just above the walls.

If you're sleeping in or near the Old Town, **parking** is tricky. The handiest place to park long-term is the Old Town garage, which you'll pass on the right as you head toward the Old Town (10 kn/hr, 120 kn/day, half-price Oct–May). From here, it's about a 10-minute downhill walk to the Old Town, or you can take a shuttle bus (2/hr, free if you're paying to park here). If you'd like to be closer to the Old Town, you can take your chances on finding a spot—either on the street directly behind and above the town walls (pay at meter), or in the convenient but often-crammed pay lot nicknamed "the tennis court," just behind the wall (10 kn/hr). Another option is to drive to this area near the Old Town to unload your bags, then leave your car at the Old Town garage (or a cheaper, more distant one) for the duration of your visit. When in doubt, ask your *soba* host or hotel for parking tips.

If you're sleeping at Lapad or Boninovo Bay, you'll have an easier time finding parking at or near your hotel—ask.

Helpful Hints

Festivals: Dubrovnik is most crowded during its Summer Festival, a month and a half of theater and musical performances held annually from July 10 to August 25 (www.dubrovnik-festival .hr). This is quickly followed by the "Rachlin & Friends" classical music festival in September (www.julianrachlin.com). For other options, see "Entertainment in Dubrovnik," later.

Crowd-Beating Tips: Dubrovnik has been discovered—especially by cruise ships (800 of which visit each year). Cruise-ship crowds descend on the Old Town on most summer days, roughly between 8:30 and 14:00 (the streets are most crowded 9:00–13:00). In summer, try to avoid the big sights—especially walking around the wall—during these peak times, and hit the beach or take a siesta midday, when the town is hottest and most crowded. On very busy days, as many as 9,000 cruise-ship day-trippers deluge Dubrovnik (three big ships' worth). If you're caught off-guard, it can be miserable. For others, it's entertaining to count the dozens of tour guides toting numbered paddles through the Old Town, and to watch the blocky orange transfer boats going back and forth to the ships moored offshore.

Wine Shop: For the best wine-tasting selection in a cool bar atmosphere, don't miss **d'vino Wine Bar** (described on page 284). If you want to shop rather than taste, **Vinoteka Miličić** offers a nice variety of local wines and helpful advice for choosing one—though they do tend to push their own wines (daily 9:00–23:00 in peak season, shorter hours off-season, near the Pile end of the Stradun, tel. 020/321-777).

Internet Access: You'll see signs all over town for Internet cafés with similar rates (around 5 kn/10 min). In the Old Town, my favorite is the modern **Netcafé,** with several speedy terminals right on Prijeko street, the "restaurant row" (daily 9:00–24:00, Prijeko 21, tel. 020/321-025). When staying in the Pile neighborhood, I use the **Dubrovnik Internet Centar** inside the Pile TI (May–Sept daily 8:00–24:00; Oct–April Mon–Sat 8:00–21:00, closed Sun; Branitelja Dubrovnika 7). There are plans to provide free Wi-Fi throughout the Old Town—if you're traveling with a laptop, ask the TI or your *sobe* host about this. Otherwise, Dubrovnik Internet Centar sells vouchers to get online at hotspots around the Old Town (including the Stradun and Old Port; 50 kn/1 day, 100 kn/3 days).

English Bookstore: The **Algoritam** shop, right on the Stradun, has a wide variety of guidebooks (including this one), non-fiction books about Croatia and the former Yugoslavia, novels, and magazines—all in English (July–Aug Mon–Sat 9:00–23:00, Sun 10:00–13:00 & 18:00–22:00; June and Sept Mon–Sat 9:00–21:00, Sun 10:00–13:00; Oct–May Mon–Fri 9:00–20:30, Sat 9:00–15:00, Sun 9:00–13:00; Placa 8).

Laundry: Hotels charge a mint to wash your clothes; *sobe* hosts are cheaper, but often don't have the time (ask). The best afford-able option is the full-service **launderette** near the hotels at Boninovo Bay, a 20-minute uphill walk or five-minute bus trip from the Pile Gate (90 kn for wash and dry in about 3 hours, no self-service, Mon–Fri 9:00–13:00 & 15:00–18:00, Sat 9:00–15:00, closed Sun, across from the big seafront Hotel Bellevue at Pera Čingrije 8, tel. 020/333-347).

Car Rental: The big international chains, such as **Avis** (tel. 020/313-633), have offices both at the airport and near the Port Gruž embankment where the big boats come in. In addi-tion, the many travel agencies closer to the Old Town also have a line on rental cars. Figure €50–60 per day, including taxes, insurance, and unlimited mileage (at the bigger chains, there's usually no extra charge for drop-off elsewhere in Croatia). Be sure the agency knows if you're crossing a border (such as Bosnia-Herzegovina or Montenegro) to ensure you have the proper paperwork.

Travel Agency: You'll see travel agencies all over town. At any of them, you can buy seats on an excursion, rent a car, book a room, buy Jadrolinija ferry tickets, and pick up a pile of bro-chures. The most established company is **Atlas,** with an office just outside the Pile Gate from the Old Town—though the location might change (June–Sept Mon–Sat 8:00–21:00, Sun 8:00–13:00; Oct–May Mon–Fri 8:00–20:00, Sat 8:00–15:00, closed Sun; down the little alley at Sv. Đurđa 4, otherwise look for signs to new location around the bus-stop area, tel. 020/442-574, fax 020/323-609, www.atlas-croatia.com, atlas.pile@atlas.hr). They also have an office at the ferry terminal building at Port Gruž (May–Sept only).

Best Views: Walking the **Old Town walls** late in the day, when the city is bathed in rich light, is a treat. The **Fort of St. Lawrence,** perched above the Pile neighborhood cove, has great views over the Old Town. A stroll up the road east of the city walls offers nice views back on the Old Town (best light early in the day).

Better yet, if you have a car, head south of the city in the morning for gorgeously lit Old Town views over your right shoulder; various turn-offs along this road are ideal photo stops. The best one, known locally as the **"panorama point,"** is where the road leading up and out of Dubrovnik meets the main road that passes above the town (look for the pull-out on the right, with tour buses). Even if you're heading north, in good weather it's worth a quick detour south for this view. For the highest vantage point without wings, head up to the fortress atop **Mount Srđ,** directly above the Old Town, which also houses a museum about the recent war (described later, under "Sights in Dubrovnik").

Getting Around Dubrovnik

If you're staying in or near the Old Town, everything is easily walkable. But those sleeping on Boninovo Bay or the Lapad Peninsula will want to get comfortable using the buses. Once you understand the system, commuting to the Old Town is a breeze.

By Bus: Libertas runs Dubrovnik's public buses. Tickets, which are good for an hour, are cheaper if you buy them in advance from a newsstand or your hotel (8 kn, ask for *autobusna karta,* ow-toh-BOOS-nah KAR-tah) than if you buy them from the bus driver (10 kn). A 24-hour ticket costs 25 kn, and a ticket for 20 rides costs 120 kn (only sold at special bus-ticket kiosks, such as the one near the Pile Gate bus stop).

When you enter the bus, validate your ticket in the machine next to the driver (orange arrow in, white side up). Because most tourists can't figure out how to validate their tickets, it can take a long time to load the bus (which means drivers are understandably grumpy, and locals aren't shy about cutting in line).

All buses stop near the Old Town, just in front of the Pile Gate (buy tickets at the newsstand or bus-ticket kiosk right by the stop). From here, they fan out to just about anywhere you'd want to go (hotels on Boninovo Bay, Lapad Peninsula, and the ferry terminal and long-distance bus station). You'll find bus schedules and a map in the TI booklet (for more information, visit www.libertasdubrovnik.hr).

By Taxi: Taxis start at 25 kn, then charge 8 kn per kilometer. The handiest taxi stand for the Old Town is just outside the Pile Gate. The biggest operation is Radio Taxi (tel. 020/970).

Tours in Dubrovnik

Walking Tours—Two companies—**Dubrovnik Walking Tours** and **Dubrovnik Walks**—offer similar one-hour walking tours of the Old Town daily at 10:00, and sometimes again in the afternoon (90 kn, also other departures and topics—look for fliers at TI). These tours are pricey and brief, touching lightly on the same basic information explained in this chapter.

Local Guide—For an in-depth look at the city, consider hiring your own local guide. **Štefica Curić** really knows her stuff and can give you an insider's look at the city (480 kn/2 hrs, mobile 091-345-0133, dugacarapa@yahoo.com). If Štefica is busy, she can refer you to another good guide for the same price. The TI can also suggest guides.

Bus-plus-Walking Tours—Two big companies (**Atlas** and **Elite**) offer expensive tours of Dubrovnik (about 220 kn, 2 hrs).

From Dubrovnik

Package Excursions—For information on tour boats and guided big-bus excursions from Dubrovnik to nearby destinations, see the next chapter.

Hire Your Own Driver—I enjoy renting my own car to see the sights around Dubrovnik (see "Helpful Hints," earlier). But if you're more comfortable having someone else do the driving, consider hiring a driver. While the drivers listed here are not official tour guides, they speak great English and offer ample commentary as you roll, and can help you craft a good day-long itinerary to Mostar, Montenegro, Korčula, or anywhere else near Dubrovnik (typically departing around 8:00 and returning in the early evening). Friendly **Pepo Klaić,** a veteran of the 1991 war, enjoys surprising my readers with worthwhile detours—go along with his suggestions (€250/day, €125 for half-day trip to nearer destinations, airport transfer for about 200 kn—cheaper than a taxi, these prices for up to 4 people—more expensive for bigger group, mobile 098-427-301, http://pepoklaic.pondi.hr, pepoklaic@yahoo.com). For €70, Pepo can drive you to the fortress at Mount Srđ up above the Old Town, with sweeping views of the entire area (about 1–1.5 hours round-trip). **Petar Vlašić** can do similar tours for similar prices, and specializes in wine tours to the Pelješac Peninsula, with stops at various wineries along the way (220-kn airport transfers, mobile 091-580-8721, www.dubrovnikriviera tours.com, meritum@du.t-com.hr). **Pero Carević,** who runs the recommended Villa Ragusa guest house, also drives travelers on excursions (similar prices, mobile 098-765-634, villa.ragusa@du .t-com.hr; see "Sleeping in Dubrovnik," later).

Self-Guided Walk

▲▲▲Welcome to Dubrovnik: Strolling the Stradun

Running through the heart of Dubrovnik's Old Town is the 300-yard-long Stradun promenade—packed with people and lined with sights. This walk offers an ideal introduction to Dubrovnik's charms. It takes about a half-hour, not counting sightseeing stops.

• Begin at the busy square in front of the west entrance to the Old Town, the Pile (PEE-leh) Gate.

Pile Neighborhood

This bustling area is the nerve center of Dubrovnik's tourist industry—it's where the real world meets the fantasy of Dubrovnik (for details on services offered here, see "Orientation to Dubrovnik," earlier). Near the modern, mirrors-and-TV-screens monument is a leafy café terrace. Wander over to the edge of the terrace and

take in the imposing walls of the Pearl of the Adriatic. The huge, fortified peninsula just outside the city walls is the **Fort of St. Lawrence** (Tvrđava Lovrijenac), Dubrovnik's oldest fortress and one of the top venues for the Dubrovnik Summer Festival. Shakespearean plays are often performed here, occasionally starring Goran Višnjić, the Croatian actor who became an American star on the TV show *ER*. You can climb this fortress for great views over the Old Town (20 kn, or covered by same ticket as Old Town walls on the same day).

• Cross over the moat (now a shady park) to the round entrance tower in the Old Town Wall. This is the...

Pile Gate (Gradska Vrata Pile)

Just before you enter the gate, notice the image above the entrance of **St. Blaise** (Sveti Vlaho in Croatian) cradling Dubrovnik in his arm. You'll see a lot more of Blaise during your time here—we'll find out why later on this walk.

Inside the outer wall of the Pile Gate and to the left, a white **sign** shows where each bomb dropped on the Old Town in the recent war. Once inside town, you'll see virtually no signs of the war—demonstrating the townspeople's impressive resilience in rebuilding so well and so quickly.

Passing the rest of the way through the gate, you'll find a lively little square surrounded by landmarks. To the left, a steep stairway leads up to the imposing **Minčeta Tower**. This is a good starting point for Dubrovnik's best activity, walking around the top of the wall (described later, under "Sights in Dubrovnik").

Next to the stairway is the small **Church of St. Savior** (Crkva

DUBROVNIK

Dubrovnik's Old Town

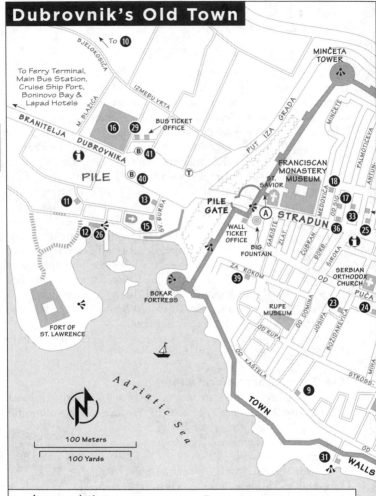

To Ferry Terminal,
Main Bus Station,
Cruise Ship Port,
Boninovo Bay &
Lapad Hotels

MINČETA
TOWER

BJELOKOSIĆA
To 10

IZMEĐU VRTA

M. BLAŽIĆA

BRANITELJA

DUBROVNIKA

PILE

PUT IZA GRADA

MINČETE

PALMOTIĆEVA

ANTUN

16   29

BUS TICKET
OFFICE

B 41

B 40

11

13

SV. ĐURĐA

12 26

15

PILE
GATE

WALL
TICKET
OFFICE

A

FRANCISCAN
MONASTERY
MUSEUM

ST.
SAVIOR

18

MEDVIĆA

OD SIG

17

STRADUN

33

36

25

GARIŠTE

ZLAT.

ČUBRAN.

ĐORĐ.

ŠIROKA

SERBIAN
ORTHODOX
CHURCH

PUČA

24

BIG
FOUNTAIN

ZA ROKOM

39

OD DOMINA

OD

RUPE
MUSEUM

JOSIPA

23

BOKAR
FORTRESS

OD RUPA

BOŽIDAREVIĆA

FORT OF
ST. LAWRENCE

OD KAŠTELA

STROSS.

MIHA

Adriatic Sea

N

TOWN

9

100 Meters

100 Yards

31

WALLS

OD

Accommodations

1 Villa Ragusa & Apts. Paviša
2 Apartments Martecchini
3 Raič Apartments
4 Plaza Apartments
5 Karmen Apartments
6 Apartments Amoret (3)
7 Apartments Placa
8 Renata Zijadić Rooms
9 Fresh Sheets Hostel
10 To Jadranka Benussi Rooms
11 Paulina Čumbelić Rooms

12 Rest. Orhan Guest House
13 Nedjeljka Benussi Rooms
14 Villa Adriatica
15 Atlas Travel Agency
16 Hilton Imperial Dubrovnik
17 Hotel Stari Grad

Restaurants, Bars & Groceries

18 Nishta Restaurant
19 Dubrovački Kantun
20 Konoba Kamenice
21 Lokanda Peskarija

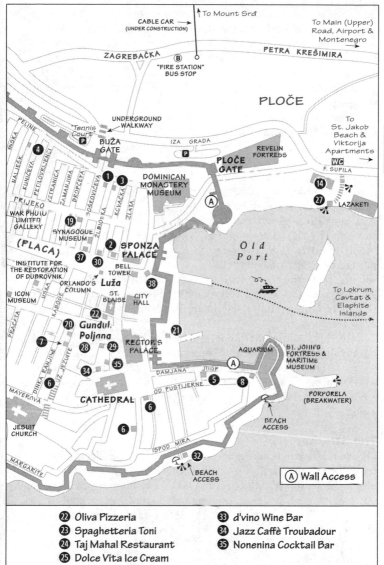

To Mount Srđ

CABLE CAR
(UNDER CONSTRUCTION)

To Main (Upper)
Road, Airport &
Montenegro

ZAGREBAČKA

PETRA KREŠIMIRA

(B) "FIRE STATION" BUS STOP

PLOČE

To
St. Jakob
Beach &
Viktorija
Apartments

PELINE

UNDERGROUND
WALKWAY

"Tennis
Court"

P

BUŽA
GATE

IZA GRADA

REVELIN
FORTRESS

PLOČE
GATE

WC

F. SUPILA

INSKA

NALJEŽI

KUNIČEVA

PETILOVRIJENCI

ŽMANJINA

PROPPEVA

BOŽIDAREVIĆA

KOVAČKA

ZLATA

DOMINICAN
MONASTERY
MUSEUM

(A)

LAZAKETI

PRIJEKO

ZELIDREKA

(14)

(27)

WAR PHOTO
LIMITED
GALLERY

(19)

SYNAGOGUE
MUSEUM

(PLACA)

(PLACA)

(2)

SPONZA
PALACE

Old
Port

INSTITUTE FOR
THE RESTORATION
OF DUBROVNIK

(37)

(30)

BELL
TOWER

(38)

To Lokrum,
Cavtat &
Elaphite
Islands

ICON
MUSEUM

ORLANDO'S
COLUMN

Luža

ST.
BLAISE

CITY
HALL

USKA

KABOGE

PRAČICA

DINKA RANJINE

(20)

(7)

Gundul.
Poljana

(28)

(29)

(22)

(35)

(21)

ST. JOHN'S
FORTRESS &
MARITIME
MUSEUM

RECTOR'S
PALACE

AQUARIUM

(A)

MAYEROVA

(6)

IZ JEZUITE

(34)

DAMJANA

JUDE

(5)

(8)

PORPORELA
(BREAKWATER)

OD PUSTIJERNE

JESUIT
CHURCH

CATHEDRAL

(6)

BEACH
ACCESS

ISPOD MIRA

(6)

MARGARITE

(32)

BEACH
ACCESS

(A) Wall Access

---

(22) Oliva Pizzeria	(33) d'vino Wine Bar
(23) Spaghetteria Toni	(34) Jazz Caffè Troubadour
(24) Taj Mahal Restaurant	(35) Nonenina Cocktail Bar
(25) Dolce Vita Ice Cream	
(26) Orhan Restaurant	**Other**
(27) Komarda Restaurant	(36) Vinoteka Miličić Wine Shop
(28) Produce Market	(37) Algoritam Bookshop
(29) Konzum Groceries (2)	(38) Sloboda Cinema
(30) Dubrava Bistro	(39) Jadran Cinema
(31) Cold Drinks "Buža" II	(40) Arriving Bus Stop
(32) Cold Drinks "Buža" I	(41) Departing Bus Stop

Svetog Spasa). Appreciative locals built this votive church to thank God after Dubrovnik made it through a 1520 earthquake. When the massive 1667 quake destroyed the city, this church was one of the only buildings left intact. And during the recent war, the church survived another close call when a shell exploded on the ground right in front of it (you can still see faint pockmarks from the shrapnel).

The giant, round structure in the middle of the square is **Onofrio's Big Fountain** (Velika Onofrijea Fontana). In the

Middle Ages, Dubrovnik had a complicated aqueduct system that brought water from the mountains seven miles away. The water ended up here, at the town's biggest fountain, before continuing through the city. This plentiful supply of water, large reserves of salt (a key source of Dubrovnik's wealth, from the town of Ston—see page 307), and a massive granary (now the Rupe Ethnographic Museum, described under "Sights in Dubrovnik") made little, independent Dubrovnik very siege-resistant.

The big building on the left just beyond the small Church of St. Savior is the **Franciscan Monastery Museum.** This building, with a delightful cloister and one of Europe's oldest pharmacies, is worth touring (described later, under "Sights in Dubrovnik").

• *When you're finished taking in the sights on this square, continue along...*

The Stradun

Dubrovnik's main promenade—officially called the Placa, but better known as the Stradun—is alive with locals and tourists alike. This is the heartbeat of the city: an Old World shopping mall by day

and sprawling cocktail party after dark, when everybody seems to be doing the traditional evening stroll—flirting, ice-cream-licking, flaunting, and gawking. A coffee and some of Europe's best people-watching in a prime Stradun café is one of travel's great $3 bargains.

When Dubrovnik was just getting its start in the seventh century, this street was a canal. Romans fleeing from the invading Slavs lived on the island of Ragusa (on your right), and the

Slavs settled on the shore. In the 11th century, the canal separating Ragusa from the mainland was filled in, the towns merged, and a unique Slavic-Roman culture and language blossomed. While originally much more higgledy-piggledy, this street was rebuilt in the current, more straightforward style after the 1667 earthquake.

During your time in Dubrovnik, you'll periodically hear the rat-a-tat-tat of a drum echoing through the streets from the Stradun. This means it's time to head for this main drag to get a glimpse of the colorfully costumed "town guards" parading through (and a cavalcade of tourists running alongside them, trying to snap a clear picture). You may also see some of these characters standing guard outside the town gates. It's all part of the local tourist board's efforts to make their town even more atmospheric.

• *Branching off from this promenade are several museums and other attractions—all described later, under "Sights in Dubrovnik." At the end of the Stradun is a passageway leading to the Ploče Gate. Just before this passage is the lively Luža Square. Its centerpiece is...*

Orlando's Column (Orlandov Stup)

Columns like this were typical of towns in northern Germany. Dubrovnik erected the column in 1417, soon after it had shifted allegiances from the oppressive Venetians to the Hungarians. By putting a northern European symbol in the middle of its most prominent square, Dubrovnik decisively distanced itself from Venice. Anytime a decision was made by the Republic, the town crier came to Orlando's Column and announced the news. The step he stood on indicated the importance of his message—the higher up, the more important the news. It was also used as the pillory, where people were publicly punished. The thin line on the top step in front of Orlando is exactly as long as the statue's forearm. This mark was Dubrovnik's standard measurement—not for a foot, but for an "elbow."

• *Now stand in front of Orlando's Column and orient yourself with a...*

Luža Square Spin-Tour

Orlando is looking toward the **Sponza Palace** (Sponza-Povijesni Arhiv). This building, from 1522, is the finest surviving example of Dubrovnik's Golden Age in the 15th and 16th centuries. It's a combination of Renaissance (ground-floor arches) and Venetian Gothic (upstairs windows). Houses up and down the main promenade used to look like this, but after the 1667 earthquake, they were replaced with boring

uniformity. This used to be the customs office *(dogana)*, but now it's an exhaustive archive of the city's history, with temporary art exhibits and a war memorial. The poignant **Memorial Room of Dubrovnik Defenders** (on the left as you enter) has photos of dozens of people from Dubrovnik who were killed fighting Yugoslav forces in 1991. A TV screen and images near the ceiling show the devastation of the city. Though the English descriptions are (perhaps unavoidably) slanted to the Croat perspective, it's compelling to look in the eyes of the brave young men who didn't start this war...but were willing to finish it (free, long hours daily in peak season, shorter hours off-season). Beyond the memorial room, the impressive **courtyard,** which generally displays temporary exhibits, is worth a peek (20 kn).

To the right of Sponza Palace is the town's **Bell Tower** (Gradski Zvonik). The original dated from 1444, but it was rebuilt when it started to lean in the 1920s. The big clock may be an octopus, but only one of its hands tells time. Below that, the circle shows the phase of the moon. At the bottom, the old-fashioned digital readout tells the hour (in Roman numerals) and the minutes (in five-minute increments). At the top of each hour (and again three minutes later), the time is clanged out on the bell up top by two bronze bell ringers, Maro and Baro. (If this all seems like a copy of the very similar clock on St. Mark's Square in Venice, locals are quick to point out that this clock predates that one by several decades.) The clock still has to be wound every two days. Notice the little window between the moon phase and the "digital" readout: The clock-winder opens this window to get some light. During the 1991–1992 siege, the clock-winder's house was destroyed—with the winding keys inside. For days, the clock bell didn't run. But then, miraculously, the keys were discovered lying in the street. The excited Dubrovnik citizens came together in this square and cheered as the clock was wound and the bell chimed, signaling to the soldiers surrounding the city that they hadn't won yet.

The big building to the right of the Bell Tower is the **City Hall** (Vijećnica). Next to that is **Onofrio's Little Fountain** (Mala Onofrijea Fontana), the little brother of the one at the other end of the Stradun. Beyond that is the **Gradska Kavana,** or "Town Café." This hangout—historically Dubrovnik's favorite spot for gossiping and people-watching—has pricey drinks and seating all the way through the wall to the Old Port. Just down the street from the Town Café is the Rector's Palace, and then the cathedral (for more on each, see "Sights in Dubrovnik").

Behind Orlando is **St. Blaise's Church** (Crkva Sv. Vlaha), dedicated to the patron saint of Dubrovnik. You'll see statues and paintings of St. Blaise all over town, always holding a model of the

city in his left hand. According to legend, a millennium ago St. Blaise came to a local priest in a dream and warned him that the up-and-coming Venetians would soon attack the city. The priest alerted the authorities, who prepared for war. Of course, the prediction came true. St. Blaise has been a Dubrovnik symbol—and locals have resented Venice—ever since.

• Your tour is finished. From here, you've got plenty of sightseeing options (all described in the next section, "Sights in Dubrovnik"). As you face the Bell Tower, you can go up the street to the right to reach the Rector's Palace and cathedral; you can walk through the gate straight ahead to reach the Old Port; or you can head through the gate and jog left to find the Dominican Monastery Museum. Even more sights— including an old synagogue, an Orthodox church, two different exhibits of war photography, and the medieval granary—are in the steep streets between the Stradun and the walls.

Sights in Dubrovnik

Nearly all of Dubrovnik's sights are inside the Old Town's walls.

Combo-Tickets: The Rector's Palace, Maritime Museum, and Rupe Granary and Ethnographic Museum—which normally cost 40 kn apiece—are covered by a combo-ticket (45 kn to visit any two, 50 kn to visit all three, tickets sold at all three sights, valid for three days). If you're visiting any one of these sights, you might as well buy the three-sight ticket and poke into the others, since it costs just slightly more than an individual entry. The TI's bigger combo-ticket—which covers the same three sights, plus the City Walls and a few lesser attractions—won't save the casual sightseer any money (100 kn/1 day).

▲▲▲Town Walls (Gradske Zidine)

Dubrovnik's single best attraction is strolling the scenic mile-and-a-quarter around the city walls. As you meander along this lofty perch—with a sea of orange roofs on one side, and the actual sea on the other—you'll get your bearings and snap pictures like mad of the ever-changing views. Bring your map, which you can use to

The Siege of Dubrovnik

In June 1991, Croatia declared independence from Yugoslavia. Within weeks, the nations were at war (for more on the war, see the Understanding Yugoslavia chapter). Though warfare raged in the Croatian interior, nobody expected that the bloodshed would reach Dubrovnik.

As refugees from Vukovar (in northeastern Croatia) arrived in Dubrovnik that fall, telling horrific stories of the warfare there, local residents began fearing the worst. Warplanes from the Serb-dominated Yugoslav National Army buzzed threateningly low over the town, as if to signal an impending attack.

Then, at 6:00 in the morning on October 1, 1991, Dubrovnik residents awoke to explosions on nearby hillsides. The first attacks were focused on Mount Srđ, high above the Old Town. First the giant cross was destroyed, then a communications tower (both have been rebuilt and are visible today). This first wave of attacks cleared the way for Yugoslav land troops—mostly Serbs and Montenegrins—who surrounded the city. The ragtag, newly formed Croatian army quickly dug in at the old Napoleonic-era fortress at the top of Mount Srđ, where just 25 or 30 soldiers fended off a Yugoslav takeover of this highly strategic position.

At first, shelling targeted military positions on the outskirts of town. But soon, Yugoslav forces began bombing residential neighborhoods, then the Pearl of the Adriatic itself: Dubrovnik's Old Town. Defenseless townspeople took shelter in their cellars, and sometimes even huddled together in the city wall's 15th-century forts. It was the first time in Dubrovnik's long history that the walls were actually used to defend against an attack.

Dubrovnik resisted the siege better than anyone expected. The Yugoslav forces were hoping that residents would flee the town, but the people of Dubrovnik stayed. Though severely out-gunned and outnumbered, Dubrovnik's defenders managed to hold the fort atop Mount Srđ, while Yugoslav forces controlled the nearby mountaintops. All supplies had to be carried up to the fort by foot or by donkey. Dubrovnik wasn't prepared for war, so they had to improvise their defense. Many brave young locals lost their lives when they slung old hunting rifles over their shoulders and, under cover of darkness, climbed the hills above Dubrovnik to meet Yugoslav soldiers face-to-face.

pick out landmarks and get the lay of the land.

There have been walls here almost as long as there's been a Dubrovnik. As with virtually all fortifications on the Croatian Coast, these walls were beefed up in the 15th century, when the Ottoman navy became a threat. Around the perimeter are several substantial forts, with walls rounded so that cannonballs would glance off harmlessly. These stout forts intimidated would-be invaders during the Republic of Dubrovnik's Golden Age, and

After eight months of bombing, Dubrovnik was liberated by the Croatian army, which attacked Yugoslav positions from the north. By the end of the siege, 100 civilians were dead, as well as more than 200 Dubrovnik citizens who lost their lives actively fighting for their hometown (much revered today as "Dubrovnik Defenders"). More than two-thirds of Dubrovnik's buildings had been damaged, and more than 30,000 people had to flee their homes—but the failed siege was finally over.

Why was Dubrovnik—so far from the rest of the fighting—dragged into the conflict? Yugoslavia wanted to catch the city and surrounding region off-guard, gaining a toehold on the southern Dalmatian Coast so they could push north to Split. They also hoped to ignite pro-Serb (and pro-Yugoslav) passions in the nearby Serb-dominated areas of Bosnia-Herzegovina and Montenegro. But perhaps most of all, Yugoslavia wanted to hit Croatia where it hurt—its proudest, most historic, and most beautiful city, the tourist capital of a nation dependent on tourism. (It seems their plan backfired. Locals now say, "When Yugoslavia attacked Dubrovnik, they lost the war"—because images of the historic city under siege swayed international public opinion *against* Yugoslavia.)

The war initially devastated the tourist industry. Now, to the casual observer, Dubrovnik seems virtually back to normal. Aside from a few pockmarks and bright, new roof tiles, there are scant reminders of what happened here nearly two decades ago. But even though the city itself has been repaired, the people of Dubrovnik are forever changed. Imagine living in an idyllic paradise, a place that attracted and awed visitors from around the world...and then watching it gradually blown to bits. It's understandable if Dubrovnik citizens are a little less in love with life than they once were.

Dubrovnik has various low-key attractions related to its recent war, including the Memorial Room of Dubrovnik Defenders in the Sponza Palace on Luža Square; the Institute for the Restoration of Dubrovnik, a few blocks away across the Stradun; and the museum in the ruined fortress atop Mount Srđ. Another sight, War Photo Limited, expands the scope to war photography from around the world. All of these sights are described in this chapter.

protected local residents during the 1991–1992 siege.

Walking the walls also offers the best illustration of the damage Dubrovnik sustained during the recent siege. It's easy to see that nearly two-thirds of Dubrovnik's roofs were replaced after the bombings (notice the new, bright-orange tiles—and how some buildings salvaged the old tiles, but have 20th-century ones underneath). Looking over this gorgeous panorama, ponder that the pristine-seeming Old Town was rebuilt using exactly

the same materials and methods with which it was originally constructed.

The highest point is the empty Minčeta Tower, above the Pile Gate at the west end of town. The tower rewards those who climb to its top with a fine view.

Posted signs send wall-walkers counterclockwise. Therefore, if you begin at the main Pile Gate entrance, you'll reach the Minčeta Tower last. Speed demons with no cameras can walk the walls in about an hour; strollers and shutterbugs should plan on longer. Because it can be very hot up top, with almost no shade, it's essential to bring sunscreen, a hat, and water. Take your time: There are several steep stretches, and you'll be climbing up and down the whole way around. A few scant shops and cafés along the top of the wall (mostly on the sea side) sell water and other drinks, but it's safest to bring what you'll need with you. Because your ticket is electronically scanned as you enter, you can't leave and re-enter the wall later.

Cost and Entrance: 50 kn to enter walls, also includes the St. Lawrence Fort outside the Pile Gate. The main entrance to the walls is just inside the Pile Gate: As you enter the Old Town through the gate, the stairs up to the top of the wall are directly to your left; but first, you have to buy your ticket at the office, tucked in the corner to your right. You can also buy tickets and enter the walls at two other points: near the Dominican Monastery north of the Ploče Gate, and by the Maritime Museum south of the Old Port.

Hours: July–Aug daily 8:00–19:30, progressively shorter hours off-season until mid-Nov–mid-March 10:00–15:00. Since the hours change with the season, confirm them by checking signs posted at the entrance (essential if you want to time your wall walk to avoid the worst crowds—explained below). Note that posted closing time indicates when the walls shut down, *not* the last entry—ascend at least an hour before this time if you want to make it all the way around. Attendants begin circling the walls about 30 minutes after the posted closing time to lock the gates. There's talk of eventually illuminating the walls at night, in which case the hours would be extended until after dark.

Audioguide: You can rent a 40-kn audioguide, separate from the admission fee, for a dryly narrated circular tour of the walls (look for vendors near the entry points). But I'd rather just enjoy the views and lazily pick out the landmarks with my map.

Crowd Control: Because this is Dubrovnik's top attraction, it's extremely crowded. Your best strategy is to avoid the walls during the times when the cruise ships are in town. On days when the walls open at 8:00, try to get started around that time. The walls are the most crowded from about 8:30 until 11:00, when the cruise ships are docked. There's generally an afternoon lull in the crowds (11:00–15:00), but that's also the hottest time to be atop the walls. Crowds pick up again in the late afternoon (starting around 15:00), peaking about an hour before closing time (18:30 in high season). So your options are either early, crowded, or hot.

The "Other" Wall Climb: Your ticket for the Old Town Walls also includes the Fort of St. Lawrence just outside the Old Town (valid same day only; fort described on page 261). If you've already bought a 20-kn ticket there, show it when buying your main wall ticket and you'll pay only the difference.

Near the Pile Gate

This museum is just inside the Pile Gate.

▲**Franciscan Monastery Museum (Franjevački Samostan-Muzej)**—In the Middle Ages, Dubrovnik's monasteries flourished. While all you'll see here are a fine cloister and a one-room museum in the old pharmacy, it's a delightful space. Enter through the gap between the small church and the big monastery (30 kn, daily April–Oct 9:00–18:00, Nov–March 9:00–17:00, Placa 2, www.malabraca.hr). Just inside the door (before the ticket-seller), a century-old pharmacy still serves residents.

Explore the peaceful, sun-dappled **cloister.** Examine the capitals at the tops of the 60 Romanesque-Gothic double pillars. Each one is different. Notice that some of the portals inside the courtyard are made with a lighter-colored stone—these had to be repaired after being hit during the 1991–1992 siege. The damaged 19th-century frescoes along the tops of the walls depict the life of St. Francis, who supposedly visited Dubrovnik in the early 13th century.

In the far corner stands the monastery's original medieval **pharmacy.** Part of the Franciscans' mission was to contribute to the good health of the citizens, so they opened this pharmacy in 1317. The monastery has had a pharmacy in continual operation ever since. On display are jars, pots, and other medieval pharmacists' tools. The sick would come to get their medicine at the little window (on left side), which limited contact with the pharmacist and reduced the risk of passing on disease. Around the room, you'll also find some relics, old manuscripts, and a detailed painting of early 17th-century Dubrovnik.

Near Luža Square

These sights are at the far end of the Stradun (nearest the Old Port). As you stand on Luža Square facing the Bell Tower, the

Rector's Palace and cathedral are up the wide street called Pred Dvorom to the right, and the Dominican Monastery Museum is through the gate by the Bell Tower and to the left.

Rector's Palace (Knežev Dvor)—In the Middle Ages, the Republic of Dubrovnik was ruled by a rector (similar to a Venetian

doge), who was elected by the nobility. To prevent any one person from becoming too powerful, the rector's term was limited to one month. Most rectors were in their 50s—near the end of the average life span and when they were less likely to shake things up. During his term, a rector lived upstairs in this palace. Because it's been plundered twice, this empty-feeling museum isn't as interesting as most other European palaces—but it does offer a glimpse of Dubrovnik in its glory days (40 kn, covered by 45-kn or 50-kn combo-ticket, daily May–Oct 9:00–18:00, Nov–April 9:00–16:00, some posted English information, 6-kn English booklet is helpful, Pred Dvorom 3).

The **exterior** is decorated in the Gothic-Renaissance mix (with particularly finely carved capitals) that was so common in Dubrovnik before the 1667 earthquake.

Standing at the main door, you can generally get a free peek into the palace's impressive **courtyard**—a venue for the Summer Festival, hosting music groups ranging from the local symphony to the Vienna Boys' Choir. In the courtyard (and also visible from the door) is the only secular statue created during the centuries-long Republic. Dubrovnik republicans, mindful of the dangers of hero-worship, didn't believe that any one citizen should be singled out. They made only one exception—for Miho Pracat (a.k.a. Michaeli Prazatto), a rich citizen who donated vast sums to charity and willed a fleet of ships to the city. But notice that Pracat's statue is displayed in here, behind closed doors, not out in public.

The palace collection, which requires a ticket, is skippable. But if you'd like to go **inside,** proceed to the ticket desk, then tour a few ground-floor exhibits. You'll see some old prison cells, which supposedly were placed within earshot of the rector's quarters, so he would hear the moans of the prisoners...and stay honest. Leaving the prison, you'll enter the courtyard described earlier, where you can get a better look at the Pracat statue.

On the mezzanine level (stairs near the main entrance), you'll find a decent display of furniture, a wimpy gun exhibit, a ho-hum coin collection, and an interesting painting of "Ragusa" in the early

17th century—back when it was still bisected by a canal.

Head back down to the courtyard and go to the upper floor (using the staircase across from mezzanine stairs, near the Pracat statue—notice the "hand" rails). Upstairs, you'll explore old apartments that serve as a painting gallery. The only vaguely authentic room is the red room in the corner, decorated more or less as it was in 1500, when it was the rector's office. Mihajlo Hamzić's exquisite *Baptism of Christ* painting, inspired by Italian painter Andrea Mantegna, is an early Renaissance work from the "Dubrovnik School" (see "Dominican Monastery Museum" listing, later).

▲**Cathedral (Katedrala)**—Dubrovnik's original 12th-century cathedral was funded largely by the English King Richard the

Lionhearted. On his way back from the Third Crusade, Richard was shipwrecked nearby. He promised God that if he survived, he'd build a church on the spot where he landed—which happened to be on Lokrum Island, just offshore. At Dubrovnik's request, Richard agreed to build his token of thanks inside the city instead. It was the finest Romanesque church on the Adriatic...before it was destroyed by the 1667 earthquake. This version is 18th-century Roman Baroque. Inside, you'll find a painting from the school of Titian *(Assumption of the Virgin)* over the stark contemporary altar, and a quirky treasury *(riznica)* packed with 187 relics (church: free, daily 8:00–20:00; treasury: 15 kn, generally open same hours as church; both have shorter hours off-season).

Examining the **treasury** collection, notice that there are three locks on the treasury door—the stuff in here was so valuable, three different VIPs (the rector, the bishop, and a local aristocrat) had to agree before it could be opened. On the table near the door are several of St. Blaise's body parts (pieces of his arm, skull, and leg—all encased in gold and silver). In the middle of the wall directly opposite the door, look for the crucifix with a piece of the True Cross. On a dig in Jerusalem, St. Helen (Emperor Constantine's mother) discovered what she believed to be the cross that Jesus was crucified on. It was brought to Constantinople, and the Byzantine czars doled out pieces of it to Balkan kings. Note the folding three-paneled altar painting (underneath the cross). Dubrovnik ambassadors packed this on road trips (such as their annual trip to pay off the Ottomans) so they could worship wherever they traveled. On the right side of the room, the silver casket supposedly holds the actual swaddling clothes of the Baby Jesus (or, as some locals call it somewhat less reverently, "Jesus' nappy"). Dubrovnik bishops secretly passed these clothes down from generation to generation... until a nun got wind of it and told the whole town. Pieces of the cloth were cut off to miraculously heal the sick, especially new mothers recovering from a difficult birth. No matter how often it was cut, the cloth always went back to its original form. Then someone tried to use it on the wife of a Bosnian king. Since she was Muslim, it couldn't help her, and it never worked again. True or not, this legend hints at the prickly relationships between faiths (not to mention the male chauvinism) here in the Balkans.

▲**Dominican Monastery Museum (Dominikanski Samostan-Muzej)**—You'll find many of Dubrovnik's art treasures—paintings, altarpieces, and manuscripts—gathered around the peaceful

Dominican Monastery cloister inside the Ploče Gate (20 kn, art buffs enjoy the 50-kn English book, daily May–Sept 9:00–18:00, Oct–April 9:00–17:00). Historically, this was the church for wealthy people, while the Franciscan Church (down at the far end of the Stradun) was for poor people. Services were staggered by 15 minutes to allow servants to drop off their masters here, then rush down the Stradun for their own service.

Work your way clockwise around the cloister. The room in the far corner from the entry contains paintings from the **"Dubrovnik School,"** the Republic's circa-1500 answer to the art boom in Florence and Venice. Though the 1667 earthquake destroyed most of these paintings, about a dozen survive, and five of those are in this room. Don't miss the triptych by Nikola Božidarović with St. Blaise holding a detailed model of 16th-century Dubrovnik (left panel)—the most famous depiction of Dubrovnik's favorite saint. You'll also see reliquaries shaped like the hands and feet that they hold.

Continuing around the courtyard, duck into the next room. Here you'll see a painting by **Titian** depicting St. Blaise, Mary Magdalene, and the donor.

At the next corner of the courtyard is the entrance to the striking **church** at the heart of this still-active monastery. Step inside. The interior is decorated with modern stained glass, a fine 13th-century stone pulpit that survived the earthquake (reminding visitors of the intellectual approach to scripture that characterized the Dominicans), and a precious 14th-century Paolo Veneziano crucifix hanging above the high altar. The most memorable piece of art in the church is the *Miracle of St. Dominic,* showing the founder of the order bringing a child back to life (over the altar to the right, as you enter). It was painted in the Realist style (late 19th century) by Vlaho Bukovac.

Near the Old Port (Stara Luka)

The picturesque Old Port, carefully nestled behind St. John's Fort, faces away from what was Dubrovnik's biggest threat, the

Venetians. At the port, you can haggle with captains selling excursions to nearby towns and islands (described in the next chapter) and watch cruise-ship passengers coming and going on their transfer boats. The long seaside building across the bay on the left is the Lazareti, once the medieval quarantine house. In those days, all visitors were locked in here for 40 days before entering town. (Today it hosts folk-dancing shows—described later, under "Entertainment in Dubrovnik.") A bench-lined harborside walk leads around the fort to a breakwater, providing a peaceful perch. From the breakwater, rocky beaches curl around the outside of the wall.

Maritime Museum (Pomorski Muzej)—By the 15th century, when Venice's nautical dominance was on the wane, Dubrovnik emerged as a maritime power and the Mediterranean's leading shipbuilding center. The Dubrovnik-built "argosy" boat (from "Ragusa," an early name for the city) was the Cadillac of ships, frequently mentioned by Shakespeare. This small museum traces the history of Dubrovnik's most important industry with contracts, maps, paintings, and models—all well-described in English. The main floor takes you through the 18th century, and the easy-to-miss upstairs covers the 19th and 20th centuries. Boaters will find the museum particularly interesting (40 kn, covered by 45-kn or 50-kn combo-ticket, 5-kn English booklet, hours depend on demand—usually March–Oct Tue–Sun 9:00–18:00, closed Mon, shorter hours Nov–Feb, upstairs in St. John's Fort, at far/south end of Old Port, tel. 020/323-904).

Aquarium (Akvarij)—Dubrovnik's aquarium, housed in the cavernous St. John's Fort, is an old-school place, with 31 tanks on one floor. A visit here allows you a close look at the local marine life and provides a cool refuge from the midday heat (30 kn, kids-10 kn, English descriptions, daily July–Aug 9:00–21:00, progressively shorter hours off-season until 9:00–13:00 Nov–March, ground floor of St. John's Fort, enter from Old Port).

Between the Stradun and the Mainland

These two museums are a few steps off the main promenade toward the mainland.

▲**Synagogue Museum (Sinagoga-Muzej)**—When Jews were forced out of Spain in 1492, a steady stream of them passed through here en route to today's Turkey. Finding Dubrovnik to be a flourishing and relatively tolerant city, many stayed. Žudioska ulica ("Jewish Street"), just inside Ploče Gate, became the ghetto in 1546. It was walled at one end and had a gate (which would be locked at night) at the other end. Today, the same street is home to the second-oldest continuously functioning synagogue in Europe (after Prague's), which contains Croatia's only Jewish museum. The top floor houses the synagogue itself. Notice the lattice windows that separated the women from the men (according to Orthodox Jewish tradition). Below that, a small museum with good English descriptions gives meaning to the various Torahs (including a 14th-century one from Spain) and other items—such as the written orders *(naredba)* from Nazi-era Yugoslavia, stating that Jews were to identify their shops as Jewish-owned and wear armbands. (The Ustaše—the Nazi puppet government in Croatia—interned and executed not only Jews and Roma/Gypsies, but also Serbs and other people they considered undesirable; see page 44.) Of Croatia's 24,000 Jews, only 4,000 survived the Holocaust. Today Croatia has about 2,000 Jews, including 12 Jewish families who call Dubrovnik home (15 kn, 10-kn English booklet; May–mid-Nov daily 10:00–20:00; mid-Nov–April Mon–Fri 10:00–13:00, closed Sat–Sun; Žudioska ulica 5, tel. 020/321-028).

War Photo Limited—If the tragic story of wartime Dubrovnik has you in a pensive mood, drop by this gallery with images of warfare from around the world. The brainchild of photojournalist Wade Goddard, this thought-provoking museum—with well-displayed exhibits on two floors—attempts to show the ugly reality of war through raw, often disturbing photographs taken in the field. A permanent exhibit depicts the wars in the former Yugoslavia through photography and video footage. Each summer, the gallery also houses two different temporary exhibits. Note that the focus is not solely on Dubrovnik, but on war anywhere and everywhere (30 kn; June–Sept daily 9:00–21:00; May and Oct Tue–Sat 9:00–15:00, Sun 10:00–14:00, closed Mon; closed Nov–April; Antuninska 6, tel. 020/322-166, www.warphotoltd.com).

Between the Stradun and the Sea

▲**Institute for the Restoration of Dubrovnik (Zavod za Obnovu Dubrovnika)**—This small photo gallery is the closest thing Dubrovnik has to a museum about the eight-month siege of the city from late 1991 to mid-1992 (see "The Siege of Dubrovnik" sidebar, earlier). The front two rooms display images of bombed-out Dubrovnik, each one juxtaposed with an image of the same building after being restored. The back room offers rotating exhibits about efforts to restore Dubrovnik to its pre-siege glory. The photos are too few, but still illuminating. The highlight of the exhibit is a video showing a series of breathless news reports from a British journalist stationed here during the siege. As you watch shells devastating this glorious city, and look in the eyes of its desperate citizens at their darkest hour, you might just begin to grasp what went on here not so long ago (free; June–Sept Mon–Fri 10:00–14:00, closed Sat–Sun; Oct–May the same space is used for rotating exhibits on other topics; Zuzorić 6, tel. 020/324-060).

▲**Serbian Orthodox Church and Icon Museum (Srpska Pravoslavna Crkva I Muzej Ikona)**—Round out your look at Dubrovnik's faiths (Catholic, Jewish, and Orthodox) with a visit

to this house of worship—one of the most convenient places in Croatia to learn about Orthodox Christianity. Remember that people from the former Yugoslavia who follow the Orthodox faith are, by definition, ethnic Serbs. With all the (perhaps understandably) hard feelings about the recent war, this church serves as an important reminder that all Serbs aren't bloodthirsty killers.

Dubrovnik never had a very large Serb population (an Orthodox church wasn't even allowed inside the town walls until the mid-19th century). During the recent war, most Serbs fled, created new lives for themselves elsewhere, and saw little reason to return. But some old-timers remain, and Dubrovnik's dwindling, aging Orthodox population is still served by this church. The candles stuck in the sand and water (to prevent fire outbreaks) represent prayers: The ones at knee level are for the deceased, while the ones higher up are for the living. The gentleman selling candles encourages you to buy and light one, regardless of your faith, so long as you do so with the proper intentions and reverence (free entry, good 20-kn English book explains the church and the museum, daily May–Sept 8:00–20:00, Oct–April 8:00–15:00, short services daily at 8:30 and 19:00, longer liturgy Sundays at 9:00, Od Puča 8).

A few doors down, you'll find the **Icon Museum** (10 kn; May–Oct Mon–Sat 9:00–14:00, closed Sun; Nov–April Mon–Fri 9:00–14:00, closed Sat–Sun). This small collection features 78 different icons (stylized paintings of saints, generally on a golden

DUBROVNIK

The Serbian Orthodox Church

The emphasis of this book is on the Catholic areas of the former Yugoslavia, but don't overlook the rich diversity of faiths in this region. Dubrovnik's Serbian Orthodox Church—as well as several Orthodox churches in Kotor, Montenegro (see page 366) and one in Ljubljana (page 416)—offer an invaluable opportunity to learn about a faith that's often unfamiliar to visitors.

As you explore an Orthodox church, keep in mind that these churches carry on the earliest traditions of the Christian faith. Orthodox and Catholic Christianity came from the same roots, so the oldest surviving early-Christian churches (such as the stave churches of Norway) have many of the same features as today's Orthodox churches.

Notice that there are no pews. Worshippers stand through the service, as a sign of respect (though some older parishioners sit on the seats along the walls). Women stand on the left side, men on the right (equal distance from the altar—to represent that all are equal before God). The Orthodox Church uses essentially the same Bible as Catholics, but it's written in the Cyrillic alphabet, which you'll see displayed around any Orthodox church. Following Old Testament Judeo-Christian tradition, the Bible is kept on the altar behind the iconostasis, the big screen in the middle of the room covered with curtains and icons (golden paintings of saints), which separates the material world from the spiritual one. At certain times during the service, the curtains or doors are opened so the congregation can see the Holy Book.

Unlike many Catholic church decorations, Orthodox icons are not intended to be lifelike. Packed with intricate symbolism, and cast against a shimmering golden background, they're meant to remind viewers of the metaphysical nature of Jesus and the saints rather than their physical form, which is considered irrelevant. You'll almost never see a statue, which is thought to overemphasize the physical world...and, to Orthodox people, feels a little too close to violating the commandment, "Thou shalt not worship graven images." Orthodox services generally involve chanting (a dialogue that goes back and forth between the priest and the congregation), and the church is filled with the evocative aroma of incense.

The incense, chanting, icons, and standing up are all intended to heighten the experience of worship. While many Catholic and Protestant services tend to be more of a theoretical and rote consideration of religious issues (come on—don't tell me you've never dozed through the sermon), Orthodox services are about creating a religious experience. Each of these elements does its part to help the worshipper transcend the physical world and enter communion with the spiritual one.

background—a common feature of Orthodox churches) from the 15th through the 19th centuries, all identified in English. In the library—crammed with old shelves holding some 12,000 books—look for the astonishingly detailed calendar, with portraits of hundreds of saints. The gallery on the ground floor, run by Michael, sells original icons and reproductions (open longer hours than museum).

▲**Rupe Granary and Ethnographic Museum (Etnografski Muzej Rupe)**—This huge, 16th-century building was Dubrovnik's biggest granary. *Rupe* means "holes"—and it's worth the price of entry just to peer down into these cavernous underground grain stores, designed to maintain the perfect temperature to preserve the seeds (63 degrees Fahrenheit). When the grain had to be dried, it was moved upstairs—where today you'll find a surprisingly well-presented Ethnographic Museum, with tools, jewelry, clothing, instruments, painted eggs, and other folk artifacts from Dubrovnik's colorful history. Borrow the free English information guide at the entry (40 kn, covered by 45-kn or 50-kn combo-ticket, Wed–Mon 9:00–16:00, closed Tue). The museum hides several blocks uphill from the main promenade, toward the sea (climb up Široka—the widest side street from the Stradun—which becomes Od Domina on the way to the museum).

Above Dubrovnik

▲**Mount Srđ**—After adding Dubrovnik to his holdings, Napoleon built a fortress atop the hill behind the Old Town to keep an eye on his new subjects (in 1810). During the city's 20th-century tourism heyday, a cable car was built to effortlessly whisk visitors to the top so they could enjoy the fine views from the fortress and the giant cross nearby. But when war broke out in the 1990s, Mount Srđ became a crucial link in the defense of Dubrovnik—the only high land that locals were able to hold. The fortress was shelled and damaged, and the cross and cable car were destroyed. Minefields and

unexploded ordnance left the hilltop a dangerous no-man's land.

But today, with the landmines cleared (see "Warning," later) and reconstruction of the cable car underway, Mount Srđ is reclaiming its status as a major tourist attraction. There are two reasons to visit: for the sweeping views, and for a ragtag new museum about the war. However, until the cable car starts running again, this trip is only worth it for those who have a healthy interest and plenty of time (given the expense and/or time it takes to summit the mountain—explained later, under "Getting There").

The bird's-eye **view** is truly spectacular, looking straight down to the street plan of Dubrovnik's Old Town. From this lofty perch, you can see north to the Dalmatian islands (the Elaphite, Mljet, and beyond); south to Montenegro; and east into Bosnia-Herzegovina.

The **cross** was always an important symbol in this very Catholic town. After it was destroyed, a temporary wooden one was erected to encourage the townspeople who were waiting out the siege below. During a visit in 2003, Pope John Paul II blessed the rubble from the old cross; those fragments are now being used in the foundations of the city's newest churches.

The **fortress** houses a humble but interesting exhibit called "Dubrovnik During the Homeland War (1991–1995)." Photos, video clips, documents, and artifacts tell the story (with some English descriptions) of the overarching war with Yugoslavia and how the people defended this fortress. You'll see actual items used in the fighting: basic, rusty rifles that the Croatians used for their improvised defense, and mortar shells and other projectiles that Yugoslav forces hurled at the fortress and the city. Look for the wire-guided Russian rockets. After being launched at their target, the rockets would burrow into a wall, waiting to be detonated once their operators saw the opportunity for maximum destruction. The explanations are, perhaps unavoidably, slanted to the Croat perspective—with talk of "Serb-Montenegrin aggression" and statements such as, "This senseless attack...showed the full hate towards the Croatian people." Though the museum feels hastily assembled and a bit basic, it's fascinating to learn about this historical moment in a place that played such a major role in the events (15 kn, daily 10:00–18:30, maybe until 20:00 in summer).

After seeing the exhibit, climb up a few flights of stairs to the **rooftop** for the view. The giant communications tower overhead flew the Croatian flag during the war, to inspire the besieged residents below. At the other end of the fortress are the haunting remains of a simpler time: a badly damaged, light-up dance floor from the disco era, back when the fortress hosted not Napoleonic or Croatian soldiers, but a popular dance club for locals and tourists. You might see some charred trees around here—these were claimed not by the war, but more recently, by forest fires. (Fear of landmines and other explosives prevented locals from fighting the wildfires as aggressively as they might otherwise, making these fires more dangerous than ever.)

Warning: While this area has officially been cleared of land-mines, nervous locals remind visitors that this was a war zone. Be sure to stay on clearly defined paths and roads.

Getting There: Work has begun to rebuild the **cable car,** which will conveniently zip visitors up to the fortress from just above the Buža Gate at the top of the Old Town. Ask around—if the cable car is up and running, it's easily the best option. Until then, reaching the top of Mount Srđ is a bit of a hassle.

If you have a **car,** you can drive up. From the high road above the Old Town, watch for the turnoff to Bosanka, which leads you to that village, then up to the fortress and cross—follow signs for *Srđ* (it's twisty but not far—figure a 20-minute drive from the Old Town area). If you're coming south from the Old Town, once you reach the main road above, you'll have to turn left and backtrack a bit to reach the Bosanka turnoff.

An easier option is to hire a **taxi,** but it's very expensive (figure €50–70 round-trip, including some waiting time at the top). Some cabbies will provide a little informal commentary during your visit. Or for €70, recommended driver Pepo Klaić will take you to the summit while sharing his firsthand experiences defending the fortress (listed on page 260).

Public **bus** #17 brings you from outside the Old Town's Ploče Gate most of the way up, but the frequency is limited (roughly every 2 hrs, 25 min). From the bus stop, you'll still have to hike nearly a mile uphill, with almost no shade. For **hikers,** a switchback trail (used to supply the fortress during the siege) connects the Old Town to the mountaintop—but it's very steep and provides minimal shade. (If you're in great shape and it's not too hot, you could ride the bus up, then hike down.)

Activities in Dubrovnik

Swimming and Sunbathing—If the weather's good and you've had enough of museums, spend a sunny afternoon at the beach. There are no sandy beaches on the mainland near Dubrovnik, but there are lots of suitable pebbly options, plus several concrete perches. The easiest and most atmospheric place to take a dip is right off the Old Town. From the Old Port and its breakwater, uneven steps clinging to the outside of the wall lead to a series of great sunbathing and swimming coves (and even a showerhead

sticking out of the town wall). Another delightful rocky beach hangs onto the outside of the Old Town's wall (at the bar called Cold Drinks "Buža" I; for more on this bar, and how to find it, see next page). Locals prefer to swim on Lokrum Island, because there are fewer tourists there; for details on taking a boat to Lokrum, see page 301. Other convenient public beaches are Banje (just outside Ploče Gate, east of Old Town) and the beach in the middle of Lapad Bay (near Hotel Kompas).

My favorite hidden beach—**St. Jakob**—takes a lot longer to reach, but if you're up for the hike, it's worth it to escape the crowds. Figure about a 25-minute walk (each way) from the Old Town. Go through the Ploče Gate at the east end of the Old Town, and walk along the street called Frana Supila as it climbs uphill above the waterfront. At Hotel Argentina, take the right (downhill) fork and keep going  on Vlaha Bukovca. Eventually you'll reach the small church of St. Jakob. You'll see the beach—in a cozy protected cove—far below. Curl around behind the church and keep an eye out for stairs going down on the right. Unfortunately, these stairs are effectively unmarked, so it might take some trial and error to find the right ones. (If you reach the rusted-white gateway of the old communist-era open-air theater, you've gone too far.) Hike down the very steep stairs to the gentle cove, which has rentable chairs and a small restaurant for drinks (and a WC). Enjoy the pebbly beach and faraway views of Dubrovnik's Old Town.

Shopping in Dubrovnik

Most souvenirs sold in Dubrovnik—from lavender sachets to plaster models of the Old Town—are pretty tacky. Whatever you buy, prices are much higher along the Stradun than on the side streets.

A classy alternative to the knickknacks is a type of local jewelry called *Konavoske puce* ("Konavle buttons"). Sold as earrings,  pendants, and rings, these distinctive and fashionable filigree-style pieces consist of a sphere with several small posts. Though they're sold around town, it's least expensive to buy them on Od Puča street, which runs parallel to the Stradun two blocks toward the sea (near the Serbian

Orthodox Church). The high concentration of jewelers along this lane keeps prices reasonable. You'll find the "buttons" in various sizes, in both silver (affordable) and gold (pricey).

You'll also see lots of jewelry made from red coral, which can only be legally gathered in small amounts from two small islands in northern Dalmatia. If you see a particularly large chunk of coral, it's likely imported. To know what you're getting, shop at an actual jeweler instead of a souvenir shop.

Entertainment in Dubrovnik

Musical Events

Dubrovnik annually hosts a full schedule of events for its Summer Festival (July 10–Aug 25, www.dubrovnik-festival.hr). Lovers of classical music enjoy the "Rachlin & Friends" festival in September (www.julianrachlin.com), and historians delight in the Renaissance-oriented Historical Festival in late September (www.ragvsevm.hr). But the town also works hard to offer traditional music outside of festival time. Spirited folk-music concerts are performed for tourists twice weekly in the Lazareti (old quarantine building) just outside the Old Town's Ploče Gate (80 kn, usually at 21:30). About one night per week through the winter, you can watch the Dubrovnik Symphony Orchestra (usually at the Rector's Palace in good weather, or Dominican Monastery in bad weather). And since Dubrovnik is trying to become a year-round destination, the city also offers tourist-oriented musical events most nights throughout the winter (often at a hotel). For the latest on any of these festivals and concerts, check the events listings in the *Best in Dubrovnik Riviera* brochure, or ask the TI.

Nightlife

Dubrovnik's Old Town is one big, romantic parade of relaxed and happy people out strolling. The main drag is brightly lit and packed

with shops, cafés, and bars, all open late. This is a fun scene. And if you walk away from the crowds or out on the port, you'll be alone with the magic of the Pearl of the Adriatic. Everything feels—and is—very safe after dark.

If you're looking for a memorable bar after dark, consider these:

▲▲▲**Drinks with a View**—**Cold Drinks "Buža"** offers, without a doubt, the most scenic spot for a drink. Perched on a cliff above the sea, clinging like a barnacle to the outside of the city walls, this is a peaceful, shaded getaway from the bustle of the Old Town...the

DUBROVNIK

perfect place to watch cruise ships disappear into the horizon. *Buža* means "hole in the wall"—and that's exactly what you'll have to go through to get to this place. There are actually two different Bužas, with separate owners. My favorite is Buža II (which is actually the older and bigger of the pair). Filled with mellow tourists and bartenders pouring wine from tiny screw-top bottles into plastic cups, Buža II comes with castaway views and Frank Sinatra ambience. This is supposedly where Bill Gates hangs out when he visits Dubrovnik (25–40-kn

drinks, summer daily 9:00–into the wee hours, closed mid-Nov–Jan). Buža I is more casual, plays hip rather than romantic music, and has concrete stairs leading down to a beach on the rocks below (18–45-kn drinks). If one Buža is full, check the other one.

Getting There: Both Bužas are high above the bustle of the main drag, along the seaward wall. To reach them from the cathedral area, hike up the grand staircase to St. Ignatius' Church, then go left to find the lane that runs along the inside of the wall. To find the classic Buža II, head right along the lane and look for the *Cold Drinks* sign pointing to a literal hole in the wall. For the hipper Buža I, go left along the same lane, and locate the hole in the wall with the *No Toples No Nudist* graffiti.

Wine Tasting—d'vino Wine Bar, just a few steps off the main drag, is the handiest place in Dalmatia to taste and learn about Croatian wines. Run by Canadian transplant Cameron Wilson, this cozy bar (with a few outdoor tables) sells more than 50 wines by the glass and lots more by the bottle. The emphasis is on Croatian wines, but they also have vintages from Italy, France, Spain, the US, Australia, and South America. Each wine is well-described on the menu, and the staff is happy to guide you through your options—just tell them what you like (18–80-kn glasses—most around 25–35 kn, 40-kn wine flights, daily June–Sept 12:00–24:00, Oct–May 17:00–24:00, Palmotićeva 4a, tel. 020/321-223).

Cocktails and People-Watching—Jazz Caffè Troubadour is a cool place, owned by a former member of the Dubrovnik Troubadours—Croatia's answer to the Beatles (or, perhaps more accurately, the Turtles). On balmy evenings, 50 chairs with tiny tables are set up theater-style in the dreamy alley facing the musicians. Step inside to see old 1970s photos of the band (40–65-kn cocktails, daily 9:00–24:00, live jazz nightly from about 22:00 or whenever the boss shows up, often live piano at other times, next to cathedral at Bunićeva Poljana 2, tel. 020/323-476).

Nonenina, a few steps from the cathedral on Pred Dvorom, is an outdoor lounge with big, overstuffed chairs at a fine vantage point for people-watching. They brag that they serve 180 different types of cocktails (50–80 kn, daily 9:00–2:00 in the morning, shorter hours off-season, across from Rector's Palace).

Movies

The Old Town has a pair of movie theaters showing American blockbusters (usually in English with Croatian subtitles, unless the film's animated or for kids). The **Sloboda** cinema, right under the Bell Tower on Luža Square, is nothing special. But in good weather, head for the fun outdoor **Jadran** cinema, where you can lick ice cream (B.Y.O.) while you watch a movie with a Dubrovnik-mountaintop backdrop. This is a cheap, casual, and very Croatian scene, where people smoke and chat, and the neighbors sit in their windowsills to watch the movie (most nights in summer only, shows begin shortly after sundown; in the Old Town near the Pile Gate). To find out what's playing, look for posters around town.

Sleeping in Dubrovnik

You basically have two options in Dubrovnik: a centrally located room in a private home (soba); or a resort hotel on a distant beach, a bus ride away from the Old Town. Since Dubrovnik hotels are generally a poor value, I highly recommend giving the sobe a careful look. For locations, see the map on page 262.

Be warned that the Old Town is home to many popular discos. My listings are quieter than the norm, but if you're finding a place

---

Sleep Code

(€1 = about $1.40, 5 kn = about $1, country code: 385, area code: 020)

S = Single, **D** = Double/Twin, **T** = Triple, **Q** = Quad, **b** = bathroom. The modest tourist tax (7 kn or €1 per person, per night, lower off-season) is not included in these rates. Hotels generally accept credit cards and include breakfast in their rates, while most soba accept only cash and don't offer breakfast. Everyone listed here speaks English.

To help you sort easily through these listings, I've divided the rooms into three categories based on the price for a standard double room with bath in peak season:

$$$ Higher Priced—Most rooms 700 kn (€95) or more.

$$ Moderately Priced—Most rooms between 400–700 kn (€55-95).

$ Lower Priced—Most rooms 400 kn (€55) or less.

on your own, you may discover you have a late-night soundtrack—particularly if you're staying near the Stradun.

No matter where you stay, prices are much higher mid-June through mid-September, and highest in July and August. Reserve ahead for these peak times, especially during the Summer Festival (July 10–Aug 25 every year). Some accommodations prefer to list their rates in euros (and I've followed suit), but you'll pay in kunas.

Sobe (Private Rooms): A Dubrovnik Specialty

In Dubrovnik, you'll almost always do better with a *soba* than with a hotel. Before you choose, carefully read the information on page 25. All of my favorite *sobe* are run by friendly English-speaking Croatians and are inside or within easy walking distance of the Old Town. There's a range of places, from simple and cheap rooms where you'll share a bathroom, to downright fancy places with private facilities and satellite TV, where you can be as anonymous as you like. Most *sobe* don't include breakfast, so I've listed some suggestions later, under "Eating in Dubrovnik."

Book direct—middleman agencies tack on fees, making it more expensive for both you and your host. Note that many Dubrovnik *sobe* hosts might ask you to send them a deposit to secure your reservation. Sometimes they'll accept your credit-card number; others might want you to mail them a check or traveler's check (the better option) or wire them the money (which can be expensive). While it's a bit of a hassle, this request is reasonable and part of the experience of sleeping at a *soba*. Remember that you'll usually need to pay your bill in cash, not with a credit card.

In the Old Town, Above the Stradun Promenade

These are some of my favorite accommodations in Dubrovnik. All are located at the top of town, high above the Stradun, and all are excellent values. The first three are within a few steps of each other, along a little block dubbed by some "Rickova ulica." If you don't mind the very steep hike up, you'll find this to be a wonderful enclave of hospitality. When one of these places is full, they work together to find space for you. The last listing is a few blocks over, and equally nice (and equally steep). Because all of these hosts live off-site, be sure to let them know when you'll arrive so they can let you in.

$$ Villa Ragusa offers my favorite rooms for the price in the Old Town. Pero and Valerija Carević have renovated a 600-year-old house at the top of town that was damaged during the war. The five comfortable, modern rooms come with atmospheric old wooden beams, antique furniture, and thoughtful touches. There are three doubles with bathrooms (including a top-floor room with breathtaking Old Town views for no extra charge—request when you reserve) and two singles that share a bathroom (July–Aug: S-€40, Db-€80; May–June and Sept–Oct: S-€30, Db-€70; Nov–April: S-€25, Db-€50; 30 percent more for 1- or 2-night stays, €8 breakfast can be eaten here or at nearby Stradun café, cash only, air-con, lots of stairs with no elevator, Žudioska ulica 15, tel. 020/453-834, mobile 098-765-634, http://villaragusa.netfirms.com, villa .ragusa@du.t-com.hr). Pero offers his guests airport transfers for a reason-

able €30, and can drive you on an all-day excursion (such as to Montenegro or Mostar) for €250—if you can split this cost with other guests, it's a good value (same price for up to 6 people).

$$ Apartments Paviša, next door to Villa Ragusa and run by Pero and Davorka Paviša, has three good rooms at the top of the Old Town (July–Aug: Db-€100; May–June and Sept–Oct: Db-€70; Nov–April Db-€50; 10 percent discount if you book direct with this book, no breakfast, cash only, air-con, lots of stairs, Žudioska ulica 19, mobile 098-427-399 or 098-175-2342, www .apartmentspavisa.com, davorka.pavisa@du t-com.hr). They have two more rooms in the **Viktorija** neighborhood, about a 20-minute mostly uphill walk east of the Old Town. While it's a long-but-scenic walk into town, the views from these apartments are spectacular (same prices as in-town rooms, Frana Supila 59, bus stop nearby). Pero and Davorka also manage **Apartments Martecchini,** these are a bit closer to the main drag in the Old Town (July–Aug: small apartment-€100, bigger apartment-€110, biggest apartment-€120; May–June and Sept–Oct: small apartment-€70, bigger apartment-€80, biggest apartment-€90; Nov–April: small apartment-€50, bigger apartment-€50, biggest apartment-€60; 10 percent discount if you book direct with this book, prices depend on size and views, www.apartmentsmartecchini.com).

$$ Anita and Ivana Raič are sisters renting three new-feeling apartments with kitchenettes and air-conditioning (July–Aug: Db-€90; June and Sept–Oct: Db-€70; Nov–May: Db-€50-60; no extra charge for 1- or 2-night stays, no breakfast, cash only, air-con, Žudioska ulica 16, mobile 098-996-0858, www.apartments -raic.com, ivanaraic@gmail.com).

$$ Plaza Apartments, run by Lidija and Maro Matić, rents three clean, well-appointed apartments on a plant-filled lane— the steepest and most appealing stretch of stairs leading up from the Stradun. Lidija's sweet personality is reflected in the cheerful rooms, which are a great value if you don't mind the hike (July–Aug:

Db-€70; May–June and Sept: Db-€55; Oct: Db-€50; Nov–April: Db-€40; these special prices for Rick Steves readers, no breakfast, cash only, air-con, free Wi-Fi, climb the stairs past Dolce Vita gelato shop to Nalješkovićeva 22, tel. 020/321-493, mobile 091-517-7048, www.dubrovnik-online.com/apartment_plaza, lidydu @yahoo.com).

In the Old Town, near the Cathedral and St. John's Fort

The following places are south of the Stradun, mostly clustering around the cathedral and St. John's Fort, at the end of the Old Port. To find the Karmen and Zijadić apartments from the cathedral, walk toward the big fort tower along the inside of the wall (follow signs for *akvarji*).

$$$ Karmen Apartments are well-run by a Brit named Marc and his Croatian wife Silva, who offer four apartments just inside the big fort. The prices are very high, and they're in all the guidebooks, but the apartments are big, well-equipped, and homey-feeling, each with a bathroom and kitchen. The decor is eclectic but tasteful, and Marc and Silva are good hosts (May–Sept: smaller apartment-€90, bigger apartment-€145; April and Oct–Nov: smaller apartment-€70, bigger apartment-€110; less Dec–March, 20 percent more for 1- or 2-night stays, no breakfast, cash only, air-con, free Wi-Fi, near the aquarium at Bandureva 1, tel. 020/323-433, www.karmendu.com, apartments@karmendu.tk).

$$$ Apartments Amoret, run by Branka Dabrović and her husband Ivica, are in all the guidebooks. The pricey but good apartments are in three different buildings: two over Amoret Restaurant in front of the cathedral (at Restićeva 2); eight more sharing an inviting terrace on a quiet, untouristy lane a few blocks east (at Dinka Ranjine 5); and two more nearby (at Ilije Sarake 4). The furnishings are a tasteful mix of traditional and modern. Since Branka doesn't live on-site, arrange a meeting time and place when you reserve (July–Aug: Db-€90–120; June and Sept: Db-€80–110; May and Oct: Db-€70–90; Nov–April: Db-€50–80; price depends on size, 30 percent more for 1-night stays, 20 percent more for 2-night stays, 10 percent more for 3-night stays, no breakfast, cash only, air-con, free Wi-Fi, mobile 091-530-4910, tel. & fax 020/324-005, www.dubrovnik-amoret.com, dubrovnik@post.t-com.hr).

$$ Apartments Placa (PLAH-tsah; not to be confused with Plaza Apartments, described earlier) is run by Tonči (TOHN-chee). He rents three apartments overlooking the market square in the heart of the Old Town. You might get some early-morning noise from the market set-up, but the double-paned windows help, and the location is wonderfully central (July–Aug: Db-€90; June and Sept: Db-€80; May and Oct: Db-€70; Nov–April: Db-€60;

no breakfast, cash only, no extra charge for 1- or 2-night stays, several flights of stairs, air-con, Gundulićeva poljana 5, mobile 091-721-9202, www.dubrovnik-online.com/apartments_placa, tonci .korculanin@du.t-com.hr).

$$ Renata Zijadić, a friendly mom who speaks good English, offers four well-located rooms with slanting floors, funky colors, and over-the-top antique furniture. A single and a double (both with great views) share one bathroom; another double features an ornate old cabinet, air-conditioning, and its own bathroom; and the top-floor apartment comes with low ceilings, air-conditioning, and fine vistas (July–Aug: S-220 kn, D-330 kn, Db-440 kn, apartment-600 kn; June and Sept: S-200 kn, D-300 kn, Db-365 kn, apartment-550 kn; cheaper Oct–May, no extra charge for 1- or 2-night stays, no breakfast, cash only, free Wi-Fi, follow signs for wall access and walk up the steps marked *ulica Stajeva* going over the street to find Stajeva 1; tel. 020/323-623, www.dubrovnik-online.com/house_renata, renatadubrovnik@yahoo.com).

$ Fresh Sheets, a bright, stylish, and appealingly funky hostel run by the former owners of Dubrovnik's hippest (now-closed) expat bar, is your best youth hostel option in the Old Town. The 22 bunks (four beds per room, two rooms and one bathroom per floor, plus one double room) sit above a tight but enjoyable common area. Located at the very top of town just inside the town walls, it's a steep hike up from the main drag, but worth it if you enjoy youthful backpacker bonding (€25/bed, likely open only April–mid-Nov, free breakfast, free Internet access and Wi-Fi, lockers, kitchen, laundry service, Smokvina 15, mobile 091-799-2086, www.igotfresh.com, beds@igotfresh.com).

In the Pile Neighborhood, Just Outside the Old Town

There's a concentration of good *sobe* just outside the Old Town's Pile Gate. The Pile (PEE-leh) neighborhood offers all the conve-

niences of the modern world (grocery store, bus stop, post office, travel agency, etc.), just steps from Dubrovnik's magical Old Town. The first place is up the hill (away from the water) from the Pile Gate's bus stop; the rest cluster around a quiet, no-name cove near Restaurant Orhan. From the bus stop area in front of Pile Gate, various lanes lead down toward this cove.

$$ Jadranka and Milan Benussi, a middle-aged professional couple, rent four rooms in a quiet, traffic-free neighborhood. Their stony-chic home, complete with a leafy terrace, is a steep 10-minute hike above the Old Town—close enough to be convenient, but far enough to take you away from the bustle and into a calm residential zone. Jadranka speaks good English, enjoys visiting with her guests, and gives her place a modern Croatian class unusual for *sobe* (July–Aug: small Db-440 kn, big Db-520 kn, small apartment-680 kn, big apartment with balcony-740 kn; June and Sept: small Db-400 kn, big Db-480 kn, small apartment-630 kn, big apartment-700 kn; cheaper Oct–May, 20 percent more for stays less than 4 nights, no breakfast, cash only, all rooms have air-con and kitchenettes, Miha Klaića 10, tel. 020/429-339, mobile 098-928-1300, www.dubrovnik-benussi.com, jadranka @dubrovnik-benussi.com). To find the Benussis, go to the big Hilton Hotel just outside the Pile Gate (across from the TI). Walk up the little stepped lane called Marijana Blažića at the upper-left corner of the Hilton cul-de-sac. When that lane dead-ends, go left up ulica Don Iva Bjelokosića (more steps) until you see a little church on the left. The Benussis' house is just before this church.

$ Paulina Čumbelić is a kind, gentle woman renting four old-fashioned rooms in her homey, clean, and peaceful house (July–Sept: S-200 kn, D-300 kn, T-450 kn; shoulder season: S-170 kn, D-260 kn, T-350 kn; 20 percent more for 1- or 2-night stays, no breakfast, cash only, closed in winter, Od Tabakarije 2, tel. 020/421-327, mobile 091-530-7985).

$ Restaurant Orhan Guest House allows hotel anonymity at *sobe* prices. Its 11 simple rooms—in a couple of different buildings around the corner from the restaurant—are well-located and quiet, with modern bathrooms (some also have air-con). As the rooms are an afterthought to the restaurant, don't expect a warm welcome (Sb or Db-400 kn, 100 kn more for 1-night stays, breakfast-50 kn, cash only, Od Tabakarije 1, tel. & fax 020/414-183, www.restaurant -orhan.com, restoran.orhan@yahoo.com). Their restaurant is also a good spot for a scenic meal (described later, under "Eating in Dubrovnik").

$ Nedjeljka Benussi, the sister-in-law of Jadranka Benussi (listed earlier), rents three modern, straightforward rooms sharing two bathrooms and a pretty view (May–Oct: D-400 kn, T-550 kn; Nov–April: D-300, T-450 kn; no extra charge for 1-night stays, no breakfast, cash only, fans but no air-con, Sv. Đurđa 4, tel. 020/423-062, mobile 098-170-5699).

Beyond the Ploče Gate, East of the Old Town

To reach these options, you'll go through the Ploče Gate and walk along the road stretching east from the Old Town (with fine views back on the Old Port). This area is shared by giant waterfront luxury hotels and residential areas, so it has a bit less character than the Pile and Old Town listings (which I prefer).

$$ Apartments Paviša, described on page 287, has two fine apartments in the Viktorija neighborhood about a 20-minute walk or short bus ride from town.

$$ Villa Adriatica has four old-fashioned rooms above a travel agency and a family home just outside the Ploče Gate, a few steps from the Old Town. The rooms share a terrace with priceless Old Port views (the main reason to consider staying here), plus a common living room and kitchen furnished with museum-piece antiques. Likeable Teo manages the rooms; ask for him at the Perla Adriatic travel agency, just outside the Ploče Gate (July–Aug: Db-€85–95; June and Sept: Db-€80–90; May and Oct: Db-€75–85; Nov–April: Db-€55–60; price depends on size and view, 20 percent more for 1- or 2-night stays, no breakfast, cash only, air-con, free Wi-Fi in some areas, Frana Supila 4, mobile 098-377-954, tel. 020/411-962, fax 020/422-766, www.dubrovnik-online.com /villa_adriatica, miroslav.tomsic@du.t-com.hr, Tomšić family).

Sobe-Booking Websites and Agencies

Several websites put you in touch with Dubrovnik's *sobe* and apartments. Of course, you'll save yourself and your host money if you book direct, but these sites are convenient. For example, www .dubrovnikapartmentsource.com, run by an American couple, offers a range of carefully selected, well-described accommodations. You can browse a variety of options, then reserve your choice and pay a nonrefundable deposit by credit card. Another, bigger operation—with a wider selection but less personal attention—is www.adriatica.net.

If you arrive without a reservation and the TI isn't too busy, they might be able to call around and find you a *soba* for no charge. Otherwise, just about any travel agency in town can help you, on the spot or in advance...for a fee. **Atlas** is the biggest company (figure Db-€50 and apartment-€60–80 in June–Sept, €10 less in shoulder season; for more on Atlas, see page 258).

Hotels

If you must stay in a hotel, you have only a few good options. There are just two hotels inside the Old Town walls—and one of them charges $500 a night (Pucić Palace, www.thepucic palace.com). Any big, resort-style hotel within walking distance of the Old Town will run you at least €200. These inflated prices drive most visitors to Boninovo Bay or the Lapad Peninsula, a bus ride west of the Old Town. In the mass-tourism tradition, many European visitors choose to take the half-board option at their hotel (i.e., dinner in the hotel restaurant). This can be convenient and a good value—especially considering the relatively low quality of Dubrovnik's restaurants (explained later, under "Eating in

Dubrovnik")—but the Old Town is a much more atmospheric place to dine.

In and near the Old Town

$$$ Hilton Imperial Dubrovnik, sitting regally just outside the Pile Gate, is the closest big hotel to the Old Town. This grand 19th-century building was recently overhauled to create 147 plush rooms. If you want predictable Hilton comfort a short walk from the Old Town, this is the place (July–Aug: Db-€300, actual rate generally closer to Db-€200; less off-season, €55 extra for sea view, €65 extra for balcony but no view, €120 extra for balcony and view, includes breakfast but not the 10 percent tax, elevator, air-con, pay cable Internet, parking-200 kn/night, Marijana Blažića 2, tel. 020/320-320, fax 020/320-220, www.hilton.com, sales .dubrovnik@hilton.com).

$$$ Hotel Stari Grad knows it's the only real hotel option inside the Old Town—and charges accordingly. It has eight modern yet nicely old-fashioned rooms a half-block off the Old Town's main drag. The rooftop breakfast terrace (summer only) enjoys a grand view over orange tiles. This place books up fast, so reserve early (July–Sept: Sb-€165, Db-€221; April–June and Oct: Sb-€125, Db-€180; Nov–March: Sb-€91, Db-€130; plus silly "insurance" charge of 8 kn/person per night, 10 percent more for 1- or 2-night stays, air-con, lots of stairs with no elevator, pay Wi-Fi in lobby, Od Sigurate 4, tel. 020/322-244, fax 020/321-256, www .hotelstarigrad.com, info@hotelstarigrad.com).

Near Boninovo Bay

Boninovo Bay is your best bet for an affordable and well-located hotel. Above this bay are Dubrovnik's only three-star hotels within walking distance of the Old Town (not to mention the city's only official youth hostel). These places offer slightly better prices and closer proximity to the Old Town than the farther-out Lapad Bay resorts. Boninovo Bay is an uphill 20-minute walk or five-minute bus ride from the Old Town (straight up Branitelja Dubrovnika). Once you're comfortable with the buses, the location is great: Any bus that leaves the Pile Gate stops first at Boninovo Bay. You'll see the bay on your left as you climb the hill, then get off at the stop after the traffic light (or stay on bus #4, which stops even closer to the hotels). To reach the hotels from the Boninovo bus stop, go up Pera Čingrije (the busy road running along the top of the cliff overlooking the sea). There's a super little bakery, Pekarnica Klas, on the right (across the street from Hotel Bellevue).

$$$ Hotel Bellevue has a striking location, with its back against the cliff rising up from Boninovo Bay and an elevator plunging directly to its own pebbly beach. Completely gutted and rebuilt just a few years ago, its 93 top-notch rooms—all with sea views, many with balconies—offer upscale wood-grain elegance (July–Aug: standard Db-generally €250; less off-season, very flexible rates, €50 more for balcony, air-con, elevator, free Wi-Fi, Pera Čingrije 7, tel. 020/330-000, fax 020/330-100, www.hotel -bellevue.hr, welcome@hotel-bellevue.hr).

$$$ **Hotel R,** a homey enclave with just 10 rooms, feels friendlier and less greedy than all the big resort hotels. Well-run by the Rešetar family, it's a good small-hotel value (June–Sept: Sb-€70, Db-€107; May and Oct: Sb-€56, Db-€84; Easter–April: Sb-€48, Db-€74; closed Nov–Easter, 10 percent more for balcony, half-board-€13, air-con, free Wi-Fi, just beyond the big Hotel Lero at Iva Vojnovića 16, tel. 020/333-200, fax 020/333-208, www.hotel-r.hr, helpdesk@hotel-r.hr).

$$$ **Hotel Lero,** 250 yards up the street from the bus stop, has 140 recently renovated rooms. Choose between sea views with some road noise, or quieter back rooms (soft rates, but generally early July–late Sept: Sb-€110, Db-€140; May–early July and late Sept–mid-Oct: Sb-€85, Db-€106; even less in winter; in busy times, you may be quoted more than these rates—try asking for a better deal; air-con, elevator, pay Internet access, free Wi-Fi in lobby, half-board-€6, Iva Vojnovića 14, tel. 020/341-333, fax 020/332-123, www.hotel-lero.hr, sales@hotel-lero.hr).

$ Dubrovnik's official **Youth Hostel** is quiet, modern, and well-run by proud manager Laura. It's institutional, with 82 beds in 19 fresh, woody dorms and few extra hostel amenities (bunk in 4- to 6-bed dorm—July–Aug: 125 kn; June and Sept: 115 kn; May and Oct: 105 kn; Nov–April: 95 kn; 10 kn more for nonmembers, includes sheets, breakfast-5 kn; reception open daily June–Oct 7:00–2:00 in the morning, Nov–May 8:00–14:00 & 18:00–20:00; 2:00 a.m. curfew in summer, none in winter; up the steps at ulica bana Jelačića 15–17, tel. 020/423-241, fax 020/412-592, www.hfhs .hr, dubrovnik@hfhs.hr). From the Boninovo bus stop, go down Pera Čingrije toward Hotel Bellevue, but take the first right uphill onto ulica bana Jelačića and look for signs up to the hostel on your left, on ulica Vinka Sagrestana. Several houses nearby rent rooms to those who prefer a double...and pick off would-be hostelers as they approach.

In Lapad

For a real resort-style vacation (at premium prices), many travelers call the touristy area around Lapad Bay home. The main drag running through the middle of this scene, called Šetalište Kralja Zvonimira, is a nicely pedestrianized people zone buzzing with tourists, restaurants, cafés, and mild diversions. From the bus stop, the main drag leads to a pleasant pebble beach good for swimming and a romantic bayside path. While I much prefer sleeping near the Old Town, this is an appealing place to be on vacation (even if the Old Town weren't just a short bus ride away). To get here from the Old Town's Pile Gate, pile onto bus #6 with all the other tourists and get off at the Pošta Lapad stop (poorly marked—after bus turns left away from the big harbor, watch for low-profile yellow *pošta* sign on left; 4–6 buses/hr until 24:30, 15 min). A taxi costs about 60 kn.

$$$ *Small Hotels in Lapad:* In this area, I like three new-ish, interchangeable small hotels. While not affiliated with each other, each one has similar amenities—air-con, elevator (except Hotel Dubrovnik), Internet access either in lobby or in room—and similar prices (July–Sept: around Db-1,000–1,400 kn, but prices are very soft and can flex with demand, season, and length of stay; check online for the latest, and ask for a deal when you reserve). **Hotel Aquarius,** hiding a block off the main drag, has 24 comfortable, plush-feeling rooms and an inviting terrace out front (Mata Vodopića 8, tel. 020/456-111, fax 020/456-100, www.hotel-aquarius.net, stjepanka@hotel-aquarius.net). **Hotel Perla,** right on the main drag, has 25 modern rooms (tel. 020/438-244, fax 020/438-245, www.perla-dubrovnik.com, info@perla-dubrovnik.com). **Hotel Dubrovnik,** two doors up from the Perla, has 25 simpler rooms (tel. 020/435-030, fax 020/435-999, www.hotel dubrovnik.hr, info@hoteldubrovnik.com).

Eating in Dubrovnik

Dubrovnik disappoints diners with high prices, surly service, and mediocre quality. With the constant influx of deep-pocketed tourists corrupting greedy restaurateurs, places here tend to go downhill faster than a game of marbles on the *Titanic*. Promising new restaurants open all the time, but most quickly fade, and what's great one year can be miserable the next. Therefore, lower your expectations, take my suggestions with a grain of salt, and ask around locally for what's good this month. Don't bother looking for a "local" favorite anywhere

near the Old Town—people who live here eat out at restaurants in the 'burbs. The good news is that it's atmospheric. Anywhere you dine, breezy outdoor seating is a no-brainer, and scrawny, adorable kittens beg for table scraps. In general, seafood restaurants are good only at seafood; if you want pasta, go to a pasta place.

In the Old Town

Nishta, featuring a short menu of delicious vegetarian fusion cuisine with Asian flair, offers a welcome change of pace from the Dalmatian seafood-pasta-pizza rut. Busy Swiss owner/chef Gildas cooks, while his wife Ruža serves. This tiny place—which, in my experience, is the only reliably good eatery in town—has just a few indoor and outdoor tables. Even if you're not a vegetarian, it's worth a visit (55–80-kn main courses, Mon–Sat 12:00–15:00 & 18:00–22:00, closed Sun, on the restaurant-clogged Prijeko street—near the Pile Gate end of the street, mobile 098-186-7440).

Dubrovački Kantun ("Dubrovnik's Nook") serves up typical, traditional Dalmatian specialties in a cozy eight-table interior that's ideal on rainy days. For now, this is one of the Old Town's more reputable options for good food. Despite its lack of outdoor seating, I'd give it a serious look (hearty 25-kn soups, 65–70-kn pastas, 70–120-kn main courses, daily 12:00–16:00 & 18:00–24:00, near the corner of Boškovićeva and Prijeko, tel. 020/331-911, Andrej).

Konoba Kamenice, a no-frills fish restaurant, is a local institution offering inexpensive, fresh, and good meals on a charming market square, as central as can be in the Old Town. On the limited menu, the seafood dishes are excellent (try their octopus salad, even if you don't think you like octopus), while the few non-seafood dishes are uninspired. Some of the waitstaff are notorious for their playfully brusque service, but loyal patrons happily put up with it. Arrive early, or you'll have to wait (35–70-kn main courses, daily 8:00–23:00, until 22:00 off-season, Gundulićeva poljana 8, tel. 020/323-682).

Lokanda Peskarija enjoys an enticing setting, with a sea of tables facing the Old Port. Servings are hearty and come in a pot, "home-style." The 60-kn seafood risotto easily feeds two, and sharing is no problem. The menu's tiny—with only seafood options, and not much in the way of vegetables. Locals complain that the quality has taken a nosedive ever since the restaurant's following has grown and its idyllic setting expanded to the hilt. But for reasonably priced seafood dishes on the water, this remains an acceptable option (most main courses 55–80 kn, daily 12:00–24:00, very limited indoor seating fills up fast, plenty of outdoor tables—which can also fill up, tel. 020/324-750, no reservations taken in summer). Notice that the tables farthest from the main restaurant have a different menu, focused on Balkan-style grilled meats; if that's what you want, skip this place and head for Taj Mahal instead (described later).

Pizza: Dubrovnik seems to have a pizzeria on every corner. Little separates the various options—just look for a menu and outdoor seating option that appeals to you. I've eaten well at

Oliva Pizzeria, just behind St. Blaise's Church (35–65-kn pizzas, Lučarica 5, daily 10:00–24:00, tel. 020/324-594). Around the side is a handy take-out window for a bite on the go.

Pasta: **Spaghetteria Toni** is popular with natives and tourists. While nothing fancy, they offer good pastas at reasonable prices. Choose between the cozy 10-table interior, or the long alley filled with outdoor tables (45–80-kn pastas, 40–60-kn salads, daily in summer 11:00–23:00, closed Sun in winter, closed Jan, Nikole Božidarevića 14, tel. 020/323-134).

Bosnian Cuisine: For a break from Croatian fare, consider the grilled meats and other tasty Bosnian dishes at the misnamed **Taj Mahal.** Though the service can be lacking, the menu offers an enticing taste of the Turkish-flavored land to the east. Choose between the tight interior, which feels like a Bosnian tea house, or tables out on the alley (50-kn salads, 45–115-kn main courses, daily 10:00–24:00, Nikole Gučetića 2, tel. 020/323-221). For a primer on Bosnian food, see "Balkan Flavors" on page 31.

Ice Cream: Dubrovnik has lots of great *sladoled*, but locals swear by the stuff at **Dolce Vita** (daily 9:00–24:00, a half-block off the Stradun at Nalješkovićeva 1A, tel. 020/321-666).

The Old Town's "Restaurant Row," Prijeko Street: The street called Prijeko, a block toward the mainland from the Stradun promenade, is lined with outdoor, tourist-oriented eateries—each one with a huckster out front trying to lure in diners. (Many of them aggressively try to snare passersby down on the Stradun, as well.) Don't be sucked into this vortex of bad food at outlandish prices. The only place worth seeking out here is Nishta (described earlier); the rest are virtually guaranteed to disappoint. Still, it can be fun to take a stroll along here—the atmosphere is lively, and the sales pitches are entertainingly desperate.

Just Outside the Old Town, with a View

Orhan Restaurant, overlooking the tranquil cove at the Pile neighborhood outside the Old Town, feels just beyond the tourist crush. It features disinterested service and unremarkable food, but great views on a large terrace (reserve a seat here in advance). Watch the people walk the Old Town walls across the cove (55–105-kn pastas, 80–180-kn main courses, daily 10:00–23:00, basic breakfast from 9:00, cash only, Od Tabakarije 1, tel. 020/414-183).

Komarda serves up forgettable food on a memorably romantic terrace, with views of Dubrovnik's walls and Old Port. Tables are scattered around a tranquil garden just above the sea and a concrete beach. As there's no point eating here unless you have a good view, consider dropping by early in the day to pick out and reserve the table of your choice for dinner (50–80-kn pastas, 65–120-kn main courses, 60-kn lunch special, daily 7:00–2:00 in the morning, reservations essential in summer, mobile 098-428-239). To find it, exit the Old Town through the Ploče Gate (east). After walking through the final fortification, you'll reach a block of travel agencies. Once you pass these, look for the stairs down to Komarda, on the right.

Picnic Tips

Dubrovnik's lack of great restaurant options makes it a perfect place to picnic. You can shop for fresh fruits and veggies at the open-air produce market (each morning near the cathedral, on the square called Gundulićeva Poljana). Supplement your picnic with grub from the cheap **Konzum grocery store** (one location near the bus stop just outside Pile Gate: Mon–Sat 7:00–21:00, Sun 8:00–14:00; another on the market square near the produce vendors. Mon–Sat 7:00–21:00, Sun 7:00–13:00). Good picnic spots include the shaded benches overlooking the Old Port; the Porporela breakwater (beyond the Old Port and fort—comes with a swimming area, sunny no-shade benches, and views of Lokrum Island); and the green, welcoming park in what was the moat just under the Pile Gate entry to the Old Town.

Breakfast

If you're sleeping in a *sobu*, you'll likely be on your own for breakfast. Fortunately, you have plenty of cafés and pastry shops to choose from, and your host probably has a favorite she can recommend. In the Pile neighborhood, I like **Restaurant Orhan**, right on the cove (described earlier; 50 kn for omelet or continental breakfast, served daily 9:00–11:00). In the Old Town, **Dubrava Bistro**—nicknamed "Snack Bar" by locals—has great views and fine outdoor seating at the most colorful end of the Stradun (basic 35–45-kn egg dishes, 18-kn caffè lattes; you'll pay a few extra kunas to sit outside—listed on the menu as *taraci*—but it's worth it; daily 8:00–24:00, Placa 6, tel. 020/321-229). Some of the other restaurants listed in this section (including Kamenice) also serve breakfast. Not many places serve before 9:00 or 10:00; if you'll be departing early, stock up on groceries the night before.

On Lapad Bay

If you want a break from the Old Town, consider venturing to Lapad Bay. The ambience is pleasant and Lapad is worth an evening stroll (for details on getting here, see page 293 under "Sleeping in Dubrovnik"). This area's main drag, **Šetalište Kralja Zvonimira,** is an amazingly laid-back pedestrian lane where bars have hammocks, Internet terminals are scattered through a forested park, and a folksy Croatian family ambience holds its own against the better-funded force of international tourism. Stroll from near Hotel Zagreb to the bay, marked by Hotel Kompas. From Hotel Kompas, a romantic walk—softly lit at night—leads past some splurge restaurants along the bay through the woods, with plenty of private little stone coves for lingering.

Dubrovnik Connections

Note that the boats listed here leave from Dubrovnik's Port Gruž, a bus ride away from the Old Town (described earlier, under "Arrival in Dubrovnik—By Car Ferry or Catamaran").

From Dubrovnik by Big Jadrolinija Car Ferry: The big boats leave Dubrovnik in the morning and go to **Korčula** (5/week July–Sept, 4/week June, 2/week Oct–May, 3–4 hrs), **Stari Grad** on Hvar Island (2/week year-round, 6.5 hrs), **Split** (2/week year-round, 8–9.25 hrs), and **Rijeka** (2/week year-round, 21 hrs including overnight from Split to Rijeka). Boat schedules are subject to change—confirm your plans at a local TI, or see www.jadrolinija.hr.

From Dubrovnik by Speedy *Nona Ana* Catamaran: This handy service connects Dubrovnik to popular islands to the north (Mljet, Korčula, and Lastovo). This schedule is subject to change from year to year, so carefully confirm the details before planning your trip. In the summer (June–Sept), the boat departs Dubrovnik each morning and heads for **Sobra** and **Polače** (1.75 hrs, 50 kn one-way) on Mljet Island. In the peak months of July and August, it sometimes continues on to **Korčula** (4/week, 2.75 hrs, 55 kn) and **Lastovo Island** (2/week, 4 hrs, 60 kn). In the winter (Oct–May), the boat goes daily to **Sobra** on Mljet (but not to Polače, Korčula, or Lastovo). The catamaran leaves from Dubrovnik's Port Gruž (buy tickets at the kiosk next to the boat, ticket window opens 1 hour before departure; in peak season, it's smart to show up about an hour ahead to be sure you get on the boat). Confirm schedules at the Dubrovnik TI, or check www.gv-line.hr.

By Bus to: Split (almost hourly, generally at the top of each hour, less off-season, 5 hrs), **Korčula** (peak season: 2/day, 3.5 hrs; off-season: Mon–Sat 1/day, Sun 2/day; also consider the shuttle-bus service described below), **Rijeka** (2/day, 12 hrs), **Zagreb** (7/day including some overnight options, 10 hrs), **Mostar** in Bosnia-Herzegovina (2–5/day depending on season, 4–5 hrs), **Kotor** in Montenegro (2–3/day, 2.5 hrs), **Pula** and **Rovinj** (nightly, 15 hrs to Pula, 16 hrs to Rovinj). For bus information, call 060-305-070 (a pricey toll line, but worth it).

By Shuttle Bus to Korčula: Korčula-based Korkyra Tours Travel Agency runs a handy door-to-door shuttle service from your Dubrovnik accommodations to Korčula (125 kn one-way plus 10 kn/bag; departs Mon–Fri at 14:00 year-round, Sat–Sun by request only; 2 hrs, reserve ahead, mobile 091-571-4355, www.korkyra .info, info@korkyra.info).

By Plane: To quickly connect remote Dubrovnik with the rest of your trip, consider a cheap flight (see "Getting to the Dalmatian Coast," page 170.) For information on Dubrovnik's airport, see "Arrival in Dubrovnik—By Plane," earlier.

By Car: For tips on driving along the Dalmatian Coast between Dubrovnik and Split, see page 204 in the Split chapter.

Can I Get to Greece from Dubrovnik? Not easily. Your best bet is to fly (though there are no direct flights, aside from the occasional charter flight from Dubrovnik to Athens—you'll generally have to transfer elsewhere in Europe). Even though Croatia and Greece are nearly neighbors, no direct boats connect them, and the overland connection is extremely long and rugged.

What About Italy? Flying is the easiest option, though there are only two direct flights (on Croatia Airlines to Rome, or on easy-Jet to Milan). You can take a direct night boat from Dubrovnik to Bari, or head to Split for more boat connections (for more on all of these boats, see page 202). The overland connection is overly long (figure 5 hrs to Split, then 5 hrs to Zagreb, then 7 hrs to Venice).

NEAR DUBROVNIK

Excursions from Dubrovnik's Old Port • Trsteno Arboretum • Pelješac Peninsula • Mljet National Park

Stretching up and down the glimmering Dalmatian Coast from Dubrovnik are a variety of worthwhile getaways. Just offshore from the city's Old Town—and accessible via scenic boat trip from its historic port—are enticing islands and villages, where time stands still for lazy vacationers: the playground islet of Lokrum, the sights-studded archipelago of the Elaphite Islands, and the serene resort town of Cavtat. To the north is a lush and diverse arboretum called Trsteno, with a playful fountain, a 600-year-old aqueduct, a villa, a chapel...and, of course, plants galore. Poking into the Adriatic is the vineyard-covered Pelješac Peninsula, anchored by the mighty little town of Ston. And out at sea is the sparsely populated island called Mljet, a third of which is carefully protected as one of Croatia's most appealing national parks, where you can hike, bike, boat, and swim to your heart's content. Best of all, there's no better place to "come home to" than Dubrovnik—after a busy day exploring the coastline, strolling the Stradun to unwind is particularly sweet.

Planning Your Time

Give yourself at least a full day and two nights to experience Dubrovnik itself. But if you can spare the time, set up in Dubrovnik for several nights and use your extra days for some of these excursions. (This also gives you the luxury of keeping an eye on the weather reports and saving the most weather-dependent activities for the sunniest days.) For suggestions on how much time to allow per destination, see the sidebar on page 302. Use a map to strategically line up these attractions—for example, you can easily do Trsteno, Ston, and the Pelješac Peninsula on a drive between Dubrovnik and Korčula.

I've listed these day trips in order of ease from Dubrovnik—the farther down the list, the more difficult to reach (with Montenegro and Bosnia-Herzegovina—the most time-consuming—covered in their own chapters). Choose the trips that sound best to you, and ask locals and other travelers for their impressions...or for new leads.

Getting There

Lokrum, Cavtat, and the Elaphite Islands are easy to reach by **excursion boat** from Dubrovnik's Old Port. The other desti-

nations are farther afield, best reached by **boat** (Mljet) or by **car** or **bus** (Montenegro, Bosnia-Herzegovina, Trsteno, Pelješac Peninsula). I've listed public transportation options for each, but consider renting a car for the day—or even splurging for your own private driver (see page 260).

Alternatively, the big Atlas Travel Agency in Dubrovnik offers **guided excursions** (by bus and/or boat) to nearby destinations. Popular itineraries include everything mentioned in this chapter, plus Korčula, Albania, and others (figure €30–100/person, depending on the itinerary; book tickets at Atlas in Dubrovnik—see page 258—or at other travel agencies; Atlas tel. 020/442-574, www.atlas-croatia.com). While these excursions can be a convenient way to see otherwise difficult-to-reach destinations, the experience is generally disappointing. I've been on two of these trips, and have gotten reports about several others. The consensus is that the buses are packed, the guides are uninspired (reading from a dull script—often in multiple languages), and quality time at the destinations is short. If you have no other way to reach a place you're dying to visit, guided excursions can still be worth considering. But I'd exhaust my other options first—consider renting a car for the day or hiring your own driver (expensive, but less so if you can split the cost with other travelers).

Excursions run by **other companies** can be smaller, more personalized, and more satisfying than Atlas' big-bus tours. Unfortunately, since this scene is constantly evolving, it's difficult to recommend one company in particular. Look around for flyers and ask locals for their best tips—but be aware that many smaller agencies simply sell seats on the big Atlas trips.

Dubrovnik Day Trips at a Glance

The international excursions to Bosnia-Herzegovina and Montenegro—which are worth considering for overnight stops—are covered in the next two chapters.

In Bosnia-Herzegovina

▲▲▲Mostar The side-trip with the highest degree of cultural hairiness—but, for many, also the most rewarding—lies

to the east, in Bosnia-Herzegovina. With its iconic Old Bridge, intriguing glimpse of European Muslim lifestyles, and still-vivid examples of war damage, Mostar is unforgettable. Though not for everyone, this trip is a must for adventurous travelers interested in Islam or in recent history. Allow a full day or more (best reached by bus or car).

Međugorje Devout Catholics may want to consider a trip to this pilgrimage site in Bosnia-Herzegovina, with a holy hill that some believe is visited regularly by an apparition of the Virgin Mary. Allow a full day or more (best reached by car or bus).

In Montenegro

▲▲The Bay of Kotor For rugged coastal scenery that arguably rivals anything in Croatia, head south of the border to Montenegro. The Bay of Kotor is a dramatic, fjord-like inlet crowned by the historic town of Kotor, with twisty Old World lanes, one of Europe's best town walls, and oodles of atmosphere. Allow a full day or more (best reached by car or bus).

The Montenegrin Interior A visit to Montenegro's scruffy but historic former capital, Cetinje, comes with a twisty drive up a mountain road and across a desolate, forgotten-feeling plateau. Allow a full day or more (best reached by car).

Budva Riviera Montenegro's best stretch of sandy beaches isn't worth a special trip, but it's a fun excuse for a drive if you've got extra time to kill. The highlight is the famous resort peninsula of Sveti Stefan. Allow a full day or more (best reached by car).

On the Mainland North of Dubrovnik

▲**Trsteno Arboretum** Plant-lovers will enjoy this surprisingly engaging botanical garden just outside Dubrovnik, punctuated by a classical-style fountain and aqueduct. Allow a half-day (best reached by bus or car).

Ston A small town with giant fortifications, Ston (on the Pelješac Peninsula) is worth a short stop to scramble up its extensive walls. Allow an hour (best reached by car or bus).

Pelješac Peninsula This long, narrow spit of land—between the main coastal road and Korčula Island—is a favorite of wine-lovers. Allow a half-day to a full day (best reached by car).

Off the Coast of Dubrovnik

▲**Mljet National Park** While this largely undeveloped island is time-consuming to reach from Dubrovnik, Mljet offers an opportunity to romp on an island without all those tacky tourist towns. This is for serious nature-lovers eager to get away from civilization. Allow a full day (best reached by boat).

Lokrum Island The most convenient excursion from Dubrovnik, this little island—just a short hop offshore from the Old Port—is a good chance to get away from (some of) the tourists. Allow a few hours (best reached by boat).

Elaphite Islands This inviting archipelago offers a variety of island experiences without straying too far from Dubrovnik. With more time, Korčula (for a small town) or Mljet (for a back-to-nature experience) is better, but the "Elafiti" (as they're known) are more convenient. Allow a half-day to a full day (best reached by boat).

Cavtat A charming resort/beach town en route to the Montenegrin border, Cavtat is more handy than must-see. Allow a few hours (best reached by boat or bus).

Excursions from Dubrovnik's Old Port

At Dubrovnik's salty Old Port, local captains set up tiny booths to hawk touristy boat trips. It's fun to chat with them, page through their sun-faded photo albums, and see if they can sell you on a short cruise. The basic option is a 50-minute "panorama cruise" out into the water and back again (75 kn, departures every hour). Among your vessel choices is the **Sv. Ivan,** a cargo boat dating from 1878. Or consider visiting one of the following destinations.

Lokrum Island

This island, just offshore from the Old Town, provides a handy escape from the city. Lokrum features a monastery-turned-Habsburg-palace, a small botani-cal garden, an old military fort, hiking trails, a café, some rocky beaches, and a little lake called the "Dead Sea" (Mrtvo More) that's suitable for swimming. Since the 1970s, when Lokrum became the "Island of Love," it's been known for its nude sunbath-ing. If you'd like to (carefully)  subject skin that's never seen the sun to those burning rays, follow the *FKK* signs from the boat dock for about five minutes to the slabs of waterfront rock, where naturists feel right at home. Boats run regularly from Dubrovnik's Old Port (40 kn round-trip, 10 kn for a map, runs April–Sept, 2/hr, 9:00–17:00, mid-June–Aug until 19:00, none Oct–March).

Elaphite Islands (Elafiti)

This archipelago, just north of Dubrovnik, is popular among day-trippers because you can hit three different islands in a single day. The main island, **Lopud,** has most of the attractions: a lively little town, boat and bike rental, and some rare sandy beaches. The other two islands—**Koločep** and **Šipan**—are less developed and (for some) a bit boring. Along the way, you'll discover fishing ports, shady forests, and forgotten escape mansions of old Dubrovnik aristocracy. The easiest way to cruise the Elafiti is to buy an excur-sion at Dubrovnik's Old Port, which includes a "fish picnic" cooked up by the captain as you cruise (about 250 kn with lunch, 180 kn without, several boats depart daily around 10:30–11:00, return around 18:00–18:30; so they can buy enough food, companies prefer you to reserve and pay a 50-kn deposit the day before). You generally spend about three hours on Lopud and about an hour each on Koločep and Šipan, with about 2.5 hours on the boat. To get to the Elaphite Islands without a tour (on a cheap ferry), you'll sail from Dubrovnik's less convenient Port Gruž. Note that if you're going to Korčula or Hvar, this trip is redundant—skip it unless you've got time to kill, need a break from Dubrovnik's crowds, and want a lazy day cruising Dalmatia.

Cavtat

This sleepy little resort town—just 12 miles to the south, near the Montenegrin border—offers a milder alternative to bustling Dubrovnik (www.tzcavtat-konavle.hr). Best known as a handy spot to find a room when Dubrovnik's booked up, Cavtat's biggest appeal is that it's a fun excuse to take a cruise somewhere. Holiday-makers who can look past the concrete resort hotels enjoy Cavtat's small-town ambience, people-filled seafront promenade, and inviting beaches. Meanwhile, sightseers find a few diversions to keep them busy: a mausoleum with eclectic flair designed by Croatian sculptor Ivan Meštrović (see page 188); a monastery with some fine Renaissance paintings; the Baltazar Bogišić Collection, with a large library and other items once belonging to a wealthy lawyer; and a museum displaying early-Modernist paintings by Cavtat-born portraitist Vlaho Bukovac.

Getting There: Boats to Cavtat leave every 30–60 minutes from Dubrovnik's Old Port (80 kn round-trip, 50 kn one-way, about 45 min each way, hourly return boats from Cavtat). Note that a round-trip ticket is cheaper, but you'll have to return with the same company (rather than whichever boat is leaving next). You can also reach Cavtat by public **bus** #10, which leaves from Dubrovnik's "former main bus station" and also stops at the "fire station" bus stop above the Old Town (about 2/hr, 30–40 min, 12 kn). For variety, consider going to Cavtat by boat (buy a one-way ticket), then returning by bus.

Trsteno Arboretum

Take a stroll through the shaded, relaxing botanical garden in Trsteno (worth ▲), just up the coast from Dubrovnik. Non-gardeners may find it a bit dull, but Trsteno is a horticulturalist's heaven. Spread over 63 acres on a bluff overlooking the sea, this arboretum features hundreds of different Mediterranean, Asian, and American plants (each one labeled in six languages, including English). The whole complex is laced with easy footpaths and sprinkled with fun attractions—a column-studded Renaissance Garden, a desolate villa, a little chapel, an old mill and olive-oil press, and a seaview pavilion.

As you wander, the world melts away and you're alone with the sounds of nature: wind, water, birds, and frogs. The garden's centerpiece is the whimsical 18th-century Neptune Fountain, featuring the god of the sea flanked by water-spouting nymphs and fishes, and holding court over a goldfish-stocked, lily-padded pond. Circling around behind the fountain, you'll discover that it's fed by an impressive 15th-century, 230-foot-long aqueduct (30 kn, daily May–Oct 8:00–19:00, Nov–April 8:00–16:00, tel. 020/751-019).

Getting There: Trsteno works best with a car, particularly if you're taking your time driving to Dubrovnik from the north (the

main coastal road goes through the town of Trsteno, right past the well-marked arboretum). You also have two bus options from Dubrovnik (around 20 kn, 20–30 min). Any long-distance northbound bus can drop you in Trsteno—ask about the next bus at the main station. Alternatively, the slower local bus #12 or #15, which depart from a bit closer to the Old Town (at the "former main bus station"), also reaches Trsteno. Coming back from Trsteno to Dubrovnik is trickier: Wait at the bus stop with the glass canopy by the park entrance and wave down any Dubrovnik-bound bus that passes (at least hourly).

Pelješac Peninsula

North of Trsteno, the skinny, 55-mile-long Pelješac (PEHL-yeh-shahts) Peninsula—practically an honorary island—splits off from the Croatian coastline as if about to drift away to Italy. (The far tip of Pelješac comes within a stone's throw of Korčula island.) This peninsula, famous for its rugged terrain—and the grapes that thrive here—is worth a detour only for wine-lovers. But its heavily fortified town of Ston, just a short side-trip from the main coastal road, merits a stretch-your-legs visit for anyone.

Getting There: Buses between Dubrovnik and Korčula traverse the Pelješac Peninsula, but drivers have the option of stopping where they like (such as at Ston or a winery). Some public buses also stop at Ston.

Ston

The town of Ston, at the base of the peninsula, is the gateway to Pelješac. This "Great Wall of Croatia" town is famous for the

impressive wall that climbs up the mountain behind it (about a half-mile encloses the town itself, while another three miles clamber up the hillsides). The unassuming town was heavily fortified (starting in 1333) for two reasons: to defend its strategic location, where mountains and bays create a bottleneck along the road from Dubrovnik to Pelješac, near the Republic of Dubrovnik's northern boundary; and to protect its impressive salt pans, which still produce salt. While nothing special today, these pans provided Dubrovnik with much of its wealth, back in the days when salt was worth more than its weight in gold. Today, the sleepy town—with more than its share of outdoor cafés and restaurants—is notable only for the chance to scramble up its massive fortifications (free, always open to walk up on top of the walls—though some sections may be closed for restoration work). The town's deserted feel is a result of a devastating 1996 earthquake, from which Ston is still rebuilding.

From Ston, the walls scamper over a ridge to its little sister, the bayside village of **Mali Ston** ("Small Ston"). Surrounded by a similar, but smaller, fortified wall, Mali Ston is known for its many mussel and oyster farms, and for its good restaurants. A local favorite is **Kapetanova Kuća,** a memorable restaurant with a fine location on Mali Ston's waterfront. The food is unpretentious but delicious, made with fresh produce from the restaurant's own

A Bridge Too Far?

If you're driving along the coast between Split and Dubrovnik, you might spot the controversial Pelješac Bridge project, which has been in flux for the last few years. Looking at a map, you'll notice that Bosnia-Herzegovina actually extends all the way to the sea (to the Bosnian resort town of Neum), cutting into a short stretch of the Dalmatian Coast. For years, coastal Bosnians and their Croatian neighbors have coexisted, albeit tensely at times. Prices for hotel rooms, groceries, and other staples are slightly cheaper in Neum, underselling the Croatian alternatives nearby.

As Croatia extends its expressway southward, the most logical approach would be a route through Bosnia to Dubrovnik. But some Croatian politicians have been looking for a way to avoid Neum altogether. One solution is to build a 1.5-mile-long bridge from just north of Neum to the Pelješac Peninsula, then re-join the coastal road back in Croatia, just south of Neum—effectively bypassing Bosnian territory. Environmentalists worry about the impact the bridge will have on the ecosystem around Mali Ston. But, because of the proposed bridge's popularity with a certain segment of the voting population, work actually began on this project prior to a recent election (notice that one mountaintop on Pelješac has already been cleared). But after the election—and with the global economic crisis—plans were put on hold. It remains to be seen whether this very expensive project will ever happen... and if so, whether the bridge will be completed before Croatia and Bosnia both join the EU and open their borders anyway.

garden (75–100-kn pastas, 100–130-kn seafood and meat dishes, daily 9:00–23:00, tel. 020/754-264, Kralj family).

Pelješac Wine Country

Farther along, the sparsely developed Pelješac Peninsula is blanketed with vineyards, and wine is the area's main draw. For a primer, see "Croatian Wine" on page 49. To really do the peninsula justice, consider hiring a driver/guide to take you on a spin around Pelješac (Dubrovnik-based Petar Vlašić is good—see page 260). The vineyards that are best set up for visitors are Matuško, Rosso, and Grgić. On Pelješac, the best area for growing wine is Dingač, with rocky soil facing the sea.

Mljet National Park

Carefully protected against modern development, the island hideaway of Mljet National Park offers a unique back-to-nature escape. With ample opportunities for hiking, swimming, biking, and boating—and without a nightclub, tacky T-shirt, or concrete "beach" pad in sight—Mljet (muhl-YET) is a potential highlight for active, outdoorsy travelers.

Though Mljet Island is one of Dalmatia's largest, it has fewer than 1,500 residents. Nearly three-quarters of the island is covered in forest, leaving it remarkably untamed. Aside from its beautiful national park, Mljet has inspired some of the most memorable tales of the Croatian coast—the poet Homer, his protagonist Ulysses, and the Apostle Paul all spent time here...or so the locals love to boast.

Many Croatians rave about Mljet. Take it with a grain of salt. The park, while enjoyable, is a bit overrated. One jaded local told me, "Mljet is basically Hvar or Korčula with no towns." But if that sounds like your kind of scene, make the trip.

Planning Your Time

Thanks to a handy catamaran connection, Mljet works perfectly as a full-day side-trip from Dubrovnik. But because of inconvenient boat schedules to other destinations, it's challenging to splice it into a one-way itinerary (say, between Korčula and Dubrovnik). So if you want to visit Mljet, either do it as a day trip on your own from Dubrovnik, or buy a package day-trip excursion from Korčula, Hvar, or Split. For details, see "Mljet Connections," at the end of this chapter.

No matter how you arrive, one day is plenty for Mljet. I've suggested a day-trip plan under "Sights on Mljet."

Be warned that everything's very seasonal and weather-dependent, so visiting outside of peak season (June–Sept) may come with some frustration.

Orientation to Mljet

The island of Mljet is long (23 miles) and skinny (less than two miles wide). The national park occupies the western third of the island. You're likely to reach Mljet via one of three port towns. **Polače** (POH-lah-cheh) and **Pomena** (POH-meh-nah) are handy entry points into the national park, while **Sobra** (SOH-brah) is much less convenient (a 1.25-hour bus trip across the island from the park). The *Nona Ana* catamaran from Dubrovnik puts in at Polače and Sobra; most excursions use Pomena; and the car ferries

NEAR DUBROVNIK

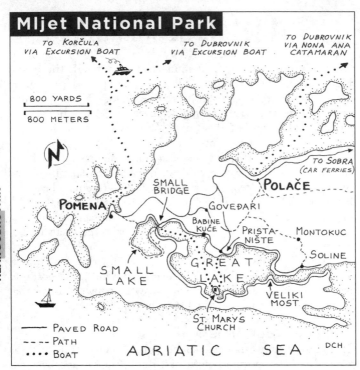

Mljet National Park

TO KORČULA VIA EXCURSION BOAT

TO DUBROVNIK VIA EXCURSION BOAT

TO DUBROVNIK VIA NONA ANA CATAMARAN

800 YARDS
800 METERS

TO SOBRA (CAR FERRIES)

SMALL BRIDGE

POLAČE

POMENA

GOVEĐARI

BABINE KUĆE

PRISTANIŠTE

MONTOKUC

G R E A T L A K E

SOLINE

S M A L L L A K E

VELIKI MOST

ST. MARY'S CHURCH

——— PAVED ROAD
- - - - PATH
• • • • BOAT

A D R I A T I C   S E A   DCH

(the big Jadrolinija Korčula–Dubrovnik car ferry, plus smaller ferries to the mainland) use Sobra.

Polače and Pomena flank the heart of the national park, a pair of saltwater "lakes" called simply **Great Lake** (Veliko Jezero) and **Small Lake** (Malo Jezero). The two bodies of water meet at a cute little bridge, appropriately named **Small Bridge** (Mali Most), where you can rent kayaks and bikes and catch a boat out to the little **island** in the Great Lake. A 15-minute walk around the Great Lake from the Small Bridge brings you to **Pristanište** (meaning, roughly, "transit hub"), where you can also catch a boat to the island or a shuttle bus to Polače. The nearby cliff-climbing town of **Goveđari** is home to many of the people who work at the park, but is not interesting to tourists.

Everything's well-signed, and there are enough landmarks that it's difficult to get really lost. Even so, I bought the detailed park map (at the entry kiosk) and was glad I had it.

Tourist Information

The **TI** is in Polače, just across from where the *Nona Ana* catamaran from Dubrovnik docks (mid-June–Aug daily 8:00–20:00; early June and Sept daily 8:00–13:00 & 17:00–20:00; Oct–May

Mon–Fri 8:00–13:00, closed Sat–Sun; tel. 020/744-086). The island's lone hotel, the **Hotel Odisej** in Pomena, acts as a second tourist information point. The hotel is a hub of services for visitors (whether you stay there or not): bike, scooter, car, and boat rentals; scuba diving and sailing lessons; walking tours around the island; cruises to some of the island's caves; and even help finding private accommodations. For more on the hotel, see "Sleeping and Eating on Mljet," later in this chapter.

The general-information website for the island (which covers the towns, Hotel Odisej, *sobe* and apartments, and more) is www.mljet.hr; for information on the national park, visit www.np -mljet.hr.

Arrival in Mljet

At Polače: Arriving on the *Nona Ana* catamaran from Dubrovnik, exit the boat to the right, walk a few steps, and look for the TI on your left. A few minutes' walk up the coast (near the Roman ruins) is a kiosk where you can buy your park entry ticket and catch a minibus to the Pristanište transit hub at the Great Lake (runs hourly, scheduled to coincide with boat arrival). From Pristanište, you can take a boat out to the island in the Great Lake (about hourly), or walk around the lake toward the Small Bridge, Small Lake, and on to Pomena.

At Pomena: If you arrive at Pomena, you're most likely on a package excursion, in which case your park entry ticket is included and you'll probably stick with your guide for a while. But in case you're on your own, exit the boat to the left (passing Hotel Odisej) and buy your park entry ticket at the kiosk. A few steps up the road beyond the kiosk, you'll see a shortcut to the right that takes you up and down some steps on your way to the Small Lake; once at the lake, bear left and continue to the Small Bridge, where you can catch the boat to the island in the Great Lake or rent a bike or kayak.

Note that there's no official bus between Polače and Pomena, but Hotel Odisej operates a shuttle to coincide with the Dubrovnik catamaran. Several informal minibus-taxis can also take you for a fee.

At Sobra: If you come on a car ferry, you're in for a long haul over to Polače and Pomena—about a 1.25-hour bus trip on twisty roads. Avoid arriving via Sobra unless you're desperate.

Sights on Mljet

▲Mljet National Park

All of the following attractions are inside the park. The steep 90-kn entry fee includes the shuttle bus from Polače to the Great Lake and a boat ride to the lake's island. The park is open daily

NEAR DUBROVNIK

The Tales of Mljet

For a mostly undeveloped island, Mljet has had a surprisingly busy history. Home to Illyrians, Greeks, Romans, Slavs, Venetians, Habsburgs, Yugoslavs, and now Croatians, the island has hosted some interesting visitors (or supposed visitors) that it loves to brag about.

Around the eighth century B.C., the Greek epic poet Homer possibly spent time here. He was so inspired by Mljet that he used it as the setting for one of the adventures of his hero Ulysses (a.k.a. Odysseus). This is the island where Ulysses fell in love with a beautiful nymph named Calypso and shacked up with her in a cave for seven years. Today there's a much-vaunted "Ulysses' Cave" (Odisejeva Spilja), a 40-minute hike below the island's main town, Babino Polje (at the far end of the island—skip it unless you're a Ulysses groupie).

Flash forward nearly a millennium, when a real-life traveler found his way to Mljet. According to the Bible (Acts 28), the Apostle Paul was shipwrecked on an island called "Melita"—likely this one—for three months. While on the island, Paul was bitten by a deadly snake, which he threw into a fire. The natives were amazed that he wasn't affected by the poison, and he proceeded to cure their ailments. This event was long believed to have happened on the similarly named isle of Malta, in the Mediterranean Sea. But more recently, many historians believe Paul was on Mljet. The most convincing argument: Malta never had poisonous snakes. Incidentally, Mljet no longer does, either—the Habsburgs imported an army of Indian mongooses to rid the island of problematic serpents. Because of this historical footnote, people from Mljet are nicknamed "mongooses" by other Croatians.

The heroics continue with today's "mongooses." There have been more than 100 fires on the island in the last 20 years (most caused by lightning, some by careless visitors), but only three have spread and caused significant destruction. That's because the people of Mljet—well aware of the fragility of the island that provides their income—are also a crack volunteer firefighting force, ready to spring into action and save their island at the first wisp of smoke.

May–mid-Oct 7:00–19:00, shorter hours in shoulder season, closed Nov–Feb; park information tel. 020/744-041.

Day-Trip Plan: If you're doing the trip on your own from Dubrovnik, try this itinerary: From Polače, take the minibus to Pristanište, where you can catch the boat to the island in the Great Lake. Take the boat back to Mali Most (Small Bridge), where you can rent a bike for a ride along the shore of the Great Lake. If you're heating up, take a dip in the Small Lake at the beach near the Small Bridge. When you're ready for a bit of civilization, walk into Pomena and relax by the seaside, then take the hotel's shuttle bus or a minibus-taxi back to Polače to catch the catamaran back home to Dubrovnik. With more energy, skip Pomena and hike up to Montokuc (you can hike down to Polače on the other side).

The Lakes—The "Great Lake" and "Small Lake" are technically saltwater bays—fed by the sea and affected by ocean currents (as you'll clearly see if you're at the little channel by the Small Bridge at the right time of day). Scientists love these lakes, which contain various shellfish species unique to Mljet.

The Island—The main activity in the park is taking a boat out to the Great Lake's little island-in-an-island (boats depart about hourly from the Small Bridge and from Pristanište). The tiny island's main landmark is St. Mary's Church (Sv. Marija) and the attached monastery, left behind by Benedictine monks who lived on Mljet starting in the 12th century. Though the monastery complex has been modified over the ages, fragments of the original Romanesque structure still survive. You can hike the easy trail up to the top of the island, passing remains of fortifications and old chapels, and look for the island's only permanent residents: a handful of goats, donkeys, and chickens. You'll have about an hour on the island, but it only takes half that to see everything—then relax with an overpriced drink at the restaurant by the boat dock.

Biking—The Great Lake is surrounded by a paved, mostly level road that's good for an hour or two of pedaling (unfortunately, you can't go all the way around because the path is broken by the channel connecting the lakes to the sea). The unpaved path around the Small Lake is rough and rocky, making biking there more difficult. The handiest place to rent a bike for a quick ride around the Great Lake is right at the lake itself, by the Small Bridge. Other bike rental points are scattered around the island, including in both Polače and Pomena. But those towns are separated from the lakes—and from each other—by steep hills, making cycling from either town to the lakes a headache for casual bikers.

Swimming—Options are everywhere, most temptingly at the Great Lake and Small Lake. In fact, even though it's fed by seawater, the Small Lake is always about seven degrees Fahrenheit warmer than the sea. The beach by the Small Bridge is particularly handy (but there are no showers or WCs).

Boating—You can rent kayaks at the Small Bridge. Motorized boats—except for the occasional local resident's dinghy—aren't allowed on the island's lakes.

Hiking to Montokuc—The most rewarding hike takes you up to the national park's highest point, Montokuc. At 830 feet above sea level, this is a serious, steeply uphill hike—skip it unless you're in good shape, and be sure to bring water (allow at least one hour round-trip at a steady pace). The trail runs between Polače, at the north end of the island, and the village of Soline, beyond the far end of the Great Lake (past the old, broken bridge called Veliki Most). If you're doing this or any other hike, the park map is essential (sold at park entry kiosks and other merchants).

Sleeping and Eating on Mljet

(€1 = about $1.40, country code: 385, area code: 020)

$$$ Hotel Odisej, the only hotel on the island, has more charm than most renovated communist hotels. Sitting right on the waterfront, with 157 rooms, it's a predictably comfortable home base (July–Aug: non-view Sb-€80–90, Sb with sea view and balcony-€95–110, non-view Db-€100–120, Db with sea view or balcony-€120–145, Db with sea view and balcony-€140–160; cheaper in shoulder season, no extra charge for 1- or 2-night stays, closed mid-Oct–mid-April, air-con, elevator, tel. 020/362-111, fax 020/744-042, www.hotelodisej.hr, info@hotelodisej.hr).

$–$$ Sobe *and Apartments:* Mljet has a wide range of private accommodations, with a few in each town or village. *Sobe* run about €15–20 per person in peak season, or €10–15 off-season; for apartments, figure €40–60 for two people in peak season, €25–40 off-season (20 percent more for 1- or 2-night stays). If you arrive without a room, the TI in Polače or Hotel Odisej in Pomena can help you find something. If you're looking in advance, check out the island website, www.mljet.hr. I'd choose a place in the population centers of Polače or Pomena (for their easy access to the park) or in the cute Great Lake–front village of Babine Kuće (near the Small Bridge). To really get away from it all, little end-of-the-road Soline (near the channel connecting the Great Lake to the sea) is rustic and remote, and has several options.

For **eating,** many good restaurants are scattered around the island. There isn't one that's particularly worth seeking out—just eat when it fits your itinerary (or bring a picnic).

Mljet Connections

To Dubrovnik and Korčula by Catamaran: The speedy, made-for-day-trippers catamaran called *Nona Ana* runs daily in each direction between Dubrovnik and Mljet. In the summer (June–Sept), it goes every morning from **Dubrovnik** to **Sobra,** then on to **Polače** (the best stop for the national park, 50 kn, 1.75 hrs). In the peak months of July and August, it sometimes continues to **Korčula** town (1 hr beyond Polače, 4/week) and **Lastovo Island** (2.25 hrs beyond Polače, 2/week). In the afternoon, it returns to Dubrovnik via the same route, bringing tired but happy side-trippers back to the city. It's less handy in the winter (Oct–May), when it goes daily from Dubrovnik only to Sobra (but not Polače, Korčula, or Lastovo). Confirm the schedule at www.gv-line.hr, and double-check your plans with the Dubrovnik TI. To be sure you get a ticket in peak season, show up early (up to an hour before the boat leaves).

Even though this boat works perfectly for day-tripping from Dubrovnik to Mljet National Park, it doesn't work as well for connecting to Korčula, since it just goes there on some mornings and is handy only if you're heading north after spending the night on Mljet.

Between Mljet and Other Destinations: All other destinations (including Hvar, Split, and day-tripping from Korčula) are more conveniently connected to Mljet by **excursion** than by public transit. The approximately €50 price tag for an all-day excursion seems high, but remember that it includes the 90-kn (€12) park admission fee and saves you the hassle of getting to the island on your own. Otherwise, you can reach Mljet only by the **car ferry** that stops at Sobra (2–3/week in peak season going between Dubrovnik and Korčula, plus other connections from the mainland).

There's no good, straightforward way to visit Mljet in a single day en route between destinations (say, on the way from Dubrovnik to Korčula). But it might work if you're lucky, flexible, and adventurous. If the excursion boats aren't full—and they rarely are—you can buy a last-minute, one-way ticket for a fraction of the full price. So, for example, you can take the morning catamaran from Dubrovnik to Mljet, enjoy the park, then continue on to Korčula in the evening on one of the day-trip boats. (It works vice versa, too: Pay for a morning excursion from Korčula to Mljet, then continue to Dubrovnik on the public catamaran.) Call the staff at Hotel Odisej—who know which excursions are coming to town—the night before to see if they have any ideas. The downside: You can't arrange this in advance, and there's always a chance the boat will be full—and you'll be stranded on Mljet for the night.

BOSNIA-HERZEGOVINA

BOSNIA-HERZEGOVINA

Mostar • Međugorje

The early 1990s weren't kind to Bosnia-Herzegovina: War. Bloodshed. Destruction. But apart from its tragic separation from Yugoslavia, the country has long been—and still remains—a remarkable place, with ruggedly beautiful terrain, a unique mix of cultures and faiths, kind and welcoming people who pride themselves on their hospitality, and some of the most captivating sightseeing in southeastern Europe. After all, little Bosnia-Herzegovina—with fewer than four million people—is a country with three faiths, three languages, and two alphabets.

While there's a lot to see in this country, two destinations are particularly safe, stable, and within easy reach of the Dalmatian Coast: the Turkish-flavored city of Mostar and the Catholic pilgrimage site of Međugorje. These places are worth considering as a detour—both geographical and cultural—from the Croatian mainstream.

Mostar, still scarred by war, has restored its famous 16th-century Old Bridge—one of Europe's most inspirational sights. Mostar also offers an illuminating and unique glimpse of a culture that's both devoutly Muslim and fully European. In the cobbled Old Town surrounding the bridge, you can poke into several mosques, tour old-fashioned Turkish-style houses, shop your way through a bazaar of souvenir stands, and hear the call to prayer echoing across the rooftops.

Međugorje, where six residents have reported seeing visions of the Virgin Mary, is of interest mostly to pilgrims. While other visitors scratch their heads and say, "Is that all there is?", many observant Catholics find something powerful here.

Nervous travelers might be tempted to give Bosnia-Herzegovina a miss. While Mostar and Međugorje are generally considered safe for tourists, they can be unsettling, because of the in-your-face war damage and an exotic mélange of cultures that seems atypical for Europe. But to me, for exactly these reasons, Mostar is easily one of the most rewarding destinations in this region—overcome your jitters and dive in. Bosnia-Herzegovina presents a jarring but fascinating contrast to what you'll see in Croatia or Slovenia. Yet, somehow it still fits with those places, giving inquisitive visitors a more complete understanding of the former Yugoslavia.

Getting Around Bosnia-Herzegovina

The destinations I've covered in this chapter aren't as easy to reach as they could be from the Dalmatian Coast, but connections are workable.

By Car: Coming with your own car gives you maximum flexibility, but you may find Mostar—which has poor signage—stressful to drive in. For specific route information, see "Route Tips for Drivers" on page 344. If you do plan to drive here, let your car-rental company know in advance to ensure you have the appropriate paperwork for crossing the border. If you're not up for driving yourself, consider splurging on a driver to bring you here (for drivers based in Dubrovnik, see page 260; for a Mostar-based driver, see page 326).

By Bus: Especially if you're spending the night in Mostar, bus connections with destinations on the Dalmatian Coast (especially Split and Dubrovnik) are workable. For details, see "Mostar Connections," later.

By Package Tour: Taking a package excursion from a Dalmatian resort town seems like an efficient way to visit Mostar or Međugorje. Unfortunately, in reality it can be less rewarding than doing it on your own—count on lots and lots of hours on a crowded bus, listening to a lackluster, multilingual tour guide reading from a script, and relatively little time in the destinations themselves. But if you just want a quick one-day look at these places, it's worth considering. These all-day tours are sold from Split, Hvar, Korčula, Dubrovnik, and other Croatian coastal destinations for about €50–60. The best tours max out their time in Mostar itself (it still won't be enough); avoid the tours that include a pointless boat trip on the Neretva River. Those that add a quick visit to the worthwhile town of Počitelj are a better deal. Atlas is the biggest operation (www.atlas-croatia.com); ask for details at any travel agency in Dalmatia.

Bosnia-Herzegovina Almanac

Official Name: Bosna i Hercegovina (abbreviated "BiH"); the *i* means "and"—Bosnia *and* Herzegovina (the country's two regions). The tongue-twisting name "Herzegovina" (hert-seh-GOH-vee-nah) comes from the German word for "dukedom" (*Herzog* means "duke").

Snapshot History: Bosnia-Herzegovina's early history is similar to the rest of the region: Illyrians, Romans, and Slavs (oh, my!). The country's story parts ways with Croatia's in the late 15th century, when Turkish rulers from the Ottoman Empire began a 400-year domination of the country. Many of the Ottomans' subjects converted to Islam, and their descendants remain Muslims today. After the Habsburgs forced out the Ottomans in 1878, Bosnia-Herzegovina became part of the Austro-Hungarian Empire, then Yugoslavia, until it declared independence in October of 1991. The bloody war that ensued came to an end in 1995. (For details, see the Understanding Yugoslavia chapter.)

Population: About 4.6 million. (There were about 100,000 identified casualties of the war, but many estimates of total casualties are double that number.) Someone who lives in Bosnia-Herzegovina, regardless of ethnicity, is called a "Bosnian." A southern Slav who practices Islam is called a "Bosniak." Today, about half of all Bosnians are Bosniaks (Muslims), a little more than a third are Orthodox Serbs, and about 15 percent are Catholic Croats. Traditionally, Bosniaks lived in the towns and cities, while Serbs and Croats farmed the countryside.

Political Divisions: As a part of the Dayton Peace Accords that ended the conflict here in 1995, the nation is divided into three separate regions: the Federation of Bosnia and Herzegovina (FBiH, shared by Bosniaks and Croats, very roughly in the western and central parts of the country), the Republika Srpska (RS, dominated by Serbs, generally to the north and east), and the Brčko District (BD, a tiny corner of the country, with a mix of the ethnicities). For the most part, each of the three native ethnic groups stay in "their" part of this divided country, but tourists can move freely between them.

Language: Technically, Bosnia-Herzegovina has three languages—Bosnian, Serbian, and Croatian. But all three are mutually intelligible dialects of what was until recently considered a single language: Serbo-Croatian. Bosniaks and Croats use basically the same Roman alphabet we do, while Serbs generally use the Cyrillic alphabet. You'll see both alphabets on currency and other official documents. Many people also speak English.

Area: 19,741 square miles (like Vermont and New Hampshire combined, or slightly larger than Slovakia).

Geography: Bosnia and Herzegovina are two distinct regions that share the same mountainous country. Bosnia constitutes the majority of the country (in the north, with a continental climate), while Herzegovina is the southern tip (about a fifth of the total area, with a hotter Mediterranean climate). Mostar is the biggest city and unofficial capital of Herzegovina—so saying you're in "Bosnia" while you're here is technically incorrect.

Red Tape: To enter Bosnia-Herzegovina, Americans and Canadians need only a passport (no visa required).

Economy: The country's economy has struggled since the war—the per capita GDP is $6,500, and the official unemployment rate is around 29 percent.

Currency: The official currency is the Convertible Mark (Konvertibilna Marka, abbreviated KM locally, BAM internationally). The official exchange rate is $1 = about 1.30 KM. But merchants in these destinations are willing to take euros or Croatian kunas, roughly converting prices with a simple formula:

2 KM = €1 = 8 kn (= about $1.40)

Even though you can get by without Convertible Marks, consider making a small withdrawal to get a sense of them. Notice that to satisfy the country's various factions, the currency uses both the Roman and the Cyrillic alphabets, and bills have different figureheads and symbols (some bills feature Bosniaks, others Serbs).

Telephones: Bosnia-Herzegovina's country code is 387. If calling from another country, first dial the international access code (00 in Europe, 011 in the US), then 387, then the area code (minus the initial zero), then the number.

Flag: The flag of Bosnia-Herzegovina, adopted after the recent war, is a blue field with a yellow triangle along the top edge. The three points of the triangle represent Bosnia-Herzegovina's three peoples (Bosniaks, Croats, Serbs), and the triangle also resembles the physical shape of the country. A row of white stars underscores the longest side of the triangle. These stars—and the yellow-and-blue color scheme—resemble the flag of the European Union (a nod to the EU's efforts to bring peace to the region). While this compromise flag sounds like a nice idea, almost no Bosnian embraces it as his or her own; each group has its own unofficial but highly prized symbols and flags (such as the fleur-de-lis for the Bosniaks, the red-and-white checkerboard shield for the Croats, and the cross with the four S's for the Serbs)—many of which offend the other groups.

Mostar

Mostar (MOH-star) represents the best and the worst of Yugoslavia. During the Tito years, it was an idyllic mingling of cultures—Catholic Croats, Orthodox Serbs, and Muslim Bosniaks living together in harmony, their differences spanned by an Old Bridge that epitomized an optimistic vision of a Yugoslavia where ethnicity didn't matter. And yet, as the country unraveled in the early 1990s, Mostar was gripped by a gory three-way war among those same peoples...and that famous bridge crumbled into the Neretva River.

More than any other destination in this book, Mostar rearranges your mental furniture. Most startling are the vivid and thought-provoking signs of the war. A few years ago, much of the city was destroyed; today, while still easy to find, the ruins aren't quite as in-your-face as before. Still, especially outside of the tourist zone, burned-out husks of buildings, unmistakable starburst patterns in the pavement, and bullet holes in walls are a constant reminder that the city is still recovering—physically and psychologically. In an age when we watch TV news coverage of conflicts abroad with the same detachment we give Hollywood blockbusters, Mostar provides an unpleasant but essential reminder of how real and how destructive war truly is.

Western visitors may also be struck by the immediacy of the Muslim culture that permeates Mostar. Here at a crossroads of civilizations, minarets share the skyline with church steeples. During the Ottomans' 400-year control of this region, many Slavic subjects converted to Islam (see sidebar on page 334). And, although they retreated in the late 19th century, the Ottomans left

behind a rich architectural, cultural, and religious legacy that has forever shaped Mostar. Five times each day, loudspeakers on minarets crackle to life, the call to prayer warbles through the streets, and Mostar's Muslim residents flock into the mosques. In many parts of the city, you'd swear you were in Turkey.

If these factors intrigue you, read on—Mostar has so much more to offer. Despite the scars of war, its setting is stunning: straddling the banks of the gorgeous Neretva River, with tributaries and waterfalls carving their way through the rocky landscape. The sightseeing—mosques, old Turkish-style houses, and that spine-tingling Old Bridge—is more engaging than much of what

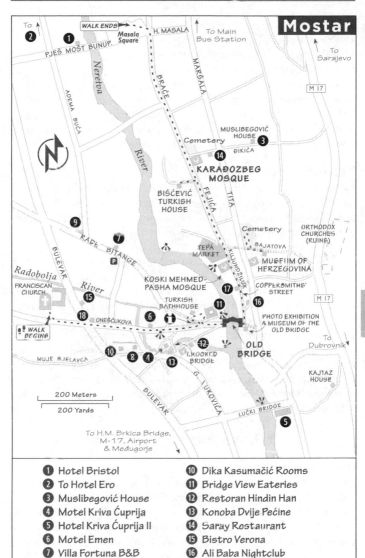

1. Hotel Bristol
2. To Hotel Ero
3. Muslibegović House
4. Motel Kriva Ćuprija
5. Hotel Kriva Ćuprija II
6. Motel Emen
7. Villa Fortuna B&B
8. Pansion Botticelli
9. Pansion Most
10. Dika Kasumačić Rooms
11. Bridge View Eateries
12. Restoran Hindin Han
13. Konoba Dvije Pećine
14. Saray Rostaurant
15. Bistro Verona
16. Ali Baba Nightclub
17. Fortuna Tours
18. Future Synagogue Site

you'll find in Croatia or Slovenia. And it's cheap—hotels, food, and museums are less than half the prices you'll pay in Croatia.

While a visit to Mostar just a few years ago was depressing, these days, more and more, it's uplifting. The city is rebuilding at an impressive pace, and local entrepreneurs are working hard to make Mostar tourist-friendly. Before long, Mostar will reclaim its status as one of the premier destinations in the former Yugoslavia. Visit now, while it still has its rough-around-the-edges charm—and you'll have seen it before it really took off.

Planning Your Time

Because of its cultural hairiness, a detour into Bosnia-Herzegovina feels like a real departure from a Dalmatian vacation. But actually, Mostar is easier to reach from Dubrovnik or Split than many popular Dalmatian islands (it's within a three-hour drive or bus ride from either city).

The vast majority of tourists in Mostar are day-trippers from the coast, which means the Old Town is packed midday, but empty in the morning and evening. You can get a good feel for Mostar in just a few hours, but a full day gives you time to linger and ponder.

You have three basic options: take a package tour from Dalmatia; rent a car for a one-day side-trip into Mostar; or (my favorite) spend the night here en route between Croatian destinations. To work a Mostar overnight into your itinerary, consider a round-trip plan that takes you south along the coast, then back north via Bosnia-Herzegovina (for example, Split–Hvar–Korčula–Dubrovnik–Mostar–back to Split).

Orientation to Mostar

(country code: 387; area code: 036)

Mostar—a mid-sized city with just over 100,000 people—is situated in a basin surrounded by mountains and split down the middle by the emerald-green Neretva River. Bosniaks live mostly on the east side of the river and Croats on the west (though increasingly the populations are mixing again). Visitors move freely throughout the city, and most don't even notice the division. The cobbled, Turkish-feeling Old Town (called the "Stari Grad" or—borrowing a Turkish term—the "Stara Čaršija") surrounds the town's centerpiece, the Old Bridge. Timid tourists feel most comfortable in the Old Town sector, and that's where I've focused my sightseeing, hotel, and restaurant recommendations.

The skyline is pierced by the minarets of various mosques, but none is as big as the two major Catholic (Croat) symbols in town, both erected since the recent war: the giant white cross on the hilltop (placed where Croat forces shelled the Bosniak side of the river, including the Old Bridge); and the enormous (almost 100-foot-tall) bell tower of the Franciscan Church of Sts. Peter and Paul. A monumental Orthodox cathedral once stood on the hillside across the river, but it was destroyed in the war when the Serbs were forced out. Funds are now being collected to rebuild it.

A note about safety: Mostar is as safe as any city its size, but it doesn't always *feel* safe. You'll see bombed-out buildings everywhere, even in the core of the city. Some are marked with *Warning! Dangerous Ruin* signs, but for safety's sake, never wander into any building that appears damaged or deserted.

Tourist Information

The virtually worthless TI shares a building with a tour office, but it does give out a free town map and a few other brochures on Mostar and Herzegovina (sporadic hours, generally open June–Oct daily 9:00–17:00, maybe later in busy times, likely closed Nov–May, just a block from the Old Bridge on Rade Bitange street, tel. 036/580-275, www.bhtourism.ba).

Arrival in Mostar

By Bus or Train: As with many things in Mostar, bus service is divided; most Bosniak (Muslim) buses, and some Croat ones, use the main bus station on the east side of town, while other Croat buses use a different stop, on the west side of town. (For details on this confusing system, see "Mostar Connections," later.)

The main bus station, which is combined with the train station, is north of the Old Town on the east side of the river (about a 10-KM taxi trip). At the station, you'll find ticket windows in the lobby facing the bus stalls. But you're better off visiting the English-speaking and generally helpful Autoprevoz "tourist agency" (to the left as you face the station, tel. 036/551-900, www.autoprevoz-bus.ba; note that they have good information for Bosniak bus companies, but not necessarily for Croat ones). To find your way to town center, walk through the bus stalls and parking lot and turn left at the big road, which leads you to the Old Town area in about 15 minutes.

By Car: For tips on driving to Mostar from the Dalmatian Coast, see page 344.

Helpful Hints

Local Cash: Need Convertible Marks? The most convenient ATM in town is to the left of Fortuna Tours' door, right at the top of Coppersmiths' Street (but remember that Croatian kunas and euros are also accepted here).

Travel Agency: The handy **Fortuna Tours** travel agency, right in the heart of the Old Town (at the top of Coppersmiths' Street), sells all the tourist stuff, can book you a local guide, and answers basic questions (open long hours daily, Kujundžiluk 2, tel. 036/551-887, main office tel. 036/552-197, fax 036/551-888, www.fortuna.ba, fortuna_mostar1@bih.net.ba).

Local Guides: Hiring a guide is an excellent investment to help you understand Mostar. I've enjoyed working with **Alma Elezović,** a warm-hearted Bosniak who loves sharing her city with visitors (€20 per person up to €70 per group for 2–3-hour tour, includes entries into a Turkish house and a mosque, tel. 036/550-514, mobile 061-467-699, aelezovic@gmail.com). If Alma is busy, various companies around town can arrange for a local guide at extremely reasonable prices (€40/2-hour tour); try **Fortuna Tours,** listed previously.

    If someone approaches you offering to be your guide, ask the price in advance (they often charge ridiculously high rates). If they seem cagey or overpriced, decline politely. The official guides are better anyway.

Local Driver: Ermin Elezović, the husband of local guide Alma Elezović, is a friendly, English-speaking driver who enjoys taking visitors on day trips from Mostar. You can also hire him for a transfer between Mostar and destinations anywhere in Croatia (small car for up to 3 people: €100 for transfer to Split, Dubrovnik, or Sarajevo, or €150 for an all-day excursion; bigger van for up to 8 people: €150 for transfer to Split, Dubrovnik, or Sarajevo, or €200 for all day; tel. 036/550-514, mobile 061-908-597, elezovicermin@gmail.com).

Sights in Mostar

Mostar's major sights line up along a handy L-shaped axis. I've laced them together as an enjoyable orientation walk: From the Franciscan Church, you'll walk straight until you cross the Old Bridge. Then you'll turn left and walk basically straight (with a couple of detours) to the big square at the far end of town.

• *Begin at the...*

▲Franciscan Church of Sts. Peter and Paul

In a town of competing religious architectural exclamation points, this spire is the tallest. The church, which adjoins a working Franciscan monastery, was built after the fighting subsided in 1997 (the same year as the big cross on the hill). The tower, which looks at first glance like a minaret on steroids, is actually modeled after the typical Croatian/Venetian campanile bell towers. Step inside to see how the vast and coarse concrete shell awaits completion. In the meantime, the cavernous interior is already hosting services. (Sunday Mass here is an inspiration.)

• *The church fronts the busy boulevard called...*

▲Bulevar

This "Boulevard" was once the modern main drag of Mostar. In the early 1990s, this city of Bosniaks, Croats, and Serbs began to

fracture under the pressure of politicians' propaganda. In October 1991, Bosnia-Herzegovina—following Croatia's and Slovenia's example, but without the blessing of its large Serb minority—declared independence from Yugoslavia. Soon after, the Serb-dominated Yugoslav National Army invaded. Mostar's Bosniaks and Croats joined forces to battle the Serbs and succeeded in claiming the city as their own and forcing out the Serb residents.

But even as they defended their city from the final, distant bombardments of Serb forces, the Bosniaks and Croats began to squabble. Neighbors, friends, and even relatives took up arms against each other. As fighting raged between the Croat and Bosniak forces, this street became the front line—and virtually all of its buildings were destroyed. Then as now, the area to the east of here (toward the river) was held by Bosniaks, while the western part of town was Croat territory.

While many of the buildings along here have been rebuilt, some damage is still evident. Stroll a bit, imagining the hell of a split community at war. Mortar craters in the asphalt leave poignant scars. (In Sarajevo, these have been filled with red resin to create monuments called "Sarajevo roses.") During those dark war years, the Croats on this side of the city laid siege to the Bosniaks (Muslims) on the other side, cutting off electricity, blocking roads, and blaring Croatian rabble-rousing pop music and Tokyo Rose-type propaganda speeches from loudspeakers. Through '93 and '94, when the Bosniaks dared to go out, they sprinted past exposed places, for fear of being picked off by a sniper. Local Bosniaks explain, "Night was time to live" (in black clothes). When people were killed along this street, their corpses were sometimes left here for months (because it wasn't safe to retrieve the bodies). Tens of thousands fled (Scandinavian countries were the first to open their doors, but many Bosnians ended up elsewhere in Europe, the US, and Canada).

The stories are shocking, and it's difficult to remain impartial. But looking back on this complicated war, I try not to broadly cast one side as the "aggressors" and another as the "victims." The Bosniaks were victimized in Mostar, just as the Croats were victimized during the siege of Dubrovnik (explained on page 268). And, as the remains of a destroyed Orthodox cathedral on the hillside above Mostar (not quite visible from here) attest, the Serbs also took their turn as victims. Every conflict has many sides, and tragically it's the civilians who often pay the highest toll—no matter their affiliation.

Cross the boulevard and head down Onešćukova street. A few steps down on the left, the vacant lot with the menorah-ornamented metal fence will someday be the Mostar Synagogue. While the town's Jewish population has dwindled to a handful of families since World War II, many Jews courageously served as aid workers and intermediaries when Croats and Bosniaks were killing each other. In recognition of their loving help, the community of Mostar gave them this land for a new synagogue.

• *Continue past the synagogue site, entering the Old Town and following the canyon with the small river...*

Radobolja River Valley

The creek called Radobolja winds over waterfalls and several mills on its way to join the Neretva. As you step upon cobbles, you suddenly become immersed in the Turkish heritage of Mostar. From the arrival of the Ottomans all the way through the end of World War II, Mostar had fewer than 15,000 residents. This compact central zone was pretty much all there was to the city until it became industrialized and grew like crazy during the Tito years. The historic core is cobbled with smooth, ankle-twisting river stones. Until 2004, the stones were simply embedded in loose sand, but now they're held together with concrete. As you explore, survey the atmospheric eateries clinging to the walls  of this canyon—and choose one for a meal or drink later in the day (I've noted a couple under "Eating in Mostar," later).

Walk straight ahead until you reach a square viewpoint platform on your right. It's across from a charming little mosque and above a stream. The mosque is one of 10 in town. Before the recent war, there were 36. Many mosques were actually damaged or destroyed in World War II, but were never repaired or replaced (since Tito's communist Yugoslavia discouraged religion). But the recent war inspired Muslims to finally rebuild. Each of the town's newly reconstructed mosques has been financed by a Muslim nation or organization (this one was a gift from an international association for the protection of Islamic heritage). Around you are several fine examples of Mostar's traditional heavy limestone-shingled roofs.

• *Spanning the river below the mosque is the...*

▲Crooked Bridge (Kriva Ćuprija)

This miniature Old Bridge was built nearly a decade before its more famous sibling, supposedly to practice for the real deal. Damaged— but not destroyed—during the war, the bridge was swept away several years later by floods. The bridge you see today is a recent reconstruction.

• *Continue deeper on the same street into the city center. After a few steps, a street to the left (worth a short detour) leads to the TI, then a copper-domed hammam, or Turkish bathhouse, which was destroyed in World War II and only recently rebuilt. A happening nightlife and restaurant scene tumbles downhill toward the river from here, offering spectacular views of the Old Bridge.*

Back on the main drag, continue along the main shopping zone, past several market stalls, to the focal point of town, the...

▲▲▲Old Bridge (Stari Most)

One of the most evocative sights in the former Yugoslavia, this iconic bridge confidently spanned the Neretva River for more than

four centuries. Mostarians of all faiths love the bridge and speak of "him" as an old friend. Traditionally considered the point where East meets West, the Old Bridge is as symbolic as it is beautiful. Dramatically arched and flanked by two boxy towers, the bridge is striking—even if you don't know its history.

Before the Old Bridge, the Neretva was spanned only by a rickety suspension bridge, guarded by *mostari* ("watchers of the bridge"), who gave the city its name. Commissioned in 1557 by the Ottoman Sultan Süleyman the Magnificent, and completed just nine years later, the Old Bridge was a technological marvel for its time..."the longest single-span stone arch on the planet." (In other words, it's the granddaddy of the Rialto Bridge in Venice.) Because of its graceful keystone design—and the fact that there are empty spaces inside the structure—it's much lighter than it seems. And yet, nearly 400 years after it was built, the bridge was still sturdy enough to support the weight of Nazi tanks that rolled in to occupy

Mostar. Over the centuries, it became the symbol for the town and region—a metaphor in stone for the way the diverse faiths and cultures here were able to bridge the gaps that divided them.

All of that drastically changed in the early 1990s. When the city became engulfed in war, the Old Bridge frequently got caught in the crossfire. Old tires were slung over its sides to absorb some of the impact from nearby artillery or shrapnel. In November 1993, Croats began shelling the bridge from the top of the mountain (where the cross is now—you can just see its tip peeking over the hill from the top of the bridge). Several direct hits caused the venerable Old Bridge to lurch, then tumble in pieces into the river. The mortar inside, which contained pink bauxite, turned the water red as it fell in. Locals said that their old friend was bleeding.

The decision to destroy the bridge was partly strategic—to cut off a Bosniak-controlled strip on the west bank from Bosniak forces on the east. (News footage from the time shows Bosniak soldiers scurrying back and forth over the bridge.) But there can be no doubt that, like the siege of Dubrovnik, the attack was also partly symbolic: the destruction of a bridge representing the city's Muslim legacy.

After the war, city leaders decided to rebuild the Old Bridge. Chunks of the original bridge were dredged up from the river. But the stone had been compromised by soaking in the water for so long, so it couldn't be used (you can still see these pieces of the old Old Bridge on the riverbank below). Staying true to their pledge to do it authentically, restorers quarried new stone (a limestone called *tenelija*) from the original quarry, and each stone was hand-carved.

Then they assembled the stones with the same technology used by the Ottomans 450 years ago: Workers erected wooden scaffolding and fastened the stones together with iron hooks cast in lead. The project cost over $13 million, funded largely by international donors and overseen by UNESCO.

It took longer to rebuild the bridge in the 21st century than it did to build it in the 16th century. But on July 23, 2004, the new Old Bridge was inaugurated with much fanfare and was immediately embraced by both the city and the world as a sign of reconciliation. Feel the shivers run down your spine as you walk over the Old Bridge today, and ponder its troubled yet inspirational past.

On a lighter note: One of Mostar's favorite traditions is for young men to jump from the bridge 75 feet down into the Neretva (which remains icy cold even in summer). Done both for the sake of tradition and to impress girls, this custom was carried on even during the time when the destroyed bridge was temporarily replaced by a wooden one. Now the tower on the west side of the bridge houses the office of the local "Divers Club," a loosely run organization that carries on this long-standing ritual. On hot summer days, you'll see divers making a ruckus and collecting donations at the top of the bridge. They tease and tease, standing up on the railing and pretending they're about to jump...then getting down and asking for more money. (If he's wearing trunks rather than Speedos, he's not a diver—just a teaser.) Once they collect about €30, one of them will take the plunge.

Before moving on, see how many of the town's 10 mosques you can spot from the top of the bridge (I counted eight minarets).

• *If you'd like to see one of the best* **views** *in town—looking up at the Old Bridge from the riverbank below—backtrack the way you came into the shopping zone, take your first left (at Šadran restaurant—a good place to try the powerful "Bosnian coffee"), then find the steps down to the river on the left.*

When you're ready to continue, hike back up to the Old Bridge and cross to the other side. After the bridge on the right are two different exhibits that are worth a quick visit. First is a good, free **photo exhibition** *of powerful images of war-torn Mostar, displayed inside a former mosque for soldiers who guarded the bridge. Just beyond that, tucked into the corner on the right, look for the stairs leading up to the...*

Museum of the Old Bridge (Muzej Stari Most)

Located within one of the Old Bridge's towers, this museum features a film and photos about the reconstruction of the bridge, archaeological findings, and a few other paltry exhibits about the history of the town and bridge, all in English (5 KM, daily 10:00–18:00, lots of stairs, Bajatova 4, tel. 036/551-602). First you'll climb up the stairs just after the bridge and buy your ticket, before hiking the rest of the way up to the top of the tower, where you'll enjoy fine views through grubby windows. Then you'll go around below to the archaeological exhibit. The museum offers more detail than most casual visitors need; consider just dropping into the smaller, free photo exhibition described previously, then moving along.

• *After the Old Bridge, the street swings left and leads you along...*

▲▲Coppersmiths' Street (Kujundžiluk)

This lively strip, with the flavor of a Turkish bazaar, offers some of the most colorful shopping this side of Istanbul. You'll see Mostar's characteristic bridge depicted in every possible way, along with blue-and-white "evil eyes" (believed in the Turkish culture to keep bad spirits at bay), old Yugoslav army kitsch, and hammered-copper decorations (continuing the long tradition that gave the

street its name). Partway up, the homes with the colorfully painted facades double as galleries for local artists. The artists live and work upstairs, then sell their work right on this street. Pop into the *atelier d'art* ("Đul Emina") on the right to meet Sead Vladović and enjoy his impressive iconographic work (daily 9:00–20:00). This is the most touristy street in all of Bosnia-Herzegovina, so don't expect any bargains. Still, it's fun. As you stroll, check out the fine views of the Old Bridge.

• *Continue uphill. About halfway along this street, on the left-hand side, look for the entrance to the...*

▲Koski Mehmed-Pasha Mosque (Koski Mehmed-Paša Džamija)

Mostar's Bosniak community includes many practicing Muslims. Step into this courtyard for a look at one of Mostar's many mosques (4 KM to enter mosque, 4 KM more to climb minaret, daily April–Oct 9:00–18:00, until 19:00 at busy times, Nov–March 9:00–15:00). This mosque, dating from the early 17th century, is notable for its cliff-hanging riverside location, and because it's particularly accessible for tourists. The following information generally applies to the other mosques in Mostar, as well.

The fountain *(šadrvan)* in the courtyard allows worshippers to wash before entering the mosque, as directed by Islamic law. This practice, called ablution, is both a literal and a spiritual cleansing in preparation for being in the presence of Allah. It's also refreshing in this hot climate, and the sound of running water helps worshippers concentrate.

The minaret—the slender needle jutting up next to the dome—is the Islamic equivalent of the Christian bell tower, used to call people to prayer. In the old days, the *muezzin* (prayer leader) would climb the tower five times a day and chant, "There is only one God, and Muhammad is his prophet." In modern times, loudspeakers are used instead. Climbing the minaret's claustrophobic staircase is a memorable experience, rewarding you with a grand view at the top (entrance to the right of mosque entry).

Because this mosque is accustomed to tourists, you don't need to take off your shoes to enter (there's a special covering on the floor), women don't need to wear scarves, and it's fine to take photos inside. Near the front of the mosque, you may see some of the small, overlapping rugs that are below this covering (reserved for shoes-off worshippers).

Once inside, notice the traditional elements of the mosque. The niche *(mihrab)* across from the entry is oriented toward Mecca

(the holy city in today's Saudi Arabia)—the direction all Muslims face to pray. The small stairway *(mimber)* that seems to go nowhere is symbolic of the growth of Islam—Muhammad had to stand higher and higher to talk to his growing following. This serves as a kind of pulpit, where the cleric gives a speech, similar to a sermon or homily in Christian church services. No priest ever stands on the top stair, which is symbolically reserved for Muhammad.

The balcony just inside the door is traditionally where women worship. For the same reason I find it hard to concentrate on God at aerobics classes, Muslim men decided prayer would go better without the enjoyable but problematic distraction of bent-over women between them and Mecca. These days, women can also pray on the main floor with the men, but they still must avoid physical contact.

Muslims believe that capturing a living creature in a painting or a sculpture is inappropriate. (In fact, depictions of Allah and the prophet Muhammad are strictly forbidden.) Instead, mosques are filled with ornate patterns and calligraphy (of the name "Muhammad" and important prayers and sayings from the Quran). Some of the calligraphy is in Arabic, and some is in Bosnian. You'll also see some floral and plant designs, which you'd never see in a more conservative, Middle Eastern mosque.

Before leaving, ponder how progressive the majority of Mostar's Muslims are. Most of them drink alcohol, wear modern European clothing (you'll see virtually no women wearing head scarves or men with beards), and almost never visit a mosque to pray. In so many ways, these people don't fit our preconceived notions of Islam...and yet, they consider themselves Muslims all the same.

The mosque's courtyard is shared by several merchants. When you're done haggling, head to the terrace behind the mosque for the best view in town of the Old Bridge.

• *Just beyond this mosque, the traffic-free cobbles of the Old Town end. Take a right and leave the cutesy tourists' world. Walk up one block to the big...*

▲▲New Muslim Cemetery

In this cemetery, which was a park before the war, every tomb is dated 1993, 1994, or 1995. As the war raged, more exposed cemeteries were unusable. But this tree-covered piece of land was

The Muslims of Mostar

While recent Muslim immigrants are becoming a fixture in most European cities, Bosnia-Herzegovina is one place where Muslims have continuously been an integral part of the cultural tapestry for centuries.

During the more than 400 years that Mostar was part of the Ottoman Empire, the Muslim Turks (unlike some Catholic despots at the time) did not forcibly convert their subjects. However, it was advantageous for non-Turks to adopt Islam (for lower taxes and better business opportunities), so many Slavs living here became Muslims. In fact, within 150 years of the start of Ottoman rule, half of the population of Bosnia-Herzegovina was Muslim.

The Ottomans became increasingly intolerant of other faiths as time went on, and uprisings by Catholics and Orthodox Christians eventually led to the end of Ottoman domination in the late 19th century. But even after the Ottomans left, many people in this region continued practicing Islam, as their families had been doing for centuries. These people constitute an ethnic

group called "Bosniaks," and many of them are still practicing Muslims today (following the Sunni branch of the Muslim faith). Keep in mind that most Bosniaks are Slavs—of the same ethnic stock as Croats and Serbs—and look pretty much the same as their neighbors, although some Bosniaks have ancestors who married into Turkish families, and they may have some Turkish features.

Due to the recent actions of a small but attention-grabbing faction of Muslim extremists, Islam is

relatively safe from Croat snipers. As the casualties mounted, locals buried their loved ones here under cover of darkness. Many of these people were soldiers, but some were civilians. Strict Muslim graves don't display images of people, but here you'll see photos of war dead who were young, less-

traditional members of the Muslim community. The fleur-de-lis shape of many of the tombstones is a patriotic symbol for the nation of Bosnia. The Arabic squiggles are the equivalent of an American having Latin on his or her tombstone—old-fashioned and formal.

burdened with a bad reputation in the Western world. But judging Islam based on Osama bin Laden and al-Qaeda is like judging Christianity based on Timothy McVeigh and the Ku Klux Klan. Visiting Mostar is a unique opportunity to get a taste of a fully Muslim society, made a bit less intimidating because it wears a more-familiar European face.

Here's an admittedly basic and simplistic outline (written by a non-Muslim) designed to help travelers from the Christian West understand a very rich but often misunderstood culture worthy of respect:

Muslims, like Christians and Jews, are monotheistic. They call God "Allah." The most important person in the Islamic faith is Muhammad, Allah's most important prophet, who lived in the sixth and seventh centuries A.D.

The "five pillars" of Islam are the same among Muslims in Bosnia-Herzegovina, Turkey, Iraq, Indonesia, the US, and everywhere else. Followers of Islam should:

1. Say and believe, "There is only one God, and Muhammad is his prophet."

2. Pray five times a day, facing Mecca. Modern Muslims explain that it's important for this ritual to include several elements: washing, exercising, stretching, and thinking of God.

3. Give to the poor (one-fortieth of your wealth, if you are not in debt).

4. Fast during daylight hours through the month of Ramadan. Fasting is a great social equalizer and helps everyone to feel the hunger of the poor.

5. Visit Mecca. This is interpreted by some Muslims as a command to travel. Muhammad said, "Don't tell me how educated you are, tell me how much you've traveled."

Good advice for anyone, no matter what—or if—you call a higher power.

• *Go up the wide stairs to the right of the cemetery (near the mosque). At #4 on the right, just before and across from the bombed-out tower, you'll find the...*

Museum of Herzegovina (Muzej Hercegovine)

This humble but worthwhile little museum holds fragments of this region's rich history, including historic photos and several items from its Ottoman period. There are sparse English descriptions, but without a tour guide the exhibits are a bit difficult to appreciate. Topics include the Turkish period, Herzegovina under the Austro-Hungarian Empire, village life, and local archaeology. One small room commemorates the house's former owner, Dzemal Bijedić, who was Tito's second-in-command during the Yugoslav period until he was killed in a mysterious plane crash in 1977. (If Bijedić had lived, many wonder whether he might have succeeded Tito... and succeeded in keeping Yugoslavia together.)

But the museum is made worthwhile by a deeply moving **film**, rated ▲▲, that traces the history of the town through its Old Bridge: fun circa-1957 footage of the diving contests; harrowing scenes of the bridge being pummeled, and finally toppled, by artillery; and a stirring sequence showing the bridge's reconstruction and grand reopening on that day in 2004—with highfives, Beethoven's *Ode to Joy*, fireworks, and more divers (5-KM museum entry includes 12-min film, no narration—works in any language, ask about "film?" as you enter, daily 8:00–16:00, Bajatova 4—walking up these stairs, it's the second door that's marked for the museum, under the overhanging balcony, www .muzejhercegovine.com).

• *Backtrack to where you left the Old Town. Notice the* **Tepa Market***, with locals buying produce, in the area just beyond the pedestrian zone. Now walk (with the produce market on your left) along the lively street called* **Braće Fejića***. (There's no sign, but the street is level and busy with cafés.) You're in the "new town," where locals sit out in front of boisterous cafés sipping coffee while listening to the thumping beat of distinctly Eastern-sounding music.*

Stroll down this street for a few blocks. At the palm trees (about 50 yards before the minaret), you can side-trip a block to the left to reach...

▲Bišćević Turkish House (Bišćevića Kuća)

Mostar has three traditional Turkish-style homes that are open for tourists to visit. The Bišćević House is the first and most conve-

nient for a quick visit, but two others are described at the end of this listing. Dating from 1635, the Bišćević House is typical of old houses in Mostar, which mix Oriental style with Mediterranean features (4 KM, daily March–Oct 8:00–20:00, Nov– Feb 9:00–15:00, Bišćevića 13).

Notice that the house is surrounded by a high wall—protection from the sun's rays, from thieves... and from prying eyes. First you'll step through the outer (or animals')

garden, then into the inner (or family's) garden. Notice how the smooth river stones are set in geometrical forms in the floor (for example, the five-sided star), and keep an eye out for the house's pet turtles. It's no coincidence that the traditional fountain *(šadrvan)* resembles those at the entrance to a mosque—a reminder of the importance of running water in Muslim culture. The little white building is a kitchen—cleverly located apart from the house so that the heat and smells of cooking didn't permeate the upstairs living area.

Buy your ticket and take off your shoes before you climb up the wooden staircase. Imagine how a stairway like this one could be pulled up for extra protection in case of danger. The cool, shady, and airy living room is open to the east—from where the wind rarely blows. The overhanging roof also prevented the hot sun from reaching this area. The loom in the corner was the women's workplace—the carpets you're standing on would have been woven there. The big chests against the wall were used to bring the dowry when the homeowner took a new wife. Study the fine wood carving and the heavy stonework of the roof.

Continue back into the main gathering room *(divanhan)*. This space—whose name comes from the word "talk"—is designed in a circle so people could face each other, cross-legged, for a good conversation while they enjoyed a dramatic view overlooking the Neretva. The room comes with a box of traditional costumes—great for photo fun. Put on a pair of baggy pants and a fez and really lounge.

Other Turkish Houses: If you're intrigued by this, consider dropping by Mostar's two other Turkish houses. The **Muslibegović House** (Muslibegovića Kuća) feels newer because it dates from 1871, just a few years before the Ottomans left town. This homey house—which also rents out rooms to visitors (see "Sleeping in Mostar," later)—has many of the same features as the Bišćević House. If she's not too busy, Sanela can give you an English tour (4 KM, mid-April–mid-Oct daily 10:00–18:00, closed to visitors off-season, just two blocks uphill from the Karađozbeg Mosque at Osman Dikica 41, tel. 036/551-379, www.muslibegovichouse .com). To find it, go up the street between the Karađozbeg Mosque and the cemetery, cross the busy street, and continue a long block uphill on the alley. The wall with the slate roof on the left marks the house.

The **Kajtaz House** (Kajtazova Kuća), hiding up a very residential-feeling alley a few blocks from the Old Bridge, feels lived-in because it still is (in the opposite direction from most of the other sights, at Gaše Ilića 21).

• *Go back to the main café street and continue to the...*

▲Karađozbeg Mosque (Karađozbegova Džamija)

The city's main mosque was completed in 1557, the same year work began on the Old Bridge. This mosque, which welcomes visitors, feels less touristy than the one back in the Old Town (4 KM to

enter mosque, 4 KM more to climb minaret, daily May–Sept 9:00–19:30, Oct–April
10:00–15:00). Before entering the gate into
the complex, look for the picture showing
the recent war damage sustained by this
mosque (which has since been repaired).
You'll see that this mosque has most of the
same elements as the Koski Mehmed-Pasha
Mosque (described earlier). But here, some
of the decorations are original. Across the
street is another cemetery with tombstones
from that terrible year, 1993.

• *Now continue into modern, urban Mostar
along the street in front of the Karađozbeg Mosque. This grimy, mostly
traffic-free street is called...*

▲Braće Fejića

Walking along the modern town's main café strip, enjoy the
opportunity to observe this workaday Bosniak town. You'll see the
humble offices of the ragtag B&H Airlines; a state-run gambling
office taxing its less-educated people with a state lottery; and lots
of cafés that serve drinks but no food. People generally eat at home
before going out to nurse an affordable drink. (Café ABC has good
cakes and ice cream; the upstairs is a popular pizza hangout for
students and families.)

Obituary announcements are tacked to trees by the mosque,
listing the bios and funeral times for locals who have recently died.
A fig tree grows out of the minaret in the small mosque—just
an accident of nature illustrating how that plant can thrive with
almost no soil.

Walking farther, you see a few ruins—still ugly nearly two
decades after the war. There's a messy confusion about who owns
what. Surviving companies have no money. Yugo Bank, which held
the mortgages, is defunct. No one will invest until clear ownership
is established. Until then, the people of Mostar sip their coffee and
rip up their dance clubs in the shadow of these jagged reminders of
the warfare that wracked this town not so long ago.

Near the end of the pedestrian zone, through the parking lot
on the right, look for the building with communist-era reliefs of
Bogomil tomb decor from the 12th century—remembering the
indigenous culture before the arrival of the Ottomans.

When you finally hit the big street (with car traffic), head left
one block to the big **Masala Square** (literally, "Place for Prayer").
Historically this was where pilgrims gathered before setting off for
Mecca on their hajj. This is a great scene on balmy evenings, when
it's a rendezvous point for the community.

• *For a finale, you can continue one block more out onto the bridge to survey the town you just explored. From here, you can backtrack to linger in the places you found most inviting.*

Nightlife in Mostar

Be sure to enjoy the local scene after dark in Mostar. Though the town is touristy, it's also a real urban center with a young popula-

tion riding a wave of raging hormones. The meat market in the courtyard next to the old Turkish bathhouse near the TI is fun to observe. The Old Bridge is a popular meeting place for locals as well as tourists (and pickpockets).

A stroll from the Old Bridge down the Braće Fejića café-lined boulevard, to the modern Masala Square at the far end of town (described earlier), gives a great peek at Mostarians socializing.

Ali Baba is an actual cave featuring a fun, atmospheric, and youthful party scene. Order a cocktail or try a Turkish-style

hubbly-bubbly (*šiša*, SHEE-
shah). Ask to have one of
these big water pipes fired
up for you and choose your
flavored tobacco: apple, cap-
puccino, banana, or lemon
(20 KM per pipe per group,
8-KM cocktails, open late
daily; look for low-profile,

cave-like entrance along Coppersmiths' Street, just down from the Old Bridge—watch for "Open Sesame" sign tucked down a rocky alley).

Sleeping in Mostar

My first two listings are big, full-service hotels, but a bit farther from the charming Old Town. The rest are small, friendly, accessible, affordable guest houses in or very near the Old Town. Mostar's Old Town can be very noisy on weekends, with nightclubs and outdoor restaurants rollicking into the wee hours. If you're a light sleeper, consider Villa Fortuna and the Muslibegović House, which are quieter than the norm.

$$$ Hotel Bristol is the only business-class place near central Mostar, overlooking the river a 10-minute walk from the heart of the Old Town. While it's on a busy street, the windows

BOSNIA-HERZEGOVINA

Sleep Code

(€1 = about $1.40, country code: 387, area code: 036)
S = Single, **D** = Double/Twin, **T** = Triple, **Q** = Quad, **b** = bathroom. Unless otherwise noted, prices include breakfast. To help you sort easily through these listings, I've divided the rooms into three categories based on the price for a standard double room with bath in peak season:

$$$ Higher Priced—Most rooms €80 or more.
$$ Moderately Priced—Most rooms between €40–80.
$ Lower Priced—Most rooms €40 or less.

---

in its 47 rooms are good (Sb-€60, Db-€100, apartment-€115, extra bed-€16, air-con, elevator, pay Internet access, Mostarskog Bataljona, tel. 036/500-100, fax 036/500-502, www.bristol.ba, info @bristol.ba).

$$$ Hotel Ero, a 20-minute walk north of the Old Town, is a good big-hotel option, with 140 fine rooms and a professional staff. This was one of the only big buildings in the center not damaged during the war, since it hosted journalists and members of the international community and was therefore off-limits (Sb-€50, Db-€85, suite-€110, air-con, elevator, some traffic noise, ulica Dr. Ante Starčevića, tel. 036/386-777, fax 036/386-700, www.ero.ba, hotel.ero@tel.net.ba).

$$ The Muslibegović House, a Bosnian national monument that also invites tourists in to visit during the day, is in an actual Turkish home dating from 1871. The complex houses nine homey rooms and two suites, all of which combine classic Turkish style (elegant old beds, old floors, carpets, sofas; guest remove shoes at the outer door) with modern comforts (air-con, free Wi-Fi). Situated on a quiet residential lane just above  the bustle of Mostar's main pedestrian drag and Old Town zone, this is the most enticing deal in town and a memorable experience (Sb-€50, Db-€70, "pasha suite"-€95, all prices €15 more in July–Aug, price includes tour of house, 2 blocks uphill from the Karađozbeg Mosque at Osman Dikica 41, tel. 036/551-379, www .muslibegovichouse.com).

$$ Motel Kriva Ćuprija ("Crooked Bridge"), by the bridge of the same name, is tucked between waterfalls in a picturesque valley a few steps from the Old Bridge. It's an appealing oasis with seven rooms, three apartments, and a restaurant with atmospheric outdoor seating (Sb-€39, Db-€65, apartment-€70, extra bed-€20, 10 percent discount with this book, can be noisy, air-con, free Wi-Fi, Kriva Ćuprija 2, tel. 036/550-953, mobile 061-135-286, www.motel-mostar.ba, info@motel-mostar.ba, Sami). Their second location—called **Hotel Kriva Ćuprija II**—offers 10 rooms in a Habsburg-style building overlooking the river in a modern neighborhood about 200 yards to the south (same prices, discount, amenities, and contact information as main hotel; Maršala Tita 186, next to the Lučki Bridge).

$$ **Motel Emen** has six modern, sleek rooms overlooking a busy café street a few cobbled blocks from the Old Bridge (Sb-€40, Db-€60, bigger Db with balcony-€70, air-con, free Internet access and Wi-Fi, Onešćukova 32, tel. 036/581-120, www.motel-emen .com, info@motel-emen.com).

$ **Villa Fortuna B&B,** in a nondescript urban neighborhood a few minutes' walk farther away from the Old Bridge, has nine tasteful, modern, air-conditioned rooms. The rooms are just above the main office of Fortuna Tours, and you'll reserve through them. There's free, secure parking on the courtyard in front, and a pleasant garden in back (Sb-€30, Db-€40, breakfast-€5, tel. 036/552-197, mobile 063-315-017, fax 036/551-888, fortuna_headoffice @bih.net.ba). Fortuna Tours can also put you in touch with locals renting rooms and apartments.

$ **Pansion Botticelli,** overlooking a charming waterfall garden just up the valley from the Crooked Bridge, has five colorful rooms (Sb-€30, Db-€40, Tb-€60, breakfast-€3, air-con, Muje Bjelavca 6, enter around back along the alley, mobile 063-319-057, botticelli@bih.net.ba, Snježana and Zoran).

$ **Pansion Most** rents eight small, older-feeling rooms a few minutes' walk farther from the Old Bridge, above a sportsbook and a travel agency. I'd consider this a last resort for budget travelers (Sb-€25, Db-€38, air-con, Adema Buća 100, tel. 036/552-528, www.pansionmost.dzaba.com, pansion_most@yahoo.com).

$ **Dika Kasumačić** has five basic, inexpensive rooms on a quiet lane just above the Crooked Bridge action (S-€15, D-€30, cash only, air-con, follow green *pansion* signs from near Pansion Botticelli to Kapetanovina 16, mobile 061-506-443, sanjink @hotmail.com).

Eating in Mostar

Most of Mostar's tourist-friendly restaurants are conveniently concentrated in the Old Town. If you walk anywhere that's cobbled, you'll stumble onto dozens of tempting restaurants charging about the same reasonable prices and serving rustic, traditional

BOSNIA-HERZEGOVINA

Bosnian food. In my experience, the menu at most places is about the same—though quality and ambience can vary greatly. Grilled meats are especially popular—read "Balkan Flavors," on page 31, before you dine. Another specialty here is *dolma*—a pepper stuffed with minced meat, vegetables, and rice. Sarajevsko Pivo beer is on tap.

On the Embankment, with Old Bridge Views

For the best atmosphere, find your way into the several levels of restaurants that clamber up the riverbank with perfect views of the Old Bridge. To reach these, go over the Old Bridge to the west side of the river, and bear right on the cobbles until you get to the old Turkish bathhouse, or *hammam* (with the copper domes on the roof). To the right of the bathhouse is the entrance to a lively courtyard surrounded with cafés and restaurants. Continuing

toward the river from the courtyard, stairs lead down to several riverfront terraces. While you'll have menus pushed in your face as you walk, don't hesitate—poke around to find your favorite bridge view before settling in for a drink or a meal. If you want a good perch, it's fun and smart to drop by earlier in the day and personally reserve the table of your choice. In terms of the setting and views, this is the most memorable place to dine in Mostar—but be warned that the quality of the food along here is uniformly low.

Away from the Old Bridge

While they lack the Old Bridge views, these places serve food that's generally a step up. The first two places are in the atmospheric Old Town, while the last two are in the modern part of town.

Restoran Hindin Han is pleasantly situated on a woody terrace over a rushing stream. It's respected locally for its good cooking and fair prices (big 10–15-KM salads, 6–12-KM grilled dishes, 10–20-KM fish and other main dishes, Sarajevsko beer on tap, daily 11:00–24:00, Jusovina 10, tel. 036/581-054). To find it, walk west from the Old Bridge, bear left at the Šadrvan restaurant, cross the bridge, and you'll see it on the left.

Konoba Dvije Pećine ("The Two Caves") is a mom-and-pop place woven into a tangle of terraces over a rushing little stream facing the Crooked Bridge. It's known for its home-cooking (*domaća*—"homemade"—is the key word), and the food does taste a cut above the norm (6–18-KM plates, splittable mixed grill for 16 KM, daily 11:00–24:00, on Jusovina street at the end of the

Crooked Bridge, mobile 061-558-228, Nuna and Jusa Dizdarević and Cako the charming head waiter).

Saray is a nondescript little eatery just uphill from the Karađozbeg Mosque in the modern part of town. They have a basic menu of very tasty grilled meats—specializing in the classic *ćevapčići* (little sausage-shaped meat patties)—and outdoor seating overlooking a playground that offers good people- and kid-watching while you eat (5–8-KM grilled meat dishes, big 6–7-KM salads, daily 9:00–17:00, mobile 061-529-320).

Bistro Verona sits along the bombed-out but increasingly revitalized Bulevar, in the shadow of the towering Franciscan Church. While as charming as a strip mall diner, it's a great chance to eat—indoors or out—surrounded by a humble, friendly, and perfectly local scene without a hint of tourism (6–10-KM grilled meat dishes and pastas, Husnije Rebca 3, mobile 062-432-260).

Mostar Connections

By Bus

Not surprisingly for a divided city, Mostar has two different bus terminals, each served by different companies. On the east (Bosniak/Muslim) side of the river, you'll find the main bus station (called "Autobusna Stanica"; about a 15-minute walk north of the Old Town—for details, see "Arrival in Mostar," earlier). On the west (Croat/Catholic) side, the situation is less predictable: Some buses leave from a bus stop near the Franciscan Church, while others use a bus station (called "Kolodvor") on Vukovarska street.

Most Bosniak buses are operated by Autoprevoz (tel. 036/551-900, www.autoprevoz-bus.ba). Many Croat buses are run by Globtour (www.globtour.com). And local or regional buses are operated by Mostar Bus, whose buses depart from across the street from the main bus station (www.mostarbus.ba).

Tracking down reliable **schedule** information in Mostar is next to impossible. There's still tension between the Bosniak and Croat companies, which means there's often a lack of communication and therefore no single, reliable place where you can go to be sure you know all of your options. Start by checking the websites above, but realize that schedules can change unexpectedly. The Autoprevoz "tourist agency" at the main bus station (described earlier, under "Arrival in Mostar") is English-speaking and generally helpful, but they don't have dependable information about Croat-run buses. It's not unheard-of for someone to ride a bus here in the morning from Dubrovnik, expecting to take a late-afternoon bus back the same day—only to find that the day's last departure leaves just a few minutes after they arrive. While this sounds intimidating, it's workable. Just do your best to double-check schedules at both ends to be sure your connection lines up—especially if you'll be cutting it close. Note that buses to seasonal destinations (such as along the Dalmatian Coast) run more frequently in peak season, roughly June through mid-September.

From Mostar by Bus to: Međugorje (7/day Mon–Fri, 3/day Sat, none Sun, 50 min, mostly from the west side, 3 KM), **Sarajevo** (about hourly, 2.5 hrs, from main bus station, 15 KM), **Zagreb** (daily at about 9:00, 8 hrs, plus 1 night bus/day, 9.5 hrs, 70 KM), **Split** (4–7/day depending on season, 4–4.5 hrs, can be from either side—ask locally about your specific bus, 20–30 KM), **Dubrovnik** (2–5/day depending on season, 4–5 hrs, from main bus station, 20–30 KM—but note that except for some weekends, most Dubrovnik buses leave early in the day, making an afternoon return from Mostar to Dubrovnik impossible). Service to **Korčula** is sporadic—sometimes once per week, sometimes none at all.

By Train

Mostar is on the train line that runs from Ploče (on the Croatian coast between Split and Dubrovnik) to Zagreb, via Mostar and Sarajevo. This train—which leaves from next to the main bus station—generally runs once daily, leaving **Ploče** soon after 6:00 in the morning, with stops at **Mostar** (1.5 hours), **Sarajevo** (4.25 hours), and **Zagreb** (13.5 hours; bus is faster). Going the opposite direction, the train leaves Zagreb at about 9:00 in the morning.

Route Tips for Drivers

You have two ways to drive between Mostar and Dubrovnik: easy and straightforward, or adventurous and off the beaten path.

Between Mostar and the Main Coastal Road

The most convenient entry point into Bosnia-Herzegovina from the Dalmatian Coast is the town of **Metković,** about halfway between Dubrovnik and Split. (If you're driving there from Dubrovnik or Korčula, you'll actually cross into Bosnia-Herzegovina twice—including the short stretch of coastline that Bosnia-Herzegovina still controls, with the town of **Neum.** For more details, see page 205.)

Near Metković, the main coastal road jogs away from the coast and around the striking **Neretva River Delta**—the extremely fertile "garden patch of Croatia," which produces a significant portion of Croatia's fruits and vegetables. The Neretva is the same river that flows under Mostar's Old Bridge upstream—but in Metković, it spreads out into 12 branches as it enters the Adriatic, flooding a vast plain and creating a bursting cornucopia in the middle of an otherwise rocky and arid region. Enjoying some of the most plentiful sunshine on the Croatian coast, as well as a steady supply of water

---

Enter the Dragon

Reconciliation works in strange and unexpected ways. In the early 2000s, idealistic young Mostarians formed the Urban Movement of Mostar, which searched for a way to connect the still-feuding Catholic and Muslim communities. As a symbol of their goals, they chose Bruce Lee, the deceased kung-fu movie star, who is beloved by both Croats and Bosniaks for his characters' honorable struggle against injustice. A life-size bronze statue of Lee was unveiled with fanfare in November 2005 in Veliki Park. Unfortunately, soon after, the statue was damaged. Whether or not the vandalism was ethnically motivated is unclear, but many locals hope the ideals embodied in the statue will continue to bring the city together.

---

for irrigation, the Neretva Delta is as productive as it is beautiful.

After passing through Metković, you'll cross the border into **Bosnia-Herzegovina,** then continue straight on the main road (M-17) directly into Mostar. As you drive, you'll see destroyed buildings and occasional roadside memorials bearing the likenesses of fresh-faced soldiers who died in the recent war.

Along the way are a few interesting detours: In Čapljina, you can turn off toward **Međugorje** (described later in this chapter).

Soon after, a mountaintop castle tower on the right side of the road marks the medieval town of **Počitelj**—an artists' colony with a compelling mix of Christian and Muslim architecture, including a big mosque and a multi-domed bathhouse. It's well worth pulling over and strolling around this steep village (pictured here).

With extra time, just before Mostar (in Buna), you can detour a few miles along the Buna River into **Blagaj**—the historical capital of the region until the arrival of the Ottomans. This is the site of a mountain called Hum, which is topped by the ruins of a hilltop castle that once belonged to Herzog ("Duke") Stjepan, who gave Herzegovina its name. Deep in Blagaj is an impressive cliff face with a scenic house marking the source of the Buna River. The building, called the Tekija, is actually a former monastery for Turkish dervishes (an order that emphasizes poverty and humility, and is famous for the way they whirl when in a worshipful trance); inside is a modest museum with the graves of two important dervishes. Today the area is surrounded by gift shops and a big restaurant with fine views over the river and cliff.

Approaching **Mostar** on M-17, you'll pass the airport, then turn left at your first opportunity to cross the river. After crossing the bridge, bear right onto Bulevar street, and continue on that main artery for several blocks (passing several destroyed buildings). At the street called Rade Bitange (just after the giant church bell tower), turn right to find the public parking lot—less than a 10-minute walk from the Old Bridge. Be warned that signage is poor; if you get lost, try asking for directions to "Stari Most" (STAH-ree most)—the Old Bridge.

Rugged-but-Scenic Backcountry Route through Serbian Herzegovina

If you're visiting Mostar round-trip from Dubrovnik, consider coming back a different route, mostly through Herzegovina. This feels much more remote and takes an hour or two longer, but the roads are good and the occasional gas station and restaurant break up the journey. Since this route takes you through the Republika Srpska part of Herzegovina, most road signs are exclusively in the Cyrillic alphabet—though, interestingly, much of the advertising you'll see uses the more familiar Roman alphabet. (Because this road goes through the Serbian part of Herzegovina, it's not popular among Bosniaks or Croats—in fact, locals might tell you this road "does not exist." It does.)

This route is narrated from Dubrovnik to Mostar, but you can do it in reverse—just hold the book upside-down. If you want a little taste of Republika Srpska, consider just day-tripping into Trebinje—especially on Saturday, when the produce market is at its liveliest.

From Dubrovnik, head south toward Cavtat, the airport, and Montenegro. Shortly after leaving Dubrovnik, watch for signs on the left directing you to *Gornji Brgat*. Follow this road to the border of Bosnia-Herzegovina, cross the border, and carry on about 20 minutes into **Trebinje** (Требиње). Consider stopping for a break in Trebinje, a pleasant and relatively affluent town with a leafy main square that hosts a fine Saturday market. Overlooking the town  from its hilltop perch is the striking Orthodox Church of Nova Gračanica, built to resemble the historically important Gračanica Monastery in Kosovo. If you have time, drive up to the church's viewpoint terrace for great views over Trebinje and the valley.

From Trebinje, you have two options. One is to drive along the very pretty valley via **Ljubinje** (Љубиње) and **Stolac** (Столац), on the Serb-Muslim boundary, then to **Počitelj** (described earlier) and on to Mostar.

Or, for a longer, more remote, middle-of-nowhere adventure, consider this alternate route: From Trebinje, drive north toward **Bilećko Lake**—a vast, aquamarine lake you'll see on your right (the Vikiovac Restaurant offers a great viewpoint). Then you'll go through the town of **Bileća** (Билећа), turning west at the gloomy industrial town of **Gacko** (Гацко, with a giant coal mine), and onward to the humble but proud little town of **Nevesinje** (Невесиње). From Nevesinje, it's a quick drive up over the mountains, then down into Mostar—passing more familiar Roman-alphabet road signs, then spectacular views of Herzog Stjepan's imposing castle over the town of Buna. Follow signs on into Mostar.

Međugorje

Međugorje is an unassuming little village that ranks with Lourdes, Fátima, and Santiago de Compostela as one of the most important pilgrimage sites in all of Christendom. To the cynical non-Catholic, it's just a strip of crassly commercial hotels, restaurants, and rosary shops leading up to a dull church, all tied together by a silly legend about a hilltop apparition. But as you look into the tear-filled eyes of the pilgrims who've journeyed here, it's clear that to some, there's so much more than what's on the surface.

For true believers, Međugorje represents a once-in-a-lifetime opportunity to tread on sacred soil: a place where, over the last three decades, the Virgin Mary has appeared to six local people. Even though the Vatican has declined to recognize the apparitions, that doesn't stop hundreds of thousands of Catholics from coming here each year. More than 30 million pilgrims have visited Međugorje since the sightings began—summer and winter, war (which didn't touch Međugorje) and peace, rain and shine. People from Ireland, Italy, Germany, Spain, the US, and just about everywhere that has Catholics make the trek here.

Planning Your Time

Unless you're a pilgrim (or think you might be a pilgrim), skip Međugorje—it's an experience wasted on nonbelievers. (The only "attractions" are an unexceptional modern church, a couple of hill-top hikes, and pilgrim-spotting.)

If you do go, the easiest way is to take a day-trip excursion from the Dalmatian Coast (sold from Split, Dubrovnik, and Korčula). By public bus, you can day-trip into Međugorje from Split, but not from Dubrovnik. Consider spending the night here, or sleep in Mostar two nights and day-trip into Međugorje.

Orientation to Međugorje

(country code: 387; area code: 036)
Međugorje (MEDGE-oo-gor-yeh, sometimes spelled "Medju-gorje" in English) is basically a one-street town—most everything happens in the half-mile between its post office (where the bus stop is) and the main church, St. James (Crkva Sv. Jakova). On the hills behind the church are two trails leading to pilgrimage sites. Many travel agencies line the main strip; at any of these, you can find a room, rent a car, hire a local guide, buy ferry tickets for Croatia, and use the Internet.

By the way, Međugorje is clearly a "Croat" sight. While this may seem odd (after all, you're in Bosnia-Herzegovina, not Croatia), remember that any Catholic from the former Yugoslavia is called a Croat. Virtually every local person you'll meet in Međugorje is, strictly speaking, a Bosnian Croat.

Sights in Međugorje

The center of pilgrim activity is **St. James' Church** (Crkva Sv. Jakova), which was built before the apparitions. The exterior and interior are both pretty dull, but that doesn't stop pilgrims from worshipping here at all times of day (inside and outside). Out in front of the church are posted maps that are useful for getting oriented and a white statue of the Virgin Mary that attracts a lot of attention from pilgrims.

As you face the church, you'll see two trails leading up to the hills. Behind and to the left of the church is **Apparition Hill** (at Podbrdo), where the sightings occurred (a 1-mile hike, topped by a statue of Mary). Directly behind the church is the **Great Hill** (Križevac, or "Cross Mountain"), where a giant hilltop cross, which predates the visions, has become a secondary site of pilgrimage (1.5-mile hike). Note that the paths up to the hilltops are embedded with rocks. If you wonder why they don't make it easier to climb up, remember that an act of pilgrimage is supposed to be challenging. In fact, pilgrims often do one or both of these hikes barefoot, as a sign of penitence.

Around back of the church is a makeshift amphitheater with

Međugorje Mary

What compels millions to flock to this little village in the middle of nowhere? The official story goes like this: On the evening of June 24, 1981, two young women were gathering their sheep on the hillside above Mostar. They came across a woman carrying a baby who told them to come near. Terrified, they fled, only to realize later that this might have been a vision of the Virgin Mary. They returned the next night with some friends and saw the apparition again.

In the nearly three decades since, six different locals (including the two original seers) claim to have seen the vision, and some of them even say they see it regularly to this day. They also say that Mary has given them 10 secrets—predictions of future events that will portend Judgment Day. Written on a piece of parchment, these are kept safely at the home of one of the seers. They have said they will reveal each of these secrets, 10 days before the event occurs, to the local parish priest, who will then alert the world.

But official representatives of the Vatican are not among the believers. According to Catholic law, such visions must be "certified" by the local bishop—and the one around here didn't buy it. One cause for suspicion is that the six seers, before witnessing the visions, were sometimes known to be troublemakers. (In fact, they later admitted that they went up the hill that fateful night not to chase wayward sheep, but to sneak a smoke.) One investigator even suggested that they invented the story as a prank, only to watch it snowball out of control once they told it to the local priest. Today the Vatican takes a wishy-washy stance on the issue, refusing either to accept or deny the claims of the seers. (Priests are allowed to accompany pilgrimages to Međugorje, but not to *lead* them.)

Whether or not the story is true is, to a certain extent, beside the point—that people *believe* it's true is why they come here.

benches, used for outdoor services. Beyond that is a path. You'll pass some Stations of the Cross, then (on the right) a giant statue of the **Resurrected Savior** (Uskrsli Spasitelj), also known as the "Weeping Knee." While the elongated, expressionistic sculpture—exemplifying Christ's suffering—is striking in itself, the eternal dampness of its right knee attracts the most attention from pilgrims. Miraculously (or not), it's always wet—go ahead and touch the

spot that's been highly polished by worshippers and skeptics alike.

Believers and nonbelievers both appreciate the parade of kitsch that lines the **main street** leading up to the church. While rosaries are clearly the big item, you can get basically anything you want stamped with Catholic imagery (Mary is particularly popular, for obvious reasons).

Sleeping in Međugorje

The main street has dozens of hotels and pensions catering to pilgrims.

$ Hotel Martin, well-run by Martin Ilić, is set back slightly from the main road. With 40 comfortable rooms, it's an easy choice (Db-€44, cash only, air-con, elevator, tel. 036/651-541, fax 036/651-505, www.martin.ba, martin.ilic@tel.net.ba). Don't confuse this with the Pansion Martin, much farther out of town.

Eating in Međugorje

The main street is lined with straightforward, crank-'em-out eateries catering to tour groups. For something a little more atmospheric and fun, head for **Gardens Restaurant** (near the post-office end of the main drag). This place—with a lively bar and wine cellar on the ground floor, a classy dining room upstairs, and the namesake garden terrace out back—serves tasty international cuisine. Somewhat youthful, but still respectable, it's a nice place to unwind at the end of a long pilgrimage (10–12-KM pastas, 15–20-KM main courses, daily 9:00–23:30, Antunovića 66, tel. 036/311-645, www.medjugorje-gardens.com).

BOSNIA-HERZEGOVINA

MONTENEGRO

MONTENEGRO

*The Bay of Kotor • Kotor • The Montenegrin Interior •
The Budva Riviera*

If Dubrovnik is the grand finale of a Croatian vacation, then Montenegro is the encore. One of Europe's youngest nations awaits just south of the border, with dramatic scenery, a refreshing rough-around-the-edges appeal, and the excitement of a new independence. If you're looking for the "next Croatia," this is it.

Montenegro is generally Orthodox, and shares a strong cultural affinity with Serbia. But while landlocked Serbia can feel businesslike, Montenegro boasts an easygoing seaside spice. With its laid-back Mediterranean orientation, sparkling coastline, and more than its share of Catholic churches (left behind by past Venetian and Austrian rulers), Montenegro also has a lot in common with Croatia.

And yet, crossing the border, you know you've left sleek, prettified-for-tourists Croatia for a place that's grittier, raw, and a bit exotic. While Croatia's showpiece Dalmatian Coast avoided the drab, boxy dullness of the Yugoslav era, less affluent Montenegro wasn't so lucky. Between the dramatic cliffs and historic villages, you'll drive past grimy, broken-down apartment blocks and some truly unfortunate concrete architecture. Montenegro is also a noticeably poorer country than its northern neighbor...with all that entails.

Today Montenegro finds itself in an awkward position: trying to cultivate an image as a high-roller luxury paradise, while struggling to upgrade what is—in places—a nearly Third World infrastructure. Glittering new €500-a-night boutique hotels are built, then suffer power and water outages. It sometimes feels as if Montenegro is skipping right past an important middle step in its tourist development (that of a fledgling, moderately priced destination). I guess what I'm saying is...lower your expectations, and don't expect a fancy facade and high prices to come with predictable quality.

Still, nothing could mar the natural beauty of Montenegro's  mountains, bays, and forests. For a look at the untamed Adriatic, a spin on the winding road around Montenegro's steep and secluded Bay of Kotor is a must. The area's main town, also called Kotor, has been protected from centuries of would-be invaders by its position at the deepest point of the fjord—and by its imposing town wall, which scrambles in a zigzag line up the mountain behind it. Wander the enjoyably seedy streets of Kotor, drop into some Orthodox churches, and sip a coffee at an al fresco café.

With more time, romantic historians can corkscrew up into the mountains to visit the remote original capital of the country at Cetinje, beach bums will head for the Budva Riviera, and celebrity-seekers can daydream about past glories at the striking hotel-peninsula of Sveti Stefan.

Getting to Montenegro

This chapter is designed for travelers day-tripping to Montenegro from Dubrovnik; all of the sights are within about a three-hour drive of Dubrovnik, and within about an hour of each other.

By Car: Driving is easily the best option, giving you maximum flexibility for sightseeing. I've narrated a handy self-guided driving tour of the Bay of Kotor, and another for the most accessible slice of the Montenegrin interior. Even if you don't have a rental car during your Dubrovnik visit, consider renting one just for the day to visit Montenegro. Perhaps most satisfying—but very expensive—is to hire your own Dubrovnik-based driver to bring you here (my favorites are recommended on page 260). While this is pricey (€250 for the day), you can try to team up with other travelers to split the cost.

By Bus: Bus service between Dubrovnik and Montenegro—discontinued for years after the war—has resumed (generally 2/day each way between Dubrovnik and Kotor town, 2.5 hrs). Unfortunately, the bus schedules don't line up conveniently for a day trip—you can take a morning bus from Dubrovnik to Kotor (departing Dubrovnik around 10:30), then take an early-afternoon bus back to Dubrovnik (departing Kotor at 14:45)—leaving you very little time in the town itself. And, of course, if you ride the bus you can't stop to explore the sights along the way. As the

Montenegro Almanac

Official Name: After being part of "Yugoslavia," then "Serbia and Montenegro," the Republic of Montenegro (Republika Crna Gora) officially declared its independence on June 3, 2006. Montenegro—or Crna Gora in the native language—means "Black Mountain." It might have gotten its name from sailors who saw darkly forested cliffs as they approached, or it may have been named for a mythical mountain in the country's interior.

Snapshot History: Long overshadowed by its Croatian and Serbian neighbors, Montenegro has gone quietly about its own business for centuries, well-insulated from the outside world's influence by its inhospitable terrain. Only in 2006 did the country finally achieve independence, in a landmark vote to secede from Serbia, its influential and sometimes overbearing "big brother."

Population: Montenegro is home to 670,000 people. Of these, the vast majority are Eastern Orthodox Christians (43 percent Montenegrins, 32 percent Serbs), with minority groups of Muslims (including Bosniaks and Albanians, about 13 percent total) and Catholics (1 percent).

Area: 5,415 square miles (slightly smaller than Connecticut).

Red Tape: Americans and Canadians need only a passport (no visa required) to enter Montenegro. Drivers must pay a €10 "eco-tax" at the border.

Geography: Montenegro is characterized by a rugged, rocky terrain that rises straight up from the Adriatic and almost immediately becomes a steep mountain range. The country has 182 miles of coastline, about a third of which constitutes the Bay of Kotor. The only real city is the dreary capital in the interior, Podgorica (137,000 people). Each of Yugoslavia's six republics had a town called Titograd...and Podgorica was Montenegro's.

MONTENEGRO

schedule is always in flux, it's important to confirm times carefully at the Dubrovnik TI or bus station.

By Excursion: As a last resort, consider taking a package excursion that follows basically the same route covered in this chapter (sold at Atlas Travel; see page 301).

Planning Your Time

Assuming you have your own car, for a straightforward one-day plan, drive to Kotor and back (figure about eight hours, including driving time). To really stretch your time, you can add as much Montenegro as you like. Get an early start (to avoid lines at the border, I'd leave Dubrovnik at 7:30 in the morning). It takes about two hours to drive from Dubrovnik to Kotor (add 1.5 hours if you stop in Perast for the boat trip out to the island). Kotor is

Economy: Upon declaring independence in 2006, Montenegro's economy was weak. But the privatization of its economy (including its dominant industry, aluminum) and the aggressive development of its tourist trade (such as soliciting foreign investment to build new luxury hotels) have turned things around. In fact, in 2008, Montenegro had the most foreign investment, per capita, of any country in Europe. Its unemployment rate has dropped from the high-20s to a more respectable 15 percent. But it's still a poor place: Montenegro's per capita GDP is just $10,100—a fraction of Croatia's or Slovenia's.

Currency: Though it's not a member of the European Union, Montenegro uses the euro as its currency: €1 = about $1.40.

Alphabet: The official language is Serbian, but the local dialect is known informally as Montenegrin. While you'll occasionally see signs using the Cyrillic alphabet—particularly in the interior—many Montenegrins use the same Roman alphabet as Croatia and Slovenia.

Telephones: Montenegro's country code is 382. When calling from another country, first dial the international access code (00 from Europe, 011 from the US), then 382, then the area code (minus the initial zero), then the number. Note that Montenegro recently changed its area codes. If you see the former code for the Bay of Kotor area, 082, you'll have to replace it with the new one: 032.

Flag: It's a red field surrounded by a gold fringe. In the middle is the national seal: a golden, two-headed Byzantine eagle topped with a single crown, holding a scepter in one hand and a ball in the other. This symbolizes the balance between church and state. The eagle's body is covered by a shield depicting a lion with one paw raised (representing the resurrected Christ).

worth two or three hours. From Kotor, you can return directly to Dubrovnik (about 1.5 hours if you use the ferry shortcut—see page 365); or drive another hour up to Cetinje in the Montenegrin interior, or a half-hour to the Budva Riviera (from either place, figure about 3 hours back to Dubrovnik). To cram everything into one extremely long day, you can do Dubrovnik-Kotor–Cetinje–Budva Riviera–Dubrovnik. If you're taking the bayside road home (not the ferry shortcut) and don't mind getting to Dubrovnik late, consider stopping for dinner at the recommended Konoba Ćatovića Mlini restaurant.

Helpful Hints

Border Delays: Crossing the Croatian-Montenegrin border (at a place called Debeli Brijeg) is relatively straightforward, though you will need to stop, show your passport (and potentially your rental car's proof of insurance, or "green card"), and pay a one-time "eco-tax" of €10. While I've gotten across this border within about 15 or 20 minutes on each visit, on busy days it's possible you'll be delayed. You'll most likely encounter long waits (of an hour or more) on Saturdays and Sundays in August, and to a lesser degree in July and early September. Locals suggest trying to reach the border by 8:00 (leaving Dubrovnik around 7:30 or 7:45) to beat the tour buses. While this is an early start, it buys you even more time to enjoy Montenegro once across the border. In a pinch, there's a second crossing (called Konfin) that rarely has a line; to reach it coming from Dubrovnik, branch off to the right soon after Gruda and before the main border. After detouring through the villages of Pločice and Vitaljina, you'll loop along the water and cross the border. While this road takes longer, it can be faster if you know there's a long line at the main crossing.

Local Guide: While many Dubrovnik-based driver/guides can bring you to Montenegro, if you really want the Montenegrin perspective, consider hiring a local guide here. I spent a great day learning about this area from **Stefan Đukanović,** a young, energetic, knowledgeable guide who speaks good English and has an infectious enthusiasm for his homeland. Hiring Stefan is a great value. The catch is that he can't come and get you in Dubrovnik, so it works best if you drive yourself and pick him up when you get to Montenegro (€60/half-day, €80/day, mobile 069-297-221, tel. 032/330-832, djukan@t-com.me).

The Bay of Kotor

With dramatic cliffs rising out of the glimmering Adriatic, ancient towns packed with history and thrilling vistas, an undeveloped ruggedness unlike anything in Croatia, and a twisty road to tie it all together, the Bay of Kotor represents the best of Montenegro. To top it off, it's easy to reach by car from Dubrovnik.

Self-Guided Driving Tour

▲▲ Bay of Kotor Day Trip (from Dubrovnik)

The Bay of Kotor (Boka Kotorska—literally the "Mouth of Kotor"; sometimes translated as "Boka Bay" in English) is Montenegro's most enjoyable and most convenient attraction for those based in Dubrovnik.

This self-guided driving tour narrates the drive from the Croatian border to the town of Kotor, in the Bay of Kotor's deepest corner. The Montenegrin border is about 45 minutes south of Dubrovnik (simply follow the main coastal road south, past Cavtat and the airport—don't forget your passport). Note that as you cross the border, you'll pay a one-time "**eco-tax**" of €10. (Your rental car might already have a toll sticker for this tax on it—ask when you pick up your car.)

From the border, you can make it to Kotor in about an hour without stopping, but with all the diversions en route you should plan for much more time. Coming back, you can trim a good halfhour off the drive by crossing the fjord at its narrowest point, using the Lepetani–Kamenari ferry (described on page 365). Navigating on this tour is really simple: It's basically the same road, no turnoffs, from Dubrovnik to Kotor.

• *From the Croatian border, you'll approach the coast at the town called...*

Igalo

Driving through Igalo, keep an eye out (on the right) for a big concrete hotel called **Institut Dr. Simo Milošević** (no relation to Slobodan). This internationally regarded spa, especially popular among Scandinavians, offers treatment for arthritis and other nerve disorders. Capable of hosting more than 1,000 patients at once, this complex boasts that it's one of the world's premier treatment facilities for these conditions. Yugoslav Presidentfor-Life Tito had a villa nearby and took treatments here (www.igalospa.com).

• *A couple of miles beyond Igalo, you enter the biggest city you'll see today...*

Herceg Novi

The drab economic and industrial capital of the Bay of Kotor, Herceg Novi (with 25,000 people), is hardly the prettiest introduction to this otherwise striking landscape. Herceg Novi flourished during the Habsburg boom of the late 19th century, when a railroad line connected it to Dubrovnik, Sarajevo, and Vienna. Back then, Austrians vacationed here—but more recent development has been decidedly less elegant than the Habsburgs'. While there is a walled Old Town core to Herceg Novi, it's not worth stopping to see—Kotor town (at the end of this drive) is better by far.

As you drive through Herceg Novi, watch for **banana trees.** Locals pride themselves on their particularly mild climate, kept warm year-round thanks to the natural protection provided by the surrounding fjord. Supposedly, "it never drops below 50 degrees Fahrenheit." While these banana trees are just decorative (the fruit

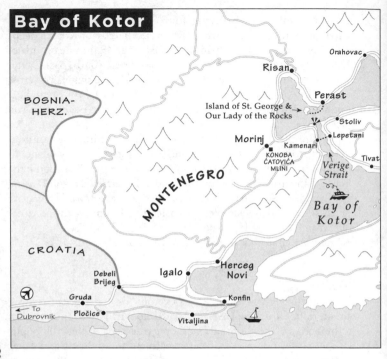

Bay of Kotor

Orahovac

Risan

Perast

BOSNIA-HERZ.

Island of St. George &
Our Lady of the Rocks

Stoliv

Lepetani

Morinj   Kamenari

KONOBA
ČATOVIĆA
MLINI

Tivat

Verige
Strait

MONTENEGRO

Bay of
Kotor

CROATIA

Debeli
Brijeg   Igalo   Herceg
Novi

← To
Dubrovnik   Gruda

Pločice   Konfin

Vitaljina

MONTENEGRO

they produce is too small to eat), they're a local symbol. So is the mimosa flower, which blooms all winter long, and is the inspiration for the town's annual Mimosa Festival—held each February, when much of Europe (including most of Montenegro) is under a layer of snow.

Also keep an eye out for Herceg Novi's stout 15th-century fortress, which was built by the Ottomans—who controlled this area, but never made it deeper into the bay.

Other than the banana trees and mimosas, Herceg Novi is basically a mess. (Don't worry—the drive gets better.) Why so much ugliness compared to Croatia? For one thing, Tito viewed Croatia's Dalmatian Coast as a gold mine of hard Western currency—so he was inclined to keep it Old World–charming. And Croatia remained in the cultural and political orbit of Zagreb, which was motivated to take good care of its historic towns. But Belgrade, which exerted more influence on Montenegro, didn't offer it the same degree of TLC. And because Montenegro has traditionally been poorer than Croatia, its officials are more susceptible to bribery and corruption. ("Would a few thousand dinar convince you to ignore my new hotel's code violations?") From an architectural point of view, it's a sad irony that gorgeous Dubrovnik was devastated by bombs and the gritty cities of Montenegro survived the

war essentially unscathed. To this day, locals aren't crazy about the Serbs who flock here in summer for as-cheap-as possible beach holidays. Instead, Montenegrins are encouraging the construction of new, high-class resort hotels to lure high rollers from around the world (such as James Bond, who played poker in the 2006 movie version of *Casino Royale* in "Montenegro"—though it was actually filmed in the Czech Republic).

• *As you go through Herceg Novi, follow signs for Kotor. Soon you'll emerge into a more rustic setting. This fjordside road is lined with fishing villages, some now developed as resorts (including a few with severe communist-era touches). You'll pass through the town of **Kamenari** (which has a handy ferry—described later—that you could use to shave time off your return trip to Dubrovnik). Two minutes after leaving Kamenari, watch for a convenient gravel pull-out on the right (likely packed with tour buses, by the small white lighthouse). Pull over to check out the narrowest point of the fjord, the...*

Verige Strait

This tight bottleneck at the mouth of the bay is the secret to the Bay of Kotor's success: Any would-be invaders had to pass through here to reach the port towns inside. It's narrow enough to carefully monitor (not even a quarter-mile wide), but deep enough to

The History of Kotor

With evidence of prehistoric settlements dating back to 2500 B.C., the Bay of Kotor has been a prized location for millennia. Its unique bottleneck shape makes the Bay of Kotor the single best natural harbor between Greece and Venice.

One of the earliest known civilizations in Kotor (third century B.C.) was that of the Illyrians, whose Queen Teuta held court here until her lands were conquered by the Romans. Later, when the Roman Empire split (fourth century A.D.), Montenegro straddled the cultural fault line between West (Roman Catholic) and East (Orthodox). As Rome crumbled in the sixth and seventh centuries, the Slavs moved in. Initially rejecting Roman culture, many later converted to Christianity (some Orthodox, some Catholic).

By the 10th century, Montenegro's Slavs had organized into a sovereign state, affiliated with but partially independent from the Byzantine (Eastern Roman) Empire. Thanks to its protected location, medieval Kotor became a major city of the salt trade.

The Bay of Kotor further flourished in the 14th century, under the Serbian emperor Dušan the Mighty. Notorious for his aggressive law enforcement—chopping off the hand of a thief, lopping off the nose of a liar—Dušan made the Bay of Kotor a particularly safe place to do business. One of his strategies was making the nobility responsible for safe passage. If a visiting merchant was robbed, the nobleman who controlled that land would be ruthlessly punished. Soon 2,000-horse caravans could pass without a worry along this fjord. During storms, ships would routinely seek protection in this secluded bay.

But the Serbian Empire went into steep decline after Dušan. As the Ottomans threatened to invade in the 15th century, Kotor's traders turned to Venice for help. The Venetian Republic would control this bay for the next 450 years, and it was never taken by enemies. In fact, Montenegro managed to evade Ottoman rule entirely...unlike its neighbors Albania, Kosovo, Serbia, and Bosnia-Herzegovina.

In the late 19th century, when Venice fell to Napoleon, the Bay of Kotor came briefly under the control of France, then Austria. Feudal traditions fell by the wayside, industry arrived, and the area's old-fashioned economy went into a sharp decline. As trading wealth dried up, the Bay of Kotor entered a period of architectural stagnation. But thanks to this dark spell in Montenegrin history, today's visitors can enjoy some wonderfully preserved time-warp towns.

MONTENEGRO

allow even today's large ships through (more than 130 feet deep). Because this extremely narrow strait is relatively easy to defend, whoever controlled the inside of the fjord was allowed to thrive virtually unchecked.

Centuries before Christ, even before the flourishing of Roman culture, the Bay of Kotor was home to the Illyrians—the mysterious ancestors of today's Albanians. In the third century B.C., Illyrian Queen Teuta spanned this strait with an ingenious ship-wrecking mechanism to more effectively collect taxes. To this day, many sunken ships litter the bottom of this bay. (Teuta was a little too clever for her own good—her shrewdness and success attracted the attention of the on-the-rise Romans, who seized most of her holdings.)

In later times, the Venetians came up with an even more elaborate plan: Place cannons on either side of the strait, with a clear shot at any entering ships. Looking across the wide part of the bay, notice the town of Perast (by the two islands). Perast—our next stop—was also equipped with cannons that could easily reach across the bay. Thanks to this extensive defense network, Ottomans or any other potential invaders were unlikely to penetrate the bay, either by sea or by land.

• *Continue driving around the fjord. If you're ready for a meal, consider stopping in the town of **Morinj** for the fine food and gorgeous setting of the recommended Konoba Ćatovića Mlini restaurant (see page 375). Otherwise, continue around the bay.*

*After going through Morinj and some other small villages, you'll pass through the larger resort town of **Risan**. Back in Greek times, when the Bay of Kotor was known as "Sinus Rhizonicus," Risan was the leading town of the bay. Later, during the Illyrian Queen Teuta's brief three-year reign, Risan was her capital. Today the town is still home to the scant remains of Teuta's castle (on the hilltop just before town), but it's mostly notable for its giant communist eyesore hotel—named, appropriately enough, Hotel Teuta.*

*Continue on to **Perast**. As you approach the town, take the right fork (marked with brown sign) directly down into Perast; or you can first pass above town (left fork) for sweeping views over the bay, then backtrack down into the town center. Park for free along the water in front of the church.*

Perast

This second-most appealing town on the fjord (after Kotor) is considered the "Pearl of Venetian Baroque." It's worth taking some time to wander and explore its buildings and enjoy its relaxed small-town feel (minus the bustle of bigger Kotor).

Remember that Perast, with its cannons aimed at the Verige Strait across the bay, was an essential link in the Bay of Kotor's

Montenegro: Birth of a Nation

Montenegro, like Croatia and Slovenia, was one of the six republics that constituted the former Yugoslavia. When these republics began splitting away in the early 1990s, Montenegro—always allied closely with Serbia, and small enough to slip under the radar—decided to remain in the union. When the dust had settled, four of the six Yugoslav republics had seceded (Croatia, Slovenia, Bosnia-Herzegovina, and Macedonia), while only two remained united as "Yugoslavia": Serbia and Montenegro.

At first, Montenegrin Prime Minister Milo Đukanović was on friendly terms with Serbia's Slobodan Milošević. But in the late 1990s, as Milošević's political stock plummeted, Montenegro began to inch away from its big brother Serbia. Eager to keep its access to the coast, Serbia made concessions that allowed Montenegro to gradually assert its independence. In 1996, Montenegro boldly adopted the German mark as its official currency to avoid the inflating Yugoslav dinar.

By 2003, the country of Yugoslavia was no more, and the loose union was renamed "Serbia and Montenegro." Thus began a three-year "transition period" that allowed Montenegro to test the waters of real independence. During this time, "Serbia and Montenegro" were united only in defense—legislation, taxation, currency, and most governmental functions were separate. And it was agreed that after three years, Montenegro would be allowed to hold a referendum for full independence.

That fateful vote took place on May 21, 2006. In general, ethnic Montenegrins tended to favor independence, while ethnic Serbs (who felt that Serbs and Montenegrins were basically the same anyway) wanted to stay united with Serbia. To secede, Montenegro needed 55 percent of the vote. By the slimmest of margins—half a percent, or just 2,300 votes—the pro-independence faction won. On June 3, 2006, Montenegro officially declared independence. (To save face, two days later, Serbia also "declared independence" from Montenegro.)

Today's Montenegrins are excited to have their own little country and enthusiastic about eventually joining the European Union. Serbia's greatest concern was that in losing Montenegro, it would also lose its lone outlet to the sea—both for shipping and for holiday-making. The Serbs also feared that Montenegrin independence might inspire similar actions in the Serbian province of Kosovo (which did, in fact, declare independence from Serbia less than two years later).

But for many people in both countries, independence is an epilogue rather than a climax. Shortly after the referendum, I asked a Montenegrin when the countries would officially separate. He chuckled and said, "Three years ago."

MONTENEGRO

fortifications. In exchange for this important duty, Venice rewarded Perast with privileged tax-free status. Perast became extremely wealthy. Ornate mansions proliferated during its heyday, the 17th and 18th centuries. But after Venice fell to Napoleon, and the Bay of Kotor's economy changed, Perast's singular defensive role disappeared. With no industry, no hinterland, and no natural resources, Perast stagnated—leaving it a virtual open-air museum of Venetian architecture.

Go to the tallest steeple in town, overlooking a long and narrow harborfront square. Perast is centered on its too-big (and incomplete) church, **St. Nicholas**—dedicated to the patron saint of fishermen. It was originally designed to extend out into the sea (the old church, still standing, was to be torn down). But Napoleon's troops came marching in before the builders got that far, so the plans were abandoned—and this massive partial-church was instead simply grafted on to the existing, modest church.

Go inside (free, €1 to enter treasury, sporadic hours, generally open April–Nov daily 9:00–18:00, July–Aug until 19:00, closed

during Mass, closed Dec–March except by request—ask locals around the church if someone can let you in). Beyond the small sanctuary, you'll find a treasury with relics and icons. Past that is what was to be the main apse (altar area) of the unfinished massive church (notice it's at a right angle to the actual, in-use altar of the existing smaller church). The rough, unadorned brick walls are a reminder that they didn't get very far. Check out the model of the ambitious never-built church, and the priceless crucifix from the Tiepolo school. The Baroque main altar is by Bernini's student Francesco Cabianca, who lived in this area and was always trying to earn money to pay off his gambling debts.

If you have the time and energy, pay €1 to climb the **church tower** for the view.

Perast's only other "sight" is its **Town Museum,** skippable unless you've got time to kill (€2.50, Mon–Sat 9:00–18:00, Sun 9:00–14:00, along the water near the start of town, in the ornate building with the arcade and balcony).

For an enjoyable drink or meal, consider the well-shaded **Konoba Milinović** restaurant, filling a pier on the bay in the middle of town.

• *Before leaving Perast, take a close look at the two islands just offshore (and consider paying them a visit).*

St. George (Sv. Đorđe) and Our Lady of the Rocks (Gospa od Škrpjela)

These twin islands—one natural, the other man-made—come with a fascinating story.

The **Island of St. George** (the smaller, rocky island with trees and a monastery—closed to tourists), named for the protector of

Christianity, was part of the fortification of the Bay of Kotor. This natural island had a small underwater reef nearby. According to legend, two fishermen noticed a strange light emanating from this reef in the early-morning fog. Rowing out to the island, they discovered an icon of Our Lady. They attempted to bring it ashore, but it kept washing back out again to the same spot. Taking this celestial hint, local seamen returning home from a journey began dropping rocks into the sea in this same place. The tradition caught on, more and more villagers dropped in rocks of their own, and eventually more than a hundred old ships and other vessels were filled with stones and intentionally sunk in this spot. And so, over two centuries, an entire island was formed in the middle of the bay.

Flash forward to today's **Our Lady of the Rocks** (the flat island with the dome-topped Catholic church). In the 17th century, locals built a Baroque **church** on this holy site and filled it with symbols of thanks for answered prayers. Step inside (free entry) to explore the collection: silver votive plaques—many of them with images of ships in storms or battles—given by appreciative sailors who survived; 1,700 silver and gold votive plaques from other grateful worshippers; 68 canvases by local Baroque painter Tripo Kokolja; and a huge collection of wedding bouquets given by those who had nothing else to offer (the church is a popular place for weddings).

The adjacent **museum** is an entertaining mishmash of items, and the entry price includes a fun little tour by Davorka or Nešo (€1, June–Oct daily 9:00–19:00, April–May and Nov opens spo-radically with boat arrival, closed Dec–March). You'll see a wide range of ancient artifacts, 65 paintings of ships commissioned by local sailors (notice that most have a saintly image of Mary and the Baby Jesus hovering nearby), and other gifts given through the ages. Upstairs, near the gift shop counter, look for the amazing embroidery made by a local woman who toiled over it

MONTENEGRO

for more than 25 years. She used her own hair for the hair of the angels—which you can see fade from brown to gray as she aged. As you closely observe the image's hair clockwise, beginning at around 3 o'clock, you'll see the subtle change in color.

Getting There: Boats to Our Lady of the Rocks leave from in front of St. Nicholas' Church in Perast—look for the guys milling around the harborfront with boats ready to go (€5 per person round-trip, try to negotiate a better deal if you're traveling with a larger group).

• *When you're ready to move on, continue driving around the fjord. After the large town of Orahovac, you'll see part of the bay roped off for a mussel farm. These farms do best when located where mountain rivers spill into the bay. And a hundred or so yards later, you cross a bridge spanning the don't-blink-or-you'll-miss-it...*

LJuta River

According to locals, this is the "shortest river in the world"—notice that the source (bubbling up from under the cliff) is just to the left of the bridge, and it meets the sea just to the right. Short as it is, it's hardly a trickle—in fact, its name means "Angry River" for its fierce flow during heavy rains. The river actually courses underground for several miles before it gets here. Like the Karst area south of Ljubljana, this is a karstic landscape—limestone that's honeycombed with underground rivers, caves, and canyons. Many other waterfalls and streams feed the Bay of Kotor with snowmelt from the surrounding mountains. Because of this steady natural flushing, locals brag that the bay's water is particularly clear and clean.

• *Continuing along the fjord, as you pass through the town of Dobrota, look across the bay to the village of...*

Prčanj

This town is famous as the former home of many centuries' worth of wealthy sea captains. When the Bay of Kotor was part of the Austrian Empire, Emperor Franz Josef came to Prčanj. Upon being greeted by some 50 uniformed ship captains, he marveled that such a collection of seafarers had been imported for his visit... not realizing that every one of them lived nearby.

• *Keep on driving. When you see the giant moat with the town wall, and the smaller wall twisting up the hill above, you'll know you've arrived in* **Kotor** *(described next).*

After visiting Kotor (and the Montenegrin interior or the Budva Riviera, if you choose), it'll be time to head...

Back to Croatia: Lepetani–Kamenari Ferry Shortcut

When you're ready to return to Dubrovnik, you can go back the way you came. Or, for a quicker route, consider the ferry that cuts across the narrow part of the fjord (between the towns of Lepetani and Kamenari). On the Kotor side of the bay, the boat departs from the town of Lepetani. From Kotor, you have two options to reach the ferry: The easiest option is to leave Kotor and take the tunnel toward Budva. Once through the tunnel, follow signs into Tivat, and continue straight through Tivat on the main road to reach Lepetani, which is a few miles beyond the end of town. Or, for a more challenging but more scenic route, you can simply continue driving on the waterfront road clockwise around the bay (through Prčanj and Stoliv) until you land in Lepetani. But be warned that this road is extremely narrow (one lane with an Adriatic shoulder) and can be exhausting if there's much oncoming traffic.

No matter how you approach, remember that "ferry" is *trajekt* (it's also signed for Herceg Novi—the big city across the bay). The boat goes continuously, and the crossing takes just four minutes (it takes longer to load and unload all the cars than it does to cross). A small car and its passengers pay €4 each way.

Kotor

MONTENEGRO

Butted up against a steep cliff, cradled by a calm sea, naturally sheltered by its deep-in-the-fjord position, and watched over by an imposing network of fortifications, the town of Kotor is as impressive as it is well-protected. Though it's enjoyed a long and illustrious history, today's Kotor is a time-capsule retreat for travelers seeking a truly unspoiled Adriatic town.

There's been a settlement in this location at least since the time of Christ. The ancient town of Catarum—named for the Roman word for "contracted" or "strangled," as the sea is at this point in the gnarled fjord—was first mentioned in the first century A.D. Like the rest of the region, Kotor's next two millennia were layered with history as it came under control of a series of foreign powers: Illyrians, Romans, Serbs, Venetians, Napoleonic soldiers, Austrians, Tito's Yugoslavia...and now, finally, Montenegrins. Each group left its mark, and Kotor has its share of both Catholic and Orthodox churches, plus monuments and reminders of plenty of past colonizers and conquerors.

Through all those centuries, Kotor avoided destruction by warfare. But it was damaged by earthquakes—including the same 1667 quake that leveled Dubrovnik (known here as the "Great Shaking"), as well as a devastating 1979 earthquake that the city is still cleaning up from. While only 3,000 people live within the Old Town walls, "greater Kotor" has a population of about 12,000.

With an extremely inviting Old Town that seems custom-built for aimless strolling, Kotor is an idyllic place to while away a few hours. Though it's sometimes called a "little Dubrovnik," Kotor is more low-key, less ambitious, and much smaller than its more famous neighbor. And yet, with its own special spice that's exciting to sample, Kotor is a hard place to tear yourself away from.

Orientation to Kotor

Kotor (or Cattaro in Italian) has a compact Old Town shaped like a triangle. The two sides facing the bay are heavily fortified by a thick wall, and the third side huddles under the cliff face. A meandering defensive wall climbs the mountainside directly behind and above town.

The Old Town's mazelike street plan is confusing, but it's so small and atmospheric that getting lost is more fun than frustrating. Note that locals virtually ignore addresses, including the names of streets and squares. Most Old Town addresses are represented simply as "Stari Grad," then a number (useless if you're trying to navigate by streets). To make matters worse, a single square can have several names—so one map labels it Trg od Katedrale (Cathedral Square), while another calls it Pjaca Sv. Tripuna (Piazza of St. Tryphon). My advice: Don't fret about street or square names. Simply navigate with a map and by asking locals for directions. Thanks to the very manageable size of the Old Town, this is easier than it sounds.

Tourist Information

The TI is in a kiosk just outside the Old Town's main entrance gate (generally May–Oct daily 8:00–20:00; Nov–April Mon–Sat 8:00–15:00, closed Sun; tel. 032/325-950, www.tokotor.com). Pick up the free map and browse the collection of guidebooks and souvenirs. They can help you find a room for no fee.

Arrival in Kotor

By Car: Approaching town, you'll first see Kotor's substantial wall overlooking a canal. You can park in one of two pay lots: immediately across from the main gate (more expensive but convenient, to the right just after crossing the bridge by the wall); or in the lot across the canal (on the left just before the bridge by the wall—you'll be sent back here if the first lot is full). Either is a quick walk from the Old Town entrance. Be sure you've parked legally; some of my readers report having been towed and fined for parking in what they thought were legal spaces.

By Bus: The bus station is about a half-mile south of the Old Town. Arriving here, simply exit to the right and walk straight up the road—you'll run into the embankment and town wall in 10 minutes.

Sights in Kotor

Because of its tangled alleys and irregular street plan, Kotor feels bigger than it is. But after 10 minutes of wandering, you'll discover you're going in circles and realize it's actually very compact. (In fact, aimless wandering is Kotor's single best activity.) How such a cute town manages to be so delightfully lazy and traffic-free, without being utterly overrun by tourists, I'll never know.

As you ramble, keep an eye out for these key attractions. I've listed them roughly in the order of a counterclockwise route through town, beginning outside the main entrance gate.

▲**Main Town Gate (Glavna Gradska Vrata)**—The bustling square fronting the bay and waterfront marina now welcomes visitors. But for centuries, its purpose was exactly the opposite. As the primary point of entry into this heavily fortified town, it was the last line of defense. Before the embankment was built, the water came directly to this door, and there was only room for one ship to tie up at a time (near where the cannons are today). If a ship got this far (through the gauntlet we saw back at the Verige Strait), it was carefully examined here again (and taxes were levied) before its passengers could disembark. This may seem paranoid, but realize that pirates could fly the flag of a friend to get through the strait, only to launch a surprise attack once here. By the way, pirates' primary booty wasn't silver or gold, but men—kidnapped for ransom, or, if ransom wasn't paid, as slaves to row on ships.

Check out the pinkish gate itself. The oldest parts of this gate date from 1555. It once featured a Venetian lion, then the double-headed eagle of the Habsburg Empire. But today, most of the symbolism touts Tito's communism (notice the stars and the old Yugoslav national seal at the top). The big date (November 21, 1944) commemorates when this area was liberated from the Nazis by Tito's homegrown Partisan Army. The Tito quote *(tuđe nećemo svoje nedamo)* means, roughly, "Don't take what's ours, and we won't take what's yours"—a typically provocative statement in these troubled Balkans.

• *Notice the TI in the kiosk just to the left of the gate. You'll emerge into the...*

Square of Arms (Trg od Oržja)—Do a quick spin-tour of the square, which is ringed with artifacts of the city's complex history. Looking to the left, you'll see a long building lined with cafés, ATMs (which dispense euros), and a small casino. The building was once the palace of the rector, who ruled Kotor on behalf of

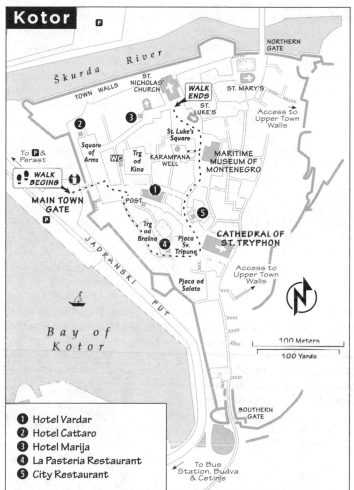

Kotor

Škurda River

TOWN WALLS

ST. NICHOLAS' CHURCH

NORTHERN GATE

ST. MARY'S

WALK ENDS

ST. LUKE'S

Access to Upper Town Walls

❷

❸

Square of Arms

WC

Trg od Kina

St. Luke's Square

KARAMPANA WELL

MARITIME MUSEUM OF MONTENEGRO

To 🅿 & Perast

WALK BEGING

MAIN TOWN GATE

🅿

POST

❶

❺

JADRANSKI PUT

Trg od Braina

❹

Pjaca Sv. Tripung

CATHEDRAL OF ST. TRYPHON

Access to Upper Town Walls

Pjaca od Salate

N

Bay of Kotor

100 Meters

100 Yards

SOUTHERN GATE

To Bus Station, Budva & Cetinje

❶ Hotel Vardar
❷ Hotel Cattaro
❸ Hotel Marija
❹ La Pasteria Restaurant
❺ City Restaurant

MONTENEGRO

Venice; princes could watch the action from their long balcony overlooking the square, which served as the town's living room.

Later, the palace became the Kotor Town Hall. Beyond that, two buildings poke out into the square (on either side of the lane leading out of the square). The one on the right is the Venetian arsenal, the square's namesake. The one on the left is the "French Theater," named for its purpose during the time this area was under Napoleon's control. Directly across from the gate you just came through, you'll see the town's Bell Tower, one of Kotor's symbols. The odd triangular structure at its base was once the town pillory. Wrongdoers would be chained to this with their transgression printed on a placard hanging from their neck, open to public ridicule of the rudest kind imaginable. In the little recessed square just right of that, you'll spot the recommended, copper-roofed Hotel Vardar.

• *Walk down the long part of the square directly ahead of where you entered (toward Hotel Vardar). About 20 yards in front of the hotel, take the broad lane angling off to the right, which leads past mansions of Kotor's medieval big shots. Turn left down the little lane next to the Montenegro Airline office. Soon you'll hit Pjaca Sv. Tripuna (a.k.a. Trg od Katedrale), home to the...*

▲**Cathedral of St. Tryphon (Katedrala Sv. Tripuna)**—Even though most Kotorians are Orthodox, Kotor's most significant church is Catholic. According to legend, in A.D. 809, Venetian merchants were sailing up the coast from Nicea (in today's Turkey) with the relics of St. Tryphon—a third-century martyr and today's patron saint of gardeners. A storm hit as they approached the Bay of Kotor, so they took shelter here. Every time they tried to leave, the weather worsened...so they finally got the message that St. Tryphon's remains should remain in Kotor.

The earliest, Romanesque parts of this church, dating from the mid-12th century, are made of limestone from the Croatian island of Korčula. But the church has been rebuilt after four different earthquakes—most extensively after the 1667 quake, when it achieved its current Renaissance-Baroque blend. This 1667 earthquake, which also contributed to Dubrovnik's current appearance, destroyed three-quarters of Kotor's buildings. A fire swept the city, and all of the dead bodies attracted rats (and with them, the plague)—a particularly dark chapter in Kotor's history.

Why are the two towers different? There are plenty of legends, but the most likely is that restorers working after 1667 simply ran out of money before they finished the second one. Notice the Church of Our Lady of Health way up on the hill above this church—built in thanks to God by survivors of the plague (it also serves as part of the town fortifications—described later).

Go inside the cathedral (€1.50, daily 9:00–19:00 in peak season, until 17:00 in shoulder season, until 15:00 in winter). The main part of the church is marginally interesting: stout columns;

MONTENEGRO

surviving Byzantine-style frescoes under the arches—all that's left of paintings that once covered the church; and a fine 15th-century silver-and-gold altar covered by a delicate canopy. But the best part is the reliquary upstairs. Find the stairs at the rear and walk up to the chapel. Behind the Baroque altar (by Bernini's student Francesco Cabianca, whose work we saw in Perast) and the screen, you'll see 48 different relics. In the center is St. Tryphon—his bones in a silver casket and his head in the golden chalice to the right. Just to the right of the screen, examine the fascinating icon of the Madonna and Child from the 15th century. The painting (like the icons above) exemplifies this town's position as a bridge between Western and Eastern Christianity: The faces, more lifelike, are Western-style (Catholic) Gothic; the stiff, elongated bodies are more Eastern (Orthodox) and Byzantine-style.

• *Exit the church. Notice the recommended* **La Pasteria** *restaurant immediately across from the cathedral, with good Italian style fare and scenic al fresco tables. When you're ready to continue, face the cathedral facade and exit the square to your left (at the back-left corner of the square). In a block, you'll wind up on a little square that's home to the...*

Maritime Museum of Montenegro (Pomorski Muzej Crne Gore)—Like so many Adriatic towns, Kotor's livelihood is tied to the sea. This humble museum explores that important heritage. As you climb the stairway, notice the evocative maps and etchings of old Kotor. Portraits of salty swashbucklers, traditional costumes, and 98 coats of arms representing aristocratic families who have lived here (ringing the main room upstairs) are all reminders of the richness of Kotor's history. You'll see a display of rifles and swords (some with fun ornamental decorations illustrating the art of killing) and lots of model ships (€4, includes English audioguide, July–Aug daily 9:00–23:00, progressively shorter hours off-season, on Trg Grgurina, tel. 032/304-720). The museum is housed in the Gregorina Palace, one of dozens of aristocratic mansions that dot the Old Town—yet another reminder of the historically high concentration of wealth and power in this little settlement.

• *Facing the museum, go around the left side. After 10 yards, you'll pass a well on your left called the...*

Karampana—This well served as Kotor's only public faucet until the early 20th century (swing the pendulum to get things flowing). As such, it was also the top place in town for gossip, like the office water cooler. It's said that if your name is mentioned here, you know you've arrived. Today, though the chatter is no longer raging on this square, the town's gossip magazine is called *Karampana*.

• *Continue straight past the well into the next square...*

St. Luke's Square (Trg Svetog Luke)—There are two Serbian Orthodox churches on this pretty square, each with the typical

Orthodox church features: a squat design, narrow windows, and portly domes. Little **St. Luke's Church** (Crkva Sv. Luka), in the middle of the square, dates from the 12th century. During the Venetian era, it did double duty as both an Orthodox and a Catholic church (usually closed to visitors; if you'd like to go inside, try asking at St. Nicholas' Church to be let in). The bigger and much newer **St. Nicholas' Church** (Crkva Sv. Nikola), at the far corner, was built in the early 20th century—because of its Neo-Byzantine design, has similarly spherical domes and slit-like windows (undergoing extensive renovation; when finished, it's generally open daily 8:00–12:00 & 17:00–20:00).

Notice how the crosses on the steeples of St. Nicholas' Church differ from Western Christian churches. In addition to the arms

of the cross, Orthodox crosses often have a second, smaller crossbar near the top (representing the *I.N.R.I.* plaque that was displayed above Jesus' head). Sometimes Orthodox crosses also feature a third, angled crossbar at the bottom. Many believe that rather than being nailed directly to the cross, Jesus' feet were nailed to a crossbar like this one to prolong his suffering. The slanted angle represents Jesus' forgiveness of the thief crucified to his right (the side that's pointing up)...and suggests where the unrepentant thief on his left ended up.

Stepping into these (or any other Orthodox) churches, you'll immediately notice some key differences from Catholic churches: no pews (worshippers stand through the service as a sign of respect), tall and skinny candles (representing prayers), and a screen of icons, called an iconostasis, in the middle of the sanctuary to separate the material world from the holy world (where the Bible is kept). For more about Orthodox worship, see the sidebar on page 278.

• *If you go down the street to your left as you face St. Nicholas, you'll wind up back at the Square of Arms. But first try getting lost, then found again, in Kotor's delightful maze of streets. The town's final attraction is above your head.*

▲▲**Town Walls (Gradske Zidine)**—Kotor's fortifications begin as stout ramparts along the waterfront, then climb up the sheer cliff face behind town in a dizzying zigzag line. If there's a more elaborate city wall in Europe, I haven't seen it. A proud Kotorian bragged to me, "These fortifications cost more to build than any palace in Europe."

Imagine what it took to create this "Great Wall of Kotor": nearly three miles long, along an extremely inaccessible terrain. It

was built in fits and starts over a millennium (9th–19th centuries, though most of it was during the Venetian occupation in the 17th and 18th centuries). Its thickness varies from 6 to 50 feet, and the tallest parts are 65 feet high. Sections higher on the hill—with thinner walls, before the age of gunpowder—are the oldest, while the thick walls along the water are most recent. It was all worth it: The fortified town survived many attacks, including a two-month Ottoman siege in 1657.

If you're in great shape, consider scrambling along the walls and turrets above the Old Town (you'll pay €2 to enter the walls if you visit May–Oct daily 8:00–20:00; otherwise they're free). This involves climbing 1,500 steps (an elevation gain of more than 700 feet)—so don't overestimate your endurance or underestimate the heat. ("Am-I-*that*-out-of-shape?" tourists routinely find themselves winded and stranded high above town.) It's best to tackle the walls clockwise. (Even if you're not doing the hike, you can visually trace this route.) Find the entrance at the back-left corner of town (near St. Mary's Church, through the alley with the two arches over it, including one with a Venetian lion). Pay the entry fee and begin hiking up.

Climb as high as the **Church of Our Lady of Health** (Crkva Gospe od Zdravlj). While some believe this church has miraculous healing powers, most everyone agrees it offers some of the best views down over Kotor. From this church, you can either cut back down toward the Old Town, or—if you're not exhausted yet—keep hiking up to the tippy-top **Fortress of St. John** (marked by the red-and-gold national flag of this new country). Built on the remains of fortifications from the Illyrians (you can scan the third-century B.C. remains just beyond the fort), this was the headquarters for the entire wall network below it. Then head back down, enjoying your reward: a downhill walk with head-on views of the Bay of Kotor.

Sleeping in Kotor

Kotor's hotels are a poor value, and they feel very "Balkan" (a mix of colorful, tacky, and chaotic). You'll sleep cheaper in Dubrovnik, but Kotor might seduce you into spending the night. My recommendations are all inside the Old Town. Be warned that loud nightclubs can bother light sleepers, especially in summer.

MONTENEGRO

Sleep Code

(€1 = about $1.40, country code: 382, area code: 032)
S = Single, **D** = Double/Twin, **T** = Triple, **Q** = Quad, **b** = bathroom.
To help you sort easily through these listings, I've divided the rooms into two categories based on the price for a standard double room with bath in peak season:

$$ Higher Priced—Most rooms €100 or more.
$ Lower Priced—Most rooms less than €100.

Most of the town's cheaper *sobe* are outside the city walls (ask for details at TI).

$$ Hotel Vardar has 24 rooms smack dab in the middle of the Old Town. This classic old copper-roofed hotel was recently renovated from top to bottom, leaving it mod but not gaudy. While convenient, the dead-central location can come with some noise, especially on weekends—request a quieter room (July–Aug: Sb-€125, Db-€185; mid-May–June and Sept: Sb-€115, Db-€155; Oct–mid-May: Sb-€95, Db-€125; 20 percent less Fri–Sat nights for two people, pricier and larger apartments have views on the square, elevator, air-con, free Wi-Fi in lobby, Stari Grad 476, tel. 032/325-054, www.hotelvardar.com, info@hotelvardar.com).

$$ Hotel Cattaro offers 20 newish, Balkan-plush rooms—with dark wood and bold old-meets-new decor—above a casino right on the Square of Arms (June–Sept: Sb-€90, Db-€120; Oct–May: Sb-€69, Db-€99; pricier suites, air-con, elevator, pay Wi-Fi, tel. 032/311-000, fax 032/311-080, www.cattarohotel.com, cattarohotel@t-com.me).

$ Hotel Marija, a throwback on an Old Town square, offers 17 rooms and wood-paneled halls. Rooms overlooking the square come with noise and the windows are thin, so request a quieter room in the back. Communicating with the staff can be challenging but is workable (Sb-€65, Db-€90, Tb-€103, on Trg od Kina, tel. 032/325-062, hotel.marija.kotor@t-com.me).

Eating in Kotor

There's no shortage of dining options in Kotor's Old Town; even locals suggest simply wandering the streets and squares, following your nose, and choosing the ambience you like best. I've eaten well and scenically at **La Pasteria,** with good pizzas and pastas, and breezy outdoor tables facing St. Tryphon's Cathedral (€6–8 pizzas and pastas, €11–15 main courses, daily 8:00–1:00 in the morning, Pjaca Sv. Tripuna/Trg od Katedrale, tel. 032/322-269). Locals also

MONTENEGRO

like the **City Restaurant,** which lacks cathedral views but offers a fine, shady perch—its well-varnished picnic tables are set within the little forest in the Old Town, and more tables fill a small square out front (€6–9 pizzas and pastas, €7–15 main courses, daily 8:00–1:00 in the morning, mobile 069-378-167).

Near the Verige Strait, in Morinj

Konoba Ćatovića Mlini is a memorable restaurant worth going out of your way to reach. Hiding in a sparse forest off the main

fjordside road, this oasis is situated amidst a series of ponds, streams, waterfalls, and bubbling springs. The traditionally clad waiters are stiffly formal, and the cuisine is good and surprisingly affordable. Choose between several different seating options, stony indoors and out. Family-run for 200 years, this place is a local institution, yet it feels like a well-kept secret (despite the crowds in summer). Reservations are essential (€8–10 pastas, €8–12 meat dishes, €8–22 fish dishes, extensive wine list—Vranac is a popular local dry red, daily 11:00–23:00, tel. 032/373-030). The best plan might be to dine here on your way back to Dubrovnik from Kotor.

Getting There: At the town of Morinj, watch for burgundy *Konoba Ćatovića Mlini* signs leading away from the water. You'll make several turns, but signs will lead you right to the restaurant.

The Montenegrin Interior

Although Montenegro is trying to cultivate a glitzy beach-break cachet, for most of its history it has been thought of as a rugged mountain kingdom. While the coast—the focus of most of this chapter—was traditionally Venetian or Austrian, it was behind the sheer wall of mountains shooting up from that seafront that the real heart of Montenegro beat. Romantics, caught up in out-dated Balkan fantasies, still think of this inland area as the "real" Montenegro.

While the Bay of Kotor is the most accessible and appealing part of the country, with more time consider a joyride up into the mountains. For a quick look at this area, the easiest loop takes you to the historic capital of Cetinje—a dull little town in its own right, but a fine excuse for a mountain drive. You could do this whole loop in about two and half hours without stopping (about an hour from Kotor to Cetinje, then another hour to Budva, then a half-hour back to Kotor), but if you want to stretch your legs in Njeguši or Cetinje, allow more time.

Self-Guided Driving Tour

The Road into the Mountains

The road to Cetinje twists you up the mountain face that stretches high above Kotor—it's an incredibly scenic, white-knuckle drive.

From Kotor, leave town toward Budva. At the edge of Kotor, before the big tunnel, take a right (marked for *Cetinje*) and begin your ascent. Cresting the first hill, you can either head right to go back down to the coast toward Budva (see "The Budva Riviera," later), or left to get to Cetinje (also marked for *Njeguši*).

Taking the left turn, you wind up and up (past a small Roma encampment) on 25 numbered switchbacks. The road is a souvenir from the Habsburg era (1884)—while Venetian rule brought sea trade, Austrian rule brought fortresses and infrastructure. After switchback #13, you'll pass an old customs house marking the former border between the Austro-Hungarian Empire and the Kingdom of Montenegro—a reminder that the coastline was not historically an integral part of Montenegrin cultural identity. As you near the top, look across the canyon to the left to spot the impossibly rough little donkey path that once was Cetinje's connection with the coast—like a tenuous umbilical cord tethering the mountainous interior to the outside world.

As you crest the hill, the vegetation changes—you're high above the Adriatic, with commanding views of Kotor and its bay (and great photo-op pull-outs—the best is just after switchback #25). Continuing inland, you find yourself in another world: poor, insular, and more Eastern (you'll see more Cyrillic lettering). Country farmhouses sell smoked ham, mountain cheese, and *medovina* (honey brandy). Before long, you reach a broad plain and the hamlet of...

Njeguši

The humble-seeming village of Njeguši (NYEH-goo-shee) is actually well-known among Montenegrins, with two very important claims to fame. This was the hometown of the House of Petrović-Njegoš, the dynasty that ruled Montenegro for much of its history (1696–1918). The family's favorite son was Petar II Petrović-Njegoš (1813–1851). Aside from ruling the country, Petar II is remembered most fondly as a great poet and playwright...sort of the Montenegrin Shakespeare.

Njeguši is also famous for producing its own special type of air-dried ham, called *Njeguški pršut*. Locals explain that, because this meadow overlooks the sea on one side, and the mountains on the other, the wind changes direction 10 times each day, alternating between dry mountain breeze and salty sea air—perfect for seasoning and drying ham hocks. For good measure, the *pršut* is also smoked with beech wood. The blocky, white buildings lining the road that look like giant Monopoly houses are actually smokehouses, jammed with five layers of hanging ham hocks—thousands of euros worth—silently aging. (More industry than you realize hides out in sleepy villages.) A couple of traditional restaurants at the heart of the village are happy to serve passing tourists a lunch of this local specialty. For more on *pršut*, see the sidebar on page 392.

From Njeguši to Cetinje

Continuing through Njeguši toward Cetinje, you'll twist up into more mountains—soon arriving in an even more rugged and inhospitable landscape than the road that brought you here from the coast. Eyeing this desolate scenery, you can understand why the visiting Lord Byron said of this place, "Am I in paradise or on the moon?" Along the mountain road that drops you down into Cetinje, each rock has the phone number of a vulture-esque road repair service *(auto slep)* spray-painted onto it. Low-profile plaques mark the site of Tito-era ambush assassinations.

Keep an eye out (on the horizon to the right) for the pointy peak of the mountain called **Lovćen,** which is capped by an elaborate mausoleum, designed by the great Croatian sculptor Ivan Meštrović, and devoted to King Petar II Petrović-Njegoš (explained earlier). With more time, you could actually drive up to the top of this mountain for sweeping views across Montenegro.

When you get into Cetinje, take a right when you hit a fork and find a place to park. To find your way into the old center, ask "guh-DEH yeh TSEHN-tar?"

Cetinje

Cetinje (TSEH-teen-yeh)—the historic capital of Montenegro—is a fine but fallen-on-hard-times little burg that sits cradled in a desolate valley surrounded by mighty peaks. Run-down as Cetinje is, it's still more pleasant than the current, drab capital, Podgorica.

Observing Cetinje from afar, it seems made to order as the historic capital of a remote and rustic people. It was the home of the Montenegrin king since the 15th century, but has always been pretty humble. In fact, it's said that when the Ottomans conquered it and moved in ready to rampage, they realized there wasn't much to pillage and plunder—so they just destroyed the town and moved out. The town was destroyed several other times, as well—and each time, its locals rebuilt.

This "Old Royal Capital," once the leading city in the realm, is today a victim of Tito's quirky economic program for Yugoslavia. It used to provide shoes and refrigerators for the country, but when Yugoslavia disintegrated, so did the viability of Cetinje's economy. As you explore the two-story town today, it seems there's little more than a scruffy dollop of tourism to keep its 17,000 people housed and fed. Many of its younger generation have left for employment along the coast in the tourism industry.

Stroll the main street (Njegoševa) past kids on bikes, old-timers with hard memories, and young adults with a metabolism as low as the town's. At the end of this drag is the main square (Balšića Pazar), surrounded by low-key sights with sporadic opening hours: the **Ethnographic Museum** (traditional costumes and folk life), **Historical Museum** (tracing the story of Montenegro), **Njegoš Museum** (dedicated to the beloved poet-king Petar II Petrović-Njegoš), and **National Museum,** which honors King Nikola I, who ruled from 1860 until 1918. While his residence is as poor and humble a royal palace as you'll see in Europe, Nikola I thought big. He married off five of his daughters into the various royal families of Europe.

A short walk from the palace is the birthplace of the town, **Cetinje Monastery.** It's dedicated to St. Peter of Cetinje, a legendary local priest who carried a cross in one hand and a sword in the other, established the first set of laws among Montenegrins, and inspired his people to defend Christianity against the Muslims. The monastery also holds the supposed right hand of St. John the Baptist. You are free to wander respectfully through the courtyard and church of this spiritual capital of Serbian Orthodox Montenegro.

From Cetinje Back to the Coast

To avoid backtracking down the same twisty road you came up, consider heading more directly back toward the coast from Cetinje. Just follow signs for *Budva*. A few miles outside of Cetinje along this road, look for the good **Restoran Konak,** which serves up tasty traditional dishes with indoor and outdoor seating (open long hours daily, tel. 041/761-011).

Continuing along this road, you'll pop out high above the **Budva Riviera.** Looking out to sea, you'll spot the distinctive peninsula of Sveti Stefan off to the left, and the town of Budva to the right. If you have even more time, linger along the coast to visit these sights (described next). Otherwise, head right to return to Kotor or Dubrovnik.

The Budva Riviera

Montenegrins boast, "Croatia's got islands, but we've got beaches!" Surrounding the resort town of Budva, just south of Kotor, are long swaths of coarse-sand and fine-pebble beaches. This 15-mile stretch of coast, called the "Budva Riviera," is unappealingly built up, with endless strings of cheap resort hotels (and quite a few new five-star ones)—making it pale in comparison to the jagged saltiness of the Bay of Kotor or the romantic tidiness of Dalmatia. But the area isn't without its charm. Aside from the pleasant Old Town of the region's unofficial capital, Budva, you'll discover a near-mythical haunt of the rich and famous: the highly exclusive resort peninsula of Sveti Stefan. For me, more time in Kotor or an earlier return to Dubrovnik would be more satisfying than the trek to the Budva Riviera. But beach lovers who have plenty of time and a spirit of adventure will find this area merits a look.

Getting to the Budva Riviera

Budva is about a 30-minute drive south of **Kotor**. The easiest approach is to continue past Kotor along the fjord, then through the tunnel (following *Budva* signs). For a more scenic route, take a right for the upper road to Budva that twists over the mountain (described earlier, under "The Montenegrin Interior"). After winding up several switchbacks (with giddy views back over the Bay of Kotor) and cresting the hill, go right (again following *Budva* signs). You'll coast down into a valley, through the town of Lastva, then back over another mild hill that deposits you above the beaches of Budva.

First you'll reach the town of **Budva** (turn right at traffic light, following brown *Stari Grad* signs to the Old Town; parking well-marked in modern complex next to Old Town). Continuing around the bay, you'll pass the busy, modern resort cluster of Bečići before reaching **Sveti Stefan.**

Sights on the Budva Riviera

Between the strings of resort hotels are two towns that deserve a quick visit.

Budva—The Budva Riviera's best Old Town has charming Old World lanes crammed with souvenir shops and holiday-making Serbs. While far less appealing than Kotor (and Dalmatian towns such as Korčula, Hvar, and Trogir), Budva at least offers a taste of romance between the resort sprawl.

Budva's ancient history (dating back at least to the fifth century B.C.) is arguably more illustrious than Kotor's. It began as an "emporium" (market and trading center) for Greek seamen, and

extremely valuable jewelry uncovered here indicates that some pretty important people spent time in Budva. And yet, Budva isn't about history; it's about today. As in many Mexican vacation areas, the Old Town is just one more part of the resort experience—it's basically treated as a backdrop for outdoor dining and nightclubs.

A 10-minute stroll tells you all you need to know about Budva. The layout is simple and intuitive—a peninsula (flanked by beaches) with a big Venetian-style bell tower. From the parking lot, simply go through the Old Town walls and wander up the main drag, Njegoševa; near the end of the street on the right is the **TI** (open long hours daily in summer, tel. 033/452-750). Out at the tip of town, you'll find several churches, including the Holy Trinity Church, with gorgeous and colorful Orthodox Serb decorations inside (daily 8:00–12:00 & 17:00–20:00 in summer, 8:00–12:00 & 16:00–19:00 in winter). You'll also see a huge citadel that's been turned into a restaurant (€2 entry, free with drink or meal purchase).

▲**Sveti Stefan**—Like a mirage hovering just offshore, the resort peninsula of Sveti Stefan beckons curious travelers. Once an actual, living town (connected to the mainland only by a narrow, natural causeway), Sveti Stefan was virtually abandoned after World War II. The Yugoslav government developed it into a giant resort hotel in the 1950s. As old homes were converted to hotel rooms, the novelty of the place—and its sterling location, surrounded by pebbly beaches and lush scenery—began to attract some seriously wealthy guests.

During this resort's heyday in the 1960s and 1970s, it ranked with Cannes or St-Tropez as *the* place to see or be seen on Europe's beaches. You could rent a room, a house, an entire block of houses, or even the entire peninsula. Anonymity was vigilantly protected, as the nicest "rooms" had their own private pools (away from public scrutiny), lockable gates, and security guards. Lured by Sveti Stefan's promise of privacy,

celebrities, rock stars, royalty, and dignitaries famously engaged in bidding wars to decide who'd be granted access to the best suites: Whoever put the most money in a sealed envelope and slipped it to the manager, won. (According to local legend, Sly Stallone's money talked.) Guests were pampered—indulged no matter how outrageous their requests. Sophia Loren, Kirk Douglas, Doris Day, and Claudia Schiffer are just a few of the big names who basked on Sveti Stefan's beaches.

In recent years, Sveti Stefan has experienced a dramatic decline. Warfare in nearby places (such as Dubrovnik and Kosovo) kept visitors away, its cachet faded, and the resort grew a bit rough around the edges. International investors drew up ambitious plans to restore the island to its former status as one of the world's most exclusive, crème-de-la-crème resorts. But the global financial crisis put those plans on hold—which means the complex may not be open during your visit. As of this writing, they were charging €12 to park at the mainland to walk along the beach, but it wasn't possible to actually walk across to the island itself.

When it's open, visitors find that Sveti Stefan is exactly what it sounds like: a peninsular old-town-turned-hotel. Though totally lacking the charm of an actual town, and less impressive than it sounds, Sveti Stefan is undeniably cool. If you're able to visit, circle your way around the "hotel" clockwise. Stroll through the dead town, peeking through gates, hoping to spot a withered old celebrity who forgot to go home. Notice the varying degrees of privacy (each more expensive than the last): no fence, small fence, big fence. At the far end is the biggest and most famous "suite," where guests have an entire corner of the peninsula to themselves. At the top of the peninsula is a big Russian Orthodox church and a smaller Serbian Orthodox church—though both are little more than hotel decorations today. Continuing clockwise around the peninsula, find your way down to the big café terrace and look back to the mainland. You'll spot one of Tito's former vacation villas across the water, on its own little cove. If you're ready for a hike after leaving Sveti Stefan, walk over the small hill (on the left as you come across the causeway) to this villa for a look around (and more views back on Sveti Stefan).

Getting to Sveti Stefan: Sveti Stefan is just three miles (5 km) beyond Budva. Coming around the bay from Budva (following signs toward *Bar*), skip the first turnoff to the right that leads into Sveti Stefan. Instead, pass above the peninsula on the main road, watching for the pull-out on the right that offers great views over the resort. After snapping your photos, backtrack to the access road and head down to the town, twisting through a more recent commercial sprawl to the pay parking lot near the causeway.

From Sveti Stefan to Dubrovnik: Figure two hours to the Croatian border (if you go via Tivat—rather than Kotor—and use the shortcut ferry across the Bay of Kotor, described on page 365), then another 45 minutes to Dubrovnik.

SLOVENIA

SLOVENIA

Slovenija

Tiny, overlooked Slovenia is one of Europe's most unexpectedly charming destinations. At the intersection of the Slavic, German, and Italian worlds, Slovenia is an exciting mix of the best of each culture. Though it's just a quick trip away from the tourist throngs in Venice, Munich, Salzburg, and Vienna, Slovenia has stayed off the tourist track—a handy detour for in-the-know Back Door travelers.

Today, it seems strange to think that Slovenia was ever part of Yugoslavia. Both in the personality of its people and in its landscape, Slovenia feels more like Austria. Slovenes are more industrious, organized, and punctual than their fellow former Yugoslavs...yet still friendly, relaxed, and Mediterranean. Locals like the balance. Visitors expecting minefields and rusting Yugo factories are pleasantly

surprised to find Slovenia's rolling countryside dotted instead with quaint alpine villages and the spires of miniature Baroque churches, with breathtaking, snowcapped peaks in the distance.

Only half as big as Switzerland, but remarkably diverse for its size, Slovenia can be easily appreciated on a brief visit. Travelers can hike on alpine trails in the morning and explore some of the world's best caves in the afternoon, before relaxing with a seafood dinner on the Adriatic.

Slovenia enjoys a powerhouse economy—the healthiest of all of Europe's former communist countries. The Austro-Hungarian Empire left it with a strong industrial infrastructure, which the Yugoslav government expanded. By 1980, 60 percent of all Yugoslav industry was in little Slovenia (which had only 8 percent of Yugoslavia's population and 8 percent of its territory). With independence, Slovenia continued this trend, pushing their mighty little economy into the future. Of the 12 new nations that

have joined the European Union since 2004, Slovenia was the only one rich enough to be a net donor (with a higher per-capita income than the average), and the first one to join the euro currency zone (it adopted the euro in January 2007). Thanks to its long-standing ties to the West and can-do spirit, Slovenia already feels more "Western" than any other destination in this book.

The country has a funny way of making people fall in love with it. Slovenes are laid-back, easygoing, stylish, and fun. They won't win any world wars (they're too well-adjusted to even try)... but they're exactly the type of people you'd love to chat with over a cup of coffee. Many of today's American visitors are soldiers who participated in the conflict in nearby Bosnia and have good memories of their vacations here in Slovenia. Now they're bringing their families back with them.

The Slovenian language is as mellow as the people. While Slovenes use Serb and German curses in abundance, the worst they can say in their native tongue is, "May you be kicked by a horse." For "Darn it!" they say, "Three hundred hairy bears!"

Coming from such a small country, locals are proud of the few things that are distinctly Slovenian, such as the roofed hayrack. Foreigners think that Slovenes' fascination with these

Slovenia Almanac

Official Name: Republika Slovenija, or simply Slovenija.

Snapshot History: After being dominated by Germans for centuries, Slovenian culture proudly emerged in the 19th century. In the aftermath of World War I, Slovenia merged with its neighbors to become Yugoslavia, then broke away and achieved independence for the first time in 1991.

Population: Slovenia's two million people (a count similar to Nevada's) are 83 percent ethnic Slovenes who speak Slovene, plus a smattering of Serbs, Croats, and Muslim Bosniaks. The majority of the country is Catholic.

Latitude and Longitude: 46° N and 14° E (latitude similar to Lyon, France; Quebec, Canada; or Bismarck, North Dakota).

Area: At 7,800 square miles, it's about the size of New Jersey, but with one-fourth the population.

Geography: Tiny Slovenia has three extremely different terrains and climates: the warm Mediterranean coastline (just 29 miles long—about one inch per inhabitant); the snow-capped, forested alpine mountains in the northwest (including 9,400-foot Mount Triglav); and the moderate-climate, central limestone plateau that includes Ljubljana and the cave-filled Karst region. If you look at a map of Slovenia and squint your eyes a bit, it looks like a chicken running toward the east.

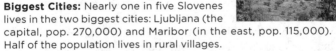

Biggest Cities: Nearly one in five Slovenes lives in the two biggest cities: Ljubljana (the capital, pop. 270,000) and Maribor (in the east, pop. 115,000). Half of the population lives in rural villages.

Economy: With a Gross Domestic Product of $55 billion and a GDP per capita of $30,000, Slovenia's economy is much stronger than the average Eastern European country. Slovenia's wealth comes largely from manufactured metal products (trucks and machinery) traded with a diverse group of partners.

Currency: Slovenia uses the euro: €1 = about $1.40.

Government: The country is led by the prime minister (currently Borut Pahor), who heads the leading vote-getting party in legislative elections. He governs along with the figurehead president (currently Danilo Türk). Slovenia's relatively peaceful succession is credited largely to former Prime Minister Milan Kučan, who remains a popular figure. The National Assembly consists of about 90 elected legislators; there's also a second house of parliament, which has much less power. Despite the country's small size, it is divided into some 200 municipalities.

Flag: Three horizontal bands of white (top), blue, and red. A shield in the upper left shows Mount Triglav, with a wavy-line sea below and three stars above.

The Average Slovene: The average Slovene skis, in this largely alpine country, and is an avid fan of team handball (yes, handball). He or she lives in a 250-square-foot apartment, earns $1,400 a month, watches 16 hours of TV a week (much of it in English with Slovene subtitles), and enjoys a drink-and-a-half of alcohol every day.

Notable Slovenes: A pair of prominent Ohio politicians—perennial presidential candidate Dennis Kucinich and Senator George Voinovich, both from the Cleveland area—are each half-Slovene. (In 1910, Cleveland had the biggest Slovenian population of any city in the world—just ahead of Trieste and Ljubljana.) Classical musicians might know composers Giuseppe Tartini and Hugo Wolf. Even if you haven't heard of architect Jože Plečnik yet, you'll hear his name a hundred times while you're in Slovenia—especially in Ljubljana (see page 419). Perhaps most famous of all is the illustrious Melania Knauss—a GQ cover girl who's also Mrs. Donald Trump.

Sporty Slovenes: If you follow alpine sports or team handball, you'll surely know some world-class athletes from Slovenia. NBA fans might recognize basketball players Primož Brezec and Bostjan Nachbar, as well as some lesser players. The athletic Slovenes—perhaps trying to compensate for the miniscule size of their country—have accomplished astonishing feats: Davo Karničar has skied down from the summits of some of the world's tallest mountains (including Everest, Kilimanjaro, and McKinley). Benka Pulko became the first person ever to drive a motorcycle around the world (that is, all seven continents, including Antarctica; total trip: 118,000 miles in 2,000 days—also the longest solo motorcycle journey by a woman; www.benka pulko.com). Dušan Mravlje ran across all the continents (www .dusanmravlje.si). And ultra-marathon swimmer Martin Strel has swum the entire length of several major rivers, including the Danube (1,775 miles), the Mississippi (2,415 miles), the Yangtze (3,915 miles), and the Amazon (3,393 miles; for more, see www .martinstrel.com).

hayracks is strange...until they visit and see them absolutely everywhere (especially in the northwest). Because of the frequent rainfall, the hayracks are covered by a roof that allows the hay to dry thoroughly. The most traditional kind is the *toplar,* consisting of two hayracks connected by one big roof. It looks like a skinny barn with open, fenced sides. Hay hangs on the sides to dry; firewood, carts, tractors, and other farm implements sit on the ground inside; and dried hay is stored in the loft above. But these wooden *toplarji* are firetraps, and a stray bolt of lighting can burn one down in a flash. So in recent years, more farmers are moving to single hayracks *(enojni);* these are still roofed, but have posts made of concrete, rather than wood. You'll find postcards and miniature wooden models of both kinds of hayracks (a fun souvenir).

Another good (and uniquely Slovenian) memento is a creatively decorated front panel from a beehive *(panjske končnice).* Slovenia has a strong beekeeping tradition, and beekeepers once believed that painting the fronts of the hives made it easier for bees to find their way home. Replicas of these panels are available at gift shops all over the country.  (For more on the panels and Slovenia's beekeeping heritage, see page 460.)

Slovenia is also the land of polka. Slovenes claim it was invented here, and singer/accordionist Slavko Avsenik—from the village of Begunje near Bled—cranks out popular oompah songs that make him bigger than the Beatles (and therefore, presumably, Jesus) in Germany. You'll see the Avsenik ensemble and other oompah bands on Slovenian TV, where hokey Lawrence Welk-style shows are a local institution.

To really stretch your euros, try one of Slovenia's more than 200 farmhouse B&Bs, called "tourist farms" *(turistične kmetije).* These are actual, working farms (often organic) that sell meals and/or rent rooms to tourists to help make ends meet. You can use a tourist farm as a home base to explore the entire country—remember, the farthest reaches of Slovenia are only a day trip away. A comfortable, hotelesque double with a private bathroom—plus a traditional Slovenian dinner and a hearty breakfast—costs as little as $50. Request a listing from the Slovenian Tourist Board (see page 549), or find information at www.slovenia.info.

Most visitors to Slovenia are, in my experience, completely charmed by the place. With all it has going for it, it's hard to believe that Slovenia is not already overrun with tourists. Somehow, this little country continues to glide beneath the radar. Exploring its mountain trails and meeting its friendly locals, you'll feel like you're in on a secret.

Helpful Hints

Sunday Closures: Slovenia can be extremely sleepy on Sundays, even in the larger towns and cities, where virtually all shops are closed. Plan ahead. Fortunately, many restaurants remain open, plus a select few grocery stores.

Smoking Ban: Smoking is prohibited in public places, unless it's a specially designated (and well-ventilated) smoking room. Larger hotels still have some "smoking" rooms, but smoking isn't allowed in public areas.

Euro Conversion: Even though Slovenia has used the euro currency since January 2007, some locals still think in terms of the previous currency, the *tolar* (which you might see on menus or price lists). There were about 190 tolars in one dollar, and about 240 tolars in one euro.

Telephones: Insertable phone cards, sold at newsstands and kiosks everywhere, get you access to the modern public phones.

When calling locally, dial the seven-digit number. To make a long-distance call within the country, start with the area code (which begins with 0). To call a Slovenian number from abroad, dial the international access number (00 if calling from Europe, 011 from the United States or Canada) followed by 386 (Slovenia's country code), then the area code (without the initial 0) and the seven-digit number. To call out of Slovenia, dial 00, the country code of the country you're calling (see chart in appendix), the area code if applicable (may need to drop initial zero), and the local number.

Slovenian phone numbers beginning with 080 are toll-free; 090 and 089 denote expensive toll lines. Most mobile phone numbers begin with 031, 041, 051, 040, or 070.

Toll Sticker: To drive on Slovenia's expressways *(avtocesta)*, you'll need to display a toll sticker *(vinjeta,* veen-YEH-tah; €15/week, €30/month). Your rental car might come with one; otherwise, you can buy one at a gas station, post office, or some newsstands.

Slovenian History

Slovenia has a long and unexciting history as part of various larger empires. Charlemagne's Franks conquered the tiny land in the eighth century, and, ever since, Slovenia has been a backwater of the Germanic world—first as a holding of the Holy Roman Empire and later, the Habsburg Empire. Slovenia seems as much German as Slavic. But even as the capital, Ljubljana, was populated by

Slo-what?-ia

The only thing I know about Slovakia is what I learned first-hand from your foreign minister, who came to Texas.

—George W. Bush, to a Slovak journalist (Bush had actually met with Dr. Janez Drnovšek, who was then Slovenia's prime minister)

Maybe it's understandable that many Americans confuse Slovenia with Slovakia. Both are small, mountainous countries that not too long ago were parts of bigger, better known, now defunct nations. But anyone who has visited Slovenia and Slovakia will set you straight—they feel worlds apart.

Slovenia, wedged between the Alps and the Adriatic, is a tidy, prosperous country with a strong economy. Until 1991, Slovenia was one of the six republics that made up Yugoslavia. Historically, Slovenia has had very strong ties with Germanic culture—so it feels like its neighbor to the north, Austria.

Slovakia—two countries away, to the northeast—is slightly bigger. Much of its territory is covered by the Carpathian Mountains, most notably the dramatic, jagged peaks of the High Tatras. In 1993, the Czechs and Slovaks peacefully chose to go their separate ways, so the nation of Czechoslovakia dissolved into the Czech Republic and the Slovak Republic (a.k.a. Slovakia).

To make things even more confusing, there's also **Slavonia.** This is the thick, inland "panhandle" that makes up the northeast half of Croatia, along Slovenia's southeast border. Much of the warfare in Croatia's 1991–1995 war took place in Slavonia (including Vukovar; see the Understanding Yugoslavia chapter).

I won't tell on you if you mix them up. But if you want to feel smarter than a former president, do a little homework and get it right.

Austrians (and called Laibach by its German-speaking residents), the Slovenian language and cultural traditions survived in the countryside.

Ljubljana rose to international prominence for half a decade (1809–1813) when Napoleon named it the capital of his "Illyrian Provinces," stretching from Austria's Tirol to Croatia's Dalmatian Coast. During this time, the long-suppressed Slovene language was used for the first time in schools and the government. Inspired by the patriotic poetry of France Prešeren, national pride surged.

The last century saw the most interesting chapter of Slovenian history. Some of World War I's fiercest fighting occurred at the Soča (Isonzo) Front in northwest Slovenia—witnessed by young Ernest Hemingway, who drove an ambulance (see sidebars on pages 472 and 480). After the war, from 1918 to 1991, Slovenia was Yugoslavia's smallest, northernmost, and most affluent republic. Concerned about Serbian strongman Slobodan Milošević's nationalistic politics, Slovenia seceded in 1991. Because more than 90 percent of the people here were ethnic Slovenes, the break with Yugoslavia was simple and virtually uncontested. Its war for independence lasted just 10 days and claimed only a few dozen lives. (For more details, see the Understanding Yugoslavia chapter, page 532.)

After centuries of looking to the West, Slovenia became the first of the former Yugoslav republics to join the European Union in May of 2004. The Slovenes have been practical about this move, realizing it's essential for their survival as a tiny nation in a modern world. But there are trade-offs, and "Euroskeptics" are down on EU bureaucracy. As borders disappear, Slovenes are experiencing more crime. Traditional farms are grappling with strict EU standards. Slovenian businesses are having difficulty competing with big German and other Western European firms. Before EU membership, only Slovenes could own Slovenian land. But now wealthy foreigners are buying property, driving up the cost of real estate.

Yet EU membership seems to be agreeing with the Slovenes. Slovenia became the first post-communist country to adopt the euro currency in January of 2007. Despite the worldwide economic crisis, business here is booming. As throughout their history, the Slovenes are adjusting to the 21st century with their characteristic sense of humor and easygoing attitude.

Slovenian Food

Slovenian cuisine offers more variety and better quality than Croatian fare. Slovenes brag that their cuisine melds the best of

Italian and German cooking—but they also embrace other international influences, especially French. Like Croatian food, Slovenian cuisine also features some pan-Balkan elements: The savory phyllo-dough pastry *burek* is the favorite fast food here, and when Slovenes host a backyard barbecue, they grill up *čevapčići* and *ražnjići*, topped off with the eggplant-and-red-bell-pepper condiment *ajvar* (see "Balkan Flavors," page 31). Slovenia enjoys Italian-style fare, with a pizza or pasta restaurant on seemingly every corner. Hungarian food simmers in the northeast corner of the country (where many Magyars reside). And in most of the country, traditional Slovenian food

Pršut

In Slovenia, Croatia, and Montenegro, *pršut* (purr-SHOOT) is one of the essential food groups. This air-cured ham (like Italian prosciutto) is soaked in salt and sometimes also smoked. Then it hangs in open-ended barns for up to a year and a half, to be dried and seasoned by the howling Bora wind. Each region produces a slightly different *pršut*. In Dalmatia, a layer of fat keeps the ham moist; in Istria, the fat is trimmed, and the *pršut* is dryer.

Since Slovenia joined the European Union, strict new standards have swept the land. Separate rooms must be used for the slaughter, preparation, and curing of the ham. While this seems fair enough for large producers, small family farms that want to produce just enough *pršut* for their own use—and maybe sell one or two ham hocks to neighbors—find they have to invest thousands of euros to be compliant.

has a distinctly Germanic vibe—including the "four S's": sausages, schnitzels, strudels, and sauerkraut.

Traditional Slovenian dishes are prepared with groats—a grainy mush made with buckwheat, barley, or corn. Buckwheat, which thrives in this climate, often appears on Slovenian menus. You'll also see plenty of *štruklji* (dumplings), which can be stuffed with cheese, meat, or vegetables. *Repa* is turnip prepared like sauerkraut. Among the hearty soups in Slovenia is *jota*—a staple for Karst peasants, made from *repa*, beans, and vegetables.

The cuisine of Slovenia's Karst region (the arid limestone plain south of Ljubljana) is notable. The small farms and wineries of this region have been inspired by Italy's Slow Food movement—their owners believe that cuisine is meant to be gradually appreciated, not rushed—making the Karst a destination for gourmet tours. Karstic cuisine is similar to France's nouvelle cuisine—several courses in small portions, with a focus on unusual combinations and preparations—but with a Tuscan flair. The Karst's tasty air-dried ham *(pršut),* available throughout the country, is worth seeking out (see sidebar). Istria (the peninsula just to the south of the Karst, in southern Slovenia and Croatia) produces truffles that, locals boast, are as good as those from Italy's Piedmont (see page 141).

Voda is water, and *kava* is coffee. Radenska, in the bottle with the three little hearts, is Slovenia's best-known brand of mineral water—good enough that the word *Radenska* is synonymous with bottled water all over Slovenia and throughout the former

Yugoslavia. It's not common to ask for (or receive) tap water, but you can try requesting *voda iz pipe*.

Adventurous teetotalers should forego the Coke and sample Cockta, a Slovenian cola with an unusual flavor (which supposedly comes from berry, lemon, orange, and 11 herbs). Originally called "Cockta-Cockta," the drink was introduced during the communist period, as an alternative to the difficult-to-get Coca-Cola. This local variation developed a loyal following...until the Iron Curtain fell, and the real Coke became readily available. Cockta sales plummeted. But in recent years—prodded by the slogan "The Taste of Your Youth"—nostalgic Slovenes are drinking Cockta once more.

To toast, say, *"Na ZDROW-yeh!"*—if you can't remember it, think of "Nice driving!" The premier Slovenian brand of *pivo* (beer) is Union (OO-nee-ohn), but you'll also see a lot of Laško (LASH-koh), whose mascot is the Zlatorog (or "Golden Horn," a mythical chamois-like animal).

Slovenia produces some fine *vino* (wine). The Celts first made wine in Slovenia; the Romans improved the process and spread it throughout the country. Slovenia has three primary wine regions. Podravje, in the northeast, is dominated by *laški* and *renski riesling*. Posavje, in the southeast, produces both white and red wines, but is known mostly for the light, russet-colored *cviček* wine. Primorska, in the southwest, has a Mediterranean climate and produces mostly reds. One of the most popular is *teran*, made from *refošk* grapes, which grow in iron-rich red soil *(terra rossa)*—infusing them with a high lactic acid content that supposedly gives the wine healing properties.

Slovenia's national dessert is *potica*, a rolled pastry with walnuts and sometimes also raisins. For more tasty treats, see the "Bled Desserts" sidebar on page 456. Locals claim that Ljubljana has the finest gelato outside of Italy—which, after all, is just an hour down the road.

Slovenian Language

Slovene is surprisingly different from languages spoken in the other former Yugoslav republics. While Serbian and Croatian are mutually intelligible, Slovene is gibberish to Serbs and Croats. Most Slovenes, on the other hand, know Serbo-Croatian because, a generation ago, everybody in Yugoslavia had to learn it.

Linguists have identified some 250 dialects of Slovene. Locals can tell which city—or sometimes even which remote mountain valley—someone comes from by their accent.

The tiny country of Slovenia borders Italy and Austria, with important historical and linguistic ties to both. For self-preservation, Slovenes have always been forced to function in many different languages. All of these factors make them excellent linguists. Most young Slovenes speak effortless, flawless English—then admit that they've never set foot in the United States or Britain, but love watching American movies and TV shows (which are always subtitled, never dubbed).

Remember, *c* is pronounced "ts" (as in "cats"). The letter *j* is pronounced as "y"—making "Ljubljana" easier to say than it looks (lyoob-lyee-AH-nah). Slovene only has one diacritical mark: the *strešica*, or "little roof." This makes *č* sound like "ch," *š* sound like "sh," and *ž* sound like "zh" (as in "measure"). The letter *v* is pronounced like "u"—so the Slovenian word *avto* sounds like "auto."

The only trick: As in English, which syllable gets the emphasis is unpredictable. Slovenes use many of the same words as Croatians, but put the stress on an entirely different place.

Learn some key Slovenian phrases (see "Slovenian Survival Phrases," page 583). You'll make more friends and your trip will go more smoothly.

SLOVENIA

LJUBLJANA

Slovenia's capital, Ljubljana (lyoob-lyee-AH-nah), with a lazy Old Town clustered around a castle-topped mountain, is often likened to Salzburg. It's an apt comparison—but only if you inject a healthy dose of breezy Adriatic culture, add a Slavic accent, and replace favorite son Mozart with local architect Jože Plečnik.

Ljubljana feels smaller than its population of 270,000. While big-league museums are in short supply, the town itself is an idyllic place that sometimes feels too good to be true. Festivals fill the summer, and people enjoy a Sunday stroll any day of the week. Fashion boutiques and al fresco cafés jockey for control of the Old Town, while the leafy riverside promenade crawls with stylishly dressed students sipping *kava* and polishing their near-perfect English. Laid-back Ljubljana is the kind of place where graffiti and crumbling buildings seem elegantly atmospheric instead of shoddy. For better or worse, Ljubljana has been sprucing up lately—be prepared for lots of torn-up streets during your visit.

Batted around by history, Ljubljana has seen cultural influences from all sides—most notably Prague, Vienna, and Venice. This has left the city a happy hodgepodge of cultures. Being the midpoint between the Slavic, Germanic, and Italian worlds gives Ljubljana a special spice. People often ask me: What's the "next Prague"? And I have to answer Kraków. But Ljubljana is the *next* "next Prague."

Planning Your Time

Ljubljana deserves a full day. While there are few must-see sights, the city's biggest attraction is its ambience. You'll spend much of your time strolling the pleasant town center, exploring the

The Story of Ljubljana

In ancient times, Ljubljana was on the trade route connecting the Mediterranean (just 60 miles away) to the Black Sea (toss a bottle off the bridge here, and it can float to the Danube and, eventually, all the way to Russia). Legend has it that Jason and his Argonauts founded Ljubljana when they stopped here for the winter on their way home with the Golden Fleece. The town was Romanized (and called Emona) before being over-run by Huns, only to be resettled later by Slavs.

In 1335, Ljubljana fell under the jurisdiction of the Habsburg emperors (who called it Laibach). After six centuries of Habsburg rule, Ljubljana still feels Austrian—especially the abundant Austrian Baroque and Viennese Art Nouveau architecture—but with a Mediterranean flair.

Napoleon put Ljubljana on the map when he made it the capital of his Illyrian Provinces, a realm that stretched from the Danube to Dubrovnik, from Austria to Albania (for only four years, 1809–1813). For the first time, the Slovene language was taught in schools, awakening a newfound pride in Slovenian cultural heritage. People still look back fondly on this very brief era, which was the first (and probably only) time when Ljubljana rose to prominence on the world stage. After more than 600 years of being part of the Habsburg Empire, Ljubljana has no "Habsburg Square"...but they do have a "French Revolution Square."

In the mid-19th century, the railway connecting Vienna to the Adriatic (Trieste) was built through town—and Ljubljana boomed. But much of the city was destroyed by an earth-quake in 1895. It was rebuilt in the Art Nouveau style so popular in Vienna, its capital at the time. A generation later, architect Jože Plečnik bathed the city in his distinctive, artsy-but-sensible, classical-meets-modern style.

In World War II, Slovenia was occupied first by the Italians, then by the Nazis. Ljubljana had a thriving resistance movement that the Nazis couldn't suppress—so they simply fenced off the entire city and made it a giant prison for three years, allowing only shipments of basic food supplies to get in. But the Slovenes—who knew their land far better than their oppressors did—continued to slip in and out of town unde-tected, allowing them to agitate through the end of the war.

In 1991, Ljubljana became the capital of one of Europe's youngest nations. Today the city is filled with university stu-dents, making it a very youthful-feeling town. Ljubljana has always felt free to be creative, and recent years—with unprec-edented freedoms—have been no exception. This city is on the cutting edge when it comes to architecture, public art, fashion, and trendy pubs. But the scintillating avant-garde culture has soft edges—hip, but also nonthreatening and user-friendly.

many interesting squares and architectural gems, shopping at the boutiques, and sipping coffee at sidewalk cafés along the river.

Here's the best plan for a low-impact sightseeing day: Begin on Prešeren Square, the heart of the city. Cross the Triple Bridge and wander through the riverside produce market before joining the town walking tour at 10:00 (at 11:00 in Oct–March). After the tour, wander along the Ljubljanica River to Jože Plečnik's National and University Library, French Revolution Square, and on to my favorite Ljubljana museum, the Jože Plečnik House (this sight might be closed for renovation, and even when open, it has limited hours—call or ask the TI to confirm the opening times, and plan accordingly). In the afternoon, Ljubljana is a great place to squander a few hours. Go window-shopping at colorful boutiques, commit some quality time to people-watching at a riverside café, or consider some more sightseeing: Wander through the museum zone west of Prešeren Square, dip into the Serbian Orthodox Church, and stroll through Tivoli Park (paying a visit to the good Contemporary History Museum in the park, or any others that interest you). It's also worth the 10-minute walk northeast of Prešeren Square to visit the excellent Slovenian Ethnographic Museum.

Plenty of good day trips are a short distance from Ljubljana. With a second day, visit Lake Bled (see next chapter), or head for one of the two impressive caves (Škocjan or Postojna) and nearby sights in the Karst region south of the city (see The Karst chapter).

Ljubljana is dead and disappointing on Sundays (virtually all shops are closed and the produce market is quiet, but museums are generally open, a modest flea market stretches along the riverfront, and the TI's walking tour still runs). The city is also relatively quiet in August, when the students are on break and many locals head to beach resorts. They say that in August, even homeless people go to the coast.

Orientation to Ljubljana

(area code: 01)

Ljubljana—with narrow lanes, architecture that mingles the Old World and contemporary Europe, and cobbles upon cobbles of wonderful distractions—can be disorienting for a first-timer. But the charming central zone is compact, and with a little wandering, you'll quickly get the hang of it.

The Ljubljanica River—lined with cafés, restaurants, and a buzzing

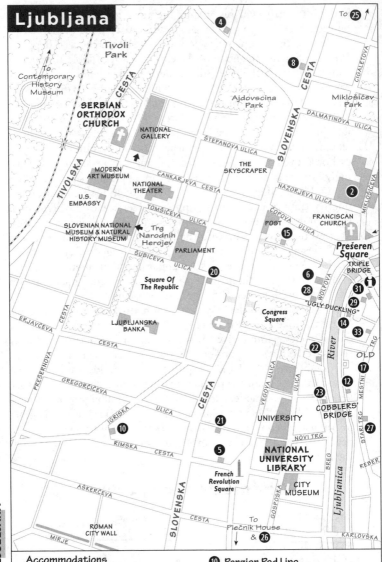

Ljubljana

Accommodations

1. Antiq Hotel
2. Grand Hotel Union
3. Central Hotel
4. Slamič B&B
5. Pri Mraku Guesthouse
6. Hotel Emonec & Laundry
7. B&B Petra Varl
8. Hotel Center
9. Stari Tišler Rooms
10. Penzion Pod Lipo
11. Hostel Celica
12. Alibi CN27 Hostel
13. Alibi M14 Hostel

Eateries

14. Zlata Ribica Restaurant
15. Gostilna As Rest. & Lounge
16. Ribca Restaurant
17. Old Town Main-Drag Eateries

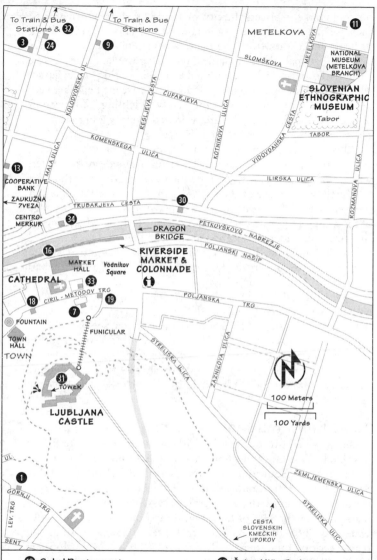

18 Sokol Restaurant
19 Vodnikov Hram
20 DaBuDa Restaurant
21 Pizzeria Foculus
22 Ljubljanski Dvor Pizzeria
23 Paninoteka Sandwiches
24 Nobel Burek
25 To Olympia Burek
26 To Pri Škofu & Harambaša

27 Čajna Hiša Teahouse
28 Zvezda Kavarna
29 Abecedarium Restaurant
30 Rustika Choc. & Ice Cream

Services
31 Rustika Gallery Shops (2)
32 To Kod & Kam Map Store
33 Dom Trgovina Shops (2)
34 Internet Café

outdoor market—bisects the city, making a 90-degree turn around the base of a castle-topped mountain. Most sights are either along or just a short walk from the river. Visitors enjoy the distinctive bridges that span the Ljubljanica, including the landmark Triple Bridge (Tromostovje) and pillared Cobblers' Bridge (Čevljarski Most)—both designed by Jože Plečnik. Between them is a very plain wooden bridge dubbed the "Ugly Duckling." The center of Ljubljana is Prešeren Square, watched over by a big statue of Slovenia's national poet, France Prešeren.

I've organized the sights in this chapter based on which side of the river they're on: the east (castle) side of the river, where Ljubljana began, with more medieval charm; and the west (Prešeren Square) side of the river, which has a more Baroque/Art Nouveau feel and most of the urban sprawl. At the northern edge of the tourist's Ljubljana is the train station; at the southern edge is the garden district of Krakovo and the Jože Plečnik House.

Ljubljana's Two Big Ps: You'll hear the following two easy-to-confuse names constantly during your visit. Mind your Ps, and your visit to Ljubljana becomes more meaningful:

Jože Plečnik (YOH-zheh PLAYCH-neek, 1872–1957) is the architect who shaped Ljubljana, designing virtually all of the city's most important landmarks. For more information, see page 422.

France Prešeren (FRAHN-tseh preh-SHAY-rehn, 1800–1849) is Slovenia's greatest poet and the namesake of Ljubljana's main square. Some civic-minded candy shops—trying to imitate the success of Austria's "Mozart Ball" chocolates—sell chocolate "Prešeren Balls."

Tourist Information

Ljubljana's helpful, businesslike TI has a useful website (www.visitljubljana.si) and four branches: at the **Triple Bridge,** across from Prešeren Square (daily June–Sept 8:00–21:00, Oct–May 8:00–19:00, Stritarjeva ulica 1, tel. 01/306-1215); at the upper corner of the **market** (with pay Internet access, bike rental, and information about the rest of Slovenia; daily June–Sept 8:00–21:00, Oct–May 8:00–19:00, Krekov trg 10, tel. 01/306-4575); at the **train station** (June–Sept daily 8:00–22:00; Oct–May Mon–Fri 10:00–19:00, Sat 8:00–15:00, closed Sun; Trg O.F. 6, tel. 01/433-9475); and at the **airport** (hours depend on flight schedule, generally daily 11:00–19:00).

At any TI, pick up a pile of free resources: the big city map, the Tourist Guide, the monthly *Where to?* events guide, and a wide range of informative brochures. The TI also offers a free room-finding service. Skip the **Ljubljana City Card,** which includes access to public transportation and free entry or discounts at some city museums (€13/72 hrs).

Arrival in Ljubljana

By Train: Ljubljana's modern, user-friendly train station (Železniška Postaja) is at the northern edge of the city center. Emerging from the passage up to track 1a, turn right and walk under the long canopy along the train tracks to find the yellow arrivals hall. Everything is well-signed in English, including a **TI,** the handy train-information office next door (with useful handouts outlining trips to several domestic and international destinations, daily 5:30–21:30), and—near the front of the station—a big **ticket office** with clearly marked ticket windows and an **ATM** (office open daily 5:00–22:00). Arrivals are *prihodi*, departures are *odhodi*, and track is *tir*.

The main square is an easy 10-minute **walk** from the station; you can walk to any of my recommended hotels within about 20 minutes (often less). To reach Prešeren Square at the city's center, leave the arrivals hall to the right and walk a long block along the busy Trg Osvobodilne Fronte (or "Trg O.F." for short, with the bus station in the middle). After passing all of the bus stalls, turn left across Trg O.F. and go down Miklošičeva, at the building with the round red-brick columns. This takes you past some of Ljubljana's most appealing architecture to Prešeren Square.

Unscrupulous **taxis** crouch in front of the station, waiting to spring on unsuspecting tourists. The fair metered rate to any of my recommended hotels is around €3 (maybe up to €4–5 in heavy traffic or after hours). But most of the train-station cabbies are crooks accustomed to charging you whatever they want without using the meter. To avoid these jerks, call for a taxi instead (dial 041-731-831 or 041-240-200; the train station TI is willing to call for you, if they're not too busy). If you do use the taxi stand, ask the price up front, and *never* pay more than €5. For more on taxis—and how to avoid rip-offs—see "Getting Around Ljubljana—By Taxi," later.

By Bus: Ljubljana's bus station (Autobusna Postaja) is a low-profile building (with ticket windows, Internet access, a bakery, and newsstands) in the middle of Trg O.F., right in front of the train station. To get into the city center, see "By Train," above.

By Car: As you approach Ljubljana on the expressway, the toll road ends. Once you're on the ring road, simply follow signs for *Center*. Once you get into the city center, you'll begin to see directional signs to individual hotels. Ask your hotel about parking—most have some available, usually for a price. If you need to gas up your rental car before returning it, you'll find a huge gas station on Tivolska Cesta (just west of the train station, near the big Union brewery). Otherwise, your options in the center are limited—it's better to look for a gas station on the expressway as you approach the city.

By Plane: See "Ljubljana Connections," at the end of this chapter.

Helpful Hints

Pedestrian Safety: Many Ljubljana residents commute by bike. As a pedestrian, I've had many close calls with bikes whizzing by. Keep your eyes open and stay out of the designated bike lanes on the sidewalks (often marked in red).

Closed Days: Most Ljubljana museums (except the castle and a few less-important museums) are closed on Mondays. The recommended Jože Plečnik House is closed Sundays, Mondays, and Fridays, and might be closed entirely for restoration during your visit (for details, see page 421).

Markets: In addition to the regular **market** that sprawls along the riverfront (described under "Sights in Ljubljana"), a colorful **flea market** hops along the castle side of the Ljubljanica River (south of the TI) every Sun 8:00–14:00.

Money: Most banks are open Mon–Fri 8:00–12:00 & 15:00–17:00, a few also open Sat 9:00–12:00, closed Sun.

Internet Access: Most hotel lobbies have Internet access for guests. The TI at the upper end of the market has several terminals (€1/30 min, see "Tourist Information," earlier). **Cyber Café Xplorer** is twice as expensive but has longer hours (Mon–Fri 10:00–22:00, Sat–Sun 14:00–22:00, across the river from the market at Petkovškovo nabrežje 23).

Post Office: The main post office *(pošta)* is in a beautiful yellow Art Nouveau building a block up Čopova from Prešeren Square, at the intersection with the busy Slovenska cesta (Mon–Fri 8:00–19:00, Sat 8:00–13:00, closed Sun).

Architecture Guidebooks: Ljubljana is a turn-on for architecture buffs. If you want to learn more about this city's quirky buildings, consider the excellent €13.50 architecture guidebook, or the €17 book about Jože Plečnik's work (sold at the Jože Plečnik House, some TIs, and many bookstores).

Map Store: **Kod & Kam** has a huge selection of maps, English guidebooks, and other books about Slovenia (Mon–Fri 8:00–20:00, Sat 8:00–13:00, closed Sun, near the train station at Miklošičeva cesta 34).

Laundry: Most hotels can do your laundry, but it's pricey. **Hostel Celica** serves as the town's self-serve launderette (€7/load, not very central at Metelkova 8, hostel guests have priority for using the machines; described later, under "Sleeping in Ljubljana"). Or try **Chemoexpress,** where you can drop your laundry off in the morning and pick it up in the afternoon (€4.20/kilo, figure about €20–25 for a full load, Mon–Fri 7:00–18:00, closed Sat–Sun, hiding in a courtyard at Wolfova

Ljubljana Essentials

English	Slovene	Pronounced
Ljubljana Castle	Ljubljanski Grad	lyoob-lyee-AHN-skee grahd
Prešeren Square	Prešernov trg	preh-SHEHR-nohv turg
Congress Square	Kongresni trg	kohn-GREHS-nee turg
French Revolution Square	Trg Francoske Revolucije	turg frant-SOH-skeh reh-voh-LOOT-see-yeh
Square of the Republic	Trg Republike	turg-reh-POOB lee-keh
Triple Bridge	Tromostovje	troh-moh-STOHV-yeh
Cobblers' Bridge	Čevljarski Most	chehv-LAR-skee mohst
Dragon Bridge	Zmajski Most	ZMAY-skee mohst
Jože Plečnik, the architect	Jože Plečnik	YOH-zheh PLAYCH-neek
France Prešeren, the poet	France Prešeren	FRAHN-tseh preh-SHAY-rehn

12, tel. 01/231-0782).

Car Rental: Figure about €60 per day (includes tax and insurance, no extra charge for drop-off elsewhere in Slovenia). Handy options include **Europcar** (in City Hotel at Dalmatinova 15, mobile 031-382-052, www.europcar.si) and **Avis** (Čufarjeva 2, tel. 01/430-8010, www.avis.si).

Best Views: If The Skyscraper's observation deck is open to visitors, it offers the best views in town (see page 418). Views from the castle are nearly as good. At street level, my favorite views are from the wooden bridge called the "Ugly Duckling" (between the Triple and Cobblers' bridges), especially at night. On sunny, blue-sky days, the colorful architecture on and near Prešeren Square pops, and you'll take photos like crazy along the river promenade.

Getting Around Ljubljana

By Bus: Virtually all of Ljubljana's sights are easily accessible by foot, so public transportation probably isn't necessary. And it's a bit of a headache: To ride a bus, you first have to buy a plastic card, called the "Urbana," for €2 (nonrefundable), which you then load with credit to pay for rides. A ride costs €0.80, but you can't pay the driver—you have to use the card (shareable by up to three people). You can buy the Urbana card at the TI, bus station, and some newsstands. Transit info: www.lpp.si.

By Taxi: While there are several companies charging different rates, taxis usually start at about €1.50, and then charge €1 per kilometer. Additional "surcharges" (such as for luggage) are bogus—and are often tacked on as a surprise after you reach your destination. Crooked cabbies are a big problem in Ljubljana (especially those hanging out at the train station). A ride within the city center (such as from the station to a hotel) should run only a few euros, generally less than €5. Your best strategy is to ask for an estimate up front. The cabbie will probably want to just take you for a flat price without using the meter. This is the easiest solution, but realize you'll probably wind up paying a euro or two more than you would if he used the meter. (If you're feeling stingy and feisty, try insisting on the meter.) Another common trick is to charge you the "Sunday and holidays" *(nedelja in počitnice)* rate even on weekdays. If you're suspicious, ask your cabbie to explain why he's chosen the tariff. Your odds of getting an honest cabbie are better if you call for a taxi, and it's always cheaper than hailing one on the street. Don't be intimidated—dispatchers generally speak some English, and your hotel, restaurant, or maybe the TI (if they're not too busy) can call a cab for you. **Yellow Taxi** is more reputable than the norm (mobile 041-731-831); **Metro Taxi** is known for being inexpensive (mobile 041-240-200).

By Bike: Ljubljana is a cyclist's delight, with lots of well-marked bike lanes. A few hotels have rental or loaner bikes, or you can rent bikes at the market square TI (€1/2 hrs, €5/day; see "Tourist Information," earlier).

Tours in Ljubljana

Most of Ljubljana's museums are disappointing; the town's ambience, architecture, and public art are its best attraction. To help you appreciate it all, taking a walking tour—either through the TI or by hiring your own local guide—is worth ▲▲.

Walking Tour—The TI organizes excellent two-hour guided town walks of Ljubljana in English, led by knowledgeable guides. In summer, the walk also includes either a trip up to the castle (by funicular or tourist train) or a 30-minute boat ride on the river. From April through September, there are three tours daily: at 10:00, 14:00, and 17:00. From October through March, the walking tour goes daily at 11:00 (€10, meet at Town Hall around corner from Triple Bridge TI).

Local Guides—Having an expert show you around his or her hometown for two hours for €50 has to be the best value in town. Ljubljana's hardworking guides lead tours on a wide variety of topics and can tailor their tour to your interests (figure €50/2 hrs, 50 percent more for same-day booking, contact TI for details, arrange at least 24 hours before). **Marijan Krišković,** who leads tours for me throughout Europe, is an outstanding guide (mobile 040-222-739, kriskovic@yahoo.com). **Barbara Jakopič,** soft-spoken and extremely knowledgeable, is also good (mobile 040-530-870, b_lucky2@yahoo.com). **Minka Kahrič,** who's traveled solo to the North Pole, also leads tours closer to home—including walks around Ljubljana and excursions into the countryside (€50/2-hour walking tour; driving: €80/up to 4 hours, €120/up to 8 hours; mobile 041-805-962, polarnimedo@yahoo.com).

Boat Cruise—Consider seeing the town from the Ljubljanica River. You have two options for your one-hour cruise: with English commentary from a live guide (€10, 2/day in summer), or unguided (€8, hourly in summer 10:00–20:00). For details, check with the TI (weather permitting, few or no cruises Nov–March, departs from near the Triple Bridge—about one block along the embankment away from the market). Because Ljubljana is a small town that's easily seen by foot, this trip is more romantic than informative.

Bike Tour—The TI offers a bike tour of the city by request (€15, 2 hours, 2-person minimum, arrange at least 24 hours ahead, get details at TI).

Self-Guided Spin-Tour

▲▲Prešeren Square

The heart of Ljubljana is lively Prešeren Square (Prešernov trg). It's always been bustling, but now it's more people-friendly than ever, since the mayor recently outlawed buses and taxis here.

The city's meeting point is the large **statue of France Prešeren,** Slovenia's greatest poet, whose works include the lyrics to the Slovenian national anthem (and whose silhouette adorns Slovenia's €2 coin). The statue shows Prešeren, an important catalyst of 19th-century Slovenian nationalism, being inspired from overhead by a Muse. This statue provoked a scandal and outraged the bishop when it went up a century ago—a naked woman sharing the square with a church! To ensure that nobody could be confused about

Ljubljana at a Glance

▲▲▲**People-Watching** Ljubljana's single best activity is sitting at an outdoor café along the river and watching the vivacious, stylish, fun-loving Slovenes strut their stuff. **Hours:** 24/7.

▲▲**Riverside Market** Lively market area in the Old Town with produce, clothing, souvenirs—even wild boar salami. **Hours:** Best in the morning, especially Sat; market hall open Mon–Fri 7:00–16:00, Sat 7:00–14:00, closed Sun.

▲▲**Serbian Orthodox Church of Sts. Cyril and Methodius** Beautifully decorated house of worship giving insight into the Orthodox faith. **Hours:** Tue–Sun 9:00–12:00 & 14:00–18:00, closed Mon.

▲▲**National and University Library** Jože Plečnik's pièce de résistance, with an intriguing facade, piles of books, and a bright reading room. **Hours:** Main stairwell open Mon–Fri 9:00–20:00, Sat 9:00–14:00, closed Sun; student reading room open to the public mid-July–mid-Aug Mon–Fri 14:00–20:00.

▲▲**Jože Plečnik House** Final digs of the famed hometown architect who shaped so much of Ljubljana, explained by an enthusiastic guide. **Hours:** English tours begin at the top of each hour Tue–Thu 10:00–18:00, Sat 9:00–15:00, last tour departs one hour before closing, closed Sun–Mon and Fri, and possibly closed at other times while undergoing renovation—call ahead.

the woman's intentions, she's conspicuously depicted with typical Muse accessories: a laurel branch and a cloak. Even so, for the first few years they covered the scandalous statue with a tarp each night. And the model who posed for the Muse was so disgraced that no one in Slovenia would hire her—so she emigrated to South America and never returned.

Stand at the base of the statue to get oriented. The bridge crossing the Ljubljanica River is one of Ljubljana's most important landmarks, Jože Plečnik's **Triple Bridge** (Tromostovje). The middle (widest) part of this bridge already existed, but Plečnik added the two side spans to more efficiently funnel the six streets of traffic on this side of the bridge to the one street on the other side. The bridge's Venetian vibe is intentional: Plečnik recognized that Ljubljana, located midway between Venice and then-capital Vienna, is itself a bridge between the Italian and Germanic worlds. Across the bridge is the TI, WCs, ATMs, market and cathedral (to the left), and the Town Hall (straight ahead).

Now turn 90 degrees to the right, and look down the first

▲▲**Slovenian Ethnographic Museum** Engaging, well-presented collection celebrating Slovenian culture. **Hours:** Tue–Sun 10:00–18:00, closed Mon.

▲**Dragon Bridge** Distinctive Art Nouveau bridge adorned with the city's mascot. **Hours:** Always roaring.

▲**Ljubljana Castle** Tower with good views and so-so 3-D film. **Hours:** Grounds open daily May–Sept 9:00–23:00, Oct–April 10:00–21:00; castle open daily May–Sept 9:00–21:00, Oct–April 10:00–18:00, film plays all day on the half-hour.

▲**Contemporary History Museum** Baroque mansion in Tivoli Park, with exhibit highlighting Slovenia's last 100 years. **Hours:** Tue–Sun 10:00–18:00, closed Mon.

▲**City Museum of Ljubljana** Modern, high-tech exhibit on the city's history. **Hours:** Tue–Sun 10:00–18:00, closed Mon.

▲**Cobblers' Bridge** Columned bridge that epitomizes Jože Plečnik's distinctive architectural style. **Hours:** Always open.

▲**Architectural Museum of Ljubljana** Castle with Plečnik exhibit on the edge of town. **Hours:** Mon–Fri 9:00–15:00, Sat 10:00–18:00, Sun 10:00–15:00.

street after the riverbank. Find the pale woman in the picture frame on the second floor of the first yellow house. This is **Julija,** the unrequited love of Prešeren's life. Tour guides spin romantic tales about how the couple met. But the truth is far less exciting: He was a teacher in her father's house when he was in his 30s and she was four. Later in life, she inspired him from afar—as she does now,

from across the square—but they never got together. She may have been his muse, but when it came to marriage, she opted for wealth and status.

In 1895, a devastating earthquake destroyed half the city. While tragic, it allowed Ljubljana to rebuild in style. Today Ljubljana—especially the streets around this square—is an architecture-lover's paradise. The **Hauptmann**

House, to the right of Julija, was the only building on the square to survive the quake. A few years later, the owner redecorated it in the then-trendy Viennese Art Nouveau style you see today, using bright colors (since his family sold dyes). All that remains of the original is the little Baroque balcony above the entrance.

Just to the right of the Hauptmann House is a car-sized **model** of the city center—helpful for orientation. The street next to it (with the McDonald's) is **Čopova,** once the route of Ljubljana's Sunday promenade. A century ago, locals would put on their Sunday best and stroll from here to Tivoli Park, listening to musicians and dropping into cafés along the way. Plečnik called it the "lifeline of the city," connecting the green lungs of the park to this urban center. Today, busy Slovenska avenue and railroad tracks cross the route, making the promenade less inviting. But in the last decade, Ljubljana has been trying to recapture its golden age, and some downtown streets are pedestrian-only on weekends once again. The new evening *paseo* thrives along the river between the Triple Bridge and Cobblers' Bridge.

Continue looking to the right, past the big, pink landmark Franciscan Church of St. Mary. The characteristic glass awning

marks **Centromerkur**—the first big post-quake department store, today government-protected. At the top of the building is Mercury, god of commerce, watching over the square that has been Ljubljana's commercial heart since the city began. (If you look carefully, you can see the mustachioed face of the building's owner hiding in the folds of cloth by Mercury's left foot.) Since this area was across the river from medieval Ljubljana (beyond the town's limits...and the long arm of its tax collector), it was the best place to sell and buy goods. Today it's the heart of Ljubljana's boutique culture.

The street between Centromerkur and the pink church is **Miklošičeva cesta,** which connects Prešeren Square to the train station. When Ljubljana was rebuilding after the 1895 earthquake, town architects and designers envisioned this street as a showcase of its new, Vienna-inspired Art Nouveau image.

Up Miklošičeva street and on the left is the prominent **Grand Hotel Union,** with a stately domed spire on the corner. When these buildings were designed, Prague was the cultural capital of the Slavic world. The new look of Ljubljana paid homage to "the golden city of a hundred spires" (and copied Prague's romantic image). The city actually had a law for several years that new corner buildings had to have these spires. Even the trees you'll see around town were part of the vision. When the architect Plečnik designed the Ljubljanica River embankments a generation later, he planted tall, pointy poplar trees and squat, rounded willows—imitating the spires and domes of Prague.

Detour a block up Miklošičeva cesta to see two more architectural gems of that era (across from the Grand Hotel Union): First is

a Secessionist building—marked **Zadružna Zveza**—with classic red, blue, and white colors (for the Slovenian flag). Next is the noisy, pink, zigzagged **Cooperative Bank.** The bank was designed by Ivan Vurnik, an ambitious Slovenian architect who wanted to invent a distinctive national style after World War I, when the Habsburg Empire broke up and Eastern Europe's nations were proudly emerging for the first time.

Prešeren Square is the perfect springboard to explore the rest of Ljubljana. Now that you're oriented, visit some of the areas listed next.

Sights in Ljubljana

East of the River, Under the Castle: The Market and Old Town

The castle side of the river is the city's most colorful and historic quarter, packed with Old World ambience.

▲▲**Riverside Market (Tržnice)**—In Ljubljana's thriving Old Town market, big-city Slovenes enjoy buying directly from the producer. Prices go down as the day gets late and as the week goes on. The market, worth an amble anytime, is best on Saturday mornings, when the townspeople take their time wandering the stalls. In this tiny capital of a tiny country, you may even see the president searching for the perfect melon.

Begin your walk through the market at the Triple Bridge (and TI). The riverside **colonnade,** which echoes the long-gone medieval city wall, was designed by (who else?) Jože Plečnik. This first stretch—nearest the Triple Bridge—is good for souvenirs: wood-carvings, miniature painted frontboards from beehives, honey products (including honey brandy), and lots of colorful candles (bubbly Marta will gladly paint a special message on your candle for no extra charge).

Farther in, the market is almost all local, and the colonnade is populated by butchers, bakers, fishermen, and lazy cafés. Peek down at the actual river and see how the architect wanted the town and river to connect. The lower arcade is a people zone, with easy access from the bridge, public WCs, inviting cafés, and a stinky fish market *(ribarnica)* offering a wide variety. The recommended restaurant just below, **Ribca,** serves fun fishy plates, beer, and coffee with great riverside seating (open Mon–Fri 8:00–16:00, Sat 8:00–14:00, closed Sun).

Across from the stairs down into the fish market, about where the souvenir stands end, you reach the first small market square. On your right, notice the 10-foot-tall concrete **cone.** Plečnik wanted to make Ljubljana the "Athens of the North" and imagined a huge hilltop cone crowning the center of a national acropolis—a complex for government, museums, and culture. This ambitious plan didn't make it off the drawing board, but part of Plečnik's Greek idea came true: this marketplace, based on an ancient Greek *agora.* Plečnik's cone still captures the Slovenes' imaginations...and adorns Slovenia's €0.10 coin.

At the top of this square, you'll find the 18th-century **cathedral** *(stolnica)* standing on the site of a 13th-century Romanesque church. The cathedral is dedicated to St. Nicholas, protector against floods and patron saint of the fishermen and boatmen who have long come to sell their catch at the market. Go under the high arch, then take a close look at the intricately decorated side door on the left. This remarkable door was created for Pope John Paul II's visit here in 1996. Buried deeply in the fecund soil of their ancient and pagan history, the nation's linden tree of life sprouts with the story of the Slovenes. The ceramic pots represent the original Roman settlement here. Just to the left, above the tree, are the Byzantine missionaries Cyril and Methodius, who came here to convert the Slavs to Christianity in the ninth century. Just above, Crusaders and Ottomans do battle. Near the top, see the Slovenes going into the cave—entering the dark 20th century (World War I, World War II, and communism). At the top is Pope John Paul II (the first Slavic pontiff, who also oversaw the fall of communism). Below him are two men who are on track for becoming Slovenia's first saints; the one on the right is Frederic Baraga, a 19th-century bishop who became a missionary in Michigan and codified Chippewa grammar (notice the Native American relief on the book he's holding). In the upper right-hand corner is a sun, which has been shining since Slovenia gained its independence in 1991. Around back of the cathedral is a similar door, carved with images of the six 20th-century bishops of Ljubljana.

The cathedral's interior is stunning Italian Baroque (free, open long hours daily but closed 12:00–15:00). The transept is surrounded by sculptures of four bishops of Roman Ljubljana (when it was called Emona, or Aemon). The bust on the right depicts Anton Vovk, a 20th-century bishop who's one miracle shy of beatification. Left of the main altar, notice the distinctive chair. This was designed by the very religious Jože Plečnik, whose brother was a priest here. Look up over the nave to enjoy the recently restored, gorgeous ceiling fresco.

The building at the end of the first market square is the seminary palace. In the basement is a **market hall,** with vendors selling cheeses, meats, baked goods, dried fruits, nuts, and other goodies (Mon–Fri 7:00–16:00, Sat 7:00–14:00, closed Sun). This place is worth a graze. Most merchants are happy to give you a free sample (point to what you want, and say *probat, prosim*—"a taste, please").

When you leave the market hall, continue downstream into the big **main market square,** packed with produce and clothing stands. (The colorful flower market hides behind the market hall.) The row of vendors nearest the colonnade sell fruit from all over, but the ones located deeper in the market sell only locally grown produce. These producers go out of their way to be old-fashioned—a few of them still follow the tradition of pushing their veggies on wooden carts (called *cizas*) to the market from their garden patches in the suburbs. Once at the market, they simply display their goods on top of their cart, turning it into a sales kiosk. Tell the vendor what you want—it's considered rude for customers to touch the fruits and vegetables before they're bought. Over time, shoppers develop friendships with their favorite producers. On busy days, you'll see a long line at one stand, while the other merchants stand bored. Your choice is simple: Get in line, or eat subpar produce.

Near the market hall, look for the little **scales** in the wooden kiosks marked *Kontrolna Tehtnica*—allowing buyers to immediately check whether the producer cheated them (not a common problem, but just in case). The Habsburg days left locals with the old German saying, "Trust is good; control is better."

At the corner of this market square (toward Prešeren Square), you'll notice a big gap along the riverfront colonnade. This was to be the site of a huge, roofed **Butchers' Bridge** designed by Jože Plečnik, but those plans never materialized. Aware of Plečnik's newfound touristic currency, a few years back some town politicians dusted off the old plans and proposed building the bridge. (In fact, at one point an overzealous politician even placed a cornerstone for the project.) But after all that talk, the new bridge on this site is based on modern designs (not Plečnik's).

Just beyond the end of the market colonnade is the...

▲**Dragon Bridge (Zmajski Most)**—The dragon has been the symbol of Ljubljana for centuries, ever since Jason (of Argonauts

and Golden Fleece fame) supposedly slew one in a nearby swamp. This is one of the few notable bits of Ljubljana architecture not by Plečnik (but by Jurij Zaninović, a fellow student of Vienna architect Otto Wagner). While the dragon is the star of this very photogenic Art Nouveau bridge, the bridge itself was officially dedicated to the 40th anniversary of Habsburg Emperor Franz Josef's reign (see the dates on the side: 1848–1888). Tapping into the emp's vanity got new projects funded—vital as the city rebuilt after its devastating earthquake of 1895. But the Franz Josef name never stuck; those dragons are just too darn memorable.

▲**Town Square (Mestni Trg) and the Old Town**—Ljubljana's Town Square, just across the Triple Bridge and up the street from Prešeren Square, is home to the **Town Hall** (Rotovž), highlighted by its clock tower and pillared loggia. Step inside the Renaissance courtyard to see artifacts and a map of late 17th-century Ljubljana. Studying this map, notice how the river, hill, and wall worked together to fortify the town. Courtyards like this (but humbler) are hidden throughout the city. As rent in these old places is cheap, many such courtyards host funky and characteristic little businesses. Be sure to get off the main drag and poke into Ljubljana's nooks and crannies.

In the square is a recent replica of the **Fountain of Three Carniolian Rivers,** inspired in style and theme by Rome's many fountains. (The original is in a museum.) The figures with vases represent this region's three main rivers: Ljubljanica, Sava, and Krka. This is one of many works in town by Francesco Robba, an Italian who came to Ljubljana for one job, fell in love with a Slovene, and stayed here the rest of his life—decorating the city's churches with beautiful Baroque altars.

In the early 19th century, Ljubljana consisted mainly of this single street, running along the base of Castle Hill (plus a small "New Town" across the river). Stretching south from here are two other "squares"—Stari trg (Old Square) and Gornji trg (Upper Square)—which have long since grown together into one big, atmospheric promenade lined with quaint boutiques, great restaurants, and cafés (perfect for a stroll). Virtually every house along this drag has a story to tell, of a famous resident or infamous incident. As you walk, keep your eyes open for Ljubljana's mascot dragon—it's everywhere. At the end of the pedestrian zone (at Gornji trg), look uphill and notice the village charms of some of the oldest buildings in town (four medieval houses with rooflines slanted at the ends, different from the others on this street).

▲**Ljubljana Castle (Ljubljanski Grad)**—The castle above town offers enjoyable views of Ljubljana and the surrounding

countryside. There has probably been a settlement on this site since prehistoric times, though the first fortress here was Roman. The 12th-century version was gradually added on to over the centuries, until it fell into disrepair in the 17th century. Today's castle was rebuilt in the 1940s, renovated in the 1970s, and is still technically unfinished (subject to ongoing additions). The castle houses a restaurant, a gift shop, temporary exhibition halls, and a Gothic chapel with Baroque paintings of the coat of arms of St. George (Ljubljana's patron saint, the dragon-slayer). Above the restaurant are two wedding halls—Ljubljana's most popular places to get married (free for locals). While the castle and its attractions are ho-hum, the views are worth the trip.

It's free to enter the castle grounds (daily May–Sept 9:00–23:00, Oct–April 10:00–21:00, tel. 01/232-9994). Inside are two optional activities you have to pay for (€3.50 covers both, daily May–Sept 9:00–21:00, Oct–April 10:00–18:00): the **castle tower,** with 92 steps leading to one of the best views in town; and a 23-minute **3-D film** about the history of Ljubljana (touted as a "virtual museum," but barely worth your time; plays all day on the half-hour).

Tours of the castle in Slovene and English leave from the entry bridge daily June through mid-September at 10:00, 11:00, 14:00, and 16:00 (€5, tour lasts 1–1.5 hours). The castle is also home to the Ljubljana Summer Festival, with **concerts** throughout the summer (tel. 01/426-4340, www.festival-lj.si).

Getting to the Castle: A slick **funicular** whisks visitors to the top in a jiff (€1.80 one-way, €3 round-trip, every 10 min, 1-min ride, daily May–Sept 9:00–23:00, Oct–April 10:00–21:00, catch it at Krekov trg, across the street from the market square TI). From the top, you'll find free WCs and a few easy flights of stairs up into the heart of the castle complex (or take the elevator). Another sweat-free route to the top is via the **tourist train** that leaves at the top of each hour (or more frequently, with demand) from in front of the Triple Bridge TI (€3 round-trip, daily in summer 9:00–21:00, shorter hours off-season, doesn't run in snow or other bad weather). There are also two handy **trails** to the castle. The steeper-but-faster route begins near the Dragon Bridge (find Študentovska lane, just past the statue of Vodnik in the market). Slower but a bit less steep is Reber, just off Stari trg (Old Square), a few blocks south of the Town Hall. Walk up to the top of Reber; at the dead end, turn right and start climbing up the stairs. From here on out, always bear left, then go right when you're just under the castle (follow *Grad* signs).

West of the River, Beyond Prešeren Square: The Museum Zone and Tivoli Park

The Prešeren Square (west) side of the river is the heart of modern Ljubljana, and home to several prominent squares and fine museums. These sights are listed roughly in order from Prešeren Square and can be linked to make an interesting walk.

• *Leave Prešeren Square in the direction the poet is looking, bear to your left (up Wolfova, by the picture of Julija), and walk a block to...*

Congress Square (Kongresni Trg)—This grassy, tree-lined square is ringed by some of Ljubljana's most important buildings: the University headquarters, the Baroque Ursuline Church of the Holy Trinity, a classical mansion called the Kazina, and the Philharmonic Hall. At the top end of the square, by the entry to a pedestrian underpass, a Roman sarcophagus sits under a gilded statue of a **Roman citizen**—a replica of an artifact from 1,700 years ago, when this town was called Emona. The busy street above you has been the main trading route through town since ancient Roman times. This square hosts the big town events. Locals remember how, when President Clinton visited, tens of thousands packed the square.

• *Take the underpass beneath busy Slovenska avenue (the town's main traffic thoroughfare), then continue straight through the shopping mall into the...*

▲Square of the Republic (Trg Republike)—This unusual square is essentially a parking lot ringed by an odd collection of buildings. While hardly quaint, the Square of the Republic gives you a good taste of a modern corner of Ljubljana. And it's

historic—this is where Slovenia declared its independence in 1991.

The **twin office towers** (with the world's biggest digital watch, flashing the date, time, and temperature) were designed by Plečnik's protégé, Edvard Ravnikar. As harrowing as these seem, imagine if they had followed the original plans—twice as tall as they are now, and connected by a bridge, representing the gateway to Ljubljana. These buildings were originally designed as the Slovenian parliament, but they were scaled back when Tito didn't approve (since it would have made Slovenia's parliament bigger than the Yugoslav parliament in Belgrade). Instead, the **Slovenian Parliament** is across the square, in the strangely low-profile office building with the sculpted entryway. The carvings are in the Socialist Realist style, celebrating the noble Slovenian people conforming to communist ideals for the good of the entire society. Completing the square are a huge conference center (Cankarjev Dom, the white building behind the skyscrapers), a shopping mall, and some public art.

• *Just a block north, through the grassy park (Trg Narodni Herojev), you'll find the...*

Slovenian National Museum (Narodni Muzej Slovenije) and Slovenian Museum of Natural History (Prirodoslovni Muzej Slovenije)

—These two museums share a single historic building facing a park behind the Parliament. While neither collection is particularly good, they're both worth considering if you have a special interest or if it's a rainy day (€3 for each museum, or €5 for both, some English descriptions, daily 10:00–18:00, Thu until 20:00, Muzejska 1, tel. 01/241-4400, www.narmuz-lj.si and www.pms-lj.si).

The **National Museum** occupies the ground floor, featuring a lapidarium with carved-stone Roman monuments and exhibits on Egyptian mummies. (Temporary exhibits are also on this level.) Upstairs and to the right are more exhibits of the National Museum, with archaeological findings ranging from old armor and pottery to the museum's two prized possessions: a fragment of a 45,000-year-old Neanderthal flute, supposedly the world's oldest musical instrument; and the "figural situla," a beautifully decorated bronze bucket from 500 B.C. (The National Museum also has a newer branch in the Metelkova district, described later.)

Upstairs and to the left is the **Natural History** exhibit, featuring the flora and fauna of Slovenia. You'll see partial skeletons of a mammoth and a cave bear, plenty of stuffed reptiles, fish, and birds, and an exhibit on "human fish" (*Proteus anguinus*—long, skinny, pale-pink amphibians).

• *At the far end of the building is a glassed-in annex displaying Roman stone monuments (free). Turning left around the museum building and walking one block, you'll see the...*

US Embassy—This pretty yellow chalet (with brown trim and a red roof, at Prešernova cesta 31) wins my vote for quaintest embassy building in the world. Resist the urge to snap a photo... those guards are all business.

• *Just up Prešernova street from the embassy are two decent but skippable art museums.*

National Gallery (Narodna Galerija)—This museum has three parts: European artists, Slovenian artists, and temporary exhibits. Find the work of Ivana Kobilca, a late 19th-century Slovenian Impressionist. Art-lovers enjoy her self-portrait in *Summer*. If you're going to Bled, you can get a sneak preview with Marko Pernhart's huge panorama of the Julian Alps (€7, more for special exhibits, permanent collection free first Sun of the month, open Tue–Sun 10:00–18:00, closed Mon, enter through old-fashioned facade at Cankarjeva 20, another entrance is at big glass box between two older buildings at Prešernova 24, tel. 01/241-5418, www.ng-slo.si).

Museum of Modern Art (Moderna Galerija Ljubljana)—This museum has a ho-hum permanent collection of modern and contemporary Slovenian artists, as well as temporary exhibits by both Slovenes and international artists. Having recently undergone an extensive renovation, it might be open in time for your visit (if open: likely €4, Tue–Sun 10:00–18:00, closed Mon, Tomšičeva 14, tel. 01/241-6800, www.mg-lj.si).

• *By the busy road near the art museums, look for the distinctive Neo-Byzantine design (tall domes with narrow slits) of the...*

▲▲Serbian Orthodox Church of Sts. Cyril and Methodius—Ljubljana's most striking church interior isn't Catholic, but Orthodox. This church was built in 1936, soon after the Slovenes joined a political union with the Serbs. Wealthy Slovenia attracted its poorer neighbors from the south—so it built this church for that community. Since 1991, the Serb population continues to grow, as people from the struggling corners of the former Yugoslavia flock to prosperous Slovenia.

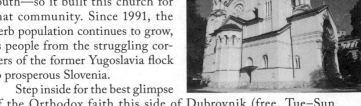

Step inside for the best glimpse of the Orthodox faith this side of Dubrovnik (free, Tue–Sun 9:00–12:00 & 14:00–18:00, closed Mon). The church is colorfully

decorated without a hint of the 21st century, mirroring a very conservative religion. You'll see Cyrillic script in this building, which feels closer to Moscow than to Rome. Notice that there are no pews, because worshippers stand throughout the service. On the left, find the little room with tubs of water, where the faithful light tall, skinny beeswax candles (purchased at the little window in the back corner). The painted screen, or iconostasis, is believed to separate our material world from the spiritual realm behind it. Ponder the fact that several centuries ago, before the Catholic Church began to adapt to a changing world, all Christians worshipped this way. For more on the Orthodox faith, see the sidebar on page 278.
• *On the other side of the busy street is...*

Tivoli Park (Park Tivoli)—This huge park, just west of the center, is where Slovenes relax on summer weekends. The easiest access is

through the graffiti-covered underpass from Cankarjeva cesta (between the Serbian Orthodox Church and the Museum of Modern Art). As you emerge, the Neoclassical pillars leading down the promenade clue you in that this part of the park was designed by Jože Plečnik. Along this "main boulevard" of the park, various changing photographic exhibitions are displayed.

• *Aside from taking a leisurely stroll, the best thing to do in the park is visit the...*

▲Contemporary History Museum (Muzej Novejše Zgodovine)—In a Baroque mansion (Cekinov Grad) in Tivoli Park, a well-done exhibit called "Slovenians in the 20th Century" traces the last hundred years of Slovenia—essentially from the end of World War I to independence in 1991. Out front is a T-55 Yugoslav tank that was commandeered by the Slovenes during their war for independence. Inside, the ground floor displays temporary exhibits, and upstairs you'll find several rooms using models, dioramas, and light-and-sound effects to creatively tell the story of one of Europe's youngest nations. It's a little difficult to fully appreciate, even with the good English descriptions. But the creativity and the spunky spirit of the place are truly enjoyable. The "Slovenia 1945–1960" exhibit outlines both the good and the bad of the early Tito years (including a photo album with Tito's visits to Slovenia). But the most evocative room has artifacts from the Slovenes' brave declaration of independence from a hostile Yugoslavia in 1991. The well-organized Slovenes had only to weather a 10-day skirmish to gain their freedom. Camouflage-clad mannequins represent the two sides that stared each other down during this tense standoff—the ragtag but determined Slovenian militia (on the left) and the well-equipped but unmotivated Yugoslav National Army (on the right). It's chilling to think that bombers were en route to level this gorgeous city. The planes were called back at the last minute, by a Yugoslav National Army officer with allegiances to Slovenia (€3.50, permanent exhibit free first Sun of the month, open Tue–Sun 10:00–18:00, closed Mon, in Tivoli Park at Celovška cesta 23, tel. 01/300-9610, www.muzej-nz.si).

Getting There: The museum is a 20-minute walk from the center, best combined with a wander through Tivoli Park. The fastest approach: As you emerge from the Cankarjeva cesta underpass into the park, climb up the stairs, then turn right and go straight ahead for five minutes. You'll continue straight up the ramp, then turn left after the tennis courts and look for the big pink-and-white mansion on the hill.

• *Hungry? Straight ahead and down the stairs from the museum, look for the "Hot Horse" food kiosk, selling €4 horseburgers (no joke). A local institution, this is a popular place to get together with friends and neighbors. The giant, modern, blocky, light-blue building across the busy road is the Pivovarna Union—the brewery for Ljubljana's favorite brew.*

On your way back to the center, consider stopping by...

The Skyscraper (Nebotičnik)—This 1933 Art Deco building was the first skyscraper in Slovenia, for a time the tallest building in Central Europe, and one of the earliest European buildings that was clearly influenced by American architecture. The Skyscraper's observation deck offers the best view of Ljubljana's skyline; unfortunately, it's been closed to the public for years. However, an investor is carrying out an extensive renovation project, and hopes to open it to visitors in early 2010 (ask TI for details; The Skyscraper is 2 blocks from Prešeren Square at Štefanova ulica 1).

• *A few blocks south, near several Jože Plečnik sights (see next section) at the river end of French Revolution Square, you'll find the...*

▲City Museum of Ljubljana (Mestni Muzej Ljubljana)—This thoughtfully presented museum, located in the recently restored Auersperg Palace, offers a high-tech, in-depth look at the "Faces of Ljubljana." You'll begin your visit in the cellar, with Roman ruins (including remains of the original Roman road and sewer system, found right here and displayed *in situ*) and layers of medieval artifacts. Touchscreens provide more information.

Then you'll head up to the first floor, which traces the social history of Ljubljana through the eyes of its participants: men (see the creatively painted shooting targets, from the "country clubs" of the late 18th-century aristocracy); women (with stories and artifacts of six women who've had an impact on the city); children (who were hidden from the authorities during the Nazi occupation); and youth (specifically in the 1960s and 1970s, when Ljubljana's Šumi bar was Yugoslavia's answer to Haight-Ashbury).

Various themed exhibits fill the second floor. One traces how the city's role has evolved over time. In another room, pay close attention to Slovenia's short-lived currency, the *tolar* (1991–2006). Rather than heads of state and generals, all of the notables pictured on these bills were artists and scientists. The most interesting exhibit ("From State to State") explains how Ljubljana has belonged to 10 different states over the last 200 years, ranging from the genteel Habsburg Empire to the oppressive Nazi regime to membership in the benevolent EU. Another exhibit examines the modern woes of traffic, including noise and air pollution, and gives you the opportunity to sit in a mustard-yellow, communist-era Fiat Fičko car.

Rounding out the collection is a relaxing 15-minute movie and a range of special exhibits on the ground floor. Though everything is well-described in English, a student on the museum's staff might be able to show you around if it's not too busy—ask (entry-€4, Tue–Sun 10:00–18:00, closed Mon, kid-friendly, Gosposka 15, tel. 01/241-2500, www.mestnimuzej.si).

• *If visiting the museum, don't miss the nearby National University Library and French Revolution Square—both described in the next section.*

South of Prešeren Square: Jože Plečnik's Architecture

Jože Plečnik is to Ljubljana what Antoni Gaudí is to Barcelona: a homegrown and amazingly prolific genius who shaped his town with a uniquely beautiful vision. And, as in Barcelona, Ljubljana has a way of turning people who couldn't care less about architecture into huge Plečnik fans. There's plenty to see. In addition to the Triple Bridge, the riverside market, and the sights listed here, Plečnik designed the embankments along the Ljubljanica and Gradaščica Rivers in the Trnovo neighborhood; the rebuilt Roman wall along Mirje street, south of the center; the Church of St. Francis, with its classicist bell tower; St. Michael's Church on the Marsh; Orel Stadium; Žale Cemetery; and many more buildings throughout Slovenia.

Some of the best Plečnik sights are near the river, just south of Congress and Prešeren squares. I've linked them up in the order of a short self-guided walk.

• *From Prešeren Square, stroll south along the river. After the plain wooden bridge called the "Ugly Duckling," you'll come to the...*

▲**Cobblers' Bridge (Čevljarski Most)**—Named for the actual cobblers (shoemakers) who set up shop along the river in olden times, the bridge encapsulates Plečnik's style perhaps better than

any other structure: simple, clean lines adorned with classical columns. Ideal for people-watching (with the castle hovering scenically overhead), this is one of Ljubljana's most appealing spots.

• *Continue past the Cobblers' Bridge on the right side of the river. After about a block, turn right up the parked-up street called Novi trg. At the top of this street, on the left, is a red-brick building embedded with gray granite blocks in an irregular checkerboard pattern. This is the...*

▲▲National and University Library (Narodna in Univerzitetna Knjižnica, or NUK)—Widely regarded as Plečnik's

masterpiece, this building is a bit underwhelming...until an understanding of its symbolism brings it to life. On the surface, the red-and-gray color scheme evokes the red soil and chunks of granite of the Karst region, south of Ljubljana. But on a deeper level, the library's design conveys the message of overcoming obstacles to attain knowledge. The odd-sized and -shaped blocks in the facade represent a complex numerological pattern that suggests barriers on the path to enlightenment. The sculpture on the river side is Moses—known for leading his people through 40 years of hardship to the Promised Land. On the

right side of the building, find the horsehead doorknobs—representing the winged horse Pegasus (grab hold, and he'll whisk you away to new levels of enlightenment). Step inside. The main staircase is dark and gloomy—modeled after an Egyptian tomb. But at the top, through the door marked *Velika Čitalnica*, is the bright, airy main reading room: the ultimate goal, a place of learning. The top-floor windows are shaped roughly like open books.

Aside from being a great work of architecture, the building also houses the most important library in Slovenia, with more than two million books (about one per Slovene). The library is supposed to receive a copy of each new book printed in the country. In a freaky bit of bad luck, this was the only building in town damaged in World War II, when a plane crashed into it. But the people didn't want to see their books go up in flames—so hundreds of locals formed a human chain, risking life and limb to get the books out of the burning building.

You can easily duck into the main stairwell (free, Mon–Fri 9:00–20:00, Sat 9:00–14:00, closed Sun). The quiet student reading room is officially open for visitors during very limited hours, when it's technically closed to students (mid-July–mid-Aug Mon–Fri 14:00–20:00). If you're not here during that one-month span, and you're really determined to see the room, you can try sticking close to a student going inside—but note that the guards frown on uninvited visitors. To get out, follow another student—or push gently on the door (it'll likely open easily).

• *Directly behind the library is a mellow square with an obelisk in the middle. This is...*

French Revolution Square (Trg Francoske Revolucije)—

Plečnik designed the **obelisk** in the middle of the square to commemorate Napoleon's short-lived decision to make Ljubljana the capital of his Illyrian Provinces. It's rare to find anything honoring Napoleon outside of Paris, but he was good to Ljubljana. Under his rule, Slovenian culture flourished, schools were established, and roads and infrastructure were improved. The monument contains ashes of the unknown French soldiers who died in 1813, when the region went from French to Austrian control.

The Teutonic Knights of the Cross established the nearby **monastery** (Križanke, ivy-capped wall and gate, free entry) in 1230. The adaptation of these monastery buildings into the Ljubljana Summer Theatre was Plečnik's last major work (1950–1956).

• *From here, it's a scenic 10-minute walk to the next sight. From the obelisk, walk down Emonska toward the twin-spired church. You'll pass (on the left) the delightful Krakovo district—a patch of green countryside in downtown Ljubljana. Many of the veggies you see in the riverside market come from these carefully tended gardens. When you reach the Gradaščica stream, head over the bridge (also designed by Plečnik) and go around the left side of the church to find the house.*

▲▲Jože Plečnik House (Plečnikova Zbirka)—Ljubljana's

favorite son lived here from 1921 until his death in 1957. He added on to an existing house, building a circular bedroom for himself and filling the place with bric-a-brac he designed, as well as

artifacts, photos, and gifts from around the world that inspired him as he shaped Ljubljana. Living a simple, almost monastic lifestyle, Plečnik knew what he liked, and these tastes are mirrored in his house.

Today the house is decorated exactly as it was the day Plečnik

Jože Plečnik
(1872–1957)

There is probably no other single architect who has shaped one city as Jože Plečnik (YOH-zheh PLAYCH-neek) shaped Ljubljana. From libraries, office buildings, cemeteries, and stadiums to landscaping, riverside embankments, and market halls, Plečnik left his mark everywhere. While he may not yet register very high on the international Richter scale of important architects, the Slovenes' pride in this man's work is understandable.

Plečnik was born in Ljubljana and trained as a furniture designer before his interest turned to architecture. He studied in Vienna under the Secessionist architect Otto Wagner. His first commissions, done around the turn of the 20th century in Vienna, were pretty standard Art Nouveau stuff. Then Tomáš Masaryk, president of the new nation of Czechoslovakia, decided that the dull Habsburg design of Prague Castle could use a new look to go with its new independence. But he didn't want

an Austrian architect; it had to be a Slav. In 1921, Masaryk chose Jože Plečnik, who sprinkled the castle grounds with his distinctive touches. By now, Plečnik had perfected his simple, eye-pleasing

died, containing much of his equipment, models, and plans. The house can be toured only with a guide, whose enthusiasm brings the place to life. There are very few barriers, so you are in direct contact with the world of the architect. Still furnished with unique, Plečnik-designed furniture, one-of-a-kind inventions, and favorite souvenirs from his travels, the house paints an unusually intimate portrait of an artist.

While the house initially underwhelms some visitors, it's worth ▲▲▲ for those who get caught up in Ljubljana's idiosyncratic sense of style. As you tour the place, be patient. Listen to its stories. Appreciate the subtle details. Notice how reverently your guide (and other Slovenes) speak of this man. Contrast the humbleness of Plečnik's home with the dynamic impact he had on the cityscape of Ljubljana and the cultural heritage of Slovenia. Wandering Plečnik's hallways, it's hard not to be tickled by this man's sheer creativity and by the unique world he forged for himself to live in. As a visitor to his home, you're in good company. He invited only his closest friends here—except during World War II, when Ljubljana was occupied by Nazis and the university was style, which mixes modern and classical influences, with lots of columns and pyramids—simultaneously austere and playful.

By the time Plečnik finished in Prague, he had made a name for himself. His prime years were spent creating for the Kingdom of Yugoslavia (before the ideology-driven era of Tito). Plečnik returned home to Ljubljana and set to work redesigning the city, both as an architect and as an urban planner. He lived in a humble house behind the Trnovo Church (now a tourable and recommended museum), and on his walk to work every day, he pondered ways to make the city even more livable. Wandering through town, notice how thoughtfully he incorporated people, nature, the Slovenian heritage, town vistas, and symbolism into his works—it's feng shui on a grand urban scale.

For all of Plečnik's ideas that became reality, even more did not. After World War II, the very religious Plečnik fell out of favor with the new communist government and found it more difficult to get his projects completed. (It's fun to imagine how this city might look if Plečnik had always gotten his way.) After his death in 1957, Plečnik was virtually forgotten by Slovenes and scholars alike. His many works in Ljubljana were taken for granted.

But in 1986, an exposition about Plečnik at Paris' Pompidou Center jump-started interest in the architect. Within a few years Plečnik was back in vogue. Today, scholars laud him as a genius who was ahead of his time…while locals and tourists enjoy the elegant simplicity of his works.

closed, Plečnik allowed his students to work with him here.

Possible Closure: As the house is slated to be closed for restoration sometime soon, it's important to ask the TI, check the website, or call the museum to be sure it's open before making the trek out here.

Cost, Hours, Information: €4, Tue–Thu 10:00–18:00, Sat 9:00–15:00, 30-min English tours begin at the top of each hour, last tour departs one hour before closing, closed Sun–Mon and Fri, tel. 01/280-1600, www.aml.si, pz@aml.si. It's well-run by Ana and Natalija, who sometimes lead the tours.

Getting There: It's directly behind the twin steeples of the Trnovo Church, at Karunova ulica 4. The 15-minute stroll from the center—the same one Plečnik took to work each day—is nearly as enjoyable as the house itself. You can either walk south along the river, then turn right onto Gradaška and stroll along the stream to the church; or, from French Revolution Square, head south on Emonska. Either way, you'll pass through the garden-patch district of Krakovo, where pea patches and characteristic Old World buildings gracefully cohabitate. On the way to or from the museum, consider getting a meal in Krakovo (two great restaurants—Pri Škofu and Harambaša—are described later, under "Eating in Ljubljana").

• *The final sight is on the outskirts of town.*

▲**Architectural Museum of Ljubljana (Arhitekturni Muzej Ljubljana)**—If your visit to Ljubljana has infected you with Plečnik fever, you can trek out to this interesting museum, located in Fužine Castle on the outskirts of Ljubljana. The permanent exhibit features parts of the 1986 Paris exhibition that made Plečnik famous all over again. Downstairs is a display of plans and photos from Plečnik's earlier works in Vienna and Prague, and upstairs, you'll find an exhibit on his works in Slovenia, including some detailed plans and models for ambitious projects he never completed (like the huge, cone-shaped parliament building atop Castle Hill). It's worthwhile, but a bit of a hassle to reach—only true enthusiasts should pay a visit (€3, Mon–Fri 9:00–15:00, Sat 10:00–18:00, Sun 10:00–15:00, last entry 30 min before closing, Pot na Fužine 2, tel. 01/540-9798, www.aml.si). Take bus #20 or #22 from near Congress Square (direction: Fužine) to the end of the line (about 20 min).

Museums in Metelkova, Northeast of Prešeren Square

These two museums, in the dull but up-and-coming district of Metelkova, face each other on a slick modern plaza next to the park called Tabor. They are about a 10-minute walk northeast of Prešeren Square.

▲▲**Slovenian Ethnographic Museum (Slovenski Etnografski Muzej)**—Housed in a brand-new facility, this delightful museum is Ljubljana's most underrated attraction. At the core of the collection is an exhibit that strives to explain what it is to be Slovene, with well-presented and well-described cultural artifacts from around the country (many English descriptions posted, others are borrowable). A good but slow-moving film visits the four major regions of Slovenia. One exhibit ponders how people half a world away—in Slovenia and in North America—simultaneously invented a similar solution (snowshoes) for a common problem. Another exhibit deconstructs Slovenian clichés (including this country's odd fascination with its traditional hayracks). The collection is displayed to emphasize the evolution of an increasingly complicated civilization, from basic farming tools to ceramics to modern technology. The children's section features an A-to-Ž array of engaging, hands-on activities. The museum also houses a collection of non-European cultures (with more photos and prose and fewer artifacts), as well as high-quality temporary exhibits. The newest permanent exhibit, called "I, We, and Others," encourages visitors to examine their place in the world. If you've caught the Slovenian folk culture itch, this is the place to scratch it (€4.50, free last Sun of month, Tue–Sun 10:00–18:00, closed Mon, great café, Metelkova 2, tel. 01/300-8745, www.etno-muzej.si).

Slovenian National Museum-Metelkova (Narodni Muzej Slovenije)—Having decided to bring its collection out of storage, Slovenia's National Museum recently moved the contents of its attics and cellars to two floors of this brand-new facility, right next to the Ethnographic Museum. This very pretty historical bric-a-brac is neatly presented without much context—it's just an excuse to get a bunch of interesting stuff out into public view. Each room has a different collection: furniture, pottery and ceramics, church vestments, weapons and armor, and more. The painting gallery is nicely organized by century and style. Everything's labeled in English, and on weekday afternoons and all day weekends, a guide on their staff can show you around, if they're not too busy (€3, Tue–Sun 10:00–18:00, closed Mon, Maistrova 1, tel. 01/241-4400).

Shopping in Ljubljana

Ljubljana, with its easygoing ambience and countless boutiques, is made to order for whiling away an afternoon shopping. It's also a fun place to stock up on souvenirs and gifts for the folks back home. Popular items include wood carvings and models (especially of the characteristic hayracks that dot the countryside), different flavors of schnapps (the kind with a whole pear inside—cultivated to actually grow right into the bottle—is considered a particularly classy gift), honey mead brandy (*medica*—sweet and smooth), and those adorable painted frontboard panels from beehives (described on page 461). Rounding out the list of traditional Slovenian items are wrought-iron products from Kropa, crystal from Rogaska, lace from Idrija, salt from Piran, and Peko shoes (similar to high-fashion Italian models, but cheaper; the name is an abbreviation of its founder's name: Peter Kozina).

Souvenirs: The most atmospheric trinket-shopping is in the first stretch of the **market colonnade,** along the riverfront next to the Triple Bridge (described earlier, under "Sights in Ljubljana"). A souvenir shop with a wide variety is **Dom Trgovina,** with two locations: One is a block across the Triple Bridge from Prešeren Square and facing the Town Hall (Mon–Fri 9:00–19:00, Sat 9:00–15:00, closed Sun, Mestni trg 24, tel. 01/241-8390), and the other is across from the TI on the main market square (Mon–Fri 8:00–19:00, Sat 8:00–15:00, closed Sun, Ciril-Metodov trg 5). If you're looking for serious handicrafts rather than trinkets, drop by the **Rustika** gallery, just over the Triple Bridge (on the castle side). In addition to beehive panels, they also have lace, painted chests and boxes, and other tasteful local-style mementos (Mon–Fri 9:00–19:00, Sat 10:00–19:00, Sun 10:00–14:00, Stritarjeva ulica 9, mobile 031-459-509). There's another location up at the castle courtyard.

Boutiques and Galleries: Of the many fun and funky boutique streets in town, my two favorites are along the main drag through the **Old Town** (Mestni trg/Stari trg/Gornji trg), and along **Trubarjeva street,** a block up from the river (easy to find from Prešeren Square).

Sleeping in Ljubljana

Ljubljana has a good range of accommodations in all price ranges. I've focused my listings in or within easy walking distance of the city center. To get the best value, book ahead. The most expensive hotels raise their prices even more during conventions (Sept–Oct, and sometimes also June). The TI can give you a list of cheap private rooms *(sobe)*. To locate the following accommodations, see the map on page 398.

$$$ Antiq Hotel is a family-run boutique hotel idyllically situated on a cobbled square in Ljubljana's Old Town. Its 16 overpriced, idiosyncratically decorated rooms sprawl through two buildings with lots of stairs and a mazelike floor plan (small S-€61, Sb-€113–133, small D-€77, Db-€144–168, price depends on size, air-con, free Internet access and Wi-Fi, some rooms have low beams and doors, Gornji trg 3, tel. 01/421-3560, fax 01/421-3565, www.antiqhotel.si, info@antiqhotel.si).

$$$ Grand Hotel Union is Ljubljana's top address, as much an Art Nouveau landmark as a hotel. You'll pay dearly for its Old World elegance, hundred years of history, professional staff, big pool, and perfect location (right on Prešeren Square). While their rack rates are outrageously high, you can often snare a great deal in the summer (July–Aug), winter, and on many weekends. The 194 plush "Executive" rooms are in the main building (official rates: Sb-€194, Db-€224; in slow times maybe as low as Sb-€110, Db-€120; air-con, non-smoking floors, elevator, free cable Internet, Miklošičeva cesta 1, tel. 01/308-1270, fax 01/308-1015, www.gh -union.si, hotel.union@gh-union.si). Its 133 "Business" rooms next door are less luxurious, almost as expensive, and a lesser value (official rates: Sb-€178, Db-€208; same potential deals as "Executive" rooms, air-con, non-smoking floors, elevator, free cable Internet, Miklošičeva cesta 3, tel. 01/308-1170, fax 01/308-1914, www.gh -union.si, hotel.business@gh-union.si). Both have access to a pool and sauna in the Business branch, and a free Internet terminal and parking (€17/day) in the Executive branch. Because of a noisy nearby disco, request a quieter room at either building if you're here on a weekend.

$$$ Central Hotel, technically part of the Grand Hotel Union up the street, has 74 rooms similar to (but slightly smaller than) the "Business" rooms at the main hotel, but cheaper and in a friendlier, less-pretentious package. The hotel is conveniently situated between Prešeren Square and the train station (official rates: Sb-€139, Db-€167; much lower prices likely July–Aug, in winter, and on weekends—maybe as low as Sb-€75, Db-€90; extra bed-€27, non-smoking rooms, elevator, free Internet access and cable Internet, parking garage €19/day, Miklošičeva cesta 9, tel. 01/308-4300, fax 01/230-1181, www.centralhotel.si, central.hotel @gh-union.si).

$$ Slamič B&B has 11 modern rooms with hardwood floors and tasteful decor. Over an upscale café in a nondescript neighborhood, this is a fine spot for affordable elegance (Sb-€65–75, Db-€95–99, price depends on size; suite: Sb-€135, Db-€165; free Wi-Fi, no elevator, Kersnikova 1, tel. 01/433-8233, fax 01/433-8022, www.slamic.si, info@slamic.si). As the café hours are limited (Mon–Thu 7:30–22:00, Fri 7:30–21:00, Sat 9:00–16:00, closed Sun), clearly communicate your arrival time.

$$ Pri Mraku Guesthouse has 36 comfortable, slightly over-priced rooms in a pleasant neighborhood near French Revolution Square. While it's a bit rough around the edges and not without its quirks, this trusty old place is my sentimental favorite in Ljubljana (Sb-€70–74, Db-€106, ground-floor and top-floor rooms have air-con and cost about €15 more, 8 percent discount for Rick Steves readers if you reserve ahead, extra bed-€20, cheaper mid-Oct–March, non-smoking floor, free Internet access and Wi-Fi, lunch restaurant with terrace under an old vine, Rimska 4, tel. 01/421-9650, fax 01/421-9655, www.daj-dam.si, mrak@daj-dam.si).

$$ Hotel Emonec (eh-MOH-nets), with some of the most centrally located cheap beds in Ljubljana, hides just off Wolfova lane between Prešeren and Congress squares. Its 41 sleek rooms—in two buildings across a courtyard from each other—feel institutional and characterless, with cramped bathrooms, but the price is right. As it's near a noisy disco, light sleepers should try requesting a quiet room (Sb-€64, small Db-€69, bigger "standard" Db-€77, Tb-€96, Qb-€111, pay Internet access, free Wi-Fi, free loaner bikes for guests, Wolfova 12, tel. 01/200-1520, fax 01/200-1521, www.hotel-emonec.net, hotelemonec@siol.net).

$ B&B Petra Varl offers comfortable, affordable, nicely appointed rooms on a courtyard across from the bustling riverside market. Petra, who's an artist and speaks good English, will help you feel at home. This place is an appealing budget option for non-hostelers, so book early (Db-€60, extra bed-€10, includes kitchenette with basic do-it-yourself breakfast, cash only, air-con, free cable Internet, go into courtyard at Vodnikov trg 5 and look for *B&B* sign at 5A, mobile 041-389-470, petra @varl.si).

$ Hotel Center (not to be confused with "Central Hotel," listed earlier) is a particularly good value. Marko's eight new, small, modern rooms deliver on his promise of "three-star furnishings at two-star prices," and the location—just across the busy Slovenska road from the main part of town—is convenient for the price (Db-€66, breakfast-€3, free Wi-Fi, some traffic noise on streetside rooms—ask for quieter courtyard room, down the passage at Slovenska cesta 51 and around back, mobile 041-263-347, www. hotelcenter.si, info@hotelcenter.si).

$ Stari Tišler ("Old Carpenter") is a good budget option in a characteristically old, time-warp house immersed in a commercial zone a 10-minute walk from Prešeren Square. Its four modern rooms—which are nicely appointed for this price range—share two toilets and one shower, keeping prices low. It's above a restaurant that's popular at lunchtime with local businesspeople (D-€44, T-€66, breakfast-€5, up 2 flights of stairs, free Wi-Fi, Kolodvorska 8, tel. 01/430-3370, www.stari-tisler.com, info@stari-tisler.com, Sandra).

$ Penzion Pod Lipo, a lesser value, has 10 rooms above a restaurant in a mostly residential area about a 12-minute walk from Prešeren Square. While the rooms are old and simple, this is an acceptable budget option (Db-€58, Tb-€69, Qb-€92, breakfast in restaurant-€3.50 extra, cash only, reception open 8:00–24:00, nonsmoking, guest kitchen, free Internet access, free cable Internet, tel. 01/251-1683, mobile 031-809-893, www.penzion-podlipo.com, ko.mar2@siol.net, Marjan).

Hostels

Ljubljana has several good hostels. The ones listed here are particularly well-established.

$ Hostel Celica, a proud, innovative, and lively place, is
funded by the city and run by a nonprofit student organization.
This former military prison's 20 cells *(celica)* have been converted
into hostel rooms—each one unique, decorated by a different
designer (tours of the hostel daily at 14:00). The top floor features
more typical hostel rooms (each with its own bathroom, for 3–12
people). The building also houses an art gallery, tourist information, Internet access and Wi-Fi, self-serve laundry (€7/load), good
restaurant, and shoes-off "Oriental café" (all prices listed are per
person—cell rooms: S-€47, D-€28, T-€23; bed in top-floor rooms
with bathrooms: 3- to 5-bed room-€26, 6- to 7-bed dorm-€23,
12-bed dorm-€21; includes breakfast, sheets, towels, and tax; no
curfew, non-smoking, bike and car rental, active excursions around
Slovenia, Metelkova 8, a dull 15-min walk to Prešeren Square, 8
min to the train station, tel. 01/230-9700, fax 01/230-9714, www
.hostelcelica.com, recepcija@souhostel.si). Light sleepers take note:
The hostel hosts live music events about two nights per week until
around 24:00, but otherwise maintains "quiet time" after 23:00.
However, the surrounding neighborhood—a bit run-down and
remote, but safe—is a happening nightlife zone, which can make
for noisy weekends.

$ Alibi Hostel, an official IYHF hostel creatively run by
Gorazd, has two very different branches. For a grungy, funky
backpacker scene, head for **Alibi CN27,** with 100 beds (including five private rooms). The rooms are colorful and scruffy, and
it's ideally located right on Ljubljana's main riverfront-café drag.
The imaginative graffiti murals—featuring a stripper with memorable piercings and a certain cowboy president—are guaranteed to
offend just about anyone over 30 (dorm bed-€17, or €19 Fri–Sat;
D-€50, or €60 Fri–Sat; includes sheets and tax, cheaper Oct–May,
no breakfast, lockers, free Internet access and Wi-Fi, Cankarjevo
nabrežje 27, tel. 01/251-1244, www.alibi.si). When backpackers
grow a bit older and more sedate, they're more interested in comfort
than socializing—and it's time to head for **Alibi M14,** across the
street from Grand Hotel Union, a few steps off Prešeren Square.
With five small but well-appointed private rooms, a 10-bed dorm
(sharing one bathroom), and a pleasant kitchen—but not a lot of
rowdy hangout areas—it's a good compromise (dorm bed-€18,
or €20 Fri–Sat; D-€50, or €60 Fri–Sat; Db-€60, or €70 Fri–Sat;
cheaper Oct–May, includes sheets and towels, coin-op laundry,
lockers, free Internet access and Wi-Fi, Miklošičeva cesta 14, tel.
01/232-2770, www.alibi.si, m14@alibi.si).

Eating in Ljubljana

At this crossroads of cultures (and cuisines), Italian and French flavors are just as "local" as meat-and-starch Slovenian food. This cosmopolitan city also dabbles in other cuisines; you'll find Thai, Indian, Chinese, Mexican, and more. To locate these restaurants, see the map on page 398.

Zlata Ribica ("Golden Fish") is along the castle side of the embankment, with pricey food but the best riverfront view in town. The menu features modern and traditional Slovenian cuisine and delicious pastas, especially the gnocchi (€9–15 pastas, €12–24 main courses, daily 9:00–24:00, between the Triple and Cobblers' bridges at Cankarjevo nabrežje 5–7, tel. 01/241-2680).

Gostilna As ("Ace"), tucked into a courtyard just off Prešeren Square, offers fish-lovers the best blowout in town. It's dressy, pricey, and pretentious (waiters ignore the menu and recommend what's fresh). Everything is specially prepared each day and beautifully presented. It's loosely based on the Slow Food model: Servings are small, and you're expected to take your time and order two or three courses (mostly fish and Italian, €11–22 starters, €22–45 main courses, daily 12:00–24:00, reservations smart, Čopova ulica 5A, or enter courtyard with *As* sign near image of Julija on Wolfova ulica, tel. 01/425-8822). For cheaper food from the same kitchen, eat at their attached **As Lounge.** This much livelier, more casual spot features drinks, €8–11 salads and sandwiches, €7–10 pastas, and €11–19 main courses. You'll sit in the leafy courtyard or the glassed-in winter garden (food served daily 12:00–23:00, longer hours for drinks). The courtyard also has a couple of other fun eateries—and, in the summer only, live music and a much-loved gelato stand.

Ribca ("Fish")—not to be confused with Zlata Ribica, described earlier—hides under the first stretch of market colonnade near the Triple Bridge. This is your best bet for a relatively quick and cheap riverside lunch. Choose between the two straightforward menus: grilled fillets or fried small fish. With the fragrant fish market right next door, you know it's fresh. If you just want to enjoy sitting along the river below the bustling market, this is also a fine spot for a coffee or beer (€6 salads, €5–8 main courses, Mon–Fri 8:00–16:00, Sat 8:00–14:00, closed Sun).

In the Old Town: The main drag through the Old Town (which starts at the Town Hall and changes names as it goes: Mestni trg, then Stari trg, then Gornji trg) is lined with inviting eateries. Tables spill into the cobbled pedestrian street, filled with happy diners. While I list no specific restaurants here, it's only because I've tried several and they're uniformly good. (The across-the-street duet of Romeo and Julija, about halfway along this stretch, are both excellent; I've also enjoyed a great salad lunch at the Čajna Hiša tea house—described later, under "Coffee, Tea, and Treats.") If you're at a loss for where to eat, stroll here to survey your options, then pick your favorite menu and ambience.

Traditional Slovenian: Two restaurants in central Ljubljana serve up stick-to-your-ribs Slovenian fare. Because Slovenes head into the countryside when they want this sort of food, both of these places cater mostly to tourists—so don't expect top quality or a great value. But if you want a taste of traditional Slovenia, these are your handiest options in town. **Sokol,** with brisk, traditionally clad waiters, fills a fun, sprawling Slovenian-village interior with jaunty polka on the soundtrack and a very central location. It's in all the guidebooks and deluged by tourists, so don't expect an authentic experience (€8–22 main courses, veggie options, Mon–Sat 7:00–23:00, Sun 10:00–23:00, on castle side of Triple Bridge at Ciril-Metodov trg 18, tel. 01/439-6855). A few blocks away, across from the main market square, **Vodnikov Hram** has an Old World interior and outdoor tables overlooking a parking lot. While a variation on the same theme as Sokol, it's marginally less touristy, and has slightly lower prices (€7–8 pastas, €7–25 main courses, Mon–Sat 9:00–24:00, Sun 18:00–24:00, Vodnikov trg 2, tel. 01/234-5260).

Asian Fusion: **DaBuDa** is the best spot in Ljubljana for Asian cuisine, featuring good Thai dishes (salads, curries, wok meals, and noodles) in a very mod, dark-wood, split-level setting frequented by hip young professionals (good-value €6–7 lunch specials, €8–13 main courses at dinner, Mon–Fri 11:00–23:00, Sat–Sun 12:00–23:00, also a few outdoor tables, between Congress Square and Square of the Republic at Šubičeva 1A, tel. 01/425-3060).

Pizzerias

Ljubljana has lots of great sit-down pizza places. Expect to pay €5–10 for an average-sized pie (wide variety of toppings).

Pizzeria Foculus, tucked in a boring alleyway a few blocks up from the river, has a loyal local following, a happening atmosphere, an innovative leafy interior, a few outdoor tables, and Ljubljana's best pizza (over 50 types for €5–9, €4–6 salads, Mon–Fri 10:00–24:00, Sat–Sun 12:00–24:00, just off French Revolution Square across the street from Plečnik's National and University Library at Gregorčičeva 3, tel. 01/251-5643).

Ljubljanski Dvor enjoys the most convenient and scenic location of any pizzeria in town. On a sunny summer day, the outdoor riverside terrace is unbeatable. The interior has a simple pizza parlor downstairs (€5–11 pizzas and pastas), with a more refined dining room upstairs (selling the same pizzas and pastas, plus €12–20 Italian main courses; pizza parlor open daily 10:00–24:00, upstairs restaurant opens at 12:00 and is closed Sun in winter, just 50 yards from Cobblers' Bridge at Dvorni trg 1, tel. 01/251-6555). They also have a cheap pizza take-out window (listed in the next section).

Fast and Cheap

Paninoteka serves tasty €3–4 grilled sandwiches, €4–6 wraps, and €6–7 salads right along the river. The outdoor seating—a prime people-watching vantage point, with the Cobblers' Bridge and the castle above—is particularly inviting on a sunny day (order at the display case for take-away, or sit at a table to be waited on; great vegetarian options, casual service, Mon–Sat 8:00–1:00 in the morning, Sun 9:00–23:00, fine outdoor seating, Jurčičev trg 3, mobile 059-018-455).

Burek, the typical Balkan phyllo-dough snack (see "Balkan Flavors" on page 31), can be picked up at street stands around town. Most are open 24 hours and charge about €2 for a hearty portion. An easy choice is **Nobel Burek,** next to Miklošičeva cesta 30; but many locals prefer **Olympia Burek,** around the corner at Pražakova ulica 14 (across from the post office).

Pizza Slices: **Ljubljanski Dvor,** listed earlier, has a walk-up window selling cheap pizza by the slice; from the riverfront, go around back to the walk-up window on Congress Square (€2 slices to go, picnic in the park or down on the river—plenty of welcoming benches, Mon–Sat 9:00–24:00, closed Sun).

In Krakovo

The Krakovo district—just south of the city center, where garden patches nearly outnumber simple homes—is a pleasant area to wander. It's also home to a pair of tasty restaurants. Consider combining a meal here with your trip to the Jože Plečnik House (which is just beyond Krakovo).

Pri Škofu ("By the Bishop") is a laid-back, informal place with mostly outdoor seating and a focus on freshness, serving international cuisine with a Slovenian flair. There's no menu—the waiter tells you what's good today...and it is. They'll ask what kind of pasta or meat you want, then help you narrow down your options (sauces, sides, etc.) to get to your ideal meal. This hidden gem is deliciously memorable and worth seeking out. Reservations are essential (creative €3 soups, €7–8 lunches, €7–17 main courses at dinner, homemade €3 desserts, Mon–Fri 10:00–24:00, Sat–Sun 12:00–24:00, Rečna 8, tel. 01/426-4508).

Harambaša is the closest thing to a ticket to Sarajevo. Serving Balkan grilled meats, this popular-with-students eatery has Bosnian-flavored decor, old pictures, and cuisine reminiscent of the Bosnian capital. For a refresher on the meat dishes, see "Balkan Flavors" on page 31. The menu is limited, which makes ordering easy. Their handy €6.50 *pola-pola* combo-plate—with lotsa meat combined with chopped onions, *kajmak* (a buttery spread), and *lepinja* (bread)—makes for a simple but filling lunch. Also consider the Turkish coffee (a high-octane brew with "mud" at the bottom) and baklava. Vegetarians need not apply (€5–7 main courses, Mon–Fri 10:00–22:00, Sat 12:00–22:00, Sun 12:00–18:00, Vrtna ulica 8, mobile 041-843-106).

Coffee, Tea, and Treats

Riverfront Cafés: Enjoying a coffee, beer, or ice-cream cone along the Ljubljanica River embankment (between the Triple and

Cobblers' bridges) is Ljubljana's single best experience —worth ▲▲▲. Tables spill into the street, and some of the best-dressed, best-looking students on the planet happily fill them day and night. (A common question from first-time visitors to Ljubljana: "Doesn't anybody here have a job?") This is some of the top people-watching in Europe. Rather than recommend a particular place (they're all about the same), I'll leave you to explore and find the spot with the breezy ambience you like best. When ordering, the easiest choice is a *bela kava*—"white coffee," basically a caffè latte.

Tea House: If coffee's not your cup of tea, go a block inland to the teahouse **Čajna Hiša.** They have a shop (called "Cha") with over 100 varieties of tea, plus porcelain teapots and cups from all over (Mon–Fri 9:00–20:00, Sat 9:00–13:30, closed Sun). The café serves about 50 different types of tea, light food (including great salads), and desserts (€3 cakes and sandwiches, €5–8 salads, Mon–Fri 9:00–22:30, Sat 9:00–15:00 & 18:00–22:00, closed Sun, on the atmospheric main drag in the Old Town a few steps from Cobblers' Bridge at Stari trg 3, tel. 01/252-7010).

Cakes: **Zvezda Kavarna,** a trendy, central place at the bottom of Congress Square, is a local favorite for cakes, pastries, and ice cream (decadent €3–4 cakes, Mon–Sat 7:00–23:00, Sun 10:00–20:00, a block up from Prešeren Square at Wolfova 14, tel. 01/421-9090). **Abecedarium** (ah-beh-tseh-dah-ree-oom, like the alphabet) serves up delicious €4 Nutella-banana cake (and other food) with indoor or outdoor seating near the Triple Bridge. It's located in the oldest house in town, named for a work by one of Slovenia's greatest thinkers, who also lived in the house (daily 8:00–24:00, Ribji trg 2, tel. 01/426-9514).

Chocolates and Ice Cream: **Rustika** is a local chain that sells tasty homemade chocolates (€3.50/100 grams), cookies (including one with three different kinds of chocolate), and a wide variety of unusual and delicious artisan ice cream flavors. The menu changes from day to day, but highlights can include balsamic vinegar with vanilla or strawberry, very dark chocolate, Kanada (with maple syrup and walnuts), and Greek yogurt with honey and nuts. The handiest location is about an eight-minute walk from Prešeren Square, and comes with a delightful stroll along colorful Trubarjeva street (€1/scoop, Mon–Fri 8:00–20:00, Sat 9:00–14:00, closed Sun, Trubarjeva 44, mobile 059-935-730).

More Ice Cream: Ljubljana is known for its Italian gelato–style ice cream. You'll see fine options all along the Ljubljanica River embankment. Favorites include the courtyard garden at **Gostilna As** (summer only) and **Zvezda Kavarna** (both described earlier).

Ljubljana Connections

As Slovenia's transportation hub, Ljubljana is well-connected to both domestic and international destinations. When checking schedules, be aware of name variations: In Slovene, Vienna is "Dunaj" and Budapest is "Budimpešta."

Getting to Croatia

To reach **Istria** by public transportation, you have two relatively straightforward options: In summer (June–late Sept), a direct bus departs Ljubljana for Rovinj each day (around 13:45, 5.5 hrs, €22, no buses off-season; also stops en route in Piran and Poreč). Mondays through Fridays year-round, there's also a train connection to Pula (departs around 13:20, 3.5 hrs, changes in Divača, Slovenia, and Buzet, Croatia); once in Pula, you can connect by bus to other Istrian destinations. On off-season weekends, you might have to get creative (try connecting through Rijeka).

If connecting directly to Croatia's **Dalmatian Coast,** you have three options: Train to Zagreb (2.5 hrs), where you can catch a cheap Croatia Air flight or a bus (see "Zagreb Connections" on page 73); take the long, once-daily train connection from Ljubljana to Split (8 hrs, requires a change in Zagreb); or, much slower, take the train to Rijeka, then cruise on a boat down the coast from there. (For specifics on flights, buses, and boats, see "Getting to the Dalmatian Coast," page 170.)

By Train

From Ljubljana by Train to: Lesce-Bled (roughly hourly, 40–60 min—but bus is better because it goes right to Bled town center), **Postojna** (nearly hourly, 1 hr), **Divača** (close to Škocjan Caves and Lipica, nearly hourly, 1.75 hrs), **Sežana** (close to Lipica, nearly hourly, 2 hrs), **Piran** (direct bus is better—see below; otherwise allow 4 hours, train to Koper, 5/day, 2.5 hrs; then bus to Piran, 7/day, 30 min), **Maribor** (hourly, 2–3 hrs, more with a transfer in Zidani Most), **Ptuj** (3/day, 2.5 hrs, more with transfer in Pragersko), **Zagreb** (8/day, 2.5 hrs), **Rijeka** (2–3/day direct, 2.5 hrs), **Pula** (1/day Mon–Fri, none Sat–Sun, 3.5 hrs, transfer in Divača, Slovenia, and Buzet, Croatia), **Split** (1/day, 9 hrs, transfer in Zagreb), **Vienna** (that's *Dunaj* in Slovene, 1/day direct, 6 hrs; otherwise 6/day with transfer in Villach, Maribor, or Graz, 6–7 hrs), **Budapest** (that's *Budimpešta* in Slovene; 6/day, 8–9 hrs, 1–2 changes, night train departs Ljubljana around 2:00 in the morning), **Venice** (1/day direct, 4 hrs; plus 1/day with a change to a bus in Villach, 6.75 hrs), **Salzburg** (4/day direct, 5 hrs), **Munich** (3/day direct, 6 hrs, including 1 night train; otherwise transfer in Salzburg). Train info: tel. 01/291-3332, www.slo-zeleznice.si.

By Bus

The bus station is a low-profile building in front of the train station. Buses depart from the numbered stalls in the middle of the street. For any bus, you have to buy tickets at the bus station ticket windows, not from the driver. Bus info: www.ap-ljubljana.si, tel. 090 4230 (toll number—about €0.75/min).

By Bus to: Bled (Mon–Sat hourly—usually at the top of each hour, fewer on Sun, 1.25 hrs, €6.30), **Postojna** (at least hourly, 1 hr, €6), **Divača** (close to Škocjan Caves and Lipica, about every 2 hrs, 1.5 hrs, €7.90), **Piran** (6/day, 2.5 hrs, €12), over the **Vršič Pass** to **Bovec** (1/day July–Aug, departs Ljubljana 6:30, arrives Bovec 10:45, €13.10; off-season only Sat–Sun), **Rovinj** (1/day June–late Sept, departs Ljubljana around 13:45, 5.5 hrs, €22, no buses off-season), **Rijeka** (2/day, 2.5 hrs).

By Plane

Slovenia's only **airport** (airport code: LJU) is 14 miles north of Ljubljana, about halfway to Bled. Confusingly, the airport goes by three names: Ljubljana Airport (the international version); Brnik (for the town that it's near); and Jože Pučnik Airport (a politician for whom it was controversially renamed in 2007). Most flights are operated by Slovenia's national airline, Adria Airways (www.adria-airways.com), but others are run by easyJet (www.easyjet.com), Wizz Air (www.wizzair.com), Czech Airlines (www.csa.cz), and others. There's a TI in the airport's arrivals hall. If you're killing time here, follow signs (around to the right as you face the outside of the terminal) to *Razgledna Terasa* and ride the elevator up to the rooftop terrace (with a café). Here you can sip a coffee while you watch planes land and take off. Airport info: tel. 04/206-1000, www.lju-airport.si.

Getting Between Downtown Ljubljana and the Airport: Two kinds of buses connect the airport with Ljubljana's bus station: **public bus** #28 (to the right as you exit the airport; Mon–Fri hourly until 20:00, only 7/day Sat–Sun, 45 min, €4.10), and a **minibus** (to the left as you exit the airport, scheduled to depart after various arriving flights—look for schedule posted near bus stop). Two different companies run the minibus transfers, which take about 30 minutes: Markun (€5 to train station, €9 to your hotel, mobile 041-792-865) and Marko Nowotny (€8 regardless of your destination, mobile 040-771-771, www.airport-shuttle.si). I'd take whichever one is departing first. For a transfer *to* the airport, your hotel can make arrangements with one of these companies a day or so in advance (same price). Unfortunately, certain evening arrivals don't coordinate well with either the bus or the minibus, so you might have to wait a while or take a pricey **taxi** (figure €20–25 to the airport, but more like €42 *from* the airport—since you have to use the pricey taxi stand out front).

The Austrian Alternative: Since Ljubljana's airport is the only one in the country and thus charges extremely high taxes and airport fees, many Slovenes prefer to fly out of Austria. The airport in **Klagenfurt** (airport code: KLU, also known as "Alpe-Adria Airport"), just over the Austrian border to the north, is subsidized by the local government to keep prices low and compete with Ljubljana's airport. Especially if you're connecting to Bled, it's somewhat handy to reach (from Ljubljana or Bled, take the train to Villach, then to Klagenfurt's Annabichl station, which is a 5-min walk from the airport; total trip 3 hrs from Ljubljana, or 2 hrs from Bled; www.klagenfurt-airport.com). A taxi transfer to Bled runs a hefty €120 and takes about an hour (see "By Taxi" on page 444). Austrian Airlines (www.aua.com) flies from Klagenfurt, as do low-cost carriers such as Ryanair (www.ryanair.com), TUIfly (www.tuifly.com), Germanwings (www.germanwings.com), and Air Berlin (www.airberlin.com).

LAKE BLED

Lake Bled—Slovenia's leading mountain resort—comes complete with a sweeping alpine panorama, a fairy-tale island, a cliff-hanging medieval castle, a lazy lakeside promenade, and the country's most sought-after desserts. While Bled has all the modern resort-town amenities, its most endearing qualities are its stunning setting, its natural romanticism, and its fun-loving wedding parties.

Since the Habsburg days, Lake Bled (locals pronounce it "blayd") has been *the* place where Slovenes wow visiting diplomats. Tito had one of his vacation homes here (today's Hotel Vila Bled), and more recent visitors have included Prince Charles, Madeleine Albright, and Laura Bush. But above all, Lake Bled feels like a place that Slovenes enjoy alongside their visitors.

Lake Bled has plenty of ways to idle away an afternoon. While the lake's main town, also called Bled, is more functional than quaint, it offers postcard views of the lake and handy access to the region. Hike up to Bled Castle for intoxicating vistas. Make a wish and ring the bell at the island church. Wander the dreamy path around the lake. Sit on a dock, dip your feet in the water, and feed some of the lake's resident swans. Then dive into some of Bled's famous cakes while you take in the view of Triglav, Slovenia's favorite mountain (see "Mount Triglav" sidebar on page 471). Bled quiets down at night—no nightlife beyond a handful of pubs—giving hikers and other holiday-makers a chance to recharge. Bled is also a great jumping-off point for a car trip through the Julian Alps (see next chapter).

Planning Your Time

Bled and its neighboring mountains deserve two days. With one day, spend it in and around Bled (or, to rush things, spend the morning in Bled and the afternoon day-tripping). With a second day and a car, drive through the Julian Alps using the self-guided tour in the next chapter. The circular route takes you up and over the stunning Vršič Pass, then down the scenic and historic Soča River Valley. Without a car, skip the second day, or spend it doing nearby day trips: Bus or bike to Radovljica to see the bee museum, hike to Vintgar Gorge, or visit the more rustic Lake Bohinj (all described under "Near Lake Bled," at the end of this chapter).

Orientation to Lake Bled

(area code: 04)
The town of Bled is on the east end of 1.5-mile-long Lake Bled.
The lakefront is lined with cafés
and resort hotels. A 3.5-mile path
meanders around the lake. As no
motorized boats are allowed, Lake
Bled is particularly peaceful.

The tourists' center of Bled
is a cluster of big resort hotels,
dominated by the giant, red Hotel
Park (dubbed the "red can"). The
busy street called **Ljubljanska cesta** leads out of Bled town toward
Ljubljana and most other destinations. Just up from the lakefront,
across Ljubljanska cesta from Hotel Park, is the modern **commercial center** (Trgovski Center Bled), with a travel agency, grocery
store, ATM, shops, and a smattering of lively cafés. Nicknamed
"Gaddafi" by the people of Bled, the commercial center was
designed for a Libyan city, but the deal fell through—so the frugal
Slovenes built it here instead. Just up the road from the commercial
center, you'll find the post office and library (with Internet access).

Bled's less-touristy Old Town is under the castle, surrounding
the pointy spire of St. Martin's Church. There you'll find the bus
station, some good restaurants, a few hostels, and more locals than
tourists.

The mountains poking above the ridge at the far end of the lake
are the Julian Alps, crowned by the three peaks of Mount Triglav.
The big mountain behind the town of Bled is Stol ("Chair"), part
of the Karavanke range that defines the Austrian border.

Tourist Information

Bled's helpful TI is in the long, lakefront casino building across
the street from the big, red Hotel Park (as you face the lake, the

TI is hiding around the front at the far left end, overlooking the lake). Pick up the good map (with the lake on one side and the whole region on the other) and the free Bled information booklet. Get advice on hikes and day trips, confirm transit schedules, and if you're doing any serious hiking, spring for a good regional map (July–Aug Mon–Sat 8:00–21:00, Sun 9:00–17:00; May–June and Sept Mon–Sat 8:00–19:00, Sun 11:00–17:00; Oct–April Mon–Sat 8:00–18:00, Sun 8:00–13:00; Cesta Svobode 10, tel. 04/574-1122, www.bled.si). The TI can give you a list of accommodations, but they can't find you a room (book direct or use Kompas Bled Travel Agency's room-booking service—see "Helpful Hints," later).

For more details on hiking in Triglav National Park, pay a visit to the new **Triglav National Park Information Center** on the main road out of town (free information, maps and guidebooks for sale, possible charge for exhibition, Tue–Sun 10:00–18:00, closed Mon, Ljubljanska cesta 27, tel. 04/578-0200, www.tnp.si).

Arrival in Bled

By Train: Two train stations have the name "Bled." The **Bled Jezero** ("Bled Lake") station is across the lake from Bled town and is used only by infrequent, slow, tourist-oriented trains into the mountains. You're much more likely to use the **Lesce-Bled** station in the nearby village of Lesce. The Lesce-Bled station is on the main line and has far better connections to Ljubljana and international destinations. So if you're buying a train ticket or checking schedules, request "Lesce-Bled" rather than just "Bled." (This is so important, I'll remind you again later.)

The small **Lesce-Bled station** is in the village of Lesce, about 2.5 miles from Bled. The nearest ATM is upstairs in the shopping center across the street (at the Gorenjska Banka on the third floor, across the parking lot from Mercator supermarket). From the Lesce station, you can take the bus into Bled town (2/hr, 10 min, €1.30, catch it across the street from the train station); or pay about €10 for a taxi into town. If taking the train out of Lesce-Bled, you can buy tickets at this station or on the train—nobody in Bled town sells tickets.

By Bus: Bled's main bus station is just up from the lake in the Old Town. To reach the lake, walk straight downhill on Cesta Svobode. Note that many buses also stop on the way into town, along Ljubljanska cesta; this stop is handier for walking to many of my recommended accommodations (for details, see "Sleeping in Bled," later).

By Car: Coming from Ljubljana, you'll wind your way into Bled on Ljubljanska cesta, which rumbles through the middle of town before swinging left at the lake. Ask your hotel about parking. Also see "Route Tips for Drivers" on page 458.

Bled Town

To Podhom &
Vintgar Gorge

To Zasip

POLJSKA POT

PARTIZANSKA CES.

REČIŠKA CESTA

CESTA

GRAJSKA CESTA

GRAJSKA

15

10

9

13

14 **16**

OLD TOWN

ST. MARTIN

18

P

CASTLE

8

P

SWIMMING POOLS & BOAT RENTALS

To Rowing Center & Campground

Lake Bled

To Island & Church

N

300 Meters

300 Yards

To Mlino & Bohinj &

11

To Luge Ride

LAKE BLED

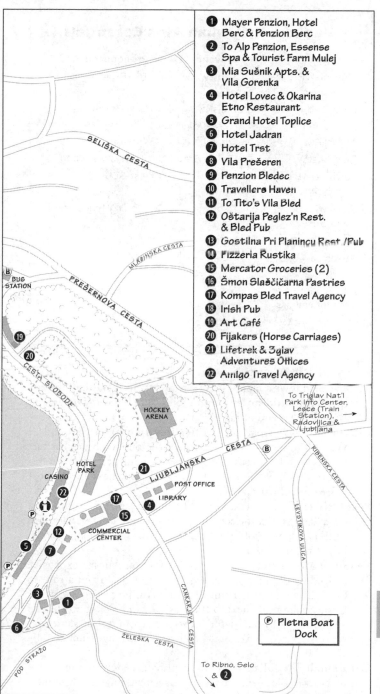

1 Mayer Penzion, Hotel Berc & Penzion Berc
2 To Alp Penzion, Essense Spa & Tourist Farm Mulej
3 Mia Sušnik Apts. & Vila Gorenka
4 Hotel Lovec & Okarina Etno Restaurant
5 Grand Hotel Toplice
6 Hotel Jadran
7 Hotel Trst
8 Vila Prešeren
9 Penzion Bledec
10 Travellers Haven
11 To Tito's Vila Bled
12 Oštarija Peglez'n Rest. & Bled Pub
13 Gostilna Pri Planincu Rest./Pub
14 Pizzeria Rustika
15 Mercator Groceries (2)
16 Šmon Slaščičarna Pastries
17 Kompas Bled Travel Agency
18 Irish Pub
19 Art Café
20 Fijakers (Horse Carriages)
21 Lifetrek & 3glav Adventures Offices
22 Amigo Travel Agency

SELIŠKA CESTA

MLAŠINSKA CESTA

B BUS STATION

PREŠERNOVA CESTA

CESTA SVOBODE

HOCKEY ARENA

To Triglav Nat'l Park Info Center, Lesce (Train Station), Radovljica & Ljubljana →

LJUBLJANSKA CESTA

B

RIBENSKA CESTA

HOTEL PARK

CASINO

POST OFFICE

LEVSTIKOVA ULICA

LIBRARY

P i

COMMERCIAL CENTER

CANKARJEVA CESTA

P Pletna Boat Dock

POD STRAŽO

ŽELEŠKA CESTA

To Ribno, Selo & 2

LAKE BLED

Bled and the Julian Alps Essentials

English	Slovene	Pronounced
Slovenia's Biggest Mountain	Triglav	TREE-glahv
Lake Bled	Blejsko Jezero	BLAY-skoh YAY-zay-roh
The Island	Otok	OH-tohk
Bled Castle	Blejski Grad	BLAY-skee grahd
Town near Bled with Train Station	Lesce	lest-SEH
Town with Bee Museum	Radovljica	rah-DOH-vleet-suh
Gorge near Bled	Vintgar	VEENT-gar
Rustic Lake near Bled	Bohinj	BOH-heen
Scenic High-Mountain Pass	Vršič	vur-SHEECH
Historic River Valley	Soča	SOH-chah

Helpful Hints

Money: Bled town's handiest ATMs are at **SKB Banka** (upstairs in round building at commercial center) and **Gorenjska Banka** (at far end of Hotel Park).

Internet Access: Most hotels offer free Internet access and/or Wi-Fi for their guests. In a pinch, the public library has terminals with fast access (free up to one hour per day, Mon–Fri 10:00–19:00, Sat 8:00–12:00, closed Sun, next to the post office on Ljubljanska cesta).

Post Office: If you're coming up from the lake on Ljubljanska cesta, it's just past the commercial center and library (Mon–Fri 8:00–19:00, Sat 8:00–12:00, closed Sun, slightly longer hours July–Aug, tel. 04/575-0200).

Laundry: Most hotels can do laundry for you, but it's expensive (priced by the piece). You'll get a better deal from a can-do local: Drop off your laundry at the Amigo travel agency (at Cesta Svobode 15, next to the Casino), and pick it up cleaned and folded 24 hours later (€15/load, €5 more for same-day express service, Anže Štalc, call first to arrange, mobile 041-575-522).

Car Rental: The Julian Alps are ideal by car. Several big chains rent cars in Bled—figure €60 per day, including tax, insurance, and unlimited mileage (generally no extra charge for drop-off elsewhere in Slovenia). Various major companies have branches in Bled, including **Europcar** (mobile 031-382-055), **Budget** (tel. 04/578-0320), **National** (mobile 041-400-980), and **Sixt** (tel. 04/578-0120), but as the offices tend to move around, inquire in Bled about the current locations.

Travel Agency: Kompas Bled Travel Agency, in the commercial center, rents bikes, sells books and maps, offers a room-booking service (including many cheap rooms in private homes—though most are away from the lake), and sells various tours around the region (Mon–Sat 8:00–19:00, Sun 8:00–12:00 & 16:00–19:00, June–Sept until 20:00, Ljubljanska cesta 4, tel. 04/572-7500, www.kompas-bled.si, kompas.bled@siol.net).

Massage: If you're here to relax, consider a massage at the **Essense** wellness center at the recommended Alp Penzion. This modern, classy facility—hiding in the countryside about a 15-minute walk or 5-minute taxi ride above the lake— offers a wide range of spa treatments, including pedicure, Thai massage, and Indian ayurveda massage (with warm oils). A standard 50-minute massage will run you about €30 (call first to arrange, Cankarjeva cesta 20A, tel. 04/576-7450, www.alp-penzion.com).

Getting Around Lake Bled (Literally)

By Bike: You can rent a mountain bike at the TI or at Kompas Bled Travel Agency (both listed earlier) for the same rates (€3.50/hr, €6/3 hrs, €8/half-day, €11/day). While walking around the lake is slo-mo bliss, biking it is also enjoyable. For a longer pedal, ask for the TI's excellent biking map, with various great bike trips clearly marked and described. The bike path to the nearby town of Radovljica (and its bee museum) is about four miles one-way (get details at the TI).

By Horse and Buggy: Buggies called *fijakers* are the romantic, expensive, and easy way to get around the lake. You'll see them along the lakefront between Hotel Park and the castle (around the lake-€30, one-way up to castle-€30, round-trip to castle with 30-min wait time-€40, mobile 041-710-970).

By Tourist Train: A little train makes a circuit around the lake every 40 minutes in summer (€3, daily 9:00–21:00 in peak season, shorter hours off-season, weather-dependent, mobile 051-337-478).

By Tourist Bus: A handy shuttle bus passes through Bled once daily in summer. It leaves the bus station at 10:00, stops at a few hotels (including Grand Hotel Toplice), then goes up to the castle and on to the Vintgar Gorge entrance (€3.50, mid-June–Sept only, confirm schedule at TI or bus station).

By Taxi: Your hotel can call a taxi for you. Or contact **Bled Tours,** run by friendly, English-speaking driver Sandi Demšar and his girlfriend Cvetka (€10 to the castle or to Lesce-Bled train station, €14 to Radovljica, €50 to Ljubljana airport, €120 to Klagenfurt airport in Austria, mobile 031-205-611, info@bled tours.si).

By Boat: For information on renting your own boat, see "Boating," page 450. For details on riding the characteristic *pletna* boats, see "Getting to the Island," page 447.

By Private Plane: If you have perfect weather and deep pockets, there's no more thrilling way to experience Slovenia's high-mountain scenery than from a small propeller plane soaring over the peaks. Flights depart from a grass airstrip near the village of Lesce, a 10-minute drive or taxi ride from Bled. Expensive...but unforgettable (€75 for 15-min hop over Lake Bled only, €135 for 30-min flight that also buzzes Lake Bohinj, €195 for deluxe 45-min version around the summit of Triglav, arrange at least a day in advance, tel. 04/532-0100, www.alc-lesce.si, info@alc-lesce.si).

Tours at Lake Bled

Local Guides—Tina Hiti and **Sašo Golub** are excellent guides who enjoy sharing the town and region they love with American visitors. Hiring one of them can add immeasurably to your enjoyment and understanding of Bled (€30/2 hrs, arrange several days in advance; Tina: mobile 040-166-554, tinahiti@gmail.com; Sašo: mobile 040-524-774, sasogolub@gmail.com). Either one can drive you in their car on a long day tour into the Julian Alps—or anywhere in Slovenia—for €120. (This price is for two people; it's more expensive for three or more people, since they have to rent a van.) I've spent great days with both Tina and Sašo and was thankful they were behind the wheel. If these two are busy, they might send Tina's father, Gorazd—a former Yugoslav Olympian (in ice hockey) who brings the older generation's perspective to the trip (and speaks fine English).

Excursions—To hit several far-flung day-trip destinations in one go, you could take a package tour from Bled. Destinations range from Ljubljana and the Karst region to the Austrian Lakes to Venice. For example, an all-day Julian Alps trip to the Vršič Pass and Soča Valley runs about €35 (sold by various agencies, including Kompas Bled). This tour is handy, but two people can rent a car for the day for about the same price and do it at their own pace using the self-guided driving tour in the next chapter.

Adventure Trips—Various Bled-based companies specialize in taking tourists on active, outdoorsy excursions into the surrounding countryside and mountains. One popular, all-day trip is white-water rafting on the Soča River (around €90). Other options include canyoning, river tubing, mountain biking, paragliding, rock climbing, and more. Various outfits cluster near the commercial center; these include **3glav Adventures** (just above commercial center at Ljubljanska cesta 1, mobile 041-683-184, www.3glav-adventures.com), **Lifetrek Adventures** (next to 3glav at Ljubljanska cesta 1, mobile 040-508-853, www.lifetrek-slovenia.com), and **Amigo** (next to the Casino at Cesta Svobode 15, tel. 05/597-3250, www.amigo.si). Note that these companies tend to attract a young, sometimes rowdy crowd that enjoys lubricating their adventures with plenty of alcohol.

Sights at Lake Bled

Bled doesn't have many "sights," but there are plenty of rewarding and pleasant activities.

▲▲▲**Walk Around the Lake**—Strolling the 3.5 miles around the lake is enjoyable, peaceful, and scenic. At a leisurely pace, it takes about an hour and a half...not counting stops to snap photos of the ever-changing view. On the way, you'll pass some great villas, mostly from the beginning of the 19th century. The most significant one was a former residence of Marshal Tito—today the Hotel Vila Bled, a great place to stop for a coffee and pretend Tito invited you over for a visit (described next). For the more adventurous, hiking paths lead up into the hills surrounding the lake (ask TI for details and maps; or hike to Vintgar Gorge, described on page 462).

▲**Tito's Vila Bled**—Before World War II, this villa on Lake Bled was the summer residence for the Yugoslav royal family. When Tito ran Yugoslavia, the part-Slovene communist leader took over the place and had it renovated using plans from the architect Jože Plečnik. During his heyday, Tito entertained international guests here (big shots from the communist and non-aligned world, from Indira Gandhi to Nikita Khrushchev to Kim Il Sung to Raúl Castro). Since 1984, it's been a classy hotel and restaurant, offering guests grand Lake Bled views and James Bond ambience. The garden surrounding the villa is filled with exotic trees, brought here by Tito's guests from distant lands.

The terrace has a restaurant that welcomes visitors to drop in for a meal, a piece of cake, or just a cup of coffee. Tito fans might want to splurge for an overnight (standard Db-€210, tel. 04/579-1500, www.vila-bled.com). But even if you're not a guest here, the hotel's staff is generally tolerant of curious tourists poking around the public areas inside. From the marbled lobby, head upstairs. This is where Tito fans have a nostalgic opportunity to send an email from Tito's desk, sip tea in his lounge, and gawk at his **Socialist Realist wall murals.** Those murals, decorating the upper walls of a vast ballroom on the second floor, are a fascinating peek at the propaganda of the time. Follow the rousing story of the origins of postwar Yugoslavia, starting on the upper left as you enter: First you see the Nazi destruction of Belgrade in 1941, a dark moment that inspired the South Slavs to band together to fight these foreign occupiers. See Tito raising his ragtag army, then leading them into pivotal battles in Bosnia-Herzegovina (notice the minaret and the destroyed bridge over the Neretva River), followed by a winter spent enduring hardship. At the end of this long wall, Tito's victorious Partisans crush the final vestiges of the Nazis; in the upper-right corner, the spring blossoms represent a promising future for the people of Yugoslavia. The large panel at the end of the room trumpets the idealized postwar world that Tito envisioned: proud workers from all walks of life coming together for the betterment of Yugoslavia. In the shadow of a mighty factory—a symbol of heavy industry, which communists embraced as the way of the future—notice that  the ironworker and the farmer are literally holding hands in unity. The room's focal point is the mother hoisting a young child with one arm, and the flag of the nascent Socialist Federal Republic of Yugoslavia with the other.

Getting There: The villa is a 20-minute lakeside walk from the town of Bled at Cesta Svobode 26 (it's the big, white villa with the long staircase at the southern end of the lake, just beyond the village of Mlino). You can also ask your *pletna* gondolier to drop you off here after visiting the island. Those hiking around the lake will pass the gate leading up through Tito's garden to the restaurant and lobby.

▲▲**The Island (Otok)**—Bled's little island—capped by a super-cute church—nudges the lake's quaintness level over the top. Locals call it simply "The Island" *(Otok).* While it's pretty to look at from afar, it's also fun to visit.

The island has long

been a sacred site with a romantic twist. On summer Saturdays, a steady procession of brides and grooms, cheered on by their entourages, heads for the island. Ninety-nine steps lead from the island's dock up to the Church of the Assumption on top. It's tradition for the groom to carry—or try to carry—his bride up these steps. About four out of five are successful (proving themselves "fit for

marriage"). During the communist era, the church was closed, and weddings were outlawed here. But the tradition re-emerged—illegally—even before the regime ended, with a clandestine ceremony in 1989.

An eighth-century Slavic pagan temple dedicated to the goddess of love and fertility once stood here; the current Baroque version (with Venetian flair—the bell tower separate from the main church) is the fifth to occupy this spot. Go inside (€3, daily May–Sept 9:00–19:00, Oct and April until 18:00, Nov–March until 16:00) and find the rope for the church bell, hanging in the middle of the aisle just before the altar. A local superstition claims that if you can get this bell to ring three times with one big pull of the rope, your dreams will come true. Worth a try.

If you're waiting for a herd of tourists to ring out their wishes, pass the time looking around the front of the church. When the church was being renovated in the 1970s, workers dug up several medieval graves (you can see one through the glass under the bell rope). They also discovered Gothic frescoes on either side of the altar, including, above the door on the right, an unusual ecclesiastical theme: the *bris* (Jewish circumcision ritual) of Christ.

A café (with a WC) and souvenir shop (with an exhibit of nativity scenes) are near the church at the top of the steps.

To descend by a different route, walk down the trail behind the church, then follow the path around the island's perimeter back to where your *pletna* boat awaits.

Getting to the Island: The most romantic route to the island is to cruise on one of the distinctive *pletna* boats (€12 per person round-trip, includes 30-min wait time at the island; catch one at several spots around the lake—most convenient from in front of Grand Hotel Toplice or just below Hotel Park, might have to wait for more passengers to fill the boat, generally run from dawn until around 20:00 in summer, stop earlier off-season, replaced by enclosed electric boats in winter—unless the lake freezes, mobile 031-316-575). For more on these characteristic little vessels, see the

Pletna Boats

The *pletna* is an important symbol of Lake Bled. In addition to providing a pleasant way to reach the island, these boats

also carry on a tradition dating back for generations. In the 17th century, Habsburg Empress Maria Theresa granted the villagers from Mlino—the little town along the lakefront just beyond Bled—special permission to ferry visitors to the island. (Since Mlino had very limited access to farmland, the people needed another source of income.) Mlino residents built their *pletnas* by hand, using a special design passed down from father to son for centuries—like the equally iconic gondolas of Venice. Eventually, this imperial decree and family tradition evolved into a modern union of *pletna* oarsmen, which continues to this day.

Today *pletna* boats are still hand-built according to that same centuries-old design. There's no keel, so the skilled

oarsmen work hard to steer the flat-bottomed boat with each stroke—boats piloted by an inexperienced oarsman can slide around on very windy days. There are 21 official *pletnas* on Lake Bled, all belonging to the same union. The gondoliers dump all of their earnings into one fund, give a cut to the tourist board, and divide the rest evenly among themselves. Occasionally a new family tries to break into the cartel, underselling his competitors with a "black market" boat that looks the same as the official ones. While some see this as a violation of a centuries-old tradition, others view it as good old capitalism. Either way, competition is fierce.

"*Pletna* Boats" sidebar. You can also **rent your own boat** to row to the island (see "Boating," later). It's even possible to **swim** to the island, especially from the end of the lake nearest the island (see "Swimming," later), but you're not allowed into the church in your swimsuit.

▲**Bled Castle (Blejski Grad)**—Bled's cliff-hanging castle, dating in one form or another from 1,000 years ago, was the seat of the Austrian Bishops of Brixen, who controlled Bled in the

Middle Ages. Your castle admission includes a newly spruced-up castle museum (with interesting videos, creaky rooms, and good English descriptions); a small theater continuously showing a fun 20-minute movie about Bled (under the restaurant); a tiny chapel with 3-D frescoes that make it seem much bigger than it is; and a rampart walk with an "herbal gallery" (gift shop of traditional-meets-modern herbal brandies, cosmetics, and perfumes). While these attractions are nothing exciting, the real reason to come up here is to bask in the sweeping views over Lake Bled and the surrounding mountainscapes (€7, daily May–Oct 8:00–20:00, Nov–April 9:00–17:00, tel. 04/572-9782).

In addition, the castle is home to a pair of interesting, old-fashioned shops: You can visit a working replica of a **printing press** *(grajsku tiskarna)* from Gutenberg's time and print your own custom-made souvenir certificate for €5–10 (in the castle's oldest tower—from the 11th century). Or, at the **wine cellar** *(grajska klet de Adami)*, bottle and cork your own bottle of wine (€10–15). These attractions are manned by a pair of gregarious guys, one dressed as a medieval printer and the other as a monk. Both men happen to be named Andrej (they switch costumes sometimes for a change of pace). Both shops are generally open daily in summer 10:00–18:00 (less off-season; if one of the shops is closed, the other should be open).

Eating at the Castle: The **restaurant** at the castle is fairly expensive, but your restaurant reservation gets you into the castle grounds for free (international cuisine and some local specialties, €10–20 main courses, tel. 04/579-4424). Better yet, there's a scenic little **picnic spot** in the castle courtyard, with fine tables and views (buy sandwiches at the Mercator grocery store in the commercial center before you ascend—described later, under "Eating in Bled").

Getting to the Castle: To really earn those views, you can **hike** up the steep hill (20–30 min). The handiest trails are behind big St. Martin's Church: Walk past the front door of the church with the lake at your back, and look left after the first set of houses for the *Grad* signs marking the steepest route up (on this trail, bear uphill—or right—at the benches); or, for a longer but less steep route, continue past the church on the same street about five minutes, bearing uphill (left) at the fork, and find the *Grad* sign just after the Pension Bledec hostel on the left. Once you're on this second trail, don't take the sharp-left uphill turn at the fork (instead, continue straight up, around the back of the hill). If you'd rather skip the hike, you can take the 10:00 **tourist bus** (see "Getting Around Lake Bled," earlier), your **rental car,** a taxi (around €10), or—if you're wealthy and romantic—a **horse and buggy** (€30, €10 extra to wait 30 min and bring you back down). However, these options take you only to the parking lot, from which it's a steep and slippery-when-wet five-minute hike up to the castle itself.

Boating—Bled is the rowing center of Slovenia. Town officials even lengthened the lake a bit so it would perfectly fit the standard two-kilometer laps, with 100 meters more for the turn. Three world championships have been held here. The town has produced many Olympic medalists, winning gold in Sydney and silver in Athens. You'll notice that local crew team members are characters—with a tradition of wild and colorful haircuts. You'll likely see them running or rowing. This dedication to rowing adds to Bled's tranquility, since no motorized boats are allowed on the lake.

If you want to get into the action, you'll find **rental rowboats** at the swimming pool under the castle (small 3-person boat: first hour-€12, additional hours-€6.50 each; bigger 5-person boat: first hour-€14, additional hours-€7.50 each; daily in summer 10:00–18:00). Two other places farther from Bled town also rent rowboats (4-person boat-€10/hr, closed in bad weather and off-season): Pension Pletna in Mlino (a 15-minute walk around the lake past Grand Hotel Toplice) and the campground on the far end of the lake.

Swimming—Lake Bled has several suitable spots for a swim. The swimming pools under the castle are filled with lake water and routinely earn the "blue flag," meaning the water is top-quality (swim all day-€6.50, less for afternoon only, June–Sept daily 8:00–19:00, closed Oct–May and in bad weather, tel. 04/578-0528). Bled's two beaches are at the far end of the lake. Both are free; the one at the campground (southwest  corner) has lots of tourists, while locals prefer the one at the rowing center (northwest corner). If you swim to the island, remember that you can't get into the church in your swimsuit.

Luge Ride (Polento Sankanje)—Bled's "summer toboggan" luge ride, atop Mount Straža overlooking the lake, allows you to scream down a steep, curvy metal rail track on a little plastic sled. A chairlift takes you to the top of the track, where you'll sit on your sled, take a deep breath, and remind yourself: Pull back on the stick to slow down, push forward on the stick to go faster. You'll drop 480 feet in altitude on the 570-yard-long track, speeding up to about 25 miles per hour as you race toward the lake. You'll see the track on the hillside just south of town, beyond the Grand Hotel Toplice (€6/ride, cheaper for multiple rides, chairlift only-€3, weather-dependent—if it rains, you can't go; mid-June–Aug daily 11:00–20:00; May–mid-June and Sept Sat–Sun only

11:00–18:00, closed Mon–Fri; Oct Sat–Sun only 11:00–16:30; most of April Sat–Sun only 11:00–17:00; closed Nov–early April).

Day Trips—For details on some easy and enjoyable nearby side-trips—including a quirky bee museum, a scenic gorge hike, and a more remote lake experience—see "Near Lake Bled" at the end of this chapter.

Nightlife in Bled

Bled Pub Crawl

Bled is quiet after hours. However, the town does have a few fun bars that are lively with a young crowd (all open nightly until 2:00 in the morning). Since many young people in Bled are students at the local tourism school, they're likely to speak English...and eager to practice with a native speaker. Try a "Smile," a Corona type Slovenian lager. *Šnops* (schnapps) is a local specialty—popular flavors are plum *(slivovka)*, honey *(medica)*, blueberry *(borovničevec)*, and pear *(hruškovec)*.

Kick things off with the fun-loving local gang at **Gostilna Pri Planincu** near the bus station (described later, under "Eating in Bled"). Then head down Cesta Svobode toward the lake; just below Hotel Jelovica, you'll find the rollicking **Irish Pub** (a.k.a. "The Pub"), with Guinness and indoor or outdoor seating. For a more genteel atmosphere, duck across the street and wander a few more steps down toward the lake to find the **Art Café**, with a mellow ambience reminiscent of a Van Gogh painting. Around the lake near the commercial center, **Bled Pub** (a.k.a. "The Cocktail Bar" or "Troha"—for the family that owns it) is a trendy late-night spot where bartenders sling a dizzying array of mixed drinks to an appreciative crowd (between the commercial center and the lake, above the recommended Oštarija Peglez'n restaurant). If you're still standing, several other, more low-key bars and cafés percolate in the commercial center.

Sleeping in Bled

Bled is dominated by a few giant, gradually decaying, communist-era convention hotels. Some have been nicely renovated, but most are stale, outmoded, and overpriced. (It's a strange, incestuous little circle—the majority of the town's big hotels and restaurants are owned by the same company.) Instead, I prefer staying in smaller, countryside, pension-type accommodations—many of them just a short walk above the lake. These quaint little family-run pensions book up early with Germans and Brits; reserve as far ahead as possible. I've listed the high-season prices (May–Oct). Off-season, prices are typically 10–20 percent lower. For even cheaper beds,

Sleep Code

(€1 = about $1.40, country code: 386, area code: 04)
S = Single, **D** = Double/Twin, **T** = Triple, **Q** = Quad, **b** = bathroom. Unless otherwise noted, credit cards are accepted. Everyone speaks English, and all of these accommodations include breakfast. Bled levies a €1.01 tourist tax per person, per night (not included in below prices unless noted).

To help you sort easily through these listings, I've divided the rooms into three categories based on the price for a standard double room with bath:

$$$ Higher Priced—Most rooms €100 or more.
$$ Moderately Priced—Most rooms between €60–100.
$ Lower Priced—Most rooms €60 or less.

consider one of the many *sobe* (rooms in private homes) scattered around the lake (about €25 per person in peak season, often with a hefty 30 percent surcharge for stays shorter than three nights). Kompas Bled Travel Agency can book you a *soba* (see page 443), but be sure the location is convenient before you accept.

Above the Lake

These friendly, cozy, characteristic accommodations are Bled's best values. The only catch is that they're perched on a hilltop a steep five- to ten-minute climb up from the lake (easier than it sounds). There are two ways to find them from the town center: Walk around the lake to Grand Hotel Toplice, then go up the stairs around the right side of the Hotel Jadran (on the hill across the street from Grand Hotel Toplice). Or, from the main road into town (Ljubljanska cesta), take the small service road just above the commercial center (in front of Hotel Lovec), and loop up around the big Kompas and Golf hotels. Some buses (including those to Ljubljana) stop at a bus stop higher up on Ljubljanska cesta, just above the traffic light. This stop is handier to these hotels than Bled's main bus station. From the bus stop, you can walk down Ljubljanska cesta and take the road just above the post office, which leads up to this area.

If you're sleeping up here, Mayer Penzion's restaurant is the easiest choice for dinner (described later, under "Eating in Bled").

$$ Mayer Penzion, thoughtfully run by the Trseglav family, comes with 13 great-value rooms, a helpful staff, a tasty restaurant, an atmospheric wine-tasting cellar, and beautifully handcrafted Slovenian woodwork inside and out. They book up fast in summer with return clients, so reserve early (Sb-€55, Db-€80, €5 less for 3 nights or more, extra bed-€20, family deals, elevator, Wi-Fi, Želeška cesta 7, tel. 04/576-5740, fax 04/576-5741, www.mayer-sp.si, penzion@mayer-sp.si). They also rent a cute, newly restored two-story Slovenian farm cottage next door (Db-€120, Tb/Qb-€150).

$$ Hotel Berc and **Penzion Berc** (pronounced "berts"), run by the Berc brothers, are next door to Mayer Penzion. Both have cozy public spaces, free Internet access and Wi-Fi, and free loaner bikes, and are worth reserving ahead (both cash only, www.berc -sp.si). The new hotel building has 15 rooms with pleasantly woody decor (Sb-€40–50, Db-€70–80; price depends on size, season, and length of stay; all rooms have balconies, Pod Stražo 13, tel. 04/576-5658, fax 04/576-5659, hotel@berc-sp.si, run by Luka). The older, adjacent *penzion* offers 11 cheaper, older, but nearly-as-nice rooms (Sb-€35, Db-€60, €5 more for 1-night stays, 10 percent cheaper off-season, most rooms have balconies, closed in Nov and sporadically off-season, Želeška cesta 15, tel. 04/574-1838, fax 04/576-7320, penzion@berc-sp.si, run by Miha).

$$ Alp Penzion is in a tranquil countryside setting amid hayfields. It's a long hike beyond the others listed here, but still within a 15-minute walk of the lake (better for drivers or for those who don't mind the walk). With 11 rooms, this place is enthusiastically run by the Sršen family, who offer lots of fun extras, including a tennis court and summer barbecue grill/outdoor pub (Sb-€55, Db-€80–85—higher price is for balcony, Tb-€100, 3 percent cheaper if you pay cash, cheaper Oct–April, family rooms, half-board for just €5 extra per person, free Internet access and Wi-Fi, free loaner bikes, Cankarjeva cesta 20A, tel. 04/574-1614, fax 04/574-4590, www.alp-penzion.com, bled@alp-penzion.com). Just next door is the relaxing Essense spa (described earlier, under "Helpful Hints").

$ Mia Sušnik, who is friendly and speaks English, rents out two comfortable apartments. Modern, tidy, and equipped with kitchens, these are a good budget choice for families (Db-€57, 20 percent extra for fewer than 3 nights, no breakfast, cash only, laundry service-€10, free Wi-Fi, free parking, Želeška cesta 3, tel. 04/574-1731, www.bled-holiday.com, susnik@bled-holiday.com). It's just toward the lake from the bigger pensions, with a big crucifix out front. Her sister Ivanka also rents apartments, but they're farther from the lake.

$ Tourist Farm Mulej, farther out of town than my other listings and better for drivers, is a new but traditional farmhouse in a tranquil valley about a half-mile from the lake (1.5 miles from Bled town). Damjana and Jože, who run a working farm, rent out eight modern rooms and four apartments—all with balconies—and serve breakfasts and dinners made with food they produce (Db-€60, or €80 with dinner; €30 per extra person in apartments, or €40 with dinner; 20 percent extra for 1- or 2-night stays in June–Aug, cash only, family rooms, free cable Internet, free loaner bikes, horseback riding, Selo pri Bledu 42a, tel. & fax 04/574-4617, www.mulej-bled.com, info@mulej-bled.com). It's in the farm village of Selo—drive along the lakeside road south from Bled, then turn off in Mlino toward Selo, and look for the signs (to the right) once in the village.

$ Vila Gorenka is your non-hostel, low-budget option. The Žerovec family's old-fashioned house has 10 basic, faded, musty rooms sharing two bathrooms upstairs from their home (S-€20, D-€36, cash only, no extra charge for 1-night stays, no breakfast, free Internet access and Wi-Fi, just below the bigger pensions at Želeška cesta 9, mobile 051-369-070, http://freeweb.siol.net/mz2, vila.gorenka@siol.net, Martin).

Near the Lake

You'll pay a premium to be closer to the lake—but it's hard to argue with the convenience.

$$$ Hotel Lovec (LOW-vets), a Best Western Premier, sits in a convenient (but non-lakefront) location just above the commercial center. Gorgeously renovated inside and out, and run by a helpful and friendly staff, it's a welcoming, cheery, well-run alternative to Bled's many old, dreary communist hotels. Its 60 plush rooms come with all the comforts (Sb-€128, Db-€151, €20 more for a lake-view balcony, very soft rates fluctuate with demand—email to ask for best price, cheaper Nov–Feb, family and "executive" suites available, delicious breakfast, elevator, free Internet access and cable Internet, indoor pool, free parking garage for guests, Ljubljanska cesta 6, tel. 04/620-4100, fax 04/576-8625, www.lovechotel.com, booking@kompas-lovec.eu).

$$$ Grand Hotel Toplice (TOHP-leet-seh) is the grande dame of Bled, with 87 high-ceilinged rooms, parquet floors, an elegant view lounge, posh decor, all the amenities, and a long list of high-profile guests—from Madeleine Albright to Jordan's King Hussein to Slovene-by-marriage Donald Trump (ask to see their "wall of fame"). Rooms in the back are cheaper, but have no lake views and overlook a noisy street—try to get one as high up as possible (non-view: Sb-€150, Db-€170; lake view: Sb-€180, Db-€220; suites with lake views-€280; 15–20 percent less Nov–April, elevator, air-con, free one-hour boat rental for guests, free Internet access and cable Internet, free parking, Cesta Svobode 12, tel. 04/579-1000, fax 04/574-1841, www.hotel-toplice.com, ghtoplice @hotelibled.com). The hotel's name—*toplice*—means "spa"; guests are free to use the hotel's swanky, natural-spring-fed indoor swimming pool (a chilly 72 degrees Fahrenheit). This hotel also runs two smaller, far less luxurious hotels nearby with very dated and faded rooms and lower rates (Hotel Trst and Hotel Jadran, details at Toplice's website).

$$$ Vila Prešeren has eight stylish, pricey rooms above a popular restaurant right on the lake (Sb-€112, Db-€150, apartment-€200–214 depending on size, cheaper mid-Oct–early May, no reception—check in at the restaurant, air-con, free Wi-Fi, Veslaška promenada 14, tel. 04/575-2510, www.vilapreseren.si, vila preseren@sprtinaresrots.si).

$ Penzion Bledec (BLED-ets), an official IYHF hostel, is just below the castle at the top of the Old Town. Each of the 13 rooms has its own bathroom, and some can be rented as doubles (though "doubles" are actually underutilized triples and quads, with separate beds pushed together—so they might not be reservable July–Aug or at other busy times). The friendly staff is justifiably proud of the bargain they offer (bed in 4- to 7-bed dorm-€21, Db-€54, Tb-€63, cheaper Nov–April, members pay 10 percent less, includes sheets and breakfast, great family rooms, free Internet access and Wi-Fi, full-service laundry for guests-€9/load, restaurant, Grajska 17, tel. 04/574-5250, fax 04/574-5251, www.mlino.si, bledec@mlino.si).

$ Travellers Haven is a low-key hostel run by Mirjam and Karmen. The 27 beds fill six rooms in a nicely renovated hundred-year-old villa in the Old Town (€19 for a bunk in a 4–6-bed room, D-€48, no breakfast but guest kitchen, tight bathrooms offer little privacy, reception open 8:00–13:00 & 16:00–23:00; free Internet access, Wi-Fi, laundry machines, and loaner bikes; Riklijeva cesta 1, mobile 031-704-455 or 041-396-545, www.travellers-haven.si, travellers-haven@t-2.net).

Eating in Bled

Bled has several good restaurants, but most everything is quite similar. For variety, wait for Ljubljana.

Okarina Etno, run by charming, well-traveled Leo Ličof, serves a diverse array of cuisines, all of them well-executed: international fare, traditional Slovenian specialties, and Indian (Himalayan) dishes. Leo has a respect for salads and vegetables and a passion for fish. Creative cooking, fine presentation, friendly service, and an atmosphere as tastefully eclectic as the food make this place a great splurge (€9–14 pastas, €10–22 main courses, plus a few pricier splurges, Mon–Fri 18:00–24:00, Sat–Sun 12:00–24:00, next to Hotel Lovec at Ljubljanska cesta 8, tel. 04/574-1458). In the back of the menu, look for the copy of the guest book page

Bled Desserts

While you're in Bled, be sure to enjoy the town's specialty, a cream cake called **kremna rezina** (KRAYM-nah ray-ZEE-nah; often referred to by its German-derived name, **kremšnita,** KRAYM-shnee-tah). It's a layer of cream and a thick layer of vanilla custard artfully sandwiched between sheets of delicate, crispy crust. Heavenly. Slovenes travel from all over the country to sample this famous dessert.

Slightly less renowned—but just as tasty—is **grmada** (gur-MAH-dah, "bonfire"). This dessert was developed by Hotel Jelovica as a way to get rid of their day-old leftovers. They take yesterday's cake, add rum, milk, custard, and raisins, and top it off with whipped cream and chocolate syrup.

Finally, there's *prekmurska gibanica*—or just **gibanica** (gee-bah-NEET-seh) for short. Originating in the Hungarian corner of the country, *gibanica* is an earthy pastry filled with poppy seeds, walnuts, apple, and cheese, and drizzled with rum.

These desserts are typically enjoyed with a lake-and-mountains view—the best spots are the terrace at Vila Prešeren, the Panorama restaurant by Grand Hotel Toplice, and the terrace across from the Hotel Park (figure around €5 for cake and coffee at any of these places). For a more local (but non-lake view) setting, consider Šmon Slaščičarna (only slightly cheaper; see below).

with Paul McCartney's visit from May 2005. Around the left side of the building is **Leo's Balkan Grill,** serving up typical grilled meat dishes (see "Balkan Flavors" on page 31; €6–10 dishes, open summer only).

Oštarija Peglez'n ("The Old Iron"), conveniently located on the main road between the commercial center and the lake, cooks up tasty Slovenian and Mediterranean meals, with an emphasis on fish. Choose between the delightful Slovenian cottage interior or the shady streetside terrace. Reservations are smart in summer (€7–9 salads and pastas, €12–25 main courses, daily 12:00–23:00, fun family-style shareable plates, Cesta Svobode 19A, tel. 04/574-4218).

Vila Prešeren is the best choice for lakeside dining, with a giant terrace reaching all the way down to the lakefront path. Featuring mod decor and international cuisine, this is a great spot for a meal, a drink, or a classic Lake Bled dessert (€9–11 salads, €7–10 pastas, €12–28 main courses, daily 7:00–23:00, Veslaška promenada 14, tel. 04/575-2510).

Mayer Penzion, just up the hill from the lakefront, has a dressy restaurant with good traditional cooking that's worth the short hike. This is where a Babel of international tourists come to swap hiking tips and day-trip tales. As this is the only real restaurant in the pension neighborhood, it can be very busy—reserve ahead (€8–21 main courses, Tue–Sun 18:00–24:00, closed Mon, indoor or outdoor seating, above Hotel Jadran at Želeška cesta 7, tel. 04/576-5740).

Gostilna Pri Planincu ("By the Mountaineers") is a homey, informal bar coated with license plates and packed with fun-loving and sometimes rowdy natives. A larger dining area sprawls behind the small, local-feeling pub, and there's outdoor seating out front and on the side patio. The menu features huge portions of stick-to-your-ribs Slovenian pub grub, plus Balkan grilled-meat specialties (€7–16 main courses, fish splurges up to €25). Ask about their €5–7 daily specials—huge, home-style traditional dishes. Upstairs is a timbered pizzeria selling €4–8 wood-fired pies (daily 9:00–23:00, pizzeria open from 11:00, Grajska cesta 8, tel. 04/574-1613). The playful cartoon mural along the outside of the restaurant shows different types of mountaineers (from left to right): thief, normal, mooch ("gopher"), climber, and naked (...well, almost).

Pizzeria Rustika, in the Old Town, offers good wood-fired pizzas and salads. Its upstairs terrace is relaxing on a balmy evening (€5–8 pizzas, Tue–Sun 12:00–22:00, Mon 15:00–22:00—but opens at 12:00 in peak season, service can be slow when it's busy, Riklijeva cesta 13, tel. 04/576-8900).

The **Mercator** grocery store, in the commercial center, has the makings for a bang-up picnic. They sell pre-made sandwiches for about €3, or will make you one to order (point to what you want). This is a great option for hikers and budget travelers (Mon–Fri 7:00–19:00, Sat 7:00–15:00, Sun 8:00–12:00). There's another location closer to the Old Town and castle.

Dessert: While tourists generally gulp down their cream cakes on a hotel restaurant's lakefront terrace, local residents know the best desserts are at **Šmon Slaščičarna** (a.k.a. the "Brown Bear," for the bear on the sign). It's nicely untouristy, but lacks the atmosphere of the lakeside spots (€2–3 cakes, daily 7:30–21:00, near bus station at Grajska cesta 3, tel. 04/574-1616).

Lake Bled Connections

The most convenient train connections to Bled leave from the Lesce-Bled station, about 2.5 miles away (see details under "Arrival in Bled," earlier). Remember, when buying a train ticket to Lake Bled, make it clear that you want to go to the Lesce-Bled station (not the Bled Jezero station, which is poorly connected to the main line). No one in the town of Bled sells train tickets; buy them at the station just before your train departs (open Mon–Fri 5:30–21:00, Sat 7:00–14:00, Sun 13:30–19:30). If the ticket window there is closed, buy your ticket on board from the conductor (who will likely waive the €2.50 additional fee).

Note that if you're going to **Ljubljana,** the bus (which leaves from Bled town itself) is better than the train (which leaves from the Lesce-Bled train station).

From Lesce-Bled by Train to: Ljubljana (roughly hourly, 40–60 min—but bus is better since it leaves from Bled town), **Salzburg** (5/day, 4 hrs), **Munich** (3/day, 6 hrs), **Vienna** (that's *Dunaj* in Slovene, 5/day, 6 hrs, transfer in Villach, Austria), **Venice** (3/day with transfer in Villach, 6 hrs), **Zagreb** (5/day, 3.5 hrs).

By Bus to: Ljubljana (Mon–Sat hourly—usually at :30 past the hour, fewer on Sun, 1.25 hrs, €6.30), **Radovljica** (Mon–Fri at least 2/hr, Sat hourly, Sun almost hourly, 15 min, €1.60), **Lesce-Bled train station** (2/hr, 10 min, €1.30), **Lake Bohinj** (hourly, 40 min and €3.60 to Bohinj Jezero stop, 50 min and €4.10 to Bohinj Vogel or Bohinj Zlatorog stop), **Podhom** (15-min hike away from Vintgar Gorge, Mon–Fri 5/day in the morning, 1/day Sat, none Sun, 15 min, €1.30), **Spodnje Gorje** (also 15-min hike from Vintgar Gorge, take bus in direction of Krnica, hourly, 15 min, €1.30). Confirm times at the TI or using the schedules posted at the unstaffed Bled bus station. Buy tickets on the bus.

By Plane: Ljubljana Airport is between Lake Bled and Ljubljana, about a 45-minute drive from Bled. Connecting by taxi costs around €50 (set price up front—since it's outside of town, they don't use the meter). The bus connection from Bled to the airport is cheap (total cost: about €5) but complicated and time-consuming: First, go to Kranj (Mon–Fri 12/day, Sat–Sun 8/day, 35 min), then transfer to a Brnik-bound bus (at least hourly, 20 min). Many Bled residents prefer to fly from Klagenfurt, Austria. For details on both the Ljubljana and Klagenfurt airports, see page 435.

Route Tips for Drivers: Bled is less than an hour north of Ljubljana. The new A-2 expressway zips you almost all the way there; a bridge and a tunnel might not yet be completed for your visit (due to be done by sometime in 2011). Watch for signs to *Bled;* the Bled exit will take you directly to the lake (where the road becomes Ljubljanska cesta).

To reach Radovljica (bee museum) or Lesce (train station), drive out of Bled on Ljubljanska cesta toward the expressway. Watch for the turnoff to those two towns on the right. They're on the same road: Lesce first (to reach train station, divert right when entering town), then Radovljica.

Near Lake Bled

The countryside around Bled offers several day trips that can be done easily without a car (bus connection information is described in each section). The three listed here are the best (one small-town/museum experience, two hiking/back-to-nature options). They're more convenient than can't-miss, but each is worthwhile on a longer visit, and all give a good taste of the Julian Alps. For a self-guided driving tour through farther-flung (and even more striking) parts of the Julian Alps, see the next chapter.

Radovljica

The town of Radovljica (rah-DOH-vleet-suh) is larger than Bled, perched on a plateau above the Sava River. The town itself is noth-ing exciting, though its old center pedestrian zone, Linhartov trg, makes for a pleasant stroll (TI tel. 04/531-5300). But the town is home to a fascinating and offbeat beekeeping museum—which, with only a few rooms, still ranks as  one of Europe's biggest on the topic. Skip the town on Mondays, when the museum is closed (and be aware that the museum closes for a three-hour lunch break in shoulder season).

Getting to Radovljica: Buses to Radovljica generally leave Bled every half-hour (fewer on weekends, €1.60, buy ticket from driver, trip takes about 15 min). **Drivers** leave Bled on Ljubljanska cesta, then turn right at the sign for *Radovljica* and go through the village of Lesce; the road dead-ends at Radovljica's pedestrian zone, where you'll find a parking lot and rustic garage. From here, it's a short walk to the bee museum (see directions below). A handy **bike** path scenically and peacefully connects Bled with Radovljica (about 4 miles, get details at TI).

Arrival in Radovljica: To reach the old town square and the bee museum from the bus station, leave the station going straight ahead, cross the bus parking lot and the next street, then turn left down the far street (following brown sign for *Staro Mesto*). In five minutes, you'll get to the pedestrianized Linhartov trg (TI on right just before you enter pedestrian zone). At the end of this square on the left is the big, yellow Baroque mansion that houses the bee museum (upstairs).

Near Lake Bled

Sights in Radovljica

▲Apicultural Museum (Čebelarski Muzej)

This museum celebrates Slovenia's long beekeeping heritage. Since the days before Europeans had sugar, Slovenia has been a big honey producer. Slovenian farmer Anton Janša is considered the father of modern beekeeping and was Europe's first official teacher of beekeeping (in Habsburg Vienna).

The first two rooms of the museum trace the history of beekeeping, from the time when bees were kept in hollowed-out trees to the present day. Notice the old-fashioned **tools** in the second room. When a new queen bee is born, the old queen takes half the hive's bees to a new location. Experienced beekeepers used the long, skinny instrument (a beehive stethoscope) to figure out when the swarm would fly the coop. Then, once the bees had moved to a nearby tree, the beekeeper used the big spoons to retrieve the queen—surrounded by an angry ball of her subjects—from her new home before she could get settled in. The beekeeper transported the furious gang into a manmade hive designed for easier, more sanitary collection of the honey. You can also see the tools beekeepers used to create smoke, which makes bees less aggressive. Even today, some of Slovenia's old-fashioned beekeepers simply light up a cigarette and blow smoke on any bees that get ornery.

The third room features the museum's highlight: whimsically painted beehive **frontboards** (called *panjske končnice*). Nineteenth-century farmers, believing these paintings would help the bees

find their way home, developed a tradition of decorating their hives with religious, historical, and satirical folk themes (look for the devil sharpening a woman's tongue on a wheel). The depiction of a hunter's funeral shows all the animals happy...except his dog. There's everything from portraits of Habsburg emperors, to a "true crime" sequence of a man murdering his family as they sleep, to proto-"Lockhorns" cartoons of marital strife, to 18th-century erotica (one with a woman showing some leg and another with a flip-up, peek-a-boo panel).

The life-size wooden statues were used to "guard" the beehives—and designed to look like fearsome Ottoman and Napoleonic soldiers.

You'll also find an interactive multimedia exhibit, a good video in English, temporary exhibitions, and—in the summer only—an actual, functioning beehive (try to find the queen). The gift shop is a good place for souvenirs, with hand-painted replicas of frontboards, honey brandy, candles, ornaments, and other bee products (museum entry-€2.50, good English descriptions, free sheet of English info, €1.60 English guidebook is a nice souvenir; May–Oct Tue–Sun 10:00–18:00, closed Mon; March–April and Nov–Dec Wed and Sat–Sun 10:00–12:00 & 15:00–17:00, Tue and Thu–Fri 8:00–15:00, closed Mon; Jan–Feb Tue–Fri 8:00–15:00, closed Sat–Mon; upstairs at Linhartov trg 1, tel. 04/532-0520, www.muzeji-radovljica.si).

Eating in Radovljica

Several Radovljica restaurants near the bee museum have view terraces overlooking the surrounding mountains and valleys.

Lectar offers pricey, hearty Slovenian fare in a rural-feeling setting with a user-friendly, super-traditional menu. Its several heavily decorated rooms are often filled with tour groups, but in good weather, don't miss the terrace out back. The restaurant is known for its heart-shaped gingerbread cookies (called *lect*), inscribed with messages of love. In the cellar is a €1 "museum" where you can watch costumed bakers make and decorate these hearts according to the traditional recipe (€9–18 main courses, Wed–Mon 12:00–22:00, closed Tue, family-friendly,

Linhartov trg 2, tel. 04/537-4800).

The cheaper **Grajska Gostilnica** dishes up good, basic pub grub (salads, pizza, pastas, open long hours daily, across from the bus station and to the left, inside Hotel Grajski Dvor at Kranjska 2, tel. 04/531-5585).

Vintgar Gorge

Just north of Bled, the river Radovna has carved this mile-long, picturesque gorge into the mountainside. For hikers, Vintgar (VEENT-gar) Gorge is worth ▲▲. Boardwalks and bridges put you right in the middle of the action of this "poor man's Plitvice." You'll cross over several waterfalls and marvel at the clarity of the water. The easy hike is on a board-walk trail with handrails (sometimes nar-row and a bit slippery). At the end of the gorge, you'll find a snack stand, WCs, and a bridge with a fine view. Go back the way you came, or take a prettier return to Bled (see "Scenic Hike Back to Bled," later). The gorge is easily reachable from Bled by bus or foot and is the best option for those who are itching for a hike but don't have a car

(€4 to enter gorge, open daily May–late Oct 8:00–19:00 or until dusk, June–Aug maybe until 20:00, closed late Oct–April, tel. 04/572-5266).

Getting to Vintgar Gorge: The gorge is 2.5 miles north of Bled. You can walk (at least one hour) or bus (15-min ride plus 15-min walk, or 30-min ride on summer tourist bus) to the gorge entrance.

Walkers leave Bled on the road between the castle and St. Martin's Church and take the uphill (left) road at the fork. Just after the little yellow chapel, turn right on the road with the big tree, then immediately left at the Mercator grocery store. When the road swings left, continue straight onto Partizanska (marked for *Podhom* and a walking sign for *Vintgar;* ignore the bus sign for *Vintgar* pointing left). At the fork just after the little bridge, go left for Podhom, then simply follow signs for *Vintgar.*

In summer, the easy **tourist bus** takes you right to the gorge entrance in 30 minutes (see "Getting Around Lake Bled," page 443). Otherwise, you can take a **local bus** to one of two stops: Podhom (Mon–Fri 5/day in the morning, 1/day Sat, none Sun, 15 min, €1.30) or Spodnje Gorje (take bus in direction of Krnica, hourly, 15 min, €1.30). From either the Podhom or the Spodnje Gorje bus stop, it's a 15-minute walk to the gorge (follow signs for *Vintgar*).

Drivers follow signs to *Podhom*, then *Vintgar* (see walking instructions).

Scenic Hike Back to Bled: If you still have energy once you reach the end of the gorge, consider this longer hike back with panoramic views. Behind the snack stand, find the trail marked *Katarina Bled*. You'll go uphill for 25 strenuous minutes (following the red-and-white circles and arrows) before cresting the hill and enjoying beautiful views over Bled town and the region. Continue straight down the road 15 minutes to the typical, narrow, old village of Zasip, then walk (about 30 min) or take the bus back to Bled.

Lake Bohinj

The pristine alpine Lake Bohinj (BOH-heen), 16 miles southwest of Bled, enjoys a quieter scene and (in clear weather) even better vistas of Triglav and the surrounding mountains. This is a real back-to-nature experience, with just a smattering of hotels and campgrounds, rather than the well-oiled resort machine of Bled. Some people adore Bohinj; others are bored by it. If you think Bled is too touristy to allow you to really enjoy the nature, go to Bohinj.

Getting to Lake Bohinj: From Bled, hourly **buses** head for Bohinj, stopping at three different destinations: Bohinj Jezero

(the village of Ribčev Laz, 40 min, €3.60), then Bohinj Vogel (a 10-minute walk from the base of the Vogel Mountain cable car, 50 min, €4.10), and finally a few hundred yards more to Bohinj Zlatorog (Hotel Zlatorog and the one-hour hike to the Savica waterfall trailhead, 50 min, €4.10). Off-season, there are fewer buses—confirm times before you depart. **Drivers** leave Bled going south along the lakefront road, Cesta Svobode; in the village of Mlino, you'll peel off from the lake and follow signs to *Boh Bistrica* (a midsize town near Lake Bohinj). Once in the town of Bohinjska Bistrica, turn right, following *Bohinj Jezero* signs. The road takes you to the village of Ribčev Laz and along the lakefront road with all the attractions.

Sights at Lake Bohinj

A visit to Bohinj has three parts: a village, a cable car (and nearby cemetery), and a waterfall hike. I've listed them as you'll reach them along the main road from Bled, which runs along the south side of the lake.

Ribčev Laz Village—Coming from Bled, your first views of Bohinj will be from the little village called Ribčev Laz (loosely translated as "Good Fishin' Hole") at the southeast corner of the lake. Here you'll find a TI, a handful of hotels and ice-cream stands, and the Bohinj Jezero bus stop. The town's main landmark is its church, **St. John the Baptist** (to your right as you face the lake, past the distinctive stone bridge; not open to visitors).

In the other direction, a five-minute stroll down the lakefront road, is a dock where you can catch an electric **tourist boat** to make a silent circuit around the lake (€10 round-trip, €7 one-way, daily 10:00–18:00, 2/hr, less off-season). The boat stops at the far end of the lake, at Camp Zlatorog—a 10-minute walk from the Vogel cable car (see below). Across from the Ribčev Laz dock is a fun concrete 3-D model of Triglav (compare to the real thing, hovering across the lake). Finally, a few more steps down the road, just beyond a boat rental dock, you'll see a statue of Zlatorog, the "Golden Horn"—a mythical chamois-like creature native to the Julian Alps. Continuing down the road, you'll reach the next attraction.

Vogel Mountain Cable Car—For a mountain perch without the sweat, take the cable car up to Vogel Mountain, offering impressive panoramic views of Mount Triglav and the Julian Alps (€13 round-trip, runs every 30 min, daily 7:00–19:00 in summer, 8:00–18:00 in winter, shorter hours and less frequent departures in spring and fall—confirm schedule before you make the trip, closed Nov, www.vogel.si). The top is a ski-in-winter, hike-in-summer area with fine views and a chairlift experience. The alpine hut Merjasec ("Wild Boar") offers tasty strudel and a wide variety of local brandies (including the notorious "Boar's Blood"—a concoction of several different flavors guaranteed to get you snorting). To reach the cable-car station, drivers follow signs to *Vogel* (to the left off the main lakefront road); by bus, get off at the Bohinj Vogel stop (request this stop from driver) and hike about 10 minutes up the steep road on the left (away from the lake).

World War I Cemetery—Back down below the cable car, on the main road just beyond the cable-car station and Bohinj Vogel bus stop, look for the metal gate on the left marking a World War I cemetery—the final resting place for some Soča Front soldiers (see sidebar on page 480). While no fighting occurred here (it was mostly on the other side of these mountains), injured soldiers were brought to a nearby hospital. Those who didn't recover ended up here. Notice that many of the names are not Slovenian, but Hungarian, Polish, Czech, and so on—a reminder that the entire multiethnic Austro-Hungarian Empire was involved in the fighting. If you're walking down from the cable-car station, the cemetery makes for a poignant detour on your way to the main road (look for it through the trees).

Savica Waterfall (Slap Savica)—Up the valley beyond the end of the lake is Bohinj's final treat, a waterfall called Slap Savica (sah-VEET-seh). Hardy hikers enjoy following the moderate-to-strenuous uphill trail (including 553 stairs) to see the cascade, which dumps into a remarkably pure pool of aquamarine snow-melt (€2.40, daily in summer from 8:00 until dusk, allow about 90 min for the round-trip hike). Drivers follow the lakefront road to where it ends, right at the trailhead. Without a car, getting to the trailhead is a hassle. If you take the public bus from Bled, or the boats on the lake, they'll get you only as far as the Bohinj Zlatorog stop—the end of the line, and still a one-hour hike from the trailhead (from the bus stop, follow signs to *Slap Savica*). In summer, a sporadic shuttle bus takes you right to the trailhead. But frankly, it's not worth it if you don't have a car.

THE JULIAN ALPS

Vršič Pass • Soča River Valley • Bovec • Kobarid

The countryside around Lake Bled is plenty spectacular. But to crescendo your Slovenian mountain experience, head for the hills. The northwestern corner of Slovenia —within yodeling distance of Austria and Italy—is crowned by the Julian Alps (named for Julius Caesar). Here, mountain culture has a Slavic flavor.

The Slovenian mountainsides are laced with hiking paths, blanketed in a deep forest, and speckled with ski resorts and vacation chalets. Beyond every ridge is a peaceful alpine village nestled around a quaint Baroque steeple. And in the center of it all is Mount Triglav—ol' "Three Heads"—Slovenia's symbol and tallest mountain.

The single best day in the Julian Alps is spent driving up and over the 50 hairpin turns of the breathtaking Vršič Pass (vur-SHEECH, open May–Oct) and back down via the Soča (SOH-chah) River Valley, lined with offbeat nooks and Hemingway-haunted crannies. As you curl on twisty roads between the cut-glass peaks, you'll enjoy stunning high-mountain scenery, whitewater rivers with superb fishing, rustic rest stops, thought-provoking World War I sights, and charming hamlets.

A pair of Soča Valley towns holds watch over the region. Bovec is all about good times (it's the whitewater adventure-sports hub), while Kobarid attends to more serious matters (WWI history). Though neither is a destination in itself, both Bovec and Kobarid are pleasant, functional, and convenient home bases for exploring this gloriously beautiful region.

Getting Around the Julian Alps

The Julian Alps are best by **car**. Even if you're doing the rest of your trip by train, consider renting a car here for maximum mountain day-trip flexibility. I've included a self-guided driving tour incorporating the best of the Julian Alps (Vršič Pass and Soča Valley).

It's difficult to do the Vršič Pass and Soča Valley without your own wheels. Hiring a **local guide** with a car can be a great value, making your time not only fun, but also informative. Cheaper but less personal, you could join a day-trip **excursion** from Bled. (Both options are explained under "Tours at Lake Bled," page 444.) A public **bus** follows more or less this same route, leaving Ljubljana each morning at 6:30, arriving in Bovec at 10:45 (daily July–Aug, Sat–Sun only Sept–June). Or stay closer to Bled, and get a taste of the Julian Alps by taking advantage of easy and frequent bus connections to more convenient day-trip destinations (Radovljica, the Vintgar Gorge, and Lake Bohinj— all described under "Near Lake Bled" in the previous chapter).

Julian Alps Self-Guided Driving Tour

This all-day, self-guided driving tour, rated ▲▲▲, takes you over the highest mountain pass in Slovenia, with stunning scenery and a few quirky sights along the way. From waterfalls to hiking trails, World War I history to queasy suspension bridges, this trip has it all.

Orientation to the Julian Alps

Most of the Julian Alps are encompassed by the Triglav National Park (Triglavski Narodni Park). (Some sights near Lake Bled—such as Lake Bohinj and the Vintgar Gorge—are also part of this park, but are covered in the previous chapter.) This drive is divided into two parts: the Vršič Pass and the Soča River Valley. While not for stick-shift novices, all but the most timid drivers will agree the scenery is worth the many hairpin turns. Frequent pull-outs offer plenty of opportunity to relax, stretch your legs, and enjoy the vistas.

Planning Your Time: This drive can be done in a day, but consider spending the night along the way for a more leisurely pace. You can start and end in Bled or Ljubljana. For efficient sightseeing, I prefer to begin in Bled (after appreciating the mountains from afar for a day or two) and end in the capital.

Length of This Tour: These rough estimates do not include stops: Bled to the top of Vršič Pass—1 hour; Vršič Pass to Trenta (start of Soča Valley)—30 min; Trenta to Bovec—30 min; Bovec to Kobarid—30 min; Kobarid to Ljubljana or Bled—2 hours (remember, it's an hour between Ljubljana and Bled). In other words, if you started and ended in Bled and drove the entire route without stopping, you'd make it home in less than five hours...but you'd miss so much. It takes at least a full day to really do the region justice.

Tourist Information: The best sources of information are the Bled TI (see page 438), the Triglav National Park Information Centers in Trenta (page 473) and Bled (page 439), and the TIs in Bovec and Kobarid (both listed in this chapter).

Maps: Pick up a good map before you begin (available at local TIs, travel agencies, and gas stations). The all-Slovenia *Autokarta Slovenija* or the TI's *Next Exit: Goldenhorn Route* map both include all the essential roads, but several more detailed options are also available. The 1:50,000 Kod & Kam *Posoče* map covers the entire Vršič Pass and Soča Valley (but doesn't include the parts of the drive near Bled and Ljubljana).

OK...let's ride.

Part 1: Vršič Pass

From Bled or Ljubljana, take the A-2 expressway north, enjoying views of Mount Triglav on the left as you drive. About 10 minutes past Bled, you'll approach the industrial city of **Jesenice,** whose iron- and steelworks— once called the "Detroit of Yugoslavia"— filled this valley with multicolored smoke until most of them closed in the 1980s. The city plans to convert these old factories into a sort of theme park.

Just after the giant smokestack with the billboards, the little gaggle of colorful houses on the right (just next to the freeway) is **Kurja Vas** ("Chicken Village"). This unassuming place is locally famous for producing hockey players: 18 of the 20 players on the 1971 Yugoslav hockey team—which went to the World Championships—were from this tiny hamlet.

As you zip past Jesenice, keep your eye out for the exit marked

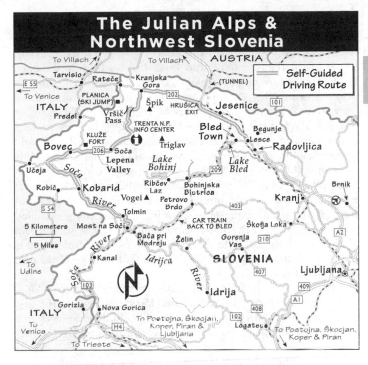

Jesenice-zahod, Trbiž/Tarvisio, Kr. Gora, and *Hrušica* (it's after the gas station, just before the tunnel to Austria). When you exit, turn left toward *Trbiž/Tarvisio* and *Kranjska Gora* (yellow sign).

Just after the exit, the big, blue building surrounded by tall lights was the former border station (the overpass you'll go under leads into Austria). Locals have fond memories of visiting Austria during the Yugoslav days, when they smuggled home forbidden Western goods. Some items were simply not available back home (VCRs, Coca-Cola, designer clothes); other goods were simply better over there (chocolate, coffee, dishwasher soap).

Slovenes brag that their country—"with 56 percent of the land covered in forest"—is Europe's second-greenest. As you drive toward Kranjska Gora, take in all this greenery...and the characteristic Slovenian hayracks (recognized as part of the national heritage and now preserved; see page 385). The Vrata Valley (on the left) is a popular starting point for climbing Mount Triglav. Paralleling the road on the left is a rails-to-trails bike path that loops from here through Italy and Austria, allowing bikers to connect three countries in one day. On the right, watch for the statue of Jakob Aljaž, who actually bought Triglav, back when such a thing was possible (he's pointing at his purchase). Ten minutes later, in Gozd Martuljek, you'll cross a bridge and enjoy a great head-on view of Špik Mountain.

Entering Kranjska Gora (once Yugoslavia's leading winter resort and still popular with Croatian skiers), you'll see a turnoff to the left marked for *Bovec* and *Vršič*. This leads up to the pass, but winter sports fanatics may first want to take a 15-minute detour to see the biggest ski jump in the world, a few miles ahead (stay straight through Kranjska Gora, then turn left at signs for **Planica,** the last stop before the Italian border). Every year, tens of thousands of sports fans flock here to watch the ski-flying world championships. This is where a local boy was the first human to fly more than 100 meters (328 feet) on skis. Today's competitors routinely set new world records (currently 784 feet—that's 17 seconds in the air). From the ski jump, you're a few minutes' walk from Italy or Austria. This region—spanning three nations—lobbied unsuccessfully under the name Senza Confini (Italian for "without borders") to host the 2006 Winter Olympics. This philosophy is in tune with the European Union's vision for a Europe of regions, rather than nations.

Back in Kranjska Gora, follow the signs for *Vršič*. Before long, you'll officially enter **Triglav National Park** and come to the first of this road's 50 hairpin turns (24 up, then 26 down)—each one numbered and labeled with the altitude in meters. Notice that they're cobbled to provide better traction. If the drive seems daunting, remember that 50-seat tour buses routinely conquer this pass... if they can do it, so can you. (Better yet, imagine the bicyclists who routinely pedal to the top. The best can do it in less than 30 minutes—faster than driving.)

After switchback #8, with the cute waterfall, park your car on the right and hike up the stairs on the left to the little **Russian chapel**. This road was built during World War I by at least 10,000 Russian POWs of the Austro-Hungarian Empire to supply the front lines of the Soča Front. The POWs lived and worked in terrible conditions, and several hundred died of illness and exposure. On March 8, 1916, an avalanche thundered down the mountains, killing hundreds more workers. This chapel was built where the final casualty was found. Take a minute to pay your respects to the men who built the  road you're enjoying today. Because it's a Russian Orthodox chapel, notice that the crosses topping the steeples have three crossbars. (For more on the Orthodox faith, see page 278.)

Back on the road, after #17, look as high as you can on the cliff face to see sunlight poking through a **"window"** in the rock. This

Mount Triglav

Mount Triglav ("Three Heads") stands watch over the Julian Alps and all of Slovenia. Slovenes say that its three peaks are the guardians of the water, air, and earth. This mountain defines Slovenes, even adorning the nation's flag: Look for the national seal, with three peaks. The two squiggly lines under it represent the Adriatic. Or take a look at one of Slovenia's €0.50 coins.

From the town of Bled, you'll see Triglav peeking up over the ridge on a clear day. (You'll get an even better view from nearby Lake Bohinj.)

It's said that you're not a true Slovene until you've climbed Triglav. One native took these words very seriously and climbed the mountain 853 times...in one year. Climbing to the summit—at 9,396 feet—is an attainable goal for any hiker in decent shape. If you're here for a while and want to become an honorary Slovene, befriend a local and ask if he or she will take you to the top.

If mountain climbing isn't your style, relax at an outdoor café with a piece of cream cake and a view of Triglav. It won't make you a Slovene...but it's close enough on a quick visit.

natural formation, a popular destination for intrepid hikers, is big enough for the Statue of Liberty to crawl through.

After #22, at the pullout for Erjavčeva Koča restaurant, you may see tour-bus groups making a fuss about the mountain vista. They're looking for a ghostly face in the cliff wall, supposedly belonging to the mythical figure **Ajda**. This village girl was cursed by the townspeople after correctly predicting the death of the Zlatorog (Golden Horn), a magical, beloved, chamois-like animal. Her tiny image (with a Picasso nose) is just above the tree line, a little to the right—try to get someone to point her out to you (you

can see her best if you stand at the signpost near the road).

After #24, you reach the **summit** (5,285 feet). Consider getting out of the car to enjoy the views (in peak season, you'll pay an attendant to park here). Hike up to the hut for a snack or drink on the grand view terrace. On the right, a long gravel

Hemingway in the Julian Alps

It was against the scenic backdrop of the Slovenian Alps that a young man from Oak Park, Illinois, first came to Europe—the continent with which he would forever be identified. After graduating high school in 1917 and working briefly as a newspaper reporter, young Ernest Hemingway wanted to join the war effort in Europe. Bad vision kept him out of the army, but he craved combat experience—so he joined the Red Cross Ambulance Corps instead.

After a short detour through Paris, Hemingway was sent to the Italian Front. On his first day, he was given the job of retrieving human remains—gruesomely disfigured body parts—after the explosion of a munitions factory. Later he came to the Lower Piave Valley, not far from the Soča Front. In July 1918, his ambulance was hit by a mortar shell. Despite his injuries, he saved an Italian soldier who was also wounded. According to legend, he packed his own wound with cigarette butts to stop the flow of blood.

Sent to Milan to recuperate, Hemingway fell in love with a nurse, but she later left him for an Italian military officer. A decade later, Hemingway wrote about Kobarid (using its Italian name, Caporetto), the war, and his case of youthful heartbreak in the novel *A Farewell to Arms*.

chute gives hikers a thrilling glissade down. (From the pullout just beyond #26, it's easy to view hikers "skiing" down.)

As you begin the descent, keep an eye out for old WWI debris. A lonely guard tunnel stands after #28, followed by a tunnel marked *1916* (on the left) that was part of the road's original path. Then you'll see abandoned checkpoints from when this was the border between Italy and the Austro-Hungarian Empire. At #48 is a statue of **Julius Kugy,** an Italian botanist who wrote books about alpine flora.

At #49, the road to the right (marked *Izvir Soče*) leads to the **source of the Soča River.** If you feel like stretching your legs after all that shifting, drive about five minutes down this road to a restaurant parking lot. From here, you can take a challenging 20-minute uphill hike to the Soča source. This is also the starting point for a new, well-explained Soča Trail (Soška Pot) that leads all the way to the town of Bovec, mostly following the road we're driving on today. With plenty of time and a hankering to hike rather than drive, consider taking this trail (about 12 miles one-way).

Nearing the end of the switchbacks, follow signs for *Bovec*. Crossing the Soča River, you begin the second half of this trip.

Part 2: Soča River Valley

During World War I, the terrain between here and the Adriatic made up the Soča (Isonzo) Front. As you follow the Soča River south, down what's nicknamed the "Valley of the Cemeteries," the scenic mountainsides around you tell the tale of this terrible warfare. Imagine a young Ernest Hemingway driving his ambulance through these same hills (see sidebar).

But it's not all so gloomy. There are plenty of other diversions—interesting villages and churches, waterfalls and suspension bridges, and lots more. Perhaps most impressive is the remarkable clarity and milky-blue color of the Soča itself, which Slovenes proudly call their "emerald river."

The last Vršič switchback (#50) sends you into the village of **Trenta**. You'll pass a church and a botanical garden of alpine plants (Alpinum Juliana), then go over a bridge. Immediately after the bridge on the right is the parking lot for the Mlinarica Gorge. While the gorge is interesting, the bridge leading to it was damaged in a severe storm and hasn't yet been rebuilt—so it's best left to hardy hikers.

As you get to the cluster of buildings in Trenta's "downtown," look on the left for the **Triglav National Park Information Center,** which also serves as a regional TI (daily May–Oct 10:00–18:00, Dec–April 10:00–14:00, closed Nov, tel. 05/388-9330, www.tnp.si). The humble €4 museum here provides a look (with English explanations) at the park's flora, fauna, traditional culture, and mountaineering history. A poetic 15-minute slideshow explains the wonders and fragility of the park (included in museum entry, ask for English version as you enter).

After Trenta, you'll pass through a tunnel; then, on the left, look for a classic **suspension bridge.** Pull over to walk out for a bounce, enjoying the river's crystal-clear water and the spectacular mountain panorama.

About five miles beyond Trenta, in the town of Soča, is the **Church of St. Joseph** (with red onion dome, hiding behind the big tree on the right). The church was damaged in the earthquakes of 1998 and 2004, so the interior is likely covered with scaffolding. But if it's not covered, you'll see some fascinating art. During World War II, an artist hiding out in the mountains filled this church with patriotic symbolism. The interior is bathed in Yugoslav red, white, and blue—a brave statement made when such nationalistic sentiments were dangerous. On the ceiling is St. Michael (clad in Yugoslav colors) with Yugoslavia's three WWII enemies at his feet: the eagle (Germany), the wolf (Italy), and the serpent (Japan). The tops of the walls along the nave are lined with saints, but these are Slavic, not Catholic. Finally, look carefully at the Stations of the Cross and find the

faces of hated Yugoslav enemies: Hitler (fourth from altar on left) and Mussolini (first from altar on right). Behind the church, the stylized cross on the hill marks a World War I **cemetery**—the final resting place of some 600 Austro-Hungarian soldiers who were killed in action.

For another good example of how the Soča River cuts like God's band saw into the land, stop about two minutes past the church at the small gravel lot (on the left) marked *Velika Korita Soče* ("Grand Canyon of Soča"). Venture out onto the suspension bridge over the gorge...and bounce if you dare. Just beyond this bridge is the turnoff (on the left) to the Lepena Valley, home of the recommended Pristava Lepena pension—and their Lipizzaner horses (described later, under "Sleeping in Bovec").

Roughly five miles after the town of Soča, you exit the National Park, pass a WWI graveyard (on the left), and come

to a fork in the road. The main route leads to the left, through Bovec. But first, take a two-mile detour to the right (marked *Trbiž/ Tarvisio* and *Predel/Kluže*), where the WWI **Kluže Fort** keeps a close watch over the narrowest part of a valley leading to Italy (€3; July–Aug daily 9:00–20:00; June and Sept Sun–Fri 9:00–17:00, Sat 9:00–18:00; May and Oct Sat–Sun 10:00–18:00, closed Mon–Fri; closed Nov–April). In the 15th century, the Italians had a fort here to defend against the Ottomans. Half a millennium later, during World War I, it was used by Austrians to keep Italians out of their territory. Notice the ladder rungs fixed to the cliff face across the road from the fort—allowing soldiers to quickly get up to the mountaintop.

Back on the main road, continue to **Bovec.** This town, which saw some of the most vicious fighting of the Soča Front, was hit hard by earthquakes in 1994 and 1998 (and another tremor in 2004). Today, it's been rebuilt and remains the adventure-sports capital of the Soča River Valley—also known as the "Adrenaline Valley," famous for its whitewater activities. (Since the water comes from high-mountain runoff, the temperature of the Soča never goes above 68 degrees Fahrenheit.) For a good lunch stop in Bovec, take the turnoff as you first reach the town, and you'll pass a pair of inviting restaurant terraces on the right (Martinov Hram, then Letni Vrt; for details, see "Eating in Bovec," later). But if you're not eating or spending the night in Bovec, you could skip the town (continue along the main road to bypass the town center).

Heading south along the river—with water somehow both perfectly clear and spectacularly turquoise—watch for happy kayakers. When you pass the intersection at Žaga, you're just four miles from Italy. Along the way, you'll also pass a pair of waterfalls: the well-known Boka ("Slovenia's second-longest waterfall," on the right just before Žaga) and the hidden gem Veliki Kozjak (unmarked, on the left just before Kobarid). For either, you'll have to park your car and hike uphill to see the falls.

Signs lead to the town of **Kobarid**, home to a sleepy main square and some fascinating WWI sights. Even if you don't think you're interested in the Soča Front, consider dropping in the Kobarid Museum. Driving up to the Italian mausoleum hovering over the town is a must. (These sights are described later, under "Sights in Kobarid.")

Leaving Kobarid, continue south along the Soča to **Tolmin**. Before you reach Tolmin, decide on your route back to civilization...

Finishing the Drive

To Ljubljana: From Tolmin, you have two possible driving routes to the capital. Either option brings you back to the A-1 expressway south of Ljubljana, and will get you to the city in about two hours (though the second route has fewer miles).

The option you'll encounter first (turnoff to the right before Tolmin) is the smoother, longer route southwest to **Nova Gorica**. This fairly dull city is divided in half by the Italian border (the Italian side is called "Gorizia"). Because Italians aren't allowed to gamble in their home towns, Nova Gorica is packed with casinos catering to Italian gamblers. In fact, it's home to Europe's biggest casino. Rocks spell out the name "TITO" on a hillside above town—a strange relic of an earlier age. From Nova Gorica, you can hop on the H-4 expressway, which links easily to the main A-1 expressway. Also notice that the road from Nova Gorica to Ljubljana takes you through the heart of the Karst region—if you have time and daylight to spare, you could tour a cave, castle, or Lipizzaner stud farm on your way back up to Ljubljana (see the Karst chapter).

I prefer the more rural second option: Continue through

Tolmin, then head southeast through the hills back toward Ljubljana. Along the way, you could stop for a bite and some sightseeing at the town of **Idrija** (EE-dree-yah), known to all Slovenes for three things: its tourable mercury mine, fine delicate lace, and tasty *žlikrofi* (like ravioli). Back at the expressway (at Logatec), head north to Ljubljana or on to Bled.

To Bled: The fastest option is to load your car onto a **"Car Train"** (Autovlak) that cuts directly through the mountains. The train departs at 18:30 from Most na Soči (just south of Tolmin, along the Idrija route described above) and arrives at Bohinjska Bistrica, near Lake Bohinj, at 19:14 (€12 for the car; confirm schedule at the Bled TI before making the trip). From Bohinjska Bistrica, it's just a half-hour drive back to Bled. No reservations are necessary, but arrive at the train station about 30 minutes before the scheduled departure to allow time to load the car.

To **drive** all the way back, the fastest route (about 2 hours) is partially on a twisty, rough, very poor-quality road (go through Tolmin, turn off at Bača pri Modreju to Podbrdo, then from Petrovo Brdo take a very curvy road through the mountains into Bohinjska Bistrica and on to Bled). For timid drivers, it's more sane and not too much longer to start out on the Idrija route toward Ljubljana (described above), but turn off in Želin (before Idrija) toward Skofja Loka and Kranj, then on to Bled. Or take one of the two routes described above for Ljubljana, then continue on the expressway past Ljubljana and back up to Bled (allow 3 hours).

Bovec

The biggest town in the area, Bovec (BOH-vets) has a happening main square and all the tourist amenities. It's best known as a hub for whitewater adventure sports. While not exactly quaint, Bovec is charming enough to qualify as a good lunch stop or overnight home base. If nothing else, it's a nice jolt of civilization wedged between the alpine cliffs.

Orientation to Bovec

(area code: 05)
Tourist Information
The helpful TI on the main square offers fliers on mountain biking and water sports (flexible hours, generally June–Sept daily 8:30–20:30, shorter hours off-season, Trg Golobarskih Žrtev 8, tel. 05/389-6444, www.bovec.si).

Arrival in Bovec

The main road skirts Bovec, but you can turn off (watch for signs on the right) to take the road that goes through the heart of town, then rejoins the main road farther along. As you approach the city center, you can't miss the main square, Trg Golobarskih Žrtev, with the TI and a pair of good restaurants (described later, under "Eating in Bovec").

Sleeping in Bovec

$$$ Dobra Vila is a gorgeous hotel with classy traditional-meets-contemporary decor that feels out of place in little, remote Bovec. Not that I'm complaining. Its 12 rooms are swanky, and the public spaces (including a sitting room/library, breakfast room/restaurant, wine cellar, winter garden porch, and terrace with cozy mountain-view chairs) are welcoming. Enthusiastically run by Andreja and Sebastian Kovačič, it's a winner (high season: Db-€127–134, Db with balcony-€137–172; low season: Db-€112–119, Db with balcony-€122–157; Sb-€20 less than Db rate, price depends on size of room, 10 percent extra for 1-night stays, includes breakfast and dinner, fun old-fashioned elevator, on the left just as you enter town on the main road from the Vršič Pass at Mala Vas 112, tel. 05/389-6400, fax 05/389 6404, www.dobra-vila-bovec.com, welcome@dobra-vila-bovec.com).

$$ Martinov Hram has 11 nondescript modern rooms over a popular restaurant a few steps from Bovec's main square. While the rooms are an afterthought to the busy restaurant (reception at the bar), they're comfortable (very flexible rates, in peak season figure Sb-€40, Db-€70, a few euros less off-season, no extra charge

---

Sleep Code

(€1 = about $1.40, country code: 386, area code: 05)
S = Single, **D** = Double/Twin, **T** = Triple, **Q** = Quad, **b** = bathroom. Unless otherwise noted, breakfast is included and credit cards are accepted. Everyone speaks English and all of these accommodations include breakfast. These prices don't include the €1.01 tourist tax per person, per night.

To help you sort easily through these listings, I've divided the rooms into three categories based on the price for a standard double room with bath:

$$$ Higher Priced—Most rooms €100 or more.
$$ Moderately Priced—Most rooms between €50-100.
$ Lower Priced—Most rooms €50 or less.

for 1-night stays, Trg Golobarskih Žrtev 27, tel. 05/388-6214, sara .berginc@volja.net).

Near Bovec

$$$ Pristava Lepena is a relaxing oasis hiding out in the Lepena Valley just north of Bovec. Well-run by Milan and Silvia Dolenc, this place is its own little village: a series of rustic-looking cabins, a restaurant, and a sauna/outdoor swimming pool. Hiding behind the humble split-wood shingle exteriors is surprising comfort: 13 cozy apartments (with wood-burning stoves, TV, telephone, and all the amenities) that make you feel like relaxing. This place whispers "second honeymoon" (July–Aug: Db-€138; May–June and Sept: Db-€122; early Oct and late April: Db-€106; closed in winter, multi-night stays preferred, 1-night stays may be possible for 20 percent extra, dinner-€19, lunch and dinner-€31, nonrefundable 30 percent advance payment when you reserve; just before Bovec, turn left off the main road toward Lepena, and follow the white horses to Lepena 2; tel. 05/388-9900, fax 05/388-9901, www .pristava-lepena.com, pristava.lepena@siol.net). The Dolences also have three Welsh ponies and four purebred Lipizzaner horses (two mares, two geldings) that guests can ride (in riding ring-€16/hr, on trail-€20/hr, riding lesson-€24; non-guests may be able to ride for a few euros more—call ahead and ask).

$ Tourist Farm Pri Plajerju, on a picturesque plateau at the edge of Trenta (the first town at the bottom of the Vršič Pass road), is your budget option. Run by the Pretner family, this organic farm raises sheep and goats, and rents four apartments and one room in three buildings separate from the main house. While not quite as tidy as other tourist farms I recommend, it's the best one I found in the Soča Valley (July–Aug: Db-€38–50; Sept–June: Db-€34–45; price depends on size of room or apartment, breakfast-€6, dinner-€10, watch for signs to the left after passing through the village of Trenta, Trenta 16a, tel. & fax 05/388-9209, www.eko-plajer .com, info@eko-plajer.com).

Eating In Bovec

Martinov Hram, run by the Berginc family, has an inviting outdoor terrace under a grape trellis. Inside, the nicely traditional decor goes well with Slovenian specialties focused on sheep (good homemade bread, €6–9 pastas, €9–15 main courses, closed Mon, on the main road through Bovec, just before the main square on the right at Trg Golobarskih Žrtev 27, tel. 05/388-6214).

Letni Vrt Pizzeria, dominating the main square, is the busiest place in town—with pizzas, pastas, salads, and more (closed Sun, Trg Golobarskih Žrtev 12, tel. 05/388-6335).

Kobarid

Kobarid (KOH-bah-reed) feels older, and therefore a bit more appealing, than its big brother Bovec. This humble settlement was immortalized by a literary giant, Ernest Hemingway, who drove an ambulance in these mountains during World War I. He described Kobarid as "a little white town with a campanile in a valley. It was a clean little town and there was a fine fountain in the square." Sounds about right. Even though Kobarid loves to tout its Hemingway connection, historians believe that Papa did not actually visit Kobarid until he came back after the war to research his book.

Aside from its brush with literary greatness, Kobarid is known as a hub of Soča Front information (with an excellent WWI museum, a hilltop Italian mausoleum, and walks that connect the nearby sights). You won't find the fountain Hemingway wrote about—it's since been covered up by houses (though the town government hopes to excavate it as a tourist attraction). You will find a modern statue of Simon Gregorčič (overlooking the main intersection), the beloved Slovenian priest-slash-poet who came from and wrote about the Soča Valley.

Orientation to Kobarid

(area code: 05)
The main road cuts right through the heart of little Kobarid, bisecting its main square (Trg Svobode). The Kobarid Museum is along this road, on the left before the square. To reach the museum from the main square, simply walk five minutes back toward Bovec.

Tourist Information
The TI has good information on the area and Internet access (daily July–Sept 9:00–19:00, Oct–April 10:00–13:00 & 14:00–15:00, May–June 9:00–13:00 & 14:00–18:00, tel. 05/380-0490, on the main square at Trg Svobode 16, www.lto-sotocje.si and www.kobarid.si).

The Soča (Isonzo) Front

The valley in Slovenia's northwest corner—called Soča in Slovene and Isonzo in Italian—saw some of World War I's fiercest fighting. While the Western Front gets more press, this eastern border between the Central Powers and the Allies was just as significant. In a series of 12 battles involving 22 different nationalities along a 60-mile-long front, 300,000 soldiers died, 700,000 were wounded, and 100,000 were declared MIA. In addition, tens of thousands of civilians died. A young Ernest Hemingway, who drove an ambulance for the Italian army in nearby fighting, would later write the novel *A Farewell to Arms* about the battles here (see "Hemingway in the Julian Alps" sidebar on page 472).

On April 26, 1915, Italy joined the Allies. A month later, it declared war on the Austro-Hungarian Empire (which included Slovenia). Italy unexpectedly invaded the Soča Valley, quickly taking the tiny town of Kobarid, which it planned to use as a home base for attacks deeper into Austro-Hungarian territory. For the next 29 months, Italy launched 10 more offensives against the Austro-Hungarian army on the mountain-tops. All of these Italian offensives were unsuccessful, even though the Italians outnumbered their oppo-  nents three to one. This was unimaginably difficult warfare—Italy had to attack uphill, waging war high in the mountains, in the harshest of conditions. Trenches were carved into rock instead of mud, and many unprepared conscripts—brought here from faraway lands and unaccustomed to the harsh winter conditions atop the Alps—froze to death. During one winter alone, some 60,000 soldiers were killed by avalanches.

Visitors take a look at this tight valley, hemmed in by seemingly impassible mountains, and wonder: Why would people fight so fiercely over such an inhospitable terrain? At the time, Slovenia was the natural route from Italy to the Austro-Hungarian capital at Vienna. The Italians believed that if they could hold this

Sights in Kobarid

▲▲▲**Kobarid Museum (Kobariški Muzej)**—This modest but world-class museum, offering a haunting look at the tragedy of the Soča Front, was voted Europe's best museum in 1993. The tasteful exhibits, with fine English descriptions and a pacifist tone, take an even-handed approach to the fighting—without getting hung up on identifying the "good guys" and the "bad guys." The museum's focus is not on the guns and heroes, but on the big picture of the valley and push over the mountains, Vienna—and victory—would be theirs. Once committed, they couldn't turn back, and the war devolved into one of exhaustion—who would fall first?

In the fall of 1917, Austro-Hungarian Emperor Karl appealed to his ally Germany, and the Germans agreed to assemble an army for a new attack to retake Kobarid and the Soča Valley. In an incredible logistical puzzle, they spent just six weeks building and supplying this new army by transporting troops and equipment high across the mountaintops under cover of darkness...over the heads of their oblivious Italian foes dozing in the valley.

On October 24, Austria-Hungary and Germany launched a downhill attack of 600,000 soldiers into the town of Kobarid. This crucial 12th battle of the Soča Front, better known as the Battle of Kobarid, was the turning point—and saw the introduction of battlefield innovations that are commonplace in the military today. German field commanders were empowered to act independently on the battlefield, reacting immediately to developments rather than waiting for approval. Also, for the first time ever, the Austrian-German army used elements of a new surprise-attack technique called *Blitzkrieg*. (One German officer, Erwin Rommel, made great strides in the fighting here, and later climbed the ranks to become famous as Hitler's "Desert Fox" in North Africa.)

The attack caught the Italian forces off-guard, quickly breaking through three lines of defense. Within three days, the Italians were forced to retreat. (Because the Italian military worked from the top down, the soldiers were sitting ducks once they were cut off from their commanders.) The Austrians called their victory the "Miracle at Kobarid." But Italy felt differently. The Italians see the battle of Caporetto (the Italian name for Kobarid) as their Alamo. To this day, when an Italian finds himself in a mess, he says, "At least it's not a *Caporetto*."

A year later, Italy came back—this time with the aid of British, French, and US forces—and easily retook this area. On November 4, 1918, Austria-Hungary conceded defeat. After more than a million casualties, the fighting at Soča was finally over.

front and on the stories of the common people who fought and died here.

Cost, Hours, Location: €4, good €8 *Soča Front* book; April–Sept Mon–Fri 9:00–18:00, Sat–Sun 9:00–19:00; Oct–March Mon–Fri 10:00–17:00, Sat–Sun 9:00–18:00; Gregorčičeva 10, tel. 05/389-0000, www.kobariski-muzej.si.

❂ **Self-Guided Tour:** The entry is lined with hastily made cement and barbed-wire gravestones, flags representing all the nationalities involved in the fighting, and pictures of soldiers and nurses from diverse backgrounds who were brought together here (for example, the men wearing fezzes were from Bosnia-Herzegovina, annexed by the Austro-Hungarian Empire shortly before the war).

Buy your ticket and ask to watch the English version of the 19-minute film on the history of the Soča Front (informative but dry, plays on top floor).

The first floor up is divided into several rooms. The White Room, filled with rusty crampons, wire-cutters, pickaxes, and shovels, explains wintertime conditions at the front. What looks like a bear trap was actually used to trap enemy soldiers. The Room of the Rear shows the day-to-day activities away from the front line, from supplying troops to more mundane activities (milking cows, washing clothes, getting a shave, playing with a dog). The Black Room is the museum's most somber, commemorating the more than one million casualties of the Soča Front. These heartbreaking exhibits honor the common people whose bodies fertilized the battlefields of Europe. Horrific images of war injuries are juxtaposed with a display of medals earned by soldiers such as these—prompting the question, was it worth it? The little altar was purchased by schoolchildren, who sent it to the front to offer the troops some solace.

Through the door marked *Room of the Krn Range* (also on the first floor up), find your way to the Kobarid Rooms, which trace the history of this region from antiquity to today. High on the wall, look for the timelines explaining the area's turbulent history. The one in the second room shows wave after wave of invaders (including Ottomans, Habsburgs, and Napoleon). In the next room, above a display case with military uniforms, another timeline shows the many flags that flew over Kobarid's main square in the 20th century.

On the top floor, across from the room where the film plays (described above), you'll see a giant model of the surrounding mountains, painstakingly tracing the successful Austrian-German *Blitzkrieg* attack during the Battle of Kobarid.

▲▲**Italian Mausoleum (Kostnica)**—The 55 miles between here and the Adriatic are dotted with more than 75 cemeteries, reminders of the countless casualties of the Soča Front. One of the most dramatic is this mausoleum, overlooking Kobarid. The access road, across Kobarid's main square from the side of the church, is marked by stone gate towers (with the word *Kostnica*—one tower is topped with a cross and the other with a star for the Italian army).

Take the road up Gradič Hill—passing Stations of the

Cross—to the mausoleum. Built in 1938 (when this was still part of Italy) around the existing Church of St. Anthony, this octagonal pyramid holds the remains of 7,014 Italian soldiers. The stark, cold, Neoclassical architecture is pure Mussolini. Names are listed alphabetically, along with mass graves for more than 1,700 unknown soldiers *(militi ignoti)*.

Walk behind the church and enjoy the **view.** Find the WWI battlements high on the mountain's rock face (with your back to church, they're at 10 o'clock). Incredibly, the fighting was done on these treacherous ridges; civilians in the valleys only heard the distant battles. Looking up and down the valley, notice the "signal churches" evenly spaced on hilltops, each barely within view of the next—an ancient method for spreading messages or warnings across long distances quickly.

If the **church** is open, go inside and look above the door to see a brave soldier standing over the body of a fallen comrade and fending off enemies with nothing but rocks.

When Mussolini came to dedicate the mausoleum, local revolutionaries plotted an assassination attempt that couldn't fail. A young man planned to suicide-bomb Mussolini as he came back into town from this hilltop. But as Mussolini's car drove past, the would-be assassin looked at his fellow townspeople around him, realized the innocent blood he would also spill, and had a last-minute change of heart. Mussolini's trip was uneventful, and fascism continued to thrive in Italy.

World War I Walks—At the Kobarid Museum (and local TIs), you can pick up a free brochure outlining the **"Kobarid Historical Walk"** tracing WWI sites in town and the surrounding countryside (3 miles, mostly uphill, allow 3–5 hours; or you can just do a shorter stretch along the river, 1–2 hours). A newer **"Walk of Peace"** links several WWI sights all along the Soča Valley (details and map at TI). History buffs can also call ahead to arrange a private guide (€15/hr, tel. 05/389-0000).

Sleeping in Kobarid

(€1 = about $1.40, country code: 386, area code: 05)

My first listing is right on the main square. The other two hide on side streets about a block off the main road through town, between the museum and the main square (about a 3-min walk to either).

$$$ Hotel Hvala is the only real hotel in town. Run by the Hvala family, its 31 contemporary rooms are comfortable, and the location can't be beat. The mural on the wall in the elevator shaft tells the story of the Soča Valley as you go up toward the top floor (mid-July–Aug: Sb-€76, Db-€112; April–mid-July and Sept–mid-Nov: Sb-€72, Db-€104; cheaper off-season; pricier superior Db with air-con and sleek new decor-€160–200, hotel closed Feb and most of Nov, elevator, Trg Svobode 1, tel. 05/389-9300, fax 05/388-5322, www.hotelhvala.si, topli.val@siol.net).

$ Picerija Fedrig is a pizzeria that rents five simple but fine rooms upstairs (Db-€40, less for more than 1 night, 10 percent more in Aug, between the main square and the Kobarid Museum at Volaričeva 11, tel. 05/389-0115, jernej.grahli@volja.net).

$ Apartma-Ra has four rooms and three apartments in a cozy, family-friendly house (D-€30, Db-€40–50, apartment-€80–110, cash only, also runs a rafting company, Gregorčičeva 6C, mobile 041-641-899, apartma-ra@siol.net).

Eating in Kobarid

Topli Val ("Heat Wave"), Hotel Hvala's restaurant, is pricey but good, with a menu that emphasizes fish (€9–15 pastas, €10–30 main courses, lengthy list of Slovenian wines, daily 12:00–15:00 & 18:00–23:00, Trg Svobode 1, tel. 05/389-9300).

Kotlar Restaurant, across the square from Hotel Hvala, is similarly priced and well-regarded (Thu–Mon 12:00–23:00, closed Tue–Wed, Trg Svobode 11, tel. 05/389-1110). Kotlar also rents rooms if you're in a pinch.

Picerija Fedrig (also listed under "Sleeping in Kobarid," above) serves up good €5–7 pizzas (Tue–Sun 12:00–22:00, closed Mon, Volaričeva 11, tel. 05/389-0115).

LOGARSKA DOLINA
and the NORTHERN VALLEYS

The Julian Alps around Lake Bled are Slovenia's most accessible and most famous pincushion of peaks. But the high-mountain thrills don't end there. Stretching to the east, along the border with Austria, is the Kamniško-Savinjske range—home to several very remote valleys. One particularly inviting nook between the cut-glass peaks is the time-passed valley called Logarska Dolina. To get way, way, way off the beaten track—with gravel roads, unpasteurized milk, and the few Slovenes who still don't speak English—head to Logarska Dolina, its surrounding valleys, and the breathtaking Panoramic Road above them all. Slovenes like to keep this getaway a secret; it's one of their favorite escapes from the daily grind (and, along with Lake Bled, one of the country's most popular places to get married). Travelers who find Lake Bled too touristy prefer Lake Bohinj (see page 463). But travelers who think Bohinj is too touristy...love Logarska Dolina.

Logarska Dolina—very loosely translated as "Woodsman's Valley"—is best left to adventurous drivers, true back-to-nature nuts, and those intrigued by old-fashioned farming lifestyles...or, better yet, someone who's all three. Most of all, Logarska Dolina is the ideal excuse for a long drive on high-mountain roads to one of Slovenia's most traditional corners.

Planning Your Time
A trip to Logarska Dolina can be done as a long full-day circular drive from either Bled or Ljubljana. With more time, you could spend the night. If you're heading between Ljubljana/Bled and Ptuj/Maribor on the A-1 expressway, Logarska Dolina is roughly on the way (though it's still an hour off the expressway).

LOGARSKA DOLINA

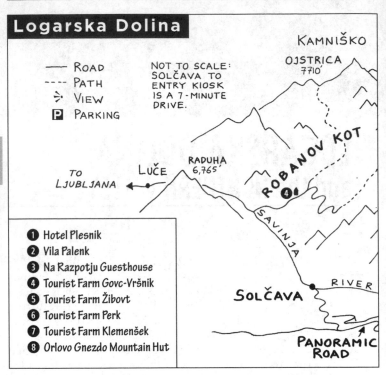

Getting to Logarska Dolina

I'd skip this region without a car. Public transportation to the northern valleys is extremely time-consuming. In summer only, one **bus** a day goes from the city of Celje to Solčava, then on to Logarska Dolina. But once you're there, many of the region's best attractions (such as the Panoramic Road) are unreachable by public bus.

On the other hand, Logarska Dolina is made to order by **car.** The valley is nearly due north from Ljubljana. But because of the mountains that lie between them, you'll boomerang substantially to the east to get there. From Ljubljana, take the A-1 expressway east (toward Celje) to the Šentrupert exit. From here, most of the route is well-marked with *Log Dolina* signs (usually brown). Head north on road 225 along the Savinja River, past Mozirje and Nazarje, then continue northwest on road 428 through Ljubno, Luče, and Solčava. (For details on getting around the valleys once you're in Solčava, see "Route Tips for Drivers," later.) Figure about an hour from Ljubljana to the Šentrupert exit, then another hour to Solčava.

A good, detailed map is essential. The *Avtokarta Slovenija* map will do, but consider getting one with even more detail for

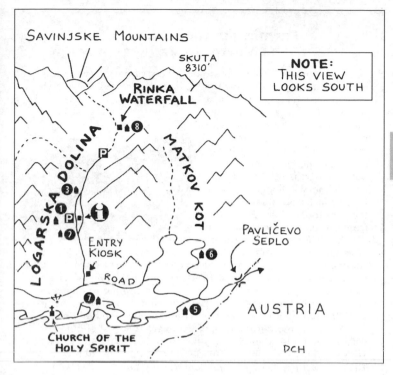

SAVINJSKE MOUNTAINS

SKUTA
8310'

RINKA
WATERFALL

NOTE:
THIS VIEW
LOOKS SOUTH

LOGARSKA DOLINA

P

MATKOV KOT

3

1
P

2

ENTRY
KIOSK

PAVLIČEVO
SEDLO

6

ROAD

7

5

AUSTRIA

CHURCH OF THE
HOLY SPIRIT

DCH

(vertical right margin) LOGARSKA DOLINA

this region (such as the 1:50,000 *Zgornja Savinjska Dolina* map, available locally).

The route I've described previously is the best. Detailed maps will show some seeming "shortcuts" that appear to take you more directly between Ljubljana and Logarska Dolina—but actually cost you time. I've tried both of the most likely options: the easier version, through Kamnik, then over the mountains via Gornji Grad to pick up the main road into Solčava (near Ljubno); and the off-road version of this route, cutting the corner from Krivčevo north (on unpaved roads—impassable outside of summer) through Podvolovljek to Luče. These alternatives come with some beautiful scenery and save you miles, but they are very time-consuming. Another seeming shortcut via Kranj—dipping into Austria on the impossibly twisty Jezersko-Pavličevo Sedlo road, through Vellach—is also possible, but time-consuming.

Orientation to Logarska Dolina

(area code: 03)
The region is tucked in the northern corner of Slovenia, just a few miles from Austria. This chapter's sights branch off from an

Farming in (and Above) the Northern Valleys

For many visitors, the most striking thing about a visit to this region is the ingenious way the intrepid locals have learned to eke out a living in such an inhospitable land. Just as throughout the Alps, the valleys and plateaus here are carefully manicured, creating cow-filled pastures wherever there's a flat patch of earth. But what's special in Logarska Dolina is the way farmers also cultivate the land at the very tops of hills. Especially from the Panoramic Road, you can see that the highest points  of various ridges and foothills are shaved bare—rounded hilltops sticking up here and there like bald heads in a crowd. Cows graze even on this sharply angled land. Locals joke that these farms are so steep that cows' front legs are shorter than their rear legs to make it easier for them to climb uphill—and dogs have to hang on to the grass with their teeth and bark through their rear ends.

You'll see more traditional houses here than just about anywhere else in the country. Many have wooden roofs and siding. These shingles are generally made of hard, durable larch wood. The boards are not cut, but split. Each house has a tiled stove for

east–west axis formed by the valley of the Savinja River. The main attraction here is the valley called **Logarska Dolina,** which cuts through the mountainscape south from the Savinja River Valley. Roughly parallel to Logarska Dolina are two smaller valleys: gentle **Robanov Kot** to the east and rugged **Matkov Kot** to the west. (*Dolina* means "valley;" *kot*—literally, "corner"—is a short valley.) Running along the top of the Podolševa ridge above the Savinja River is the rough, gravelly **Panoramic Road** (Panoramska Cesta)—with spectacular views over the entire region.

Tourist Information

Logarska Dolina has a modest TI kiosk, across the parking lot from Hotel Plesnik (described later, under "Sleeping in Logarska Dolina"). The TI can help you find a room or plan a hike and can arrange activities such as guided hikes, bike rental, horseback riding, rock climbing, archery, and paragliding (very flexible hours but generally May–Oct daily 9:00–15:00, closed Nov–April and in bad weather, take left fork to hotel after you enter Logarska Dolina to Logarska Dolina 9, tel. 03/838-9004, www.logarska-dolina.si).

heat, and a patch of grass to feed livestock.

It's a rough lifestyle. A farming family's primary source of income is their animals—mostly cows used for milk and meat, but also pigs and goats. Some of the farms in the Savinja River Valley raise yaks imported from Scotland, which are bred for their meat. A second source of income is forestry: The trees on a farm's property can be harvested and sold. Finally, they make a living from you and me, in the form of overnights or meals eaten at their farms.

All the tourist farms in this region are a recent phenomenon. During the Yugoslav era, people who lived here stopped farming and moved or commuted into nearby towns in the valley to work in factories. But Slovenia's industry was designed to work as a cog in the Yugoslav machine—other regions provided raw materials, and a large, ready-made market to buy the finished product. After the Slovenes declared independence from Yugoslavia, many of their factories closed, and their farmers turned workers returned to ancestral farming ways. To supplement their income, many families have converted their working farms into tourist farms, inviting guests to visit, stay, and dine with them, and appreciate their unique lifestyles. (I've listed several tourist farms under "Sleeping in Logarska Dolina" and "Eating in Logarska Dolina," later.) Even though many of the farms in Logarska Dolina seem as though they could be generations old, some date from only the mid-1990s.

If it's closed—as is the case off-season—the nearby Hotel Plesnik also provides basic tourist information. There are also TIs along the main road in Luče (tel. 03/839-3555) and in Solčava (tel. 03/839-0710). Both have similar hours to the Logarska Dolina TI.

Sights in Logarska Dolina

The road along the Savinja River, and the Panoramic Road up above, are connected at both ends—forming a handy loop that allows drivers to see everything efficiently. I suggest driving the Panoramic Road first, to get a good overview of the region, then winding down along the Savinja River to see the valleys. (If you have bad morning weather that looks like it may clear up in the afternoon, do the opposite.)

Route Tips for Drivers: The town of Solčava is the gateway to the region. In Solčava, you can twist up to the Panoramic Road (follow signs to *Podolševa*). At the far (west) end of this sky-high road, you'll come to a fork: Going left drops you directly down into Logarska Dolina, while going right takes you toward the Austrian border at Pavličevo Sedlo, and a very rugged, gravelly loop around the top, then bottom, of Matkov Kot (easy to miss—follow signs for tourist farms).

After visiting Logarska Dolina, take the Savinja River road back to Solčava. If you have time, you can detour into the valley of Robanov Kot when you head south from Solčava.

▲▲▲**Panoramic Road (Panoramska Cesta)**—The Logarska Dolina valley itself (described later) is beautiful. But the region's spectacular highlight is the Panoramic Road twisting along the top of the cliff above it. At an altitude of around 4,000 feet (compared to about 2,500 feet in Logarska Dolina), this road offers one thrilling drive.

As you rattle along the rough road, all around you are vast swaths of mountain forests, broken only by hilltops covered with patches of green grass. Each of these hills is its own farm, which raises grass to feed livestock (see sidebar). Several stretches of the Panoramic Road are what Slovenes poetically call "white road"—that is, gravel (no pavement). Realize that you're just an avalanche's tumble from the Austrian border.

About halfway along the Panoramic Road, the late-19th-century **Church of the Holy Spirit** (Sveti Duh) hovers on a

hilltop above the hamlet of Podolševa. Climb up to the church for sweeping views over Logarska Dolina. If the church is open, duck inside and find a very unusual relief of three men representing the Holy Trinity. God is in the center, Jesus is on the left, and on the right, it's...the Holy Spirit, depicted not as a dove but as a balding man.

The Panoramic Road is lined with inviting tourist farms *(turistična kmetija)*, offering beds and meals to travelers—just follow the views to the farm of your choice (Tourist Farm Klemenšek, listed under "Eating in Logarska Dolina," is one good option). Some farms, such as Tourist Farm Žibovt (near the end of the Panoramic Road, listed under "Sleeping in Logarska Dolina"), serve *kislo mleko,* or "soured milk"...which is exactly what it sounds

like (about €3 per bowl). Fresh, unpasteurized milk is set out in the open air, usually in a darkened room. The fat rises to the top and forms a skin on top. The bottom of the milk is like yogurt, white and relatively flavorless. Meanwhile, the yellowish top layer comes with a kick: a pungent barnyard aftertaste. I tried it—once—and enjoyed it...the experience, if not the flavor.

▲▲**Logarska Dolina**—This valley, 4.5 miles long and about a quarter-mile wide, is the region's main draw. A flat, broad meadow surrounded on all sides by sheer alpine cliffs, it's an idyllic place for a drive, hike, or bike ride. Various sights—caves, waterfalls, old

log cabins, and so on—surround the valley, but it's most appealing simply as a place to commune with gorgeous Slovenian nature.

Though you can enter the valley year round, you'll have to pay a €5 entry fee per car April through October (at other times, or if there's bad weather and the entry kiosk is closed, it's free).

After the valley entrance, the road forks. Take the left fork to reach the TI (see "Tourist Information," earlier) and hotels; or take the right fork to bypass them (the two forks rejoin after a while).

At the far end of the valley, you'll find a parking lot with some snack stands. From here, you can follow the *Slap Rinka—10 min* signs up the moderately strenuous path to the **Rinka Waterfall.** Relax at the little mountain hut called Orlovo Gnezdo ("Eagle's Nest") and enjoy a drink with a view of the falls, which plunge 300 feet down from the adjacent cliffs.

With more time, Logarska Dolina offers an inviting, mostly level place to go for a longer **hike,** surrounded by cow-filled meadows and towering peaks. The "Nature-Ethnographic Trail" is a two-hour, four-mile (one-way) hike that starts near the entrance of the valley and leads to the end of the valley. As you enter Logarska Dolina, pick up the brochure that narrates the route. This brochure and information on more adventurous hikes up into the mountains around Logarska Dolina are also available at the TI.

Robanov Kot and Matkov Kot—These smaller, sleepier valleys, dotted with traditional farm buildings, flank Logarska Dolina. They offer the same surrounded-by-mountains feeling, but are less cultivated and less crowded than Logarska during the peak season. With extra time, poke into one or both of these mini-valleys simply to enjoy the peaceful views. **Robanov Kot,** near Solčava, is more accessible, with better and more level roads (well-marked with a brown sign just south of Solčava; home to recommended Tourist Farm Govc-Vršnik). The **Matkov Kot** road is more rugged, with cliff-hanging gravel roads (it's easy to miss this poorly marked valley—look for signs to the tourist farms; home to recommended Tourist Farm Perk).

Sleeping in Logarska Dolina

The accommodations listed here are in four very different settings. The hotel/villa and guesthouse are in the heart of the Logarska Dolina valley; the first tourist farm is in the side-valley called Robanov Kot; the second tourist farm is on the Panoramic Road, capping the ridge above the valleys; and the last farm is in the side-valley called Matkov Kot.

$$ Hotel Plesnik and **Vila Palenk,** both part of the only big hotel outfit in the area, sit proudly in the middle of Logarska Dolina. The hotel, with lively public spaces and 30 modern rooms with traditional farmhouse furnishings, is a big, classy, overpriced splurge (Sb-€96, Db-€154, €5 cheaper without balcony, elevator). The nearby, smaller Vila Palenk has 11 rustic rooms with more character (Sb-€79, Db-€126, no elevator, breakfast at the main hotel). The staff at both places speak English. Reservations for both are handled through the same office (no extra charge for 1-night stays, €14 per person for lunch or dinner at hotel restaurant, check online for weekend deals, indoor swimming pool, Logarska Dolina 10, tel. 03/839-2300, fax 03/839-2312, www.plesnik.si, info@plesnik.si). After entering Logarska Dolina, you'll come to a fork; bear left to reach the hotel.

Near Logarska Dolina

$$ Na Razpotju Guesthouse, affiliated with the hotel, has 10 straightforward rooms. It's family-friendly and a better value than the hotel, but communication can be challenging (Sb-€50, Db-€80, a quarter-mile from Hotel Plesnik toward the far end of the valley, tel. 03/839-1650, razpotje@siol.net).

$ Tourist Farm Govc-Vršnik, the most modern and accessible of my tourist farm listings, is in the smaller, relaxing valley of Robanov Kot, a 15-minute drive from Logarska Dolina. This working farm, run by the English-speaking Vršnik family, has a traditional beehive and 10 cozy rooms with bright, woody decor (Db-€58, or €70 with dinner, €6 less mid-Sept–June, cash only, free Wi-Fi, Robanov Kot 34, tel. 03/839-5016, fax 03/839-5017, www.govc-vrsnik.com, govc.vrsnik@siol.net). As you enter the valley of Robanov Kot (just south of Solčava), just watch for signs (it's the second tourist farm on the left).

$ Tourist Farm Žibovt is dramatically situated at the far end of the Panoramic Road, a few minutes' walk from the Austrian border. It perches on a ledge with fine views of a tranquil meadow that

---

Sleep Code

(€1 = about $1.40, country code: 386, area code: 03)
S = Single, **D** = Double/Twin, **T** = Triple, **Q** = Quad, **b** = bathroom. These accommodations include breakfast. The hotel accepts credit cards, but the tourist farms are cash only and charge 20–30 percent extra for stays of fewer than three nights. These prices don't include the €1.01 tourist tax per person, per night.

To help you sort easily through these listings, I've divided the rooms into two categories based on the price for a standard double room with bath:

$$ Higher Priced—Most rooms €60 or more.
$ Lower Priced—Most rooms less than €60.

---

ends at a sheer cliff plunging to the bottom of Logarska Dolina. In addition to renting six cheery rooms, the Poličnik family serves meals and turns out a wide range of dairy products—including the unforgettable *kislo mleko* ("soured milk"). Near this farm is a modest marble quarry (Db-€52, or €68 with dinner, cash only, minimal English spoken, Logarska Dolina 24, tel. 03/584-7118, www.slovenia.info/zibovt, kmetija.zibovt@gmail.com, Žarko and Martina). The farm is well-marked at the far end of the Panoramic Road (near the Austrian border crossing at Pavličevo Sedlo).

$ Tourist Farm Perk is the most rustic of my listings, with seven rooms (some of which have a private bathroom on the hall). It's scenically perched on the particularly remote-feeling gravel road high above Matkov Kot (D/Db-€48, or €56 with dinner, cash only, Logarska Dolina 23, tel. 03/584-7120, mobile 041-282-485, www.tkperk-krivec.si, krivec.neza@siol.net, Krivec family).

Eating in Logarska Dolina

Many of the region's tourist farms *(turistična kmetija)* serve full meals to passersby in summer and light food and snacks at other times.

Tourist Farm Klemenšek, perched on a grassy ridge with spectacular views, has the classic Logarska Dolina setting, home cooking, and indoor or outdoor tables (July–Aug daily 11:00–21:00; May–June and Sept–mid-Oct only Sat–Sun 11:00–21:00; closed mid-Oct–April; halfway between Sveti Duh and the end of the Panoramic Road, tel. 03/838-9024, www.na-klemencem.si).

Hotel Plesnik and **Na Razpotju Guesthouse,** listed earlier, also serve food to non-guests. But the best option is to bring a **picnic** with you and eat whenever you find the scenic perch you like best. You'll find small grocery stores along the main road in both Luče and Solčava, but few opportunities to buy groceries once in the valley.

Near Logarska Dolina: Velenje Castle

This scenic, 700-year-old, hill-capping castle seems out of place over the modern industrial town of Velenje (which was once named "Titovo Velenje" for the Yugoslav dictator, Tito). Even more unusual is the eclectic, extensive, and endearing museum it houses. While it's not worth going far out of your way to see, a trip to the castle makes a good rainy-day activity or a fine diversion if you've got extra time at the end of your Logarska Dolina day.

You'll find a surprising diversity of exhibits surrounding the tranquil castle courtyard: replicas of a circa-1930s general store and pub; a Czech professor's three-room collection of African art and everyday items; a survey of regional history through the Middle Ages, including a replica of a countryside home; a city history overview (the town was founded only after World War II, so much of the story dates from Tito's Yugoslav era); various Slovenian paintings and sculptures; and temporary exhibits. Separate buildings house a collection of Baroque church art and an exhibit on mastodons (the remains of two of these woolly mammoth-like creatures were found near here in 1964).

Only some of the exhibits are described in English, but you can borrow the good one-page English descriptions when you enter. If the guides aren't busy, one of them can show you around (included in ticket). Better yet, call ahead to see if an English tour is scheduled, or to request a tour for yourself (€2.50, Tue–Sun 10:00–18:00, closed Mon, Ljubljanska cesta 54, tel. 03/898-2630, www.muzej-velenje.si).

Getting There: Velenje Castle is easy to visit en route to or from Logarska Dolina, especially if you're headed east on the expressway. From the road connecting Logarska Dolina to the expressway, you can detour east just south of Mozirje (via Gorenje) into Velenje, where you'll look for easy-to-miss brown signs to turn off for the castle. From Velenje, you can head south straight to the expressway.

PTUJ and MARIBOR

The vast majority of Slovenia's attractions are concentrated in the western third of the country: the mountains, the sea, the capital city, and the Karst. East of Ljubljana, the mountains gradually merge into plains, the towns and cities become less colorful, and "oh, wow!" turns into "so what?" But there's hope, in the form of Slovenia's oldest town (and winner of the "funniest name" award): Ptuj (puh-TOOey—the "P" is almost silent; and yes, it really does sound like someone spitting).

With a storied past, a much-vaunted castle, and easygoing locals who act like they've never met a tourist, Ptuj charms. Populated since the Early Stone Age, Ptuj has a long and color-ful history that reads like a Who's Who of Central Europe: Celts and Romans, Dominican friars and Habsburg counts, Nazis and Yugoslavs...not to mention a fuzzy monster named Kurent. The people of Ptuj are particularly proud of their Roman era, when "Poetovio" was a bustling metropolis of 40,000 people. But even as it clings to its noble past, today's Ptuj is refreshingly real, with a sleepy small-town ambience and an interesting castle museum.

While it hosts plenty of visitors (mostly Germans and Austrians, who call it "Pettau"), Ptuj is hardly a tourist town. Real people, not nightclubs or T-shirt shops, populate the Old Town. If this makes Ptuj feel a bit less polished than the big-name sights in western Slovenia, so much the better—think of it as a diamond in the rough.

For a big-city complement to Ptuj, drop into Maribor—the country's second city, and the de facto capital of eastern Slovenia (described at the end of this chapter).

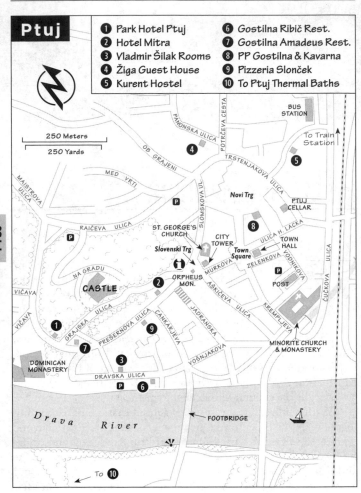

Ptuj

1 Park Hotel Ptuj
2 Hotel Mitra
3 Vladmir Šilak Rooms
4 Žiga Guest House
5 Kurent Hostel
6 Gostilna Ribič Rest.
7 Gostilna Amadeus Rest.
8 PP Gostilna & Kavarna
9 Pizzeria Slonček
10 To Ptuj Thermal Baths

PTUJ

Planning Your Time

With a week or more in Slovenia and a desire to delve into the less-touristed areas of the country, Ptuj deserves a short visit. A few hours are enough to feel you've mastered the town; if you're a restless sightseer, it's tough to fill an entire day here. Begin by touring the castle, then enjoy a wander through the Old Town and consider Ptuj's other museums. Let your pulse slow and take a mini-vacation from your vacation. If you can't sit still that long, consider a side-trip into Maribor.

Ptuj is conveniently located on the train network, easy to reach from Ljubljana and Maribor, as well as international destinations like Zagreb and Budapest.

Orientation to Ptuj

(area code: 02)

Ptuj is squeezed between its historic castle and the wide Drava River. With just 11,000 people (23,000 in greater Ptuj), it still ranks as Slovenia's eighth-largest town. The Old Town is shaped roughly like a triangle, with the castle and the two monasteries as its points. You can walk from one end of the Old Town to the other in about 10 minutes, but since the town slopes uphill from the river to the castle, there's a bit of up and down.

Tourist Information

Ptuj's TI shares the square called Slovenski trg with its landmark City Tower. Pick up the information magazine, which contains a city map marked with sights, hotels, and restaurants. The TI also publishes an events guide and has free Internet access (daily May–Sept 9:00–20:00, Oct–April 9:00–18:00, Slovenski trg 5, tel. 02/779-6011, www.ptuj-tourism.si).

Arrival in Ptuj

The humble **train** station is about a 10-minute walk from the center. Exit the station to the left, then cross the busy road to the **bus** station. From the bus station, the Old Town is just on the other side of the big commercial center. **Drivers** will find a handy parking lot on the riverfront, next to the recommended Gostilna Ribič restaurant.

Helpful Hints

Internet Access: The town has a few Internet cafés, but the easiest access is at the free terminal inside the TI (see above).

Local Guide: To arrange your own private guide, contact the **Ptujske Vedute agency** (€40 for up to a 90-min tour of the Old Town, tel. 02/778-8780, ptuj@vedute.si). The TI can also help you find a guide.

Sights in Ptuj

▲▲Ptuj Castle (Ptujski Grad)

The modest castle is Ptuj's top sight, and proudly claims to be Slovenia's most-visited museum. Overlooking the town from its perch over the Drava River, it's less than thrilling from afar. But the horseshoe-shaped castle complex hosts a series of surprisingly rich and engaging exhibits.

Cost, Hours, Information: €4, daily 9:00–17:00, until 18:00 May–mid-Oct, until 20:00 Sat–Sun in high season, tel. 02/748-0360, www.pok-muzej-ptuj.si. Good English descriptions are posted in some rooms. English tours are rare, but you can call to ask if one is scheduled that you can join (included in €4 entry fee). Or you can call ahead to arrange your own private tour for €10 extra (depends on guide availability, call at least one day ahead). But my self-guided tour, below, covers the highlights. For more in-depth information, pick up the €2.50 booklet or the thorough €8 guidebook.

Getting There: You can't miss the castle, sitting over the city. It's about a 10-minute cobbled hike above the Old Town. Several different trails lead up from the Old Town, all well-marked with *Grad* signs (easiest to find is the lane called Grajska ulica, near the TI).

❷ Self-Guided Tour: The core of the Ptuj Castle collection shows off the lifestyles of the castle's historic residents, while other exhibits display weapons, musical instruments, and traditional costumes used for the annual Kurentovanje festival. You'll follow a one-way route. The entrances to each exhibit are not all well-marked, but attendants are always around to direct you to what you want to see. Touring the whole shebang takes about two hours.

After buying your ticket, go up the stairs near the ticket office and turn right. Look over the **courtyard** for this quick history les-

son: In the 11th century, the archbishops of Salzburg built a fortress here. In the 12th century, the Lords of Ptuj, who watched over the Salzburgers' land, moved in. The LoP's died out in the mid-15th century, and from then on, the castle changed hands frequently. Over the next several centuries, Ptuj Castle gradually acquired its current appearance: a Romanesque core (part of a 14th-century fortress, barely visible now) with a Renaissance arcaded courtyard (designed by Italian experts who came to fortify the castle against the Ottomans), accentuated by an austere Baroque addition (the outermost wing, with the decorated stone window frames). Most of what you'll see in today's exhibit dates from the time of the Counts of Herberstein (1873–1945).

Now look over the door at the end of the arcade to see the **castle seal,** a hodgepodge of symbols representing previous owners. What's an English phrase doing on a seal for a castle in Slovenia? It's because of a Hungarian princess. In the Middle Ages, when a princess of Hungary moved to Scotland to be with her new husband, she took with her a particularly protective chamberlain. When the chamberlain buckled the princess to her horse for a treacherous river crossing, he'd fasten her on with three belts instead of just one, and shout "Grip fast!" when they came to any rough patches. That chamberlain's descendants took the name Leslie and eventually bought this castle in 1656. The family crest became those three buckles the chamberlain had used to protect his princess (in the left shield). You'll spot this insignia throughout the castle.

• *Going through the door, you enter the...*

Feudal Dwelling Culture Collection: This exhibit displays artifacts belonging to the castle's previous owners. The route takes you more or less clockwise in a roughly chronological order, from the 16th to the 19th centuries. In the first few rooms—where receptions were held and guests were (hopefully) impressed—you'll see several 17th-century tapestries from Brussels depicting the travels of Ulysses. Notice that nearly every big room has its own ceramic stove (fed from behind the wall by servants). Looking up, you'll see that while some of the rooms have exposed wooden-beam ceilings, others are adorned with cake-frosting stucco work—it's original, by highly skilled masters, and still intact after nearly 300 years. At the end of the first hall is a gallery of portraits of the Herbersteins, who furnished this part of the castle and were eager to establish their legitimacy as a ruling family.

• *Looping back to where you began, head down the hallway into the residential part of the castle (in the hall, notice the 700-year-old Herberstein family tree on your right). The first big room is the...*

Countess' Salon: Also called the "Chinese Salon," this room reveals the fascination many 17th- and 18th-century Europeans had for foreign cultures. But the European artists who created these works never actually visited China, instead basing their visions on stories they heard from travelers who may or may not have had firsthand experience there. The results—European depictions of imagined Chinese culture—are highly inaccurate at best, and flights of pure fantasy at worst (look around for animals and instruments that never existed). This European interest in Chinese culture is known as *chinoiserie*. We'll see a similar fixation on Turkish culture soon.

• *Head through the next few rooms (countess' bedroom, countess' dressing room, old chapel, chambermaid's room). Before entering the 14th-century core—and oldest part—of the castle, keep your head up to see a very unusual chandelier: an anatomically correct (or surgically enhanced, by the look of it) female dragon. Continue into the...*

Bedrooms: The first shows off what prim and proper 17th-century Europeans considered to be "erotic" art (with a mythical creature trying to woo a woman), while the second is decorated in Napoleonic-era Empire-style furniture. In this room, pay special attention to the stove: Water (which could be scented) was poured into the top, and emerged at the bottom in the form of

Kurentovanje

Ptuj is famous for its distinctive Mardi Gras celebration, called Kurentovanje (koo-rent-oh-VAWN-yeh). Locals dress up in elaborate costumes and parade through the streets, celebrating the end of winter and heralding the arrival of spring. Nearby villages have similar, smaller, and more traditional processions.

It seems quaint today, but in the Middle Ages, Kurentovanje was deadly serious. The winter is particularly harsh here, so when spring began to approach, the peasants wanted to offer encouragement. They'd put on frightening masks and costumes and

parade around making as much noise as possible to scare off the winter.

Kurentovanje's most notable character is Kurent, a fun-loving Slavic pagan god of hedonism—sort of the Slovenian Bacchus. A Kurent is covered with fur and has a long, red tongue, horns, a snout, whiskers, two red-ringed eyes, a wooden club with a spiny hedgehog skin wrapped around one end, and red or green socks. It wears a chain of five bells around its waist, and jumps around and swings its hips to get them clanging as loudly as possible. Kurents travel together in packs, so the combined noise can be deafening.

steam. Fancy. The third bedroom brings the survey of furniture up to date: 19th-century Biedermeier...simple, practical, comfortable, but still beautiful.

• *Going into the arcade, turn left to find the...*

Festival Hall: Then as now, this hall was a preferred place for banquets and concerts. Decorating the walls is Europe's biggest collection of *turqueries*. Like the faux-Chinese stuff we saw earlier, this is a (usually highly inaccurate) European vision of Turkish culture. After the Habsburgs militarily defeated the Ottomans and forced them out of Central Europe, the two powers began a diplomatic relationship. In the late 17th century, many Austrian officers went to Turkey and came back with souvenirs and tall tales, which were patched together to form the idiosyncratic vision of the Ottoman Empire you see here.

The left wall shows Ottoman politicians of the day—many with European features (presumably painted by artists who'd never laid eyes on an actual Turkish person). Along the back wall, we see portraits of four sultans' wives. Imagine how astonishing the notion of a harem must have been in the buttoned-down Habsburg

Traditionally the role of Kurent was played by young men of the village—they were able to pull it off physically (the costume could weigh 90 pounds) and used it as an opportunity to catch the eye of a potential wife. (As the Kurents parade through the streets, young women still toss them handkerchiefs in approval.) Leading up to the procession, the young man would make his own costume in secret. That way, the monster would be all the more frightening and impressive when it was finally revealed. Ideally, they'd use the stinkiest animal hides they could find, to make the beast smell as hideous as it looked and sounded.

These processions have evolved into modern extravaganzas. These days, men and women of any age buy their Kurent costumes in a store, and Kurentovanje's daytime parades are followed by evenings of music, celebration, and general debauchery. In recent years, in a sort of "creature exchange" program, characters from Mardi Gras celebrations in other countries have come to take part in Kurentovanje.

Imagine about 350 of these hairy beasts, each one with five huge bells clanging at top volume, stomping down Prešernova street. Or come the Sunday before Ash Wednesday, and see for yourself. For details on all the festivities, check out www.kurentovanje.net.

Kurentovanje ends at midnight on Shrove Tuesday (before Ash Wednesday), when people move into the more pensive season of Lent... confident that spring will return with ease.

days. But even though these paintings are unmistakably titillating, they're still appropriately repressed. The first woman (on left) wears two different layers of semi-transparent clothing (what's the point?). And the fourth woman (on right) reaches for some fruit (symbolic of...well, you know) and teasingly pulls open her dress so we can see what's underneath, which is...more clothes.

Finally, look on the right wall, with 17th-century Eurofied visions of people from other cultures: Africans, Native Americans, and Asians, all with exaggerated features.

This quirky collection is typical of Slovenian museums: Since they can't afford great works by famous artists, they collect items that may be obscure, but have an even more interesting story to tell.

• *Backtrack to where you entered, and go straight ahead along the arcade to the end of the hall, where you'll take the tight, medieval spiral staircase up one level. At the top, turn left into the...*

France Mihelič Archive: France Mihelič was an important Slovenian painter of the mid-20th century who donated an enormous stash of paintings to this museum. Some are displayed here, while others are carefully archived in the big steel filing cabinets. Enjoy these expressionistic works.

• *In the next room begins the...*

Sluga Collection: Donated by a local collector, this exhibit shows off more of the Biedermeier furniture that was all the rage in Central Europe during the early to mid-19th century.

• *The next two big rooms are the...*

Castle Gallery: The first room displays works of art from the Baroque period, including an army of sandstone dwarfs. The second (darkened) room highlights the Middle Ages. The first three sculptures on the left (#10–12) are especially precious, done by the greatest local masters of the day.

• *Exit to the right, and walk to the end of the arcade. And now for something completely different.*

Carnival Masks Collection: Ptuj's Mardi Gras celebration, called Kurentovanje, is well-known for its processions of fanciful masked characters (see sidebar). This exhibit—colorful as an episode of *Sesame Street*—offers an entertaining look at the complete Kurentovanje experience. The costume of the old woman carrying the old man on her back seems whimsical, but it represents a powerful theme: We carry the memory of the deceased with us always. The bear costume is a reminder of times when Roma (Gypsy) entertainers actually did bring trained bears to town. The plow is used to symbolically "wake up the soil" and set the stage for a season of bountiful crops. The horse (called Rusa) is taken by a farmer from house to house, trying to "sell" it to neighbors. But the horse is unruly and obnoxious—supposedly good luck for the health and fertility of livestock. The Kurent costumes (in the last room) are especially striking—from old homemade costumes (turn an old coat inside-out to reveal the fur lining) to today's store-bought version (they run about €500).

After the Carnival Masks Collection, you might pass through an ethnographic collection (farm implements, traditional tools, etc.), which the museum hopes to move soon to a more suitable location.

• *Head back down to the courtyard. Ask one of the attendants to direct you (across the courtyard from the ticket office) to the...*

Collection of Musical Instruments: This fun and well-presented exhibit groups instruments by type of music, which you'll hear as you enter each room. The first section celebrates Ptuj's civic marching band, a prized local tradition. The next section displays ancient Roman instruments. The tibia (in the display case), dating from the second century A.D., is the only one ever found; it had two pipes made of bone leading to a single mouthpiece (illustrated on the wall). The next section features woodwinds and strings, including a rare, preserved lute. And the last section shows off a

Bösendorfer piano and other keyboard instruments.

• *As you exit, you can ask to be directed to the anticlimactic finale (to the right), the...*

Collection of Arms: Squeezed into one corner of a huge, vaulted room is an armory collection spanning several centuries, from the 1400s through World War I. They're displayed on racks, as they would have been in a real armory.

• *Your castle visit is over. Enjoy the views, then head back down into town.*

Old Town

The sights in Ptuj's Old Town are simple and not very time-consuming. Wander around, take them in at your own pace, then reward yourself with a relaxing drink on a square.

▲**Slovenski Trg**—Once Ptuj's main square, and now its most atmospheric, Slovenski trg is fronted by the TI, Hotel Mitra, and the City Tower. Around this square are several reminders of Ptuj's Roman past.

The white marble slab in the middle of the square, known as the **Orpheus Monument,** was commissioned by a Roman mayor in the second century A.D. to honor an esteemed figure...himself. Notice the musician playing the lyre (near the top, center of slab, below the naked woman). Since the lyre is commonly associated with Orpheus, the monument's nickname stuck. When Rome fell, so did many of its structures, including this one. It became buried in history, only to reappear in the 16th century as the town pillory, where criminals were punished (secured by chains that were embedded in the holes you still see in the slab). In the Middle Ages, the town judge would come out onto the balcony over the door of his white house at the top of the square (at #6) to witness justice being served.

The **City Tower** was built in the late 16th century to defend against Ottoman invaders (who were likely to pass by here on their way to lay siege to Vienna). The tower used to be another story taller, but the top burned in a devastating fire (one of four that swept the city in the late 17th and early 18th centuries). The newly shorter tower was capped with this jaunty Baroque steeple.

Embedded in the staircase at the back of the tower are more fragments from Ptuj's Roman era. This so-called **"open-air museum"** is just a taste of the vast Roman material unearthed in Ptuj. In the middle of the staircase, make out the letters: POETOVIONA—a longer version of Ptuj's Roman name, Poetovio. (For an even more extensive Roman collection, head for the Dominican Monastery.)

Just behind the City Tower is **St. George's Parish Church** (Cerkev Svetega Jurija), which dates back before any other building in Slovenia. The current Gothic version is packed with diverse ecclesiastical art. If it's open, go inside (daily 7:00–11:00 & 18:00–18:30). As you enter, notice (on your left) the gorgeous circa-1380 statue of St. George, Ptuj's patron saint, slaying the dragon. Then go to the first big pillar on the right, where you'll see a glass-covered relief depicting throngs of admirers adoring the Baby Jes...wait—where's Jesus? (Not to mention Mary's hands?) Several years ago, Jesus was stolen from this pillar. To help prevent further vandalism, the priests reduced the opening times (notice the ridiculously long midday break).

Prešernova Street (Prešernova Ulica)—Stretching away from

the City Tower is Ptuj's main drag and oldest street. It's wider than most streets in town because it led to what was the medieval market square (now Slovenski trg), and merchants would set up market stalls all along the street. Many of the houses here have long since been renovated in Renaissance or Baroque style, making it Ptuj's most picturesque thoroughfare.

Town Square (Mestni Trg)—Today Ptuj's main square, this lively people zone (just down Murkova street from Slovenski trg) is a hub of activity. Major events and festivals—including the Kurentovanje Mardi Gras festival—take place here.

The square is watched over by the distinctive **Town Hall,** built by a visionary mayor a century ago. The three flags represent

(left to right) the European Union, Slovenia, and the Municipality of Ptuj. Over the left door (on the corner) are two statues commemorating Ptuj's Roman history: on the right, Emperor Trajan, who granted Ptuj city status in the early second century A.D.; and on the left, St. Viktorin, a Ptuj bishop who wrote scholarly works on ecclesiastical themes during the late third century A.D., until he was martyred by Emperor Diocletian.

In the middle of the square is a statue of **St. Florian,** who traditionally protects towns against fire. Ptuj was devastated by four different fires in the late 17th and early 18th centuries. This statue is a 1993 replica of one that was built here after the fourth fire, in 1744. Miraculously, the town never burned again...or maybe not so miraculously, since they rebuilt it with stone instead of wood. Largely as a result of Ptuj's frequent fires, its rival Maribor (to the north) gradually supplanted Ptuj as the region's main center of commerce and winemaking. Ptuj's fate was sealed a century later, when the rail line between Vienna and Trieste was routed through Maribor. Today Maribor has 10 times as many people as Ptuj—and 10 times the industry, congestion, and urban gloominess. Hmm... maybe Ptuj got the better end of the deal, after all.

PtuJ Cellar (Ptujska Klet)—Ptuj is highly regarded for its wines. Simple wine was produced in this region as far back as the Celts. The Romans advanced the art, only to have it disappear in the Dark Ages, then be revived in the 13th century by Minorite monks. Today this enormous cellar, branching out under the Old Town, continues this proud tradition—and holds a staggering five million liters of wine (about 85 percent whites). The cellar is also home to a "wine archive" with bottles dating back to 1917. This precious archive survived World War II because it was sealed off and hidden from the Nazis behind a giant barrel.

The cellar is most proud of their award-winning Sauvignon Blanc (€4/bottle), but their best seller—at a million bottles a year—is a local wine called Haložan (a semi-dry blend of four whites, €2/bottle).

Cellar **tours** and **wine-tastings** are only available to groups, and English tours are rare—call ahead to find out if one is scheduled that you can join. If you're determined, it's easy to join a German- or Slovene-language tour. Either way, you'll pay about €9 for the experience. The cellar tour comes with some hokey lighting effects and is followed by an even hokier audio-visual presentation during the tasting (call Tanja at mobile 041-394-896).

If you just want to pick up a bottle, stop by their **wine shop,** next door to the cellar (Mon–Fri 7:00–19:00, Sat 7:00–12:00, closed Sun, Vinarski trg 1, tel. 02/787-9810, www.ptujska-klet.si).

Minorite Church and Monastery (Minoritski Samostan)—This church, dedicated to Saints Peter and Paul, was one of the only buildings in town destroyed in World War II. (The Allies believed that the occupying Nazis were storing munitions here.) Only the foundation at the back end of the church (the part that's yellow instead of white) survived, and it was left as ruins for decades. In 1989, friars celebrated their 750th anniversary in Ptuj by rebuilding the back part of the church. About a decade later, the front (white) half was also reconstructed. They followed the original plans carefully, but something's missing: Those empty niches above the door, once occupied by statues, are a sobering reminder of wartime devastation. But step into the contemporary interior (free, daily 7:30–18:30, Minoritski trg). There, at the altar, are the original statues that once adorned the church facade.

At the chapel at the back of the church (on the right), you'll see very contemporary Stations of the Cross. Then go through the door on the right into the peaceful cloister. A handful of friars can still be seen roaming these tranquil halls, and you're welcome to stroll here, too.

Dominican Monastery (Dominikanski Samostan)—This monastery, at the opposite end of the Old Town, no longer operates, but instead hosts a wide range of Roman artifacts—many of which are displayed on the lawn. Inside you'll find more Roman fragments scattered around a cloister with sparse explanations (€4, mid-April–Nov daily 10:00–17:00, closed in winter, Muzejski trg 1, tel. 02/787-9230).

Ptuj Thermal Baths (Terme Ptuj)—This gigantic bath complex, a 15-minute walk across the river from Ptuj's Old Town, is a fun place to splash around on a longer visit. The "Thermal Park" has multiple swimming pools, whirlpools, and slides, including the "longest slide in Slovenia." The complex also offers various spa treatments (€11 to enter Thermal Park, cheaper after 15:00, Mon–Fri 7:00–22:00, Sat–Sun 8:00–22:00, Pot v Toplice 9, tel. 02/749-4100, www.terme-ptuj.si).

Sleeping in Ptuj

Central Ptuj has only a few hotels, a hostel, and a handful of *sobe/* guest houses. While the options seem limited, the rooms are generally a good value compared to the western part of the country. Several of the cheaper places don't serve breakfast, but you can get a €5 buffet breakfast at Hotel Mitra even if you're not staying there (included for guests).

$$$ Park Hotel Ptuj is doing its best to be big-time stylish in a small-time town. Its 15 rooms come with slick modern decor, but—without an elevator, and with air-conditioning in only some of the rooms—it doesn't quite live up to the high prices (Sb-€57, Db-€97–107 depending on size, free Wi-Fi, Prešernova 38, tel. 02/749-3300, fax 02/749-3319, www.parkhotel-ptuj.si, info @parkhotel-ptuj.si).

$$$ Hotel Mitra enjoys Ptuj's best location: right on its most appealing street, a few steps from the landmark City Tower. It's the closest thing in town to a business-class hotel. Each of the

Sleep Code

(€1 = about $1.40, country code: 386, area code: 02)
S = Single, **D** = Double/Twin, **T** = Triple, **Q** = Quad, **b** = bathroom.
No hotel in Ptuj has an elevator, but everyone listed here speaks English. Unless otherwise noted, credit cards are accepted, breakfast is included, and the modest tourist tax (€1.01 per person, per night) is not.

To help you easily sort through these listings, I've divided the rooms into three categories based on the price for a standard double room with bath:

$$$ Higher Priced—Most rooms €80 or more.
$$ Moderately Priced—Most rooms between €30–80.
$ Lower Priced—Most rooms €30 or less.

29 rooms has its own historical theme (Sb-€58–64, Db-€98, Db suite-€136, €10 less mid-Oct–April, lots of stairs, free Wi-Fi, Prešernova 6, tel. 02/787-7455, fax 02/787-7459, www.hotel-mitra .si, info@hotel-mitra.si).

$$ Vladmir Šilak rents seven comfortable rooms around a charming courtyard in his gorgeously renovated, circa-1513 Old Town home. If you want to sleep in a 500-year-old house with huge medieval vaults and three-foot-thick walls, this is the place (Sb-€28–30, Db-€36–42, Tb/Qb-€54–64, five-person apartment-€70–80, extra bed-€15, price depends on size of room, no breakfast, about €10 more if you want your own kitchen, no extra charge for 1-night stays, free Wi-Fi, bike rental, Dravska 13, tel. 02/787-7447, mobile 031-597-361, www.rooms-silak.com, info @rooms-silak.com).

$$ Žiga Guest House is simpler, slightly cheaper, and less memorable. Located on a nondescript street between the bus station and the Old Town, this reliable budget option has 10 outmoded rooms (Sb-€22, Db-€35, no breakfast, cash only, some noise from nearby bar on weekends, free Wi-Fi, Panonska 1, tel. 02/748-1683, fax 02/748-1684, www.prenocisca-ziga.com, prenocisce.ziga@gmail.com, run with care by the Šoštarić family).

$ Kurent Youth Hostel, an IYHF hostel, is institutional, comfortable, and clean. It has 53 bunks in two- to six-bed rooms, each with its own bathroom (€16 per bed, €1.50 less with hostel membership, breakfast €0.50 extra, Internet access, self-service laundry-€4.50/load, reception open daily 8:00–12:00 & 16:00–20:00, Osojnikova 9, tel. 02/771-0814, fax 02/771-0815, yhptuj @csod.si). It's hiding in the big, pinkish commercial center (with the Spar supermarket) near the bus station.

Eating in Ptuj

Little Ptuj isn't known for its high cuisine. You'll spot several breezy cafés and packed pizzerias, but high-quality eateries are in short supply.

Gostilna Ribič is every local's first recommendation for a splurge dinner. One of the most popular (and expensive) places in town, it has a short menu focused on fish. Sit in the classy interior or outside on the relaxing riverside terrace (€7 pastas, €10–20 main courses, Tue–Sun 10:00–22:30, closed Mon, Dravska ulica 9, tel. 02/749-0635). If you're ready for a break from Slovenian cuisine, the Chinese restaurant (Kitajski Vrt) across the street is surprisingly good.

Gostilna Amadeus serves up traditional Slovenian cuisine to tour groups, individual tourists, and a few locals. They're especially proud of their €4 *štruklji* (ravioli-like filled dumplings). The bar, with outdoor seating, is downstairs; to eat a meal, head upstairs to their nicely appointed dining room (€6 pastas, €7–15 main courses, Mon–Sat 12:00–23:00, Sun 12:00–16:00, Prešernova 36, tel. 02/771-7051).

PP is frequented by locals who enjoy its inexpensive, unpretentious, stick-to-your-ribs fare—lots of meat and potatoes, plus fried...everything. With a gaudy pub ambience, this Slovenian answer to T.G.I. Friday's is on the town's main shopping square (Novi trg), surrounded by supermarkets and malls. The Kavarna (café) has light food and outdoor seating; to eat a full meal, look for the indoor Gostilna (filling €4–9 main courses, Mon 9:00–22:00, Tue–Sat 9:00–20:00, closed Sun, Kavarna open until 22:00, Novi trg 2, tel. 02/749-0622). The name stands for Perutnina Ptuj, a chicken conglomerate that owns half the town (including this place, Gostilna Ribič, and the big wine cellar)—you'll see their logo everywhere.

Pizzeria Slonček has a great location right on Prešernova, with outdoor tables and good pizzas for less than €5 (daily 9:00–22:00, Prešernova 19, tel. 02/776-1311).

Ptuj Connections

From Ptuj by Train to: Maribor (8/day, 45–60 min), **Ljubljana** (3/day, 2.5 hrs, more with transfer in Pragersko), **Zagreb** (9/day, 3–4.5 hrs, usually requires 2 transfers), **Budapest** (4/day, 7.25–8 hrs, 2–3 changes), **Vienna** (5/day, 4.5–6.75 hrs, most require 1–2 changes). For destinations in western Slovenia, first go to Ljubljana.

Maribor

The second-biggest city in Slovenia (with 110,000 people), Maribor lives forever in the shadow of its much glitzier big sister, Ljubljana. Maribor is too small to offer an exciting big-city experience and too big to be charming. But this home of industry, business, and one of Slovenia's three universities is worth a quick look if you want to round out your Slovenian experience.

The lazy provincial town of Maribor woke up fast in 1846, when the Habsburgs built the train line from Vienna to the coast through here. It quickly modernized, losing some of its quaintness but gaining an urban, industrial flavor. However, Maribor was devastated in World War II (unlike other Slovenian cities), when it served as a headquarters for occupying Nazi forces. Since the city's factories also produced plane engines and other supplies, it became a "secondary target," where Allied warplanes—mostly Americans—would drop their bombs if unable to bomb their primary targets in Germany or Austria.

Today, rebuilt Maribor feels mellow for its size. Nestled up against a gentle vineyard-covered hill, it's almost cozy. From a tourist's perspective, the town is pleasant enough, but pretty dull—there's little to do other than wander its pedestrians-only streets. Maribor doesn't merit a detour, but it's worth a couple of hours for a stroll if you're passing through or have run out of diversions in Ptuj.

The countryside surrounding Maribor—called Mariborsko Pohorje—is an inviting recreational area, with vine-strewn hills lively with hikers and bicyclists in summer and with skiers in winter. Maribor is also the center of a thriving wine-growing region—especially popular among Austrians, who flow over the border to sample wines here, then stumble home. If you have time to spare, ask the TI for details about either of these outlying activities.

Orientation to Maribor

Maribor lines up along the bank of the Drava River. At the center of its concrete sprawl is the mostly traffic-free Old Town, with a variety of fine squares.

MARIBOR

Tourist Information

The main TI is at the northeast corner of the Old Town, on the far side of the Franciscan Church from Trg Svobode (Mon–Fri 9:00–19:00, Sat–Sun 9:00–18:00, Partizanska 6a, tel. 02/234-6611, www.maribor-pohorje.si). Pick up the handy city map and any other brochures that interest you. The TI can also give you a list of hotels or help you arrange for a local guide.

Arrival in Maribor

The train station (which has big €2 lockers) is a 10-minute walk east of the Old Town. Exit the station to the left and head up busy Partizanska cesta. Follow Partizanska as it swings right at the bus station, then continue three more blocks toward the Franciscan Church, with its twin red-brick spires. The main TI is in front of the church, and the Old Town is immediately behind the church.

Self-Guided Walk

Welcome to Maribor

Maribor's Austrian-feeling Old Town lacks big-league sights, but its squares and lanes are worth a wander. This very lightly narrated walk will give you the lay of the land. You could do it in less than a half-hour, not including stops.

Entering the Old Town from the train station (on Partizanska, near the Franciscan Church with its two red-brick spires—see "Arrival in Maribor," earlier), you find yourself on **Trg Svobode.** The oddly bulbous monument honors local Partisans (Yugoslav freedom-fighters) who were executed by Nazis during World War II. Wine cellars honeycomb the earth under this square (most can be toured only with a group—ask at the TI).

At the end of the square, with the tall tower, is the town's **castle** (Mestni Grad), which houses a good regional museum.

Adjoining Trg Svobode is a second square, **Grajski trg**— Maribor's liveliest, bustling with cafés and restaurants (including the recommended Štajerc brewpub, described later). At the top of the square is the venerable **Café Astoria,** a local landmark (open long hours daily).

Recent-history buffs may want to take a detour from here to Maribor's most interesting museum: the **Maribor National Liberation Museum** (Muzej Narodone Osvoboditve Maribor), about a five-minute walk up the street at the top of Grajski trg (between Café Astoria and the castle). This collection features a hodgepodge of items from the city's history, mostly focusing on Slovenia's turbulent 20th century. A permanent exhibit covers the early Tito years (1945–1955) and is supplemented by temporary exhibits. Enjoy the idealized Socialist Realist propaganda posters of happy Yugoslavs, eagerly pitching in to build a new nation (€2, Mon–Fri 8:00–18:00, Sat 9:00–12:00, closed Sun, Ulica Heroja Tomšiča 5).

Back on Grajski trg, follow lively **Slovenska ulica,** lined with characteristic cafés, sweet shops, and happy al fresco diners. Take a left at Gosposka, then turn right on 10 Oktobra to find the big parking-lot square called Slomškov trg, with the city **cathedral** (skip the tower climb—the view is nothing special).

From the cathedral, walk straight down toward the river, cutting through Rotovški trg. You'll wind up on the long, narrow **Glavni trg,** surrounded by historic buildings (including the City Hall) and presided over by an impressive 18th-century plague column.

If you continue down to the riverbank, you'll find yourself in the district called **Lent,** where vintners traditionally offer tastings of their wines. While it's usually pretty quiet, this area hops each summer when Maribor hosts its Lent Festival (late June–early July, http://lent.slovenija.net). Along this embankment, look for the locally revered "old vine" stretching along a railing—it's supposedly 400 years old and still produces wine.

Eating in Maribor

Štajerc is a popular local watering hole that brews its own beer and serves up heavy, starchy, traditional food. They're particularly known for their distinctive emerald-green beer, Štajerc Zeleno. Sit inside, or enjoy the outdoor seating on Maribor's most happening square, Grajski trg (€5–12 meals, closed Sun, Vetrinjska 30, tel. 02/234-4234).

Maribor Connections

From Maribor by Train to: Ptuj (8/day, 45–60 min), **Ljubljana** (hourly, 2–3 hrs, more with a transfer in Zidani Most).

THE KARST

Caves, Castles, and Horses

In Slovenia's Karst region, about an hour on the A-1 expressway south of Ljubljana, you'll find some of the most impressive cave systems on the planet, a chance to see the famous Lipizzaner stallions for a fraction of what you'd pay in Vienna, and one of Europe's most dramatically situated castles—built into the face of a mountain.

The term "karst" is used worldwide to refer to an arid limestone plateau, but Slovenia's is the original. It comes from the Slovenian word "Kras"—a specific region near the Italian border. Since this limestone terrain is easily dissolved by water, karstic regions are punctuated by remarkable networks of caves and underground rivers.

Your top Karst priority is a cave visit. Choose between Slovenia's two best caves, Škocjan or Postojna—each with a handy side-trip nearby (to help you pick, see the sidebar on page 518).

In the neighborhood of Škocjan is Lipica, where the Lipizzaner stallions strut their stuff. Just up the road from Postojna is Predjama Castle, picturesquely nestled into the side of a cliff.

Sleeping: To sleep in the heart of the Karst—a short drive from all these sights—consider

Tourist Farm Hudičevec (hoo-DEE-cheh-vets), midway between Škocjan and Postojna. This kid-friendly complex, with seven rooms and two apartments, is run by the farming Simčič family. A roomy, hotelesque, spick-

and-span double with a private bathroom—including a Slovenian dinner and farm-fresh eggs for breakfast—costs only €64 for two people (Db without dinner-€46, big apartment-€80 plus €9 per person for optional dinner, cash only, Wi-Fi, tel. 05/703-0300, fax 05/703-0320, www.hudicevec.com, info@hudicevec.si). Idyllic and remote as this place sounds, it's actually right next to the express-way (which makes it easy to reach, but also means it comes with some road noise, and large tour groups show up for dinner). Take the Razdrto exit from the expressway, turn right toward Postojna, then start looking right away for the low-profile sign directing you back under the road.

Škocjan Caves and Lipica Stud Farm

Drivers can easily combine these two attractions, which are just a short drive from each other. By public transportation, it's more challenging. The main transit hubs for this area are the towns of Divača and Sežana, both served by train and bus from Ljubljana. A shuttle bus goes between the Divača train station and Škocjan Caves (10 min, 2/day, coordinated to meet some trains—check schedules at Ljubljana TI). To reach Lipica, you'll have to take a taxi from one of the train stations.

▲▲▲Škocjan Caves (Škocjanske Jame)

Škocjan (SHKOHTS-yahn) offers good formations and a vast canyon with a raging underground river. You'll end up walking about two miles, going up and down more than 400 steps. While anyone in good shape can enjoy Škocjan, those who have trouble walking or tire easily are better off touring the Postojna Caves instead (described later).

Upon arrival, get a ticket for the next tour (they rarely fill up). You'll pass waiting time at a covered terrace with a gift kiosk, a bar serving light meals and drinks, and an interactive educational center with exhibits about the caves. At tour time, your guide (tot-ing an industrial-strength flashlight) calls everyone together, and you march silently for 10 minutes to the cave entrance. There you split into language groups and enter the cave.

The first half of the experience is the "dry caves," with a wide array of won-drous formations and what seem like large caverns. The experience builds and builds as you go into ever-more-impressive grottoes, and you

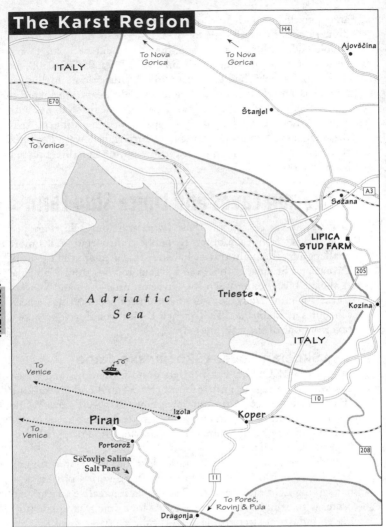

The Karst Region

think you've seen the best. But then you get to the truly colossal "finale" cavern, with a mighty river crashing through the bottom. You feel like a bit player in a sci-fi thriller. It's a world where a thousand evil *Wizard of Oz* monkeys could comfortably fly in formation. You hike high above the river for about a mile, crossing a breathtaking (but stable-feeling) footbridge 150 feet above the torrent. Far below, the scant remains of century-old trails from the early days of tourism are evocative. The cave finally widens, sunlight pours in, and you emerge—like lost creatures seeking daylight—into a lush canyon. A steep, somewhat strenuous hike

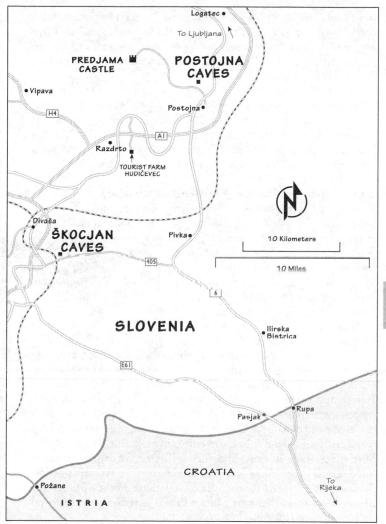

leads to a small funicular, which lifts you back to the ticket booth/café/shop.

Cost and Hours: The guided tour is mandatory, usually in English, and takes about two hours (€14, June–Sept tours daily at the top of each hour 10:00–17:00, Oct–May tours daily at 10:00 and 13:00 and sometimes also at 15:00 or 15:30, call or pick up current brochure—which you'll find everywhere in Slovenia—to confirm schedule before making the trip, tel. 05/708-2110, www.park-skocjanske-jame.si).

Getting to Škocjan: By car, take the A-1 expressway south from Ljubljana about 1.5 hours and get off at the Divača exit (also marked with brown signs for *Lipica* and *Škocjanske jame*) and follow signs for *Škocjanske jame*. (Before or after Škocjan, drivers can easily visit the Lipica Stud Farm, described next.) The caves have free and easy parking.

By public transportation, it's trickier. Take the train or bus to Divača (see "Ljubljana Connections," page 434), which is about three miles from the caves. To get from the Divača train station to the caves, you can either take the local shuttle bus (2/day); rent a bike (often possible in summer); hike about 45 minutes; or take a taxi (around €8, taxi stand in front of Divača train station).

▲Lipica Stud Farm (Kobilarna Lipica)

The Lipica (LEE-peet-suh) Stud Farm, a 10-minute drive from the Škocjan Caves, was founded in 1580 to provide horses for the Habsburg court in Vienna. Horse-loving Habsburg Archduke Charles wanted to create the perfect animal: He imported Andalusian horses from his homeland of Spain, then bred them with a local line to come up with an extremely intelligent and easily trainable breed. Charles' creation, the Lipizzaner stallions—known for their noble gait and Baroque shape—were made famous by Vienna's Spanish Riding School.

Italian and Arabian bloodlines were later added to tweak various characteristics. These regal horses have changed shape with the tenor of the times: They were bred strong and stout during wars, frilly and slender in more cultured eras. But they're always born black, fade to gray, and turn a distinctive white in adulthood. Until World War I, Lipica bred horses for Austria's needs. Now Austria breeds its own line, and these horses prance for Slovenia—a treasured part of its cultural heritage (and featured on Slovenia's €0.20 coin).

Today you can tour the Lipizzaner stables to visit the magnificent animals, whose stalls are labeled with their purebred bloodlines. Unlike in Vienna, it's cheap and easy to get tickets to see the horses perform. While the show is less polished than in Vienna, the Lipizzaners' clever routine—stutter-stepping sideways to the classical beat—still thrills visitors. This up-close horse encounter is worth a visit only if you're a horse enthusiast, or if you have a car and it fits your schedule.

By the way, the hills less than a mile away are in Italy. Aside from the horses, Lipica's big draw is its casino. Italians across the border are legally forbidden from gambling in their own town's casinos—for fear of addiction—so they flock here to Slovenia to try their luck.

Visiting the Stud Farm: There are three activities at Lipica— you can tour the farm for a look at the horses, watch a training session, and, on some days, see a more elaborate performance of the prancing stallions. If you're coming all the way to Lipica, you might as well time it so that you can do both the one-hour tour and a training session (10:00–12:00) or—better yet—a full performance. Call ahead or check online to confirm performance and tour times before you make the trip (tel. 05/739-1580, www.lipica .org). Note that in summer, Monday is the only day you can't see the horses in action (but the tour still runs).

Cost: Stud farm tour (with or without training session)-€10, tour plus performance-€17.

Tours: July–Aug daily on the hour 9:00–18:00 except 12:00; April–June and Sept–Oct daily on the hour 9:00–17:00 except 12:00 (also at 18:00 Sat–Sun); off-season daily at 10:00, 11:00, 13:00, 14:00, and 15:00 (plus 16:00 Sat–Sun in March). Note that on days when there's a 15:00 performance, you can tour the farm before (14:00) or after (16:00) the show.

Performances: April–Oct Tue, Fri, and Sun at 15:00, none Nov–March.

Training Sessions: April–Oct Tue–Sun 10:00–12:00, none Mon or Nov–March.

Getting to Lipica: The Lipica Stud Farm is in Slovenia's southwest corner (a stone's throw from Trieste, Italy). By car, exit the A-1 expressway at Divača and follow brown *Lipica* signs. (As you drive into the farm, you'll go through pastures where the stallions often roam.) It's a hassle by public transportation. You can take the train or bus from Ljubljana to Divača (about six miles from Lipica) or to Sežana (about four miles from Lipica). From those places, you can hire a taxi (€15 from Divača, €10 from Sežana) or rent a bike (often possible in summer).

Postojna Caves and Predjama Castle

These two sights are easy to connect for drivers, since they're along the same road. If you're using public transportation, a handy bus operated by the Slovenian Railway connects the train station in the town of Postojna with both the Postojna Caves and Predjama Castle (4/day, 5 min to caves, 30 min to castle, included with train ticket to Postojna, confirm schedules before making the trip).

▲▲Postojna Caves (Postojnska Jama)

Postojna (poh-STOY-nah) is the most accessible—and touristy— cave experience in the region. It's the biggest cave system in

Postojna vs. Škocjan: Which Caves to Visit?

To Postojna or to Škocjan?—that is the question. Each cave system is massive, cut into the limestone by rivers for more than two million years. Stalagmites and stalactites—in a slow-motion love story—silently work their way toward each other until that last drip never drops. Minerals picked up by the water as it seeps through various rocks create the different colors (iron makes red, limestone makes white, and so on). Both caves were excavated and explored in the mid-19th century.

Slovenes debate long and hard about which cave system is better. The formations at Postojna are slightly more abundant, varied, and colorful, with stalagmites and stalactites as tall as 100 feet. Postojna is easier to reach by public transportation and far less strenuous to visit than Škocjan—of the three-mile route, you'll walk only about a mile (the rest of the time, you're on a Disney World–type people-mover). But Postojna is also more expensive and much more touristy (they get half a million visitors each year, five times as many as Škocjan)—you'll wade through tour buses and tacky souvenir stands on your way to the entrance. Most importantly, Postojna lacks Škocjan's spectacular, massive-cavern finale. Škocjan also comes with a fairly strenuous hike, leaving you feeling like you really did something adventurous. Finally, the choice of likely side-trip might help you decide: Near Postojna is the cliff-hanging Predjama Castle, while Škocjan is closer to the Lipica Stud Farm.

No matter which cave you visit, you'll find it chilly, but not really cold (a light sweater is fine). Both caves technically forbid photography (a laughable rule that nobody takes seriously).

Slovenia (and, before borders shifted a few generations ago, it was the biggest in Italy...a fact that envious Italians still haven't forgotten).

Whether you arrive by car, tour bus, or on foot, you'll walk past a paved outdoor mall of shops, eateries, and handicraft vendors to the gaping hole in the mountain. Buy your ticket and board a train, which slings you deep into the mountain, whizzing past wonderful formations. (The ride alone is exhilarating.) Then you get out, assemble into language groups, and follow a guide on a well-lit, circular, paved path through more formations. You'll see hundred-foot-tall stalagmites and stalactites, as well as translucent "curtains" of rock and ceilings dripping with skinny "spaghetti stalactites." You'll wind up peering at the strange "human fish" (a.k.a. olm or *Proteus anguinus*)—sort of a long, skinny, pale-pink salamander with fingers and toes. The world's biggest cave-dwelling animal, these amphibians can survive up to seven years without eating (the live specimens you see here are never fed during the four months they're on display). Then you'll load back onto the train and return to the bright daylight.

Cost and Hours: Your visit, which is by tour only, costs €20 and lasts 1.5 hours. Tours leave daily at the top of each hour (July–Aug 9:00–18:00; May–June and Sept 9:00–17:00; April and Oct at 10:00, 12:00, 14:00, and 16:00; Nov–March at 10:00, 12:00, and 15:00; call to confirm schedule or pick up brochure at any TI). From mid-May through August, try to show up 30 minutes early for the morning tours (popular with tour buses); otherwise, aim for 15 minutes ahead. Information: tel. 05/700-0100, www.postojna-cave.com.

"Proteus Vivarium": This exhibit gives you the chance to learn more about karstic caves and about speleobiology—the study of cave-dwelling animal life. While troglodytes, science nuts, and those who just can't get enough of those human fish may get a charge out of this exhibit, it's basically just an attempt to wring a little more cash out of gullible tourists (€7, daily May–Sept 9:30–17:30, Oct–April 10:30–15:30).

Getting to Postojna: The caves are just outside the town of Postojna, about an hour south of Ljubljana on the A-1 expressway (Jamska cesta 30). By car, take the expressway south from Ljubljana and get off at the Postojna exit. Turn right after the tollbooth and follow the *jama/grotte/cave* signs through town until you see the tour buses. Drivers pay to park 200 yards from the cave entry. By train, you'll arrive at the train station in the town of Postojna; from here, a handy shuttle bus takes you to the caves (4/day, 5 min); otherwise, you can walk there in 20 minutes. If coming on the bus from Ljubljana, you'll be dropped just a five-minute walk from the caves.

▲Predjama Castle (Predjamski Grad)

Burrowed into the side of a mountain close to Postojna is dramatic Predjama Castle (prehd-YAH-mah), one of Europe's most scenic castles (despite its dull interior). Predjama is a hit with tourists for its striking setting, exciting exterior, and romantic legend.

Notice as you approach that you don't even see Predjama—crouching magnificently in its cave—until the last moment. The first castle here was actually a tiny ninth-century fortress embedded deep in the cave behind the present castle. Over the centuries, different castles were built here, and they gradually moved out to the mouth of the cave. While the original was called "the castle in the cave," the current one is *pred jama*—"in front of the cave."

While enjoying the view, ponder this legend: In the 15th century, a nobleman named Erasmus killed the emperor's cousin in a duel. He was imprisoned under Ljubljana Castle and spent years nursing a grudge. When he was finally released, he used his castle—buried deep inside the cave above this current version—as a home base for a series of Robin Hood–style raids on the local nobility and merchants. (Actually, Erasmus stole from the rich and kept for himself—but that was good enough to make him a hero to the peasants, who hated the nobles.)

Soldiers from Trieste were brought in to put an end to Erasmus' raids, laying siege to the castle for over a year. Back then, the only way into the castle was through the cave in the valley below—then up, through an extensive labyrinth of caves, to the top. While the soldiers down below froze and starved, Erasmus' men sneaked out through the caves to bring in supplies. (They liked to drop their leftovers on the soldiers below to taunt them, letting them know that the siege wasn't working.)

Eventually, the soldiers came up with a plan. They waited for Erasmus to visit the latrine—which, by design, had to be on the thin-walled outer edge of the castle—and then, on seeing a signal by a secret agent, blew Erasmus off his throne with a cannonball. Today, Erasmus is supposedly buried under the huge linden tree in the parking lot.

As the legend of Erasmus faded, the function of the castle changed. By the 16th century, Predjama had become a castle for hunting more than for defense—explaining its current picturesque-but-impractical design.

After driving all the way here, it seems a shame not to visit the interior—but it's truly skippable. The management (which also runs the nearby Postojna Caves) is very strict about keeping the interior 16th-century in style, so there's virtually nothing inside except 20th-century fakes of 16th-century furniture, plus a few forgettable paintings and cheesy folk displays. English descriptions are sparse, and the free English history flier is not much help. But for most, the views of the place alone are worth the drive.

Cost and Hours: €8 to go inside, daily July–Aug 9:00–19:00, May–June and Sept 9:00–18:00, April and Oct 10:00–17:00, Nov–March 10:00–16:00. Information: tel. 05/751-6015.

Cave Tours: If you're already visiting the caves at Postojna or Škocjan, a visit to the caves under this castle is unnecessary (€7, 45 min; May–Sept daily at 11:00, 13:00, 15:00, and 17:00; no tours Oct–April).

Getting to Predjama: Predjama Castle is on a twisty rural road 5.5 miles beyond Postojna Caves. By car, just continue on the winding road past Postojna, following signs for *Predjama* and *Predjamski Grad* (coming back, follow signs to *Postojna*). If using public transportation, you can take the train to the town of Postojna; from the train station there, a shuttle bus brings visitors to the castle (4/day, 30 min)—but the sparse frequency might leave you with more time at the castle than you really need. Check the return schedule carefully. If you're in a pinch, consider hitching a ride between Predjama and Postojna with a friendly tour bus or tourist's car, as most visitors do both sights.

PIRAN

Croatia's 3,600-mile-long coast gets all the press, but don't overlook Slovenia's own 29 miles of Adriatic coastline. The Slovenian coast has only a handful of towns: big, industrial Koper; lived-in and crumbling Izola; and the swanky but soulless resort of Portorož. But the Back Door gem of the Slovenian Adriatic is Piran. Most Adriatic towns are all tourists and concrete, but Piran has kept itself charming and in remarkably good repair while holding the tourist sprawl at bay. In peak season, it's overrun with Italian vacationers. But as you get to know it, Piran becomes one of the most pleasant and user-friendly seaside towns this side of Dubrovnik.

Planning Your Time

You can see everything in Piran (including a pop into the Maritime Museum and a hike up the bell tower) in a quick, hour-long walk. Then feel free to just bask in the town's ambience. Enjoy a gelato or a *kava* (coffee) on the sleek, marbled Tartini Square, surrounded by Neoclassical buildings and watched over by the bell tower. Wander Piran's piers and catch its glow at sunset.

Piran also works as a base for visiting the caves, horses, and castles of the nearby Karst region (see previous chapter). Notice, too, that it's conveniently on the way between Ljubljana/the Karst and Croatia's Istria (see "Route Tips for Drivers" at the end of this chapter).

Orientation to Piran

(area code: 05)

Piran (pee-RAHN) is small; everything is within a few minutes' walk. Crowded onto the tip of its peninsula, the town can't grow. Its population—7,500 a century ago—has dropped to about 4,200 today, as many young people find more opportunity in bigger cities.

Piran clusters around its boat-speckled harbor and main showpiece square, Tartini Square (Tartinijev trg). Up the hill behind Tartini Square is the landmark bell tower of the Cathedral of St. George. A few blocks toward the end of the peninsula from Tartini Square is the heart of the Old Town, May 1 Square (Trg 1 Maja).

From Tartini Square and the nearby marina, a concrete promenade—lined with rocks to break the storm waves and with expensive tourist restaurants to break your budget—stretches along the town's waterfront, inviting you to stroll.

Tourist Information

The TI is on Tartini Square facing the marina (daily June–Aug 9:00–20:00, Sept–May 9:00–17:00, at #2, tel. 05/673-4440, www .portoroz.si). For **Internet access,** get online at the Val Youth Hostel (described later, under "Sleeping in Piran"). You can **rent a bike** at the Maona travel agency (€6/2 hrs, €20/24 hrs, Cankarjevo nabrežje 7, tel. 05/673-4520).

Arrival in Piran

By Car: In peak season (June–early Sept), you have to park at the big harborside lot called Fornače, just outside the gate into town (€1.20/hr, €12/day, frequent shuttle buses take you right to Tartini Square, or you can walk 10 min). If you're staying in town, you can drive in to drop things off at your hotel, but you'll likely need to take your car right back to the harborside lot. Off-season, you may be able to find some marked tourist spaces inside the Old Town area, but they're expensive (€5 for the first hour, €3/hr after that, get a ticket as you enter the gate and pay as you exit)—but be careful to park only in spaces designated for tourists.

By Bus: Piran has two bus stops. Shuttle buses from the harborside parking lot and nearby towns (such as Portorož) stop right at Tartini Square; buses to long-distance destinations (such as Ljubljana) use the low-profile main bus station along the water near the entrance to town.

Sights in Piran

In Piran

▲**Tartini Square (Tartinijev trg)**—Tartini Square, with its polished marble, was once part of a protected harbor. In 1894, the

harbor smelled so bad that they decided to fill it in. Today, rather than fishing boats, it's filled with skateboarding kids.

The statue honors **Giuseppe Tartini** (1692–1770), a composer and violinist once known throughout Europe. While the Church of St. Peter has overlooked this spot since 1272, its current facade is Neoclassical, from the early 1800s. The Neo-Renaissance Town Hall dates from the 1870s.

The fine little red palace in the corner (at #4) evokes Venice.

This **"Venetian House"** (c. 1450) is the oldest preserved house on the square. Classic Venetian Gothic, it was built by a wealthy Venetian merchant and comes with a legend: The merchant fell in love with a simple local girl when visiting on business, became her sugar daddy, and eventually built her this flat. When the townsfolk began to gossip about the relationship, he answered them with the relief you see today (with the Venetian lion, between the two top windows): *Lassa pur dir* ("Let them talk").

May 1 Square (Trg 1 Maja)—This square marks the center of medieval Piran, where its main streets converged. Once the administrative center of town, today it's the domain of local kids and ringed by a few humble eateries. The stone rainwater cistern dominating the center of the square was built in 1775 after a severe drought. Rainwater was captured here with the help of drains from roofs and channeled by hardworking statues into the system. The water was filtered through sand and stored in the well, clean and ready for townspeople to draw—or, later, pump—for drinking.

Cathedral and Bell Tower of St. George (Stolna Cerkev Sv. Jurija)—Piran is proud of its many churches, numbering more than 20. While none are of any real historic or artistic importance, the Cathedral of St. George is worth a look. This cathedral dates from the 14th century and was decorated in the Baroque style by Venetian artists in the 17th century. It dominates the Old Town with its bell tower *(campanile)*, a miniature version of the more

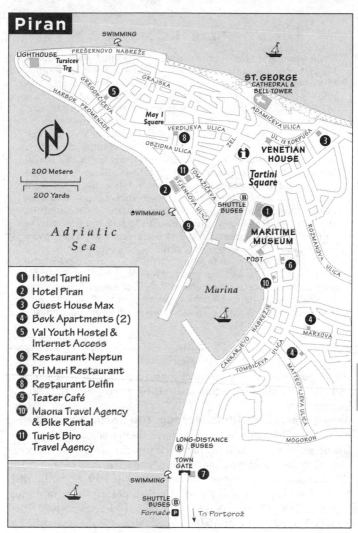

Piran

SWIMMING

PREŠERNOVO NABREŽE

LIGHTHOUSE
Tursicev Trg

GRAJSKA

GREGORČIČEVA

HARBOR PROMENADE

5

ST. GEORGE
CATHEDRAL &
BELL TOWER

ADAMIČEVA ULICA

May 1
Square

VERDIJEVA ULICA

OBZIDNA ULICA

8

ZEL

UL. IX KORPUSA

VENETIAN
HOUSE

3

*Tartini
Square*

11

TOMAŽIČEVA

STJENKOVA ULICA

2

SWIMMING

9

SHUTTLE
BUSES

B

1

MARITIME
MUSEUM

POST

ROZMANOVA ULICA

6

10

*A d r i a t i c
S e a*

200 Meters

200 Yards

Murina

CANKARJEVO NABREŽE

TOMŠIČEVA ULICA

MARXOVA

4

4

MATTEOTIJEVA ULICA

MOGORON

❶ Hotel Tartini
❷ Hotel Piran
❸ Guest House Max
❹ Bevk Apartments (2)
❺ Val Youth Hostel &
   Internet Access
❻ Restaurant Neptun
❼ Pri Mari Restaurant
❽ Restaurant Delfin
❾ Teater Café
❿ Maona Travel Agency
   & Bike Rental
⓫ Turist Biro
   Travel Agency

LONG-DISTANCE
BUSES

B

TOWN
GATE

7

SWIMMING

SHUTTLE
BUSES **B**

Fornače **P**

↓ To Portorož

PIRAN

famous one on St. Mark's Square in Venice. The tower (with bells dating from the 15th century) welcomes tourists willing to pay €1 to climb 146 rickety steps for the best view in town and a chance for some bell fun (daily 10:00–17:00, until 19:00 in summer). Stand inside the biggest bell. Chant, find the resonant frequency, and ring

Piran History

Piran was named for the fires (*pyr* in Greek) that were lit at the tip of its peninsula to assist passing ships. Known as "Pirano" in *Italiano*, the town is home to a long-standing Italian community (about 1,500 today)—so it's legally bilingual, with signs in two languages. As with most towns on the eastern Adriatic, it has a Venetian flavor. Piran wisely signed on with Venice as part of its trading empire in 933. Because of its valuable salt industry and strong trade, Piran managed some autonomy in later centuries. After plagues killed most of Piran's population in the 15th century, local Italians let Slavs fleeing the Ottomans repopulate the town. Piran's impressive walls were built to counter the growing Ottoman threat. Too much rain ruined the town's valuable salt basins, but in the 19th century, the Austrian Habsburg rulers rebuilt the salt industry (these salt fields are still open for tourist visits—see next page). With that change came a new economic boom, and Piran grew in importance once again. After World War I, this part of the Habsburg Empire was assigned to Italy, but fascism never sat well with the locals. After World War II, the region was made neutral, then became part of Yugoslavia in 1956. In 1991, with the creation of Slovenia, the Slovenes of Piran were finally independent.

the clapper ever so softly. Snap a portrait of you, your partner, and the rusty clapper. Brace yourself for *fortissimo* clangs on the quarter-hour.

Sergej Mašera Maritime Museum (Pomorski Muzej Sergej Mašera)—This humble museum faces the harbor and the square, filling an elegant old building with meager but faintly endearing exhibits—furniture, model ships, and paintings—about the "Slovenian seamen" and the town's history (€3.50, €0.50 English booklet, otherwise borrow scant English descriptions; July–Aug Tue–Sun 9:00–12:00 & 18:00–21:00, closed Mon; Sept–June Tue–Sun 9:00–12:00 & 15:00–18:00, closed Mon; Cankarjevo nabrežje 3, tel. 05/671-0040, www.pommuz-pi.si).

Harborfront Stroll—Wandering along the harborfront is a delight: almost no pesky mopeds or cars, and virtually no American or Japanese tourists—just Slovenes and Italians. Children sell shells on cardboard boxes. Husky sunbathers lie like large limpets on the rocks. Walk around the lighthouse at the tip of the town and around the corner, checking out the cafés and fish restaurants along the way.

Swimming—While there is no sandy beach, the water is warm and clean, and swimming is a major activity in Piran. There are two pebbly beaches: one just outside of town before the big parking lot, and the other at the end of the harbor promenade past the lighthouse. Two designated swimming areas are accessible from the promenade—both with very slippery concrete embankments, ladders, and showers (one in front of Hotel Piran, the other around the corner from the lighthouse).

Near Piran

▲Sečovlje Salina Nature Park (Krajinski Park Sečoveljske Soline)—A few miles south of Piran, a literal stone's throw from the Croatian border, are enormous salt fields used since the Middle Ages for harvesting salt—back when salt was more precious than gold. As you drive by on the way to Croatia, you'll wonder what this massive complex is—so why not stop for a visit? This "nature park" has two parts: **Lera,** to the north, harvests salt using modern techniques; while **Fontanigge,** to the south (closer to Croatia), is no longer in operation—except to demonstrate traditional salt-harvesting methods to tourists. I'd skip the Lera section (or visit it quickly), but make time for Fontanigge and its informative museum.

At Fontanigge (within a few feet of the Croatian border, which is just over the little river), you'll see the way salt was harvested from medieval times up until the 1960s. Well-explained by posted English information and a knowledgeable docent, the exhibit demonstrates tools and methods and explains the lifestyles of the people who eked out a hard living on these salty marshes (for example, since they all shared a communal oven, each family had their own stamp for marking their loaves of bread). If your timing's right, you may even see museum docents gathering salt the way their ancestors did. I never thought salt could be so interesting.

The catch: The museum is about a mile and a half off the main road, reached only by a 30-minute walk down a very bumpy gravel road (or an easy boat trip from Piran—see "Getting There," below).

Cost, Hours, Information: €5 covers entry to both Fontanigge and Lera salt fields and the museum; salt fields open daily 8:00–20:00 in summer, 9:00–17:00 off-season; museum open daily April–Oct 9:00–18:00, closed Nov–March; tel. 05/671-0040, www.kpss.si.

Getting There: Both salt fields are between Piran and the Croatian border. The easiest access is by the *Solinarka* **boat** from Piran (goes right to the museum, frequency depends on demand—ask at the Piran TI).

For **drivers,** reaching the museum involves a long walk: As you drive south toward Croatia (see "Route Tips for Drivers" at the end of this chapter), you'll pass the entrance to the modern Lera salt field on the right just after entering the town of Seča. For the more interesting Fontanigge—farther along this same road—it's more complicated: You'll actually have to cross the Slovenian border, then a few feet later, just before you reach the Croatian border post, you'll see a gravel road on the right, leading to the salt field. It's a five-minute drive to the gate, where you'll park and walk about 30 minutes to the museum. (Though there is a very rough gravel road to the museum, they prefer that visitors avoid driving on it, in order to protect this fragile landscape.)

Sleeping in Piran

Piran's accommodations options are limited: two comparable hotels, a colorful guest house, some youth hostels, and *sobe* (rooms in private homes). The hotels raise their rates in peak season (mid-July–late Aug). If everyone's booked up, find a *soba*.

$$$ Hotel Tartini faces the main square 50 yards from the waterfront. Its 46 rooms are jaunty, colorful, and a bit faded. Don't miss the upstairs terrace cocktail bar, with great views over Tartini Square (peak season: Sb-€88, Db-€118; shoulder season: Sb-€76, Db-€102; €10 more for seaside room with balcony; air-con, elevator, pay Wi-Fi, Tartinijev trg 15, tel. 05/671-1000, fax 05/671-1665, www.hotel-tartini-piran.com, info@hotel-tartini-piran.com).

$$$ Hotel Piran is right on the water, with a concrete "beach" directly in front of it. Its 89 rooms are more business than resort, with a complex pricing scheme (peak season: seaview Sb-€92, non-view Db-€115, seaview Db-€125; shoulder season: non-view Sb-€60, seaview Sb-€75, non-view Db-€95, seaview Db-€110; "superior" rooms have air-con, a bigger bathroom, and more soundproof windows for €15 more; prices drop Nov–mid-April, elevator, pay Internet access and Wi-Fi, €12 parking—ask when you reserve, Stijenkova 1, tel. 05/676-2100, fax 05/676-2520, www.hoteli-piran.si, marketing@hoteli-piran.si).

$$ Guest House Max is a clean-yet-funky place just under the town's bell tower. Mellow and friendly Max welcomes travelers with six simple, mod, and comfy rooms up a tight staircase over a cozy breakfast room. He enjoys sharing his long afternoon siesta (13:00–17:00) with guests in his bar. Since Max is a one-man show, it's essential to carefully settle on an arrival time with him (April–Aug: Db-€70; Sept–March: Db-€60; €10 less for Sb, cash only, no extra charge for 1-night stays, includes breakfast, fans but no air-con, free Wi-Fi, ulica 9 Korpusa #26, tel. 05/673-3436, mobile 041-692-928, www.maxpiran.com, info@maxpiran.com).

$$ Bogdan and Jana Bevk rent six good apartments in two different buildings buried in a quiet part of the Old Town (July–Aug: Db-€60–70; May–June and Sept–Oct: Db-€50–60; Nov–April: Db-€40–50; higher prices are for newer apartments

Sleep Code

(€1 = about $1.40, country code: 386, area code: 05)
S = Single, **D** = Double/Twin, **T** = Triple, **Q** = Quad, **b** = bathroom.
Unless otherwise noted, credit cards are accepted and break-
fast is included. Everyone speaks English.

To help you sort easily through these listings, I've divided
the rooms into three categories based on the price for a
standard double room with bath:

$$$ Higher Priced—Most rooms €85 or more.
  $$ Moderately Priced—Most rooms between €50–85.
   $ Lower Priced—Most rooms €50 or less.

with sauna, 50 percent more for 1–2-night stays, no breakfast, air-
con, free Wi-Fi, lots of stairs, Marxova 13 and Prežihova 4, mobile
051-623-682, tel. 05/902-2111, www.bevk.si, info@bevk.si).

$ Val Youth Hostel rents the cheapest beds in this otherwise
expensive town. It's a friendly place, a half-block off the waterfront (56 beds in 22 two-, three-, or four-bed rooms, mid-May–
mid-Sept: €25 per person; off-season: €22 per person; €2 more for
1-night stays in peak season, includes breakfast and sheets, prices
are the same regardless of room size, free self-service laundry,
kitchen; free Internet access for guests, or €1/hr for non-guests;
20 yards in from waterfront near tip of peninsula at Gregorčičeva
38A, tel. 05/673-2555, fax 05/673-2556, www.hostel-val.com,
yhostel.val@siol.net).

$ Sobe: To track down a private room, try two local travel
agencies: **Maona** (Cankarjevo nabrežje 7, tel. 05/673-4520, www
.maona.si, maona@siol.net) or **Turist Biro** (Tomažičeva 3, tel.
05/673-2509, www.turistbiro-ag.si, info@turistbiro-ag.si). As with
those who rent rooms in coastal Croatia, Piran's *sobe* hosts charge
30–50 percent extra for one- or two-night stays.

Eating in Piran

Pricey tourist bars and restaurants face the sea (figure about €20
per main course), while the laid-back, funky, and colorful local
joints seem to seek an escape from both the tourists and the sun in
the back lanes. Get off the beaten track to find one of my recommended restaurants, and you'll enjoy a seafood-and-pasta feast for
half what you'd pay in Venice (just across the sea).

Restaurant Neptun, with fresh seafood and pastas in a fish-
net-strewn dining room, is far classier than the tacky tourist fish
joints. The Grilj family and their three cooks work hard to please

six tables of diners. Everything's made to order with fish straight out of the Adriatic—nothing's frozen. I can't resist their gnocchi with scampi (€6–10 pastas, €8–18 meat and fish dishes, daily 12:00–16:00 & 18:00–24:00, open all day in summer, Župančičeva 7, tel. 05/673-4111). Don't confuse this with Neptun Café, at the waterfront bus station.

Pri Mari Restaurant is about a 10-minute walk from Tartini Square, near the entrance to town. Gregarious Mara and Tomaž will welcome you into their cheery dining room like an old friend, then treat you to tasty Venetian-style cooking (€7–12 pastas, €8–16 meat and fish dishes, Tue–Sat 12:00–22:00, Sun 12:00–18:00—or until 22:00 in July–Aug, closed Mon, Dantejeva 17, tel. 05/673-4735).

Restaurant Delfin is a crank-'em-out fish restaurant with a good reputation. Run by the Pašalić family, it has a pleasant dining room as well as tables out on the Old Town's May 1 Square (€6–7 pastas, €8–12 meat dishes, €11–18 fish dishes, daily 11:00–24:00, Kosovelova 4, tel. 05/673-2448).

Drinks: **Teater Café** is *the* place for drinks with Adriatic views and a characteristic old interior. Catching the sunset here is a fine way to kick off your Piran evening (open long hours daily, Stjenkova 1).

Piran Connections

The best way to connect Piran with **Ljubljana** is by **bus** (6/day, 2.5 hrs, €12). By **train,** the trip takes four hours (bus between Piran and Koper, then train between Koper and Ljubljana).

By **car,** Piran is about 90 minutes from Ljubljana. From Ljubljana, take the A-1 expressway south to Koper; once in Koper, follow *Portorož/Portorose* signs, then *Piran/Pirano.* For arrival and parking instructions, see "Arrival in Piran," earlier.

To Croatia's Istria: In summer (June–late Sept), a handy bus goes each afternoon from Piran to Rovinj (also stops in Poreč en route; about 2.5 hours from Piran to Rovinj; does not run off-season). Year-round, there are also buses going from Piran to Poreč and Pula (2/day Mon–Fri, 1/day Sat–Sun); from those towns, you can transfer to reach Rovinj. There are additional bus connections between Piran and Umag (at the northern end of Istria; 3/day Mon–Fri, 2/day Sat–Sun). From Umag, buses run to other destinations in Istria (including Rovinj and Pula). Additional connections into Istria depart from Portorož, the large resort town next to Piran.

About once weekly in summer, Venezia Lines runs **boats** between Piran and Istria (including Rovinj and Poreč; for details, visit www.venezialines.com).

By Boat to Venice: A boat called the *Prince of Venice*—designed for day-trippers, but also convenient for one-way transport—sails from Slovenia's coast to Venice two or three times each week in peak season. The boat generally goes from the nearby town of Izola, Slovenia. Occasionally the boat departs from Piran, stopping in the Croatian town of Umag en route to Venice (3-hr trip each way; €35–46 one-way, depending on season; departs from Izola at 8:00 or from Piran at 7:30; when boat departs from Izola, a shuttle bus picks up at Piran's Tartini Square one hour before departure; boat returns from Venice on the same day at 17:00, arriving Izola at 20:00; book through Kompas Travel Agency in nearby Portorož: tel. 05/617-8000, portoroz@kompas.si). Once a week from late May through mid-September, Italian-run **Venezia Lines** does a similar trip, departing directly from Piran (€46–50 one-way depending on season, usually departs Piran around 8:30 and arrives Venice 2.5 hours later, boat leaves from Venice same day around 17:00, Italian tel. 041-272-2646, www.venezia lines.com).

Route Tips for Drivers

Piran is a natural stopover between Ljubljana and Croatia's Istria. You can do the Karst sights on the way down (lined up conveniently along the A-1 expressway), sleep in Piran, then continue to Istria; or simply make a beeline to Piran and see the town before moving on to sleep in Istria.

From Piran to Croatia's Istria: Leaving Piran, go through Portorož, then Lucija, then follow signs to *Pula*. Just after you enter Seča, signs on the right point to the salt fields. The border is just a few minutes straight ahead. (If you want to see the salt museum, remember that it's between the Slovenian and Croatian border posts—just after leaving Slovenia, keep an eye on the right for the very easy-to-miss gravel road.) Once in Croatia, follow *Pula* signs to get on the *ipsilon* highway that zips you down through the middle of Istria.

UNDERSTANDING YUGOSLAVIA

Americans struggle to understand the complicated breakup of Yugoslavia—especially when visiting countries that rose from its ashes, such as Croatia and Slovenia. Talking to the locals can make it even more confusing: Everyone in the former Yugoslavia seems to have a slightly different version of events. A very wise Bosniak told me, "Listen to all three sides—Muslim, Serb, and Croat. Then decide for yourself what you think." That's the best advice I can offer. But since you likely won't have time for that on your brief visit, here's an admittedly oversimplified, as-impartial-as-possible history to get you started.

Balkan Peninsula 101

For starters, it helps to have a handle on the different groups who've lived in the Balkans—the southeastern European peninsula between the Adriatic and the Black Sea, stretching from Hungary to Greece. The Balkan Peninsula has always been a crossroads of cultures. The Illyrians, Greeks, and Romans had settlements here before the Slavs moved into the region from the north around the seventh century. During the next millennium and a half, the western part of the peninsula—which would become Yugoslavia—was divided by a series of cultural, ethnic, and religious fault lines.

The most important influences were three religions: **Western Christianity** (i.e., Roman Catholicism, first brought to the western part of the region by Charlemagne and later reinforced by the Austrian Habsburgs), **Eastern Orthodox Christianity** (brought to the east from the Byzantine Empire), and **Islam** (in the south, from the Ottomans).

Two major historical factors made the Balkans what they are today: The first was the **split of the Roman Empire** in the fourth century A.D., dividing the Balkans down the middle into Roman

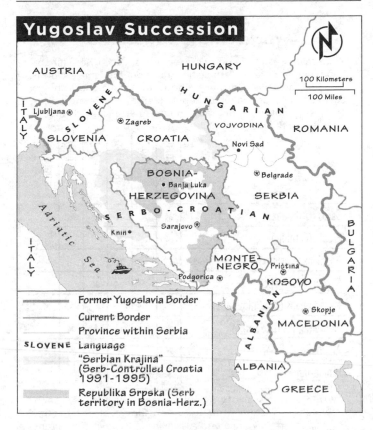

Yugoslav Succession

AUSTRIA

HUNGARY

ITALY

Ljubljana ⊛

SLOVENIA

SLOVENE

Zagreb ⊛

CROATIA

HUNGARIAN

VOJVODINA

Novi Sad ⊛

ROMANIA

100 Kilometers

100 Miles

BOSNIA-
HERZEGOVINA

Banja Luka •

SERBO-CROATIAN

Sarajevo ⊛

Knin •

Adriatic Sea

ITALY

MONTE-
NEGRO

Podgorica ⊛

Belgrade ⊛

SERBIA

Priština ⊛

KOSOVO

BULGARIA

Skopje ⊛

MACEDONIA

ALBANIAN

ALBANIA

GREECE

Former Yugoslavia Border

Current Border

Province within Serbia

SLOVENE Language

"Serbian Krajina"
(Serb-Controlled Croatia
1991-1995)

Republika Srpska (Serb
territory in Bosnia-Herz.)

Catholic (west) and Byzantine Orthodox (east)—roughly along today's Bosnian-Serbian border. The second was the **invasion of the Islamic Ottomans** in the 14th century. The Ottoman victory at the Battle of Kosovo Polje (1389) began five centuries of Islamic influence in Bosnia-Herzegovina and Serbia, further dividing the Balkans into Christian (north) and Muslim (south).

Because of these and other events, several distinct ethnic identities emerged. Confusingly, the major "ethnicities" of Yugoslavia are all South Slavs—they're descended from the same ancestors and speak essentially the same language, but they practice different religions. Catholic South Slavs are called **Croats** or **Slovenes** (mostly west of the Dinaric Mountains: Croats along the Adriatic coast and Slovenes farther north, in the Alps); Orthodox South Slavs are called **Serbs** (mostly east of the Dinaric range); and Muslim South Slavs are called **Bosniaks** (whose ancestors converted to Islam under the Ottomans, mostly living in the Dinaric Mountains). To complicate matters, the region is also home to several non-Slavic minority groups, including **Hungarians** (in the

Who's Who in Yugoslavia

Yugoslavia was made up of six republics, which were inhabited by eight different ethnicities (not counting small minorities such as Jews, Germans, and Roma). This chart shows each ethnicity, and in which republic(s) they were most concentrated. Not coincidentally, the more ethnically diverse a region was, the more conflict it experienced.

	Serbia*	Croatia	Bosnia-Herz.	Slovenia	Montenegro	Macedonia
Serbs (Orthodox)	X	X	X		X	
Croats (Catholic)		X	X			
Bosniaks (Muslims)			X			
Slovenes (Catholic)				X		
Macedonians (like Bulgarians)						X
Montenegrins (like Serbs)					X	
Albanians	X		X			X
Hungarians	X	X		X		

*Within Serbia were two "autonomous provinces," each of which was dominated by a non-Slavic ethnic group: Hungarians in Vojvodina and Albanians in Kosovo. Tito intentionally set up these two autonomous provinces to prevent Serbia from becoming too powerful. Tito was right: Slobodan Milošević's annexation of Kosovo is precisely what tipped the balance of power in Yugoslavia, sparking the Balkan wars of the 1990s.

northern province of Vojvodina) and **Albanians,** concentrated in the southern state of Kosovo (descended from the Illyrians, who lived here long before the Greeks and Romans).

Of course, these geographic divisions are extremely general. The groups overlapped a lot—which is exactly why the breakup of Yugoslavia was so contentious. One of the biggest causes of this ethnic mixing came in the 16th century. The Ottomans were threatening to overrun Europe, and the Austrian Habsburgs wanted a buffer zone—a "human shield." The Habsburgs encouraged Serbs who were fleeing from Ottoman invasions to settle along today's Croatian-Bosnian border (known as *Vojna Krajina,* or "Military Frontier"). The Serbs stayed after the Ottomans left, establishing homes in predominantly Croat communities.

After the Ottoman threat subsided in the late 17th century, some of the Balkans (basically today's Slovenia and Croatia) became part of the Austrian Habsburg Empire. The Ottomans stayed longer in the south and east (today's Bosnia-Herzegovina and Serbia)—making the cultures in these regions even more different. Serbia finally gained its independence from the Ottomans in the mid-19th century, but it wasn't long before World War I erupted...after a disgruntled Bosnian Serb nationalist killed the Austrian archduke and heir to the Habsburg throne.

South Slavs Unite

When the Austro-Hungarian Empire fell at the end of World War I, the European map was redrawn for the 20th century. After centuries of being governed by foreign powers, the South Slavs began to see their shared history as more important than their differences. A tiny country of a few million Croats or Slovenes couldn't have survived on its own. Rather than be absorbed by a non-Slavic power, the South Slavs decided that there was safety in numbers, and banded together as a single state—first called the "Kingdom of the Serbs, Croats, and Slovenes" (1918), later known as the Kingdom of Yugoslavia ("Land of the South Slavs"—*yugo* means "south"). "Yugoslav unity" was in the air, but this new union was fragile and ultimately bound to fail (not unlike the partnership between the Czechs and Slovaks, formed at the same time and for much the same reasons).

From the very beginning, the various ethnicities struggled for power within the new union of Yugoslavia. The largest group was the Serbs (about 45 percent), followed by the Croats (about 25 percent). Croats often felt they were treated as lesser partners under the Serbs. For example, many Croats objected to naming the country's official language "Serbo-Croatian"—why not "Croato-Serbian?" Serbia already had a very strong king, Alexander Karađorđević, who immediately attempted to give his nation a leading role in the federation. A nationalistic Croatian politician named Stjepan Radić, pushing for a more equitable division of powers, was shot by a Serb during a parliament session in 1928. Karađorđević abolished the parliament and became dictator. Six years later, infuriated Croatian separatists killed him.

Many Croat nationalists sided with the Nazis in World War II in the hopes that it would be their ticket to independence from Serbia. The Nazi puppet government in Croatia (under the Ustaše party) conducted an extermination campaign, murdering hundreds of thousands of Serbs (along with Jews and Roma) living in Croatia; other Serbs were forced to flee the country or convert to

Catholicism. Most historians consider the Ustaše concentration camps to be the first instance of "ethnic cleansing" in the Balkans, and the Serbs' long memory of it may go far in explaining their own harsh ethnic cleansing of the Croats in the 1990s.

At the end of World War II, the rest of Eastern Europe was "liberated" by the Soviets, but the Yugoslavs regained their independence on their own, as their communist Partisan Army forced out the Nazis. After the short but rocky Yugoslav union between the World Wars, it seemed that no one could hold the southern Slavs together in a single nation. But there was one man who could, and did: Tito.

Tito's Yugoslavia

Communist Party president and war hero Josip Broz (a.k.a. Tito) emerged as a political leader after World War II. With a Slovene for a mother, a Croat for a father, a Serb for a wife, and a home in Belgrade, Tito was a true Yugoslav. Tito had a compelling vision that this fractured union of the South Slavs could function. And, under him, it did.

Tito's new incarnation of Yugoslavia aimed for a more equitable division of powers. It was made up of six republics, each with its own parliament and president: **Croatia** (mostly Catholic Croats), **Slovenia** (mostly Catholic Slovenes), **Serbia** (mostly Orthodox Serbs), **Bosnia-Herzegovina** (the most diverse—mostly Muslim Bosniaks, but with very large Croat and Serb populations), **Montenegro** (mostly Serb-like Montenegrins), and **Macedonia** (with about 25 percent Albanians and 75 percent Macedonians—who share similarities with both Bulgarians and Serbs). Within Serbia, there were also two autonomous provinces, each one dominated by an ethnicity that was a minority in greater Yugoslavia: Albanians in **Kosovo** (to the south) and Hungarians in **Vojvodina** (to the north). Tito hoped that by allowing these two provinces some degree of independence—including voting rights—they could balance the political clout of Serbia, preventing a single republic from dominating the union.

Each republic managed its own affairs...but always under the watchful eye of president-for-life Tito, who said that the borders between the republics should be "like white lines in a marble column." Nationalism was strongly discouraged, and Tito's tight control—though sometimes oppressive—kept the country from unraveling. For more on Tito, see the sidebar on page 538.

Tito's Yugoslavia was communist, but it wasn't Soviet communism; you'll find no statues of Lenin or Stalin here. Despite strong pressure from Moscow, Tito refused to ally himself with the Soviets—and therefore received good will (and $2 billion) from the United States. Tito's vision was for a "third way," where

Yugoslavia could work with both East and West, without being dominated by either. Yugoslavia was the most free of the communist states: While large industry was nationalized, Tito's system allowed for small businesses. This experience with a market economy benefited Yugoslavs when Eastern Europe's communist regimes eventually fell. And even during the communist era, Yugoslavia remained a popular tourist destination for visitors from both East and West, keeping its standards more in line with Western Europe than the Soviet states. Meanwhile, Yugoslavs were in a unique position among communist countries of being allowed to travel to Western countries. In fact, because Yugoslavs were able to travel relatively hassle-free in both East and West, their "red passports" were worth even more on the black market than American ones.

Things Fall Apart

With Tito's death in 1980, Yugoslavia's six constituent republics gained more autonomy, with a rotating presidency. But before long, the fragile union Tito had held together started to unravel.

The breakup began in the late 1980s, with squabbles in the province of Kosovo between the Serb minority and the ethnic-Albanian majority. While technically part of Serbia, Kosovo had been awarded partial autonomy by Tito. But, even though nine out of every 10 Kosovars were Albanian, the region remained important to the Serbs, who consider Kosovo the cradle of their civilization—the site of their most important monasteries and historic sites. Most significantly, it was the location of the Battle of Kosovo Polje ("Field of Blackbirds"), an epic 14th-century battle that is considered the foundation of Serbian cultural identity...even though the Serbs lost to the Ottoman invaders (sort of the Serbian Alamo). One Serb told me, "Kosovo is the Mecca and Medina of the Serb people."

Serbian politician Slobodan Milošević saw how the conflict could be used to Serbia's (and his own) advantage. Milošević went to Kosovo, where he delivered a rabble-rousing speech, pledging that Serbia would come to the aid of its Kosovar-Serb brothers. In this one visit, Milošević upset the delicate balance that Tito had so carefully sought to attain. (He had also set the stage for his own rise to the Serbian presidency.) The end was near.

When Milošević-led Serbia annexed Kosovo soon after, other republics (especially Slovenia and Croatia) feared that he would gut their nation to create a "Greater Serbia," instead of a friendly coalition of diverse Yugoslav republics. Some of the leaders—most notably Milan Kučan of Slovenia—tried to avoid warfare by suggesting a plan for a loosely united Yugoslavia, based on the Swiss model of independent yet confederated cantons. But other parties,

YUGOSLAVIA

Tito
(1892–1980)

The Republic of Yugoslavia was the vision of a single man, who made it reality. Josip Broz—better known as Maršal Tito—

presided over the most peaceful and prosperous era in this region's long and troubled history. Three decades after his death, Tito is beloved by many of his former subjects...and yet, he was a communist dictator known for torturing and executing his political enemies. This love-him-and-hate-him autocrat is one of the most complex figures in the history of this very complicated land.

Josip Broz was born in 1892 to a Slovenian mother and a Croatian father in the northern part of today's Croatia, which then belonged to the Austro-Hungarian Empire. After growing up in the rural countryside, Tito was trained as a metalworker. He was drafted into the Austro-Hungarian army, went to fight on the Eastern Front during World War I, and was captured and sent to Russia as a prisoner of war. Freed by Bolsheviks, Broz fell in with the Communist Revolution... and never looked back.

At war's end, Broz returned home to the newly independent Yugoslavia, where he worked alongside the Soviets to build a national Communist Party. As a clandestine communist operative, he adopted the code name he kept for the rest of his life: Tito. (Some people half-joke that the name came from Tito's authoritarian style: *"Ti, to!"* means "You, do this!")

When the Nazis occupied Yugoslavia, Tito raised and commanded a homegrown, communist Partisan Army. Through guerilla tactics, Tito's clever maneuvering, and sheer determination, the Partisans liberated their country. And because they did so mostly without support from the USSR, Yugoslavia could set its own postwar course.

The war hero Tito quickly became the "president for life" of postwar Yugoslavia. But even as he introduced communism to his country, he retained some elements of a free-market economy—firmly declining to become a satellite of Moscow. He also led the creation of the worldwide Non-Aligned Movement, joining with nations in Africa, the Middle East, Asia, and Latin America in refusing to ally with the US or USSR (see page 536). Stubborn but suitably cautious, Tito expertly walked a tightrope between East and West.

There was a dark side to Tito. In the early years of his regime, Tito resorted to brutal, Stalin-esque tactics to assert his control. Immediately following World War II, the Partisan Army massacred tens of thousands of soldiers who had supported the Nazis.

Then Tito systematically routed out other Nazi supporters, arresting, trying, torturing, or executing those who did not accept his new regime (including the Croatian archbishop Alojzije Stepinac, whom Tito imprisoned for five years—see page 44).

But once he had gained full control, Tito moved away from strong-arm tactics and into a warm-and-fuzzy era of Yugoslav brotherhood. Tito believed that the disparate peoples of Yugoslavia could live in harmony. For example, every Yugoslav male had to serve in the National Army, and Tito made sure that each unit was a microcosm of the complete Yugoslavia—with equal representation from each ethnic group. This meant that Yugoslavs from diverse backgrounds were forced to work together and socialize, and as a result, they became friends.

Tito's reign is a case study in the power of the cult of personality. Rocks on hillsides throughout Yugoslavia were rearranged to spell "TITO," and his portrait hung over every family's dinner table. Each of the six republics renamed one of its cities for their dictator. The main street and square in virtually every town was renamed for Tito (and many still are). Tito also had vacation villas in all of Yugoslavia's most beautiful areas, including Lake Bled, the Brijuni Islands, and the Montenegrin Coast. People sang patriotic anthems to their Druža (Comrade) Tito: "Comrade Tito, we bow to you."

Tito died in 1980 in a Slovenian hospital. His body was loaded onto his Blue Train and went on a grand tour of the Yugoslav capitals: Ljubljana, Zagreb, Sarajevo, and Belgrade, where he was buried before hundreds of thousands of mourners, including more heads of state than any other funeral in history.

The genuine outpouring of support at Tito's death might seem unusual for a man who was, on paper, an authoritarian communist dictator. But even today, many former Yugoslavs—especially Slovenes—have forgiven him for governing with an iron fist, believing that this was a necessary evil to keep the country strong and united. The eventual balance Tito struck between communism and capitalism, and between the competing interests of his ethnically diverse nation, led to this region's most stable and prosperous era. Pictures of Tito still hang in many Croatians' homes. In a recent poll in Slovenia, Tito had a higher approval rating than any present-day politician, and 80 percent of Slovenes said they had a positive impression of him.

And yet, the Yugoslavs' respect for their former leader was not enough to keep them together. Tito's death began a long, slow chain reaction that led to the end of Yugoslavia. As the decades pass, the old joke seems more and more appropriate: Yugoslavia had eight distinct peoples in six republics, with five languages, three religions (Orthodox, Catholic, and Muslim), and two alphabets (Roman and Cyrillic), but only one Yugoslav—Tito.

YUGOSLAVIA

who wanted complete autonomy, refused. Over the next decade, Yugoslavia broke apart, with much bloodshed.

The Slovene Secession

Slovenia was the first Yugoslav republic to hold free elections, in the spring of 1990. The voters wanted the communists out—and their own independent nation. Along with being the most ethnically homogeneous of the Yugoslav nations, Slovenia was also the most Western-oriented, most prosperous, and most geographically isolated—so secession just made sense. But that didn't mean that there was no violence.

After months of stockpiling weapons, Slovenia closed its borders and declared independence from Yugoslavia on June 25, 1991. Belgrade sent in the Yugoslav National Army to take control of Slovenia's borders with Italy and Austria, figuring that whoever controlled the borders had a legitimate claim on sovereignty. Fighting broke out around these borders. Because the Yugoslav National Army was made up of soldiers from all republics, many Slovenian soldiers found themselves fighting their own countrymen. (The army had cut off communication between these conscripts and the home front, so they didn't know what was going on—and often didn't realize they were fighting their friends and neighbors until they were close enough to see them.)

Slovenian civilians bravely entered the fray, blockading the Yugoslav barracks with their own cars and trucks. Most of the Yugoslav soldiers—now trapped—were young and inexperienced, and were terrified of the ragtag (but relentless) Slovenian militia, even though their own resources were far superior.

After 10 days of fighting and fewer than a hundred deaths, Belgrade relented. The Slovenes stepped aside and allowed the Yugoslav National Army to take all of the weapons with them back into Yugoslavia and destroy all remaining military installations. When the Yugoslav National Army cleared out, they left the Slovenes with their freedom.

The Croatian Conflict

In April 1990, a historian named Franjo Tuđman—and his highly nationalistic, right-wing party, the HDZ (Croatian Democratic Union)—won Croatia's first free elections (for more on Tuđman, see page 46). Like the Slovenian reformers, Tuđman and the HDZ wanted more autonomy from Yugoslavia. But Tuđman's methods were more extreme than those of the gently progressive Slovenes. Tuđman invoked the spirit of the last group that led an "independent" Croatia—the Ustaše, who had ruthlessly run Croatia's puppet government under the Nazis. Tuđman reintroduced historical symbols that had previously been embraced by the Ustaše, including the red-and-white checkerboard flag and their currency. The 600,000 Serbs living in Croatia, mindful of their grandparents who had been massacred by the Ustaše, saw the writing on the wall and began to rise up.

The first conflicts were in the Serb-dominated Croatian city of Knin. Among Tuđman's reforms was the decree that all of Croatia's policemen wear a new uniform, which bore a striking resemblance to Nazi-era Ustaše uniforms. Infuriated by this slap in the face, and prodded by Slobodan Milošević's rhetoric, Serb police officers in Knin refused. Over the next few months, tense negotiations ensued. Serbs from Knin and elsewhere began the so-called "tree trunk revolution"—blocking important tourist roads to the coast with logs and other barriers. Meanwhile, the Croatian government—after being denied support from the United States— illegally purchased truckloads of guns from Hungary. Tensions escalated, and the first shots of the conflict were fired on Easter Sunday 1991 at Plitvice Lakes National Park, between Croatian policemen and Serb irregulars from Knin.

By the time Croatia declared its independence (on June 25, 1991—the same day as Slovenia), it was already embroiled in the beginnings of a bloody war. Croatia's more than half-million Serb residents immediately declared their own independence from Croatia. The Serb-dominated Yugoslav National Army swept in, supposedly to keep the peace between Serbs and Croats—but it soon became obvious that they were there to support the Serbs. The ill-prepared Croatian resistance, made up mostly of police- men and a few soldiers who defected from the Yugoslav National Army, were quickly overwhelmed. The Serbs gained control over the parts of inland Croatia where they were in the majority: a large swath around the Bosnian border (including Plitvice) and Croatia's inland panhandle (the region of Slavonia). They called this territory—about a quarter of Croatia—the **Republic of Serbian Krajina** (*krajina* means "border"). This new "country" (hardly rec- ognized by any other nations) minted its own money and raised its own army, much to the consternation of Croatia—which was now worried about the safety of Croats living in Krajina.

As the Serbs advanced, hundreds of thousands of Croats fled to the coast and lived as refugees in resort hotels. The Serbs began a campaign of ethnic cleansing, systematically removing Croats from contested territory—often by murdering them. The bloodi- est siege was at the town of **Vukovar,** which the Yugoslav army surrounded and shelled relentlessly for three months. By the end of the siege, thousands of Croat soldiers and civilians had mysteri- ously disappeared. Many of these people were later discovered in mass graves; hundreds are still missing, and bodies are still being found. In a surprise move, Serbs also attacked the tourist resort of **Dubrovnik** (see page 268). By early 1992, both Croatia and the Republic of Serbian Krajina had established their borders, and a tense ceasefire fell over the region.

The standoff lasted until 1995, when the now well-equipped Croatian army retook the Serbian-occupied areas in a series of two offensives—**"Lightning"** *(Blijesak)*, in the northern part of the country, and **"Storm"** *(Oluja)*, farther south. Some Croats retaliated for earlier ethnic cleansing by doing much of the same to Serbs—torturing and murdering them, and dynamiting their homes. Croatia quickly established the borders that exist today, and the Erdut Agreement brought peace to the region. But most of the 600,000 Serbs who once lived in Croatia/Krajina were forced into Serbia or were killed. While Serbs have long since been legally invited back to their ancestral Croatian homes, relatively few have returned—afraid of the "welcome" they might receive from the Croat neighbors who killed their relatives or blew up their houses just a few years ago.

The War in Bosnia-Herzegovina

Bosnia-Herzegovina declared its independence from Yugoslavia four months after Croatia and Slovenia did. But Bosnia-Herzegovina was always at the crossroads of Balkan culture, and therefore even more diverse than Croatia, as it was populated predominantly by Muslim Bosniaks (mostly in the cities) but also by large numbers of Serbs and Croats (many of them farmers).

The fighting in Bosnia-Herzegovina began for similar reasons as fighting in Croatia did: As soon as Bosnia-Herzegovina declared independence, the Bosnian Serb minority seceded as their own "state," called the Republic of the Serb People of Bosnia-Herzegovina. To legitimize their claim on this land, the Serbs began a campaign of ethnic cleansing against Bosniaks and Croats in the spring of 1992.

At first, the Bosniaks and Croats teamed up to fight against the Serbs. But even before the first wave of fighting had subsided, Croats and Bosniaks turned their guns on each other. The Croats split off their own mini-state, which they called the Croatian Republic of Herzeg-Bosnia. A bloody war raged for years between the three groups: the Serbs (with support from Serbia proper), the Croats (with support from Croatia proper), and—squeezed between them—the internationally recognized Bosniak (Muslim) government, led by President Alija Izetbegović, who desperately worked for peace.

Bosnia-Herzegovina was torn apart. Even the many mixed families were forced to choose sides. If you had a Serb mother and a Croat father, you were expected to pick one ethnicity or the other—and your brother might choose the opposite. As families and former neighbors trained their guns on each other, proud and beautiful cities such as Sarajevo and Mostar were turned to rubble, and people throughout Bosnia-Herzegovina lived in a state of constant terror.

Serb sieges of Bosnian Muslim cities—such as the notorious siege of Srebrenica in July 1995, which ended with a massacre of about 8,000 Bosniak civilians—brought the ongoing atrocities to the world's attention. The methods of the aggressors were intentionally gruesome and violent. Perhaps most despicable was the establishment of so-called "rape camps"—concentration camps where Bosniak women were imprisoned and systematically raped by Serb soldiers. It was the aggressors' goal not only to remove people from "their" land (which could have been done more peacefully), but to ensure that the various groups could never tolerate living together again.

While there were many villains in this conflict, the two men considered most responsible for the worst atrocities in Bosnia-Herzegovina were the Bosnian Serb President Radovan Karadžić and his general, Ratko Mladić.

The United Nations Protection Force (UNPROFOR)—dubbed "Smurfs" both for their light-blue helmets and for their ineffectiveness—exercised their very limited authority to try to suppress the violence. But because they were not allowed to use force, even in self-defense, they became impotent witnesses to atrocities. This ugly situation was brilliantly parodied in the film *No Man's Land* (which won the Oscar for Best Foreign Film in 2002), a very dark comedy about the absurdity of the Bosnian war.

Finally, in 1995, the Dayton Peace Accords carefully divided Bosnia-Herzegovina among the different ethnicities. According to this compromise, the country is split into three different units: the Federation of Bosnia and Herzegovina (shared by Bosniaks and Croats), the Serb-dominated Republika Srpska, and the Brčko District (a tiny corner of the country, with a mix of the ethnicities).

The Fall of Milošević

After years of bloody conflicts, public opinion among Serbs had decisively swung against their president. The transition began gradually in early 2000, spearheaded by Otpor, a nonviolent, grassroots, student-based opposition movement, and aided by similar groups. These organizations used clever PR strategies to gain support and convince Serbians that real change was possible. As anti-Milošević sentiments gained momentum, opposing political parties banded together and got behind one candidate, Vojislav Koštunica. Public support for Koštunica mounted, and when the arrogant Milošević called an early election in September 2000, he was soundly defeated. Though Milošević tried to claim that the election results were invalid, determined Serbs streamed into their capital, marched on their parliament, and—like the Czechs and Slovaks a decade before—peacefully took back their nation.

In 2001, Milošević was arrested and sent to The Hague, in the Netherlands, to stand trial before the International Criminal Tribunal for the Former Yugoslavia (ICTY). Milošević served as his own attorney as his trial wore on for five years, frequently delayed due to his health problems. Then, on March 11, 2006—as his trial was coming to a close—Milošević was found dead in his cell. Ruled a heart attack, Milošević's death, like his life, was controversial. His supporters alleged that Milošević had been denied suitable medical care, some speculated that he'd been poisoned, and others suspected that he'd intentionally worsened his heart condition to avoid the completion of his trial. Whatever the cause, in the end Milošević avoided coming to justice—he was never found guilty of a thing.

The Strange Tale of Dr. Dragan David Dabić

On July 18, 2008, Serbian police announced that they had captured Radovan Karadžić, the former leader of the Bosnian Serb state who is considered one of the worst culprits in the Serbs' brutal ethnic cleansing during the war.

Karadžić, who went into hiding shortly after the war (in 1996), had been living for part of that time in a residential neighborhood of Belgrade, posing as an alternative-medicine healer named Dr. Dragan David Dabić. (Karadžić had previously received training as a psychiatrist.) This expert on what he called "Human Quantum Energy" had his own website and even presented at conferences.

How did one of the world's most wanted men effectively disappear in plain sight for 12 years? He had grown a very full beard and wore thick glasses as a disguise, and frequented a neighborhood bar where a photo of him, in his earlier life, hung on the wall...and yet, he was undetected even by those who saw him every day. It's alleged that at least some Serb authorities knew of his whereabouts, but, considering him a hero, refused to identify or arrest him.

After his arrest, Karadžić was taken to stand trial in The Hague for war crimes including genocide. He insisted on defending himself, then boycotted the start of his trial twice until the judge appointed a defense attorney for him. As his trial wears on, at this writing, Karadžić's military leader, General Ratko Mladić, is still at large—and now individually holds the title of world's most wanted man (after, perhaps, Osama bin Laden).

Montenegro and Kosovo: Europe's Newest Nations

After the departures of Croatia, Slovenia, Bosnia-Herzegovina, and Macedonia (which peacefully seceded in 1991), by the late 1990s only two of the original six republics of Yugoslavia remained united: Serbia (which still included the provinces of Kosovo and Vojvodina) and Montenegro. But in 2003, Montenegro began a gradual, tiptoe secession process that ended when it peacefully gained its independence in 2006. (For all the details, see "Montenegro: Birth of a Nation" on page 362.)

The Yugoslav crisis concluded in the place where it began: the Serbian province of Kosovo. Kosovo's majority Albanians rebelled in 1998, only to become victims of Milošević's ethnic cleansing (until US General Wesley Clark's NATO warplanes forced the Serbian army out). For nearly a decade, Kosovo remained a UN protectorate within Serbia—still nominally part of Serbia, but for all practical purposes separate and self-governing (under the watchful eye of the UN).

The long-term plan was for Kosovo to eventually become independent. But on Sunday, February 17, 2008, Kosovo's provisional government unilaterally declared its independence as the "Republic of Kosovo"—without going through proper UN channels. (It had grown impatient that its UN bid for independence was being stalled by Russia.) The Republic of Kosovo was quickly recognized by the US, UK, France, Germany, and several other countries, but not officially endorsed by the UN. Serbia was backed in its opposition by several large countries who are involved in their own internal disputes with ethnic regions that would like to secede: Russia (areas of Georgia), China (Taiwan), and Spain (Catalunya, the Basque Country, and others).

The new Kosovo government very carefully stated it would protect the rights of its minorities, including Serbs. But the Serbs deeply believed that losing Kosovo would also mean losing their grip on their own history and culture. They also feared for the safety of the Serb minority there (and potential retribution from Albanians who had for so long been oppressed themselves). For a few tense months, international observers watched nervously, worrying that war might erupt in the region once more. There were a few scuffles, especially in some of the large Serb settlements. But as of this writing, Kosovo independence appears to be successful—representing, perhaps, the final chapter of a long and ugly Yugoslav succession. Kosovo is the seventh country to emerge from the break-up of Yugoslavia.

Finding Their Way:
The Former Yugoslav Republics

Today, Slovenia and Croatia are as stable as Western Europe, Bosnia-Herzegovina has made great strides in putting itself back together, Macedonia feels closer to Bulgaria than to Belgrade, and the sixth and seventh countries to emerge from "Yugoslavia"—Montenegro and Kosovo—are fledgling democracies.

And yet, nagging questions remain. Making the wars even more difficult to grasp is the fact that there were no clear-cut "good guys" and "bad guys"—just a lot of ugliness on all sides. When considering specifically the war between the Croats and the Serbs, it's tempting for Americans to take Croatia's "side" because we saw them in the role of victims first; because they're Catholic, so they seem more "like us" than the Orthodox Serbs; and because we admire their striving for an independent nation. But in the streets and the trenches, it was never that straightforward. The Serbs believe that *they* were the victims first—back in World War II, when their grandparents were executed in Croat-run Ustaše concentration camps. And when Croatians retook the Serb-occupied areas in 1995, they were every bit as brutal as the Serbs had been a few years before. Both sides resorted to ethnic cleansing, both sides had victims, and both sides had victimizers.

Even so, many can't help but look for victims and villains. During the conflict in Bosnia-Herzegovina, several prominent and respected reporters began to show things from one "side" more than the others—specifically, depicting the Bosniaks (Muslims) as victims. This reawakened an old debate in the journalism community: Should reporters above all be impartial, even if "showing all sides" might make them feel complicit in ongoing atrocities?

As for villains, it's easy to point a finger at Slobodan Milošević, Radovan Karadžić, Ratko Mladić, and other military leaders who are wanted or standing trial at The Hague. Others condemn the late Croatian President Franjo Tuđman, who, it's becoming increasingly clear, secretly conspired with Milošević to redraw the maps of their respective territories throughout the course of the war.

Visitors traveling in this region quickly realize that the vast majority of people they meet here never wanted these wars. And so finally comes the inevitable question: Why did any of it happen in the first place?

Explanations tend to gravitate to two extremes. Some observers say that in this inherently warlike part of the world, deep-seated hatreds and age-old tribal passions between the various ethnic groups have flared up at several points throughout history. According to these people, there's an air of inevitability about the recent wars...and about the potential for future conflict.

YUGOSLAVIA

Others believe that this theory is an insulting oversimplifica-
tion. Sure, animosity has long simmered in this region, but it takes
a selfish leader to exploit it to advance his own interests. It wasn't
until Milošević, Tuđman, and others expertly manipulated the
people's grudges that the country fell into war. By vigorously fanning the embers of ethnic discord, and carefully controlling media
coverage of the escalating violence, these leaders turned what could
have been a healthy political debate into a holocaust.

Tension still exists throughout the former Yugoslavia—
especially in the areas that were most war-torn. Croatians and
Slovenes continue to split hairs over silly border disputes, and
Serbs ominously warn that they'll take up arms to reclaim Kosovo.
When the people of this region encounter other Yugoslavs in their
travels, they immediately evaluate each other's accent to determine:
Are they one of us, or one of them?

But, with time, these hard feelings are fading. The younger
generations don't look back—teenaged Slovenes no longer learn
Serbo-Croatian, can't imagine not living in an independent
little country, and get bored (and a little irritated) when their
old-fashioned parents wax nostalgic about the days of a united
Yugoslavia. A middle-aged Slovene friend of mine thinks fondly of
his months of compulsory service in the Yugoslav National Army,
when his unit was made up of Slovenes, Croats, Serbs, Bosniaks,
Albanians, Macedonians, and Montenegrins—all of them countrymen, and all good friends. To these young Yugoslavs, ethnic
differences didn't matter. He still often visits with his army buddy
from Dubrovnik—600 miles away, not long ago part of the same
nation—and wishes there had been a way to keep it all together.
But he says, optimistically, "I look forward to the day when the
other former Yugoslav republics also join the European Union.
Then, in a way, we will all be united once again."

APPENDIX

Contents

Tourist Information

In the US

The Croatian and Slovenian national tourist offices in the US are a wealth of information. Before your trip, get the free general information packet and request any specifics you may want (such as regional and city maps and festival schedules).

Croatian National Tourist Office: Ask for their free brochures and maps. In the US, call 800-829-4416 or visit http://us.croatia.hr (cntony@earthlink.net).

Slovenian Tourist Office: They have a *Slovenia Invigorates* brochure, map, and information on various regions, hiking, biking, winter travel, and tourist farms. From the US, call Slovenian tel. 011-386-1-589-8550 or visit www.slovenia.info (info@slovenia.info).

In Croatia and Slovenia

Your best first stop in every town is generally the tourist information office—abbreviated **TI** in this book (though locally, you may see them marked TZ, for *turistička zajednica*). Throughout Croatia and Slovenia, you'll find TIs are usually well-organized and always have an English-speaking staff.

A TI is a great place to get a city map, advice on public transportation (including bus and train schedules), walking-tour information, tips on special events, and recommendations for nightlife. Many TIs have information on the entire country or at least the region, so try to pick up maps for destinations you'll be visiting later in your trip. If you're arriving in town after the TI closes, call ahead or pick up a map in a neighboring town.

Most TIs in Croatia and Slovenia are run by the government, which means their information isn't colored by a drive for profit. They're not allowed to make money by running a room-booking service—though they can almost always give you a list of local hotels and private rooms. If they're not too busy, they can call around for you to check on availability. While every major town has at least one travel agency with a room-booking service, even if there's no "fee," you'll save yourself and your host money by going direct with the listings in this book.

Communicating

Hurdling the Language Barrier

The language barrier in Croatia and Slovenia is actually smaller than in places like France, Italy, or Spain. You'll find that most people in the tourist industry—and virtually all young people—speak excellent English.

Of course, not *everyone* speaks English. You'll run into the most substantial language barriers in situations when you need to communicate with a lesser-educated clerk or service person aged 40 or above (train stations and post-office counters, maids, museum guards, bakers, and so on). Be reasonable in your expectations. Post-office clerks in Croatia are every bit as friendly and multilingual as they are in the US.

It helps to know a few words of the local language. Croatian and Slovene are closely related, but not identical. Still, they're similar enough that the same basic words work in both. For example, "hello" is *dobar dan* in Croatian, but *dober dan* in Slovene. I've listed the essential phrases at the end of this book (beginning on page 581).

Croatian and Slovene have a few letters that are pronounced differently than in English, and they add a few diacritics—little markings below and above some letters. Here are a few rules of

Europe's Best Linguists

Why do Croatians and Slovenes speak English so well?

Residents of big, powerful Western European countries, such as Germany or Italy, might think that foreigners should learn their language. But Croatians and Slovenes are as practical as Germans and Italians are stubborn. They realize that it's unreasonable to expect an American to learn Croatian (5 million speakers worldwide) or Slovene (2 million). When only a few million people on the planet speak your language, it's essential to find a common language with the rest of the world—so they learn English early and well.

In Croatia, all schoolchildren start learning English in the third grade. (I've had surprisingly eloquent conversations with Croatian grade-schoolers.) And, since American television programs here are subtitled rather than dubbed, people get plenty of practice hearing American English (with a non-stop simultaneous translation). This means Croatians and Slovenes speak not textbook English, but *real* English—and can be more proficient in slang than some Americans.

Whenever I've heard a Croatian and a foreigner (say, a Norwegian) conversing in English, it's a reminder to me that as Americans, we're lucky to speak the world's new lingua franca.

thumb for sounding out unfamiliar words:

J / j sounds like "y" as in "yellow"

C / c sounds like "ts" as in "bats"

Č / č and Ć / ć sound like "ch" as in "chicken"

Š / š sounds like "sh" as in "shrimp"

Ž / ž sounds like "zh" as in "leisure"

Đ / đ (only in Croatian) is like the "dj" sound in "jeans"

Croatian and Slovene are notorious for their seemingly unpronounceable consonant combinations. Most difficult are hv (as in *hvala*, "thank you") and nj (as in Bohinj, a lake in Slovenia). Foreigners are notorious for over-pronouncing these combinations. In the combination hv, the h is nearly silent; if you struggle with it, simply leave off the h (for *hvala*, just say "VAH-lah"; saying "huh-VAH-lah" sounds silly). When you see nj, the j is mostly silent, with a slight "y" sound that can be omitted: for Bohinj, just say BOH-heen. Listen to locals and imitate.

A few key words are helpful for navigation: *trg* (pronounced "turg," square), *ulica* (OO-leet-sah, road), *cesta* (TSEH-stah, avenue), *autocesta* (OW-toh-tseh-stah, expressway), *most* (mohst, bridge), *otok* (OH-tohk, island), *trajekt* (TRAH-yehkt, ferry), and *Jadran* (YAH-drahs, Adriatic).

Throughout Croatia and Slovenia, German can be a useful

second language (especially in Croatia, which is popular among German-speaking tourists). And a few words of Italian can also come in handy, especially in bicultural Istria.

Learn the key phrases and travel with a phrase book. Consider Lonely Planet's good *Eastern Europe Phrasebook,* which includes both Croatian and Slovene, or their in-depth, stand-alone *Croatian Phrasebook.*

Don't be afraid to interact with locals. The people of Croatia and Slovenia love visitors, and a friendly greeting in their language is an easy icebreaker. Give it your best shot. The locals will appreciate your efforts.

Telephones

Smart travelers learn the phone system and use it daily to reserve or reconfirm rooms, get tourist information, reserve restaurants, confirm tour times, or phone home. This section covers dialing instructions, phone cards, and types of phones. (If you need more in-depth information than I provide here, see www.ricksteves .com/phoning.)

How to Dial

Calling from the US to Europe, or vice versa, is simple—once you break the code. The European calling chart in this chapter will walk you through it.

Dialing Domestically Within Croatia or Slovenia

Croatia and Slovenia, like much of the US, use an area-code dialing system. This means you dial the local number when calling within a city, and add the area code (which starts with a 0) if calling long distance within the same country. For example, Dubrovnik's area code is 020, and the number of one of my recommended Dubrovnik B&Bs is 453-834. To call the B&B within Dubrovnik, just dial 453-834. To call it from Split, dial 020/453-834.

In Croatia, mobile phone numbers begin with 091, 098, or 099, and numbers beginning with 060 are pricey toll lines. Slovenian phone numbers beginning with 080 are toll-free; 090 and 089 denote expensive toll lines. Mobile phone numbers in Slovenia usually begin with 031, 041, 051, 040, or 070.

Dialing Internationally to or from Croatia and Slovenia

If you want to make an international call, follow these steps:

1. Dial the international access code (00 if you're calling from Europe, 011 from the US or Canada).

2. Dial the country code of the country you're calling (385 for Croatia, 386 for Slovenia).

3. Dial the area code (if applicable) and the local number,

keeping in mind that calling many countries requires dropping the initial zero of the area code or local number (the European calling chart lists specifics per country).

Here are some examples:

Calling from the US to Croatia: To call from the US to a recommended Dubrovnik B&B, dial 011, 385 (Croatia's country code), 20 (Dubrovnik's area code minus the initial zero), and 453-834 (local number).

Calling from any European country to the US: To call my office in Edmonds, Washington, from anywhere in Europe, I dial 00 (Europe's international access code), 1 (the US country code), 425 (Edmonds' area code), and 771-8303.

Note: You might see a + in front of a European number. When dialing the number, replace the + with the international access code of the country you're calling from (00 from Europe, 011 from the US or Canada).

Public Phones and Hotel-Room Phones

To make calls from public phones, you'll need a prepaid phone card. There are two different kinds of phone cards: insertable (usable only in pay phones) and international (usable from any phone). Coin-op phones are virtually extinct.

Insertable Phone Cards: This type of card is a convenient way to pay for calls from public pay phones and can be purchased at newsstands and post offices. Simply take the phone off the hook, insert the prepaid card, wait for a dial tone, and dial away. The price of the call (local or international) is automatically deducted while you talk. These cards only work in the country where you buy them (so your Slovenian phone card is worthless in Croatia). Insertable phone cards are a good deal for calling within Europe, but calling the US can be pricey (at least 50 cents/min). Be aware that with the prevalence of mobile phones, public phones are getting harder to find.

International Phone Cards: Although common throughout much of Europe, prepaid phone cards are relatively rare in Croatia and Slovenia, and the savings aren't that enticing (calls to the US generally cost around 25–50 cents per minute). They work from any type of phone, including your hotel-room phone (but ask at the front desk if there are any fees for toll-free calls). To use the card, you'll dial a toll-free access number, then type in your scratch-to-reveal PIN number. But a few of the cards I've tried have an access number that's not toll-free—which means that you pay both for the call, and for the time being deducted from your card. If you want to experiment with international phone cards, try looking for fliers advertising long-distance rates, or ask about the cards at Internet cafés, newsstands, souvenir shops, and youth hostels. I'd buy a low

European Calling Chart

Just smile and dial, using this key:
AC = Area Code, LN = Local Number.

European Country	Calling long distance within ...	Calling from the US or Canada to ...	Calling from a European country to ...
Austria	AC + LN	011 + 43 + AC (without the initial zero) + LN	00 + 43 + AC (without the initial zero) + LN
Belgium	LN	011 + 32 + LN (without initial zero)	00 + 32 + LN (without initial zero)
Bosnia-Herzegovina	AC + LN	011 + 387 + AC (without initial zero) + LN	00 + 387 + AC (without initial zero) + LN
Britain	AC + LN	011 + 44 + AC (without initial zero) + LN	00 + 44 + AC (without initial zero) + LN
Croatia	AC + LN	011 + 385 + AC (without initial zero) + LN	00 + 385 + AC (without initial zero) + LN
Czech Republic	LN	011 + 420 + LN	00 + 420 + LN
Denmark	LN	011 + 45 + LN	00 + 45 + LN
Estonia	LN	011 + 372 + LN	00 + 372 + LN
Finland	AC + LN	011 + 358 + AC (without initial zero) + LN	999 (or other 900 number) + 358 + AC (without initial zero) + LN
France	LN	011 + 33 + LN (without initial zero)	00 + 33 + LN (without initial zero)
Germany	AC + LN	011 + 49 + AC (without initial zero) + LN	00 + 49 + AC (without initial zero) + LN
Gibraltar	LN	011 + 350 + LN	00 + 350 + LN
Greece	LN	011 + 30 + LN	00 + 30 + LN
Hungary	06 + AC + LN	011 + 36 + AC + LN	00 + 36 + AC + LN
Ireland	AC + LN	011 + 353 + AC (without initial zero) + LN	00 + 353 + AC (without initial zero) + LN

European Country	Calling long distance within ...	Calling from the US or Canada to ...	Calling from a European country to ...
Italy	LN	011 + 39 + LN	00 + 39 + LN
Montenegro	AC + LN	011 + 382 + AC (without initial zero) + LN	00 + 382 + AC (without initial zero) + LN
Morocco	LN	011 + 212 + LN (without initial zero)	00 + 212 + LN (without initial zero)
Netherlands	AC + LN	011 + 31 + AC (without initial zero) + LN	00 + 31 + AC (without initial zero) + LN
Norway	LN	011 + 47 + LN	00 + 47 + LN
Poland	LN	011 + 48 + LN (without initial zero)	00 + 48 + LN (without initial zero)
Portugal	LN	011 + 351 + LN	00 + 351 + LN
Slovakia	AC + LN	011 + 421 + AC (without initial zero) + LN	00 + 421 + AC (without initial zero) + LN
Slovenia	AC + LN	011 + 386 + AC (without initial zero) + LN	00 + 386 + AC (without initial zero) + LN
Spain	LN	011 + 34 + LN	00 + 34 + LN
Sweden	AC + LN	011 + 46 + AC (without initial zero) + LN	00 + 46 + AC (without initial zero) + LN
Switzerland	LN	011 + 41 + LN (without initial zero)	00 + 41 + LN (without initial zero)
Turkey	AC (if there's no initial zero, add one) + LN	011 + 90 + AC (without initial zero) + LN	00 + 90 + AC (without initial zero) + LN

- The instructions above apply whether you're calling a land line or mobile phone.
- The international access codes (the first numbers you dial when making an international call) are 011 if you're calling from the US or Canada, or 00 if you're calling from virtually anywhere in Europe (except Finland, where it's 999 or another 900 number, depending on the phone service you're using).
- To call the US or Canada from Europe, dial 00, then 1 (the country code for the US and Canada), then the area code and number. In short, 00 + 1 + AC + LN = Hi, Mom!

denomination in case the card turns out to be a dud. These cards generally work only in the country where you buy them.

Hotel-Room Phones: Calling from your hotel room can be cheap for local calls (ask for the rates at the front desk first), but is often a rip-off for long-distance calls (unless you use an international phone card, explained previously). Incoming calls are free, making this a cheap way for friends and family to stay in touch (provided they have a good long-distance plan for calls to Europe—and a list of your hotels' phone numbers).

If you're sleeping in my recommended *sobe* (B&Bs), be aware that you're unlikely to have a telephone in your room.

Metered Phones: These are available in phone offices and sometimes in bigger post offices. You can talk all you want, then pay the bill when you leave—but be sure you know the rates before you have a lengthy conversation.

US Calling Cards: These cards, such as the ones offered by AT&T, Verizon, or Sprint, are the worst option. You'll nearly always save money by using a pay phone and locally purchased, insertable phone card instead.

Mobile Phones

Many travelers enjoy the convenience of traveling with a mobile phone.

Using Your Mobile Phone: Your US mobile phone works in Europe if it's GSM-enabled, tri-band or quad-band, and on a calling plan that includes international calls. For example, with a T-Mobile phone, you'll pay $1 per minute to make or receive a call, and about $0.35 apiece for text messages.

You can save money if your phone is electronically "unlocked"—then you can simply buy a **SIM card** (a fingernail-sized chip that stores the phone's information) in Europe. SIM cards, which give you a European phone number, are sold at mobile-phone stores and some newsstand kiosks for about $5–10; this usually includes some calling time (enough for a few minutes' worth of calls in that country). Simply insert the SIM card in your phone (usually in a slot behind the battery), and it'll work like a European mobile phone. When buying a SIM card, always ask about fees for domestic and international calls, roaming charges, and how to check your credit balance and buy more time.

Many **smartphones,** such as the iPhone or BlackBerry, work in Europe—but beware of sky-high fees, especially for data down-loading (checking email, browsing the Internet, watching videos, and so on). Ask your provider in advance how to avoid unwittingly "roaming" your way to a huge bill. Some applications allow for cheap or free smartphone calls over a Wi-Fi connection (see "Calling over the Internet").

Using a European Mobile Phone: Local mobile-phone shops all over Europe sell basic phones for around $50–100. You'll also need to buy a SIM card (explained above) and prepaid credit for making calls. If you remain in the phone's home country, domestic calls are reasonable, and incoming calls are free. You'll pay more if you're "roaming" in another country. If your phone is "unlocked," you can swap out its SIM card for a new one in other countries.

Calling over the Internet

Some things that seem too good to be true...actually are true. If you're traveling with a laptop, you can make calls using VoIP (Voice over Internet Protocol). With VoIP, two computers act as the phones, and the Internet-based calls are free (or you can pay a few cents per minute to call from your computer to a telephone). The major providers are Skype (www.skype.com) and Google Talk (www.google.com/talk).

Useful Phone Numbers
Emergencies

For medical or other emergencies, dial 112 in Croatia, Slovenia, and Montenegro, or 124 in Bosnia-Herzegovina. For police, dial 92 in Croatia, 113 in Slovenia, or 122 in Bosnia-Herzegovina and Montenegro.

US Embassies

In Croatia: Ulica Thomasa Jeffersona 2, Zagreb, passport services available Mon–Thu 13:00–15:00 plus Wed 9:00–11:00, tel. 01/661-2200, after business-hours tel. 01/661-2400, consular services tel. 01/661-2300, http://zagreb.usembassy.gov.

In Slovenia: Prešernova 31, Ljubljana, passport services available Mon–Fri 9:00–11:30 & 13:00–15:00, tel. 01/200-5595, after business hours tel. 01/200-5500, www.usembassy.si.

In Montenegro: Ljubljanska b.b., Podgorica, must call for appointment, tel. 020/410-500, http://podgorica.usembassy.gov.

In Bosnia-Herzegovina: Alipašina 43, Sarajevo, passport services available Mon–Fri 14:00–15:30 plus Fri 8:00–10:30, tel. 033/445-700, on weekends and after hours call the same number and press 0 after the recording, http://sarajevo.usembassy.gov. There's also a branch office in Mostar (Mostarskog Bataljona b.b., tel. 036/580-580).

Canadian Embassies and Consulates

In Croatia: Prilaz Đure Deželića 4, Zagreb, Mon–Thu 10:00–12:00 & 13:00–15:00, Fri 10:00–13:00, tel. 01/488-1200, after-hours emergencies call collect Canadian tel. 613/996-8885, www.canadainternational.gc.ca/croatia-croatie.

APPENDIX

In Slovenia: Consulate at Trg Republike 3, 12th floor, Ljubljana, Mon–Fri 9:00–13:00, tel. 01/252-4444, after-hours emergencies call collect Canadian tel. 613/996-8885, www.canadainternational .gc.ca/hungary-hongrie.

In Montenegro: Contact the Canadian Embassy in Belgrade, Serbia; from Montenegro dial 00-389-2-322-5630, after-hours emergencies call collect Canadian tel. 613/996-8885, www.canada international.gc.ca/serbia-serbie.

In Bosnia-Herzegovina: Contact the Canadian Embassy in Budapest, Hungary; from Bosnia-Herzegovina dial 00-36-1-392-3360, after-hours emergencies call collect Canadian tel. 613/996-8885, www.canadainternational.gc.ca/hungary-hongrie.

Travel Advisories

US Department of State: tel. 202/647-5225, www.travel.state.gov
Canadian Department of Foreign Affairs: Canadian tel. 800-267-6788, www.dfait-maeci.gc.ca
US Centers for Disease Control and Prevention: tel. 800-CDC-INFO (800-232-4636), www.cdc.gov/travel

Directory Assistance

Dial 988 in Croatia or Slovenia.

The Internet

The Internet can be an invaluable tool for planning your trip (researching and booking hotels, checking bus and train schedules, and so on). It's also useful to get online periodically as you travel—to reconfirm your trip plans, check the weather, catch up on email, blog or post photos from your trip, or call folks back home (explained earlier, under "Calling over the Internet").

Some hotels offer a computer in the lobby with Internet access for guests. Smaller places may sometimes let you sit at their desk for a few minutes just to check your email, if you ask politely.

Internet connections for laptop users are becoming commonplace at virtually all accommodations in Slovenia, as well as many in Croatia. Most accommodations that offer this do so for free, but some (especially fancier chain hotels) charge by the minute. You'll either access the hotel's wireless Internet (Wi-Fi), sometimes using a password provided by the hotelier; or plug your computer directly into an Internet wall socket (they can usually loan you a cable). On my last trip, I was able to get online at most Slovenian hotels in this book, and about half of my Croatian accommodations.

If your Croatian hotel or *soba* doesn't have access, ask your hotelier to direct you to the nearest place to get online. You can generally find a café with Wi-Fi or an Internet hotspot in most towns. (T-Mobile, the German-based telecommunications giant that has a virtual monopoly in Croatia, operates hotspots in many Croatian towns and big hotels—but it's usually quite pricey.)

Mail

Get stamps at the neighborhood post office, newsstands within fancy hotels, and some mini-marts and card shops. While you can arrange for mail delivery to your hotel (allow 10 days for a letter to arrive), phoning and emailing are so easy that I've dispensed with mail stops altogether.

Transportation

By Car or Public Transportation?

Cars are best for three or more traveling together (especially families with small kids), those packing heavy, and those scouring the countryside. Trains, buses, and boats are best for solo travelers, blitz tourists, and city-to-city travelers. While a car gives you more freedom—enabling you to search for hotels more easily and carrying your bags for you—trains, buses, and boats zip you effortlessly and scenically from town to town, usually dropping you in the center, often near a TI. Cars are great in the countryside, but a worthless headache in places like Ljubljana and Dubrovnik.

In some parts of Croatia and Slovenia, a car is helpful, if not essential: Istria (especially the hill towns), Rab, the Julian Alps, Logarska Dolina, the Karst, and Montenegro's Bay of Kotor. In other areas, a car is unnecessary: Ljubljana and most of the Dalmatian Coast (Dubrovnik, Split, Hvar, and Korčula). For most trips, the best plan is a combination: Use public transportation in some areas, then strategically rent a car for a day or two in a region that merits it. (I've noted which areas are best by car, and offered route and arrival instructions, throughout this book.)

Public Transportation

Throughout this book, I'll suggest whether trains, buses, or boats are better for a particular destination (in the "Connections" section at the end of each chapter). When checking timetables *(vozni red)*, arrivals are *prihodi* and departures are *odhodi; svaki dan* means "daily," but some transit doesn't run on Sundays *(nedjeljom)* or holidays *(praznikom)*. You'll notice that many posted schedules list departure times, but not the duration of the trip; try asking for this information at the ticket window.

Trains

Trains are ideal for certain routes in Croatia and Slovenia (such as between Ljubljana and Zagreb) and for connecting to other countries. But their usefulness is limited, and you'll find buses, boats,

Public Transportation in Croatia and Slovenia

- - - - - Rail
- - - - - Bus
- - - - - Jadrolinija Car Ferries
·········· Other Boats
✈ Airport

100 Kilometers

100 Miles

and flights better for most journeys (all explained later).

Schedules and Tickets: Pick up train schedules from stations as you go. To study ahead on the Web, check http://bahn.hafas .de/bin/query.exe/en (Germany's excellent all-Europe timetable). You can also check www.slo-zeleznice.si for Slovenia, and www .hznet.hr for Croatia. Buy tickets at the train station (or on board, if the station is unattended)—you rarely need a reservation.

Railpasses: While railpasses can be a good deal in some parts of Europe, they usually aren't as useful in Croatia or Slovenia. Point-to-point tickets are affordable and often the better option. If your travels are taking you beyond Croatia and Slovenia, consider the flexible Eurail Selectpass, which covers unlimited travel for up to 15 travel days (within a two-month period) in three, four, or five adjacent countries (Croatia and Slovenia are considered a single "country"). A separate combo-pass covers Hungary, Slovenia, and

Croatia, and another pass covers Austria, Slovenia, and Croatia. Again, none of these passes is likely to save you much money, but if a pass matches your itinerary, give it a look and crunch the numbers. For options and prices on pertinent Eurail passes, see www.ricksteves.com/rail.

Buses

Buses often take you where trains don't. For example, train tracks run only as far south as Split; for destinations on the Dalmatian

Coast farther south, you'll rely on buses (or boats). Even on some routes that are served by trains, buses are a better option. For instance, Ljubljana and Lake Bled are connected by both train and bus—but the bus station is right in the town center of Bled, while the train station is a few miles away. Buses can even be convenient for connecting to islands (via ferry, of course). For example, if heading from the island of Korčula to Dubrovnik, the bus connection (which crosses by ferry to the mainland, then follows the coastal road) runs more frequently than the comparable boat connection, and takes about the same amount of time.

Confusingly, a single bus route can be operated by a variety of different companies, making it difficult to find comprehensive schedules. Some big cities have handy websites listing all connections (such as www.ap-ljubljana.si for Ljubljana, www.akz.hr for Zagreb, and www.ak-split.hr for Split), but for smaller towns, the TI is your best source of information. Get creative with checking schedules: If you're going from a small town to Split, and that town doesn't have its own online timetable, try checking the "arrivals" schedules on the Split website instead. If your trip involves a connection at an intermediate station, don't be surprised if it's difficult to get the schedule details for your onward journey. Be patient, and try calling that town's TI (or the TI or bus station at your final destination) for details.

Prices vary among companies, even for identical journeys. For popular routes during peak season, drop by the station to buy your ticket a few hours—or even days—in advance to ensure getting a seat (ask the bus station ticket office or the local TI how far ahead you should arrive). There is some overhead bag storage on board, but you'll likely check your big bag under the bus (for the extra cost of about $2 per bag).

If you're headed south along the coast, sitting on the right side comes with substantially better scenery (sit on the left for northbound buses).

Boats

All along the Croatian coast, slow car ferries and speedy catamarans inexpensively shuttle tourists between major coastal cities and

quiet island towns. Boats run often in summer (June–early Sept), but frequency drops sharply off-season.

Croatians use the word **"ferry"** *(trajekt)* to describe a boat that takes cars (though walk-on passengers are also welcome). These move slowly but can run in almost any weather. While the number of cars is limited, there's virtually unlimited deck space for walk-on passengers. Watching the ferry crew scurrying around to load and unload cars and trucks onto their boat—especially if it's a small one—is a ▲▲▲ Croatian experience.

Increasingly, popular tourist destinations in Croatia are connected by much faster **catamarans,** which carry only passengers. These are efficient, but they have to slow down (or sometimes can't run at all) in bad weather. Catamarans are smaller, with limited seats, so they tend to sell out quickly. Because of the high speeds, you'll generally have to stay inside the boat while en route, rather than being outside on the deck.

Most of Croatia's boats are operated by the state-run company called Jadrolinija (yah-droh-LEE-nee-yah), which operates a variety of vessels. Most notable are the four big Jadrolinija car ferries: *Marko Polo* and *Liburnija* go all the way down the coast from Rijeka to Dubrovnik, and cross to Bari, Italy; *Dubrovnik* and *Ivan Zajc* cross between Ancona and Split. But Jadrolinija also runs smaller car ferries along the coast, as well as some faster catamarans.

Buy your ticket before boarding the boat. Each town has a Jadrolinija ticket office, which I've listed throughout this book; if the office isn't at the dock itself, there's always a small ticket kiosk that opens at the dock before each departure. The main Jadrolinija office is in Rijeka (tel. 051/666-111, fax 051/213-116, www.jadrolinija .hr). For non-Jadrolinija boats, you may have to buy the tickets at a travel agency, or you might buy

them at the Jadrolinija office. I've tried to list the correct place to buy tickets for each boat, but as this changes from year to year, you may have to ask around.

Boat rides are cheap for deck passengers. A short hop, such as from Split to the island of Hvar or Korčula, costs around $5–10 on most boats (strangely, the faster catamarans are usually cheaper than the slow car ferries). For a longer trip, such as from Split to Dubrovnik, figure $20–25. It's about $65 for a car and driver to go from Split to Dubrovnik (less for shorter trips).

Advance reservations are not necessary for walk-on passengers on car ferries; you can almost always find a seat on the deck or in the onboard café. Warning: The catamarans—which have limited space—can fill up, and tickets go on sale the morning of the day the boat departs (so it's not possible to buy your ticket the day before; the exception is Korčula where the *Krilo* boat departs very early in the morning, so tickets go on sale the prior evening between 18:30 and 20:00). If you're here at a busy time, it's worth going out of your way to buy your catamaran tickets early in the day (ask the local TI or boat ticket office what time they recommend). Then, to get a good seat on board, it's wise to show up 30–60 minutes before departure time.

Drivers cannot reserve a car space in advance on most routes. This means you'll want to arrive at the dock up to a few hours

early, especially in peak season. Again, since this flexes with the season, the local TI is your best resource for advice on how early to leave for the boat. Notice that on some islands, the car ferry port is a long drive from the main tourist town (for example, Vela Luka on Korčula Island is a 1-hour drive from Korčula town; Stari Grad on Hvar Island is a 20-minute drive from Hvar town).

You can buy food and drinks on board most boats. It's not too expensive, but it's not top quality, either. Bring your own snacks or a picnic instead.

Because Jadrolinija has a virtual monopoly on coastal ferries, their routes don't always cater to customer demand. But a few new, private companies are beginning to compete with Jadrolinija—most notably, the *Krilo* catamaran that connects Split, Hvar, and Korčula (www.krilo.hr), and the *Nona Ana* catamaran between Dubrovnik, Mljet Island, and Korčula (www.gv-line.hr). Other similar boats may be up and running when you visit—inquire locally.

The boat schedule information in this book changes every year, without fail. It's essential to confirm before you make your plans. Jadrolinija's website (www.jadrolinija.hr) is useful, but they don't post future schedules very far in advance. Once again, local TIs are the single best source of information for how their town is connected to the rest of the coast.

Renting a Car

The minimum age to rent a car in Croatia and Slovenia is 18, and you must have held your license for at least one year. Drivers under the age of 25 may incur a young-driver surcharge, and some rental companies do not rent to anyone 75 and over. If you're considered too old, look into leasing (explained later), which has less-stringent age restrictions.

Given the language barrier, it can also be helpful (and is technically required in Slovenia and Bosnia-Herzegovina) to get an International Driving Permit ahead of time at your local AAA office ($15 plus two passport-type photos, www.aaa.com). However, I've frequently rented cars in Croatia and Slovenia and traveled problem-free with just my US license.

Research car rentals before you go. It's cheaper to arrange long-term European car rentals in the US than in Europe. For short rentals of a day or two, I've had pretty good luck finding an affordable car on the spot (I've listed car-rental companies in this book)—but if your itinerary is set, it doesn't hurt to book ahead. All of the big American companies have offices throughout Croatia and Slovenia. Two reputable consolidators among many are Auto Europe (www.autoeurope.com) and Europe by Car (www.ebc travel.com). Comparison-shop on the Web to find the best deal, or ask your travel agent.

When choosing my car, I normally rent a small, inexpensive model like a Ford Fiesta or Škoda Fabia. Expect to pay about $450 to rent a small economy car for two weeks with unlimited mileage and basic insurance, plus another $100–150 to cover gas, tolls, and parking. Note that short rentals cost significantly more per day (for example, a four-day rental costs around $150). You'll pay extra for Collision Damage Waiver (CDW) insurance (described later). Be warned that dropping a car off in a different country—say, picking up in Ljubljana and dropping in Dubrovnik—can be prohibitively expensive (see the "Rental-Car Conundrum" sidebar for ways around this). Again, I prefer to connect long distances by train or bus, then rent cars for a day or two where they're most useful. But be aware that some companies have a minimum rental period (generally three days); you can keep the car for fewer days, but you'll pay for the minimum period anyway. If you want the car for just a day or two, try to find a company that allows short rentals.

Almost all rentals are manual by default, so if you need an automatic, you must request one in advance; beware that these cars are usually larger models (not as maneuverable on narrow, winding

The Rental-Car Conundrum

Virtually everyone planning a trip by car to this region runs into the same problem: International drop-off fees for rental cars are astronomical (usually several hundred dollars). Generally there's no extra charge for picking up and dropping off a car in different towns within the same country (for example, the 8.5-hour drive between Zagreb and Dubrovnik), but you'll pay through the nose to drop off across the border (such as the 2-hour drive from Zagreb to Ljubljana). This is especially frustrating when connecting some car-friendly parts of southern Slovenia (such as the Karst) with similar areas in northern Croatia (such as Istria or Plitvice Lakes National Park).

First, compare rates at various rental companies to see if one happens to offer a lower drop-off charge (it happens, but it's rare). If there's no way around the high fee, think creatively to avoid this huge and unnecessary expense.

Let's say you want to pick up a car in Ljubljana, drive through Slovenia's Karst to Istria, then continue to Split and drop your car. But you find out the fee to pick up in Ljubljana and drop off in Split is $400. Here are two possible alternatives: First, you could do a circuit around the sights of southern Slovenia, then head back up to Ljubljana (fast and easy, thanks to the short distances and speedy expressways), drop your Slovenian car there, and take public transit to northern Croatia (such as the bus to Rovinj, or the train to Zagreb, Rijeka, or Pula). After sightseeing there, you could pick up a second car for your Croatian driving (for example, take the bus from Rovinj—which doesn't generally have handy car-rental offices—to a nearby city that does, such as Pula or Poreč). Or you could begin your trip in Croatia, pick up your rental car there, then loop back up into Slovenia with the Croatian car before continuing to Croatia. There's no doubt that these solutions add some hassle to your itinerary, but they could save you hundreds of dollars.

roads). An automatic transmission adds about 50 percent to the car-rental cost over a manual transmission.

As a rule, always tell your car-rental company up front exactly which countries you'll be entering. Some companies levy extra insurance fees for trips taken with certain types of cars (such as BMWs, Mercedes, and convertibles) in certain countries. Or the company may prohibit driving the car in off-the-beaten-track destinations, such as Bosnia-Herzegovina. As you cross borders, you may need to show the proper paperwork, such as proof of insurance (called a "green card"). Double-check with your rental agent that you have all the documentation you need before you drive off.

When picking up the car, check it thoroughly and make sure

any damage is noted on your rental agreement. Find out how your car's lights, turn signals, wipers, and gas cap function, and be sure you know what type of fuel your car takes.

If you drop off your car early or keep it longer, you'll be credited or charged at a fair, prorated price. But always keep your receipts in case any questions arise about your billing.

Before returning your car, make sure you understand where the office is located (and get directions), and what time it's open. I have found rental agents to be flexible; even if you're supposed to drop off your car at the airport, they might be able to save you some time by meeting you in the town center (generally for an additional fee; call ahead to ask about your options). As gas stations can be sparse in some cities, begin looking for a chance to fill up long before you reach your drop-off point (ideally at an expressway stop on the way into town). When you turn in the car, be sure the agent verifies its condition with you.

Car Insurance Options

Accidents can happen anywhere, but when you're on vacation, the last thing you need is stress over car insurance. When you rent a car, you are liable for a very high deductible, sometimes equal to the entire value of the car. Limit your financial risk in case of an accident by choosing one of these three options: Buy Collision Damage Waiver (CDW) coverage from the car-rental company, get coverage through your credit card (free, but more complicated), or buy coverage through Travel Guard.

While each rental company has its own variation, the basic **CDW** costs $15–25 a day (figure roughly 25 percent extra above the rental rate) and reduces your liability, but does not eliminate it. When you pick up the car, you'll be offered the chance to "buy down" the basic deductible to zero (for an additional $10–30/day; sometimes called "super CDW").

If you opt for **credit-card coverage**, there's a catch. You'll technically have to decline all coverage offered by the car-rental company, which means they can place a hold on your card (which can be up to the full value of the car). In case of damage, it can be time-consuming to resolve the charges with your credit-card company. Before you decide on this option, quiz your credit-card company about how it works and ask them to explain the worst-case scenario.

Finally, you can buy car-rental insurance from **Travel Guard** ($9/day plus a one-time $3 service fee covers you up to $35,000, $250 deductible, tel. 800-826-4919, www.travelguard.com). It's valid everywhere in Europe but the Republic of Ireland, and some Italian car-rental companies refuse to honor it. Residents of Washington State aren't eligible for this coverage.

For more fine print about car-rental insurance, see www.rick steves.com/cdw.

Leasing

For trips of two and a half weeks or more, leasing (which automatically includes zero-deductible collision and theft insurance) is the best way to go. By technically buying and then selling back the car, you save lots of money on tax and insurance—but you may have to pick up and drop off the car in Germany or Italy. Leasing provides you a new car with unlimited mileage and a 24-hour emergency assistance program. You can lease for as little as 17 days to as long as six months. Car leases must be arranged from the US. One of many companies offering affordable lease packages is Europe by Car (US tel. 800-223-1516, www.ebctravel.com).

Driving

Drivers should be prepared for twisty seaside and mountain roads, wonderful views, and plenty of tempting stopovers.

On the Road: Bring your driver's license. Seat belts are required, and two beers under those belts are enough to land you

in jail. More and more European countries—including all of the countries in this book—require you to have your headlights on any time you're driving, even in broad daylight. (I've been pulled over more than once for having my lights off.) The lights on many newer cars automatically turn on and off with the engine, but others are manually controlled—ask when you pick up your car. Both Croatia and Slovenia prohibit using handheld mobile phones while driving. Keep a close eye out for bikers. You'll see scads of them on mountain roads, struggling to earn a thrilling downhill run.

Fuel: Gas is expensive—often about $6 per gallon. Diesel cars are more common in Europe than back home, so be sure you know what type of gas your car takes before you fill up. Gas pumps are color-coded for unleaded or diesel.

Tolls: Croatia and Slovenia are crisscrossed by an impressive network of expressways (*autocesta* in Croatian, *avtocesta* in Slovene). I don't call them "freeways" because they're not—you'll pay to use them.

In Croatia, you'll pay about 0.38 kunas per kilometer—so a 100-kilometer trip (60 miles), which lasts about an hour, costs 38 kunas ($7.60). You'll take a toll-ticket when you enter the expressway, then submit it when you get off (but don't lose your ticket, or

Driving: Distance & Time

To Salzburg 145m · 2.5h

To Vienna 250m · 4h

To Vienna 260m 4.5h

300m · 6h

AUSTRIA

Ptuj

35m 1h Velenje 20m .5h

Bled

Logarska Dolina 45m · 1.25h

55m · 1h

60m 2.5h

30m · 1h

65m 1.5h

40m · .75h

Sentrupert exit

Kobarid

70m · 2h

90m · 2h

220m · 5h

ITALY

70m · 1.75h

Ljubljana

SLOVENIA

Zagreb

125m · 3h

To Venice

50m · 1h

Skocjan Caves

75m 2h

100m · 2h

165m · 3h (via expressway)

35m · 1h

140m · 4h

85m · 2h

Piran

25m 1h

45m · 1.25h

Rijeka/ Opatija

90m · 2.5h

45m 1.5h

Motovun

40m 1.25h

65m 1.5h

Plitvice Lakes National Park

30m 1h

Rovinj

55m · 1.5h

Rab

65m · 2.5h

85m · 1.75h

30m .75h.

Pula

Jablanac (ferry to Rab)

60m · 3h

Zadar

100m · 2h (via expressway)

A d r i a t i c

CROATIA

ITALY

S e a

m = miles
h = hours
····· = car ferry

Note: Your times may vary based on traffic, construction, and road conditions.

you'll pay the maximum).

Slovenia has done away with its tollbooth system. Instead, drivers who use Slovenia's expressways are required to buy a toll sticker, or vignette (Slovene: *vinjeta*, veen-YEH-tah; €15/1 week, €30/1 month). Vignettes are sold at gas stations, post offices, and some newsstands. Your rental car might already come with one—ask. If you're caught driving on expressways without one, you could be fined.

While Bosnia-Herzegovina and Montenegro do not levy tolls (and, in fact, do not have expressways), you will pay a €10 eco-tax to enter Montenegro by car.

Road Conditions: Construction on superhighways is ongoing, so it's not unusual to discover that a not-yet-finished expressway unexpectedly ends, requiring a transfer to an older, slower road. For example, the wonderfully speedy A-1 express-way goes only about 100 kilometers (60 miles) south of Split; from there southward to Dubrovnik, you'll follow the winding coastal road. (Likewise, you'll sometimes discover that a much faster road has been built between major destinations since your two-year-old map was published.) For the latest on new express-ways in Croatia, see www.hac.hr and www.hak.hr; for Slovenia, see www.dars.si. Secondary roads are usually in good repair, but they can be very twisty—especially along the coast or through the mountains. If you get way off the beaten track, you might find gravel. Locals poetically describe these as "white roads." (Get it? No asphalt.)

Maps and Signage: A good map is essential (see page 572). While most roads are numbered, Croatians and Slovenes ignore these numbers, which rarely appear on signs. Instead, navigate by town name—at every major inter-section, directional signs point to nearby towns and cities. The color of the sign tells you what type of road you're approach-ing: yellow is a normal road, while blue (in Croatia) or green (in Slovenia) indicates that the route is via expressway. Brown indicates a cultural or natural attraction (such as a castle or a cave). Learn the universal road signs. As you approach any

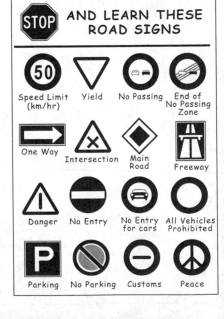

STOP AND LEARN THESE ROAD SIGNS

Speed Limit (km/hr) — Yield — No Passing — End of No Passing Zone

One Way — Intersection — Main Road — Freeway

Danger — No Entry — No Entry for cars — All Vehicles Prohibited

Parking — No Parking — Customs — Peace

town, follow the *Centar* signs (usually also signed with a bull's-eye symbol).

Bosnian Detour: If you'll be driving along the Dalmatian Coast, notice that between Split and Dubrovnik, you'll actually pass through Bosnia-Herzegovina for a few miles (through the town of Neum). Don't stress out about this international detour—it lasts about 20 minutes, and the borders are a breezy formality (you may need to show your passport, but generally you'll just be waved through).

Parking: Get parking advice from your hotel, or look for the blue-and-white *P* signs. Parking is a costly headache in big cities. You'll pay about $15–25 a day to park safely. Rental-car theft can be a problem in cities, so ask at your hotel for advice.

Cheap Flights

Each country has its own national air carrier: Croatia's is **Croatia Airlines** (www.croatiaairlines.com), while Slovenia has **Adria Airways** (www.adria-airways.com). Both airlines offer flights connecting their big cities to destinations within Croatia and Slovenia, and to most major European capitals. And both carriers sell a handful of seats on certain flights at deeply discounted promotional rates. For example, a Croatia Airlines "FlyPromo" ticket from Zagreb to Split or Dubrovnik can be as inexpensive as $50—cheaper and much faster than taking the bus. These cheap seats sell out fast, so try to book several weeks ahead.

To connect to other parts of Europe, check with the low-cost airlines. Carriers that fly to cities in Croatia or Slovenia include **easyJet** (www.easyjet.com), **Ryanair** (www.ryanair.com), **Wizz Air** (www.wizzair.com), and **Norwegian Air** (www.norwegian.no).

A visit to www.skyscanner.net sorts the numerous options offered by the many discount airlines, enabling you to see the best schedules for your trip and come up with the best deal. Other good search engines include www.mobissimo.com and www.wegolo.com.

Be aware of the potential drawbacks of flying on the cheap: nonrefundable and nonchangeable tickets, minimal customer assistance, the typical use of airports far outside town, and pricey baggage fees. Especially if you're traveling with lots of luggage, a cheap flight can quickly become a bad deal. To avoid unpleasant surprises, read the small print—especially baggage policies—before you book.

Europe by Air offers a Flight Pass, charging $99 per leg (plus taxes and airport fees) for flights within Europe. They partner with various well-established airlines, providing good coverage for low prices (most useful for Croatia Airlines flights to and from the Dalmatian Coast; tickets can be purchased only in US, www.europebyair.com, US tel. 888-321-4737).

Resources

Resources from Rick Steves

Rick Steves' Croatia & Slovenia is one of more than 30 titles in a series of **books** on European travel, which includes country guide-

books, city and regional guidebooks, and my budget-travel skills hand-book, *Rick Steves' Europe Through the Back Door*. Some of my books are available in electronic format, and selected chapters from my guide-books are reprinted as easy-to-pocket Snapshot books. My phrase books—for German, French, Italian, Spanish, and Portuguese—are practical and budget-oriented. My other books are *Europe 101* (a crash course on art and history, newly expanded and in full color), *Travel as a Political Act* (a travelogue sprinkled with advice for bringing home a global perspective), *European Christmas* (on traditional and modern-day celebrations), and *Postcards from Europe* (a fun memoir of my travels over 25 years). For a list of my major titles, see the inside of the last page of this book.

My **TV series,** *Rick Steves' Europe,* covers European destinations in 100 shows, includ-ing episodes on Croatia and Slovenia. My weekly public **radio show,** *Travel with Rick Steves,* features interviews with travel experts from around the world, including Croatia and Slovenia. All the TV scripts and radio shows (which are easy and free to download to an iPod or other MP3 player) are at www .ricksteves.com.

Maps

The black-and-white maps in this book, designed by my well-traveled staff, are concise and simple. The maps are intended to help you locate recommended places and get to local TIs, where you can pick up more in-depth maps of towns or regions (usually free). Better maps are sold at bookstores. Before you buy a map, look at it to be sure it has the level of detail you want.

Drivers will want to pick up a good, detailed map in Europe. My favorite maps of the region are by the Slovenian cartographer Kod & Kam (they have a store in Ljubljana—see page 402—but you can find these maps everywhere). Their 1:500,000-scale

Begin Your Trip at www.ricksteves.com

At our travel website, you'll find a wealth of free information on European destinations, including fresh monthly news and helpful tips from thousands of fellow travelers. You'll also find my latest guidebook updates (www.ricksteves.com/update) and my travel blog.

Our **online Travel Store** offers travel bags and accessories specially designed by Rick Steves to help you travel smarter and lighter. These include my popular carry-on bags (roll-aboard and rucksack versions), money belts, totes, toiletries kits, adapters, other accessories, and a wide selection of guidebooks, planning maps, and DVDs.

Choosing the right **railpass** for your trip—amidst hundreds of options—can drive you nutty. (If your trip involves train travel beyond Croatia and Slovenia, a railpass is worth considering.) We'll help you choose the best pass for your needs, plus give you a bunch of free extras.

Rick Steves' Europe Through the Back Door travel company offers **tours** with more than three dozen itineraries and more than 300 departures reaching the best destinations in this book...and beyond. We offer a 14-day Adriatic tour that visits Slovenia, Croatia, and a bit of Bosnia-Herzegovina, as well as a 17-day Best of Eastern Europe tour. You'll enjoy great guides, a fun bunch of travel partners (with small groups of generally around 28), and plenty of room to spread out in a big, comfy bus. You'll find European adventures to fit every vacation length. For all the details, and to get our Tour Catalog and a free Rick Steves Tour Experience DVD (filmed on location during an actual tour), visit www.ricksteves.com or call the Tour Department at 425/608-4217.

Croatia map (*Hrvaška* in Slovene, *Hrvatska* in Croatian) covers everything in this book (including Slovenia, Bosnia-Herzegovina, and most of Montenegro) with all the detail you'll need. For just Slovenia, pick up the good 1:300,000 *Autokarta Slovenija* map, sold at tourist shops everywhere (around €8, generally cheaper at TIs than at bookstores or travel agencies). Even better, the Slovenian Tourist Board publishes free excerpts of this same map, divided into three regional zones called "Next Exit"—to save some money, look for these at TIs and skip buying the big map. If you'll be hiking, especially in the Slovenian Alps, you'll find no shortage of excellent, very detailed maps locally.

Since new expressways are constantly being built in these countries, an up-to-date map is essential—it can mean the difference between choosing an old, slow road or saving an hour by finding the brand-new highway.

Other Guidebooks

If you're like most travelers, this book is all you need. But if you're heading beyond my recommended destinations, $40 for extra maps and books is money well spent. For several people traveling by car, the extra weight and expense of a small trip library are negligible.

The following books are worthwhile, though not updated annually; check the publication date before you buy. The Rough Guides, which individually cover Croatia and Slovenia, are packed with historical and cultural insight. The Lonely Planet guides (with separate Croatia and Slovenia books, and a handy *Western Balkans* book that includes Croatia, Montenegro, Bosnia-Herzegovina, and more) are similar, but are designed more for travelers than for intellectuals. If choosing between these two titles, I'd buy the one that was published most recently.

Students, backpackers, and nightlife-seekers should consider the Let's Go guides (by Harvard students, has the best hostel listings; Croatia and Slovenia are covered in their *Eastern Europe* book). Dorling Kindersley publishes snazzy Eyewitness Guides, one covering Croatia and another just on Dubrovnik and the Dalmatian Coast. While pretty to look at, these books weigh a ton and are skimpy on actual content.

The British entertainment publication *Time Out* sells a well-researched annual magazine with up-to-date coverage on Croatia, including the latest on hotels, restaurants, and nightlife (look for it at newsstands in Croatia, www.timeout.com).

If your travels take you to nearby countries, consider *Rick Steves' Eastern Europe,* which covers parts of Croatia and Slovenia, plus Hungary, Poland, the Czech Republic, and Slovakia.

Recommended Books and Movies

To learn about Croatia and Slovenia past and present, check out a few of the following books and films.

Books: Lonnie Johnson's *Central Europe: Enemies, Neighbors, Friends* is the best history overview of Croatia, Slovenia, and their neighboring countries. Rebecca West's classic, bricklike *Black Lamb and Grey Falcon* is the definitive travelogue of the Yugoslav lands (written during a journey between the two World Wars). For a more recent take, Croatian journalist Slavenka Drakulić has written a trio of insightful essay collections from a woman's perspective: *Café Europa: Life After Communism; The Balkan Express;* and *How We Survived Communism and Even Laughed.* For a thorough explanation of how and why Yugoslavia broke apart, read *Yugoslavia: Death of a Nation* (by Laura Silber and Allan Little). Joe Sacco's powerful graphic novel, *Safe Area Goražde*, describes the author's real-life experience living in a mostly Muslim town in Bosnia-Herzegovina while it was surrounded by Serb forces during the wars of the 1990s.

Films: To grasp the wars that shook this region in the early 1990s, there's no better film than the Slovene-produced *No Man's Land*, which won the 2002 Oscar for Best Foreign Film. The BBC produced a remarkable (but difficult-to-find) six-hour documentary series called *The Death of Yugoslavia*, featuring actual interviews with all of the key players (the book *Yugoslavia: Death of a Nation*, noted above, was a companion piece to this film). Croatian films worth watching include *Border Post* (2006), about various Yugoslav soldiers working together just before the war broke out, and *When Father Was Away on Business* (1985), about a prisoner on the Tito-era gulag island of Goli Otok, near Rab. Other local movies worth watching include *Armin* (2007); *How the War Started on My Island* (1996); *Underground* (1995); and *Tito and Me* (1992).

Holidays and Festivals

This is a partial list of holidays and festivals—in these countries, holidays strike without warning. As both Croatia and Slovenia are Catholic, religious holidays are a big deal—and frequent. Before planning a trip around a festival, make sure to verify the dates by checking the festival's website or contacting the national tourist office in Croatia (http://us.croatia.hr) or Slovenia (www.slovenia.info). They can also provide specifics and a more comprehensive list of festivals. Unless stated otherwise, all holidays listed here apply to both Croatia and Slovenia.

Jan 1	New Year's Day
Jan 6	Epiphany

Feb	Kurentovanje Carnival, Ptuj, Slovenia (Feb 13–23 in 2010, Feb 12–22 in 2011, www.kurentovanje.net)
Feb 8	National Day of Culture, Slovenia (celebrates Slovenian culture and national poet France Prešeren)
Late March	Ski Flying World Championships, Planica, Slovenia (3 days, www.planica.si)
Easter	(April 4 in 2010, April 24 in 2011)
April 27	National Resistance Day, Slovenia
May 1	Labor Day, Croatia and Slovenia
Ascension	(May 13 in 2010, June 2 in 2011)
Whitsunday (Pentecost) and Whitmonday	(May 23–24 in 2010, June 12–13 in 2011)
Early June	Dance Week Festival, Zagreb, Croatia (www.danceweekfestival.com)
Corpus Christi	(June 3 in 2010, June 23 in 2011)
June 22	Antifascist Struggle Day, Croatia
June 25	National Day, Slovenia; Statehood Day, Croatia
July 10–Aug 25	Dubrovnik Summer Festival, Croatia (www.dubrovnik-festival.hr)
Early July–late Aug	Ljubljana Summer Festival, Slovenia (www.ljubljanafestival.si)
Late July	Marco Polo Festival, Korčula, Croatia (3 days, www.marcopolofest.hr)
Late July	International Folklore Festival, Zagreb, Croatia (5 days, costumes, songs, dances from all over Croatia; www.msf.hr)
Aug 5	National Thanksgiving Day, Croatia
Aug 15	Assumption of Mary
Early Sept	Marco Polo Naval Battle Reenactment, Korčula, Croatia
Oct 8	Independence Day, Croatia
Oct 31	Reformation Day, Slovenia
Nov 1	All Saints' Day/Remembrance Day (religious festival, some closures)
Nov 11	St. Martin's Day (official first day of wine season)
Dec 24–25	Christmas Eve and Christmas Day
Dec 26	Boxing Day/St. Stephen's Day; Independence and Unity Day, Slovenia

Conversions and Climate

Numbers and Stumblers

- Europeans write a few of their numbers differently than we do. 1 = 1, 4 = 4, 7 = 7.
- In Europe, dates appear as day/month/year, so Christmas is 25/12/11.
- Commas are decimal points and decimals, commas. A dollar and a half is 1,50, and there are 5.280 feet in a mile.
- When counting with fingers, start with your thumb. If you hold up your first finger to request one item, you'll probably get two.
- What Americans call the second floor of a building is the first floor in Europe.
- On escalators and moving sidewalks, Europeans keep the left "lane" open for passing. Keep to the right.

Metric Conversions (approximate)

A kilogram is 2.2 pounds, and 1 liter is about a quart, or almost four to a gallon. A kilometer is six-tenths of a mile. I figure kilometers to miles by cutting them in half and adding back 10 percent of the original (120 km: 60 + 12 = 72 miles, 300 km: 150 + 30 = 180 miles).

1 foot = 0.3 meter	1 square yard = 0.8 square meter
1 yard = 0.9 meter	1 square mile = 2.6 square kilometers
1 mile = 1.6 kilometers	1 ounce = 28 grams
1 centimeter = 0.4 inch	1 quart = 0.95 liter
1 meter = 39.4 inches	1 kilogram = 2.2 pounds
1 kilometer = 0.62 mile	32°F = 0°C

Clothing Sizes

When shopping for clothing, use these US-to-European comparisons as general guidelines (but note that no conversion is perfect).

- Women's dresses and blouses: Add 30 (US size 10 = European size 40)
- Men's suits and jackets: Add 10 (US size 40 regular = European size 50)
- Men's shirts: Multiply by 2 and add about 8 (US size 15 collar = European size 38)
- Women's shoes: Add about 30 (US size 8 = European size 38.5)
- Men's shoes: Add 32–34 (US size 9 = European size 41; US size 11 = European size 45)

Climate

First line is the average daily high temperature; second line, average daily low; third line, average number of rainy days. For more detailed weather statistics for destinations in this book (as well as the rest of the world), check www.worldclimate.com.

	J	F	M	A	M	J	J	A	S	O	N	D
CROATIA • Dubrovnik												
	53°	55°	58°	63°	70°	78°	83°	82°	77°	69°	62°	56°
	42°	43°	57°	52°	58°	65°	69°	69°	64°	57°	51°	46°
	13	13	11	10	10	6	4	3	7	11	16	15
SLOVENIA • Ljubljana												
	36°	41°	50°	60°	68°	75°	80°	78°	71°	59°	47°	39°
	25°	25°	32°	40°	48°	54°	57°	57°	51°	43°	36°	30°
	13	11	11	13	16	16	12	12	10	14	15	15

Temperature Conversion: Fahrenheit and Celsius

Europe takes its temperature using the Celsius scale, while we opt for Fahrenheit. For a rough conversion from Celsius to Fahrenheit, double the number and add 30. For weather, remember that 28°C is 82°F—perfect. For health, 37°C is just right.

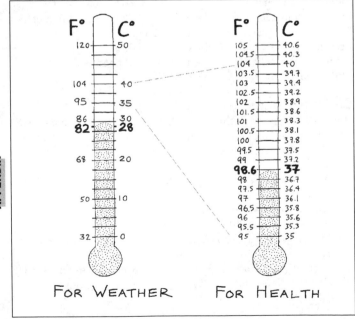

FOR WEATHER   FOR HEALTH

Essential Packing Checklist

Whether you're traveling for five days or five weeks, here's what you'll need to bring. Remember to pack light to enjoy the sweet freedom of true mobility. Happy travels!

- ❑ 5 shirts
- ❑ 1 sweater or lightweight fleece jacket
- ❑ 2 pairs pants
- ❑ 1 pair shorts
- ❑ 1 swimsuit (women only—men can use shorts)
- ❑ 5 pairs underwear and socks
- ❑ 1 pair shoes
- ❑ 1 rainproof jacket
- ❑ Tie or scarf
- ❑ Money belt
- ❑ Money—your mix of:
  - ❑ Debit card for ATM withdrawals
  - ❑ Credit card
  - ❑ Hard cash in US dollars ($20 bills)
- ❑ Documents (and back-up photocopies)
- ❑ Passport
- ❑ Printout of airline e-ticket
- ❑ Driver's license
- ❑ Student ID and hostel card
- ❑ Railpass/car rental voucher
- ❑ Insurance details
- ❑ Daypack
- ❑ Sealable plastic baggies
- ❑ Camera and related gear
- ❑ Empty water bottle
- ❑ Wristwatch and alarm clock
- ❑ Earplugs
- ❑ First-aid kit
- ❑ Medicine (labeled)
- ❑ Extra glasses/contacts and prescriptions
- ❑ Sunscreen and sunglasses
- ❑ Toiletries kit
- ❑ Soap
- ❑ Laundry soap
- ❑ Clothesline
- ❑ Small towel
- ❑ Sewing kit
- ❑ Travel information
- ❑ Necessary map(s)
- ❑ Address list (email and mailing addresses)
- ❑ Postcards and photos from home
- ❑ Notepad and pen
- ❑ Journal

If you plan to carry on your luggage, note that all liquids must be in three-ounce or smaller containers and fit within a single quart-size baggie. For details, see www.tsa.gov/travelers.

Hotel Reservation

To: _____   _____
         hotel   *email or fax*

From: _____   _____
          name   *email or fax*

Today's date: _____ /_____ /_____
                  day   *month*   *year*

Dear Hotel _____ ,
Please make this reservation for me:

Name: _____

Total # of people: _____   # of rooms: _____   # of nights: _____

Arriving: _____ /_____ /_____   My time of arrival (24-hr clock): _____
              day *month* *year*   (I will telephone if I will be late)

Departing: _____ /_____ /_____
               day *month* *year*

Room(s): Single_____   Double _____   Twin _____   Triple _____   Quad_____

With: Toilet _____   Shower_____   Bath_____   Sink only_____

Special needs: View_____   Quiet_____   Cheapest_____   Ground Floor_____

Please email or fax confirmation of my reservation, along with the type of room reserved and the price. Please also inform me of your cancellation policy. After I hear from you, I will quickly send my credit-card information as a deposit to hold the room. Thank you.

_____
Name

_____
Address

_____
City   *State*   *Zip Code*   *Country*

Before hoteliers can make your reservation, they want to know the information listed above. You can use this form as the basis for your email, or you can photocopy this page, fill in the information, and send it as a fax (also available online at www.ricksteves.com/reservation).

Croatian Survival Phrases

When using the phonetics, pronounce ī / Ī as the long I sound in "light."

Hello. (formal)	Dobar dan.	DOH-bahr dahn
Hi. / Bye. (informal)	Bog.	bohg
Do you speak English?	Govorite li engleski?	GOH-voh-ree-teh lee EHN-glehs-kee
Yes. / No.	Da. / Ne.	dah / neh
I (don't) understand.	(Ne) razumijem.	(neh) rah-ZOO-mee-yehm
Please. / You're welcome.	Molim.	MOH-leem
Thank you (very much).	Hvala (ljepa).	HVAH-lah (LYEH-pah)
Excuse me. / I'm sorry.	Oprostite.	oh-PROH-stee-teh
problem	problem	proh-BLEHM
No problem.	Nema problema.	NEH-mah proh-BLEH-mah
Good.	Dobro.	DOH-broh
Goodbye.	Do videnija.	doh veed-JAY-neeah
one / two	jedan / dva	YEH-dahn / dvah
three / four	tri / četiri	tree / CHEH-toh-ree
five / six	pet / šest	peht / shehst
seven / eight	sedam / osam	SEH-dahm / OH-sahm
nine / ten	devet / deset	DEH voht / DEH l-seht
hundred / thousand	sto / tisuća	stoh / TEE-soo-chah
How much?	Koliko?	KOH-lee-koh
local currency	kuna	KOO-nah
Write it?	Napišite?	nah-PEESH-ee-teh
Is it free?	Da li je besplatno?	dah lee yeh BEH-splaht-noh
Is it included?	Da li je uključeno?	dah lee yeh OOK-lyoo-cheh-noh
Where can I find / buy...?	Gdje mogu pronaći / kupiti...?	guh-DYEH MOH-goo PROH-nah-chee / KOO-pee-tee
I'd like / We'd like...	Želio bih / Željeli bismo...	ZHEH-lee-oh beeh / ZHEH-lyeh-lee BEES-moh
...a room.	...sobu.	SOH-boo
...a ticket to ___.	...kartu do ___.	KAR-too doh
Is it possible?	Da li je moguće?	dah lee yeh MOH-goo-cheh
Where is...?	Gdje je...?	guh-DYEH yeh
...the train station	...željeznička stanica	ZHEH-lyehz-neech-kah STAH-neet-sah
...the bus station	...autobusna stanica	OW-toh-boos-nah STAH-neet-sah
...the tourist information office	...turističko informativni centar	TOO-ree-steech-koh EEN-for-mah-teev-nee TSEHN-tahr
...the toilet	...vece (WC)	VEHT-SEH
men	muški	MOOSH-kee
women	ženski	ZHEHN-skee
left / right	lijevo / desno	LEE-yeh-voh / DEHS-noh
straight	ravno	RAHV-noh
At what time...	U koliko sati...	oo KOH-lee-koh SAH-tee
...does this open / close?	...otvara / zatvara?	OHT-vah-rah / ZAHT-vah-rah
(Just) a moment.	(Samo) trenutak.	(SAH-moh) treh-NOO-tahk
now / soon / later	sada / uskoro / kasnije	SAH-dah / OOS-koh-roh / KAHS-nee-yeh
today / tomorrow	danas / sutra	DAH-nahs / SOO-trah

In the Restaurant

I'd like to reserve…	Rezervirao bih…	reh-zehr-VEER-ow beeh
We'd like to reserve…	Rezervirali bismo…	reh-zehr-VEE-rah-lee BEES-moh
…a table for one / two.	…stol za jednog / dva.	stohl zah YEHD-nog / dvah
Non-smoking.	Za nepušače.	zah NEH-poo-shah-cheh
Is this table free?	Da li je ovaj stol slobodan?	dah lee yeh OH-vī stohl SLOH-boh-dahn
Can I help you?	Izvolite?	EEZ-voh-lee-teh
The menu (in English), please.	Jelovnik (na engleskom), molim.	yeh-LOHV-neek (nah EHN-glehs-kohm) MOH-leem
service (not) included	posluga (nije) uključena	POH-sloo-gah (NEE-yeh) OOK-lyoo-cheh-nah
cover charge	couvert	KOO-vehr
"to go"	za ponjeti	zah POHN-yeh-tee
with / without	sa / bez	sah / behz
and / or	i / ili	ee / EE-lee
fixed-price meal (of the day)	(dnevni) meni	(duh-NEHV-nee) MEH-nee
specialty of the house	specijalitet kuće	speht-see-yah-LEE-teht KOO-cheh
half portion	pola porcije	POH-lah PORT-see-yeh
daily special	jelo dana	YEH-loh DAH-nah
fixed-price meal for tourists	turistički meni	TOO-ree-steech-kee MEH-nee
appetizers	predjela	PREHD-yeh-lah
bread	kruh	krooh
cheese	sir	seer
sandwich	sendvič	SEND-veech
soup	juha	YOO-hah
salad	salata	sah-LAH-tah
meat	meso	MAY-soh
poultry	perad	PEH-rahd
fish	riba	REE-bah
seafood	morska hrana	MOHR-skah HRAH-nah
fruit	voće	VOH-cheh
vegetables	povrće	POH-vur-cheh
dessert	desert	deh-SAYRT
(tap) water	voda (od slavine)	VOH-dah (ohd SLAH-vee-neh)
mineral water	mineralna voda	MEE-neh-rahl-nah VOH-dah
milk	mlijeko	mlee-YEH-koh
(orange) juice	sok (od naranče)	sohk (ohd NAH-rahn-cheh)
coffee	kava	KAH-vah
tea	čaj	chī
wine	vino	VEE-noh
red / white	crno / bijelo	TSEHR-noh / bee-YEH-loh
sweet / dry / semi-dry	slatko / suho / polusuho	SLAHT-koh / SOO-hoh / POH-loo-soo-hoh
glass / bottle	čaša / boca	CHAH-shah / BOHT-sah
beer	pivo	PEE-voh
Cheers!	Živjeli!	ZHEE-vyeh-lee
More. / Another.	Još. / Još jedno.	yohsh / yohsh YEHD-noh
The same.	Isto.	EES-toh
Bill, please.	Račun, molim.	RAH-choon MOH-leem
tip	napojnica	NAH-poy-neet-sah
Delicious!	Izvrsno!	EEZ-vur-snoh

Slovenian Survival Phrases

When using the phonetics, pronounce ī / Ī as the long I sound in "light."
The vowel "eh" sometimes sounds closer to "ay" (depending on the speaker).

Hello. (formal)	Dober dan.	DOH-behr dahn
Hi. / Bye. (informal)	Živjo.	ZHEEV-yoh
Do you speak English?	Ali govorite angleško?	AH-lee goh-voh-REE-teh ahn-GLEHSH-koh
Yes. / No.	Ja. / Ne.	yah / neh
I (don't) understand.	(Ne) razumem.	(neh) rah-ZOO-mehm
Please. / You're welcome.	Prosim.	PROH-seem
Thank you (very much).	Hvala (lepa).	HVAH-lah (LEH-pah)
Excuse me. / I'm sorry.	Oprostite.	oh-proh-STEE-teh
problem	problem	proh-BLEHM
No problem.	Ni problema.	nee proh-BLEH-mah
Good.	Dobro.	DOH-broh
Goodbye.	Na svidenje.	nah SVEE-dehn-yeh
one / two	ena / dve	EH-nah / dveh
three / four	tri / štiri	tree / SHTEE-ree
five / six	pet / šest	peht / shehst
seven / eight	sedem / osem	SEH-dehm / OH-sehm
nine / ten	devet / deset	deh-VEHT / deh-SEHT
hundred / thousand	sto / tisoč	stoh / TEE-sohch
How much?	Koliko?	KOH-lee-koh
local currency	euro	EE-oo-roh
Write it?	Napišite?	nah-PEESH-ee-teh
Is it free?	Ali je brezplačno?	AH-lee yeh brehz-PLAHCH-noh
Is it included?	Ali je vključeno?	AH-lee yeh vuk-LYOO-cheh-noh
Where can I find / buy...?	Kje iahko najdem / kupim...?	kyeh LAH-koh NĪ-dehm / KOO-peem
I'd / We'd like...	Želel / Želeli bi...	zheh-LEEoo / zheh-LEH-lee bee
...a room.	...sobo.	SOH-boh
...a ticket to ___ .	...vozovnico do ___ .	voh-ZOHV-neet-soh doh
Is it possible?	Ali je možno?	AH-lee yeh MOHZH-noh
Where is...?	Kje je...?	kyeh yeh
...the train station	...železniška postaja	zheh-LEHZ-neesh-kah pohs-TĪ-yah
...the bus station	...avtobusna postaja	OW-toh-boos-nah pohs-TĪ-yah
...the tourist information office	...turistično informacijski center	too-REES-teech-noh een-for-maht-SEE-skee TSEHN-tehr
...the toilet	...vece (WC)	VEHT-SEH
men	moški	MOHSH-kee
women	ženski	ZHEHN-skee
left / right	levo / desno	LEH-voh / DEHS-noh
straight	naravnost	nah-RAHV-nohst
At what time...	Ob kateri uri...	ohb kah-TEH-ree OO-ree
...does this open / close?	...se odpre / zapre?	seh ohd-PREH / zah-PREH
(Just) a moment.	(Samo) trenutek.	(sah-MOH) treh-NOO-tehk
now / soon / later	zdaj / kmalu / pozneje	zuh-DĪ / kuh-MAH-loo / pohz-NEH-yeh
today / tomorrow	danes / jutri	DAH-nehs / YOO-tree

In the Restaurant

I'd like to reserve...	**Rezerviral bi...**	reh-zehr-VEE-rahl bee
We'd like to reserve...	**Rezervirali bi...**	reh-zehr-VEE-rah-lee bee
...a table for one / two.	**...mizo za enega / dva.**	MEE-zoh zah EH-neh-gah / dvah
Non-smoking.	**Za nekadilce.**	zah NEH-kah-deelt-seh
Is this table free?	**Ali je ta miza prosta?**	AH-lee yeh tah MEE-zah PROH-stah
Can I help you?	**Izvolite?**	eez-VOH-lee-teh
The menu (in English), please.	**Jedilni list (v angleščini), prosim.**	yeh-DEEL-nee leest (vuh ahn-GLEHSH-chee-nee) PROH-seem
service (not) included	**postrežba (ni) vključena**	post-REHZH-bah (nee) vuk-LYOO-cheh-nah
cover charge	**pogrinjek**	poh-GREEN-yehk
"to go"	**za s sabo**	zah SAH-boh
with / without	**z / brez**	zuh / brehz
and / or	**in / ali**	een / AH-lee
fixed-price meal (of the day)	**(dnevni) meni**	(duh-NEW-nee) meh-NEE
specialty of the house	**specialiteta hiše**	speht-see-ah-lee-TEH-tah HEE-sheh
half portion	**polovična porcija**	poh-loh-VEECH-nah PORT-see-yah
daily special	**dnevna ponudba**	duh-NEW-nah poh-NOOD-bah
fixed-price meal for tourists	**turistični meni**	too-REES-teech-nee meh-NEE
appetizers	**predjedi**	prehd-yeh-DEE
bread	**kruh**	krooh
cheese	**sir**	seer
sandwich	**sendvič**	SEND-veech
soup	**juha**	YOO-hah
salad	**solata**	soh-LAH-tah
meat	**meso**	meh-SOH
poultry	**perutnina**	peh-root-NEE-nah
fish	**riba**	REE-bah
seafood	**morska hrana**	MOHR-skah HRAH-nah
fruit	**sadje**	SAHD-yeh
vegetables	**zelenjava**	zeh-lehn-YAH-vah
dessert	**sladica**	slah-DEET-sah
(tap) water	**voda (iz pipe)**	VOH-dah (eez PEE-peh)
mineral water	**mineralna voda**	mee-neh-RAHL-nah VOH-dah
milk	**mleko**	MLEH-koh
(orange) juice	**(pomarančni) sok**	(poh-mah-RAHNCH-nee) sohk
coffee	**kava**	KAH-vah
tea	**čaj**	chī
wine	**vino**	VEE-noh
red / white	**rdeče / belo**	ahr-DEH-cheh / BEH-loh
sweet / dry / semi-dry	**sladko / suho / polsuho**	SLAHD-koh / SOO-hoh / POHL-soo-hoh
glass / bottle	**kozarec / steklenica**	koh-ZAH-rehts / stehk-leh-NEET-sah
beer	**pivo**	PEE-voh
Cheers!	**Na zdravje!**	nah ZDROW-yeh
More. / Another.	**Še. / Še eno.**	sheh / sheh EH-noh
The same.	**Isto.**	EES-toh
Bill, please.	**Račun, prosim.**	rah-CHOON PROH-seem
tip	**napitnina**	nah-peet-NEE-nah
Delicious!	**Odlično!**	ohd-LEECH-noh

Pronouncing Croatian and Slovenian Place Names

Remember that *j* is pronounced as "y," and *c* is pronounced "ts." For the special characters, č is "ch," š is "sh," ž is "zh," and đ is similar to "j."

Name	Pronounced
Bohinj	BOH-heen
Bovec	BOH-vets
Brijuni (Islands)	bree-YOO-nee
Brtonigla	bur-toh-NEEG-lah
Cetinje	TSEH-teen-yeh
Dubrovnik	doo-BROHV-nik
Grožnjan	grohzh-NYAHN
Herzegovina	hert-seh-GOH-vee-nah
Hum	hoom
Hvar	hvahr
Istria	EE-stree-ah
Jadrolinija (Ferry Company)	yah-droh-LEE-nee-yah
Kobarid	KOH-bah-reed
Korčula	KOHR-choo-lah
Lipica (Lipizzaner Stud Farm)	LEE-peet-suh
Ljubljana	lyoob-lyee-AH-nah
Međugorje	MEDGE-oo-gor-yeh
Mljet (National Park)	muhl-YET
Motovun	moh-toh-VOON
Mostar	MOH-star
Njeguši	NYEH-goo-shee
Opatija	oh-PAH-tee-yah
Otočac	OH-toh-chawts
Pelješac	PEHL-yeh-shahts
Piran	pee-RAHN
Plitvice (National Park)	PLEET-veet-seh
Polače	POH-lah-cheh
Pomena	POH-meh-nah
Poreč	poh-RETCH
Postojna (Caves)	poh-STOY-nah
Predjama (Castle)	prehd-YAH-mah
Ptuj	puh-TOOey
Pula	POO-lah
Rab	rob
Radovljica	rah-DOH-vleet-suh
Rijeka	ree-YAY-kah
Rovinj	roh-VEEN
Senj	sehn
Škocjan (Caves)	SHKOHTS-yahn
Soča (River Valley)	SOH-chah
Vršič (Pass)	vur-SHEECH
Zagreb	ZAH-grehb

INDEX

MAP INDEX

Start your trip at

▶ Plan Your Trip

Browse thousands of articles and a wealth of money-saving tips for planning your dream trip. You'll find up-to-date information on Europe's best destinations, packing smart, getting around, finding rooms, staying healthy, avoiding scams and more.

▶ Eurail Passes

Find out, step-by-step, if a rail pass makes sense for your trip—and how to avoid buying more than you need. Get a bunch of free extras!

▶ Graffiti Wall & Travelers' Helpline

Learn, ask, share—our online community of savvy travelers is a great resource for first-time travelers to Europe, as well as seasoned pros.

Rick Steves' Europe Through the Back Door, Inc.

ricksteves.com

turn your travel dreams into affordable reality

▸ Free Audio Tours & Travel Newsletter

Get your nose out of this guide-book and focus on what you'll be seeing with Rick's free audio tours of the greatest sights in Paris, Rome, Florence and Venice.

Subscribe to our free *Travel News* e-newsletter, and get monthly articles from Rick on what's happening in Europe.

▸ Great Gear from Rick's Travel Store

Pack light and right—on a budget—with Rick's custom-designed carry-on bags, roll-aboards, day packs, travel accessories, guidebooks, journals, maps and DVDs of his TV shows.

Rick Steves®

www.ricksteves.com

TRAVEL SKILLS
Europe Through the Back Door

EUROPE GUIDES
Best of Europe
Eastern Europe
Europe 101
European Christmas
Postcards from Europe

COUNTRY GUIDES
Croatia & Slovenia
England
France
Germany
Great Britain
Ireland
Italy
Portugal
Scandinavia
Spain
Switzerland

CITY & REGIONAL GUIDES
Amsterdam, Bruges & Brussels
Athens & The Peloponnese
Budapest
Florence & Tuscany
Istanbul
London
Paris
Prague & The Czech Republic
Provence & The French Riviera
Rome
Venice
Vienna, Salzburg & Tirol

PHRASE BOOKS & DICTIONARIES
French
French, Italian & German
German
Italian
Portuguese
Spanish

RICK STEVES' EUROPE DVDs
Austria & The Alps
Eastern Europe
England
Europe
France & Benelux
Germany & Scandinavia
Greece, Turkey, Israel & Egypt
Ireland & Scotland
Italy's Cities
Italy's Countryside
Rick Steves' European Christmas
Spain & Portugal
Travel Skills & "The Making Of"

PLANNING MAPS
Britain, Ireland & London
Europe
France & Paris
Germany, Austria & Switzerland
Ireland
Italy
Spain & Portugal

JOURNALS
Rick Steves' Pocket Travel Journal
Rick Steves' Travel Journal

NOW AVAILABLE

RICK STEVES APPS FOR THE iPHONE OR iPOD TOUCH

With these apps you can:

- ► Spin the compass icon to switch views between sights, hotels, and restaurant selections—and get details on cost, hours, address, and phone number.

- ► Tap any point on the screen to read Rick's detailed information, including history and suggested viewpoints.

- ► Get a deeper view into Rick's tours with audio and video segments.

Go to iTunes to download the following apps:

Rick Steves' Louvre Tour

Rick Steves' Historic Paris Walk

Rick Steves' Orsay Museum Tour

Rick Steves' Versailles

Rick Steves' Ancient Rome Tour

Rick Steves' St. Peter's Basilica Tour

Once downloaded, these apps are completely self-contained on your iPhone or iPod Touch, so you will not incur pricey roaming charges during use overseas.

Rick Steves books and DVDs are available at bookstores and through online booksellers.

Rick Steves guidebooks are published by Avalon Travel, a member of the Perseus Books Group.

Rick Steves apps are produced by Übermind, a boutique Seattle-based software consultancy firm.

Credits

Contributor
Gene Openshaw

Gene is the co-author of seven Rick Steves books. For this book, he wrote material on Europe's art, history, and contemporary culture. When not traveling, Gene enjoys composing music, recovering from his 1973 trip to Europe with Rick, and living everyday life with his daughter.

Special Thanks

The authors would like to thank our Slovenian and Croatian friends for their invaluable insights. *Hvala lepa* to Marijan Krišković, Tina Hiti, Sašo Golub, Bojan Kočar, and Gorazd Hiti.

Images

Location	Photographer
Title Page: Bled Island, Slovenia	Cameron Hewitt
Introduction: Countryside near Lake Bled, Slovenia	Cameron Hewitt
Croatia (full-page image): Rovinj	Cameron Hewitt
Zagreb: Zagreb Skyline	Cameron Hewitt
Plitvice Lakes National Park: Plitvice	Rick Steves
Istria: Motovun	Cameron Hewitt
Kvarner Gulf: Jablanac	Cameron Hewitt
Split: Riva Promenade and Old Town	Cameron Hewitt
Hvar: Hvar Harbor	Cameron Hewitt
Korčula: View of Old Town	Cameron Hewitt
Dubrovnik: View of Old Town	Cameron Hewitt
Near Dubrovnik: Neptune Fountain, Trsteno Arboretum	Cameron Hewitt
Bosnia-Herzegovina (full-page image): Old Bridge, Mostar	Cameron Hewitt
Bosnia-Herzegovina: Old Bridge, Mostar	Cameron Hewitt
Montenegro (full-page image): Perast	Cameron Hewitt
Montenegro: Perast and the Bay of Kotor	Cameron Hewitt
Slovenia (full-page image): Julian Alps	Cameron Hewitt
Ljubljana: Ljubljana Castle overlooking Prešeren Square	Cameron Hewitt
Lake Bled: *Pletna* Boat on Lake Bled	Cameron Hewitt
The Julian Alps: Mountain Hut	Cameron Hewitt
Logarska Dolina and the Northern Valleys: Logarska Dolina	Cameron Hewitt
Ptuj: View of Old Town	Cameron Hewitt
The Karst: Predjama Castle	Cameron Hewitt
Piran: Breakwater	Cameron Hewitt

Rick Steves' Guidebook Series

Country Guides

Rick Steves' Best of Europe
Rick Steves' Croatia & Slovenia
Rick Steves' Eastern Europe
Rick Steves' England
Rick Steves' France
Rick Steves' Germany
Rick Steves' Great Britain
Rick Steves' Ireland
Rick Steves' Italy
Rick Steves' Portugal
Rick Steves' Scandinavia
Rick Steves' Spain
Rick Steves' Switzerland

City and Regional Guides

Rick Steves' Amsterdam, Bruges & Brussels
Rick Steves' Athens & the Peloponnese
Rick Steves' Budapest
Rick Steves' Florence & Tuscany
Rick Steves' Istanbul
Rick Steves' London
Rick Steves' Paris
Rick Steves' Prague & the Czech Republic
Rick Steves' Provence & the French Riviera
Rick Steves' Rome
Rick Steves' Venice
Rick Steves' Vienna, Salzburg & Tirol

Rick Steves' Phrase Books

French
French/Italian/German
German
Italian
Portuguese
Spanish

Other Books

Rick Steves' Europe 101: History and Art for the Traveler
Rick Steves' Europe Through the Back Door
Rick Steves' European Christmas
Rick Steves' Postcards from Europe
Rick Steves' Travel as a Political Act

Avalon Travel
a member of the Perseus Books Group
1700 Fourth Street
Berkeley, CA 94710, USA

Portions of this book were originally published in *Rick Steves' Best of Eastern Europe* © 2009, 2007, 2006, 2005, 2004 by Rick Steves and Cameron Hewitt.

For the latest on Rick Steves' lectures, guidebooks, tours, public radio show, and public television series, contact Europe Through the Back Door, tel. 425/771-8303, fax 425/771-0833, www.ricksteves.com, rick@ricksteves.com.

ISBN 978-1-59880-106-4
ISSN 1935-7419

Europe Through the Back Door Lead Editor: Cameron Hewitt
ETBD Reviewing Editors: Tom Griffin, Jennifer Madison Davis
ETBD Editors: Gretchen Strauch, Cathy Lu, Cathy McDonald, Sarah McCormic
ETBD Managing Editor: Risa Laib
Avalon Travel Senior Editor & Series Manager: Madhu Prasher
Avalon Travel Project Editor: Kelly Lydick
Copy Editor: Naomi Adler-Dancis
Proofreader: Janet Walden
Indexer: Claire Splan
Production & Typesetting: McGuire Barber Design
Cover Design: Kimberly Glyder Design
Graphic Content Director: Laura VanDeventer
Maps & Graphics: David C. Hoerlein, Laura VanDeventer, Lauren Mills, Barb Geisler,
    Chris Markiewicz, Brice Ticen, Kat Bennett, Mike Morgenfeld
Photography: Cameron Hewitt, Rick Steves, David C. Hoerlein
Front Matter Color Photos: Page i: Bled Island, Slovenia © Cameron Hewitt
Cover Photos: Lokrum Island from the walls of Dubrovnik, Croatia © Cameron Hewitt

Distributed to the book trade by Publishers Group West, Berkeley, California